MCSA
MCSE
MCDBA
Self-Paced Training Kit

2
Second Edition

Microsoft®
SQL SERVER™ 2000
SYSTEM ADMINISTRATION

Exam 70-228

PUBLISHED BY
Microsoft Press
A Division of Microsoft Corporation
One Microsoft Way
Redmond, Washington 98052-6399

Copyright © 2003 by Microsoft Corporation

Library of Congress Cataloging-in-Publication Data
MCSA/MCSE/MCDBA Self-Paced Training Kit: Microsoft SQL Server 2000 System
    Administration, Exam 70-228 / Microsoft Corporation.--2nd ed.
        p. cm.
    Includes index.
    Rev. ed. of: MCSE training kit: Microsoft SQL Server 2000 system administration /
2001.
        ISBN 0-7356-1961-1
        1. Electronic data processing personnel--Certification. 2. Microsoft
    software--Examinations--Study guides. 3. SQL server. I. Title: Microsoft SQL Server
    2000 system administration, 70-228. II. MCSE training kit: Microsoft SQL Server 2000
    system administration. III. Microsoft Corporation.

    QA76.3.M326573   2003
    005.75'85--dc21

                                                                    2003045875

Printed and bound in the United States of America.

2 3 4 5 6 7 8 9   QWT   8 7 6 5 4

Distributed in Canada by H.B. Fenn and Company Ltd.

A CIP catalogue record for this book is available from the British Library.

Microsoft Press books are available through booksellers and distributors worldwide. For further informa-tion about international editions, contact your local Microsoft Corporation office or contact Microsoft Press International directly at fax (425) 936-7329. Visit our Web site at www.microsoft.com/mspress. Send comments to *tkinput@microsoft.com.*

Acquisitions Editor: Kathy Harding
Project Editor: Valerie Woolley

Body Part No. X09-59433

Contents

Lesson 3: Creating and Managing Logins 330
    Granting Access Using SQL Server Enterprise Manager 330
    Using the Create Login Wizard 330
    Practice: Creating a Login Using the Create Login Wizard 334
    Using SQL Server Enterprise Manager Directly to Create a Login 336
    Practice: Creating a Login Directly Using SQL Server
    Enterprise Manager 339
    Creating a User-Defined Database Role Using SQL Server
    Enterprise Manager 341
    Granting Access Using Transact-SQL Statements 342
    Windows Logins 342
    SQL Server Logins 342
    Server Roles 343
    Database Access 343
    Database Roles 344
    Practice: Granting SQL Server 2000 and Database Access
    Using Transact-SQL 345
    Viewing Access Information 346
    Using SQL Server Enterprise Manager 346
    Using Transact-SQL 350
    Practice: Viewing SQL Server 2000 Access Information 351
    Lesson Summary 354
Review 355

Chapter 11: Managing SQL Server Permissions. 357
    About This Chapter 357
    Before You Begin 357
Lesson 1: Granting Database-Specific Permissions 358
    Implementing Permissions 358
    Inherited Permissions 359
    Permission Actions and Conflicts 359
    Practice: Creating and Testing Permission Conflicts 360
    Managing Statement Permissions 361
    Creating Objects and Chain of Ownership Issues 361
    Changing Object Ownership 363
    Using SQL Server Enterprise Manager to Grant, Deny, or Revoke
    Statement Permissions 363

About This Book

Welcome to *MCSA/MCSE/MCDBA Self-Paced Training Kit: Microsoft SQL Server 2000 System Administration, Exam 70-228, Second Edition*. This book provides you with the knowledge and skills required to install, configure, administer, and troubleshoot Microsoft SQL Server 2000. The contents of this book reflect the significant changes in the product from previous versions and provide a task-oriented discussion of all of the important features that SQL Server 2000 provides for database administrators.

Note For more information on becoming a Microsoft Certified Systems Engineer or a Microsoft Certified Database Administrator, see the "The Microsoft Certified Professional Program" section later in this introduction.

Before You Begin Part 1

Each chapter in Part 1 is divided into lessons. Most lessons include hands-on procedures that allow you to practice or demonstrate a particular concept or skill. Each lesson ends with a short summary, and each chapter ends with a set of review questions to test your knowledge of the chapter material.

The "Getting Started" section of this introduction provides important setup instructions that describe the hardware and software requirements for completing the procedures in this book. Read through this section thoroughly before you start the lessons.

Intended Audience

This book has been developed for information system (IS) professionals and database administrators who need to install, administer, and support Microsoft SQL Server 2000 or who plan to take the related Microsoft Certified Professional exam 70-228: Installing, Configuring, and Administering Microsoft SQL Server 2000 Enterprise Edition.

Prerequisites

Before you begin to work with the material in the Training Kit, it is recommended that you have

- Experience using the Microsoft Windows 2000 operating system. The skills you should be comfortable with include:
  - Connecting clients running Windows 2000 to servers running Windows 2000

- Configuring the Windows 2000 environment
- Creating and managing user accounts
- Managing access to resources by using groups
- Configuring and managing disks and partitions, including disk striping and mirroring
- Securing data by using NTFS
- Securing access to Windows 2000
- Optimizing Windows 2000 server performance
- An understanding of basic relational database concepts. These concepts include:
  - Logical and physical relational database design
  - Data integrity
  - Relationships between tables and columns (primary and foreign keys, one-to-one, one-to-many, and many-to-many)
  - How data is stored in tables (rows and columns)
  - Knowledge of basic Transact-SQL syntax (*SELECT*, *INSERT*, and *UPDATE* statements)
  - An understanding of the role of a database administrator

Reference Material

You might find the following reference material useful:

- SQL Server white papers and case studies, available online at *http://www.microsoft.com/sql/techinfo/default.asp*
- SQL Server Books Online, available on the product CD-ROM

About the CD-ROM

This book contains a Supplemental Course Materials CD-ROM and a CD with a 120-day Evaluation Edition of Microsoft SQL Server 2000.

The Supplemental Course Materials CD-ROM contains files required to perform the hands-on procedures contained in the lesson material in this book.

Features of This Book

Each chapter begins with a "Before You Begin" section, which prepares you for completing the chapter. Whenever possible, lessons contain procedures that give you an opportunity to use the skills being presented. The "Review" section at the end of each chapter allows you to test what you have learned in the lesson. The Appendix, "Questions and Answers," contains all of the book's review questions and the corresponding answers.

- Characters or commands that you type appear in **bold** type.
- *Italic* in syntax statements indicates placeholders for variable information. *Italic* is also used for book titles.
- Names of files and folders appear in Title Caps, except when you are to type them directly. You can use all lowercase letters when you type a filename in a dialog box or at a command prompt.
- Acronyms appear in all uppercase.
- Monospace type represents code samples, examples of screen text, or entries that you might type at a command prompt or in initialization files.
- Square brackets [ ] are used in syntax statements to enclose optional items. For example, [*filename*] in command syntax indicates that you can choose to type a filename with the command. Type the information within the brackets, not the brackets themselves.
- Braces { } are used in syntax statements to enclose required items. Type only the information within the braces, not the braces themselves.

Keyboard Conventions

- A plus sign (+) between two key names means that you must press those keys at the same time. For example, "Press ALT+TAB" means that you hold down the ALT key while you press the TAB key.
- You can choose menu commands with the keyboard. Press the ALT key to activate the menu bar, and then sequentially press the keys that correspond to the highlighted or underlined letter of the menu command name. For some commands, you can also press a key combination listed in the menu.
- You can select or clear check boxes or option buttons in dialog boxes with the keyboard. Press the ALT key, and then press the key that corresponds to the underlined letter of the option name. Or you can press the TAB key until the option is highlighted, and then press the SPACEBAR to select or clear the check box or option button.
- You can cancel the display of a dialog box by pressing the ESC key.

Chapter and Appendix Overview

This book combines text, hands-on procedures, and review questions to teach you database administration using SQL Server 2000. It is designed to be completed from the beginning to the end, but you can choose to complete only those sections that interest you. If you choose the customized track option, see the "Before You

Begin" section in each chapter. Any hands-on procedures that require preliminary work from preceding chapters refer to the appropriate chapters.

This self-paced training book is divided into the following chapters:

- The "About This Book" contains a self-paced training overview and introduces the components of this training. Read this section thoroughly to get the greatest educational value from this self-paced training and to plan which lessons you will complete.
- Chapter 1, "Overview of SQL Server 2000," introduces SQL Server 2000. It defines some of the important characteristics of SQL Server 2000 and explains the environments in which it is designed to work. You will be introduced to the different parts of the product and given some idea as to the role played by these parts.
- Chapter 2, "Installing SQL Server 2000," explains how to install SQL Server 2000. It lists the hardware and software requirements of the program, and it explains the specific information you have to supply and the decisions you have to make during the installation process. This chapter covers using default, named, and multiple instances of SQL Server 2000. The chapter also covers performing unattended and remote installations of SQL Server 2000.
- Chapter 3, "Preparing to Use SQL Server 2000," reviews the results of installing SQL Server 2000. This chapter explains starting, stopping, and pausing SQL Server services. The chapter also covers working with OSQL, SQL Query Analyzer, and SQL Server Enterprise Manager.
- Chapter 4, "Upgrading to SQL Server 2000," shows you how to perform a version upgrade of a complete SQL Server 6.5 or 7.0 installation to SQL Server 2000. This chapter also explains how to perform an online database upgrade from SQL Server 7.0.
- Chapter 5, "Understanding System and User Databases," explains SQL Server 2000 databases. This includes the structure of a data file and the architecture of the transaction log. This chapter concludes with a discussion about system tables, including the querying of system and database catalogs.
- Chapter 6, "Creating and Configuring User Databases," teaches how to create a new user database, set database options for new or existing databases, and manage the size of data and transaction log files. This chapter concludes with a discussion about placing database files on multiple disks for recovery, fault tolerance, and performance.
- Chapter 7, "Populating a Database," discusses the population of user databases with existing data. It shows you how to transfer and transform data. This chapter focuses on the use of DTS, Bcp, and the *BULK INSERT* Transact-SQL statement.
- Chapter 8, "Developing a Data Restoration Strategy," presents an overview of the SQL Server 2000 backup and restore processes and discusses the issues that you should consider when planning a backup and restore strategy for a SQL Server 2000 installation.

■ Chapter 9, "Backing Up and Restoring SQL Server," teaches you how to perform database backups using disk and tape. It also teaches you how to perform database restorations. This chapter explains how to use SQL Server Enterprise Manager and Transact-SQL statements.

■ Chapter 10, "Managing Access to SQL Server 2000," discusses controlling access to SQL Server 2000, including the authentication process and the authorization process. The chapter concludes by showing you how to create and manage logins.

■ Chapter 11, "Managing SQL Server Permissions," shows how to grant database-specific permissions. It also discusses the use of application roles. The chapter concludes by teaching you how to design an access and permissions strategy.

■ Chapter 12, "Performing Administrative Tasks," teaches you how to perform a variety of configuration tasks and setup tasks. These include the configuration of the SQL Server service, the SQL Server Agent service, SQL Mail, SQLAgentMail, and XML. The chapter concludes with a discussion of the performance of periodic maintenance tasks.

■ Chapter 13, "Automating Administrative Tasks," shows you how to automate routine tasks using operators, jobs, and alerts. It also teaches the creation of a database maintenance plan. It concludes by teaching you to create multiserver jobs.

■ Chapter 14, "Monitoring SQL Server Performance and Activity," discusses the development of a performance monitoring methodology. This chapter introduces each of the monitoring tools and shows you how to use each tool. The chapter concludes by teaching you how to perform specific monitoring tasks, such as for memory use or slow-performing queries.

■ Chapter 15, "Using SQL Server Replication," introduces planning for, implementing, monitoring, and administering replication. This includes covering the types of replication that are available for automatically replicating data between instances of SQL Server or with heterogeneous data sources.

■ Chapter 16, "Maintaining High Availability," discusses the use of standby servers, including the use of log shipping to automate the process of maintaining a standby server. The chapter also discusses the use of SQL Server failover clusters using the Microsoft Cluster Service.

Following Part 2 you will find:

■ The Appendix, "Questions and Answers," lists all of the review questions from the book, showing suggested answers.

■ The Glossary provides definitions for many of the terms and concepts presented in this training kit.

Where to Find Specific Skills in This Book

The following tables provide a comprehensive list of the skills measured on the Microsoft Certified Professional Exam 70-228, *Installing, Configuring, and Administering Microsoft SQL Server 2000 Enterprise Edition*. The table lists the skill and indicates where in this book you will find the lesson relating to that skill. For sample questions to help gauge your readiness for exam 70-228, see Part 2, "Preparation for MCP Exam 70-228."

Note Exam skills are subject to change without prior notice at the sole discretion of Microsoft.

Table A-1.   Installing and Configuring SQL Server 2000

Skill Being Measured	Location in Book
Install SQL Server 2000	Chapter 2
Upgrade to SQL Server 2000	Chapter 4
Create a linked server	Chapter 12
Configure SQL Mail and SQLAgentMail	Chapter 12
Configure network libraries	Chapter 2
Troubleshoot failed installations	Chapter 2

Table A-2.   Creating SQL Server 2000 Databases

Skill Being Measured	Location in Book
Configure database options for performance	Chapter 6
Attach and detach databases	Chapter 6
Create and alter databases	Chapter 6

Table A-3.   Managing, Monitoring, and Troubleshooting SQL Server 2000 Databases

Skill Being Measured	Location in Book
Optimize database performance	Chapter 6, Chapter 14
Optimize data storage	Chapter 6
Modify the database schema	Chapter 5, Chapter 6
Perform disaster recovery operations	Chapter 8, Chapter 9, Chapter 15
Perform integrity checks	Chapter 12, Chapter 13
Troubleshoot transactions and locking	Chapter 14

Table A-4. Extracting and Transforming Data with SQL Server 2000

Skill Being Measured	Location in Book
Set up Internet Information Services (IIS) virtual directories to support XML	Chapter 12
Import and export data	Chapter 7
Develop and manage Data Transformation Services (DTS) packages	Chapter 7
Manage linked servers	Chapter 12
Configure, maintain, and troubleshoot replication services	Chapter 15

Table A-5. Managing and Monitoring SQL Server 2000 Security

Skill Being Measured	Location in Book
Configure mixed security modes or Windows Authentication	Chapter 2, Chapter 10
Create and manage logins	Chapter 10
Create and manage database users	Chapter 11
Create and manage security roles	Chapter 10, Chapter 11
Enforce and manage security	Chapter 10, Chapter 11
Set permissions in a database	Chapter 11
Manage security auditing	Chapter 11, Chapter 14

Table A-6. Managing, Monitoring, and Troubleshooting SQL Server 2000

Skill Being Measured	Location in Book
Create, manage, and troubleshoot SQL Server Agent jobs	Chapter 13, Chapter 15
Configure alerts and operators by using SQL Server Agent	Chapter 13
Optimize hardware resource usage	Chapter 6, Chapter 14, Chapter 16
Optimize and troubleshoot SQL Server system activity	Chapter 14

Getting Started

This self-paced training manual contains hands-on procedures to help you learn about Microsoft SQL Server 2000.

Caution   These procedures require a computer configured as a Windows 2000 domain controller. If you must perform these procedures on a server that is part of an existing domain in a larger network, you will not be able to perform some procedures at all. Other procedures will require modification of steps and scripts. Consult with your Network Administrator before you attempt any of these procedures in a larger network.

Hardware Requirements

The computer used for these hands-on procedures must have the following minimum configuration. All hardware should be on the Microsoft Windows 2000 Server Hardware Compatibility List.

Component	Requirement
Processor	Intel or compatible processor, Pentium 166 MHz or higher
Memory	128 MB minimum, 256 MB recommended
Hard disk space	400 MB of free hard disk drive space
CD-ROM drive	Required to install SQL Server 2000 from the compact disc
Network card	Optional
Sound card and speakers	Optional

Software Requirements

The following software is required to complete the procedures in this course:

- Microsoft Windows 2000 Server
- Microsoft SQL Server 2000 Evaluation Edition

A copy of the SQL Server 2000 Evaluation Edition is included with this training kit.

Note   The SQL Server 2000 Evaluation Edition provided with this training kit is provided only for the purposes of training and evaluation. Microsoft Technical Support does not support this edition. For additional support information regarding this book and the CD-ROM (including answers to commonly asked questions about installation and use), visit the Microsoft Press Technical Support Site at *http://www.microsoft.com/mspress/support/*. You can also e-mail *TKIN-PUT@MICROSOFT.COM*, or send a letter to Microsoft Press, Attn: Microsoft Press Technical Support, One Microsoft Way, Redmond, WA 98052-6399.

Setup Instructions

Configure your computer according to the following instructions.

1. Set up your computer according to the manufacturer's instructions.
2. Install Windows 2000 Server on the C drive, formatted as an NTFS partition, and using a NetBIOS name of SelfPacedCPU.
3. Configure your server as a domain controller in the SelfPacedSQL.MSFT domain.
4. Insert the Supplemental Course Materials CD-ROM into your CD-ROM drive.
5. Copy the \SelfPacedSQL folder on the CD to C:\drive. This will copy the exercise files that you will need to complete the hands-on procedures in this book.

About the eBook

The Supplemental Course Materials CD-ROM includes an electronic version of the book that you can view on screen using Adobe Acrobat Reader. For more information, see the README.TXT file included in the root folder of the Supplemental Course Materials CD-ROM.

Before You Begin Part 2

Part 2 helps you evaluate your readiness for the MCP Exam 70-228, *Installing, Configuring, and Administering Microsoft SQL Server 2000 Enterprise Edition*. When you pass this exam, you earn core credit toward Microsoft Certified Database Administrator (MCDBA) certification and elective credit toward Microsoft Certified Systems Engineer (MCSE) certification. In addition, when you pass this exam you achieve Microsoft Certified Professional status.

Note   You can find a complete list of MCP exams and their related objectives on the Microsoft Certified Professional Web site at *http://www.microsoft.com /traincert/mcp/default.asp*.

The Components of Part 2

An electronic assessment program for Exam 70-228 is provided on the Supplemental Course Material CD-ROM. This program is a practice certification test that helps you to evaluate your skills. It provides instant scoring feedback, so you can determine areas in which additional study may be helpful before you take the certification exam. Although your score on the electronic assessment does not necessarily indicate what your score will be on the certification exam, it does give you the opportunity to answer questions that are similar to those on the actual certification exam.

Part 2 is organized by the exam's objectives. Each chapter of the book pertains to one of the six primary groups of objectives on the actual exam, called the *Objective Domains*. Each Objective Domain lists the tested skills you need to master to adequately answer the exam questions. Because the certification exams focus on real-world skills, the Tested Skills and Suggested Practices lists provide practices that emphasize the practical application of the exam objectives. Each Objective Domain also provides suggestions for further reading or additional resources to help you understand the objectives and increase your ability to perform the task or skills specified by the objectives.

Within each Objective Domain, you will find the related objectives that are covered on the exam. Each objective provides you with the following:

- **Key terms** you must know to understand the objective. Knowing these terms can help you answer the objective's questions correctly.
- Several sample exam questions with the correct answers. The answers are accompanied by explanations of each correct and incorrect answer. (These questions match the questions on the electronic assessment.)

You use the electronic assessment to determine the exam objectives that you need to study, and then use Part 2 to learn more about those particular objectives and discover additional study materials to supplement your knowledge. You can also use Part 2 to research the answers to specific sample test questions. Keep in mind that to pass the exam, you should understand not only the answer to the question, but also the concepts on which the correct answer is based.

MCP Exam Prerequisites

No exams or classes are required before you take the Installing, Configuring, and Administering Microsoft SQL Server 2000 Enterprise Edition exam. However, in addition to the skills tested by the exam, you should have a working knowledge of the operation and support of hardware and software on SQL Server 2000 computers. This knowledge should include:

- Installing and configuring SQL Server 2000.
- Creating and maintaining SQL Server 2000 databases.
- Configuring and administrating replication under SQL Server 2000.
- Knowledge of SQL Server 2000 security concepts.
- Managing linked servers.
- Optimizing SQL Server performance.

Note After you determine that you are ready for the exam, use the Get MCP Information link provided on the home page of the electronic assessment tool for information on scheduling the exam. You can schedule exams up to six weeks in advance, or as late as one working day before the exam date.

Know the Products

Microsoft's certification program relies on exams that measure your ability to perform a specific job function or set of tasks. Microsoft develops the exams by analyzing the tasks performed by people who are currently working in the field. Therefore, the specific knowledge, skills, and abilities relating to the job are reflected in the certification exam.

Because the certification exams are based on real-world tasks, you need to gain hands-on experience with the applicable technology in order to master the exam. In a sense, you might consider hands-on experience in an organizational environment to be a prerequisite for passing an MCP exam. Many of the questions relate directly to Microsoft products or technology, so use opportunities at your organization or home to practice using the relevant tools.

Using the Electronic Assessment and Part 2

Although you can use the Part 2 in a number of ways, you might start your studies by taking the electronic assessment as a pretest. After completing the exam, review your results for each Objective Domain and focus your studies first on the Objective Domains for which you received the lowest scores. The electronic assessment allows you to print your results, and a printed report of how you fared can be useful when reviewing the exam material in this book.

After you have taken the electronic assessment, use the Part 2 to learn more about the Objective Domains that you find difficult and to find listings of appropriate study materials that may supplement your knowledge. By reviewing why the answers are correct or incorrect, you can determine if you need to study the objective topics more.

You can also use Part 2 to focus on the exact objectives that you need to master. Each objective in the book contains several questions that help you determine if you understand the information related to that particular skill. The book is also designed for you to answer each question before turning the page to review the correct answer.

The best method to prepare for the MCP exam is to use the Part 2 in conjunction with the electronic assessment and other study material. Thoroughly studying and practicing the material combined with substantial real-world experience can help you fully prepare for the MCP exam.

Understanding the Conventions for Part 2

Before you start using Part 2, it is important that you understand the terms and conventions used in the electronic assessment and book.

Question Numbering System

The electronic assessment and Part 2 contain reference numbers for each question. Understanding the numbering format will help you use Part 2 more effectively. When Microsoft creates the exams, the questions are grouped by job skills called *Objectives*. These Objectives are then organized by sections known as *Objective Domains*. Each question can be identified by the Objective Domain and the Objective it covers. The question numbers follow this format:

Test Number.Objective Domain.Objective.Question Number

For example, question number 70-228.02.01.003 means this is question three (003) for the first Objective (01) in the second Objective Domain (02) of the Installing, Configuring, and Administering Microsoft SQL Server 2000 Enterprise Edition exam (70-228). Refer to the "Exam Objectives Summary" section later in this introduction to locate the numbers associated with particular objectives. Each question is numbered based on its presentation in the printed book. You can use this numbering system to reference questions on the electronic assessment or in Part 2. Even though the questions in the book are organized by objective, questions in the electronic assessment and actual certification exam are presented in random order.

Notational Conventions

- Characters or commands that you type appear in **bold** type.
- Variable information and URLs are *italicized*. *Italic* is also used for book titles.
- Acronyms, filenames, and utilities appear in FULL CAPITALS.

Using the Electronic Assessment

The electronic assessment simulates the actual MCP exam. Each iteration of the electronic assessment consists of 50 questions covering all the objectives for the Installing, Configuring, and Administering Microsoft SQL Server 2000 Enterprise Edition exam. (MCP certification exams consist of approximately 50–70 questions.) Just like a real certification exam, you see questions from the objectives in random order during the practice test. Similar to the certification exam, the electronic assessment allows you to mark questions and review them after you finish the test.

To increase its value as a study aid, you can take the electronic assessment multiple times. Each time you are presented with a different set of questions in a revised order; however, some questions may be repeated.

If you have used one of the certification exam preparation tests available from Microsoft, the electronic assessment should look familiar. The difference is that this electronic assessment gives you the opportunity to learn as you take the exam.

Installing and Running the Electronic Assessment Software

Before you begin using the electronic assessment, you need to install the software. You need a computer with the following minimum configuration:

- Multimedia PC with a 75 MHz Pentium or higher processor
- 16 MB RAM for Windows 95 or Windows 98, or
- 32 MB RAM for Windows NT, or Windows Me
- 64 MB RAM for Windows 2000, or Windows XP
- 128 MB RAM for Windows Server 2003
- Internet Explorer 5.01 or later
- 17 MB of available hard disk space (additional 70 MB minimum of hard disk space to install Internet Explorer 6 from this CD-ROM)
- A double-speed CD-ROM drive or better
- Super VGA display with at least 256 colors

▶ **To install the electronic assessment**

1. Insert Supplemental Course Materials CD-ROM into your CD-ROM drive.

   A starting menu will display automatically, with links to the resources included on the CD.

   Note   If your system does not have Microsoft Internet Explorer 5.01 or later, you can install Internet 6 now by selecting the appropriate option on the menu.
   ---

2. Click the link to the exam you want to install.

   A dialog box appears indicating you will install the MCSE Readiness Review to your computer.

3. Click Next.

   The License Agreement dialog box appears.

4. To continue with the installation of the electronic assessment engine, you must accept the License Agreement by clicking Yes.

5. The Choose Destination Location dialog box appears showing a default installation folder. Either accept the default or change the installation folder if needed. Click Next to copy the files to your hard disk.

6. A Question dialog box appears asking whether you would like Setup to create a desktop shortcut for this program. If you click Yes, an icon will be placed on your desktop.

7. The Setup Complete dialog box appears. Select whether you want to view the Readme.txt file after closing the Setup program, and then click Finish.

   The electronic assessment software is completely installed. If you chose to view the Readme.txt file, it will launch in a new window. For optimal viewing, enable word wrap.

► **To start the electronic assessment**

1. From the Start menu, point to Programs, point to MCSE Readiness Review, and then click MCSE RR Exam 70-228.

    The electronic assessment program starts.

2. Click Start Test.

    Information about the electronic assessment program appears.

3. Click OK.

Taking the Electronic Assessment

The electronic assessment consists of 50 multiple-choice questions, and as in the certification exam, you can skip questions or mark them for later review. Each exam question contains a question number that you can use to refer back to Part 2 of the book.

Before you end the electronic assessment, make sure you answer all the questions. When the exam is graded, unanswered questions are counted as incorrect and will lower your score. Similarly, on the actual certification exam you should complete all questions or they will be counted as incorrect. No trick questions appear on the exam. The correct answer will always be among the list of choices. Some questions may have more than one correct answer, and this will be indicated in the question. A good strategy is to eliminate the most obvious incorrect answers first to make it easier for you to select the correct answer.

You have 75 minutes to complete the electronic assessment. During the exam you will see a timer indicating the amount of time you have remaining. This will help you to gauge the amount of time you should use to answer each question and to complete the exam. The amount of time you are given on the actual certification exam varies with each exam. Generally, certification exams take approximately 100 minutes to complete, but they can vary from 60 to 300 minutes.

Ending and Grading the Electronic Assessment

When you click the Score Test button, you have the opportunity to review the questions you marked or left incomplete. (This format is not similar to the one used on the actual certification exam, in which you can verify whether you are satisfied with your answers and then click the Grade Test button.) The electronic assessment is graded when you click the Score Test button, and the software presents your section scores and your total score.

Note   You can always end a test without grading your electronic assessment by clicking the Home button.

After your electronic assessment is graded, you can view the correct and incorrect answers by clicking the Review Questions button.

Interpreting the Electronic Assessment Results

The Score screen shows you the number of questions in each Objective Domain section, the number of questions you answered correctly, and a percentage grade for each section. You can use the Score screen to determine where to spend additional time studying. On the actual certification exam, the number of questions and passing score will depend on the exam you are taking. The electronic assessment records your score each time you grade an exam so that you can track your progress over time.

▶ **To view your progress and exam records**

1. From the electronic assessment Main menu, click View History. Each test attempt score appears.
2. Click on a test attempt date/time to view your score for each objective domain.

   Review these scores to determine which Objective Domains you should study further. You can also use the scores to determine your progress.

Using Part 2 of this Book

You can use Part 2 of this book as a supplement to the electronic assessment, or as a stand-alone study aid. If you decide to use the book as a stand-alone study aid, review the Contents or the list of objectives to find topics of interest or an appropriate starting point for you. To get the greatest benefit from the book, use the electronic assessment as a pretest to determine the Objective Domains for which you should spend the most study time. Or, if you would like to research specific questions while taking the electronic assessment, you can use the question number located on the question screen to reference the question number in Part 2 of the book.

One way to determine areas in which additional study may be helpful is to carefully review your individual section scores from the electronic assessment and note objective areas where your score could be improved. The section scores correlate to the Objective Domains listed in Part 2 of the book.

Reviewing the Objectives

Each Objective Domain in the book contains an introduction and a list of practice skills. Each list of practice skills describes suggested tasks you can perform to help you understand the objectives. Some of the tasks suggest reading additional material, whereas others are hands-on practices with software or hardware. You should pay particular attention to the hands-on practices, as the certification exam reflects real-world knowledge you can gain only by working with the software or technology. Increasing your real-world experience with the relevant products and technologies will improve your performance on the exam.

After you choose the objectives you want to study, turn to the Contents to locate the objectives in Part 2 of the book. You can study each objective separately, but you might need to understand the concepts explained in other objectives.

Make sure you understand the key terms for each objective. You will need a thorough understanding of these terms to answer the objective's questions correctly. Key term definitions are located in the Glossary of this book.

Reviewing the Questions

Each objective includes questions followed by the possible answers. After you review the question and select a probable answer, turn to the Answer section to determine if you answered the question correctly. (For information about the question numbering format, see "Question Numbering System," earlier in this introduction.)

Part 2 briefly discusses each possible answer and explains why each answer is correct or incorrect. After reviewing each explanation, if you feel you need more information about a topic, question, or answer, refer to the Further Readings section for that domain for more information.

The answers to the questions in Part 2 are based on current industry specifications and standards. However, the information provided by the answers is subject to change as technology improves and changes.

Exam Objectives Summary

Installing, Configuring, and Administering Microsoft SQL Server 2000 Enterprise Edition certification (70-228) exam measures your ability to implement, administer, and troubleshoot SQL Server 2000 Enterprise Edition.

Before taking the exam, you should be proficient with the job skills presented in the following sections. The sections provide the exam objectives and the corresponding objective numbers (which you can use to reference the questions in the electronic assessment and book) grouped by Objective Domains.

Objective Domain 1: Installing and Configuring SQL Server 2000

The objectives in Objective Domain 1 are as follows:

- Objective 1.1 (70-228.01.01)—Install SQL Server 2000.
- Objective 1.2 (70-228.01.02)—Upgrade to SQL Server 2000.
- Objective 1.3 (70-228.01.03)—Create a linked server.
- Objective 1.4 (70-228.01.04)—Configure SQL Mail and SQLAgentMail.
- Objective 1.5 (70-228.01.05)—Configure network libraries.
- Objective 1.6 (70-228.01.06)—Troubleshoot failed installations.

Objective Domain 2: Creating SQL Server 2000 Databases

The objectives in Objective Domain 2 are as follows:

- Objective 2.1 (70-228.02.01)—Configure database options for performance.
- Objective 2.2 (70-228.02.02)—Attach and detach databases.
- Objective 2.3 (70-228.02.03)—Create and alter databases.
- Objective 2.4 (70-228.02.04)—Create and manage objects.

Objective Domain 3: Managing, Monitoring, and Troubleshooting SQL Server 2000 Databases

The objectives in Objective Domain 3 are as follows:

- Objective 3.1 (70-228.03.01)—Optimize database performance.
- Objective 3.2 (70-228.03.02)—Optimize data storage.
- Objective 3.3 (70-228.03.03)—Modify the database schema.
- Objective 3.4 (70-228.03.04)—Perform disaster recovery operations.
- Objective 3.5 (70-228.03.05)—Perform integrity checks.
- Objective 3.6 (70-228.03.06)—Troubleshoot transactions and locking by using SQL Profiler, SQL Server Enterprise Manager, or Transact-SQL.

Objective Domain 4: Extracting and Transforming Data with SQL Server 2000

The objectives in Objective Domain 4 are as follows:

- Objective 4.1 (70-228.04.01)—Set up Internet Information Services (IIS) virtual directories to support XML.
- Objective 4.2 (70-228.04.02)—Import and export data.
- Objective 4.3 (70-228.04.03)—Develop and manage Data Transformation Services (DTS) packages.
- Objective 4.4 (70-228.04.04)—Manage linked servers.
- Objective 4.5 (70-228.04.05)—Convert data types.
- Objective 4.6 (70-228.04.06)—Configure, maintain, and troubleshoot replication services.

Objective Domain 5: Managing and Monitoring SQL Server 2000 Security

The objectives in Objective Domain 5 are as follows:

- Objective 5.1 (70-228.05.01)—Configure mixed security modes or Windows Authentication.
- Objective 5.2 (70-228.05.02)—Create and manage logons.

- Objective 5.3 (70-228.05.03)—Create and manage database users.
- Objective 5.4 (70-228.05.04)—Create and manage security roles.
- Objective 5.5 (70-228.05.05)—Enforce and manage security by using stored procedures, triggers, views, and user-defined functions.
- Objective 5.6 (70-228.05.06)—Set permissions in a database.
- Objective 5.7 (70-228.05.07)—Manage security auditing.

Objective Domain 6: Managing, Monitoring, and Troubleshooting SQL Server 2000

The objectives in Objective Domain 6 are as follows:

- Objective 6.1 (70-228.06.01)—Create, manage, and troubleshoot SQL Server Agent jobs.
- Objective 6.2 (70-228.06.02)—Configure alerts and operators by using SQL Server Agent.
- Objective 6.3 (70-228.06.03)—Optimize hardware resource usage.
- Objective 6.4 (70-228.06.04)—Optimize and troubleshoot SQL Server system activity.

Getting More Help

A variety of resources are available to help you study for the exam. Your options include instructor-led classes, seminars, self-paced kits, or other learning materials. The materials described here are created to prepare you for MCP exams. Each training resource fits a different type of learning style and budget.

Microsoft Official Curriculum (MOC)

Microsoft Official Curriculum (MOC) courses are technical training courses developed by Microsoft product groups to educate computer professionals who use Microsoft technology. The courses are developed with the same objectives used for Microsoft certification, and MOC courses are available to support most exams for the MCSE certification. The courses are available in instructor-led, online, or self-paced formats to fit your preferred learning style.

Self-Paced Training

Microsoft Press self-paced training kits cover a variety of Microsoft technical products. The self-paced kits are based on MOC courses, feature lessons, hands-on practices, multimedia presentations, practice files, and demonstration software. They can help you understand the concepts and get the experience you need to take the corresponding MCP exam. Part 1 is a fine example.

MCP Approved Study Guides

MCP Approved Study Guides, available through several organizations, are learning tools that help you prepare for MCP exams. The study guides are available in a variety of formats to match your learning style, including books, compact discs, online content, and videos. These guides come in a wide range of prices to fit your budget.

Microsoft Seminar Series

Microsoft Solution Providers and other organizations are often a source of information to help you prepare for an MCP exam. For example, many solution providers will present seminars to help industry professionals understand a particular product technology, such as networking.

The Microsoft Certified Professional Program

The Microsoft Certified Professional (MCP) program provides the best method to prove your command of current Microsoft products and technologies. Microsoft, an industry leader in certification, is on the forefront of testing methodology. Our exams and corresponding certifications are developed to validate your mastery of critical competencies as you design and develop, or implement and support, solutions with Microsoft products and technologies. Computer professionals who become Microsoft certified are recognized as experts and are sought after industry-wide.

The Microsoft Certified Professional program offers five certifications, based on specific areas of technical expertise:

- **Microsoft Certified Professional (MCP).** Demonstrated in-depth knowledge of at least one Microsoft operating system. Candidates may pass additional Microsoft certification exams to further qualify their skills with Microsoft BackOffice products, development tools, or desktop programs.

- **Microsoft Certified Systems Administrator (MCSA) on Microsoft Windows 2000.** Individuals who implement, manage, and troubleshoot existing network and system environments based on Microsoft Windows 2000 and Window Server 2003 operating systems.

- **Microsoft Certified Systems Engineer (MCSE).** Qualified to effectively analyze the business requirements, and design and implement the infrastructure for business solutions based on Microsoft Windows 2000 platform and Microsoft .NET Enterprise Servers.

- **Microsoft Certified Database Administrator (MCDBA).** Individuals who derive physical database designs, develop logical data models, create physical databases, create data services by using Transact-SQL, manage and maintain databases, configure and manage security, monitor and optimize databases, and install and configure Microsoft SQL Server.
- **Microsoft Certified Solution Developer (MCSD).** Qualified to design and develop custom business solutions with Microsoft development tools, technologies, and platforms, including Microsoft Office and Microsoft BackOffice.
- **Microsoft Certified Trainer (MCT).** Instructionally and technically qualified to deliver Microsoft Official Curriculum through a Microsoft Certified Technical Education Center (CTEC).

Microsoft Certification Benefits

Microsoft certification, one of the most comprehensive certification programs available for assessing and maintaining software-related skills, is a valuable measure of an individual's knowledge and expertise. Microsoft certification is awarded to individuals who have successfully demonstrated their ability to perform specific tasks and implement solutions with Microsoft products. Not only does this provide an objective measure for employers to consider; it also provides guidance for what an individual should know to be proficient. And as with any skills-assessment and benchmarking measure, certification brings a variety of benefits to the individual, and to employers and organizations.

Microsoft Certification Benefits for Individuals

Microsoft Certified Professionals receive the following benefits:

- Industry recognition of your knowledge and proficiency with Microsoft products and technologies.
- Microsoft Developer Network (MSDN) subscription. MCPs receive rebates or discounts on a one-year subscription to the Microsoft Developer Network (*http://msdn.microsoft.com/subscriptions/*) during the first year of certification. (Fulfillment details will vary, depending on your location; please see your Welcome Kit.)
- Access to technical and product information directly from Microsoft through a secured area of the MCP Web site (go to *http://www.microsoft.com/traincert /mcp/mccpsecure.asp/*).
- Access to exclusive discounts on products and services from selected companies. Individuals who are currently certified can learn more about exclusive discounts by visiting the MCP secured Web site (go to *http://www.microsoft.com/traincert /mcp/mccpsecure.asp/* and select the "Other Benefits" link) upon certification.
- MCP logo, certificate, transcript, wallet card, and lapel pin to identify you as a Microsoft Certified Professional (MCP) to colleagues and clients. Electronic files of logos and transcript may be downloaded from the MCP secured Web site upon certification.

- Invitations to Microsoft conferences, technical training sessions, and special events.

- Free access to *Microsoft Certified Professional Magazine Online*, a career and professional development magazine. Secured content on the *Microsoft Certified Professional Magazine Online* Web site includes the current issue (available only to MCPs), additional online-only content and columns, an MCP-only database, and regular chats with Microsoft and other technical experts.

- Discount on membership to PASS (for MCPs only), the Professional Association for SQL Server. In addition to playing a key role in the only worldwide, user-run SQL Server user group endorsed by Microsoft, members enjoy unique access to a world of educational opportunities (go to *http://www.microsoft.com/traincert/mcp/mcpsecure.asp/*).

An additional benefit is received by Microsoft Certified Systems Engineers (MCSEs):

- 50 percent rebate or discount off the estimated retail price of a one-year subscription to *TechNet* or *TechNet Plus* during the first year of certification. (Fulfillment details will vary, depending on your location. Please see your Welcome Kit.) In addition, about 95 percent of the CD-ROM content is available free online at the *TechNet* Web site (*http://www.microsoft.com/technet/*).

An additional benefit is received by Microsoft Certified System Database Administrators (MCDBAs):

- 50 percent rebate or discount off the estimated retail price of a one-year subscription to *TechNet* or *TechNet Plus* during the first year of certification. (Fulfillment details will vary, depending on your location. Please see your Welcome Kit.) In addition, about 95 percent of the CD-ROM content is available free online at the *TechNet* Web site (*http://mail.microsoft.com/technet/*).

- A one-year subscription to *SQL Server Magazine*. Written by industry experts, the magazine contains technical and how-to tips and advice—a must for anyone working with SQL Server.

Microsoft Certification Benefits for Employers and Organizations

Through certification, computer professionals can maximize the return on investment in Microsoft technology. Research shows that Microsoft certification provides organizations with:

- Excellent return on training and certification investments by providing a standard method of determining training needs and measuring results.

- Increased customer satisfaction and decreased support costs through improved service, increased productivity and greater technical self-sufficiency.

- Reliable benchmark for hiring, promoting and career planning.

- Recognition and rewards for productive employees by validating their expertise.
- Retraining options for existing employees so they can work effectively with new technologies.
- Assurance of quality when outsourcing computer services.

Requirements for Becoming a Microsoft Certified Professional

The certification requirements differ for each certification and are specific to the products and job functions addressed by the certification.

To become a Microsoft Certified Professional, you must pass rigorous certification exams that provide a valid and reliable measure of technical proficiency and expertise. These exams are designed to test your expertise and ability to perform a role or task with a product, and are developed with the input of professionals in the industry. Questions in the exams reflect how Microsoft products are used in actual organizations, giving them "real-world" relevance.

- Microsoft Certified Product candidates are required to pass one operating system exam. Candidates may pass additional Microsoft certification exams to further qualify their skills with other Microsoft products, development tools, or desktop applications.
- Microsoft Certified Systems Engineers are required to pass five core exams and two elective exams. Microsoft Certified Database Administrators are required to pass three core exams and one elective exam that provide a valid and reliable measure of technical proficiency and expertise.
- Microsoft Certified Systems Administrators are required to pass three core exams and one elective exam that provide a valid and reliable measure of technical proficiency and expertise.
- Microsoft Certified Database Administrators are required to pass three core Microsoft Windows operating system technology exams and one elective that provide a valid and reliable measure of technical proficiency and expertise.
- Microsoft Certified Solution Developers are required to pass three core Microsoft Windows operating system technology exams and one elective that provide a valid and reliable measure of technical proficiency and expertise.
- Microsoft Certified Trainers are required to meet instructional and technical requirements specific to each Microsoft Official Curriculum course they are certified to deliver. The MCT program requires ongoing training to meet the requirements for the annual renewal of the certification. For more information on becoming a Microsoft Certified Trainer, visit *http://www.microsoft.com /traincert/mcp/mct/*.

Technical Support

Every effort has been made to ensure the accuracy of this book and the contents of the Supplemental Course Materials CD-ROM. If you have any comments, questions, or ideas regarding this book or the Supplemental Course Materials CD-ROM, please send them to Microsoft Press, using either of the following methods:

Microsoft Press provides corrections for books through the World Wide Web at the following address:

http://www.microsoft.com/mspress/support

To query the Technical Support Knowledge Base about a question or issue that you may have, go to:

http://www.microsoft.com/support/search.asp

E-mail:

TKINPUT@MICROSOFT.COM

Postal mail:

Microsoft Press
Attn: Microsoft Training Kit Series Editor
One Microsoft Way Redmond, WA 98052-6399

SQL Server 2000 Evaluation Edition Software Support

The SQL Server 2000 Evaluation Edition included with this book is unsupported by both Microsoft and Microsoft Press, and should not be used on a primary work computer. For online support information related to the full version of SQL Server 2000 (much of which will also apply to the Evaluation Edition), you can connect to *http://www.microsoft.com/support/*.

For information about ordering the full version of any Microsoft software, please call Microsoft Sales at (800) 936-3500 or visit *http://www.microsoft.com*. Information about issues related to the use of the SQL Server 2000 Evaluation Edition with this training kit is posted to the Support section of the Microsoft Press Web site (*http://mspress.microsoft.com/support*).

PART 1

Self-Paced Training for Microsoft SQL Server 2000 System Administration

C H A P T E R   1

Overview of SQL Server 2000

About This Chapter

This chapter introduces you to the breadth of Microsoft SQL Server 2000 and sets the framework for understanding the environments in which the SQL Server 2000 installation you are administering might be running. The details of administering SQL Server 2000 and its databases are covered in the remaining chapters of this book. This chapter discusses the various components of SQL Server 2000 and the relationships between them. It discusses the editions in which SQL Server 2000 is available. It also introduces the various ways in which SQL Server 2000 is used, as well as how SQL Server 2000 integrates with the Microsoft Windows 2000 and Windows NT 4.0 operating systems. Finally, it provides an overview of the relational database and security architecture of SQL Server 2000.

Lesson 1: What Is SQL Server 2000?

SQL Server 2000 is a family of products designed to meet the data storage requirements of large data processing systems and commercial Web sites, as well as meet
the ease-of-use requirements of individuals and small businesses. At its core, SQL
Server 2000 provides two fundamental services to the emerging Microsoft .NET
platform, as well as in the traditional two-tier client/server environment. The first
service is the SQL Server service, which is a high-performance, highly scalable
relational database engine. The second service is SQL Server 2000 Analysis Services, which provides tools for analyzing the data stored in data warehouses and
data marts for decision support.

After this lesson, you will be able to

- Describe the SQL Server 2000 environment
- Describe the SQL Server 2000 relational database engine
- Describe SQL Server 2000 Analysis Services
- Describe SQL Server 2000 application support
- Describe the various editions of SQL Server 2000 and understand their differences
- Describe how SQL Server 2000 integrates with Windows 2000 and Windows
  NT 4.0
- Describe the database and security architecture of SQL Server 2000

Estimated lesson time: 45 minutes

The SQL Server 2000 Environment

The traditional client/server database environment consists of client applications
and a relational database management system (RDBMS) that manages and stores
the data. In this traditional environment, the client applications that provide the
interface for users to access SQL Server 2000 are intelligent (or thick) clients, such
as custom-written Microsoft Visual Basic programs that access the data on SQL
Server 2000 directly using a local area network.

The emerging Microsoft .NET platform consists of highly distributed, loosely connected, programmable Web services executing on multiple servers. In this distributed, decentralized environment, the client applications are thin clients, such as
Internet browsers, which access the data on SQL Server 2000 through Web services such as Microsoft Internet Information Services (IIS).

Figure 1.1 illustrates each of these types of clients accessing SQL Server 2000.

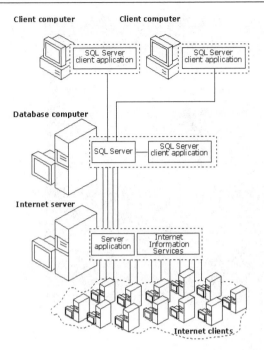

Figure 1.1.   The SQL Server 2000 environment.

SQL Server 2000 Components

SQL Server 2000 consists of numerous components. An administrator of SQL Server 2000 servers and databases must understand each of the components that comprise SQL Server 2000. Figure 1.2 illustrates the major components of SQL Server 2000 and their relationships.

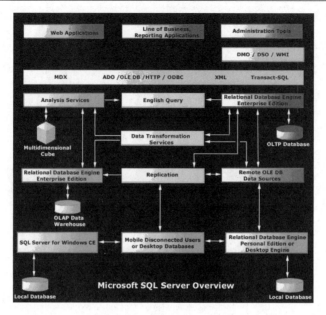

Figure 1.2.   SQL Server 2000 components.

SQL Server 2000 Relational Database Engine

The SQL Server 2000 relational database engine is an RDBMS that manages and stores data in relational tables. Each table represents some object of interest, such as customers, employees, or products. Each table has columns that represent an attribute of the object modeled by the table (such as customer number, customer name, address, and phone number), and rows that represent a single occurrence of the type of object modeled by the table (such as customer number 1374281). The relational database engine relates tables to each other when requested by an application (such as a request for a list of all customers who purchased blue trucks in 1999).

The relational database engine is designed to store detailed records of transactions generated by online transaction processing (OLTP) systems, as well as handle the online analytical processing (OLAP) requirements of data warehouses. The relational database engine is responsible for maintaining data security, providing fault tolerance, dynamically optimizing performance, using locking to provide concurrency, and ensuring data reliability.

SQL Server 2000 Analysis Services

SQL Server 2000 Analysis Services provides tools for analyzing the data stored in data warehouses and data marts on SQL Server 2000. Certain analytical processes, such as getting a summary of the monthly sales by product of all the stores in a region, take a long time if run against all the detail records of an OLTP system. To speed up these types of analytical processes, you can use SQL Server 2000 to periodically summarize and store data from an OLTP system in fact and dimension tables. This storage of summarized data for analysis is called a *data warehouse*. A subset of this data (such as for a region or a division of a company) is called a *data mart*. SQL Server 2000 Analysis Services presents the data from these fact and dimension tables as multidimensional cubes that can be analyzed for trends and other information that is important for making informed business decisions. Processing analytical queries on SQL Server 2000 Analysis Services multidimensional cubes is substantially faster than attempting the same queries on the detail data recorded in OLTP databases.

Application Support

Application developers write client applications that access SQL Server 2000 in a number of different ways.

A client application can submit Structured Query Language (SQL) statements to the relational database engine, which returns the results to the client application in the form of a tabular result set. The specific dialect of SQL supported by SQL Server 2000 is called Transact-SQL. Transact-SQL supports the Entry Level of the SQL-92 ANSI standard. Transact-SQL also supports many custom extensions, as well as some features from the Intermediate and Full Levels of SQL-92.

A client application can also submit either Transact-SQL statements or XPath queries and request that the database engine return the results in the form of an Extensible Markup Language (XML) document. XML is an emerging Internet protocol for exchanging information between systems by using self-describing data sets.

A client application can use any of the common Windows data access interfaces, such as Microsoft ActiveX Data Objects (ADO), OLE DB, or Open Database Connectivity (ODBC) to send Transact-SQL statements or XPath queries to the relational database engine using a native OLE DB provider or ODBC driver. A client application can also use Hypertext Transfer Protocol (HTTP) to send Transact-SQL statements or XPath queries to the relational database engine. A client application can also use the multidimensional extensions of either ADO or OLE DB to send Multidimensional Expressions (MDX) queries to SQL Server 2000 Analysis Services multidimensional cubes for decision support queries.

An application developer can also use any of the following administrative Application Programming Interfaces (APIs) to incorporate SQL Server 2000 administration functionality directly into a custom application to manage SQL Server 2000 and create, configure, and maintain databases, data warehouses, and data marts.

- **SQL Distributed Management Objects (SQL-DMO)**   This API is a set of Component Object Model (COM) objects that encapsulates the administration functions for all of the entities in the relational database engine and databases.
- **Decision Support Objects (DSO)**   This API is a set of COM objects that encapsulates the administration functions for all of the entities in SQL Server 2000 Analysis Services engine and multidimensional cubes.

- **Windows Management Instrumentation (WMI)**   This API is an object-oriented API that enables management applications and scripts to monitor, configure, and control the Windows operating system and devices, services, and applications in a Windows network. SQL Server 2000 provides a SQL Server 2000 WMI provider that enables WMI applications to retrieve information on SQL Server 2000 databases and instances.

Additional Components

SQL Server 2000 provides additional components to support the needs of large enterprises. As a database administrator, you will make use of the first two of these components. Application developers primarily use the last two components.

SQL Server 2000 Data Transformation Services (DTS)

You can use SQL Server 2000 Data Transformation Services (DTS) to retrieve data from one data source, perform simple or complex transformations on the data (such as summarizing data), and then store it in another data source, such as a SQL Server database or an Analysis Services multidimensional cube. DTS can work with any data source that can be accessed using OLE DB, including SQL Server, Oracle, Informix, DB2 and Microsoft Access databases, Microsoft Excel spreadsheets, and SQL Server multidimensional cubes. Using DTS, you can simplify and automate the process of building and maintaining data warehouses. You can also use DTS for the initial population of an OLTP database.

SQL Server 2000 Replication

You can use SQL Server 2000 replication to keep data close to individuals or workgroups in order to optimize performance or autonomy, while at the same time making sure that all copies of the data stored on separate computers are kept synchronized with one another. For example, a regional sales office can maintain the sales data on a local server, and replicate the sales data to a SQL Server 2000 database in the national headquarters. Mobile users using laptop computers or Windows CE devices can disconnect from the network, work throughout the day, and at the end of the day use merge replication to merge their work records back into the main database. You can also use SQL Server 2000 replication to replicate data to a data warehouse, and to replicate data to or from any data source that supports OLE DB access.

SQL Server 2000 English Query

SQL Server 2000 English Query provides a system for developing client applications that enable end users to pose questions in English instead of forming a query with a Transact-SQL statement or an XPath query. English Query can be used to access data in OLTP databases or in SQL Server 2000 Analysis Services multidimensional cubes. For example, given a car sales database, an application can send English Query a string containing the question, "How many blue trucks were sold in 1999?"

The application developer specifies database information so that English Query can process English questions about the database's particular tables, fields, objects, and data. For example, English Query must know that a question about customers is related to data in a Customers table. English Query translates a question into a Transact-SQL *SELECT* statement that is then executed against the SQL Server 2000 database to get the answer.

Meta Data Services

SQL Server 2000 Meta Data Services is a set of services that allows meta data about databases and client applications to be stored and managed. *Meta data* is information about the properties of data, such as the type of data in a column (numeric, text, and so on) or the length of a column. In a data warehouse environment, meta data can be information about the design of objects such as multidimensional cubes or dimensions, the quality and lineage of the data in the warehouse, the source and target databases, data transformations, data cleansing, data marts, and OLAP tools.

SQL Server 2000, SQL Server 2000 Analysis Services, SQL Server 2000 English Query, and Microsoft Visual Studio use Meta Data Services to store meta data, to interchange meta data with other tools, and to add versioning capability to tools that support meta data creation. Meta Data Services supports three open standards: the Meta Data Coalition Open Information Model (MDC OIM), COM interfaces, and XML encoding.

SQL Server 2000 Editions

SQL Server 2000 is available in six different editions. Four of these editions are for production systems, one edition is for application development, and one edition is for evaluation only. In addition, the SQL Server 2000 Desktop Engine component is available for distribution with applications.

SQL Server 2000 Enterprise Edition

The SQL Server 2000 Enterprise Edition supports all SQL Server 2000 features. This edition is for medium and large production database servers and scales up and out to support the performance levels required for the large Web sites, enterprise OLTP, and large data warehousing systems (OLAP).

SQL Server 2000 Standard Edition

The SQL Server 2000 Standard Edition supports many SQL Server 2000 features, but lacks the features required to scale up and out to support very large databases, data warehouses, and Web sites. This edition is for small workgroups or departments. Relational database engine features not supported on this edition are

- Failover clustering
- Failover Support in SQL Server Enterprise Manager

- Parallel CREATE INDEX
- Parallel DBCC
- Log shipping
- Enhanced read-ahead and scan
- Indexed views
- Federated Database Server
- System Area Network (SAN) Support
- Graphical utilities support for language settings

SQL Server 2000 Analysis Services features not supported on this edition are

- User-defined OLAP partitions
- Linked OLAP cubes
- Real-time OLAP
- Partition Wizard
- Relational OLAP (ROLAP) dimension support
- HTTP Internet support
- Calculated cells
- Writeback to dimensions
- Very large dimension support
- Distributed partitioned cubes

SQL Server 2000 Personal Edition

The SQL Server 2000 Personal Edition supports all of the SQL Server 2000 features supported by the SQL Server 2000 Standard Edition, except for transactional replication, which is subscriber-only supported. In addition, full-text search is not supported when this edition is installed on Windows Millennium Edition (ME) and Windows 98.

This edition is for standalone applications and mobile users requiring local data storage on a client computer. The SQL Server 2000 Personal Edition has a concurrent workload governor that limits the performance of the relational database engine when more than five batches are executed concurrently.

SQL Server 2000 Windows CE Edition

The SQL Server 2000 Windows CE Edition (SQL Server CE) is used as the data store on Windows CE devices. The memory footprint for SQL Server CE is approximately 1 MB. SQL Server CE is implemented as a set of dynamic-link libraries (DLLs) that operate as an OLE DB CE provider. This implementation allows SQL Server CE to support the ActiveX Data Objects for Windows CE (ADOCE) and OLE DB CE APIs in the Windows CE–based versions of Visual

Basic and Microsoft Visual C++. Also, it means that multiple applications running at the same time can share a common set of DLLs and save space.

Windows CE devices connected to the network can use the Remote Data Access (RDA) feature of SQL Server CE to

- Connect to instances of SQL Server 2000 on other Windows platforms
- Execute a SQL statement and pull in the result set as a recordset
- Modify a recordset and push the modifications back to an instance of SQL Server 2000 on another Windows platform
- Subscribe to merge replication as an anonymous subscriber to keep Windows CE data synchronized with a primary database

The SQL Server CE connectivity options are well suited for use on wireless networks through networking features such as data compression and messaging to reduce data transmissions, and robust recovery from lost connections.

SQL Server 2000 Developer Edition

The SQL Server 2000 Developer Edition supports all of the SQL Server 2000 features, other than graphical utilities support for language settings. This edition is for programmers developing applications that use SQL Server 2000 as their data store. This edition is licensed for use only as a development and test system, not a production server.

SQL Server 2000 Enterprise Evaluation Edition

The SQL Server 2000 Enterprise Evaluation Edition is a full-featured version available by a free download from the Web. This edition is for use in evaluating the features of SQL Server 2000 and will stop running 120 days after downloading. Support for language settings in SQL Server graphical tools is not available in the Evaluation Edition.

SQL Server 2000 Desktop Engine

The SQL Server 2000 Desktop Engine is a redistributable version of the SQL Server 2000 relational database engine. This edition is for applications to use to store data without requiring any database administration from the end user. The Desktop Engine is designed to manage its configuration and resource usage dynamically, minimizing the requirement for administration of the engine after it has been installed. The Desktop Engine does not include any of the SQL Server 2000 utilities or tools that have graphical user interfaces. Standard SQL Server 2000 APIs must be used to create and configure the database, and the application must use the SQL Server 2000 APIs to perform any needed administration.

The Desktop Engine supports the same relational database engine and replication features as the Personal Edition, other than full-text search and the graphical administration and developer tools and wizards. However, the Desktop Engine does not support SQL Server 2000 Analysis Services. The size of Desktop Engine databases cannot exceed 2 GB and the Desktop Engine has a concurrent workload governor that limits the performance of the database engine when more than five batches are executed concurrently.

Installing SQL Server Editions on Various Windows Operating Systems

Table 1.1 sets forth the operating system platforms on which each SQL Server edition may be installed.

Table 1-1.   Operating Systems Supported by SQL Server Editions

Operating System	Enterprise	Standard	Personal	Enterprise Evaluation	Desktop Engine	Developer	Windows CE
Windows 2000 Data Center	Supported	Supported	Supported	Supported	Supported	Supported	N/A
Windows 2000 Advanced Server	Supported	Supported	Supported	Supported	Supported	Supported	N/A
Windows 2000 Server	Supported	Supported	Supported	Supported	Supported	Supported	N/A
Windows 2000 Professional	N/A	N/A	Supported	Supported	Supported	Supported	N/A
Windows NT 4.0 Server, Enterprise Edition	Supported	Supported	Supported	Supported	Supported	Supported	N/A
Windows NT 4.0 Server	Supported	Supported	Supported	Supported	Supported	Supported	N/A
Windows NT 4.0 Workstation	N/A	N/A	Supported	Supported	Supported	Supported	N/A
Windows Millennium Edition	N/A	N/A	Supported	N/A	Supported	N/A	N/A
Windows 98	N/A	N/A	Supported	N/A	Supported	N/A	N/A
Windows CE	N/A	N/A	N/A	N/A	N/A	N/A	Supported

Integration with Windows 2000 and Windows NT 4.0

When an instance of SQL Server 2000 is running on any version of Windows 2000 or Windows NT 4.0, the following features and capabilities of these operating systems are leveraged and integrated.

Windows Authentication

An instance of SQL Server 2000 running on Windows 2000 or Windows NT 4.0 can use Windows authentication and allow the operating system to control access to SQL Server 2000 using only trusted connections. In this environment, a user can connect to an instance of SQL Server 2000 without providing additional authentication credentials to SQL Server 2000 if that user has successfully logged on to the Windows operating system by using a valid Windows 2000 or Windows NT 4.0 user account. Allowing the operating system to handle authentication provides additional security, including the use of Kerberos authentication.

Memory Management

An instance of SQL Server 2000 running on Windows 2000 or Windows NT 4.0 dynamically uses available physical memory as a data buffer to minimize disk I/O and maximize performance. Each instance of SQL Server 2000 coordinates with Windows 2000 or Windows NT 4.0 to dynamically acquire and release memory as needed by instances of SQL Server 2000 and other server applications running on the same computer.

SQL Server 2000 Enterprise Edition uses the Microsoft Windows 2000 Address Windowing Extensions (AWE) API to support memory up to 64 GB of RAM on Windows 2000 Data Center and up to 8 GB on Windows 2000 Advanced Server. This allows instances of SQL Server 2000 Enterprise Edition to cache large numbers of rows in memory, which reduces overhead and speeds the processing of queries.

Active Directory

When SQL Server 2000 is installed on a Windows 2000 Server computer where Active Directory directory services are available, you can publish information about SQL Server 2000 in Active Directory. This information can include information about names and locations of SQL Server 2000 systems and their database names, locations, sizes, and most recent backup dates. Replication publications can also be published. In addition, with SQL Server 2000 Analysis Services, you can publish information about available data warehouses and data marts. Client applications can be coded to search Active Directory for information that has been published.

Additionally, security account delegation is supported on an instance of SQL Server 2000 installed on a Windows 2000 computer where Active Directory directory services and Kerberos authentication are available. Security account delegation is the ability to connect to multiple servers, and with each server change, to retain the authentication credentials of the original client.

An instance of SQL Server 2000 running on Windows 2000 or Windows NT 4.0 leverages the security and encryption facilities of these operating systems to implement secure data storage. This includes the option to enable the use of Secure Sockets Layer (SSL) to encrypt all data between client applications and SQL Server 2000.

Failover Clustering

An instance of SQL Server 2000 Enterprise Edition running on Windows 2000 or Windows NT 4.0 supports failover clustering to provide immediate failover to a backup server with no disruption in operation. Windows 2000 Data Center supports up to four failover nodes.

Microsoft Distributed Transaction Coordinator

An instance of SQL Server 2000 running on Windows 2000 or Windows NT 4.0 integrates with Microsoft Distributed Transaction Coordinator (MS DTC) to provide support for distributed transactions. MS DTC allows applications to extend transactions across two or more instances of SQL Server 2000 either on the same computer or across different computers.

SMP

An instance of SQL Server 2000 running on Microsoft Windows 2000 Data Center can scale effectively on up to 32 processors, and on Windows 2000 Advanced Server can scale effectively on up to 8 processors on symmetric multiprocessor (SMP) computers.

Asynchronous and Scatter-gather I/O

An instance of SQL Server 2000 running on Windows 2000 or Windows NT 4.0 takes advantage of asynchronous I/O and scatter-gather I/O to maximize throughput to support many concurrent users. Scatter-gather I/O allows a read or a write to transfer data into or out of discontiguous areas of memory. Asynchronous I/O allows instances of SQL Server 2000 to maximize the work done by individual threads while processing a batch. The scatter-gather I/O algorithm has been significantly improved on Windows 2000. In addition, SQL Server 2000 on Windows 2000 can benefit from the use of Intelligent Input/Output (I2O) hardware to offload I/O from the system processors to a dedicated processor.

Event Logs

Instances of SQL Server 2000 running on Windows 2000 or Windows NT 4.0 use event logs to record significant system, application, and security events related to SQL Server 2000.

System Monitor Counters

Instances of SQL Server 2000 running on Windows 2000 or Windows NT 4.0 provide objects and counters that can be used by System Monitor (Performance Monitor in Microsoft Windows NT 4.0), SQL Server Enterprise Manager, and SQL Server Agent to monitor SQL Server 2000 activity.

Lesson Summary

SQL Server 2000 is a relational database management system providing services to OLTP and OLAP environments. SQL Server 2000 is available in a number of different editions to meet the needs of a variety of users and environments, and can be installed on a variety of Windows operating system platforms. It is tightly integrated with Windows 2000 and Windows NT 4.0 to fully leverage their capabilities and maximize the performance of SQL Server 2000.

Lesson 2: What Are the SQL Server 2000 Components?

SQL Server 2000 provides a number of different types of components. At the core are server components. These server components are generally implemented as 32-bit Windows services. SQL Server 2000 provides client-based graphical tools and command-prompt utilities for administration. These tools and utilities, as well as all other client applications, use client communication components provided by SQL Server 2000. The communication components provide various ways in which client applications can access data through communication with the server components. These communication components are implemented as providers, drivers, database interfaces, and Net-Libraries. An additional component is SQL Server 2000 Books Online, which is implemented as Hypertext Markup Language (HTML) pages.

After this lesson, you will be able to

- Describe the SQL Server 2000 server components, how they are implemented, and their function
- Describe the various SQL Server 2000 administrative tools and their function
- Describe SQL Server 2000 client communication components and how they are implemented
- Describe SQL Server 2000 Books Online

Estimated lesson time: 30 minutes

Server Components

The server components of SQL Server 2000 are normally implemented as 32-bit Windows services. The SQL Server and SQL Server Agent services may also be run as standalone applications on any supported Windows operating system platform.

Table 1.2 lists the server components and briefly describes their function. It also specifies how the component is implemented when multiple instances are used. Multiple instances are covered in more detail in Chapter 2.

Table 1-2.   Server Components and Their Functions

Server Component	Description
SQL Server service	MSSQLServer service implements the SQL Server 2000 database engine. There is one service for each instance of SQL Server 2000.
Microsoft SQL Server 2000 Analysis Services service	MSSQLServerOLAPService implements SQL Server 2000 Analysis Services. There is only one service, regardless of the number of instances of SQL Server 2000.
SQL Server Agent service	SQLServerAgent service implements the agent that runs scheduled SQL Server 2000 administrative tasks. There is one service for each instance of SQL Server 2000.
Microsoft Search service	Microsoft Search implements the full-text search engine. There is only one service, regardless of the number of instances of SQL Server 2000.
Microsoft (MS DTC) service	Distributed Transaction Coordinator manages distributed transactions between instances of SQL Server 2000. There is only one service, regardless of the number of instances of SQL Server 2000.

Note   The SQL Server and SQL Server Agent services must be run as applications on Windows Millennium Edition and Windows 98. The Microsoft Search service and the MS DTC service do not run on Windows Millennium Edition or Windows 98.

Client-Based Administration Tools and Utilities

The SQL Server 2000 administration tools and utilities are implemented as clients, meaning that they must establish a local or network connection to SQL Server 2000 using client communication components.

Graphical Tools

Table 1.3 lists the 32-bit graphical tools provided by SQL Server 2000 and briefly describes their function.

Table 1-3.   Graphical Tools in SQL Server 2000

Graphical Tool	Description
SQL Server Enterprise Manager	The primary server and database administration tool, it provides a Microsoft Management Console (MMC) snap-in user interface.
SQL Query Analyzer	Used for creating and managing database objects and testing Transact-SQL statements, batches, and scripts interactively.
SQL Profiler	Used to monitor and capture selected SQL Server 2000 events for analysis and replay. Supports C2 security-level auditing.
SQL Server Service Manager	A taskbar application used to start, stop, pause, or modify SQL Server 2000 services.

Table 1-3.   Graphical Tools in SQL Server 2000   (continued)

Graphical Tool	Description
Client Network Utility	Used to manage the client Net-Libraries and define server aliases containing custom server connection parameters, if needed.
Server Network Utility	Used to manage the server Net-Libraries, including enabling SSL encryption.

Command-Prompt Utilities

Table 1.4 lists the most frequently used command-prompt utilities provided by SQL Server 2000 and briefly describes their function.

Client Communication Components

Users access SQL Server 2000 through client applications. SQL Server 2000 supports two main types of client applications. The first type is relational database applications, which are the more traditional type of client applications used in two-tier client/server environments. These client applications send Transact-SQL statements to the relational database engine and receive results as relational result sets.

The second type is Internet applications, which are part of the emerging Microsoft .NET platform. These client applications send either Transact-SQL statements or XPath queries to the relational database engine and receive XML documents in return.

Table 1-4.   Command-Prompt Utilities in SQL Server 2000

Command-Prompt Utility	Description
Osql	This utility allows you to query an instance of SQL Server 2000 interactively using Transact-SQL statements, system procedures, and script files. This utility replaces Isql, which was used with editions of SQL Server before SQL Server 7.0.
Scm	This utility (Service Control Manager) is used to start, stop, pause, install, delete, or modify SQL Server 2000 services. It also can start, stop, or pause SQL Server running as an application.
Sqldiag	This utility gathers and stores diagnostic information to expedite and simplify information gathering by Microsoft Product Support Services.
Bcp	This utility copies data between an instance of SQL Server 2000 and a data file in a user-specified format.
Dtsrun	This utility executes packages created using DTS.
Sqlmaint	This utility performs a specified set of maintenance operations on one or more databases. These include performing DBCC consistency checks, backing up data and transaction log files, updating distribution statistics, and rebuilding indexes.

Each of these types of client applications connects to SQL Server 2000 in different ways. It is important for you, as the database administrator, to have a basic understanding of how client applications access SQL Server databases. Certain configuration tasks are related to client communication components that you choose during installation or configure after installation. These tasks are covered in Chapter 2 and Chapter 12.

Relational Database Application Programming Interfaces

Relational database applications access SQL Server 2000 through a database API. A database API defines how to code an application to connect to an instance of SQL Server 2000 and pass commands to a SQL Server 2000 database. SQL Server 2000 provides native support for two main classes of database APIs, OLE DB and ODBC.

OLE DB is an API that allows COM applications to consume data from OLE DB data sources. SQL Server 2000 includes a native OLE DB provider. An OLE DB provider is a COM component that accepts calls to the OLE DB API and does whatever is necessary to process that request against the data source. The provider supports applications written using OLE DB, or other APIs that use OLE DB, such as ADO.

ODBC is a Call-Level Interface (CLI) that allows C and C++ applications to access data from ODBC data sources. SQL Server 2000 includes a native ODBC driver. An ODBC driver is a DLL that accepts calls to the ODBC API functions and does whatever is necessary to process that request against the data source. The driver supports applications or components written using ODBC, or other APIs using ODBC, such as Data Access Objects (DAO), Remote Data Objects (RDO), and the Microsoft Foundation Classes (MFC) database classes. ADO is generally replacing DAO and RDO.

SQL Server 2000 also supports the DB-Library (for backward compatibility only) and Embedded SQL APIs.

Net-Libraries

The OLE DB provider or ODBC driver uses a client Net-Library to communicate with a server Net-Library on an instance of SQL Server 2000. The communication can be on the same computer or across a network. Net-Libraries encapsulate requests between clients and servers for the transmission using the underlying network protocol. The communication between client and server Net-Libraries can be encrypted using the Secure Sockets Layer (SSL). SQL Server 2000 clients and a SQL Server 2000 server can be configured to use any or all of the Net-Libraries listed in Table 1.5.

Table 1-5.   Net-Libraries Employable with SQL Server 2000

Net-Library	Description
Shared memory	Used to connect to SQL Server 2000 on the same computer using a segment of memory. This is one of the default protocols for SQL Server 2000.
Named pipes	Used to connect to SQL Server 2000 using named pipes. A pipe is a file-system mechanism used for communication between processes. This is one of the default protocols for SQL Server 2000.
TCP/IP Sockets	Used to connect to SQL Server 2000 using TCP/IP. This is one of the default protocols for SQL Server 2000.
NWLink IPX/SPX	Used in the Novell network environment, primarily legacy Novell environments that do not support TCP/IP.
VIA GigaNet SAN	Used to support the new, high-speed SAN technology on GigaNet's cLAN server farm network.
Multiprotocol	Supports any available communication method between servers using Windows NT RPCs over any available network protocol. In earlier versions of SQL Server, this Net-Library was required to enable encryption and support Windows authentication. Today, it is mainly used for backward compatibility.
AppleTalk ADSP	Used in the Macintosh and Apple network environment. ADSP enables Apple Macintosh clients to connect to SQL Server 2000 using native AppleTalk.
Banyan VINES	Used in the Banyan VINES network environment. This protocol runs at the SQL Server 7.0 level of funtionality for clients and servers running Windows NT 4.0 and will not be further enhanced.

Open Data Services

Server Net-Libraries communicate with the Open Data Services layer of the relational database engine, which is the interface between the relational database engine and the server Net-Libraries. Open Data Services transforms packets received from server Net-Libraries into events that it passes to the appropriate part of the relational database engine. The relational database engine then uses Open Data Services to send replies back to SQL Server 2000 clients through the server Net-Libraries.

Client–Server Communication

Figure 1.3 shows the client communication components when the client application and the instance of SQL Server are on the same computer.

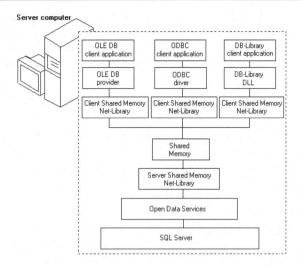

Figure 1.3.   SQL Server on the same computer as the client application.

Figure 1.4 shows a simplified version of the client communication components when the client application and the instance of SQL Server are on separate computers.

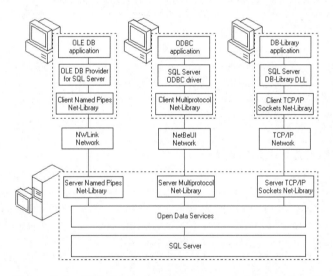

Figure 1.4.   SQL Server on a separate computer from the client application.

Internet Applications

Internet applications access SQL Server 2000 by means of a virtual root defined on an IIS server that points to an instance of SQL Server 2000. SQL Server 2000 provides an ISAPI DLL (sqlisapi.dll) that makes this possible. These applications can use a Uniform Resource Locator (URL), the ADO API, or the OLE DB API for executing XPath queries or Transact-SQL statements.

When the IIS server receives an XPath query or Transact-SQL statement, the IIS server loads the ISAPI DLL. The ISAPI DLL uses the OLE DB Provider for SQL Server (SQLOLEDB) to connect to the instance of SQL Server 2000 specified in the virtual root and pass the XPath query or Transact-SQL statement to SQL Server.

SQL Server Books Online

SQL Server Books Online is the online documentation provided with SQL Server 2000 and is implemented as HTML pages. SQL Server Books Online provides numerous methods of finding information. You can navigate through SQL Server Books Online by

- Using the contents pane
- Typing a keyword in the index
- Typing a word or phrase in the search engine
- Clicking the Help button in any of the graphical tools to bring up related information
- Pressing F1 in dialog boxes and interface elements to bring up related information
- Selecting a Transact-SQL statement, function, stored procedure, or other Transact-SQL element in SQL Query Analyzer and pressing SHIFT+F1 to view information about the selected text

---

Note   In addition to the default subsets of SQL Server Books Online provided with SQL Server 2000, you can also define custom subsets of the entire SQL Server Books Online against which to perform searches. To create a custom subset, click Define Subset on the View menu.

Lesson Summary

SQL Server 2000 has a number of server components that are normally implemented as services on Windows 2000 and Windows NT 4.0. SQL Server 2000 provides a plethora of client-based graphical and command-prompt tools and utilities to perform administration tasks. These administrative tools and utilities, as well as all other client applications, use a number of different client communication components to establish a local or a network connection to SQL Server 2000.

Lesson 3: What Is the Relational Database Architecture?

SQL Server 2000 data is stored in databases. Physically, a database consists of two or more files on one or more disks. This physical implementation is visible only to database administrators, and is transparent to users. The physical optimization of the database is primarily the responsibility of the database administrator. This topic is discussed in Chapter 6.

Logically, a database is structured into components that are visible to users, such as tables, views, and stored procedures. The logical optimization of the database (such as the design of tables and indexes) is primarily the responsibility of the database designer. The topic of logical optimization is beyond the scope of this book but is covered in *Designing Relational Database Systems* (Microsoft Press, 1999, ISBN 0-7356-0634-X) by Rebecca M. Riordan.

After this lesson, you will be able to

- Describe the SQL Server 2000 system databases
- Describe the SQL Server 2000 physical database architecture
- Describe the SQL Server 2000 logical database architecture

Estimated lesson time: 15 minutes

System and User Databases

Each instance of SQL Server 2000 has four system databases. Table 1.6 lists each of these system databases and briefly describes their function.

Table 1-6.   System Databases in SQL Server 2000

System Database	Description
master	Records all of the system-level information for a SQL Server 2000 system, including all other databases, login accounts, and system configuration settings.
tempdb	Stores all temporary tables and stored procedures created by users, as well as temporary worktables used by the relational database engine itself.
model	Serves as the template that is used whenever a new database is created.
msdb	SQL Server Agent uses this system database for scheduling alerts and jobs, and recording operators.

In addition, each instance of SQL Server 2000 has one or more user databases. The pubs and Northwind user databases are sample databases that ship with SQL Server 2000. Given sufficient system resources, each instance of SQL Server 2000 can handle thousands of users working in multiple databases simultaneously. See Figure 1.5.

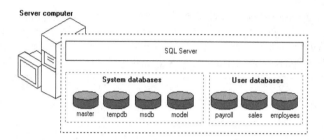

Figure 1.5.   SQL Server working with multiple user databases.

Physical Structure of a Database

Each database consists of at least one data file and one transaction log file. These files are not shared with any other database. To optimize performance and to provide fault tolerance, data and log files are typically spread across multiple drives and frequently use a redundant array of independent disks (RAID).

Extents and Pages

SQL Server 2000 allocates space from a data file for tables and indexes in 64-KB blocks called extents. Each extent consists of eight contiguous pages of 8 KB each. There are two types of extents: uniform extents that are owned by a single object, and mixed extents that are shared by up to eight objects.

A page is the fundamental unit of data storage in SQL Server 2000, with the page size being 8 KB. In general, data pages store data in rows on each data page. The maximum amount of data contained in a single row is 8060 bytes. Data rows are either organized in some kind of order based on a key in a clustered index (such as zip code), or stored in no particular order if no clustered index exists. The beginning of each page contains a 96-byte header that is used to store system information, such as the amount of free space available on the page.

Transaction Log Files

The transaction log file resides in one or more separate physical files from the data files and contains a series of log records, rather than pages allocated from extents. To optimize performance and aid in redundancy, transaction log files are typically placed on separate disks from data files, and are frequently mirrored using RAID.

Logical Structure of a Database

Data in SQL Server 2000 is organized into database objects that are visible to users when they connect to a database. Table 1.7 lists these objects and briefly describes their function.

Table 1-7.   Database Objects in SQL Server 2000

Database Object	Description
Tables	A table generally consists of columns and rows of data in a format similar to that of a spreadsheet. Each row in the table represents a unique record, and each column represents a field within the record. A data type specifies what type of data can be stored in a column.
Views	Views can restrict the rows or the columns of a table that are visible, or can combine data from multiple tables to appear like a single table. A view can also aggregate columns.
Indexes	An index is a structure associated with a table or view that speeds retrieval of rows from the table or view. Table indexes are either clustered or nonclustered. Clustering means the data is physically ordered based on the index key.
Keys	A key is a column or group of columns that uniquely identifies a row (PRIMARY KEY), defines the relationship between two tables (FOREIGN KEY), or is used to build an index.
User-defined data types	A user-defined data type is a custom data type, based on a pre-defined SQL Server 2000 data type. It is used to make a table structure more meaningful to programmers and help ensure that columns holding similar classes of data have the same base data type.
Stored procedures	A stored procedure is a group of Transact-SQL statements compiled into a single execution plan. The procedure is used for performance optimization and to control access.
Constraints	Constraints define rules regarding the values allowed in columns and are the standard mechanism for enforcing data integrity.
Defaults	A default specifies what values are used in a column in the event that you do not specify a value for the column when you are inserting a row.
Triggers	A trigger is a special class of stored procedure defined to execute automatically when an *UPDATE*, *INSERT*, or *DELETE* statement is issued against a table or view.
User-defined functions	A user-defined function is a subroutine made up of one or more Transact-SQL statements used to encapsulate code for reuse. A function can have a maximum of 1024 input parameters. User-defined functions can be used in place of views and stored procedures.

Optimizing Logical Database Design

The logical design of the database, including the tables and the relationships between them, is the core of an optimized relational database. Optimizing logical database design begins with a normalized database design. *Normalization* is the process of removing redundancies from the data. Normalization often involves breaking data from a single file into two or more logical tables in a relational database. For example, you can place customer detail information in one table and place order information in another table, and then relate the two tables based on a customer number. Transact-SQL queries can then recombine the table data by using relational join operations, when needed. By avoiding the need to update the same data in multiple places, normalization improves the efficiency of a client application and reduces the opportunities for introducing errors due to inconsistent data. Some of the benefits of normalization include

- Faster sorting and index creation
- A larger number of clustered indexes
- Narrower and more compact indexes
- Fewer indexes per table, which improves the performance of *INSERT*, *UPDATE*, and *DELETE* statements
- Fewer null values and less opportunity for inconsistency, which increase database compactness

However, there are tradeoffs to normalization. A database that is used primarily for decision support (as opposed to update-intensive transaction processing) might not have redundant updates and might be more understandable and efficient for queries if the design is not fully normalized. Nevertheless, data that is not normalized is a more common design problem in database applications than overnormalized data.

Database administrators can detect problems caused by poor database design and must work with database designers, and sometimes client and server application designers, to optimize the overall performance of a database on an instance of SQL Server 2000. Performance monitoring is discussed in Chapter 14.

Lesson Summary

SQL Server consists of system and user databases that are organized physically into data and log files for each database that are placed on one or more disks. SQL Server is organized logically into objects, such as tables, indexes, and views. Database administrators optimize the physical design and database designers optimize the logical design of databases.

Lesson 4: What Is the Security Architecture?

SQL Server 2000 uses two levels of security when validating a user. The first level of security is authentication. Authentication determines whether the user has a valid login account to connect to an instance of SQL Server 2000. The second level of security is authorization, which is also called permission validation. Authorization determines what activities the user can perform in which databases after being authenticated by SQL Server 2000. Security is discussed in Chapters 10 and 11.

After this lesson, you will be able to
- Describe the SQL Server 2000 authentication process
- Describe the SQL Server 2000 authorization process
- Describe the types of SQL Server 2000 logins, and when each is used

Estimated lesson time: 15 minutes

Authentication

A user cannot connect to an instance of SQL Server 2000 without first specifying a valid login identifier (ID). A login ID is the account identifier that controls access to an instance of SQL Server 2000. Instances of SQL Server must verify that the login ID supplied on each connection request is authorized to access the instance. Verification of the login ID is called authentication. SQL Server 2000 uses two types of authentication: Windows authentication and SQL Server authentication. When a user attempts to connect to SQL Server 2000, the user specifies the type of authentication the connection is requesting.

Windows Authentication

A database administrator can grant permission to connect to an instance of SQL Server 2000 to Windows 2000 and Windows NT 4.0 users and groups. If an attempted connection specifies Windows authentication, SQL Server 2000 uses Windows-based facilities to determine the validated network user name. SQL Server verifies the user's identity, and then permits or denies login access based on that network user name alone, without requiring a separate login name and password. This is called a trusted connection.

Windows authentication leverages the Windows 2000 and Windows NT 4.0 security system, including such features as secure validation and encryption of passwords, auditing, password expiration, minimum password length, and account lockout after multiple invalid login requests.

SQL Server Authentication

A database administrator can create SQL Server login accounts and passwords. These accounts are completely independent of any Windows 2000 or Windows NT 4.0 user account or group. If an attempted connection specifies SQL Server authentication, SQL Server 2000 performs the authentication itself by checking to see whether the SQL Server login account specified exists and whether the specified password matches the one previously recorded in SQL Server 2000.

Note   SQL Server authentication is required on instances of SQL Server 2000 installed on Windows Millennium Edition and Windows 98, and for connections by clients not being validated by Windows 2000 and Windows NT 4.0.

Authentication Modes

SQL Server 2000 can operate in two authentication modes. The default authentication mode is Windows Authentication Mode. When SQL Server 2000 is operating in this mode, a user can connect to SQL Server 2000 only with a previously authenticated Windows 2000 or Windows NT 4.0 user account. SQL Server 2000 can also operate in Mixed Mode. When SQL Server 2000 is operating in this mode, a user can connect to SQL Server 2000 with either a previously authenticated Windows 2000 or Windows NT 4.0 user account, or with a valid SQL Server login account and password. Figure 1.6 illustrates the SQL Server 2000 security decision tree.

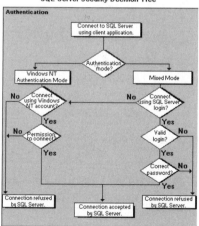

Figure 1.6.   SQL Server 2000 security decision tree.

Authorization

Once SQL Server 2000 authenticates a user, SQL Server 2000 determines whether that login ID has been authorized to perform any activities in any databases. A login ID by itself does not give a user permission to access objects in a database. It only allows a user to proceed to the next step, which is authorization or permission validation. This prevents a login from automatically accessing all databases on an instance of SQL Server 2000.

User Accounts

In general, a database administrator must associate a login ID with a user ID in a database before anyone connecting with that login ID can access objects and perform activities in that database. A database administrator applies security permissions for the objects (for example, tables, views, and stored procedures) in a database to user accounts. See Figure 1.7.

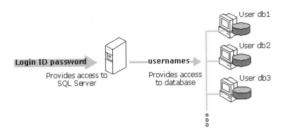

Figure 1.7.   SQL Server database access security.

Guest User Account

If a login ID has not been explicitly associated with any user ID in a database, it is associated with the guest user ID in that database, if one exists. If a database has a guest user account, the login is limited to those rights granted to the guest user. If a database has no guest user account, a login cannot access the database unless it has been associated with a valid user account. By default, all newly created user databases have no guest user account.

Roles

A database administrator uses roles to collect users into a single unit against which to set permissions. Roles are used in much the same way as Windows 2000 and Windows NT 4.0 groups. SQL Server 2000 provides fixed server roles and fixed database roles with predefined server-wide or database-specific permissions. A database administrator can also create custom user-defined database roles.

Every user in a database belongs to the public database role and has whatever permissions have been assigned to the public role, unless the user has been specifically denied certain permissions. Additional rights must be granted explicitly to the user or to a group to which the user belongs.

Lesson Summary

SQL Server uses two levels of security. The first level of security is *authentication*, which controls access to SQL Server through login IDs. Two types of authentication may be used: Windows authentication and SQL Server authentication. The second level of security is *authorization*, which controls access to each database. Login IDs are mapped to user IDs in each database. These user IDs are granted permissions to objects at the database level.

Review

Here are some questions to help you determine whether you have learned enough to move on to the next chapter. If you have difficulty answering these questions, review the material in this chapter before beginning the next chapter. The answers for these questions are located in the Appendix, "Questions and Answers."

1. You are planning to deploy SQL Server 2000 to support Internet-based sales of your products. You need this installation to handle a large volume of transactions and be available 24 X 7. Which edition of SQL Server 2000 should you choose?

2. You want to allow users to query SQL Server 2000 using their Internet browser via the Internet. What components of SQL Server 2000 are required?

3. The SQL Server 2000 database environment has a physical design component and a logical design component. As a database administrator, one of your tasks is to optimize the performance of SQL Server 2000. With respect to which type of database design do you have the most ability to affect performance?

4. You have an existing server application that uses SQL Server 2000 running on Windows 2000 servers. You have clients who access this server application using Windows 95 and Windows 98 client applications. You want to extend this server application to clients using an existing Novell network. What type of authentication decisions must you make?

C H A P T E R   2

Installing SQL Server 2000

About This Chapter

This chapter prepares you to install SQL Server 2000. This includes determining the computer hardware on which you will install SQL Server; determining which SQL Server 2000 setup configuration options to select; and learning how to perform interactive, remote, and unattended installations of default, named, and multiple instances of SQL Server 2000. It also provides you with assistance in troubleshooting SQL Server 2000 installation problems.

Before You Begin

To complete this chapter, you must have

- A computer that meets or exceeds the minimum hardware requirements listed in Table 2.1, "Hardware Requirements," in Lesson 1 of this chapter.

- Microsoft Windows 2000 Server running on your computer on an NTFS partition.
- A computer with a NetBIOS name of SelfPacedCPU, configured as a domain controller in the SelfPacedSQL.MSFT domain.
- At least 400 MB of unused hard disk space available on your computer.

Lesson 1: Planning to Install SQL Server 2000

Once you have decided to install SQL Server 2000, you need to select the appropriate computer hardware for your SQL Server 2000 installation. It is important to understand the minimum hardware requirements for each of the SQL Server 2000 editions on each supported Windows operating system edition. You must recognize, however, that these minimum hardware requirements will be insufficient in many production environments to meet either actual current or anticipated future SQL Server requirements. This knowledge will assist you in selecting appropriate computer hardware to optimize SQL Server 2000 performance to meet current needs, as well as to help eliminate costly computer upgrade decisions later.

After this lesson, you will be able to

- Describe the minimum hardware requirements for the installation of each of the SQL Server 2000 editions on each supported Windows operating system edition

- Determine which hardware resources are likely to be insufficient to meet the current and anticipated future needs of your SQL Server 2000 environment

Estimated lesson time: 15 minutes

What Is the Minimum Hardware Required?

In most SQL Server 2000 production environments, actual hardware requirements will exceed the minimum hardware requirements. However, it is still important to understand these minimum hardware requirements as a baseline. In addition, in some SQL Server 2000 desktop environments, meeting the minimum hardware requirements will be sufficient to meet the needs of these environments. Table 2.1 lists the minimum hardware requirements that are common among all SQL Server editions (other than the Windows CE edition) regardless of the Windows operating system used.

Table 2-1.   Hardware Requirements

Resource	Requirement
Computer	Intel or compatible
Processor	Pentium 166
Display	800 X 600 for SQL Server 2000 graphical tools 640 x 480 if SQL Server 2000 graphical tools are not used
Pointing Device	Microsoft Mouse or compatible
Network Card	Optional (but required for network access)
CD-ROM	Required if installing from compact disc (otherwise optional)

The minimum amount of memory required varies depending upon the SQL Server 2000 edition and the Windows operating system edition used. Table 2.2 lists the recommended minimum memory requirements based on the SQL Server edition and the Windows operating system edition used.

Table 2-2.   Recommended Minimum Memory Requirements for SQL Server

	Enterprise Edition	Standard Edition	Evaluation Edition	Developer Editions	Personal and Desktop Engine Editions
Any edition of Windows 2000 Server	256 MB (128 MB supported)	256 MB (128 MB supported)	256 MB (128 MB supported)	256 MB (128 MB supported)	256 MB (128 MB supported)
Any edition of Windows NT 4.0 Server with Service Pack5 (SP5) or later	128 MB (64 MB supported)	64 MB	128 MB recommended (64 MB supported)	64 MB	32 MB
Windows 2000 Professional	N/A	N/A	128 MB recommended (64 MB supported)	64 MB	64 MB
Windows NT 4.0 Workstation, with SP5 or later	N/A	N/A	128 MB recommended (64 MB supported)	64 MB	32 MB
Windows ME	N/A	N/A	N/A	N/A	32 MB
Windows 98	N/A	N/A	N/A	N/A	32 MB

Note   Microsoft Internet Explorer 5.0 or later is also required for all operating systems.

The amount of hard drive space required for an installation of any edition of SQL Server 2000 on any Windows operating system depends upon the installation options selected during setup. If you are upgrading from an earlier version of SQL Server, additional space will be required to update the existing user databases. Chapter 4 of this book covers the upgrading of earlier versions of SQL Server to SQL Server 2000.

Table 2.3 lists the amount of hard drive space required for the installation of various SQL Server 2000 components. These numbers assume that SQL Server must install all software required. Frequently, some of the required software, such as Microsoft Data Access Components (MDAC) 2.6, is already installed. In these cases, less actual hard drive space might be required. However, even if less actual hard drive space is required, SQL Server 2000 setup will still enforce the hard drive space requirements set forth in Table 2.3 and will require you to have at least this much free hard drive space in order to successfully complete the installation of SQL Server 2000.

Table 2-3.   Hard Drive Space Requirements for SQL Server 2000

Installation Option Selected	Hard Drive Space Required
Server and client tools	95–270 MB depending on the installation options selected
Typical installation	250 MB (178 MB on the system drive, plus 72 MB for program and data files)
Minimum installation	110 MB (73 MB on the system drive, plus 37 MB for program and data files)
Management tools	113 MB (system drive only)
Books Online	30 MB (system drive only)
Analysis Services	47 MB minimum 120 MB typical
English Query	80 MB
Desktop Engine only	44 MB

When selecting the computer hardware to use for your SQL Server 2000 installation, check the Microsoft Hardware Compatibility List (HCL). SQL Server 2000 does not have its own HCL. SQL Server 2000 will run on any hardware that is certified for the Windows operating system upon which you plan to install SQL Server 2000. To obtain the most recent HCL, go to *www.microsoft.com/hcl*. If the computer hardware used for your SQL Server 2000 installation is not on the HCL, you risk the integrity of your data (and possibly your job). Isolating and solving problems related to computer hardware and device driver failures is far easier with name-brand systems than it is with systems put together piece by piece. Any money saved through the purchase of cheap computer hardware on the front end will probably be spent many times over on the back end in resolving problems relating to computer hardware and device driver failures.

Exceeding Minimum Computer Hardware Requirements

So far, we have talked about meeting the minimum hardware requirements for various SQL Server 2000 editions and Windows operating systems editions. In most production SQL Server 2000 database environments, your computer hardware will be considerably in excess of these requirements. Even if you do not exceed these minimum hardware requirements immediately, as your databases grow, you will exceed them. It is important to understand areas in which your computer hardware will need to be more robust.

Table 2.4 describes the four primary areas in which you will probably exceed these minimum hardware requirements. Chapter 14 covers how to determine when your SQL Server 2000 environment will benefit from using more robust computer hardware. Chapters 5 and 6 cover how to optimize performance by using multiple drives and RAID.

Table 2-4.   Hardware Areas for Optimization

Hardware	Considerations
Memory	SQL Server 2000 uses memory to optimize performance. Having adequate memory is one of the most important factors in optimizing SQL Server 2000 performance. Adding more memory is generally one of the quickest ways to improve performance. The upper limit on the amount of memory you can add is generally determined by the computer hardware you select. SQL Server 2000 can address up to 64 GB of memory on appropriate computer hardware using Windows 2000 Data Center (up to 8 GB using Window 2000 Advanced Server).
Processor	SQL Server 2000 can scale out to 32 processors and can scale up to the fastest Intel processors available in the marketplace. Planning for a fast multiprocessor system is a wise investment. SQL Server 2000 can be very processor-intensive, depending on the nature of the queries being processed.
Data Storage	SQL Server 2000 can benefit from fast drives, from multiple drives for different uses, and from the use of RAID. Most large production systems use RAID to improve performance and provide fault tolerance.
Network	SQL Server 2000 can benefit from fast network adapters and from high-speed networks, including system area network (SAN) protocols for very large databases. Lack of sufficient network bandwidth can be overlooked in optimizing SQL Server 2000 performance.

Finally, beware of using write-caching disk controllers. Unless the write-caching disk controller is specifically designed for use with a database, you risk corrupting your database. SQL Server 2000 relies on the Windows operating system to notify it when an I/O operation has completed. If the write-caching disk controller notifies the Windows operating system that a write operation has completed that never actually completes, your database can become corrupt. This can occur if the power fails or the reset switch is pressed on your computer before a write operation of data that is in the cache of the disk controller has actually been written to the hard drive. Write-caching disk controllers that are designed for databases use a number of mechanisms to prevent this from occurring.

Lesson Summary

The minimum computer hardware requirements for SQL Server 2000 depend upon the SQL Server edition and Windows operating system edition you select. In addition, selecting hardware that is certified for the Windows operating system on which you plan to install SQL Server 2000 is critical. Finally, most SQL Server 2000 production databases will run on hardware that substantially exceeds the minimum hardware requirements.

Lesson 2: Deciding SQL Server 2000 Setup Configuration Options

During the installation of SQL Server 2000, you must make a number of decisions in determining the configuration of your SQL Server 2000 installation. This lesson discusses each of these decisions, and provides the information required to understand and choose the configuration option most appropriate for your SQL Server 2000 environment.

After this lesson, you will be able to

- Determine the appropriate user account for the SQL Server and SQL Server Agent services
- Choose an authentication mode for SQL Server 2000
- Determine when to modify default collation settings
- Select the network libraries to use with SQL Server 2000
- Decide on a client licensing mode

Estimated lesson time: 15 minutes

Determining the Appropriate User Account for the SQL Server and SQL Server Agent Services

Each SQL Server 2000 service runs in the security context of a user account. During SQL Server 2000 setup, you will be asked to specify the user account for the SQL Server and SQL Server Agent services. Two choices are available. You can select either the local system account or a domain user account. Generally, each of these services will use the same user account. Rarely can a case be made for using different accounts for each of these services.

The local system account is a Windows 2000 or Windows NT 4.0 operating system account with full administrator rights on the local computer. However, this account has no network access rights. This account is appropriate for use in many testing environments, as well as in production environments where SQL Server 2000 does not need to be integrated with other Microsoft server applications such as Microsoft Exchange Server or need to access any network resources, such as file shares. This account is used by default for the Distributed Transaction Coordinator service and the Microsoft Search service. Most Windows 2000 and Windows NT 4.0 operating system services also use this account.

However, in most client/SQL Server 2000 production environments, you will create and use a dedicated domain user account for the SQL Server and SQL Server Agent services. Selecting a dedicated domain user account allows these SQL

Server 2000 services to communicate with other SQL Server installations, access Microsoft Exchange Server, and access network resources (such as file shares) on other computers in your domain environment. In addition, you should generally use the same domain user account for all SQL Server installations that will need to communicate with each other. This will simplify the administration of all SQL Server 2000 computers in your domain.

Using a dedicated user account means creating a domain user account that is used solely for the SQL Server and SQL Server Agent services. This domain user account should be configured with the Password Never Expires option. The domain user account you create needs certain special access rights on the local computer, but does not need to be a member of the Administrators local group and does not need to be a domain administrator. These special access rights include the right to log on as a service, the right to access and change the SQL Server folder, the right to access and change database files, and read and write access to certain keys in the Windows registry. The SQL Server 2000 Setup program grants these rights automatically to the domain user account you specify. Certain additional rights might be required for specific tasks, such as performing certain types of jobs or registering your SQL Server 2000 installation with Active Directory directory services. These rights, and the tasks that require them, will be covered in Chapters 12 and 13. You will need to grant these additional rights manually, if you require these features.

Note   Windows ME and Windows 98 do not support the use of Windows services. SQL Server and SQL Server Agent run as executable programs on these Windows platforms. A domain user account is not required in these environments.

Practice: Creating a Dedicated Windows 2000 User Account

In this practice you use Active Directory Users And Computers to create and configure a dedicated Windows 2000 user account.

▶ **To configure a dedicated domain user account**

1. Ensure that you are logged on to the SelfPacedSQL.MSFT domain controller as Administrator.
2. Click Start, point to Programs, point to Administrative Tools, and then click Active Directory Users And Computers.
3. The Active Directory Users And Computers window appears.
4. In the console tree, expand SelfPacedSQL.MSFT.
5. Right-click Users, point to New, and then click User.
   The New Object - User dialog box appears.
6. In the First Name text box, type **SQLService**.
7. In the User Logon Name text box, type **SQLService**, and then click Next.

8. In the Password and Confirm Password text boxes, type **sql**.

9. Select the Password Never Expires check box, and then click Next.

10. Click the Finish button.

11. In the console tree, click Users.

    The details pane displays a list of all users in the Users container.

12. Verify that the SQLService domain user account has been created.

13. Close Active Directory Users And Computers.

Choosing an Authentication Mode

SQL Server 2000 supports two authentication modes, Windows Authentication Mode and Mixed Mode. The default authentication mode for SQL Server 2000 is Windows Authentication Mode. When this mode is used, the only users who can connect to SQL Server 2000 are users who have been previously authenticated by the Windows operating system. This is called *Windows Authentication*. When Windows Authentication is used, SQL Server accepts trusted connections from the Windows operating system.

The alternative authentication mode is Mixed Mode. This means that SQL Server 2000 will use one of two methods of authentication. The first method is to rely on the Windows operating system to authenticate users. The second method is for SQL Server 2000 to authenticate users directly based on the submission of a user name and password to SQL Server 2000 by the client application attempting to gain access. This is called *SQL Server Authentication*.

Note   When the Personal Edition of SQL Server 2000 is installed on Windows ME or Windows 98, SQL Server authentication must be used. This is because the server side of the trusted connection API is not supported on these Windows operating systems.

For most SQL Server 2000 environments, Windows Authentication Mode should be used. It provides the highest level of security, including password encryption, and is easier to administer in a domain environment. The SQL Server 2000 authentication mode can be changed after installation, as well as during setup. Managing SQL Server 2000 security is covered in Chapter 10. This includes a discussion of environments in which the use of Mixed Mode security might be necessary.

Determining Collation Settings

The default collation for SQL Server 2000 is defined during setup. A collation is used to determine how non-Unicode character data is stored and also governs how SQL Server 2000 sorts and compares Unicode and non-Unicode data. A SQL Server 2000 collation consists of a Windows collation and a SQL collation.

Tip   Unicode allows data from most languages to be recorded, but takes twice as much space as non-Unicode data. Non-Unicode data only supports 256 characters, and is specific to a particular language.

The place to start in understanding SQL Server 2000 collations is the Windows operating system. When you install a Windows operating system, you install a version for the language you want to use, such as English, Greek, or Russian. Different languages require different characters, and therefore different code pages (also referred to as character sets), to support these character sets and associated keyboard layouts. Based on the version of the Windows operating system that you have installed, a Windows locale is set. The Windows locale also determines settings for numbers, currencies, times, and dates. When you install SQL Server 2000, the Setup program determines a default Windows collation for SQL Server 2000 based on the Windows locale of the Windows operating system on which you are installing SQL Server 2000.

Although this might initially seem complicated, determining the Windows collation to use for SQL Server 2000 is generally quite straightforward. Allow the SQL Server 2000 Setup program to determine the default Windows collation based on the Windows locale of the Windows operating system unless:

- The primary language being supported by the SQL Server 2000 instance you are installing is different from the Windows locale of the computer on which you are installing SQL Server 2000, or
- The SQL Server 2000 instance you are installing will be participating in a replication scheme with SQL Server 2000 instances supporting a different collation. You need to ensure, in this case, that the collation selected by Setup uses the same code page as the other instances of SQL Server included in the replication scheme. In this environment, setting collation at the database level is also an option.

The next step is to understand that SQL Server 2000 uses a SQL collation to match settings used in previous versions of SQL Server. This is necessary because earlier versions of SQL Server specified code page number, character sort order, and Unicode collation separately. A SQL collation specifies three collation attributes:

- **The non-Unicode code page.**   Tells SQL Server 2000 how to store non-Unicode character data.
- **The non-Unicode sort order.**   Tells SQL Server 2000 how to sort non-Unicode character data types, such as sensitivity to capitalization.
- **The Unicode sort order.**   Tells SQL Server 2000 how to sort Unicode data types.

When the SQL Server 2000 Setup program detects that SQL Server 2000 is being installed on a computer with an English locale setting in the Windows operating system and on which no prior version of SQL Server has been installed, the Setup program automatically chooses the dictionary order, case-insensitive character sort order, for use with the 1252 character set. These match the default settings for SQL Server 7.0.

If you are installing an instance of SQL Server 2000 on a computer that has SQL Server 6.5 or 7.0 installed, the SQL Server 2000 Setup program will determine a SQL collation for SQL Server 2000 based on the code page, sort order, and Unicode collation settings in the earlier version of SQL Server (including collations that are obsolete). Most combinations of these settings are supported, but not all. Use a Custom setup to modify the collation setting selected by the SQL Server 2000 Setup program.

The final step is to understand that SQL Server collations are settable at multiple levels. You set a default collation (which consists of a Windows collation and a SQL collation) for an instance of SQL Server 2000. This default collation is the collation setting for all system databases. The model database, all user databases, and all other SQL Server 2000 objects inherit this default collation setting, unless a different collation is specified for the database or object. In international environments, having different collations for different databases can solve numerous issues involving the use of multiple languages and character sets.

Practice: Determining Your Windows Collation

In this practice, you use Control Panel to determine your Windows collation.

1. To determine your Windows collation
2. Ensure that you are logged on to the SelfPacedSQL.MSFT domain controller as Administrator.
3. Click Start, point to Settings, and then click Control Panel.

   The Control Panel window appears.
4. Double-click the Regional Options icon.
5. The Regional Options dialog box appears with the General tab selected.
6. In the Your Locale (Location) drop-down list, determine your Windows locale.

   English (United States) is the locale used by the author.
7. Click OK to close the Regional Options dialog box. Do not change your Windows locale.
8. Close the Control Panel window.

Selecting Network Libraries

SQL Server 2000 uses network libraries to send network packets between clients and a server running SQL Server 2000. These network libraries are implemented as DLLs and perform network operations using specific interprocess communication (IPC) mechanisms (such as shared memory, named pipes, and RPCs). There are client-side network libraries and server-side network libraries. These client and server network libraries support specific underlying network protocols. For example, the TCP/IP sockets network library allows SQL Server 2000 to communicate using Windows sockets as the IPC mechanism across the TCP/IP network protocol. The installation of these network protocols is part of your Windows operating system configuration and should be completed prior to installing SQL Server 2000.

A server running SQL Server 2000 monitors all configured network libraries simultaneously for incoming communication from clients seeking to gain access. By default, SQL Server 2000 installed on any Windows 2000 or Windows NT 4.0 operating system monitors TCP/IP sockets and named pipes (and shared memory for local clients). All additional network libraries are installed during setup, but are not configured for use, unless specified during a Custom setup. For a complete list of supported network libraries, see Chapter 1. If you need to configure server network libraries after setup, use the Server Network Utility from the Microsoft SQL Server program group or from the SQL Server properties dialog box in SQL Server Enterprise Manager. Configure additional server network libraries only if they are needed in your network environment, such as to support clients on a Novell network.

Note   Server-side named pipes are not supported on Windows ME and Windows 98. Clients must use TCP/IP sockets to connect to SQL Server 2000 running on these operating systems.

SQL Server 2000 clients initiate communication with a server running SQL Server 2000 using a specific network library. You can configure multiple network libraries on SQL Server 2000 clients, and you can define the order in which the Windows operating system will attempt to use each network library when connecting with SQL Server 2000. By default, all SQL Server 2000 clients running Windows 2000, Windows NT 4.0, Windows ME, or Windows 98 use the TCP/IP sockets as the primary network library and named pipes as the secondary network library. If you need to manually configure a client-side network library to communicate with a specific SQL Server installation, use the Client Network Utility from the Microsoft SQL Server program group (provided the client software has been installed on the computer).

The SQL Server 2000 client software handles the complexities of establishing a connection with a server running SQL Server 2000 automatically. The network name of the computer on which the SQL Server 2000 instance is running (and instance name if applicable) is all that is needed to establish the connection, assuming matching network libraries exist.

More Info   If a SQL Server 2000 client needs to connect to a named instance of SQL Server 2000, TCP/IP sockets, named pipes, or NWLink IPX/SPX must be used. Named instances are covered in Lesson 4 of this chapter.

You can use the Server Network Utility to enable SSL encryption over all enabled network libraries. SQL Server 2000 can then use the SSL to encrypt all data transmitted over any network library between a SQL Server 2000 client and a server running SQL Server 2000. The encryption level, 40-bit versus 128-bit, depends on the level of encryption supported by the Windows operating system involved. The multiprotocol network library supports its own encryption using the Windows RPC encryption API rather than SSL. This encryption mechanism is primarily for backward compatibility and multiprotocol encryption does not support named instances. Use the more secure SSL, rather than multiprotocol encryption, whenever possible.

Deciding on a Client Licensing Mode

SQL Server 2000 supports two client licensing modes: per processor and per seat. With per-processor licensing, you need a license on the server running SQL Server 2000 for each processor on the computer. If this client licensing mode is selected, no additional licenses are needed for any clients connecting to this installation of SQL Server 2000. This client licensing mode is intended to be most cost-effective for installations with large numbers of users, particularly anonymous Internet users.

With per-seat licensing, each client connecting to an installation of SQL Server 2000 must have a separate Client Access License (CAL). This client licensing mode is intended to be most cost-effective for installations with a small to medium number of defined users connecting to more than one server.

Lesson Summary

During the installation of SQL Server 2000, you must decide the appropriate user account to use for the SQL Server and the SQL Server Agent services. Generally, a domain user account is used if either of these services must communicate across the network. You must also decide the authentication mode for SQL Server 2000. Window Authentication Mode is the default configuration, where SQL Server 2000 will only accept trusted connections from the Windows operating system. In addition, you must decide if the default collation determined by the SQL Server 2000 Setup program is appropriate for your environment. In most cases, you will not modify the default collation. You might also want to configure additional network libraries in certain environments. Finally, you must elect to use per-processor or per-seat licensing for your SQL Server 2000 installation. Your choice will generally be determined based on the type and quantity of clients accessing your SQL Server 2000 installation.

Lesson 3: Running the SQL Server 2000 Setup Program

After you have selected your SQL Server 2000 edition, and installed the Windows operating system you have decided to use, you are ready to install SQL Server 2000 by running the SQL Server 2000 Setup program. This lesson covers running the SQL Server 2000 Setup program interactively to install an instance of SQL Server 2000 on the local computer. The details of default, named, and multiple instances are covered in Lesson 4 of this chapter. Remote and unattended installations are covered in Lesson 5 of this chapter. Upgrading from earlier versions of SQL Server is covered in Chapter 4, and installing SQL Server 2000 on a virtual server for failover clustering is covered in Chapter 16.

After this lesson, you will be able to

- Understand how to start the SQL Server 2000 Setup program
- Understand the difference between the Client Tools Only, the Server and Client Tools, and Connectivity Only installation types
- Describe the components that are installed and the software configuration options that are selected when a Typical or a Minimum setup is selected
- Determine when to select a Custom setup

Estimated lesson time: 30 minutes

Running the SQL Server 2000 Setup Program

There are several ways to start the SQL Server 2000 Setup program for an interactive installation of SQL Server 2000. The easiest way to begin is to simply insert the SQL Server 2000 compact disc into the CD-ROM drive. From the initial dialog box, you can install SQL Server 2000, Analysis Services, or English Query by clicking on SQL Server 2000 Components. The initial dialog box presents a number of additional options, including providing access to the setup/upgrade portion of Books Online, the Release Notes, and SQL Server Web site at Microsoft. Double-clicking on Autorun.exe in the root of the CD-ROM also accesses this initial dialog box. After clicking SQL Server 2000 Components, click Install Database Server to start the SQL Server 2000 Setup program. See Figure 2.1.

Note   You can also start the SQL Server 2000 Setup program by double-clicking on Setupsql.exe in the \X86\Setup folder.

Figure 2.1.   Selecting SQL Server 2000 components to install.

Understanding Installation Types

After you choose to create a new instance of SQL Server 2000 on your local computer (instances and remote installations are covered later in this chapter and upgrades are covered in Chapter 4), you can select Client Tools Only, Server and Client Tools, or Connectivity Only. MDAC 2.6 is installed with each of these installation types. MDAC 2.6 is required to connect to named instances of SQL Server 2000. Choose Connectivity Only to install network libraries for client connectivity. This requires approximately 50 MB of hard drive space. If you select this option, you have no choice to install any client management tools, Books Online, or any server components. See Figure 2.2.

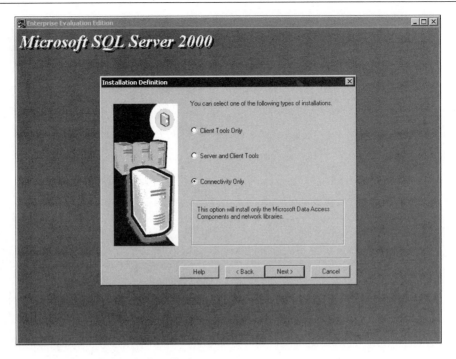

Figure 2.2.   Defining the installation type.

Choose Client Tools Only when you need to install client management tools, as well as connectivity software, to connect to and administer an existing server running SQL Server 2000. Selecting this option installs all the client management tools, the client connectivity components, Books Online, and an interface for stored procedure debugging. If you select the Client Tools Only option, you can choose to install additional development tools and code samples. You can also choose not to install Books Online or some of the client management tools. See Figure 2.3.

Choose Server and Client Tools when you need to install a server running SQL Server 2000, as well as connectivity software and client management tools. Selecting this option allows you to install SQL Server 2000 in its entirety with all available tools and components.

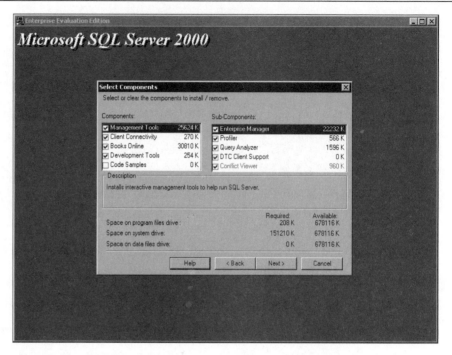

Figure 2.3. Selecting components of SQL Server.

Selecting a Setup Type

When you select an installation of Server and Client Tools, you can select to install a Typical, Minimum, or Custom setup. The default location for program and data files for each of these setup types is \Program Files\Microsoft SQL Server. If this default location is low on available hard drive space, consider moving the program and data files to another location. Click Browse to specify a new location for program files and for data files. They do not need to be in the same location. See Figure 2.4.

If you select Typical or Minimum, you are presented with these three additional choices. The SQL Server 2000 Setup program makes all other choices for you.

Choice	Options
Services Accounts	Select the local system account or a domain user account for the SQL Server and SQL Server Agent services. You can also select whether you want either or both of these services to start automatically with the operating system (Windows 2000 and Windows NT 4.0 only). See Figure 2.5.
Authentication Mode	Windows Authentication Mode (default) or Mixed Mode. If Mixed Mode is selected, you are prompted to provide a password for the *sa* login account. This account is a SQL Server login account that has full system administration privileges. You should never install SQL Server in Mixed Mode without setting (and recording in a secure location) the password for the *sa* login. See Figure 2.6.
Choose Licensing Mode	Per Seat or Processor License. See Figure 2.7.

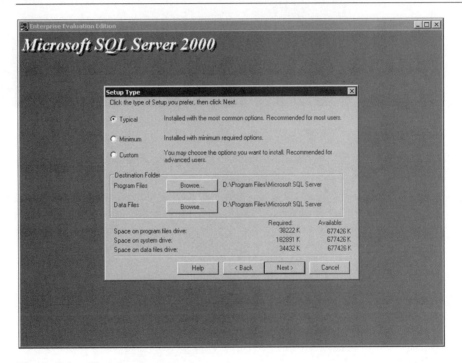

Figure 2.4.   Choosing the setup type.

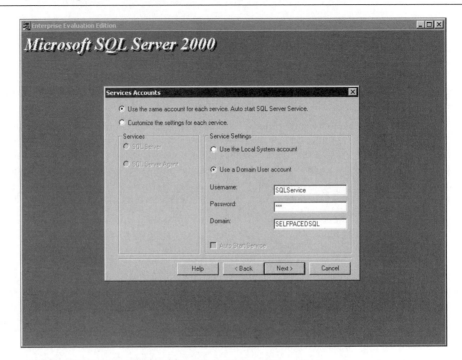

Figure 2.5.   Selecting the logon account for services.

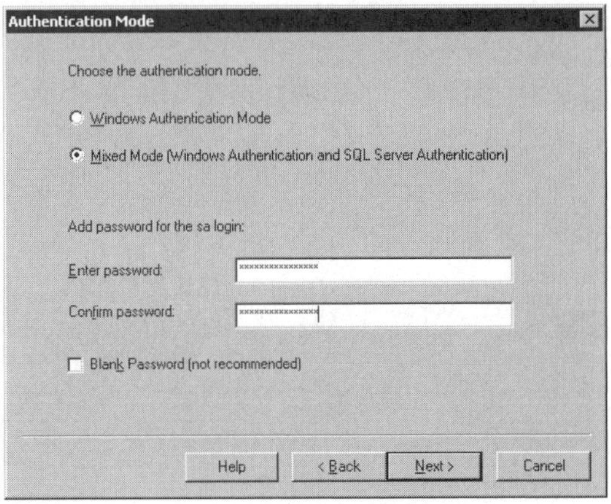

Figure 2.6.   Choosing the authentication mode.

Note   The Licensing Mode option is not available when installing the Enterprise Evaluation edition. Per seat is the licensing mode for the Enterprise Evaluation edition.

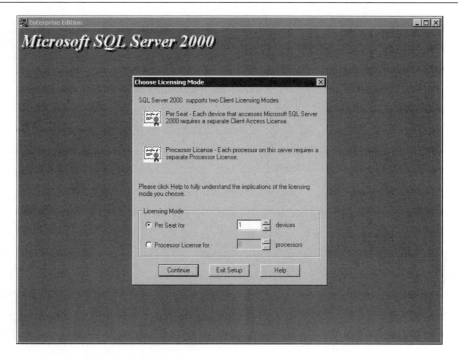

Figure 2.7.   Choosing the licensing mode.

If you choose a Custom setup, additional choices are available to you. Through the use of a Custom installation, you can

- Install additional development tools (headers and libraries, MDAC SDKs, and backup/restore APIs)
- Install code samples (15 different types of code samples are available)
- Choose specific components to install or not install
- Change the default collation settings to match the collation of another instance of SQL Server or the Windows locale of another computer
- Select and configure additional network libraries for use with a default SQL Server instance
- Change the default named pipe (default is \\ \pipe\Mssql\sql\query <file:// \\pipe\Mssql\sql\query> for the default instance)
- Change the default TCP/IP sockets port number (default is 1433 for the default instance and is dynamically assigned at startup for named instances)
- Define the proxy server address, if you set SQL Server to listen on a proxy server

See Figures 2.8, 2.9, and 2.10.

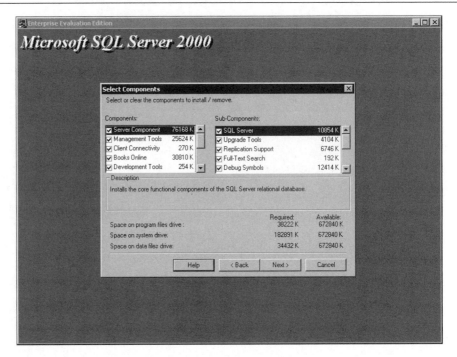

Figure 2.8.   Selecting components in a Custom setup.

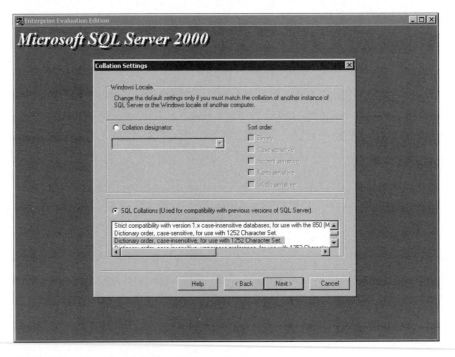

Figure 2.9.   Changing default collation settings.

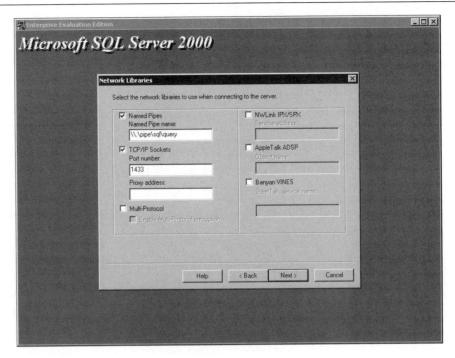

Figure 2.10.   Selecting network libraries.

Table 2.5 lists the components installed with each setup type.

Table 2-5.   Installed Components

Component	Minimum	Typical	Custom
Database server	Yes	Yes	Optional
Upgrade tools	No	Default instance only	Optional
Replication support	Yes	Yes	Optional
Full-text search	Yes	Yes	Optional
Management tools	None	Yes	Optional
Client connectivity	Yes	Yes	Optional
Books Online	No	Yes	Optional
Development tools	None	Stored procedure debugger only	Choice of tools
Code samples	None	None	Choice of samples
Collation settings	Determined by setup	Determined by setup	Choice of collation settings
Network libraries	TCP/IP sockets and named pipes	TCP/IP sockets and named pipes	Choice of additional network libraries

Practice: Installing a Default Instance of SQL Server 2000

In this practice you install a default instance of SQL Server 2000, using the Microsoft SQL Server 2000 Evaluation Edition.

▶ **To install a default instance of SQL Server 2000**

1. Ensure that you are logged on to the SelfPacedSQL.MSFT domain controller as Administrator.
2. Insert the SQL Server 2000 compact disc into the CD-ROM drive.

   The Microsoft SQL Server 2000 Evaluation Edition page appears.
3. Click SQL Server 2000 Components, and then click Install Database Server.

   The Welcome page for the Microsoft SQL Server Installation Wizard appears.
4. Click Next.

   The Computer Name page appears with Local Computer selected.
5. Click Next.

   The Installation Selection page appears with Create A New Instance Of SQL Server, Or Install Client Tools selected.
6. Click Next.

   The User Information page appears.
7. Type your name in the Name text box (if it does not already appear there), and then click Next.

   The Software License Agreement page appears displaying the 120-day Evaluation License for Microsoft SQL Server 2000.
8. Click the Yes button.

   The Installation Definition page appears with Server And Client Tools selected.
9. Click Next.

   The Instance Name page appears with the Default check box selected.
10. Click Next.

    The Setup Type page appears with Typical selected.
11. Click Next.

    The Services Accounts dialog box appears with Use The Same Account For Each Service. Auto Start SQL Server Service. selected. Use A Domain User Account is also selected.
12. In the Username text box, type **SQLService**.
13. In the Password text box, type **sql**.
14. In the Domain text box, verify *SelfPacedSQL* appears, and then click Next.

    The Authentication Mode page appears with Windows Authentication Mode selected.

15. Click Next.

    The Start Copying Files page appears.

16. Click Next.

    The SQL Server 2000 Setup program will start installing SQL Server 2000 beginning with the MDAC. When the SQL Server 2000 Setup program is complete, the Setup Complete page will appear.

17. Click the Finish button.

Lesson Summary

The SQL Server 2000 Setup program provides installation types for Client Tools Only, Server and Client Tools, and Connectivity Only. Use Connectivity Only to install only MDAC 2.6 and network libraries. Use Client Tools Only to install MDAC 2.6, client management tools, connectivity, and Books Online. Use Server and Client Tools to install a server running SQL Server 2000, MDAC 2.6, all client management tools, connectivity, and Books Online.

The SQL Server 2000 Setup program provides a Typical, Minimum, or Custom setup type when the server and client tools installation type is selected. Selecting a Typical or Minimum setup type makes most of the installation decisions for you. Select a Custom setup type if you want full control of which components are installed and how they are configured.

Lesson 4: Using Default, Named, and Multiple Instances of SQL Server 2000

SQL Server 2000 supports the installation of multiple instances (or copies) of SQL Server 2000. This capability allows you to have sets of system and user databases that are independent of each other. This capability allows you to work with earlier versions of SQL Server already installed on your computer, to test development software, and to operate instances of SQL Server 2000 independent of each other. This lesson teaches you how to install and work with default and named instances of SQL Server 2000. This lesson also covers what components are shared between instances of SQL Server.

After this lesson, you will be able to

- Install multiple named instances of SQL Server 2000
- Understand when the use of multiple instances is recommended
- Understand what components are unique between instances and what components are shared
- Work with default and named instances of SQL Server 2000

Estimated lesson time: 15 minutes

Installing Multiple Instances of SQL Server 2000

When you install SQL Server 2000, you have the option to define the installation as the default instance or as a named instance. A named instance simply means that you define a name for an instance during installation and that you access that instance using this name. You can only have one default instance, but you can have many named instances. A default instance can be an installation of SQL Server 6.5, SQL Server 7.0, or SQL Server 2000. A named instance can only be an installation of SQL Server 2000.

When you run the SQL Server 2000 Setup program, it will detect whether a default instance already exists on the computer. If a default instance is not detected, the Setup program allows you to choose to install a default or a named instance. To install a named instance, clear the Default check box. See Figure 2.11.

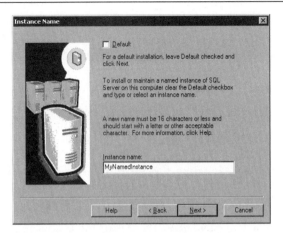

Figure 2.11.   Installing a named instance.

If a default instance already exists, you have several choices depending upon the version of SQL Server that is installed as the default instance. Upgrading from earlier versions of SQL Server is covered in Chapter 4.

- If the default instance is a SQL Server 2000 installation, you can install a named instance of SQL Server 2000.
- If the default instance is a SQL Server 7.0 installation, you can choose to upgrade the default instance to SQL Server 2000 or install a named instance of SQL Server 2000.
- If the default instance is a SQL Server 6.5 installation, you can install SQL Server 2000 as the default instance or as a named instance. If you install it as the default instance, you can use the version switch (Vswitch.exe) utility to switch between SQL Server 6.5 and SQL Server 2000. You must install SQL Server 6.5 SP5 to any instance of SQL Server 6.5 before you install an instance of SQL Server 2000 on the same machine.

Using Multiple Instances of SQL Server 2000 Effectively and Appropriately

Using multiple instances of SQL Server 2000 increases administration overhead and causes a duplication of components. These additional instances of the SQL Server and SQL Server Agent services require additional computer resources, namely memory and processing capacity. Running multiple databases in a single instance will provide superior performance compared to running a similar number of databases in multiple instances.

Using multiple instances is appropriate when testing multiple versions of SQL Server on the same computer. It is also appropriate when testing service packs and development databases and applications. Using multiple instances is also particularly appropriate when different customers each require their own system and user databases along with full administrative control of their particular instance. Finally, when the desktop engine is embedded in applications, each application can install its own instance independent of instances installed by other applications.

Understanding Shared Components Between Instances

Table 2.6 lists the components that are shared between all instances when you install multiple instances of SQL Server. These components are shared regardless of whether the default instance is SQL Server 6.5, SQL Server 7.0, or SQL Server 2000.

Understanding Unique Components Between Instances

When you install multiple instances of SQL Server 2000 (or SQL Server 2000 and either SQL Server 6.5 and 7.0), system and user databases are unique and completely independent of each other. There is no direct connection between system or user databases in one instance and system and user databases in another instance. These databases function as if they were residing on separate SQL Server installations.

Each instance has its own SQL Server and SQL Server Agent services. For the default instance, the names of these services are MSSQLServer and SQLServer-Agent. For named instances, the names of these services are MSSQL$*instancename* and SQLAgent$*instancename*. The database engine for each instance is configured completely independently of any other instance. Jobs on one instance have no knowledge of and do not interact with jobs on any other instance.

Table 2-6.   Shared Components in Multiple Instances of SQL Server

Component	Description
Client management tools and utilities (and their associated registry keys)	All instances of SQL Server on a computer share the same version of all client management tools and utilities (and their associated registry keys). These tools and utilities work with all instances. The version of the tools and utilities will be the version from the first SQL Server 2000 version installed on the computer. If SQL Server 6.5 or 7.0 is already installed on the computer that you install SQL Server 2000 on, the SQL Server 6.5 or 7.0 client management tools and utilities are upgraded to SQL Server 2000 client management tools and utilities.
Books Online	All instances of SQL Server on a computer share the same version of SQL Server Books Online and that will be the one from the first version of SQL Server 2000 installed. If instances from multiple languages are installed, Books Online will be in the language of the first SQL Server 2000 version installed. If any earlier version of SQL Server was on the computer, that version of Books Online will be upgraded.
Microsoft Search service Distributed Transaction Coordinator	There is only one instance of the Microsoft Search service. There is only one instance of the Distributed Transaction Coordinator service.

Working with Default and Named Instances of SQL Server 2000

Each instance of SQL Server 2000 listens on a unique set of network addresses. The default instance listens on the same network address as earlier versions of SQL Server. Therefore, client applications using client connectivity components from earlier versions of SQL Server can connect to SQL Server 2000 without an upgrade of those connectivity components. However, in order to connect to named instances, client applications must use the SQL Server 2000 connectivity components, or the client connectivity components must be configured to connect to alternate addresses appropriate to the particular named instance involved. The SQL Server 2000 connectivity components allow client applications to automatically detect the network libraries and network addresses required to connect to default or named instances. The only information that must be provided by the client application is the name of the computer, and the instance name if applicable.

Lesson Summary

SQL Server 2000 supports the installation of multiple instances of SQL Server 2000. This means that multiple instances of the SQL Server and SQL Server Agent services, as well as system and user databases, are supported. This allows multiple versions of SQL Server to coexist. However, only one version of SQL Server tools and utilities is supported. SQL Server 2000 tools and utilities replace tools and utilities from earlier versions of SQL Server, even if the earlier version is not upgraded. Use multiple instances only where appropriate, such as testing new versions of SQL Server or development databases and applications.

Lesson 5: Performing Unattended and Remote Installations of SQL Server 2000

SQL Server 2000 supports unattended installations of SQL Server 2000, as well as installations of SQL Server 2000 on remote computers. Each of these installation options uses the same underlying structure. This lesson teaches how to use the SQL Server 2000 Setup program to perform each of these types of installations.

After this lesson, you will be able to

- Perform an unattended installation of SQL Server 2000
- Create setup initialization files for SQL Server 2000
- Perform a remote installation of SQL Server 2000

Estimated lesson time: 45 minutes

Performing an Unattended Installation of SQL Server 2000

Performing an unattended installation of SQL Server 2000 has been made very simple with SQL Server 2000. The process involves running a batch file that calls a setup initialization (ISS) file. The .ISS file contains all setup entries for the options you require for your SQL Server 2000 installation. The command-prompt syntax for performing an unattended setup and calling a setup initialization file is as follows:

```
Start /Wait D:\X86\Setup\Setupsql.exe k=SMS -s -m -SMS -f1
"C:\Setup.iss"
```

Note The preceding command must be entered as a single line. Change the drive letter, if required, to refer to your CD-ROM drive.

Creating Setup Initialization Files for SQL Server 2000

There are three ways to create setup initialization files for SQL Server 2000 unattended installations. First, the SQL Server 2000 Setup program provides an option in the Advanced Options page to record an unattended .ISS file. If you select this option, you then proceed through the interactive Setup program and select the installation options you want. See Figure 2.12. These options are then recorded in this .ISS file and stored in the \Winnt folder.

SQL Server 2000 is not actually installed during this process. This .ISS file can later be used as is, or can be modified by any text editor. SQL Server 2000 Books Online provides detailed information regarding each entry in an .ISS file.

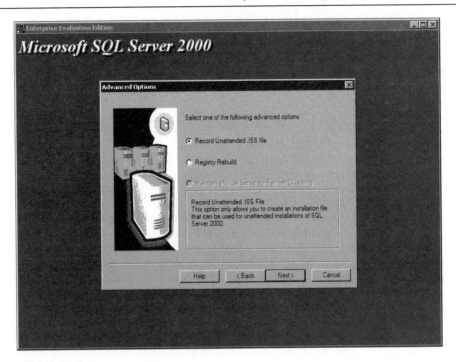

Figure 2.12.   Selecting Advanced Options.

The second way to create a setup initialization file is to use one of the three .ISS files provided on the SQL Server 2000 compact disc (in the root directory). You can use these files as is, or you can modify them using any text editor. Microsoft has provided the following files.

Setup Initialization File Name	Calling Batch File Name	Type of Installation
Sqlins.iss	Sqlins.bat	Typical installation of SQL Server 2000
Sqlcli.iss	Sqlcli.bat	Installation of client tools only
Sqlcst.iss	Sqlcst.bat	Custom installation of SQL Server 2000 including all components

The third way to create a setup initialization file is to modify the Setup.iss file that is automatically recorded each time you install SQL Server 2000. This file is placed in the \Winnt directory. This file is a complete record of the choices you made when you installed SQL Server 2000. In order to use this file, you must modify it using any text editor and add the [SdFinish-0] section. Refer to any of the setup initialization files on the SQL Server 2000 compact disc or use SQL Server 2000 Books Online for examples of how to complete this section. This corresponds to the Setup Complete dialog box in the interactive setup.

Practice: Performing an Unattended Installation of a Named Instance of SQL Server 2000

In this practice you perform an unattended installation of a named instance of SQL Server 2000.

▶ **To perform an unattended installation of a named instance of SQL Server 2000**

1. Ensure that you are logged on to the SelfPacedSQL.MSFT domain controller as Administrator.
2. Insert the SQL Server 2000 compact disc into the CD-ROM drive.

   The Microsoft SQL Server 2000 Evaluation Edition page appears.
3. Click SQL Server 2000 Components, and then click Install Database Server.

   The Welcome page for the Microsoft SQL Server Installation Wizard appears.
4. Click Next.

   The Computer Name page appears with Local Computer selected.
5. Click Next.

   The Installation Selection page appears with Create A New Instance Of SQL Server, Or Install Client Tools selected.
6. Select Advanced Options and then click Next.

   The Advanced Options page appears with Record Unattended .ISS File selected.
7. Click Next.

   The User Information page appears with your name in the Name text box.
8. Click Next.

   The Software License Agreement page appears displaying the 120-day Evaluation License for Microsoft SQL Server 2000.
9. Click the Yes button.

   The Installation Definition page appears with Server And Client Tools selected.
10. Click Next.

    The Instance Name page appears with the Default check box grayed out.
11. In the Instance name text box, type **MyNamedInstance**, and then click Next.

    The Setup Type page appears with Typical selected.
12. Click Next.

    The Services Accounts page appears with Use The Same Account For Each Service. Auto Start SQL Server Service. selected. Use A Domain User Account is also selected.
13. In the Username text box, type **SQLService**.
14. In the Password text box, type **sql**.

15. In the Domain text box, verify that *SelfPacedSQL* appears, and then click Next.

    The Authentication Mode page appears with Windows Authentication Mode selected.

16. Click Next.

    The Setup Information page appears.

17. Click Next.

18. Click Per Seat for 1 device and then click Continue.

    The Setup Complete page appears stating that the unattended installation file is ready to be created.

19. Click the Finish button.

20. Using Windows Explorer, locate the Setup.iss file in C:\Winnt.

21. Right-click Setup.iss, point to Open With, and then click Notepad.

22. Review the entries and then close Setup.iss.

23. Right-click the Windows 2000 taskbar and then click Task Manager.

    The Windows Task Manager dialog box appears.

24. Click the Performance tab to observe the CPU Usage and MEM Usage bar graphs during the installation.

25. Click Start, point to Accessories, and then click Command Prompt.

    The command Prompt window appears.

26. At the command prompt, type **start /wait d:\x86\setup\setupsql.exe k=SMS –s –m –SMS –f1 "c:\winnt\setup.iss".**

    These paths assume that your CD-ROM drive is D and that your Windows 2000 installation is C:\Winnt. If your paths are different, change the pathnames accordingly.

27. Click OK.

    A command-prompt window appears and an unattended installation of a named instance of SQL Server 2000 commences. Setup is complete when the command-prompt window closes. This should take between five and ten minutes. If the command-prompt window closes very quickly, you have typed the command incorrectly.

28. Close the Windows Task Manager dialog box when setup is complete.

Performing a Remote Installation of SQL Server 2000

SQL Server 2000 supports performing an installation of SQL Server 2000 onto a remote computer by running the SQL Server 2000 Setup program on the local computer and identifying the computer on which you want SQL Server 2000 to be installed. The remote computer is specified on the Computer Name page during installation. See Figure 2.13.

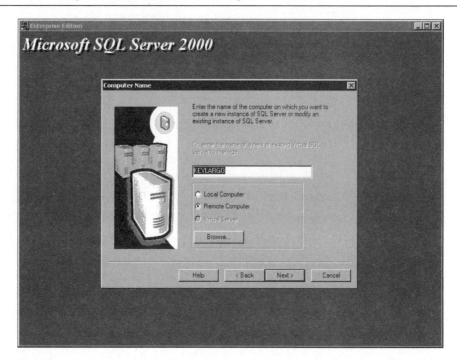

Figure 2.13.   Installing an instance of SQL Server 2000 on a remote computer.

The Setup program must be able to establish a connection to this remote computer. You must be logged on using a domain user account that has permission to access the remote computer. After the SQL Server 2000 Setup program establishes a connection to this remote computer, you must specify a logon account that has permission to install SQL Server 2000 on the remote computer, namely an account with full administrative permissions on the remote computer. You must also specify a target path for the installation files and a source path for the setup files. You enter this information on the Remote Setup Information page during installation. See Figure 2.14.

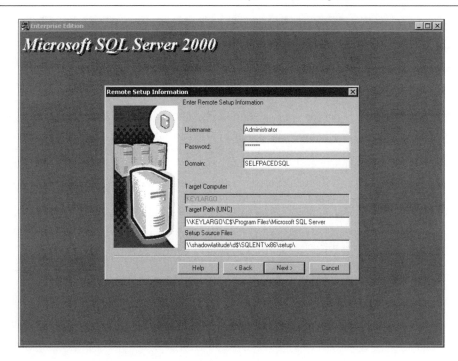

Figure 2.14. Entering Remote Setup information.

The SQL Server 2000 Setup program records all of your installation choices into a Setup.iss file. It then copies all necessary files to the remote computer and performs an unattended setup on the remote computer using this Setup.iss file. To the administrator running the Setup program, installing SQL Server 2000 on a remote computer is substantially the same as installing SQL Server 2000 on the local computer using the interactive Setup program.

Lesson Summary

SQL Server 2000 supports performing unattended installations of SQL Server 2000. This is convenient if you need to install identical (or similar) installations on numerous computers. The SQL Server 2000 Setup program provides an option to record a Custom setup initialization file for use in unattended installations. The SQL Server 2000 compact disc also provides several customized setup initialization files. SQL Server 2000 supports remote installations of SQL Server 2000 using the same structure used for unattended installations.

Lesson 6: Troubleshooting a SQL Server 2000 Installation

The SQL Server 2000 Setup program is designed to detect potential problems during installation and prompt the administrator to solve them. This includes shutting down certain programs that interfere with installation, detecting insufficient disc space, and restarting the computer if certain files are locked. The Setup program will display informational messages as necessary during setup and wait for the problem to be solved by the administrator. However, problems can still occur during an installation of SQL Server. This lesson covers where to look to find the source of these errors. This includes reviewing all relevant log files and accessing SQL Server 2000 troubleshooter information online.

After this lesson, you will be able to

- Review SQL Server 2000 Setup program log files
- Access SQL Server 2000 troubleshooting information online
- Review the SQL Server error log and Windows application log

Estimated lesson time: 15 minutes

Reviewing SQL Server 2000 Setup Program Log Files

The SQL Server 2000 Setup program generates several informational files that may be used in isolating problems relating to a failed setup. These are the Sqlstp.log, the Setup.log, and the SearchSetup.log files. Any text editor can read these files. The Sqlstp.log file is located in the \Winnt or \Windows folder and logs errors encountered during the configuration portion of the Setup program. The Setup.log file is also located in the \Winnt or \Windows folder and logs the completion or failure of setup, and records any relevant information. The SearchSetup.log file is located in the \Winnt\Temp folder and logs errors encountered during the configuration of the Microsoft Search service. These three files are primarily useful for Microsoft Product Support; however, reviewing them might give you some clue regarding where setup is failing.

Note   Installing (or partially installing) an instance of SQL Server 2000 on your computer overwrites any existing versions of these information files.

Accessing SQL Server 2000 Troubleshooting Information Online

Microsoft's Product Support Services (PSS) provides online troubleshooters that are designed to help you resolve problems you might encounter when installing an edition of SQL Server 2000. The online troubleshooter leads you through a series of questions to attempt to isolate the problem and provide you with up-to-date information regarding solving the problem. These troubleshooters cover a wide range of problems, not just problems related to setup. These online troubleshooters are available from the Microsoft Web site at *http://Support.Microsoft.com /Support/ SQL/Tshooter.asp*. The Microsoft Web site, MSDN, and TechNet also contain Knowledge Base articles that contain up-to-date information regarding SQL Server 2000 setup problems.

Reviewing the SQL Server Error Log and the Windows Application Log

The SQL Server 2000 error log is frequently the most useful place to look for error messages related to SQL Server 2000 setup problems. Many SQL Server 2000 system events and user-defined events are logged in the SQL Server 2000 error log. This includes information related to setup. The Setup program starts and stops SQL Server 2000 during installation and logs this process, including any errors. Each instance of SQL Server 2000 has its own log file. A new log file is created each time SQL Server 2000 starts. For the default instance, the current log file is \Program Files\Microsoft SQL Server\Mssql\Log\Errorlog. For a named instance, the current log file is \Program Files\Microsoft SQL Server\Mssql$*Instance-Name*\Log\Errorlog. You can view these logs using SQL Server Enterprise Manager or any text editor. By default, the six most recent error log files are saved with extension numbers reflecting the most recent file. You can modify the number of previous logs saved by right-clicking SQL Server Logs in SQL Server Enterprise Manager and then clicking Configure. You can also cycle the error log file without stopping and restarting the SQL Server service by using the *sp_cycle_errorlog* system stored procedure. This is useful on a busy system where the error log file can become quite large.

The Windows application log in Event Viewer is also a useful place to look for error messages related to SQL Server 2000 setup problems. The Windows application log records information, warning, and error messages related to applications running on the Windows operating system. Information in the Windows application log combined with information in the SQL Server 2000 error log, each of which time-stamps all recorded events, can help you narrow down and isolate the probable cause of problems. You can isolate SQL Server events in the Event Viewer application log by clicking on the View menu, pointing to Filter Events, and then selecting MSSQLSERVER in the Source list.

> **Note** It is useful to become familiar with the pattern of information in each of these logs when SQL Server 2000 has been installed successfully to quickly differentiate events that indicate a problem.

Practice: Reviewing the SQL Server Error Log and the Windows Application Log

In this practice you review the SQL Server Error log and the Windows Application log.

▶ **To review the SQL Server error log and the Windows application log**

1. Ensure that you are logged on to the SelfPacedSQL.MSFT domain controller as Administrator.
2. Using Windows Explorer, locate the Errorlog file in the C:\Program Files\Microsoft SQL Server\Mssql\Log folder.
3. Right-click Errorlog and then click Open With.

    The Open With dialog box appears.
4. Click Notepad and then click OK.

    The contents of the current error log appear in Notepad. Review the entries related to the startup of SQL Server 2000. Become familiar with typical entries.
5. Click Start, point to Programs, point to Administrative Tools, and then click Event Viewer.
6. In the console root, click Application.

    In the details pane, the contents of the Application Log appear. Review the entries related to the startup of SQL Server 2000. Become familiar with typical entries. Notice that entries for both of your SQL Server 2000 instances appear here.
7. Close Windows Explorer, Notepad, and Event Viewer.

Lesson Summary

A SQL Server installation does not fail frequently. When it does fail, several log files record information to help determine the source of the failure. The SQL Server error log and the Windows application log are the most useful of these log files to the database administrator. Microsoft also provides online troubleshooters and Knowledge Base articles to help an administrator determine and resolve problems.

Review

Here are some questions to help you determine whether you have learned enough to move on to the next chapter. If you have difficulty answering these questions, review the material in this chapter before beginning the next chapter. The answers for these questions are located in the Appendix, "Questions and Answers."

1. You have decided to install SQL Server 2000 on a test computer to evaluate the new features available. You have a Pentium III 400-MHz laptop with 96 MB of memory. Will this laptop be sufficient for testing the new features of SQL Server 2000?

2. You are installing SQL Server 2000. You want SQL Server 2000 to be able to use your Microsoft Exchange Server to notify you when jobs succeed or fail. What type of account should you use for the SQL Server and SQL Server Agent services?

3. You are installing SQL Server 2000. You have a mixed network of computers including Windows NT servers and Novell servers. Your network supports both TCP/IP and NWLink IPX/SPX. Should you perform a typical or a Custom setup?

4. You are installing SQL Server 2000. You have heard that SQL Server 2000 allows you to install SQL Server 2000 side by side with SQL Server 7.0. If you install SQL Server 2000 as a named instance, what issues should you be aware of?

5. You are installing SQL Server 2000. You plan to install identical configurations on multiple computers to test the configuration's performance on different hardware platforms. You do not want to click your way through the SQL Server 2000 interactive Setup program each time you install SQL Server 2000. What should you do?

6. You have installed SQL Server 2000 on a test computer for evaluation. You had a problem initially starting the SQL Server service due to a logon failure. You solved the problem. You want to review the SQL Server error log related to the failure to start the SQL Server service. Can you do this, and if so, how?

C H A P T E R 3

Preparing to Use SQL Server 2000

About This Chapter

This chapter prepares you to use instances of SQL Server 2000 after an installation. You will begin with reviewing the results of the installation of SQL Server 2000. Next, you learn about controlling (starting, stopping, pausing, and modifying) the SQL Server services. Finally, you learn to work with the main graphical and command-prompt administration tools. After you have completed these tasks, you will be ready to begin administering SQL Server 2000.

Before You Begin

To complete this chapter, you must have

- A computer that meets or exceeds the minimum hardware requirements listed in Table 2.1, "Hardware Requirements," in Lesson 1 of Chapter 2.
- Microsoft Windows 2000 Server running on your computer on an NTFS partition.
- A computer with a NetBIOS name of SelfPacedCPU, configured as a domain controller in the SelfPacedSQL.MSFT domain.
- Installed a default and at least one named instance of SQL Server 2000 (see Chapter 2).

Lesson 1: Reviewing the Results of Installation

After you have installed SQL Server 2000, it is important to familiarize yourself with the results of the installation. This includes reviewing the SQL Server 2000 files and folders in the file system, the SQL Server 2000 registry entries in the Windows registry, and the SQL Server 2000 programs in the Microsoft SQL Server program group on the Start menu. It also includes understanding the installation result differences between a default instance and a named instance at both the file system and the Windows registry levels. Perhaps most importantly, it is critical to understand the default security permissions set on the NTFS file system file structure and Windows registry keys. Improper or inadequate permissions can cause problems that you might need to troubleshoot.

After this lesson, you will be able to

- Use Windows Explorer to examine the files and folders added to the file system for the default or a named instance of SQL Server 2000

- Use Registry Editor to examine the registry entries that were added to the Windows 2000 registry for the default or a named instance of SQL Server 2000

- Understand the default security permissions set on folders and registry keys for the domain user account used for the SQL Server and SQL Server Agent services

- Know which SQL Server 2000 programs are available from the Start menu

Estimated lesson time: 45 minutes

What Files and Folders Were Added?

After a new installation of SQL Server 2000 (not an upgrade), the default folder location for all files and folders added to the Windows file system is the \Program Files\Microsoft SQL Server folder on the same partition as the Windows operating system. Within this folder, two subfolders are created. The first subfolder is called 80. This folder and its subfolders contain the shared files that are common between all instances of SQL Server 2000. The location for this folder cannot be changed. This folder contains tools, utilities, and SQL Server 2000 Books Online. Table 3.1 lists these shared folders and briefly describes their contents.

Note Deleting any of the files or folders listed in Table 3.1 might cause SQL Server 2000 to lose functionality or data, and might require that you uninstall and then reinstall SQL Server 2000 to regain that functionality.

Table 3-1.   Contents of the Shared Folders in the \Program Files\Microsoft SQL Server\80 Folder

Folder	Contents Description
\Program Files\Microsoft SQL Server\80\Com	Contains DLLs for COM objects, including the replication DLLs and executable programs.
\Program Files\Microsoft SQL Server\80\Com\Resources	Contains Run Length Limited (RLL) resource files used by the DLLs in the Com folder. The subfolder number within this folder will vary depending upon the localized version; 1033 is for U.S. English.
\Program Files\Microsoft SQL Server\80\Tools\Binn and \Program Files\Microsoft SQL Server\80\Tools\Binn\ Resources	Contains all of the shared SQL Server 2000 client administrative executable programs and their associated DLLs, RLLs, and Help files. It also contains a few miscellaneous shared files, such as the default SQL Server Enterprise Manager MMC console.
\Program Files\Microsoft SQL Server\80\Tools\Books	Contains SQL Server 2000 Books Online files, including SQL Server 2000 online Help files.
\Program Files\Microsoft SQL Server\80\Tools\Dev-Tools	Contains files and sample programs for use by developers. The exact contents of this folder will vary depending upon the choices you made during installation. You can choose to install additional files and programs for developers during a custom setup.
\Program Files\Microsoft SQL Server\80\Tools\Html	Contains HTML, JScript, and Graphics Interchange Format (GIF) files used by SQL Server 2000 Books Online and by SQL Server Enterprise Manager.
\Program Files\Microsoft SQL Server\80\Tools\Scripts	Contains Transact-SQL scripts by SQL Query Analyzer for object searches.
\Program Files\Microsoft SQL Server\80\Tools\Templates\Dts	Contains the DTS demonstration template file, Template Demo.dtt. This is a partially configured DTS package for copying data between an OLE DB data source and an OLE DB data destination. Templates are read-only files for use in creating packages.
\Program Files\Microsoft SQL Server\80\Tools\Templates\SQL Profiler	Contains default template files with a variety of trace definitions for use with SQL Profiler. These template files have a .tdf file extension.
\Program Files\Microsoft SQL Server\80\Tools\Templates\SQL Query Analyzer	Contains boilerplate files with Transact-SQL scripts for performing a variety of administrative tasks, such as creating a table or managing linked servers. These template files have a .tql file extension.

The SQL Server 2000 Setup program also creates a second folder containing program and data files that are unique for each SQL Server 2000 instance. The default location for this folder is \Program Files\Microsoft SQL Server; however, you can change this default during setup. This is also the default location for all newly created user databases for the SQL Server instance. The folder name for the default instance is Mssql and for a named instance is Mssql$*InstanceName*. Program file settings and databases for each instance are unique and are contained in this separate subfolder tree.

Table 3.2 lists the program and data folders that are unique to each instance and briefly describes their contents. For convenience, the folder paths for the default instance installed in the default location are used in this table. For a named instance, substitute Mssql$*InstanceName* for Mssql in the folder path.

Table 3-2.   Program and Data Folders That Are Unique to Each Instance of SQL Server 2000

Folder	Contents Description
\Program Files\Microsoft SQL Server \Mssql\	Contains information required to properly uninstall SQL Server 2000. It also includes the subfolders described below.
\Program Files\Microsoft SQL Server \Mssql\Backup	Contains all backup files that were saved to the default location.
\Program Files\Microsoft SQL Server \Mssql\Binn and \Program Files \Microsoft SQL Server\Mssql\Binn \Resources	Contains all of the unique SQL Server 2000 executable programs and their associated DLLs and RLLs. This folder also contains DLLs for extended stored procedures.
\Program Files\Microsoft SQL Server \Mssql\Data	Contains the SQL Server 2000 system and sample user database files. This is also the default location for all user-created databases.
\Program Files\Microsoft SQL Server \Mssql\Ftdata	Contains the SQL Server 2000 full-text search catalog files.
\Program Files\Microsoft SQL Server \Mssql\Install	Contains all of the Transact-SQL scripts used by the SQL Server 2000 Setup program. This includes the scripts to reinstall the Northwind or Pubs databases, if desired. It also contains a Setup.iss file that captured the interactive installation choices you made during setup.
\Program Files\Microsoft SQL Server \Mssql\Jobs	The storage location for temporary job output files.
\Program Files\Microsoft SQL Server \Mssql\Log	Contains the SQL Server and SQL Server Agent error log files. This folder contains the current logs, as well as a number of previous error log files.
\Program Files\Microsoft SQL Server \Mssql\Repldata	The default working location for replication tasks, including the storage of snapshot files used in replication tasks.

Table 3-2.   Program and Data Folders That Are Unique to Each Instance of SQL Server 2000

Folder	Contents Description
\Program Files\Microsoft SQL Server \Mssql\Repldata\Ftp	The working location for the storage of replication snapshot files when using the Internet and supporting anonymous subscribers.
\Program Files\Microsoft SQL Server \Mssql\Upgrade	Contains the files required for a version upgrade from SQL Server 6.5 to SQL Server 2000. Only the default instance contains this folder and these files.

Figure 3.1 shows the hierarchy of the folder structure explained in Table 3.2.

Figure 3.1.   Hierarchy of the program and data folders that are unique to each instance of SQL Server 2000.

What Permissions Were Set in the NTFS File System

When SQL Server 2000 is installed on an NTFS partition, the Setup program sets access permissions to the Mssql or Mssql$*InstanceName* subfolder structure that holds the program and data files for each instance. The Setup program ensures that only the SQL Server and SQL Server Agent domain user accounts and members of the local Administrators group have read or write access to this folder structure. See Figure 3.2.

The SQL Server services domain user account requires Full Control permission on all files and folders in this subfolder tree for these SQL Server services to function properly. The SQL Server services using the local system account have Full Control permission because the local system account, by design, is a member of the local Administrators group. Only the SQL Server services domain user account and members of the local Administrators group have modify, write, or delete permissions to this folder structure, so unauthorized users are prevented from tampering with the program and data files. This is another one of many good reasons to use the NTFS file system.

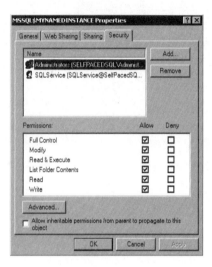

Figure 3.2.   Permissions set for the Mssql$MyNamedInstance subfolder.

Note   By default, authenticated users can read and execute all files in the Program Files folder tree, but have no permission to write, modify, or delete any of these files. The Setup program modifies this default, but only for the Program and Data Files folders, granting Full Control permissions on these folders to the domain user account used by the SQL Server services.

Practice: Reviewing the Files and Folders That Were Created

In this practice you use Windows Explorer to review the files and folders that were created by the SQL Server 2000 Setup program, and their permissions.

▶   **To review the files and folders that were created**

1. Ensure that you are logged on to the SelfPacedSQL.MSFT domain controller as Administrator.

2. Click Start, point to Programs, point to Accessories, and then click Windows Explorer.

    The Windows Explorer window appears.

3. In the console tree, expand My Computer, expand Local Disk (C), expand Program Files, and then expand Microsoft SQL Server.

    Notice that there are three subfolders named 80, Mssql, and Mssql$MyNamed-Instance. The 80 folder holds the common files. The other two folders contain the program and data files for the default instance and the named instance that we called *MyNamedInstance*.

4. In the console tree, expand 80, expand Tools, and then click Binn.

5. On the View menu, click Details.

    Notice that the full details of all files in the Binn folder appear in the details pane.

6. On the Tools menu, click Folder Options.

    The Folder Options dialog box appears with the General tab selected.

7. On the View tab, click the Like Current Folder button.

    The Folder Views message box appears.

8. Click the Yes button.

    All folders will now display all file details by default.

9. Click OK to close the Folder Options dialog box.

10. In the details pane, click the Type column to sort by type and then review the client administrative tools executable programs (applications).

    Most of these tools will be covered in detail later in this book.

11. In the console tree, expand Mssql and then click Binn.

12. In the details pane, click the Type column and then review the SQL Server 2000 executable programs (applications).

    Most of these programs will be covered in detail later in this book. Notice the Sqlservr.exe and Sqlagent.exe programs. These are the executable versions of the SQL Server and the SQL Server Agent services.

13. In the console tree, expand Mssql$MyNamedInstance.

    Compare this folder structure to the folder structure for Mssql. Notice that there is no Upgrade folder. This folder only exists for the default instance.

14. In the console tree, right-click Mssql and then click Properties.

    The Mssql Properties dialog box appears with the General tab selected.

15. Click the Security tab.

    Notice that only the SQLService domain user account that we are using as the service account for the SQL Server and SQL Server Agent services for this instance and members of the local Administrators group have permissions to this folder and its subfolders.

16. Click Cancel to close the Mssql Properties dialog box.

17. In the console tree, right-click 80 and then click Properties.

    The 80 Properties dialog box appears with the General tab selected.

18. Click the Security tab.

Notice that all authenticated users have permission to read, list, and execute files in this folder and all subfolders, but have no permission to write, modify, or delete files. This includes the SQL Server services domain user account. Only members of the Administrators and Server Operators local group, the Creator Owner group, and the System group have additional rights to this folder and its subfolders.

19. Click Cancel to close the 80 Properties dialog box, and then close Windows Explorer.

What Registry Keys Were Added

When you install SQL Server 2000, the Setup program adds registry keys to the Windows registry related to the shared files and services, and related to the unique program and data files for each instance. Registry keys related to the shared files and services are added to the following locations for all SQL Server 2000 instances:

- HKEY_LOCAL_MACHINE\SOFTWARE\Microsoft\Microsoft SQL Server\80
- HKEY_LOCAL_MACHINE\SOFTWARE\Microsoft\MSDTC
- HKEY_LOCAL_MACHINE\SYSTEM\CurrentControlSet\Services \MSSQLServerADHelper
- HKEY_LOCAL_MACHINE\SOFTWARE\Microsoft\MSSQLServer\Client

Registry keys relating to the unique program and data files for the default instance are added at and under the following locations:

- HKEY_LOCAL_MACHINE\SOFTWARE\Microsoft\MSSQLServer
- HKEY_LOCAL_MACHINE\SYSTEM\CurrentControlSet\Services \MSSQLServer

Registry keys relating to the unique program and data files for a named instance are added at and under the following locations:

- HKEY_LOCAL_MACHINE\SOFTWARE\Microsoft\Microsoft SQL Server*InstanceName*
- HKEY_LOCAL_MACHINE\SYSTEM\CurrentControlSet\Services \MSSQL$*Instancename*

Figure 3.3 shows some of these registry keys.

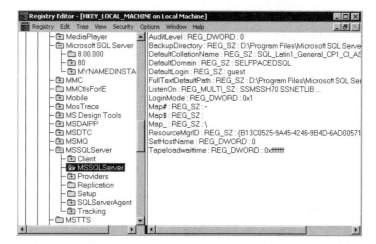

Figure 3.3.   The MSSQLServer registry key added by the SQL Server Setup program.

What Permissions Were Set on Registry Keys

When adding these registry keys, the SQL Server Setup program generally limits read or write access to these keys to the SQL Server services domain user account and members of the local Administrators group (and sometimes the System group). For certain keys, read access is granted to authenticated users and members of the local Power Users group. In addition, owners of objects may have access to sub-keys through the Creator Owner group if they are granted permission to create objects. By default, the SQL Server services domain user account and members of the local Administrators group have Full Control access to these registry keys and their subkeys. For the default instance, the Setup program specifically limits access to all registry keys at or under the following registry keys:

- HKEY_LOCAL_MACHINE\SOFTWARE\Microsoft\MSSQLServer \MSSQLServer

- HKEY_LOCAL_MACHINE\SOFTWARE\Microsoft\MSSQLServer \Providers

- HKEY_LOCAL_MACHINE\SOFTWARE\Microsoft\MSSQLServer\Setup

- HKEY_LOCAL_MACHINE\SOFTWARE\Microsoft\MSSQLServer \Replication

- HKEY_LOCAL_MACHINE\SOFTWARE\Microsoft\MSSQLServer \SQLServerAgent

- HKEY_LOCAL_MACHINE\SOFTWARE\Microsoft\MSSQLServer \Tracking

- HKEY_LOCAL_MACHINE\SYSTEM\CurrentControlSet\Services \MSSQLServer

For a named instance, the Setup program similarly limits access to all registry keys at or under the following registry keys:

- HKEY_LOCAL_MACHINE\SOFTWARE\Microsoft\ Microsoft SQL Server*InstanceName*
- HKEY_LOCAL_MACHINE\SYSTEM\CurrentControlSet\Services\ MSSQL$*InstanceName*

Note Because the registry structure for the default instance is different than for a named instance (for compatibility with previous versions of SQL Server), the Setup program has to set permissions on more individual keys for the default instance than for a named instance. For a named instance, it only has to set permissions on two keys and let the permissions flow down to all keys under those keys.

Figure 3.4 shows permissions on the MYNAMEDINSTANCE registry key.

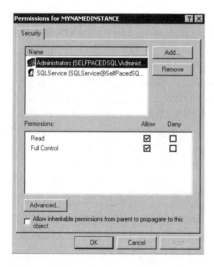

Figure 3.4.   Permissions on the MYNAMEDINSTANCE registry key.

Note You must use the Regedt32.exe version of the Registry Editor to view the permissions on registry keys, rather than the Regedit.exe version of Registry Editor.

Finally, for any instance of SQL Server 2000, the SQL Server services domain user account requires read and write access to the following existing registry keys. The Setup program grants the SQL Server services domain user account read and write permissions to all registry keys at or under the following existing registry keys:

- HKEY_LOCAL_MACHINE\SOFTWARE\Clients\Mail
- HKEY_LOCAL_MACHINE\SOFTWARE\Microsoft\Windows NT\Current-Version\Perflib

Inadequate permissions to these registry keys will cause mail-related and performance monitoring-related failures.

Practice: Reviewing Permissions on Registry Keys

In this practice you use Registry Editor to verify the permission set by the SQL Server 2000 Setup program on certain registry keys.

▶ **To review permissions on registry keys**

1. Ensure that you are logged on to the SelfPacedSQL.MSFT domain controller as Administrator.
2. Click Start and then click Run.

    The Run dialog box appears.
3. In the Open drop-down combo box, type **regedt32** and then click OK.

    The Registry Editor appears.
4. On the Window menu, click HKEY_LOCAL_MACHINE on Local Machine.
5. In the console tree, expand SOFTWARE, expand Microsoft, and then expand Microsoft SQL Server.

    Notice the 80 registry key. This key is common to the default and all named instances. This key relates to the shared files. Also notice the MyNamedInstance key. This key relates to the unique program and data files for your named instance.
6. In the console tree, click MyNamedInstance.
7. On the Security menu, click Permissions.

    The Permissions For MyNamedInstance dialog box appears. Notice that only the SQLService domain user account and the local Administrators group have full control access to this registry key.
8. Click Cancel.
9. In the console tree under SOFTWARE\Microsoft, expand Windows NT, expand CurrentVersion, and then click Perflib.
10. On the Security menu, click Permissions.

    Notice that only the local Administrators group, the SQLService domain user account, and the System group have permission to write to this registry key. The Interactive and Server Operators group has permission to read this registry key. In addition, owners of objects may have permission on subkeys through the Creator Owner group.
11. Click Cancel.
12. Close the Registry Editor.

What Programs Were Added to the Start Menu

When you install SQL Server 2000, the Setup program adds the SQL Server 2000 programs used most frequently to the Start menu. See Figure 3.5. Most of these programs were introduced in Chapter 1. Chapter 2 covered the use of the Client Network Utility and the Server Network Utility. SQL Server Service Manager, SQL Server Enterprise Manager, and SQL Query Analyzer are covered in Lessons 2 and 3 of this chapter. Configuring SQL XML support will be discussed in Chapter 12. Importing and exporting of data will be discussed in Chapter 7, and SQL Profiler will be discussed in Chapter 14.

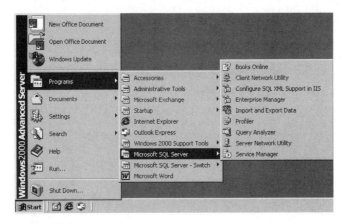

Figure 3.5.   SQL Server 2000 programs added to the Start menu by the Setup program.

Lesson Summary

The SQL Server 2000 Setup program installs SQL Server 2000 files into a number of different folder structures. One folder structure (\Program Files\Microsoft SQL Server\80) contains the files common to all SQL Server 2000 instances on the computer. Another folder structure (either \Program Files\Microsoft SQL Server\MSSQL or \Program Files\Microsoft SQL Server\Mssql$*InstanceName*) contains the program and data files unique to the particular SQL Server 2000 instance. On an NTFS partition, the Setup program secures the folder structure containing the program and data file folders by limiting access permissions to this folder structure to the SQL Server services domain user account and members of the local Administrators group. In addition, the Setup program adds and limits access to a number of keys in the Windows registry. It also ensures that the SQL Server services domain user account has write access to two existing registry keys. Finally, the Microsoft SQL Server program group is created containing shortcuts to the most commonly used SQL Server 2000 executable programs and wizards, as well as to Books Online.

Lesson 2: Starting, Stopping, Pausing, and Modifying SQL Server 2000 Services

During the installation of SQL Server 2000 on Windows 2000 or Windows NT 4.0, the SQL Server services were installed and configured. After setup is complete, it is important to familiarize yourself with the default configuration of these SQL Server services. A number of tools are provided by SQL Server 2000 as well as by Windows 2000 or Windows NT 4.0 for this purpose. These tools are also used to start, stop, pause, and modify these SQL Server services. You need to become proficient in the use of these tools. Finally, changing the SQL Server or SQL Server Agent service account after setup must be done properly, or you might have NTFS permissions problems or Windows registry permissions problems.

After this lesson, you will be able to

- Understand the default configuration for each SQL Server 2000 service
- Use several different tools to start, stop, pause, and modify SQL Server services
- Change the service account after setup

Estimated lesson time: 45 minutes

What Is the Default Configuration for Each SQL Server Service?

During the installation of SQL Server 2000, the Setup program gave you the option to define parameters for the SQL Server and SQL Server Agent services. Remember that each instance of SQL Server 2000 has its own version of each of these two services, each with its own parameters. The first parameter defined for each of these services is the startup type. By default, the SQL Server service is configured to start automatically with the Windows operating system, whereas the SQL Server Agent service is configured to be started manually. The second parameter defined for each of these services during setup is the service account for each service. By default, the same defined domain user account is used for each of these services. The domain user account of the administrator installing SQL Server 2000 is the default of the Setup program; however, using a dedicated domain user account is highly recommended.

The Setup program configures the parameters of the MS DTC and Microsoft Search services automatically. Remember that there is only one version of each of these services for all instances of SQL Server 2000. By default, each is configured to start automatically with the Windows operating system and to use the local system account. A domain user account is not required because neither of these services needs authentication beyond the local server.

Note   There is one additional service called the MSSQLServerAdHelper service. This service is used to communicate with Active Directory directory services and is covered in Chapter 12.

Starting, Stopping, and Pausing SQL Server 2000 Services

Before you can use a SQL Server 2000 service, the service must be started. The SQL Server 2000 Setup program starts the MS DTC and Microsoft Search services if they are not already running, and leaves them running. It starts the SQL Server service during installation to configure this instance of the SQL Server service, but leaves this service stopped when installation is complete. The Setup program does not start the SQL Server Agent service during installation.

Note   The terms SQL Server service and SQL Server Agent service are used to refer generically to these services, regardless of whether the services of the default instance or a named instance are being referred to. The names of these services for the default instance are MSSQLServer and SQLServerAgent. The names of these services for each named instance are MSSQL$*InstanceName* and SQLAgent$*InstanceName*.

There are several different tools to start, stop, or pause SQL Server services. SQL Server Service Manager is perhaps the most commonly used tool. SQL Server Service Manager is located in the Microsoft SQL Server program group, as well as the Windows Startup group. When this application is launched, it installs itself as a taskbar application, and appears to the left of the taskbar clock. Once started, SQL Server Service Manager will always appear on the taskbar unless you right-click its icon and click Exit. The SQL Server Service Manager always displays the state of the default service when initially started. Services are polled, by default, every five seconds to verify their current state.

When you double-click the SQL Server Service Manager taskbar tray icon, you can start, stop, or pause SQL Server services on each instance of SQL Server 2000 installed on the computer. See Figure 3.6.

Notice that by setting or clearing a check box, you can also configure whether a given service starts automatically when the Windows operating system starts. When you choose to pause or stop a service, you receive a confirmation box.

Figure 3.6.   The SQL Server Service Manager dialog box.

You can disable this confirmation box by right-clicking the icon, clicking Options, and then clearing the Verify Service Control Action check box. See Figure 3.7.

Figure 3.7.   The SQL Server Service Manager Options dialog box.

Notice that you can also change the default service that is displayed when SQL Server Service Manager starts, as well as modify the polling interval in seconds.

Note   The SQL Server Service Manager taskbar icon changes slightly to reflect the SQL Server service being displayed. Also, if you look closely, you can see a red pulse flash on and off at the lower right of its icon corresponding to how often the service is being polled.

There are a number of additional methods of controlling the state of SQL Server services. SQL Query Analyzer and SQL Profiler provide a check box option in the Connect To SQL Server dialog box to start a selected SQL Server instance if it is stopped. See Figure 3.8.

SQL Server Enterprise Manager allows you to start, stop, or pause a registered SQL Server 2000 instance by right-clicking on the instance and selecting the desired state. See Figure 3.9.

The Services MMC in Windows 2000 and the Services applet in Windows NT 4.0 also allow you to start, stop, or pause any SQL Server 2000 service. Finally, SQL Server Enterprise Manager, the Services MMC, and the Services applet also allow you to configure whether a particular SQL Server service starts automatically, as well as other configuration parameters.

Figure 3.8.   Starting a stopped SQL Server instance when connecting.

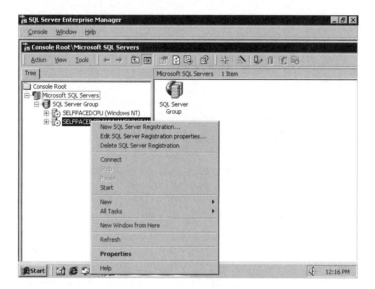

Figure 3.9.   Options on the context menu for starting, stopping, or pausing SQL Server.

You can also use the NET command to start, stop, and pause SQL Server services from a command prompt; for example, NET START MSSQLServer or NET START SQLServerAgent. You can also start an instance of SQL Server or SQL Server Agent as an application by double-clicking on it in Windows Explorer or by typing the name of the executable at a command prompt (provided it is not already running as a service). The names of these applications are: Sqlservr and Sqlagent. To stop either of these services running as an application, press CTRL+C in the Command Prompt window.

Note   Any of the preceding tools can also be used to control the state of SQL Server services on remote computers that you have permission to administer.

Practice: Starting SQL Server Services

In this practice you start several SQL Server services using different tools.

► **To start SQL Server services**

1. Ensure that you are logged on to the SelfPacedSQL.MSFT domain controller as Administrator.
2. Click Start, point to Programs, point to Microsoft SQL Server, and then click Service Manager.

    The SQL Server Service Manager dialog box appears. In the Server drop-down combo box, SelfPacedCPU appears with SQL Server displayed in the Services drop-down list as the default service. This dialog box shows that the SQL Server service is configured to auto-start when the operating system starts, and the status line indicates that it is stopped.

    Note   The service will not be stopped if you have rebooted your computer since you installed SQL Server 2000.
    ---

3. Click the Start/Continue button (green triangle) to start the SQL Server service.

    The status line indicates that the SQL Server service on your computer is starting, and then indicates that it is running.

4. In the Services drop-down list, change the displayed service to SQL Server Agent.

    The dialog box changes to display the status of the SQL Server Agent service. Notice that this service is not configured to start automatically, and that the status line indicates this service is stopped.

5. Select the Auto-Start Service When OS Starts check box.
6. Click the Start/Continue button to start the SQL Server Agent service.

    The status line indicates that the SQL Server Agent service on your computer is starting, and then indicates that it is running.

7. In the Server drop-down combo box, change the server to display your named instance.

    The dialog box changes to display the status of the SQL Server Agent service for SelfPacedCPU. The service is stopped and is not configured to start automatically.

8. Select the Auto-Start Service When OS Starts check box, but do not start the SQL Agent service.
9. Close the SQL Server Service Manager dialog box.

    Notice that the SQL Server Service Manager icon remains on the taskbar.

10. Click Start, point to Programs, point to Accessories, and then click Command Prompt.

    The Command Prompt window appears.

11. Type **net start** and then press ENTER.

    A list of all started Windows 2000 services is displayed. Notice that MSSQLSERVER and SQLSERVERAGENT are both started. Also notice that the Distributed Transaction Coordinator and Microsoft Search services are also started.

12. Type **net start sqlagent$mynamedinstance** and then press ENTER.

    Notice that the SQL Server Agent service for your named instance starts. The SQL Server service is also started because the SQL Server Agent service requires the SQL Server service to also be running. Finally, notice that the SQL Server Service Manager icon on the taskbar indicates that the SQL Server Agent service for this instance is started.

13. Close the Command Prompt window.

14. On the taskbar, right-click the SQL Server Service Manager icon, and then click Options.

    The SQL Server Service Manager Options dialog box appears.

15. Clear the Verify Service Control Action check box, and then click OK.

Changing the SQL Server or SQL Server Agent Service Account After Setup

If you want to change the service account used by the SQL Server or SQL Server Agent services after setup, you must use SQL Server Enterprise Manager to ensure the proper functioning of these SQL Server services and SQL Server 2000. You launch SQL Server Enterprise Manager by clicking Start, pointing to Programs, pointing to Microsoft SQL Server, and then clicking Enterprise Manager. When you use SQL Server Enterprise Manager to change the service account of the SQL Server or SQL Server Agent services, SQL Server Enterprise Manager ensures that proper permissions are set in the NTFS file system and in the Windows registry for this new service account. SQL Server Enterprise Manager also ensures that this service account is granted the following required user privileges: log on as a service, lock pages in memory (used for AWE), and enable trusted for delegation (required for impersonation). If you use the Services MMC in Windows 2000 or the Services applet in Windows NT 4.0, some of these permissions and privileges are not set.

Note   When you change the service account, the permissions in the NTFS file system and the Windows registry held by a domain user account previously used are not removed. You should either remove them manually, or disable (or delete) the domain user account previously used if no other service is using this domain user account.

If you are running the SQL Server service under a non-administrator account, when you attempt to change either the SQL Server or the SQL Server Agent service account (or its password), you are prompted to supply the name and password of an administrator account. This account is used to apply the required permissions and privileges to the NTFS file system and the Windows registry. See Figure 3.10.

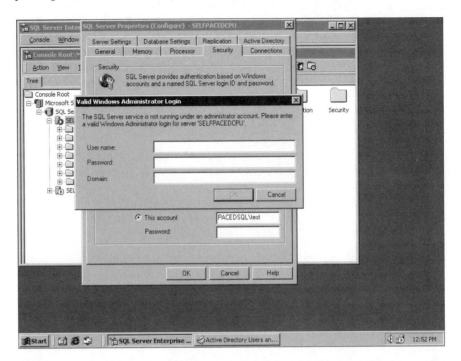

Figure 3.10.   Supplying the name, password, and domain of an administrator account.

In addition, changing the SQL Server service domain user account in SQL Server Enterprise Manager is required for proper use and administration of the Microsoft Search service by SQL Server 2000. Although this service runs in the security context of the local system account, the SQL Server service must be registered as an administrator of the Microsoft Search service for SQL Server 2000 to use and administer the Microsoft Search service. For this relationship to be maintained when a change occurs in the service account used by the SQL Server service, the change in the service account must be made using SQL Server Enterprise Manager.

Lesson Summary

The SQL Server 2000 Setup program configures the SQL Server service to start automatically when the Windows operating system starts, but configures the SQL Server Agent service to start manually. To use SQL Server 2000 after installation, you must manually start the SQL Server service (unless you restart the Windows operating system). Several tools are provided that you can use to start any of the SQL Server services. SQL Server Service Manager is the tool used most frequently. Finally, changing the service account used by the SQL Server or SQL Server Agent service should only be done using SQL Server Enterprise Manager. This ensures the proper setting of all permissions and privileges in the NTFS file system and the Windows registry.

Lesson 3: Working with Osql, SQL Query Analyzer, and SQL Server Enterprise Manager

After you have installed SQL Server 2000, reviewed the results of the installation, and started the SQL Server service, you are ready to begin working with the primary SQL Server 2000 administration tools and utilities. These are Osql, the primary command-prompt utility, and SQL Query Analyzer and SQL Server Enterprise Manager, the primary graphical tools for querying and administering SQL Server 2000. As a database administrator, you will use these tools daily and need to become very familiar with their use.

After this lesson, you will be able to

- Use Osql to connect to, query, and administer SQL Server 2000
- Use SQL Query Analyzer to connect to, query, and administer SQL Server 2000
- Use SQL Server Enterprise Manager to connect to and administer SQL Server 2000

Estimated lesson time: 45 minutes

Working with Osql

Osql is a 32-bit command-prompt utility used to query an instance of SQL Server 2000 interactively using Transact-SQL statements, system procedures, and script files. It is also used to submit batches and jobs, including operating system commands, to SQL Server 2000. Use the GO command to signal the end of a batch and tell the SQL Server service to process the batch. By default, results are formatted and returned to the console, but can also be sent to a text file. Use QUIT or EXIT to close Osql and return to a command prompt. Osql uses the ODBC API to communicate with SQL Server 2000. Osql is frequently used to test basic connectivity to SQL Server 2000.

Note   Osql replaces Isql, which was used by SQL Server 6.5 and earlier versions of SQL Server. Isql uses the DB-Library API rather than the ODBC API. Although Isql ships with SQL Server 2000, it is used mainly for backward compatibility and does not support all features supported by Osql, including named instances.

When using Osql to connect to SQL Server 2000, there are many arguments that you can pass as part of your connection string. Be aware that arguments passed to Osql are case-sensitive. Also, be aware that a dash (-) and a slash (/) are used interchangeably. SQL Server Books Online provides the syntax for all arguments supported by Osql, along with some examples. The two most important arguments for getting started are the authentication method and the server/instance to which you want to connect.

If you want to connect using Windows authentication using your Windows 2000 or Windows NT 4.0 user account, use the –E argument. Otherwise, use the –U and the –P arguments to pass a valid SQL Server user login ID and password. Be aware that both the login ID and the password are case-sensitive. If you want to use a SQL Server user login ID, SQL Server must be configured for Mixed Mode authentication. Use the –S argument to specify the server/instance to which you want to connect. If no server name is specified or no instance is specified, Osql connects to the default instance on the local server, or the named server. You can use Osql to connect to local and remote servers. Use the –L argument to display a list of all local instances and all remote instances broadcasting on the network. To connect to a named instance on a local or remote server, you must specify the server name followed by the instance name. For example, to connect to a named instance on your local computer using Windows authentication, use the following command: OSQL –E –S *YourServerName\YourInstanceName*. See Figure 3.11.

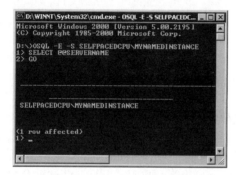

Figure 3.11.   Using the Osql command with the –E switch.

Note   You must be using the SQL Server 2000 version of Osql to connect to a named instance. The version of Osql that shipped with SQL Server 7.0 can only be used to connect to the default instance.

Practice: Using Osql to Query SQL Server 2000 Instances

In this practice you use Osql to connect to SQL Server 2000 instances.

▶ **To use Osql to connect to SQL Server 2000 instances**

1. Ensure that you are logged on to the SelfPacedSQL.MSFT domain controller as Administrator.
2. Click Start and then click Run.

    The Run dialog box appears.

3. In the Open drop-down combo box, type **cmd** and then press ENTER.

    The Command Prompt window appears.

4. Type **OSQL –E** and then press ENTER.

    Osql connects to the default instance of SQL Server 2000 on your local server (SelfPacedCPU) and then displays a 1> prompt, waiting for more input from you. If you cannot connect, you will receive an ODBC error message. A common error at this point is typing a lowercase "e" rather than an uppercase "E".

5. At the 1> prompt, type **SELECT @@SERVERNAME** and press ENTER to query the SQL Server 2000 instance using the @@*SERVERNAME* configuration function.

    Notice that the 2> prompt appears. The first command is not executed because you have not informed SQL Server 2000 of the end of a batch.

6. At the 2> prompt, type **SELECT @@VERSION** and then press ENTER to query the SQL Server 2000 instance using the @@*VERSION* configuration function.

    Notice that the 3> prompt appears. Neither command is executed.

7. At the 3> prompt, type **GO** and then press ENTER to submit the batch to SQL Server 2000 for processing.

    SQL Server 2000 is queried and returns the name of your local server (Self-PacedCPU) and the version (including the edition) of SQL Server (SQL Server 2000 – Enterprise Evaluation Edition) that is installed on your computer. In addition, the version of your Windows operating system is displayed. It also returns you to a 1> prompt for a new query.

8. Type **EXIT** and then press ENTER.

    Osql exits and returns you to a command prompt.

9. Type **OSQL –L** and then press ENTER.

    Osql returns the names of the instances of SQL Server installed on your local computer, or broadcasting on your network.

10. Type **OSQL –E –S SelfPacedCPU\MyNamedInstance** and then press ENTER.

    Osql connects to the named instance of SQL Server 2000 you installed on your local server and then displays a 1> prompt, waiting for more input from you.

11. Type **SELECT SYSTEM_USER** and then press ENTER.

    SYSTEM_USER is a niladic function used to return the current system username.

12. Type **GO** and then press ENTER.

    Osql returns your current security context within SQL Server 2000. Because you connected to SQL Server 2000 using a trusted connection, your current security context is SelfPacedSQL\Administrator. Osql then displays a 1> prompt, waiting for more input from you.

13. Type **QUIT** and then press ENTER.

14. Close the Command Prompt window.

Working with SQL Query Analyzer

SQL Query Analyzer is used for creating and managing database objects and testing Transact-SQL statements, batches, and scripts interactively. SQL Query Analyzer is one of the programs in the Microsoft SQL Server program group, and is available from the Start menu. When you launch SQL Query Analyzer, you can choose to connect to local or remote instances of SQL Server 2000 (as well as earlier versions of SQL Server). In the Connect To SQL Server dialog box, you can type or browse to select an instance of SQL Server to which to connect. This includes connecting to earlier versions of SQL Server. Be aware that (local) refers to the default instance on the local server and that using a period or a blank entry in the SQL Server drop-down combo box also refers to the default instance on the local server. After selecting the instance to which you want to connect, you select the authentication method you want to use to connect. You can choose either Windows authentication or SQL Server authentication. Finally, if the SQL Server instance to which you want to connect is not started, you can choose to start it.

After you connect to SQL Server using SQL Query Analyzer, you need to become familiar with the SQL Server Query Analyzer interface. See Figure 3.12.

Multiple query windows can be displayed. Each query window can be a connection to a different instance of SQL Server 2000 (or earlier version of SQL Server), or simply a different query window using the same connection. The title bar for each query window displays connection information specifying the instance, the database, and the user security context for the connection. Each query window contains a Query pane and a Results pane. You execute a query by clicking the Execute Query button on the toolbar or by pressing the F5 key or CTRL+E. You can highlight a specific Transact-SQL statement to execute just a selected statement from a number of statements within a query window. You can also highlight a specific Transact-SQL statement or portion thereof, and then press SHIFT+F1 to display SQL Server Books Online for that particular statement or portion of statement. The results of a query are displayed in the Results pane. The Results pane contains multiple windows. The Grids tab displays the result set or sets from the query or queries. By default, the results are displayed as a grid, but can also be displayed as free-form text. The Message tab displays information and error messages related to the query. The Query status line also provides information regarding the query, including how long it has been running if it is still running, the number of rows returned, and the current row number if you are navigating the result set.

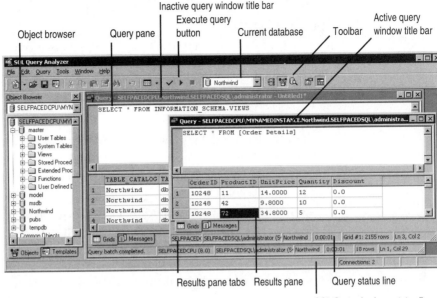

Figure 3.12.   The SQL Query Analyzer interface.

You can configure SQL Query Analyzer to display or hide the object browser. Either press the F8 key or click the Tools menu, point to Object Browser, and click Show/Hide. The Object Browser is a powerful tool used to navigate and work with the objects in a database. The Object Browser provides object scripting, stored procedure execution, and access to table and view objects. It is used primarily by database developers, but can be very useful for database administrators as well.

Each connection has connection properties. You can view the current connection properties by clicking the Current Connection Properties button on the toolbar or by clicking Options from the Tools menu. This allows you to set the connection properties for all new connections made with SQL Query Analyzer. Do not modify these properties without fully understanding the consequences. In general, the details of the connection properties are beyond the scope of this book. Use SQL Server Books Online for more information.

Practice: Using SQL Query Analyzer to Query SQL Server 2000 Instances

In this practice you use SQL Query Analyzer to query SQL Server 2000 instances.

▶ **To use SQL Query Analyzer to query SQL Server 2000 instances**

1. Ensure that you are logged on to the SelfPacedSQL.MSFT domain controller as Administrator.

2. Click Start, point to Programs, point to Microsoft SQL Server, and then click Query Analyzer.

   SQL Query Analyzer appears displaying the Connect To SQL Server dialog box.

3. Verify that Windows Authentication is selected and then click OK.

   You are connected to the default instance of SQL Server 2000 on your computer using your Windows user account. Verify this by reviewing the active query window title bar.

4. Press the F8 key to toggle the Object Browser. Leave the Object Browser visible.

5. In the Query pane, type **SELECT * FROM INFORMATION_SCHEMA.SCHEMATA**.

   This query will use information schema views to query this instance of SQL Server 2000 for all databases in this instance. Information schema views will be covered in Chapter 5. Notice the color coding. Blue indicates a keyword and gray indicates an operator. Refer to SQL Server Books Online for more information regarding color coding.

6. On the toolbar, click the Execute Query button.

   Notice that the result set from the query is displayed in the Results pane in the form of a grid. Information regarding all six databases is returned.

7. In the Object Browser, expand Master and then expand Views.

8. Right-click INFORMATION_SCHEMA.SCHEMATA and then click Open.

   Notice that the Open Table window displays the same information as the previous query.

9. Close the Open Table window.

10. In the Results pane of the original query, click the Messages tab.

    An informational message regarding the number of rows affected by the query (6 rows affected) is displayed.

11. In the Query pane, select INFORMATION_SCHEMA.SCHEMATA and then press SHIFT+F1.

    SQL Server Books Online appears displaying information regarding INFORMATION_SCHEMA.SCHEMATA in the console tree.

12. In the SQL Server Books Online console tree, double-click INFORMATION_SCHEMA.SCHEMATA view and then review the information in the details pane for Schemata.

13. Close SQL Server Books Online.

14. In the Query pane of SQL Query Analyzer, type **SELECT@@SERVERNAME** on a new line.

   Notice that the color of @@*SERVERNAME* changed to magenta when SQL Query Analyzer recognized this character string.

15. Select this new query only, and then press CTRL+E to execute just this query.

   Notice that you can select and execute a single query in a query window. The name of your server (SelfPacedCPU) is returned.

16. On the toolbar, click the Clear Window button.

   The contents of the Query pane are erased.

17. On the toolbar, click the Show Results Pane button.

   This toggles the Results pane, hiding the Results pane.

18. Press CTRL+R.

   This toggles the Results pane again, restoring the Results pane to visibility.

19. On the toolbar, click the New Query button.

   A new query window appears. Compare the two Query panes. Notice that you are connected to the same database in the same instance of SQL Server 2000 using the same security context.

20. In the active query window, type **USE Northwind** and then execute the query.

   Notice that the current database displayed on the toolbar changed to Northwind. Also notice that the active query window title bar now indicates a connection to the Northwind database rather than the Master database.

21. On the File menu, click Connect.

   The Connect To SQL Server dialog box appears.

22. Next to the SQL Server drop-down combo box, click the ellipsis (...) and select SelfPacedSQL\MyNamedInstance and then click OK.

   Notice that this named instance now appears in the SQL Server drop-down combo box.

23. Click OK to connect to your named instance.

   A new query window appears. The title bar indicates that you are connected to the Master database in your named instance. Notice that the current database on the toolbar is Master.

24. Close SQL Query Analyzer.

25. A SQL Query Analyzer message box appears.

26. Click the No To All button. Do not save any queries.

Working with SQL Server Enterprise Manager

SQL Server Enterprise Manager is the primary tool for server and database administration. SQL Server Enterprise Manager is one of the programs in the Microsoft SQL Server program group, and is available from the Start menu. When you launch SQL Server Enterprise Manager from the Start menu, a preconfigured Microsoft Management Console (MMC) console appears in user mode containing a snap-in for the administration of SQL Server 2000. If you open this MMC console in author mode, you can add additional snap-ins to this console (such as a snap-in for Event Viewer) to facilitate performing multiple common administration tasks using a single MMC console. To open the SQL Server Enterprise Manager MMC console in author mode, right-click the SQL Server Enterprise Manager.msc file in the \Program Files\Microsoft SQL Server\80\Tools\Binn folder and click Author. For more information regarding MMC consoles, use Windows 2000 Books Online.

After you open SQL Server Enterprise Manager, you need to become familiar with the interface. See Figure 3.13.

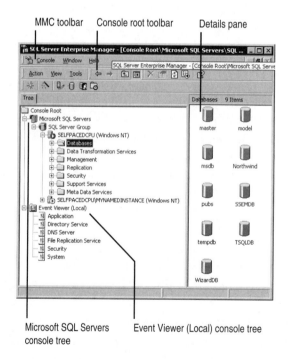

Figure 3.13.   The SQL Server Enterprise Manager interface.

The left pane of an MMC console is the console root container that contains separate console trees for each snap-in. A console tree is a hierarchical structure containing folders, extension snap-ins, monitor controls, tasks, wizards, and documentation. The SQL Server Enterprise Manager console contains the Microsoft SQL Servers console tree in the left pane. The Microsoft SQL Servers console tree contains the SQL Server Group container. This is the default group (or container) for all SQL Servers registered in this console for administration. When you install an instance of SQL Server 2000, the Setup program automatically registers that instance for administration on the local computer and places it in this default group. Each SQL Server 2000 instance has its own container. You can create separate groups containing selected servers for administrative convenience when administering many servers.

Note   Registering additional SQL Server 2000 instances is covered in Chapter 12.

When you click an object in a console tree, the right pane of the MMC console (called the details pane) displays additional subcontainers or the contents of that object, depending upon the object. You can specify and customize the view of the details pane, including modifying the items that appear on the toolbar when the object is selected. Some objects in the console tree have preconfigured taskpad views for that object. These views include preconfigured report information and shortcuts to relevant wizards to make it easier for you to perform certain tasks. Taskpad views are HTML pages. By default, the taskpad views are not enabled.

An MMC console contains two types of toolbars. The first is the MMC toolbar. This is primarily used when you are in author mode. The second type of toolbar is specific to each console tree. If your focus is within the Microsoft SQL Servers console tree, the console root toolbar (directly beneath the MMC toolbar) will contain menu items and tools specific to SQL Server Enterprise Manager. If your focus is within another console tree within the MMC console (such as Event Viewer), the console root toolbar will be specific to that console tree. The console root toolbar for SQL Server Enterprise Manager contains three context-sensitive menus: Action, View, and Tools. These menu items allow you to perform a variety of tasks, including launching other SQL Server 2000 tools, such as SQL Query Analyzer and SQL Profiler. The items that are available from each menu vary depending upon your focus within the console tree. For example, most items on the Tools menu are unavailable until your focus is on a specific instance of SQL Server 2000, because these tools act upon a particular instance.

To establish a connection to an instance of SQL Server 2000 that is registered in SQL Server Enterprise Manager, simply expand the container for that instance. You can also right-click an instance of SQL Server 2000 to start, stop, pause, or disconnect from that instance. By default, SQL Server Enterprise Manager will connect using Windows authentication and will start SQL Server 2000 if it is not already started. You can change these registration configuration defaults by right-clicking the container for an instance of SQL Server 2000 and editing the properties of the registration. For example, you can choose to connect to SQL Server 2000 using SQL Server authentication using the *sa* account. You can also choose to hide all system databases and objects as part of the registration configuration.

Finally, be aware that SQL Server Enterprise Manager connects to an instance of SQL Server 2000 as a client. By default, the SQL Server Enterprise Manager client polls the SQL Server service every 10 seconds to verify its state. In addition, changes to objects displayed in SQL Server Enterprise Manager after you establish a connection to a SQL Server 2000 instance generally will not be reflected immediately. This can include changes made by SQL Server Enterprise Manager and by SQL Query Analyzer. To update a particular object and its contents, right-click the object and click Refresh. To refresh all objects in a SQL Server instance, disconnect from the instance and then reconnect.

Practice: Working with the SQL Server Enterprise Manager MMC Console

In this practice you work with the SQL Server Enterprise Manager MMC console.

▶ **To work with the SQL Server Enterprise Manager MMC console**

1. Ensure that you are logged on to the SelfPacedSQL.MSFT domain controller as Administrator.

2. Click Start, point to Programs, point to Microsoft SQL Server, and then click Enterprise Manager.

    SQL Server Enterprise Manager appears displaying the Microsoft SQL Servers console tree in the console root. No other console trees appear.

3. On the MMC toolbar, click Console.

    Notice the only option available is Exit. No other menu options are available because SQL Server Enterprise Manager was opened in user mode.

4. Click Exit to close SQL Server Enterprise Manager.

5. Click Start, point to Search, and then click For Files Or Folders.

    The Search Results dialog box appears.

6. In the Search For File Or Folders Named: text box, type ***.msc** and then click the Search Now button.

    Notice that a plethora of preconfigured MMC consoles appear. Most are separate MMC consoles each for a specific Windows 2000 administrative task.

7. Right-click SQL Server Enterprise Manager.msc and then click Author.

    The SQL Server Enterprise Manager MMC console appears in author mode.

8. On the MMC toolbar, click Console and then click Add/Remove Snap-in.

    The Add/Remove Snap-in dialog box appears.

9. Click the Add button.

    The Add Standalone Snap-in dialog box appears displaying all of the available standalone snap-ins that may be added.

10. Select Event Viewer and then click the Add button.

    The Select Computer dialog box appears.

11. Click the Finish button to accept the default configuration, which is to always manage the local computer.

12. Click the Close button to close the Add Standalone Snap-in dialog box and then click OK to close the Add/Remove Snap-in dialog box.

    The SQL Server Enterprise Manager MMC console now displays two separate console trees, Microsoft SQL Servers and Event Viewer (Local).

13. On the Console menu, click Exit.

    A Microsoft Management Console message box appears.

14. Click the Yes button to save these new console settings to the default SQL Server Enterprise Manager MMC console.

15. Close the Search Results dialog box.

16. Click Start, point to Programs, point to Microsoft SQL Server, and then click Enterprise Manager.

    SQL Server Enterprise Manager appears displaying the Microsoft SQL Servers and the Event Viewer (Local) console trees in the console root.

17. Click the Event Viewer (Local) console tree container.

    The logs available within Event Viewer appear in the details pane. Notice that the menu items and tools on the console root toolbar change when you change console trees. The console root title bar indicates your focus within the console root.

18. Click the Microsoft SQL Servers console tree container.

    Notice that the menu items and tools on the console root toolbar specific to SQL Server Enterprise Manager appear in place of the items on the Event Viewer toolbar.

19. Expand the Microsoft SQL Servers container and then expand the SQL Server Group container.

    The default instance (*SelfPacedCPU*) and your named instance (*MyNamedInstance*) appear in the Microsoft SQL Servers console tree, each in their own container and displaying the state of the SQL Server service for that instance. Each instance also displays the authentication method used to connect to the instance, enclosed in parenthesis (namely Windows authentication).

Note   If the named instance is not registered, right-click SQL Server Group and then click New SQL Server Registration. Follow the instructions in the wizard to complete the registration.

Notice that your focus in the console tree remains the Microsoft SQL Servers container and that the contents of the details pane do not change when you expand an item in the console tree. The details pane changes only when your focus changes.

20. Click the container for your default instance.

Notice that the details pane displays the contents of this container. We will cover each of these objects in detail throughout the course of this book. Also notice that the icon indicating the state of the SQL Server service changed from a green triangle in a white circle to a white triangle in a green circle. This indicates that you have established a connection to this instance.

21. On the SQL Server Enterprise Manager toolbar, click the View menu.

Notice the available options, including Taskpad. The container object that is your current focus contains a preconfigured view.

22. Click Taskpad.

Notice that the details pane changes to display the taskpad view for this container object. The taskpad contains two tabs, General and Wizards. The General tab displays information regarding your computer and your server configuration. The Wizards tab displays the wizards that are available for your use. These wizards are also available from the Tools menu. We will use these wizards in exercises in later chapters of this book.

23. In the Microsoft SQL Servers console tree, right-click the container for your default instance and then click Edit SQL Server Registration Properties.

Notice the configured registration properties.

24. Click Cancel.

25. Close SQL Server Enterprise Manager.

Lesson Summary

SQL Server 2000 contains a number of client tools and utilities to administer SQL Server 2000. Osql is the primary command-prompt utility used for the submission of batches of Transact-SQL statements to SQL Server 2000. SQL Query Analyzer is the primary graphical tool used for interactive testing of Transact-SQL statements and batches. It is also used to create and administer objects within SQL Server 2000. SQL Server Enterprise Manager is the primary graphical tool used to graphically administer objects in SQL Server 2000. SQL Server Enterprise Manager is a preconfigured MMC console that you might want to customize. Becoming familiar with each of these tools is an essential task for a database administrator because he or she will use these tools daily.

Review

Here are some questions to help you determine whether you have learned enough to move on to the next chapter. If you have difficulty answering these questions, review the material in this chapter before beginning the next chapter. The answers for these questions are located in the Appendix, "Questions and Answers."

1. You have installed SQL Server 2000 on a test computer for evaluation. Gloria, another database administrator at your company, logged on to the SQL Server 2000 computer and attempted to review the new files that were added. She reports that she cannot view all of the files that were installed. Why might this be happening? Is there a problem?

2. You have installed SQL Server 2000 on a test computer for evaluation. During installation, you used the local system account as the service account for the SQL Server and SQL Server Agent services. You have decided you need to configure and use a dedicated domain user account for these services. How should you change the service account for these services?

3. You have installed SQL Server 2000 on a test computer for evaluation. You want to verify that you can connect to SQL Server 2000 and begin configuring objects in SQL Server 2000. What tool would you start with and why?

C H A P T E R   4

Upgrading to SQL Server 2000

About This Chapter

This chapter prepares you to upgrade an existing SQL Server 6.5 or 7.0 installation to SQL Server 2000. In this chapter, you will learn the upgrade options available to you, including how to keep an existing version of SQL Server intact and usable. You will learn the hardware and software requirements for an upgrade. You will also learn how to prepare for an upgrade. Then, you will learn two separate processes for upgrading from SQL Server 7.0, performing a version upgrade and performing an online database upgrade. Finally, you will learn how to perform a version upgrade from SQL Server 6.5.

Before You Begin

There are no prerequisites for completing the lessons in this chapter.

Lesson 1: Preparing to Upgrade

If you are using either SQL Server 6.5 or 7.0 in production, you will need to plan and prepare to upgrade your existing installation to SQL Server 2000. For this process to be successful and as painless as possible, you first need to understand the upgrade options available to you. This includes determining whether you need to keep your existing installation intact. You also need to determine how to minimize downtime. Next, you need to understand the hardware and software requirements for an upgrade. Finally, you need to prepare your existing installation for the actual upgrade.

After this lesson, you will be able to

- Work with multiple versions of SQL Server
- Choose the appropriate upgrade process and method
- Determine whether any hardware or software upgrades are necessary
- Prepare your existing installation for the actual upgrade

Estimated lesson time: 30 minutes

Working with Multiple Versions of SQL Server on the Same Computer

SQL Server 2000 is designed to support multiple versions of SQL Server simultaneously on the same computer. It accomplishes this in two different ways. The first method is through the use of version switching, and the second method is through the use of multiple instances. Through the use of these two methods, SQL Server 6.5, SQL Server 7.0, and SQL Server 2000 can coexist on the same computer, although only two versions may be running at any given time (one of which must be SQL Server 2000).

Version Switching

Version switching allows SQL Server 7.0 or SQL Server 2000 to be installed as the default instance on a computer on which SQL Server 6.5 is already installed. You can then use the Vswitch.exe utility to switch between SQL Server 6.5 and either SQL Server 7.0 or SQL Server 2000 (but not both). Using version switching allows you to switch between default instances, controlling which version of SQL Server (including any version-specific tool) is running as the default instance at any given point in time. It does not allow multiple instances or versions to run simultaneously. The Vswitch utility is available from the Start menu, in the Microsoft SQL Server – Switch program group. It is also available in the \Program Files\Microsoft SQL Server\Mssql\Binn folder.

Note   You cannot version-switch between SQL Server 7.0 and SQL Server 2000. Version switching is available only between SQL Server 6.5 and either SQL Server 2000 or SQL Server 7.0.

Named Instances

Using a named instance allows you to install and run SQL Server 2000 as a named instance on a computer on which either SQL Server 6.5 or SQL Server 7.0 is installed without performing a version upgrade of that installation. This allows you to keep your existing version of SQL Server intact and running while also running SQL Server 2000 on the same computer. Installing SQL Server 2000 as a named instance on a computer on which SQL Server 7.0 is installed is the only way to maintain the default instance of SQL Server 7.0 on that computer. When you install SQL Server 2000 as a named instance on a computer on which SQL Server 7.0 is also installed, all SQL Server 7.0 client tools are upgraded to SQL Server 2000 client tools for all instances.

Note   You can install SQL Server 6.5 or 7.0 only as default instances. Only SQL Server 2000 can be installed as a named instance.

Choosing the Appropriate Upgrade Process and Method

When you decide to upgrade SQL Server 6.5, you have only one upgrade process available. However, you have several methods to choose from. Your need to have SQL Server 6.5 running simultaneously with SQL Server 2000 after the upgrade might determine this decision. When you decide to upgrade SQL Server 7.0, you have two separate upgrade processes to choose between. Your need to migrate server and replication settings, as well as the need to minimize server downtime, might determine this choice. You must also determine whether to use a default or a named instance for your SQL Server 2000 installation. Your need to have multiple versions of SQL Server running simultaneously on the same computer might determine this choice.

SQL Server 6.5

If you are using SQL Server 6.5 and you want to upgrade your installation to SQL Server 2000, you must perform a version upgrade using the SQL Server Upgrade Wizard (this requires SQL Server 6.5 SP5). When you perform a version upgrade, you can choose to upgrade some or all of your user databases along with the system databases. The SQL Server Upgrade Wizard can transfer replication settings, SQL Executive settings, and most server configuration settings. The upgrade process includes built-in recovery methods to restart and resume an upgrade if it fails during the upgrade process. During this upgrade process, SQL Server 6.5 must be offline and unavailable to users. To perform an upgrade from SQL Server 6.5, you must also install SQL Server 6.5 SP5.

Note   If you merely want to migrate your data to SQL Server 2000 rather than upgrade your installation, you can use the DTS graphical tool, use the bulk copy program (Bcp) command-prompt utility, or perform a query between linked servers. These data transfer methods are covered in Chapter 7.

The SQL Server Upgrade Wizard can upgrade a computer running SQL Server 6.5 to SQL Server 2000 using either the local hard drive or a local tape drive. Using the local hard drive gives the best performance and is the most reliable. Use a tape drive only when you do not have sufficient hard drive space. The SQL Server Upgrade Wizard can also upgrade from one computer running SQL Server 6.5 to another computer running SQL Server 2000. Regardless of the method you choose, the SQL Server Upgrade Wizard can only upgrade to the default instance; it cannot upgrade SQL Server 6.5 to a named instance.

After the SQL Server Upgrade Wizard finishes the upgrade, you will have two independent installations of SQL Server with two independent sets of identical data (at least initially). SQL Server 6.5 is not removed during the upgrade process (although all client tools are upgraded). You should verify the success of the upgrade before you remove the SQL Server 6.5 installation.

Note   If you want to have SQL Server 6.5 running simultaneously with the SQL Server 2000 installation after the upgrade is complete (in order to verify the upgrade), you must upgrade SQL Server 6.5 from one computer to another.

SQL Server 7.0

If you are using SQL Server 7.0 and you want to upgrade your installation to SQL Server 2000, you have a choice of two processes. Your first choice is to perform a version upgrade of SQL Server 7.0 to SQL Server 2000 using the SQL Server 2000 Setup program. Version switching back to SQL Server 7.0 after the upgrade is not an option. During the version upgrade process, the Setup program replaces and overwrites your SQL Server 7.0 installation. All program files (including all tools and utilities) are upgraded and all databases are converted to SQL Server 2000. Replication settings, SQL Server Agent settings, and most server configuration settings are retained. However, SQL Server 7.0 Profiler traces and servers registered with SQL Server Enterprise Manager are not retained. During (and after) this upgrade process, SQL Server 7.0 must be offline and unavailable to users.

Your second choice is to use the Copy Database Wizard to perform an online database and associated meta data upgrade of selected SQL Server 7.0 user databases. Meta data information includes such things as logon information and user-specific objects associated with user databases. Performing an online database upgrade allows you to upgrade any or all of your user databases without having to shut down SQL Server 7.0 during the upgrade. In addition, your SQL Server 7.0 installation remains intact after the upgrade. If you plan to use this process, you can install SQL Server 2000 as a named instance on the same computer that is running

SQL Server 7.0 as the default instance. In addition, the Copy Database Wizard can upgrade databases from remote servers. Finally, you can also schedule the online database upgrade to occur at a specified time because the Copy Database Wizard creates a DTS package that is scheduled as a job. DTS packages and jobs are covered in Chapter 7.

Note   An online database upgrade does not upgrade SQL Server Agent or server configuration settings, and cannot be used with databases involved in replication.

Replication Issues

When upgrading servers involved in replication, you must upgrade the server functioning as the Distributor first, followed by the Publisher and finishing with the Subscribers. If you update servers in this sequence, you can continue to publish and replicate data during this process even though servers are running different versions of SQL Server. If you are using the immediate updating functionality or are using File Transfer Protocol (FTP), additional upgrade steps are required. Refer to "Replication and Upgrading" in SQL Server Books Online for more detail.

Note   For databases involved in replication, you must perform a version upgrade; on SQL Server 6.5, it must be a single computer version upgrade.

Determining Hardware and Software Requirements

The process of upgrading an existing SQL Server installation to SQL Server 2000 has certain hardware and software requirements, in addition to the hardware and software requirements for installing SQL Server 2000. These requirements differ depending on the version of SQL Server being upgraded, and on the type of upgrade process being performed.

SQL Server 6.5

If you are upgrading a SQL Server 6.5 installation running on Microsoft Windows NT 4.0 and plan to upgrade on the same computer, you must apply Service Pack 5 or later and Internet Explorer 5.0 or later to Windows NT 4.0 before upgrading to SQL Server 2000. You must also apply SQL Server 6.5 Service Pack 5 or later to your SQL Server 6.5 installation. However, if you are performing a computer-to-computer upgrade, you need only apply SQL Server 6.5 Service Pack 3 or later to your SQL Server 6.5 installation. Regardless of the upgrade method, the SQL Server Upgrade Wizard uses named pipes. SQL Server 6.5 and SQL Server 2000 must be set to use the default pipe (\\.\pipe\sql\query). Finally, upgrading SQL Server 6.5 to SQL Server 2000 requires available hard drive space equal to approximately 1.5 times the size of the SQL Server 6.5 user databases. This additional hard drive space is required only during the upgrade process. You can use the SQL Server Upgrade Wizard to estimate the amount of space required to complete the upgrade.

SQL Server 7.0

If you are upgrading a SQL Server 7.0 installation running on Windows NT 4.0 and plan to perform a version upgrade, you must apply Service Pack 5 or later and Internet Explorer 5.0 or later to Windows NT 4.0 before upgrading to SQL Server 2000. You do not need to apply any service packs to SQL Server 7.0 prior to upgrading to SQL Server 2000. Performing a version upgrade of SQL Server 7.0 requires the use of named pipes. SQL Server 7.0 and SQL Server 2000 must be set to use the default pipe (\\.\pipe\sql\query). However, an online database upgrade (using the Copy Database Wizard) does not require named pipes; rather, it will use any available Net-Library. Finally, an upgrade of SQL Server 7.0 to SQL Server 2000 does not require any additional hard drive space, although the Copy Database Wizard might require additional space if the database is copied rather than moved.

Preparing for the Actual Upgrade

You must perform the following tasks on your SQL Server installation prior to commencing the upgrade:

- Terminate all user activity in the database and obtain exclusive use of all files in the database.
- Back up all system and user databases (including master) to ensure recoverability.
- Run the appropriate Database Console Commands (DBCC) to ensure database consistency (such as DBCC CHECKDB).
- For SQL Server 6.5, set the tempdb system database size to at least 10 MB (25 MB is recommended).
- For SQL Server 6.5, verify that the master database has at least 3 MB of free space.
- For SQL Server 6.5, verify that the master database contains logon information for all users.
- For SQL Server 6.5, disable any startup stored procedures. If you do not disable them, the upgrade process might stop responding.
- Disable all jobs.
- Close all open applications, particularly all that are dependent on SQL Server.
- Stop replication and ensure that the replication log is empty.
- Ensure that there is enough hard disk space available to perform the upgrade.
- Make sure that you upgrade all databases that have cross-database dependencies at the same time. This will ensure that, for example, logon information for owners of objects with cross-database dependencies will be created, which, in turn, will ensure that their objects can also be created.

Lesson Summary

You can perform a version upgrade of SQL Server 6.5 to SQL Server 2000 on a single computer or between computers. You must upgrade to the default instance; you cannot upgrade to a named instance. When installing SQL Server 2000 on the same computer, you can use the version switch utility to switch between versions to verify the upgrade. You can perform either a version upgrade of SQL Server 7.0 on a single computer or an online database upgrade of one or more databases between instances on a single computer from a remote computer. If you perform an online database upgrade, SQL Server 7.0 remains available to users during the database upgrade process. However, an online database upgrade does not upgrade server settings and cannot be used when replication is involved. Finally, you need to prepare the production databases for the upgrade and make backups to ensure recoverability in case of a failure.

Lesson 2: Performing a Version Upgrade from SQL Server 7.0

When you install SQL Server 2000 on a computer running SQL Server 7.0, you are given the option during setup to upgrade your SQL Server 7.0 installation to SQL Server 2000. After installation, there are several tasks that you should perform to ensure maximum performance from your upgraded installation. Finally, you need to understand that certain items are not upgraded at all and that other items must be upgraded separately.

After this lesson, you will be able to

- Perform a version upgrade of SQL Server 7.0 to SQL Server 2000
- Understand the tasks you should perform after the version upgrade is complete
- Manually upgrade the Meta Data Services Information Models and repository database

Estimated lesson time: 15 minutes

Performing a Version Upgrade

You perform a version upgrade by running the SQL Server 2000 Setup program. When the Setup program detects an installed version of SQL Server, you are given the option to upgrade, remove, or add components to an existing instance of SQL Server on your computer. See Figure 4.1.

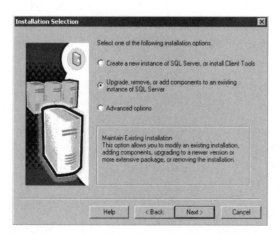

Figure 4.1.   Upgrade, remove, or add installation option.

To upgrade your SQL Server 7.0 installation, choose the default instance on your computer and then choose to upgrade your existing installation. See Figure 4.2.

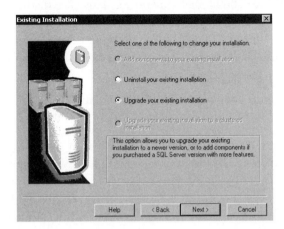

Figure 4.2.   Upgrade option.

After you choose to upgrade your SQL Server 7.0 installation, you define the authentication mode for the Setup program to use to connect to SQL Server 7.0. The Setup program verifies that it can successfully connect using this connection information (starting SQL Server 7.0 if necessary). Next, you must choose the licensing mode (see Chapter 2). Thereafter, SQL Server 7.0 is upgraded to SQL Server 2000. The system databases are upgraded using a series of scripts and the registry is updated. MDAC 2.6 and client tools are also upgraded at this point, unless a previously installed SQL Server 2000 named instance already performed this task.

Performing Post-Upgrade Tasks

After the Setup program completes the upgrade process, there are a number of tasks that the database administrator should perform. These are:

- Review the SQL Server error logs and the Sqlstp.log file if troubleshooting is necessary.
- Repopulate all full-text catalogs if full-text search is being used. The upgrade process disables all full-text catalogs because of a format change that occurs during the upgrade. Repopulation can be time-consuming, so planning an appropriate amount of time is important. Maintaining full-text catalogs is covered in Chapter 12.
- Update statistics. This process can also be time-consuming on large databases, but using SQL Server 7.0 statistics with SQL Server 2000 could result in poor query performance. Updating statistics is covered in Chapter 12.

- Register servers. Servers registered with SQL Server Enterprise Manager for SQL Server 7.0 are not registered with the new SQL Server Enterprise Manager for SQL Server 2000 (other than the local instance that was upgraded). Registering servers is covered in Chapter 12.

Manually Upgrading Meta Data Services Tables and the Repository Database

When you upgrade your SQL Server 7.0 installation to SQL Server 2000, the Meta Data Services Information Models required by DTS are not updated as part of this process. You must perform a manual update of the information to save and retrieve DTS package versions to and from Meta Data Services. This update modifies the Meta Data Services table structure to support the new functionality and features available with SQL Server 2000 and preserves existing repository data in the new table structure. The precise commands and syntax for manually upgrading the information model are available in the DTS Information model section of Books Online.

In addition, the repository database used by Meta Data Services must also be upgraded manually to take advantage of the new repository engine 3.0 installed during the upgrade to SQL Server 2000. The precise commands and syntax for manually upgrading the repository database are available in the "Upgrading and Migrating a Repository Database" section of Books Online. DTS packages, Meta Data Services, and the Meta Data Services repository are covered in Chapter 7.

Lesson Summary

The SQL Server 2000 Setup program is used to perform a version upgrade of SQL Server 7.0 to SQL Server 2000. After the upgrade is complete, SQL Server 7.0 is completely replaced by SQL Server 2000. The database administrator should update statistics and repopulate all full-text catalogs if full-text search is being used, to optimize the performance of the upgraded installation. Finally, the information models and the repository used by Meta Data Services must be upgraded manually to take advantage of the new features and functionality provided by SQL Server 2000.

Lesson 3: Performing an Online Database Upgrade from SQL Server 7.0

When you choose to perform an online database upgrade, you use the Copy Database Wizard to upgrade one or more SQL Server 7.0 databases to an instance of SQL Server 2000. You can upgrade databases from instances on the local computer or from a remote computer. The database being upgraded can be copied or moved. After installation, there are several tasks that you should perform to ensure maximum performance from your upgraded installation.

After this lesson, you will be able to

- Perform an online database upgrade from SQL Server 7.0 to SQL Server 2000
- Understand the tasks you should perform after the database upgrade is complete

Estimated lesson time: 15 minutes

Performing an Online Database Upgrade

The Copy Database Wizard is used to perform an online database upgrade. It is available from several locations within SQL Server Enterprise Manager. You can launch it from the Tools/Wizards menu, by right-clicking an instance of SQL Server 2000 and clicking All Tasks, or by clicking the Wizards tab from the task-pad (if you have enabled the taskpad). See Figure 4.3.

When you run the Copy Database Wizard, follow these steps:

1. Launch the Copy Database Wizard, using one of the methods described previously. When the Welcome To The Copy Database Wizard appears, click Next.
2. From the Select A Source Server page, select a source server from which you want to move or copy a database.

Note   Because the database upgrade process is transparent and the Copy Database Wizard is also used to copy and move SQL Server 2000 databases, terminology in the wizard only makes reference to copying and moving databases.

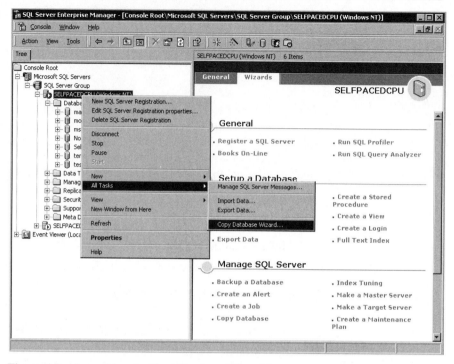

Figure 4.3. Launching the Copy Database Wizard from the All Tasks menu.

On the Select A Source Server page, you can connect to any SQL Server instance on the network (including any local instance). To list the currently active instances of SQL Server, click its associated ellipse button. When the Select Server dialog box is displayed, select the desired active server. Finally, you must connect using either a Windows or SQL Server login account that has system administrator privileges on the source server. See Figure 4.4.

3. After you have selected the source server, you must select the destination server from the Select A Destination Server page. Again, to list the currently active instances, click its associated ellipse button. The destination server does not have to be the instance of the server from which you are running the Copy Database Wizard. However, when you are copying or moving a database between servers, the service account used by the SQL Server service on the destination server must be a domain user account to have the rights to copy files over the network. The local system account has no such rights and therefore can only be used when the source and destination servers are on the same computer. Finally, you must connect using either a Windows or SQL Server login account that has system administrator privileges on the destination server. See Figure 4.5.

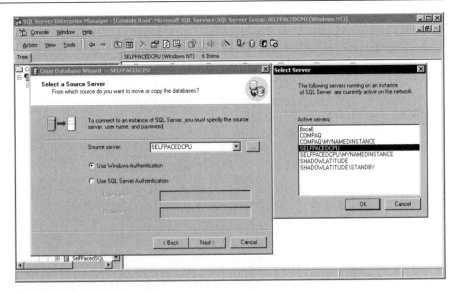

Figure 4.4.   Selecting a source server.

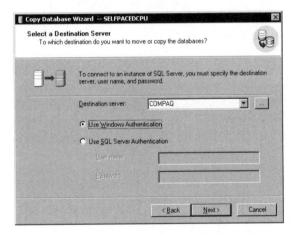

Figure 4.5.   Selecting a destination server.

4. Next, you must select a user database to move or copy on the Select The Databases To Move Or Copy page. You can move or copy multiple databases in one operation, by selecting the associated check boxes under the Move or Copy columns. However, you cannot move or copy a database if a database with the same name exists on the destination server. You must resolve any name conflicts prior to running the Copy Database Wizard, because database names cannot be renamed during a move or copy operation. In addition, you cannot move system databases (only user databases are available to be moved). See Figure 4.6.

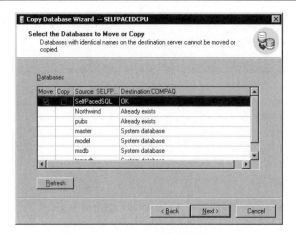

Figure 4.6.   Selecting a user database.

5. After you have selected the database you want to move or copy, you can change the default location for the data and log files on the Database File Location page. You select a new location by clicking the Modify button. When the Database Files dialog box appears, you click the ellipse button next to the destination you want to change. When the CDW dialog box appears, select the new default location for the files. You are also given the option, in the Destination Files column, to change the filename for the destination database files (but not the name of the database itself). The default location for the files is the Data folder for the instance to which the database is being copied or moved. The Database Files dialog box also informs you regarding available disk space on the destination drive. See Figure 4.7.

6. By default, all logins for the databases being copied or moved, along with all logins for stored procedures, jobs, and user-defined error messages, are copied along with the database. However, you can modify this default to selected specific logins only on the Select Related Objects page. See Figure 4.8.

7. Finally, on the Schedule The DTS Package page, you can schedule the copy or move operation to occur immediately, to run once at a specified date and time, or as a scheduled DTS package at a later time. Be aware that the DTS package must be able to place the source database in single-user mode prior to copying or moving it, or it will terminate the processing of the DTS package with an error message. If SQL Server Enterprise Manager (or any other client) is connected to the source server at the time the package runs, this open connection will prevent the package from running. See Figure 4.9.

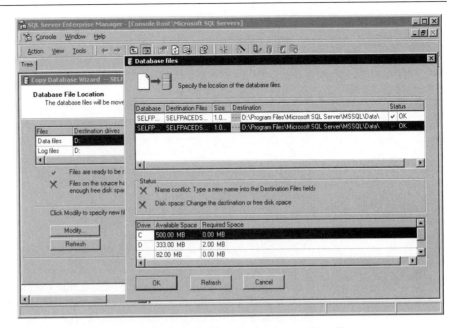

Figure 4.7.   Changing the default location for the data and log files.

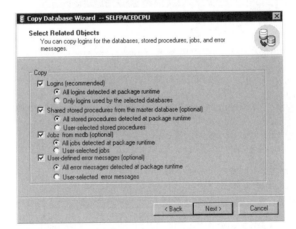

Figure 4.8.   Selecting database objects to upgrade.

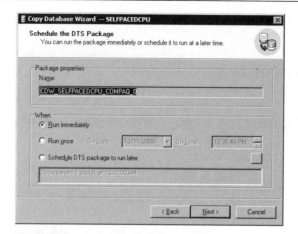

Figure 4.9.   Scheduling the DTS package.

8. Depending upon whether you are copying or moving the files, either the Completing The Copy Database Wizard page or the Completing The Move Database Wizard page appears. Verify that the options listed there are correct, and then click the Finish button. See Figure 4.10.

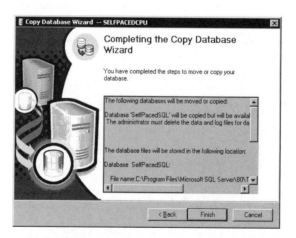

Figure 4.10.   Completing the Copy Database Wizard.

9. The Log Detail dialog box, shown in Figure 4.11, appears when the actual move or copy takes place. This dialog box displays information about the status of each file and also displays any error messages that occurred during the transfer.

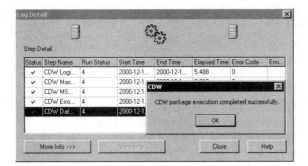

Figure 4.11.   The Log Detail dialog box displays information about the upgrade.

Note   A move between servers or disk drives does not remove the underlying data and log files from the file system, but simply detaches the database from the source server and reattaches it to the destination server.

Performing Post-Upgrade Tasks

After the Copy Database Wizard successfully completes the online database upgrade, there are a number of tasks that the database administrator should perform. You should perform the following tasks:

- Repopulate all full-text catalogs if full-text search is being used. The upgrade process disables all full-text catalogs because of a format change that occurs during the upgrade. Repopulation can be time-consuming, so planning an appropriate amount of time is important. Maintaining full-text catalogs is covered in Chapter 12.

- Update statistics. This process can also be time-consuming on large databases, but using SQL Server 7.0 statistics with SQL Server 2000 could result in poor query performance. Updating statistics is covered in Chapter 12.

- Delete the underlying data and log files after verification of the upgraded database.

Lesson Summary

The Copy Database Wizard is used to upgrade SQL Server 7.0 databases to a SQL Server 2000 installation. After the upgrade, the SQL Server 7.0 installation remains intact. The upgraded databases can be copied or moved. In the event of a move, the underlying data and log files are generally not removed and should be removed manually. Finally, the database administrator should update statistics and repopulate all full-text catalogs if full-text search is being used to optimize the performance of the upgraded installation.

Lesson 4: Performing a Version Upgrade from SQL Server 6.5

You upgrade a SQL Server 6.5 installation by running the SQL Server Upgrade Wizard on a computer that has SQL Server 2000 installed as the default instance. An upgrade from SQL Server 6.5 to SQL Server 2000 is more involved than an upgrade from SQL Server 7.0 and is therefore more likely to have objects that could not be upgraded properly. This might require some troubleshooting. Finally, you need to be aware that because of changes in features, you might need to use backward compatibility levels to make the transition to SQL Server 2000 smooth.

After this lesson, you will be able to

- Perform a version upgrade of SQL Server 6.5 to SQL Server 2000
- Troubleshoot a SQL Server 6.5 upgrade
- Specify backward compatibility levels for upgraded databases

Estimated lesson time: 30 minutes

Performing a Version Upgrade

To perform a version upgrade of SQL Server 6.5 to SQL Server 2000, you must run the SQL Server Upgrade Wizard from a computer on which you have installed SQL Server 2000 as the default instance. You start the SQL Server Upgrade Wizard from the Microsoft SQL Server – Switch program group. This wizard is available on any computer that has SQL Server 2000 installed as the default instance. This wizard (Upgrade.exe) is also in the Upgrade folder of your SQL Server 2000 installation. The upgrade folder location is \Program Files\Microsoft SQL Server\Mssql\Upgrade. See Figure 4.12.

Note You must use SQL Server authentication to connect to the SQL Server 2000 server. Because the default authentication mode of SQL Server 2000 allows only Windows authentication, you might need to change the SQL Server 2000 configuration to permit SQL Server authentication. This requires a restart of the SQL Server service. Changing authentication modes is covered in Chapter 10.

When you run the SQL Server Upgrade Wizard you perform the following steps:

1. When you start the SQL Server Upgrade Wizard, using one of the methods described above, it begins by recommending that you read the Upgrading topics online carefully. The major issues are discussed in this lesson, but you should definitely read the Upgrading topics in Books Online as well. The changes from SQL Server 6.5 to SQL Server 2000 are substantial. See Figure 4.13.

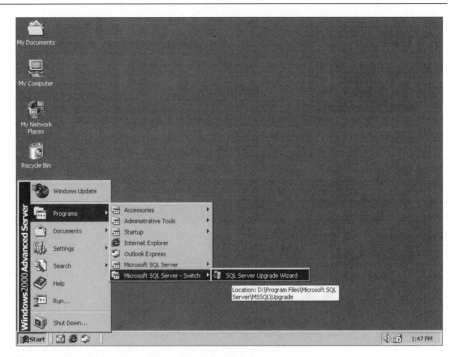

Figure 4.12.   Starting the SQL Server Upgrade Wizard.

Figure 4.13.   Welcome to the SQL Server Upgrade Wizard.

2. Next, on the Data And Object Transfer page, the wizard prompts you to select the upgrade method you will use. You can perform a direct upgrade on the same computer using either named pipes or a tape device for the transfer of data (the tape device option will be available only if a tape device is detected on the local computer). You can also choose to perform additional verification options. If you choose to have the SQL Server Upgrade Wizard validate the successful

transfer of data objects, the wizard prepares a list of all objects in the SQL Server 6.5 databases and the number of rows in each table before the upgrade and then compares this list to a similar list after the upgrade. The wizard reports any discrepancies. This verification is in addition to the reporting of any problem in the creation of database objects that is recorded by default in the output logs. Selecting this initial level of verification is highly recommended. The next level of verification is to perform an exhaustive byte-by-byte checksum verification on each column in each table to verify that no data values have changed. This level of verification substantially increases the time required for the upgrade. Errors occur only rarely, but if the time is available, this additional level of verification is also recommended. See Figure 4.14.

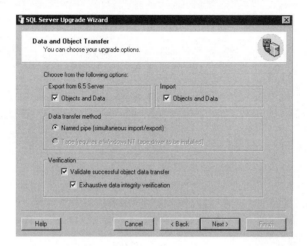

Figure 4.14.   Selecting the upgrade method and options.

3. Next, on the Logon page, you specify the name of the SQL Server 6.5 computer you want to upgrade (called the export server). The default is the computer on which you are running the wizard, but you can specify any other computer in the same domain. The server you are upgrading to must be the server on which you are running the wizard (called the import server).

Note   If you are upgrading a database involved in replication, you must perform a single computer upgrade, and the database compatibility level must be set to 70 during the upgrade.

In addition, you must specify the password for the SQL Server administrator account (sa) for both the export and the import server. You can also provide optional startup arguments for the export and the import server. See Figure 4.15.

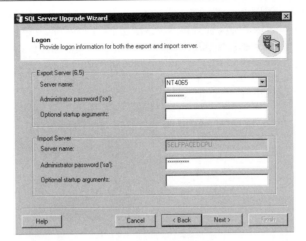

Figure 4.15.   Specifying logon information for the export and import servers.

4. After you provide the name of the server being upgraded and provide the authentication information and optional startup arguments for both the servers, the wizard displays a SQL Server Upgrade Wizard dialog box warning that both of the SQL Server installations need to be stopped and then restarted, using these authentication and startup parameters. During this verification process, the wizard also obtains the code page used by SQL Server 6.5 from the master database.

    Next, the Code Page Selection page appears. The Upgrade Wizard requires the selection of a scripting code page, which is used to create the upgrade scripts. Most users can accept the default code page. The code page used in the upgrade scripts must match the code page of the database being upgraded. See Figure 4.16.

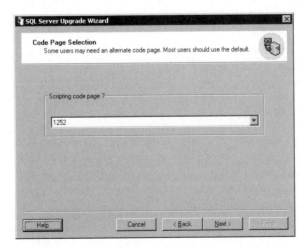

Figure 4.16.   Code page selection for upgrade scripts.

5. You then select databases to upgrade on the Upgrade Databases To SQL Server 2000 page. You can choose to upgrade some or all user databases. Notice that the master, msdb, publication, pubs, and Northwind databases are not available for selection. Only the model database and any user-created user databases can be selected for upgrading. It is recommended that you upgrade all databases at the same time. See Figure 4.17.

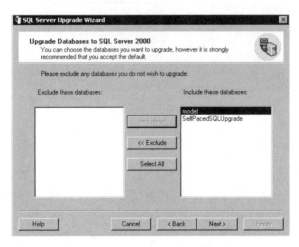

Figure 4.17.   Selecting databases to upgrade.

After you select the databases to upgrade, the wizard examines the layout of SQL Server 6.5 devices. It uses this information to create database files in SQL Server 2000.

6. Next, the Database Creation page appears. The wizard creates data and log files for the databases being upgraded. The data files are sized to hold all transferred objects and data, with no allowance for additional free space. The log files are sized based on the size of the SQL Server 6.5 log files. The locations of the data and log files are the same as for the first device for data and logs in SQL Server 6.5. If multiple devices were used in SQL Server 6.5, multiple files will be created in SQL Server 2000, but the initial file is sized to contain the objects and data with additional files sized minimally. On the Database Creation page, you can specify a custom configuration of database files and logs by editing this default configuration, using databases previously created for this purpose in SQL Server 2000, or by using Transact-SQL scripts. See Figure 4.18. When you click the Edit button on the Database Creation page, the SQL Server Upgrade Wizard dialog box appears. In this dialog box, you can modify the name, file path, and initial size of the file, as well as the autogrow increment. See Figure 4.19.

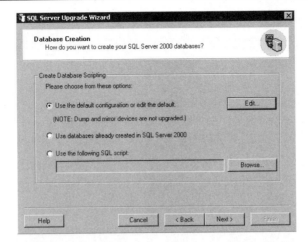

Figure 4.18. Specifying the database configuration for the upgrade.

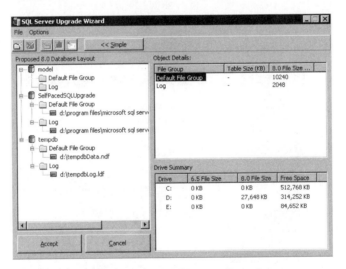

Figure 4.19. Modifying the database configuration.

7. Next, on the System Configuration page, you select system objects to transfer. These include server configuration information (such as local information and remote logon registrations), replication settings (including all articles, publications, and subscriptions) and SQL Executive settings (including all tasks and schedules). In addition, you must set the ANSI_NULLS and the QUOTED_IDENTIFIER settings. The wizard uses these settings for all database objects it creates. Refer to the topic "System Configuration" in Books Online for more information regarding these advanced settings. The choices you make for these settings will vary based on your existing SQL Server 6.5 databases and how you created objects within them. See Figure 4.20.

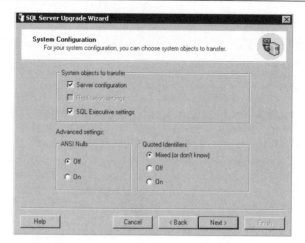

Figure 4.20.   Selecting system objects to transfer.

8. Finally, the Completing The SQL Server Upgrade Wizard page appears. A summary of your choices and any warning messages are listed here. Click the Finish button to begin the upgrade. See Figure 4.21.

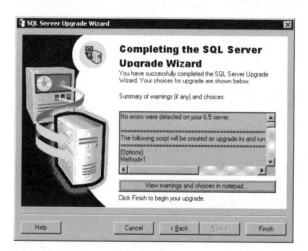

Figure 4.21.   Completing the SQL Server Upgrade Wizard.

While the upgrade is in process, the wizard displays each step in the process in the SQL Server Upgrade Script Interpreter dialog box and then notifies you when the upgrade is complete. If an error occurs, details of the error are displayed. See Figure 4.22.

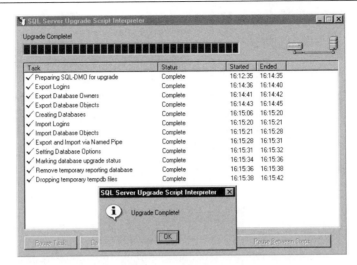

Figure 4.22.   Notification of your completed upgrade.

Troubleshooting a SQL Server 6.5 Upgrade

If the SQL Server Upgrade Wizard encounters problems during the upgrade, either you are notified during the upgrade of the problem or you must look in the upgrade logs created by the wizard specifying any problems it encounters. Typical problems are an inability to create objects and tables (you will have to create these manually after the upgrade). The possible reasons for this include:

- Text is missing from the syscomments table.

- Objects were renamed using *sp_rename* (the syscomments entry is not updated when the object is renamed).

- Stored procedures were embedded within other stored procedures (no entry exists in syscomments for these stored procedures).

- Table and views have NULL column names (the wizard cannot script these objects).

- Tables were created on behalf of a user that does not have CREATE permissions.

- A stored procedure modifies a system table or references a system table that does not exist in SQL Server 2000.

Another problem that can occur is having a computer name that does not match the server name returned by @@*SERVERNAME*. Use the *sp_dropserver* and *sp_addserver* system stored procedures to change the server name returned by @@*SERVERNAME* to match the computer name.

Specifying a Backward Compatibility Level for Upgraded Databases

When you upgrade databases from SQL Server 6.5 to SQL Server 2000, it is likely that you will have objects in the upgraded databases that use features that have changed. Most applications are not affected by the changes in behavior. However, in some cases, applications will need to be upgraded. SQL Server 2000 allows you to set a backward compatibility level to retain the earlier behavior while retaining almost all of the performance enhancements of SQL Server 2000. This allows time for applications to be upgraded. The backward compatibility setting affects only a small number of Transact-SQL statements. As always, test your applications thoroughly after the upgrade. If you need to set a backward compatibility level for an upgraded database, use the *sp_dbcmptlevel* system stored procedure. Valid levels are 60, 65, 70, and 80. You can also set the compatibility level using SQL Server Enterprise Manager by right-clicking the desired database, clicking Properties, clicking the Options tab, and then selecting the desired compatibility level.

Note   Microsoft might drop the 60 and 65 backward compatibility levels in future versions of SQL Server.

Lesson Summary

The SQL Server Upgrade Wizard allows you to upgrade a SQL Server 6.5 installation to the default instance of SQL Server 2000. The default instance can be on the same computer as the SQL Server 6.5 installation, or it can be on a second computer. After the upgrade is complete, SQL Server 6.5 will be upgraded to SQL Server 2000, and your SQL Server 6.5 installation will remain intact. This allows you to verify the upgrade. Check the upgrade logs to determine whether certain objects were not upgraded. Finally, test your applications and use backward compatibility levels where necessary until you can upgrade the applications.

Review

Here are some questions to help you determine whether you have learned enough to move on to the next chapter. If you have difficulty answering these questions, review the material in this chapter before beginning the next chapter. The answers for these questions are located in the Appendix, "Questions and Answers."

1. You are planning to upgrade your SQL Server 7.0 installation running on Windows NT 4.0 Server to SQL Server 2000. You want to test SQL Server 2000 on the same computer on which you currently have SQL Server 7.0 installed, and you need to keep the SQL Server 7.0 installation available for users. What issues do you need to consider?

2. You have recently performed a version upgrade of SQL Server 7.0 to SQL Server 2000. Although overall performance has improved, full-text searches are not working. Why might this be?

3. You have decided that you cannot afford the downtime associated with a version upgrade of your SQL Server 7.0 installation and have decided to perform an online database upgrade of your production databases. What settings and objects will you have to re-create manually?

4. You have been testing SQL Server 2000 on the same computer on which you have been running your SQL Server 6.5 installation. You decide to upgrade your SQL Server 6.5 installation. However, you cannot locate the SQL Server Upgrade Wizard. It is not located on the Start menu and you cannot find it on your hard drive. Why?

C H A P T E R   5

Understanding System and User Databases

About This Chapter

Before you begin creating and configuring user databases for your data, you need to achieve an understanding of the physical structure of SQL Server 2000 databases. Next, you need to understand how the transaction log is organized and functions. Finally, you need to become familiar with the most commonly used and queried system tables within the system and database catalogs. This includes how to query these catalogs for meta data regarding system and user databases.

Before You Begin

To complete this chapter, you must have

- A computer that meets or exceeds the minimum hardware requirements listed in Table 2.1, "Hardware Requirements," in Lesson 1 of Chapter 2.
- Microsoft Windows 2000 Server running on your computer on an NTFS partition.
- A computer configured as a server or a domain controller in the SelfPacedSQL domain.
- Installed a default and at least one named instance of SQL Server 2000 (see Chapter 2).

Lesson 1: Understanding the Database Architecture

As discussed earlier in this book, each SQL Server 2000 database (system or user) consists of at least one data file and at least one transaction log file. This lesson covers the architecture of these data files, including the allocation and management of space and the organization of data and index pages within data files.

After this lesson, you will be able to

- View the properties of data files
- Understand how SQL Server 2000 allocates and manages space within a data file
- Understand how SQL Server 2000 organizes data and index pages within a data file

Estimated lesson time: 15 minutes

Introducing Data Files

Each SQL Server 2000 database has one primary data file and can have secondary data files, each of which is used only by that database. Each data file is a separate operating system file. The primary data file generally has the .MDF filename extension (this extension is not required but is useful for identification). This primary data file stores data in tables and indexes and contains the startup information for the database. It contains system tables that track objects in the database, including file location information about all additional files in the database (secondary data files and transaction log files). Each secondary data file generally has the .NDF filename extension (this extension is also not required). Secondary data files are used primarily when a database spans multiple disk drives.

SQL Server 2000 records the locations of all the database files in two places: in the master database and in the primary file for the database. Most of the time, the database engine uses the file location information found in the master database. The exception to this rule occurs when you perform operations that cause the database engine to use the file location information found in the primary file to initialize the file location entries in the master database. These operations are upgrading from SQL Server 7.0 to SQL Server 2000, restoring the master database, and attaching a database to SQL Server 2000 using the *sp_attach_db* system stored procedure.

Each data file (primary and secondary) has a logical filename (*logical_file_name*) used in Transact-SQL statements and a physical filename (*os_file_name*) used by the Microsoft Windows operating system. The logical filename must be unique to the specified database and must also conform to the SQL Server identifier rules. For further information about logical filename identifiers, see "Using Identifiers" in SQL Server Books Online. The physical filename must conform to the rules of file-naming conventions for the particular operating system you are using.

Additional data file properties include the file ID, initial file size, file growth increment (if any), and maximum file size. These data file properties are stored in the File Header page, which is the first page of each data file. SQL Server uniquely identifies pages in a data file by file ID and page number. Pages in a data file are numbered sequentially starting at zero. Defining and altering the properties of a data file are covered in Chapter 6.

Note SQL Server data and log files cannot be stored on compressed file systems.

Practice: Viewing the Properties of a Data File

In this practice you use SQL Server Enterprise Manager to view some of the properties of a data file.

▶ **To view the properties of a data file**

1. Ensure that you are logged on to the SelfPacedSQL.MSFT domain controller as Administrator.

2. Click Start, point to Programs, point to Microsoft SQL Server, and then click Enterprise Manager.

   SQL Server Enterprise Manager appears, displaying the Microsoft SQL Servers and the Event Viewer (Local) console trees in the console root.

3. In the console tree, expand the Microsoft SQL Servers container, expand the SQL Server Group container, expand the default instance, and then expand Databases.

4. In the console tree, right-click Master and then click Properties.

   The Master Properties dialog box appears with the General tab selected, displaying various properties of the master database, such as the database status, date of last backup, and collation name.

5. Click the Data Files tab.

   The File Name column on the Data Files tab displays the logical filename of the master database.

6. Expand the width of the Location column by sliding the column bar to the right.

   The name and complete file path of the operating system file are displayed.

7. Reduce the width of the Location column so you can view the Space Allocated (MB) column.

The current space allocated is displayed. Most systems will display 12 MB. This is the initial size of the master database (which is rounded to the nearest whole number).

8. Click Cancel to close the Master Properties dialog box.

9. Close SQL Server Enterprise Manager.

Allocating Space for Tables and Indexes

Before SQL Server 2000 can store information in a table or an index, free space must be allocated from within a data file and assigned to that object. Free space is allocated for tables and indexes in units called *extents*. An extent is 64 KB of space, consisting of eight contiguous pages, each 8 KB in size. There are two types of extents, mixed extents and uniform extents. SQL Server 2000 uses mixed extents to store small amounts of data for up to eight objects within a single extent and uses uniform extents to store data from a single object.

When a new table or index is created, SQL Server 2000 locates a mixed extent with a free page and allocates the free page to the newly created object. A page contains data for only one object. When an object requires additional space, SQL Server 2000 allocates free space from mixed extents until an object uses a total of eight pages. Thereafter, SQL Server 2000 allocates a uniform extent to that object. SQL Server 2000 will grow the data files in a round-robin algorithm if no free space exists in any data file and autogrow is enabled.

When SQL Server 2000 needs a mixed extent with at least one free page, a Secondary Global Allocation Map (SGAM) page is used to locate such an extent. Each SGAM page is a bitmap covering 64,000 extents (approximately 4 GB) that is used to identify allocated mixed extents with at least one free page. Each extent in the interval that SGAM covers is assigned a bit. The extent is identified as a mixed extent with free pages when the bit is set to 1. When the bit is set to 0, the extent is either a mixed extent with no free pages, or the extent is a uniform extent.

When SQL Server 2000 needs to allocate an extent from free space, a Global Allocation Map (GAM) page is used to locate an extent that has not previously been allocated to an object. Each GAM page is a bitmap that covers 64,000 extents, and each extent in the interval it covers is assigned a bit. When the bit is set to 1, the extent is free. When the bit is set to 0, the extent has already been allocated.

Note   SQL Server 2000 can locate GAMs and SGAMs quickly because they are the third and fourth pages in the first extent allocated within a data file. The first page in the first extent is the File Header page and the second page is the Page Free Space (PFS) page.

When SQL Server 2000 allocates a page within a mixed extent or a uniform extent to an object, it uses an Index Allocation Map (IAM) page to track all pages allocated to a table or an index. Each IAM page covers up to 512,000 pages, and IAM pages are located randomly within the data file. All IAM pages for an object are linked together, the first IAM page pointing to the second IAM page, and so on.

When SQL Server 2000 needs to insert data into pages allocated for an object, it uses the PFS page to locate an allocated page with available space. PFS pages within a data file record, using a bitmap, whether a page has been allocated and the amount of free space on an allocated page (empty, 1–50 percent full, 51–80 percent full, 81–95 percent full, or more than 95 percent full). Each PFS page covers 8,000 contiguous pages. The second page in the first extent in a data file contains the first PFS page, and every 8000th page thereafter contains a PFS page.

Storing Index and Data Pages

In the absence of a clustered index, SQL Server 2000 stores new data on any unfilled page in any available extent belonging to the table into which the data is being inserted. This disorganized collection of data pages is called a *heap*. In a heap, the data pages are stored in no specific order and are not linked together. In the absence of either a clustered or a nonclustered index, SQL Server 2000 has to search the entire table to locate a record within the table (using IAM pages to identify pages associated with the table). On a large table, this complete search is quite inefficient.

To speed this retrieval process, database designers create indexes for SQL Server 2000 to use to find data pages quickly. An index stores the value of an indexed column (or columns) from a table in a B-tree structure. A B-tree structure is a balanced hierarchal structure (or tree) consisting of a root node, possible intermediate nodes, and bottom-level leaf pages (nodes). All branches of the B-tree have the same number of levels. A B-tree physically organizes index records based on these key values. Each index page is linked to adjacent index pages.

SQL Server 2000 supports two types of indexes, clustered and nonclustered. A *clustered* index forces the physical ordering of data pages within the data file based on the key value used for the clustered index (such as last name or zip code). The leaf level of a clustered index is the data level. When a new data row is inserted into a table containing a clustered index, SQL Server 2000 traverses the B-tree structure and determines the location for the new data row based on the ordering within the B-tree (moving existing data and index rows as necessary to maintain the physical ordering). See Figure 5.1.

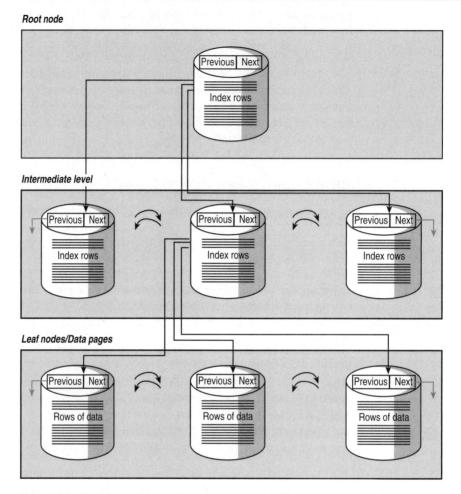

Root node

Intermediate level

Leaf nodes/Data pages

Figure 5.1.   Structure of a clustered index.

The leaf level of a *nonclustered* index contains a pointer telling SQL Server 2000 where to find the data row corresponding to the key value contained in the nonclustered index. When a new data row is inserted into a table containing only a nonclustered index, a new index row is entered into the B-tree structure, and the new data row is entered into any page in the heap that has been allocated to the table and contains sufficient free space. See Figure 5.2.

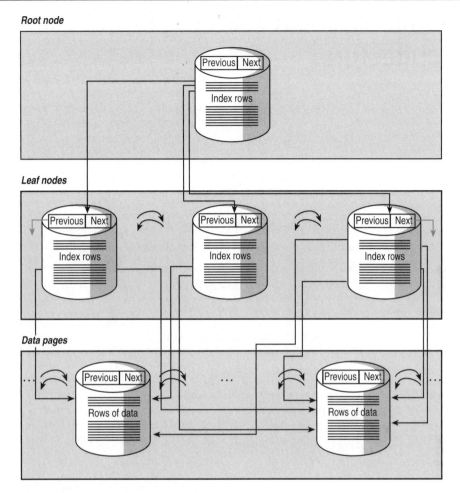

Figure 5.2.   Structure of a nonclustered index.

Lesson Summary

SQL Server 2000 uses one or more data files to store information in tables and indexes. Data files are operating system files. Tables and indexes are allocated individual pages from mixed extents or uniform extents based on the number of pages used by these objects. A number of special pages are used to track free space within a data file, the pages and extents that have been allocated to an object, and the amount of available space on allocated pages. Data pages are stored in a disorganized heap unless a clustered index exists on a table. Nonclustered indexes are used to point to data pages in a heap or in a clustered index structure. If a clustered index exists, data pages are physically ordered based on the index key and stored in a B-tree structure. Index pages are always stored in a B-tree structure.

Lesson 2: Understanding the Transaction Log Architecture

Each database contains at least one transaction log file. The transaction log records changes made to a database and stores sufficient information to allow changes to be undone (rolled back) or redone (rolled forward). This lesson covers the architecture of the transaction log, including the organization of transaction log files. This lesson also covers how the transaction log works and how the various recovery models affect the transaction log.

After this lesson, you will be able to

- Understand the organization of transaction log files
- Understand how the transaction log functions
- Understand SQL Server 2000 recovery models
- View the properties of transaction log files

Estimated lesson time: 30 minutes

Introducing Transaction Log Files

Each SQL Server 2000 database has at least one transaction log file and can have multiple transaction log files spread across a number of disks. Each transaction log file is a separate operating system file and is used by only one database. Each transaction log file generally has the .ldf filename extension (this extension is not required).

Each transaction log has a logical filename that is used in Transact-SQL statements and a physical filename that is used by the Windows operating system. Additional file properties include the file ID number, initial file size, file growth increment (if any), and maximum file size. Unlike data files that contain pages, transaction log files contain a series of transaction log records. A sequential log sequence number (LSN) identifies each transaction log record. Regardless of the number of physical log files, SQL Server 2000 treats the transaction log as one continuous log.

SQL Server 2000 logically divides each physical transaction log file into a number of virtual log files (VLFs). The number and size of virtual log files are determined dynamically based on the size of each transaction log file. Each transaction log file has at least two VLFs. Each growth increment (if any) is treated as a separate physical file with its own VLFs. The number or size of VLFs cannot be configured or set directly by the database administrator. SQL Server 2000 tries to maintain a small number of virtual file logs because it operates most efficiently with a small number of VLFs.

Tip   You should create a transaction log large enough to prevent the need for frequent growth. If automatic growth is required, you should set a reasonable growth increment to prevent many small growth increments because small growth increments will result in many small virtual log files, which can slow down recovery.

When a database is created, the logical transaction log begins at the start of the first physical log file, which is also the beginning of the first virtual log file. The logical transaction log is made up of the portion of the transaction log that is required for recovery and backup. The portion of the transaction log required for recovery and backup will vary with the recovery model chosen. Backup and restore strategies are covered in Chapter 8.

How the Transaction Log Works

SQL Server 2000 uses a buffer cache, which is an in-memory structure, into which it retrieves data pages from disk for use by applications and users. Each modification to a data page is made to the copy of the page in the buffer cache. A modified buffer page in the cache that has not yet been written to disk is called a *dirty page*. The modification is recorded in the transaction log before it is written to disk. For this reason, the SQL Server 2000 transaction log is called a *write-ahead* transaction log. SQL Server 2000 has internal logic to ensure that a modification is recorded in the transaction log before the associated dirty page is written to disk.When SQL Server writes the dirty page in the cache to the disk, it is called *flushing the page*.

A transaction log record contains sufficient information to roll any database modification back or forward if necessary, including any extent allocations or index modifications. This ensures that any modification written to disk (such as a change to a data page or the creation of a new database object) can be rolled back in case the transaction that caused the modification fails to complete for any reason (such as a server failure or a rollback command), or rolled forward in case a completed transaction is not completely written to disk for any reason (such as a server failure).

Note   Because of this rollback capacity, a backup of the transaction log allows a database to be rebuilt when a drive containing a data file fails. The rollback capacity is also the reason that the transaction log file for a database should be on a different drive than the data file.

SQL Server 2000 periodically writes dirty pages to disk from the buffer cache. These writes occur either when a database checkpoint process occurs or when an operating system thread (either an individual worker thread or a lazywriter thread) scans for dirty pages, writes the dirty pages to disk, and then clears space in the buffer cache to hold new data pages. Operating system threads may write dirty pages to disk before SQL Server 2000 knows whether the transaction is complete. However, if a transaction rolls back or never completes, the transaction log ensures that modifications made to disk by transactions that did not complete will be rolled back either via a rollback command or when the server restarts in the case of a server failure.

Checkpoint Process

The checkpoint process is designed to minimize the recovery time if the server fails, by minimizing the number of pages in the buffer cache that have not been written to disk. Checkpoints occur whenever

- A *CHECKPOINT* statement is issued.
- The *ALTER DATABASE* statement is used.
- An instance of SQL Server 2000 is stopped normally.
- An automatic checkpoint is issued. Automatic checkpoints are generated periodically based on the number of records in the active portion of the transaction log, not on the amount of time that has elapsed since the last checkpoint.

The checkpoint process records the lowest LSN that must be present for a successful rollback of an incomplete transaction. This number is called the *minimum LSN* (MinLSN). The MinLSN is based on the lowest LSN of the oldest active transaction, the beginning of the oldest replication transaction that has not been replicated yet to all subscribers, or the start of the checkpoint. The portion of the transaction log from the MinLSN to the most recent transaction log record is the active portion of the transaction log and must be present to ensure a successful rollback, if necessary. Whenever SQL Server 2000 starts (either normally or after a failure), a recovery process occurs on each database. The recovery process checks the transaction log for completed transactions that were not written to disk and rolls them forward. It also checks the transaction log for incomplete transactions and makes sure they were not written to disk. If they were written to disk, they are removed from the disk. The MinLSN from the most recent checkpoint identifies the earliest LSN that SQL Server 2000 must look at during this recovery process.

All transaction log records lower than the MinLSN are no longer active (the checkpoint ensures that records older than the MinLSN have been written to disk). To reuse this space, the transaction log records must be truncated (deleted) from the transaction log file. The smallest unit of truncation is an individual VLF file. If any part of a VLF is part of the active log, that VLF cannot be truncated. If the Simple Recovery model is used, the checkpoint process simply truncates each VLF within the inactive portion of the transaction log (allowing these VLFs to be reused). If the Full Recovery or Bulk-Logged Recovery models are used, you must back up the transaction log to truncate the inactive portion of the transaction log. Chapters 8 and 9 cover transaction log backups.

Note   Log truncations must be performed from the parts of the log before the MinLSN and can never be performed on any part of the active log.

Figure 5.3 illustrates the transaction log after a checkpoint has occurred and the inactive portion of the transaction log has been truncated. Notice that the MinLSN is earlier than the LSN of the checkpoint.

The checkpoint process frees space from the physical transaction log file so that the logical log file can reuse space when it reaches the end of the last physical transaction log file. When the end of the logical transaction log reaches the end of the last physical transaction log file, the logical transaction log wraps to the beginning of the first physical file (provided that the first VLF has been truncated). If the first VLF has not been truncated and the transaction log is not set to autogrow (or the drive is out of disk space), SQL Server 2000 cannot continue to function. Figure 5.4 illustrates this wrapping of the logical log to the beginning of the first physical transaction log file.

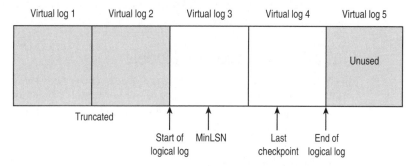

Figure 5.3.   The transaction log after truncation of the inactive portion.

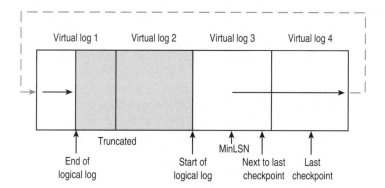

Figure 5.4.   Wrapping of the logical log.

Operating System Threads

SQL Server 2000 uses individual worker threads and a lazywriter thread to periodically scan the memory buffer, schedule dirty pages for asynchronous writes to disk, and free inactive buffer pages for reuse. A thread is an operating system component that allows multiple processes to execute using separate asynchronous execution paths. The write of each dirty page is recorded in the transaction log before the write to disk can occur. Individual worker threads are threads from other SQL Server 2000 processes, such as an asynchronous read request by a user. These individual worker threads scan the buffer cache while waiting for their primary task to complete. A SQL Server 2000 lazywriter thread also periodically scans the free buffer list. If the free buffer list is below a certain point (dependent on the size of the cache), the lazywriter thread scans the buffer cache to free buffer space. The term "lazywriter" refers to the fact that this lazywriter thread sleeps for an interval of time, awakes and scans the memory buffer, and then goes back to sleep.

Note   The individual worker threads and the lazywriter thread write most of the dirty pages to disk between checkpoints, and the checkpoint process generally finds few dirty pages to write to disk. The difference between the threads and the checkpoint process is that checkpoints do not place the buffer pages back on the free list. These three processes work together to smooth out the writing of data to disk in order to minimize disk bottlenecks and optimize performance.

Introducing Recovery Models

SQL Server 2000 provides a choice of three recovery models: Simple, Full, and Bulk-Logged. Each database has a recovery model. The model chosen affects the size of the transaction log and the backup and recovery choices. Backup and recovery strategies are covered in Chapter 8.

Full Recovery Model

The Full Recovery model gives you the ability to recover a database to the point of failure or to a specific point in time. When a database uses the Full Recovery model, all operations are fully logged. This includes full logging of all large-scale operations (such as index creation and bulk loading of data using SELECT INTO, Bcp, or BULK INSERT). These large-scale operations frequently use a substantial amount of transaction log space. If you use this recovery model, you must make sure that the transaction log does not run out of space (particularly during a large-scale operation). Regular and frequent backups of the transaction log are required to ensure that the transaction log is regularly truncated to free up space for more records.

Bulk-Logged Recovery Model

When a database uses the Bulk-Logged Recovery model, all operations except certain large-scale operations are fully logged. Index creation and bulk load operations are minimally logged. The transaction log does not record sufficient detail of these large-scale operations to recover in case of a media failure after one of these operations. This helps reduce the amount of transaction log space used, but increases exposure to data loss after these large-scale operations. A full database backup after a large-scale operation is not required for recoverability. With the Bulk-Logged Recovery model, regular backups of the transaction log are still required to truncate the transaction log to free up space for more records, but these backups need to occur less frequently than with the full recovery model.

Note   Point-in-time recovery is not supported in the Bulk-Logged Recovery model.

Simple Recovery Model

When a database uses the Simple Recovery model, all operations are fully logged (including all large-scale operations). However, because this recovery model does not rely on transaction log backups for database recovery, each checkpoint process truncates the inactive portion of the transaction log. This prevents the transaction log from running out of space in most circumstances. However, long-running transactions and unreplicated transactions marked for replication can still cause the transaction log to fill up. This recovery model is rarely used in production databases because the risk of loss of recently written changes is simply too great. When you use the Simple Recovery model, the database can be recovered only to the point of the last backup.

Note   The tempdb system database always uses the Simple Recovery model. The sample user databases, Northwind and pubs, use the Simple Recovery model by default, but this can be changed.

Practice: Viewing the Properties of a Transaction Log and a Database

In this practice you use SQL Server Enterprise Manager to view some of the properties of a transaction log file and a database.

▶ **To view the properties of a transaction log file and a database**

1. Ensure that you are logged on to the SelfPacedSQL.MSFT domain controller as Administrator.
2. Click Start, point to Programs, point to Microsoft SQL Server, and then click Enterprise Manager.

   SQL Server Enterprise Manager appears, displaying the Microsoft SQL Servers and the Event Viewer (Local) console trees in the console root.
3. In the console tree, expand the Microsoft SQL Servers container, expand the SQL Server Group container, expand the default instance, and then expand Databases.
4. In the console tree, right-click Northwind and then click Properties.

   The Northwind Properties dialog box appears, with the General tab selected, displaying various properties of the Northwind database.

5. Click the Transaction Log tab.

   The File Name column displays the logical filename of the Northwind database.

6. Expand the size of the Location column by sliding the column bar to the right.

   The name and complete file path of the operating system file are displayed.

7. Reduce the size of the Location column so you can view the Space Allocated (MB) column.

   The current space allocated is displayed. Most systems will display 1 MB. This is the initial size of the Northwind transaction log file (which is rounded to the nearest whole number).

8. Click the Options tab.

   Notice that the Northwind database is using the Simple Recovery model.

9. Click Cancel to close the Northwind Properties dialog box.

10. Close SQL Server Enterprise Manager.

Lesson Summary

SQL Server 2000 uses one or more transaction log files to record modifications made by transactions ahead of writing these data modifications to disk. This ensures that a transaction can be rolled forward or rolled back if needed, such as in the case of a server failure. SQL Server 2000 uses the checkpoint process and operating system threads to ensure that data modifications are written to disk. The checkpoint process also identifies the portion of the transaction log that is no longer active. The inactive portion of the transaction cannot be reused until it is truncated. The recovery model in use determines whether the checkpoint process truncates the inactive portion of the transaction log, or a transaction log backup is required to truncate the transaction log. Finally, the recovery model chosen determines the extent of logging for bulk operations, which dictates the frequency of transaction log backups.

Lesson 3: Understanding and Querying System and Database Catalogs

SQL Server 2000 uses a variety of system tables to manage an instance of SQL Server 2000 and its associated databases. These tables hold meta data about the system as a whole and about objects in each database. This lesson covers the most frequently used system tables, including the use of system-stored procedures, system functions, and Information Schema Views to query these tables.

After this lesson, you will be able to

- Understand the most frequently used system tables
- Use system-stored procedures to query system tables
- Use system functions to query system tables
- Use Information Schema Views to query system tables

Estimated lesson time: 15 minutes

Introducing System Tables

The system tables used by SQL Server 2000 consist of two groups of tables: the system catalog and the database catalog. Changing or deleting a system table can cause SQL Server 2000 to lose functionality, function erratically, or be unable to function at all.

Tip   System tables begin with the *sys* prefix.

System Catalog

The system catalog consists of the set of system tables SQL Server 2000 uses to manage the entire instance, and exists only in the master database. These system tables record meta data about the entire instance (such as all users and all databases) and system configuration settings (such as server configuration settings).

Table 5.1 describes some of the most frequently queried system tables in the system catalog.

Table 5-1.   Frequently Queried System Tables in the System Catalog

System Table	Description
Sysaltfiles	Contains a row of information for each file in the database, including the file ID, database ID (dbid), physical and logical filenames, location, size, and growth characteristics.
Sysconfigures	Contains a row of information for each server option set by an administrator before SQL Server 2000 started, plus dynamic configuration options set since startup.
Sysdatabases	Contains a row of information for each database, including the dbid, security identifier (SID) of the database owner, creation date, database compatibility level, location of the primary file, and database configuration options that have been set.
Sysdevices	Contains a row of information for each permanent backup device that has been created, including the physical and logical filenames, file size, and controller type for the device (such as disk or tape).
Syslockinfo	Contains a row of information for each waiting, converting, and granted lock request, including the ID of the user or process requesting the lock and the object being locked.
Syslogins	Contains a row of information for each login account, including the sid, login ID, encrypted password (may be NULL), default database, and server role.
Sysmessages	Contains a row of information for each system error or warning that SQL Server 2000 can return, including the error number, severity level, and description.
Sysperfinfo	Contains a row of information for each SQL Server performance counter, including the object name, counter name, and counter value. These counters are used in Windows System Monitor (or Windows2000 Performance Monitor) and performance condition alerts.

Database Catalog

The database catalog consists of a set of system tables used to manage a particular database. Each database has a set of these system tables. The system tables contain sufficient information for a user database to be detached from one instance of SQL Server 2000 and attached to another instance with the same or different database name. Table 5.2 describes some of the most frequently queried system tables in the database catalog.

Table 5-2. Frequently Queried System Tables in the Database Catalog

System Table	Description
Syscomments	Contains a row of information for each view, rule, default, trigger, CHECK constraint, DEFAULT constraint, and stored procedure. The text column contains the original Transact-SQL definition statement used to create the object. None of the entries in this table should be modified or removed. You can hide stored procedure definitions by using the ENCRYPTION keyword when the stored procedure is created.
Sysindexes	Contains a row of information for each index and table in the database, including the index ID (indid), type, original fill factor, and index name.
Sysobjects	Contains a row of information for each object in a database, including object name, object ID, user ID (uid) of the object owner, and creation date.
Sysusers	Contains a row of information for each Windows user, Windows group, SQL Server user, and SQL Server role in the database, including the user ID, username, group ID (gid), and creation date.

Retrieving System Information

You can query system tables directly, but querying system tables by using scripts is not recommended because Microsoft might change system tables in future releases to add new functionality. These changes in a new release of SQL Server could break any scripts that query system tables directly. SQL Server 2000 provides a number of mechanisms to query system tables that you can embed in scripts that will not be affected by future changes to system tables. These mechanisms include system stored procedures, system functions, and information schema views.

Note System tables can also be queried using OLE DB schema rowsets and ODBC catalog functions.

Practice: Querying System Tables Directly

In this practice you use SQL Query Analyzer to query system tables directly.

► **To query system tables directly**

1. Ensure that you are logged on to the SelfPacedSQL.MSFT domain controller as Administrator.
2. Click Start, point to Programs, point to Microsoft SQL Server, and then click Query Analyzer.
   SQL Query Analyzer appears displaying the Connect To SQL Server dialog box.
3. Connect to your default instance using Windows authentication.
4. SQL Query Analyzer appears, displaying a new query window.
5. In the query pane, type **SELECT * FROM sysdatabases**.

6. On the toolbar, click the Execute Query button, or press the F5 key, or press CTRL-E to execute the query.

   Notice that the results pane displays information regarding each database in this instance of SQL Server 2000.

7. On the toolbar, click the Clear Window button or press CTRL+SHIFT+DEL simultaneously.

8. In the query pane, type **SELECT * FROM sysaltfiles**.

   Notice that the results pane displays information regarding each data and transaction log file used by this instance of SQL Server 2000.

9. Close SQL Query Analyzer.

10. Click the No button if a SQL Query Analyzer dialog box appears asking if you want to save the changes.

System-Stored Procedures

System-stored procedures are prewritten Transact-SQL statements that ship with SQL Server 2000. System-stored procedures work with system tables to provide system information to and perform administrative tasks for database administrators.

Note   System-stored procedures begin with an *sp_*.

Table 5.3 describes some of the most frequently used system-stored procedures for querying system tables.

Practice: Querying System Tables Using System-Stored Procedures

In this practice you use system-stored procedures in SQL Query Analyzer to query system tables.

▶ **To query system tables using system-stored procedures**

1. Ensure that you are logged on to the SelfPacedSQL.MSFT domain controller as Administrator.

2. Click Start, point to Programs, point to Microsoft SQL Server, and then click Query Analyzer.

   SQL Query Analyzer appears, displaying the Connect To SQL Server dialog box.

3. Connect to your default instance using Windows authentication.

   SQL Query Analyzer appears, displaying a new query window.

4. In the query pane, type **sp_helpdb**.

Table 5-3.   System-Stored Procedures Used for Querying System Tables

System-Stored Procedure	Description
Sp_configure ['name', 'value']	Reports (or changes) configuration settings for a SQL Server 2000 instance.
Sp_dboption ['database', 'option', 'value']	Reports (or changes) database options for a particular database.
Sp_help ['object']	Reports information about a particular database object or data type.
Sp_depends ['object']	Reports information about dependencies of database objects, such as views or procedures that depend on a particular table.
Sp_helpdb ['database']	Reports information about a particular database (or all databases if no database is specified).
Sp_helpfile ['name']	Reports the physical names and attributes of files associated with the current database.
Sp_lock ['spid1', 'spid2']	Reports information about current locks.
Sp_monitor	Reports information about how busy SQL Server 2000 has been since it started and since *sp_monitor* was last run.
Sp_spaceused ['object', 'updateusage']	Reports information about the number of rows, disk space reserved, disk space used by a table or database, and whether the DBCC UPDATE-USAGE command should be run.
Sp_statistics ['table_name', 'owner', 'qualifier', 'index_name', 'is_unique', 'accuracy']	Reports information about all indexes and statistics on a table or view.
Sp_who ['login']	Reports information about current SQL Server 2000 users and processes, and can be filtered using the ACTIVE keyword to display only processes that are not idle.

5. On the toolbar, click the Execute Query button.

   Notice that the results pane displays information regarding each database in this instance of SQL Server 2000.

6. In the query pane, type a space and then **Northwind** to modify your query to read *sp_helpdb Northwind*.

   Notice that the results pane displays information regarding the Northwind database only, including an additional result set showing the file allocation for the Northwind database.

7. On the toolbar, click the Clear Window button.

8. In the query pane, type **sp_spaceused**.

9. On the toolbar, click the Execute Query button.

Notice that the results pane displays information regarding space used by the current database, which is master.

10. On the toolbar, click the drop-down list and then change the current database to Northwind.

11. On the toolbar, click the Execute Query button.

    Notice that the results pane displays information regarding space used by the current database, which is now Northwind.

12. In the query pane, type **'customers'** to modify your query to read *sp_spaceused 'customers'*.

13. On the toolbar, click the Execute Query button.

    Notice that the results pane now displays information regarding space used by the customers table in the Northwind database.

14. Close SQL Query Analyzer.

15. Click the No button if a SQL Query Analyzer dialog box appears asking whether you want to save the changes.

System Functions

System functions are a set of built-in functions that ship with SQL Server 2000 that query system tables from within Transact-SQL statements and return specific information about values, objects, and settings. Table 5.4 describes some of the system functions used most frequently by database administrators to query system tables.

Table 5-4.   System Functions Used to Query System Tables

System Function	Description
DATABASEPROPERTYEX ('database','property')	Returns a value regarding a database option or property (such as Recovery).
DB_ID ('database')	Returns the ID number of a database.
DB_NAME (database_id)	Returns the name of a database.
FILE_ID ('file_name')	Returns the ID number of a logical filename.
FILE_NAME (file_ID)	Returns the logical file name of a file.
FILEPROPERTY ('file_name', 'property')	Returns a value regarding a file property (such as SpaceUsed).
GETDATE ()	Returns the current system date and time in the SQL Server 2000 format for datetime values.
HOST_NAME ()	Returns the name of the host computer.
STATS_DATE (table_id, index_id)	Returns the date that statistics for an index were updated.
USER_ID ('user_name')	Returns the database ID of a user.
USER_NAME (id)	Returns the database name of a user (such as dbo).

Practice: Querying System Tables Using System Functions

In this practice you use system functions in SQL Query Analyzer to query system tables.

▶ **To query system tables using system functions**

1. Ensure that you are logged on to the SelfPacedSQL.MSFT domain controller as Administrator.

2. Click Start, point to Programs, point to Microsoft SQL Server, and then click Query Analyzer.

    SQL Query Analyzer appears displaying the Connect To SQL Server dialog box.

3. Connect to your default instance using Windows authentication.

    SQL Query Analyzer appears displaying a new query window.

4. In the query pane, type **SELECT DB_ID ('Northwind')**

5. On the toolbar, click the Execute Query button. Notice that the results pane displays the database ID for the Northwind database in this instance of SQL Server 2000.

6. On the toolbar, click the Clear Window button.

7. In the query pane, type **SELECT FILEPROPERTY ('Northwind', 'SpaceUsed')**

8. On the toolbar, click the Execute Query button.

    Notice that the results pane displays the number of pages allocated in the Northwind database.

9. On the toolbar, click the Clear Window button.

10. In the query pane, type **SELECT USER_NAME (2)**.

    Notice that the results pane displays the name for the user with a user ID of 2 (this is the Guest account).

11. Close SQL Query Analyzer.

12. Click the No button if a SQL Query Analyzer dialog box appears asking whether you want to save the changes.

Information Schema Views

Information schema views are views of system and database catalog information based on the ANSI SQL-92 standards. These views are independent of the implementation of catalogs by any particular vendor, and thus applications using information schema views are portable between heterogeneous systems that comply with ANSI SQL-92. They are also independent of any changes to the underlying system tables.

Table 5.5 describes some of the most frequently used information schema views for querying system tables.

Table 5-5.   Information Schema Views for Querying System Tables

Information Schema View	Description
Information_schema.columns	Contains a row of information for each column accessible to the current user in the current database.
Information_schema.schemata	Contains a row of information for each database in which the current user has permissions.
Information_schema.tables	Contains a row of information for each table in the current database in which the current user has permissions.
Information_schema.table_privileges	Contains a row of information for each table privilege granted to or by the current user in the current database.
Information_schema.view_table_usage	Contains a row of information for each table in the current database used in a view.

Practice: Querying System Tables Using Information Schema Views

In this practice you use information schema views in SQL Query Analyzer to query system tables.

▶ **To query system tables using information schema views**

1. Ensure that you are logged on to the SelfPacedSQL.MSFT domain controller as Administrator.

2. Click Start, point to Programs, point to Microsoft SQL Server, and then click Query Analyzer.

    SQL Query Analyzer appears displaying the Connect To SQL Server dialog box.

3. Connect to your default instance using Windows authentication.

    SQL Query Analyzer appears displaying a new query window.

4. On the toolbar, click the drop-down list and then change the current database to Northwind.

5. In the query pane, type **SELECT * FROM INFORMATION_SCHEMA.SCHEMATA**.

6. On the toolbar, click the Execute Query button.

    Notice that the results pane displays information regarding all databases in this instance of SQL Server 2000.

7. On the toolbar, click the Clear Window button.

8. In the query pane, type **SELECT * FROM INFORMATION _SCHEMA.TABLES.**

9. On the toolbar, click the Execute Query button.

Notice that the results pane displays information regarding tables in the current database.

10. On the toolbar, click the Clear Window button.

11. In the query pane, type **SELECT * FROM INFORMATION _SCHEMA.TABLE_PRIVILEGES**.

12. On the toolbar, click the Execute Query button.

Notice that the results pane displays information regarding privileges on all tables in the Northwind database.

13. Close SQL Query Analyzer.

14. Click the No button if a SQL Query Analyzer dialog box appears asking whether you want to save the changes.

Lesson Summary

The system catalog and database catalog contain system tables used by SQL Server 2000 to manage the entire instance and each particular database. Although you can query these system tables directly using SQL Query Analyzer, you should not embed direct queries into Transact-SQL scripts because the system tables might change in future releases of SQL Server. If you want to embed queries in Transact-SQL scripts, you should use one of several methods that are guaranteed to work with future versions of SQL Server. These include system-stored procedures, system functions, and information schema views.

Review

Here are some questions to help you determine whether you have learned enough to move on to the next chapter. If you have difficulty answering these questions, review the material in this chapter before beginning the next chapter. The answers for these questions are located in the Appendix, "Questions and Answers."

1. Describe the difference in the ordering of data pages from a table caused by using either a clustered index or a nonclustered index.

2. Which recovery model does not require regular backups of the transaction log?

3. Why should you not create scripts that use Transact-SQL statements to directly query system tables?

C H A P T E R   6

Creating and Configuring User Databases

About This Chapter

This chapter prepares you to create and configure user databases. The chapter begins with learning the mechanics of creating a user database, using either SQL Server Enterprise Manager or Transact-SQL statements in SQL Query Analyzer. Next you learn about the various database options that you can set and how to set them, either at the time of creation or after the database is in production. Next you learn about manual and automatic methods of managing the size of user databases, including both data and transaction log files. Finally you learn how to optimize your disk subsystem by placing data and transaction log files on multiple disks, using a combination of RAID, filegroups, and multiple disks. After you have completed these tasks, you will be ready to begin loading data into your SQL Server 2000 installation.

Before You Begin

To complete this chapter, you must have

- A computer that meets or exceeds the minimum hardware requirements listed in Table 2.1, "Hardware Requirements," in Lesson 1 of Chapter 2.
- Microsoft Windows 2000 Server running on your computer on an NTFS partition.
- A computer with a NetBIOS name of SelfPacedCPU, configured as a domain controller in the SelfPacedSQL.MSFT domain.
- Installed a default instance and at least one named instance of SQL Server 2000 (see Chapter 2).

Lesson 1: Creating a User Database

Now that you have installed SQL Server 2000, you are ready to create user databases to hold your data. In this lesson, you will learn the mechanics of creating a user database using SQL Server Enterprise Manager and using the *CREATE DATABASE* Transact-SQL statement in SQL Query Analyzer. You will also learn how to use SQL Server Enterprise Manager to generate a Transact-SQL script that will re-create a database object (for example, in a disaster recovery situation).

After this lesson, you will be able to

- Understand the process of creating a user database
- Create a user database using SQL Server Enterprise Manager
- Create a user database using the *CREATE DATABASE* Transact-SQL statement in SQL Query Analyzer
- Create a Transact-SQL script of a database object using SQL Server Enterprise Manager

Estimated lesson time: 45 minutes

Creating a User Database

When you create a new user database, you define it by selecting a database name that is unique to the current instance of SQL Server 2000. No other properties of a user database need be defined explicitly. The database name you choose should conform to SQL Server 2000 rules for identifiers (although this is not required). These rules state that for identifier names

- The first character must begin with a letter, the underscore (_), the "at" sign (@), which signifies a local variable or parameter, or the number sign (#), which signifies a temporary table or procedure.
- Subsequent characters in the name can also include numbers and the dollar sign ($).
- Embedded spaces and special characters cannot be included.
- A SQL Server 2000 reserved keyword in uppercase or lowercase (examples: BACKUP or PLAN) cannot be used.

Note   If an identifier does not follow these rules, you must reference the identifier using double quotation marks or brackets (for example, *sp_helpdb* "My Database" or *sp_helpdb* [My Database] if you use a database name that includes a space).

Additional properties that you will define frequently are the size, physical and logical filename, and physical location of both the primary data file and the initial transaction log file. You can specify multiple data files and multiple transaction log files (generally on separate disks) when you create the database (or you can add them later). You can also group data files into filegroups and change the default filegroup. Lesson 4 of this chapter covers placing database files on multiple disks, using multiple files, and creating user-defined filegroups for a database. Next, for each data file and transaction log file you create, you can specify whether the file autogrows when it runs out of space, how large each growth increment is, and the maximum size to which it can grow. Lesson 3 of this chapter covers managing database growth.

If you do not define these additional file properties, SQL Server 2000 uses default values. Table 6.1 lists the default properties for a database (in the default instance) with a database name of SelfPaced.

Table 6-1.   Example Default Database Properties for Database Name SelfPaced

Database Property	Value
Logical primary data filename	SelfPaced_Data
Physical primary data filename	SelfPaced_Data.mdf
Physical primary data file location	C:\Program Files\Microsoft SQL Server\Mssql\Data
Physical size of the primary data file	The actual size of the model data file (640 KB by default) if created with a Transact-SQL script or the actual size of the model data file rounded up to the nearest whole number (1 MB) if created with SQL Server Enterprise Manager
Physical primary data file growth properties	Autogrowth enabled, with a growth increment of 10%, and no maximum file growth size Logical transaction log filename SelfPaced_Log
Physical transaction log filename	SelfPaced_Log.ldf
Physical transaction log file location	C:\Program Files\Microsoft SQL Server\Mssql\Data
Physical size of the transaction log file	The actual size of the model transaction log file (512 KB by default) if created with a Transact-SQL script or the actual size of the model transaction log file rounded up to the nearest whole number (1 MB) if created with SQL Server Enterprise Manager
Physical transaction log file growth properties	Autogrowth enabled, with a growth increment of 10%, and no maximum file growth size

When SQL Server 2000 creates a database, it performs this task in two steps. First it copies the model database to the primary data file to initialize the new user database and its meta data. The objects that are copied include system database objects and any user-defined database objects that have been placed in the model database (such as tables, views, stored procedures, and user-defined data types). Next SQL

Server 2000 fills the rest of each data file with empty pages, except those specialized pages used to track allocation of space (such as GAMs, SGAMs, and IAMs). This primary data file must always have room to add new catalog information to the system tables. System tables are always contained in the primary data file.

Note   The tempdb database is re-created each time you start SQL Server 2000 (using the model database meta data).

In addition to inheriting database objects from the model database, each new user database inherits database option settings from the model database (tempdb does not inherit database option settings). Change these settings for the model database to change the database option settings for all new databases. You can also change these settings after a user database has been created. Setting and changing database options are covered in Lesson 2 of this chapter.

Finally, by default, each new database inherits the default collation setting from the model database. The default collation for the model database is the same as for all system databases (the default collation is defined during setup). The default collation for system databases cannot be changed easily—you must have access to all scripts and information needed to recreate the user databases and their objects, all user data must be exported, all user databases must be dropped, the system databases must be rebuilt, and all user data must be reloaded. In international environments, having user databases with collation settings that are different from each other's settings and from the system databases' settings can be quite useful. To change the default collation for a new user database, specify a different collation when you create the new database. It is also possible to change the default collation *after* you have created a user database, loaded data, and created objects, but this is not an easy task. To change the default collation at that stage, you must first export all user data, recreate all database objects, and reload all user data.

Note   You must be a member of the Sysadmin or Dbcreator role (or be specifically granted the permission) to create a user database. Permissions are covered in Chapters 10 and 11.

Using SQL Server Enterprise Manager to Create a User Database

You can create a user database in two separate ways with SQL Server Enterprise Manager. The first way is by using the Create Database Wizard. The second way is to create a database directly by right-clicking Databases and then selecting New Database in the console tree. The Create Database Wizard is useful for novices, but limits the complexity of your physical database design. If you plan to use multiple disks and multiple files, you cannot use the Create Database Wizard.

Using the Create Database Wizard

The SQL Server Enterprise Manager wizards are available from the Tools menu, and are also available from any taskpad view. Figure 6.1 displays the Select Wizard dialog box, from which you can select a variety of wizards, including the Create Database Wizard.

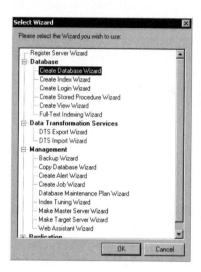

Figure 6.1.   The Select Wizard dialog box.

After you start the Create Database Wizard, you are asked to select a name for your new database in the Name The Database And Specify Its Location page. You can also choose to change the default location for the data file and the transaction log file (when you are using the Create Database Wizard, both files must be in the same location). See Figure 6.2.

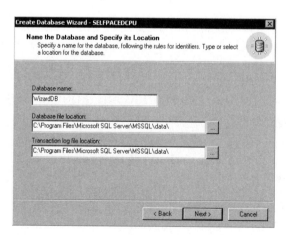

Figure 6.2.   Selecting a name and location for the database.

Next, in the Name The Database Files page, you define both the logical filename and the physical filename for each data file (when you are using the Create Database Wizard, both names must be the same). You can also add additional data files in the default location and can specify the initial size for each data file. The default is 1 MB. See Figure 6.3.

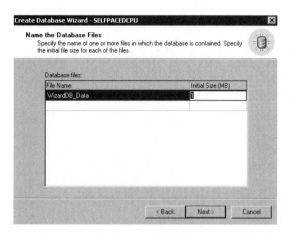

Figure 6.3.   Naming the database files.

Next, in the Define The Database File Growth page, you specify the growth characteristics of all data files. Notice that the default is to grow each data file in increments of 10 percent and to allow unlimited growth. Notice that you cannot specify different growth characteristics for each data file using the Create Database Wizard. Lesson 3 of this chapter covers setting appropriate growth characteristics. See Figure 6.4.

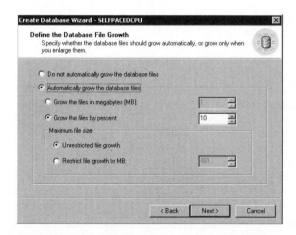

Figure 6.4.   Specifying the growth characteristics of data files.

Next, in the Name The Transaction Log Files page, you define both the logical file-name and the physical filename for the transaction log file (when you are using the Create Database Wizard, both names must be the same). You can also add additional transaction log files in the default location and can specify the initial size for each transaction log file. The default is 1 MB. See Figure 6.5.

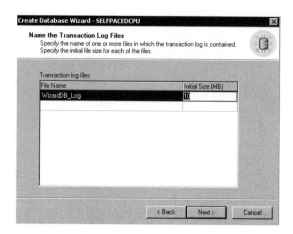

Figure 6.5.   Naming the transaction log file.

Next, in the Define The Transaction Log File Growth page, you specify the growth characteristics of all transaction log files. Notice that the default is to grow each transaction log file in increments of 10 percent and to allow unlimited growth. Notice also that you cannot specify different growth characteristics for each transaction log file when you use the Create Database Wizard. Lesson 3 of this chapter covers setting appropriate growth characteristics. See Figure 6.6.

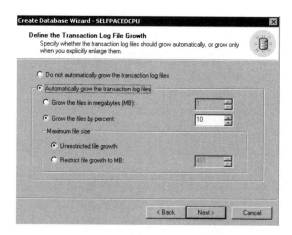

Figure 6.6.   Specifying the growth characteristics of transaction log files.

Next, in the Completing The Create Database Wizard page, you are given the opportunity to review the selections you have made before you actually create the new database. You can click the Back button to change any parameter you want to change. Click the Finish button to create the new database. See Figure 6.7.

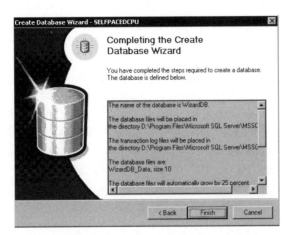

Figure 6.7.   Reviewing the database parameters that you have selected.

After the new database is successfully created, a Create Database Wizard dialog box appears to give you the opportunity to create a maintenance plan for this new database. Click the No button. Creating a maintenance plan for a database is covered in Chapter 13.

Practice: Creating a Database Using the Create Database Wizard in SQL Server Enterprise Manager

In this practice you create a database using the Create Database Wizard in the SQL Server Enterprise Manager.

▶ **To create a database using the Create Database Wizard in SQL Server Enterprise Manager**

1. Ensure that you are logged on to the SelfPacedSQL.MSFT domain controller as Administrator.

2. Click Start, point to Programs, point to Microsoft SQL Server, and then click Enterprise Manager.

   SQL Server Enterprise Manager appears displaying the Microsoft SQL Servers and the Event Viewer (Local) console trees in the console root.

3. In the console tree, expand the Microsoft SQL Servers container, expand the SQL Server Group container, and then click the default instance.

4. On the Tools menu, click Wizards.

   The Select Wizard dialog box appears.

5. Expand Database and then double-click Create Database Wizard.

   The Welcome To The Create Database Wizard page appears.

6. Click Next.

   The Name The Database And Specify Its Location page appears.

7. In the Database Name text box, type **WizardDB**.

8. Review the default locations for the database file and the transaction log file, and then click Next.

   The Name The Database Files page appears. Notice the default logical database primary data file name and default initial size for the primary data file. Also notice that you can add additional data files, but only in the default location.

9. In the Initial Size (MB) text box, type **10**, and then click Next.

   The Define The Database File Growth page appears. Notice the default settings.

10. In the Grow The Files By Percent: spin box, type **25**.

11. Click the Restrict File Growth To MB: option button, and then in the Restrict File Growth To MB: spin box, type **30**.

12. Click Next.

    The Name The Transaction Log Files page appears. Notice the default name and initial size. The default initial size is the same size as the initial data file size.

13. In the Initial Size (MB) text box, type **4** and then click Next.

    The Define The Transaction Log File Growth page appears.

14. Click the Grow The Files In Megabytes (MB): option button, and then in the Grow The Files In Megabytes (MB): spin box, type **3**.

15. Click the Restrict File Growth To MB: option button, and then in the Restrict File Growth To MB: spin box, type **15**.

16. Click Next.

    The Completing The Create Database Wizard page appears.

17. Click the Finish button.

    A Create Database Wizard message box appears letting you know that the database was successfully completed.

18. Click OK.

    A Create Database Wizard dialog box appears asking whether you want to create a maintenance plan for this database.

19. Click the No button.

20. In the SQL Server Enterprise Manager console tree, expand your default instance and then expand Databases.

    Notice that the WizardDB database appears in the list of databases.

21. Right-click WizardDB, and then click Properties.

   The WizardDB Properties dialog box appears, with the General tab selected.

22. Click the Data Files tab and review the properties of the data file for the WizardDB database.

23. Click the Transaction Log tab and review the properties of the transaction log file for WizardDB database.

24. Click Cancel to close the WizardDB Properties dialog box.

25. Do not close SQL Server Enterprise Manager.

Using SQL Server Enterprise Manager Directly

To create a database directly using SQL Server Enterprise Manager, right-click the Databases container in the console tree and then click New Database. The Database Properties dialog box appears with the General tab selected, as in Figure 6.8. Notice that you can change the collation for this new database.

On the Data Files tab, you can create multiple data files, each with differing properties. You can also create user-defined filegroups and place secondary data files in specific filegroups. Placing database files is covered in Lesson 4 of this chapter. See Figure 6.9.

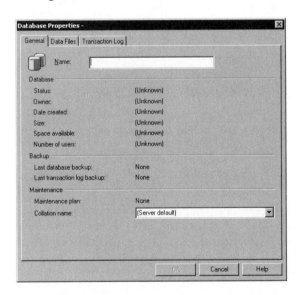

Figure 6.8.   The General tab of the Database Properties dialog box.

Figure 6.9.   The Data Files tab of the Database Properties dialog box.

On the Transaction Log tab, you can create multiple transaction log files, each with differing properties. See Figure 6.10.

Figure 6.10.   The Transaction Log tab of the Database Properties dialog box.

Practice: Creating a Database Directly Using SQL Server Enterprise Manager

In this practice you create a database directly using SQL Server Enterprise Manager.

▶ **To create a database directly using SQL Server Enterprise Manager**

1. In the SQL Server Enterprise Manager console tree, expand the Microsoft SQL Servers container, expand the SQL Server Group container, and then expand the default instance.

2. Right-click Databases and then click New Database.

   The Database Properties dialog box appears with the General tab selected.

3. In the Name text box, type **SSEMDB** and then click the Data Files tab.

   Notice the default logical filename, physical name and location, initial size, filegroup, and growth properties.

4. In the File Name column, overwrite the default primary filename by typing **SSEMDB_Data1** in the first cell of the column.

   Notice that the physical filename in the corresponding Location cell changes to SSEMDB_Data1_Data.mdf.

5. In the corresponding Initial Size (MB) cell, type **50**.

6. In the File Growth group box, type **15** in the By Percent: spin box.

7. In the Maximum File Size group box, click the Restrict File Growth (MB): option button, and then in the Restrict File Growth (MB): spin box, type **150**.

8. In the File Name column, click the second line and then type **SSEMDB_Data2**.

   Notice the default parameters for this new data file. In particular, notice that the default name for this secondary data file ends with the .NDF suffix.

9. Change the physical location for this secondary data file to C:\SSEMDB_Data2_Data.ndf.

   In a production system, you would not place a secondary data file on the same physical drive as the primary data file. If you have a second physical drive in your practice system, place this secondary file on that drive.

10. In the corresponding Initial Size (MB) cell, type **50**.

11. In the File Growth group box, type **15** in the By Percent: box.

12. In the Maximum File Size group box, click the Restrict File Growth (MB): option button, and then in the Restrict File Growth (MB): spin box, type **100**.

13. Click the Transaction Log tab.

    Notice the default parameters for this new transaction log file.

14. In the Initial Size (MB) cell, type **20** to replace the default parameter.

15. In the File Growth group box, type **25** in the By Percent: spin box.

16. In the Maximum File Size group box, click the Restrict File Growth (MB): option button, and then in the Restrict File Growth (MB): spin box, type **75**.

17. Click OK to create the new database.

    In the console tree, notice that the SSEMDB database appears in the list of databases.

18. Right-click SSEMDB, and then click Properties.

    The SSEMDB Properties dialog box appears, with the General tab selected.

19. Click the Data Files tab and review the properties of the data files for the SSEMDB database.

20. Click the Transaction Log tab and review the properties of the transaction log file for the SSEMDB database.

21. Click Cancel to close the SSEMDB Properties dialog box.

22. Do not close SQL Server Enterprise Manager.

Using the CREATE DATABASE Transact-SQL Statement to Create a User Database

The CREATE DATABASE Transact-SQL syntax for creating a user database requires only a database name. All other parameters are optional. The Transact-SQL syntax allows you to define the properties of multiple data files, create user-defined filegroups, place secondary data files in specific filegroups, and define the properties of multiple transaction log files. The CREATE DATABASE topic in SQL Server Books Online provides the complete syntax with a number of examples.

Tip   When you are first learning a new Transact-SQL command, use the examples in SQL Server Books Online to help decipher the syntax. This is frequently the easiest way to learn a new command.

Creating a Simple Database Using Transact-SQL

The following example, run in SQL Query Analyzer, creates a database called TSQLDB without specifying any data files or transaction log files.

```
CREATE DATABASE TSQLDB
```

Creating a Multiple File Database Using Transact-SQL

The following example creates a database called TSQLDB, which consists of a 100-MB primary data file, a 500-MB secondary file, and a 250-MB transaction log file. The properties of the primary data file in this example include an initial size of 100 MB, a growth increment of 25 MB, and a maximum data file size of 250 MB. The properties of the secondary data file include an initial size of 500 MB, a growth increment of 50 MB, and a maximum data file size of 1000 MB. The properties of the transaction log file in this example include an initial size of 250 MB, a growth increment of 40 percent, and a maximum transaction log size of 500 MB.

```
CREATE DATABASE TSQLDB
ON
( NAME = TSQLDB1 ,
    FILENAME = 'D:\SQL_Data\TSQLDB1.mdf' ,
    SIZE = 100 ,
    MAXSIZE = 250 ,
    FILEGROWTH = 25 ) ,
( NAME = TSQLDB2 ,
    FILENAME = 'E:\SQL_Data\TSQLDB2.ndf' ,
    SIZE = 500 ,
    MAXSIZE = 1000 ,
    FILEGROWTH = 50 )
LOG ON
( NAME = TSQLDB_Log ,
    FILENAME = 'F:\SQL_Log\TSQLDB2.ldf' ,
    SIZE = 250,
    MAXSIZE = 500 ,
    FILEGROWTH = 40% )
```

Practice: Creating a Database in SQL Query Analyzer Using the CREATE DATABASE Transact-SQL Statement

In this practice you create a database in SQL Query Analyzer using the CREATE DATABASE Transact-SQL statement in SQL Query Analyzer.

▶ **To create a database in SQL Query Analyzer using the CREATE DATABASE Transact-SQL statement**

1. On the SQL Server Enterprise Manager Tools menu, click SQL Query Analyzer.
    SQL Query Analyzer appears.
2. On the toolbar, click the Load SQL Script button or press CTRL+SHIFT+P.
    The Open Query File dialog box appears.
3. Browse to the C:\SelfPacedSQL\CH_6 folder and open the CreateDB.sql script.
4. Review this script. The script is shown below.

```
CREATE DATABASE TSQLDB
ON
( NAME = TSQLDB_DATA ,
    FILENAME =
    'C:\Program Files\Microsoft SQL Server\MSSQL\Data\TSQLDB.mdf' ,
    SIZE = 10 ,
    MAXSIZE = 25 ,
    FILEGROWTH = 5 )
LOG ON
( NAME = TSQLDB_LOG ,
    FILENAME =
    'C:\Program Files\Microsoft SQL Server\MSSQL\Data\TSQLDB.ldf' ,
    SIZE = 4 ,
```

```
                          MAXSIZE = 12 ,
                          FILEGROWTH = 40% )
```

5. Execute the CreateDB.sql script.

   Notice that the results pane displays the results of the creation of the TSQLDB database. The TSQLDB_DATA file was allocated 10 MB and the TSQLDB_LOG file was allocated 4 MB.

6. On the toolbar, click the Clear Window button.

7. In the query pane, type **EXEC sp_helpdb TSQLDB** and then press CTRL+E (to execute the query) on your keyboard.

8. Review the output in the results pane to verify the properties of the TSQLDB database.

9. On the toolbar, click the Clear Window button.

10. Minimize SQL Query Analyzer.

Scripting Databases and Database Objects Using SQL Server Enterprise Manager

Using SQL Server Enterprise Manager, you can generate a Transact-SQL script to document existing database objects (such as databases, tables, indexes, views, users, groups, and logins). You can use these scripts to re-create any of these database objects at a later time (for disaster recovery) in the same or different database. You can generate a single script that will re-create all database objects, or create separate scripts for each object.

To generate a Transact-SQL script, right-click the object for which you want to generate a script, point to All Tasks, and then click Generate SQL Script. See Figure 6.11.

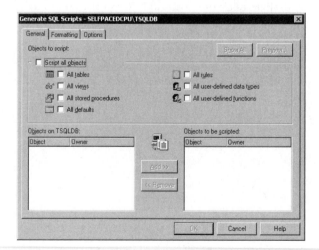

Figure 6.11.   General tab in the Generate SQL Scripts dialog box.

You can select objects to be scripted. If no objects have been created within the database, no objects will appear.

Click the Formatting tab to display formatting options. Depending on the object you are scripting, you will have a variety of scripting options. By default, the script will contain the *CREATE* and *DROP* statement for each object being scripted. See Figure 6.12.

Click the Options tab to display security scripting options, table scripting options, and file options. See Figure 6.13.

Note   You can script the database schema and all database objects into a single script or create multiple scripts for multiple objects.

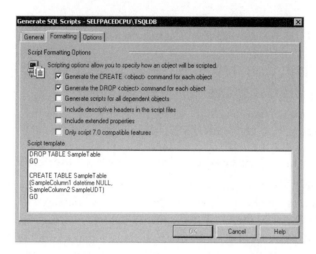

Figure 6.12.   Formatting tab in the Generate SQL Scripts dialog box.

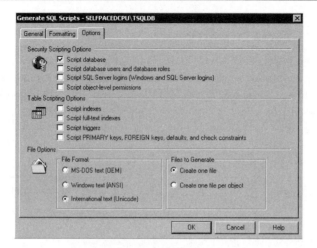

Figure 6.13.   Options tab in the Generate SQL Scripts dialog box.

Practice: Generating a Transact-SQL Script to Re-create the TSQLDB Database

In this practice you use SQL Server Enterprise Manager to generate a Transact-SQL script to re-create the TSQLDB Database.

▶ **To generate a Transact-SQL script to re-create the TSQLDB database**

1. In the SQL Server Enterprise Manager console tree, expand the Microsoft SQL Servers container, expand the SQL Server Group container, expand the default instance, and then expand Databases.

    Notice that the TSQLDB database does not appear in the database list. The reason is that this database was created by using a different client management tool.

2. Right-click Databases and then click Refresh.

    Notice that the TSQLDB database now appears in the database list.

3. Right-click TSQLDB, point to All Tasks, and then click Generate SQL Script.

    The Generate SQL Scripts – SelfPacedSQL\TSQLDB dialog box appears, with the General tab selected.

4. Click the Options tab.

5. In the Security Scripting Options group box, select the Script Database check box and then click OK.

    The Save As dialog box appears.

6. In the Save In drop-down list, change the folder to C:\SelfPacedSQL\CH_6.

7. In the File Name text box, type **TSQLDB** and then click the Save button.

8. Click OK to close the Scripting message box.

9. Switch to SQL Query Analyzer.
10. On the toolbar, click the Load SQL Script button.

    The Open Query File dialog box appears.
11. Browse to the C:\SelfPacedSQL\CH_6 folder and open the TSQLDB.sql script.

    Notice that the script begins with a *DROP DATABASE* Transact-SQL statement and a *CREATE DATABASE* Transact-SQL statement. Notice also that it contains the database option settings for the TSQLDB database. These settings will be covered in Lesson 2 of this chapter.
12. Close SQL Query Analyzer.

Lesson Summary

You can create user databases using either SQL Server Enterprise Manager or using Transact-SQL scripts in SQL Query Analyzer. If you are a novice, you can use the Create Database Wizard in SQL Server Enterprise Manager to create simple databases. To create more complex databases, use either the direct method in SQL Server Enterprise Manager or write a Transact-SQL script for execution in SQL Query Analyzer. When you create a user database, SQL Server 2000 will use default values for all data file and transaction log properties that you do not specifically define. Finally, when you create a new user database, it inherits the system and user database objects in the model database, as well as its database option settings.

Lesson 2: Setting Database Options

In addition to the properties of each data file and transaction log file in a user database, you can set a number of database options that determine various characteristics of a user database. In this lesson, you will be introduced to these settings and learn how to view and modify these settings for an existing database, including the model database.

After this lesson, you will be able to

- Describe the database options that you can set
- View the database settings
- Modify the database settings

Estimated lesson time: 15 minutes

Introducing Database Options

Database option settings for a database determine various default behaviors for the database. These settings for a user database are inherited from the model database when the user database is created. Database options fall into five categories:

- Control of certain automatic behaviors (such as automatically creating statistics, automatically updating statistics, and automatically shrinking database files)
- Cursor behavior and scope (such as local or global)
- Recovery options (Full, Bulk-Logged, or Simple)
- ANSI compliance options (such as ANSI nulls and quoted identifiers)
- State options (such as read-only and dbo access only)

In most environments, you will rarely modify more than a few of these settings. Setting the recovery model for a database and restricting the level of user access to a database are the settings that you will change periodically. Recovery settings were covered in Chapter 5 and will also be covered in Chapter 8. You restrict access to a user database to perform various administrative tasks (such as restoring a database) or to create a read-only database. Options include setting a database to read-only, allowing only database owners and members of the Dbcreator and Sysadmin server roles to connect to the database, and setting a database to allow only a single user to connect. Refer to the Setting Database Options topic in SQL Server Books Online for full details on other settings.

Viewing Database Option Settings

You view the current settings for database options using SQL Server Enterprise Manager or using the *DATABASEPROPERTYEX* system function. SQL Server Enterprise Manager displays the most commonly modified settings. To view them, right-click a database, click Properties, and then click the Options tab. See Figure 6.14.

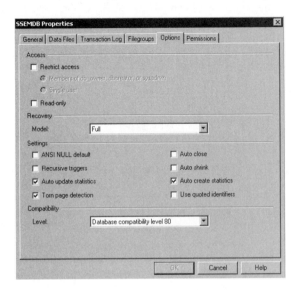

Figure 6.14.   Viewing the database option settings.

To view the current recovery model for the TSQLDB database using the *DATA-BASEPROPERTYEX* system function, use the following statement in SQL Query Analyzer.

```
SELECT DATABASEPROPERTYEX ('TSQLDB', 'RECOVERY')
```

Modifying Database Options

You set the most common database options by clicking a check box in SQL Server Enterprise Manager, or you can set any database option using the *ALTER DATABASE* Transact-SQL statement. For example, to set the TSQLDB database to Bulk-Logged Recovery model using the *ALTER DATABASE* statement, use the following statement.

```
ALTER DATABASE TSQLDB SET RECOVERY BULK_LOGGED
```

Note   The *sp_dboption* system-stored procedure can also be used to display or change certain database option settings. However, this system-stored procedure is only supported for backward compatibility with previous versions of SQL Server. It does not allow you to view (or set) options that are new to SQL Server 2000.

Lesson Summary

Database options control the default behavior of a database. These settings are inherited from the model database. In general, change only the database recovery setting or restrict access to a database to perform administrative tasks or create a read-only user database. To view the current settings of a database, use SQL Server Enterprise Manager or the *DATABASEPROPERTYEX* system function. To change these settings for all new databases, change the database option settings for the model database. To change these settings for an existing database, use SQL Server Enterprise Manager or the *ALTER DATABASE* Transact-SQL statement.

Lesson 3: Managing User Database Size

After you create a user database, you need to manage the size of the user database. Data stored in the data files normally grows over time, and systems tend to get busier over time, resulting in transaction logs that fill more rapidly. Occasionally, you will need to reduce the size of data or transaction log files. SQL Server 2000 provides a number of mechanisms for managing database growth (and shrinkage). In this lesson you learn how to use the automatic methods provided by SQL Server 2000 appropriately. You also learn how to manually increase the size of data files and transaction log files, and how to add additional files. Finally you will learn how to shrink data files and transaction log files.

After this lesson, you will be able to

- Use the autogrow capability appropriately
- Use the autoshrink capability appropriately
- Manually grow and shrink data files
- Manually grow and shrink transaction log files
- Add data files and transaction log files

Estimated lesson time: 30 minutes

Using Automatic File Growth Appropriately

When you create a user database, by default each data file and transaction log file is set to grow automatically when the particular file becomes full. Autogrowth is particularly useful for embedded applications and small installations where there is no database administrator to regularly monitor free space, such as in desktop installations. However, in a dedicated SQL Server 2000 environment, autogrowth should only be used as a safety valve because of performance issues. Each time a file must grow, your system suffers a performance hit. In addition, disk fragmentation will occur if your disk grows frequently, particularly on a drive shared with other applications and data. Rather than relying on autogrowth, you should regularly monitor your data and transaction log files and manually increase (or decrease) their size as needed at a time when the database is not busy.

Note   There is also a constant small performance hit when autogrowth is enabled because your system must continually monitor the size of each file to determine if and when it needs to grow.

In general, you should plan the size of your data and transaction log files so that autogrowth is needed rarely, if at all. If you use autogrowth, set a growth increment large enough so that growth occurs infrequently. Furthermore, you should always set a maximum size to which a file can grow so the file does not fill up the entire disk (if the file is sharing the disk with other files). To monitor file growth and available free space, you should set an alert to notify you when a file automatically grows and when free space falls below a set value. Configuring alerts is covered in Chapter 13.

Use SQL Server Enterprise Manager or the *ALTER DATABASE* Transact-SQL statement to modify autogrowth settings. For example, to disable autogrowth for the primary data file in the TSQLDB database, use the following statement.

```
ALTER DATABASE TSQLDB MODIFY FILE ( NAME = 'tsqldb_data' , FILEGROWTH =
0 )
```

Note   Setting *FILEGROWTH* equal to zero prevents the database files from expanding beyond their initial size. When the data files fill with data, no more data can be added until the existing data files are expanded or until more data files are added to the database. When the transaction log files fill with log records, no more transactions can complete until the existing transaction log files are expanded, more transaction log files are added, or the transaction log files are backed up (and truncated).

Practice: Configuring Automatic Filegrowth Settings Using SQL Server Enterprise Manager

In this practice you configure automatic filegrowth settings using SQL Server Enterprise Manager.

▶ **To configure automatic filegrowth settings using SQL Server Enterprise Manager**

1. In the SQL Server Enterprise Manager console tree, expand the Microsoft SQL Servers container, expand the SQL Server Group container, expand the default instance, and then expand Databases.

2. In the console tree, right-click Northwind and then click Properties.

   The Northwind Properties dialog box appears with the General tab selected, displaying various properties of the Northwind database.

3. Click the Data Files tab.

   Notice that the primary data file for the Northwind database is set to grow automatically in 10 percent increments. Also notice that no maximum size is set.

4. In the Maximum File Size group box, click the Restrict File Growth (MB): option button and then type **25** in the Restrict File Growth (MB): spin box.

5. Click the Transaction Log tab.

6. In the File Growth group box, click the In Megabytes: option button and then type **5** in the In Megabytes: spin box.

7. Click OK to apply these changes to the Northwind database.

Using Automatic File Shrinkage Appropriately

In addition to autogrowth, you can configure a user database to shrink automatically whenever a data file or transaction log file has a large amount of free space. By default, this database option setting is set to false (disabled). Although this option is sometimes useful for desktop installations and embedded applications, you should never set this option to true in a regular production system, for the same performance reasons discussed for autogrowth. You should plan the size of your data files and transaction log files to use an appropriate amount of space. If you need to shrink a file, you should perform that task manually at a time when your system is not busy. Also, automatically shrinking a file that will have to autogrow later is inefficient. Use SQL Server Enterprise Manager or the *ALTER DATABASE* Transact-SQL statement to modify autoshrink settings.

Controlling Data File Size Manually

Monitoring the amount of free space in your data files allows you to anticipate the need to increase the size of your data files. You can then perform this task at a time when your system is not busy. Use SQL Server Enterprise Manager or the *ALTER DATABASE* Transact-SQL statement to increase the size of a data file. For example, to set the size of the primary data file for the TSQLDB database to 15 MB, use the following statement.

```
ALTER DATABASE TSQLDB
MODIFY FILE ( NAME = 'tsqldb_data' , SIZE = 15 )
```

If you need to shrink the size of a data file manually, use SQL Server Enterprise Manager or the *DBCC SHRINKFILE* statement. For example, to reduce the size of the primary data file in the TSQLDB database, use the following statement to specify a target size of 7 MB.

```
USE TSQLDB
DBCC SHRINKFILE ( 'tsqldb_data' , 7 )
```

DBCC SHRINKFILE applies to the current database only. When you shrink a data file, the data file is shrunk from the end of the file. By default, all used pages in the part of the data file being shrunk are relocated to available free space toward the beginning of the data file to shrink the data file to the desired size. You can also shrink a data file to the last allocated extent without relocating pages, or you can relocate pages without shrinking the data file. You cannot shrink a data file smaller than the amount of data it contains or the size of the model database. *DBCC SHRINKFILE* will shrink a data file smaller than the original size. In addition, you can shrink a data file while users are working in the database, but not while the database or transaction log is being backed up.

You can use the *DBCC SHRINKDATABASE* to shrink an entire database, including all data files and all transaction log files, to a specified percent of the current size. Using *DBCC SHRINKDATABASE*, you cannot shrink a database to a size smaller than its size at creation.

Note   *ALTER DATABASE* cannot be used to shrink the size of a file (only to increase the size of a file).

Practice: Modifying Data File Size Using SQL Server Enterprise Manager

In this practice you modify the size of a data file using SQL Server Enterprise Manager.

▶   **To modify data file size using SQL Server Enterprise Manager**

1. In the SQL Server Enterprise Manager console tree, expand the Microsoft SQL Servers container, expand the SQL Server Group container, expand the default instance, and then expand Databases.

2. In the console tree, right-click Northwind and then click Properties.

   The Northwind Properties dialog box appears with the General tab selected, displaying various properties of the Northwind database.

3. Click the Data Files tab.

   In the Space Allocated (MB) column, notice that the primary data file for the Northwind database is set to 3 MB.

4. In the Space Allocated (MB) cell, type **7**.

5. Click OK to apply this change to the Northwind database.

Controlling Transaction Log File Size Manually

In addition to monitoring the amount of free space in your data files regularly, you should monitor the free space available in your transaction log files. When using the Full and Bulk-Logged Recovery models, you must perform regular transaction log backups to truncate the transaction log files to free up space for additional records. When you are using the Full Recovery model, large-scale operations and bulk load operations can fill up the transaction log quickly. If you find your transaction log files filling up more rapidly than you want, you must either perform more frequent transaction log backups, allow SQL Server 2000 to automatically grow the transaction log files whenever they run out of space (when SQL Server 2000 is already busy), or manually increase the size of your transaction log files. Use SQL Server Enterprise Manager or the *ALTER DATABASE* Transact-SQL statement to increase the size of a transaction log file in the same manner you increase the size of a data file.

Caution   If SQL Server 2000 runs out of transaction log space, SQL Server 2000 will stop.

If you need to shrink the size of a transaction log file manually, use SQL Server Enterprise Manager or the *DBCC SHRINKFILE* statement. You can use SQL Server Enterprise Manager or the *DBCC SHRINKDATABASE* statement to shrink all data files and transaction log files at once. Like a data file, a transaction log file is shrunk from the end of the file. The unit of shrinkage is the VLF. If the transaction log file being shrunk contains inactive VLFs at the end of the file, the transaction log file will be reduced by the size of these inactive VLFs at the end of the file to reduce the file to as close as possible to the requested size. The requested size is rounded up to the next highest virtual log file boundary. For example, if you specify a target size of 150 MB and the transaction log file size is currently 300 MB with six VLFs, the new size for this transaction log file will be 180 MB (if the VLFs at the end of the transaction log file are empty).

If there are not sufficient empty VLFs at the end of the transaction log file to free up the desired space, SQL Server 2000 frees up as much space as possible. It fills the last active VLF at the end of the file with dummy records so that the MinLSN can move to the beginning of the file (after long-running transactions and unreplicated transactions replicate). See Figure 6.15.

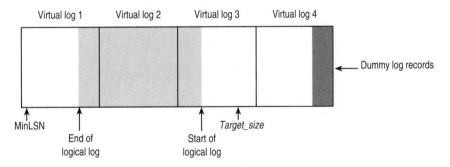

Figure 6.15.   Shrinking the transaction log by adding dummy records.

SQL Server 2000 then sends an information message telling you to perform a transaction log backup to truncate the VLFs at the end of the file. After you perform this action, you perform the DBCC command again to shrink the transaction log file to your desired size. See Figure 6.16.

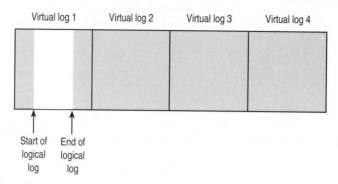

Figure 6.16.   Transaction log after shrinking.

Creating Additional Data and Transaction Log Files

If you need to create additional data files or transaction log files (either because the additional space is on a separate drive or to enhance performance by spreading database files among multiple disks), you can use SQL Server Enterprise Manager or the *ALTER DATABASE* Transact-SQL statement. When creating additional database files using SQL Server Enterprise Manager, you simply add the desired file in the Properties dialog box for the database. By default, all additional data files are added to the primary filegroup. Lesson 4 of this chapter covers the use of user-defined filegroups. See Figure 6.17.

The following example adds a file to the TSQLDB database using the *ALTER DATABASE* Transact-SQL statement.

```
ALTER DATABASE TSQLDB
ADD FILE
(NAME = 'TSQLDB2_DATA' ,
    FILENAME =
    'C:\Program Files\Microsoft SQL Server\MSSQL\Data\TSQLDB2.ndf' ,
    SIZE = 10 ,
    MAXSIZE = 25 ,
    FILEGROWTH = 5 )
```

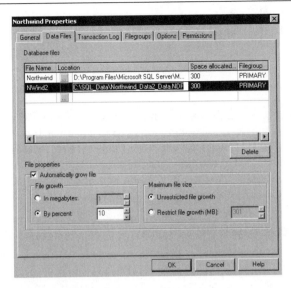

Figure 6.17.   Adding new database files.

Lesson Summary

Over time, your SQL Server 2000 installation will need additional space for data files and transaction log files. You can allow SQL Server 2000 to add this additional space automatically, but in most production environments, you should only use this as a safety valve. For better performance, you should monitor your data files to anticipate when they are getting low on available space and increase their size manually. This allows you to grow your database files when your system is not busy. If your transaction log files are running low on space, you can either increase their size or perform the transaction log backups more frequently. In addition to increasing the size of existing database files, you can add additional data files and transaction log files. You can also shrink database files automatically or manually. For best performance, shrink database files manually, if at all.

Lesson 4: Placing Database Files on Multiple Disks

Most production systems use multiple disks to ensure recoverability, increase performance, and add fault tolerance. Multiple disks are also used for maintenance reasons. This lesson covers the various options available to accomplish these goals. These options range from simply placing each of your data files and transaction log files on separate disks to utilizing a combination of RAID and filegroups for very large databases (VLDBs).

After this lesson, you will be able to

- Determine the appropriate RAID-level system to optimize performance and provide fault tolerance
- Describe how to use RAID with filegroups for VLDBs
- Plan file placement for performance and recoverability
- Move database files

Estimated lesson time: 30 minutes

Introducing RAID

A RAID system consists of two or more disk drives that provide greater performance and fault tolerance than a single large drive at a lower cost. RAID support is provided by software on the disk storage system (hardware RAID) or by the Windows operating system (software RAID). Because software RAID requires SQL Server 2000 to share processor resources with RAID, hardware RAID is generally used for maximum performance. However, software RAID will provide better performance than no RAID at all.

Note   Hardware RAID also supports hot swappable drives, which allow you to replace a faulty drive without shutting down the system. Some implementations also support hot standby drives (extra drives already installed). Also RAID 10 is only available with hardware RAID.

RAID levels 0, 1, 5, and 10 (also known as 1+0) are typically used with SQL Server 2000. A RAID system appears as a single drive to SQL Server 2000 on which a single file can be placed. Table 6.2 briefly describes each of these RAID levels and their performance characteristics.

Introducing Filegroups

There are three types of filegroups—primary, user-defined, and default. Each database can have a maximum of 256 filegroups. SQL Server 2000 always contains at least one filegroup, the primary file group. A filegroup can consist of multiple data files spread across multiple drives. Transaction log files cannot be part of a filegroup. The primary filegroup contains the primary data file containing the system tables. When you create secondary data files within a database, by default, these additional data files are placed in the primary filegroup. When you create database objects (such as tables and indexes) and add data to these objects, SQL Server 2000 uses the space within each of the data files within the filegroup proportionally, rather than allocating space from and writing data to one data file until it is full before writing to the next data file. This proportional fill method allows a database to be created that spans across multiple disks, with associated performance benefits. For example, if your SQL Server 2000 system has four disks, you could use one disk for the transaction log and the remaining three disks for the data files (one per disk).

Table 6-2.   RAID Levels and Their Performance

RAID Level	Description	Advantage/Disadvantage
0	Consists of two or more disks. Data writes are divided into blocks and spread evenly across all disks. Known as disk striping. This level is the easiest level to implement.	Fastest read and write performance; uses 100% of disk capacity. Not fault tolerant. The failure of one drive will result in all data in an array being lost. It is not advisable to use level 0 for data in mission-critical environments.
1	Generally consists of two disks (some RAID implementations support more than two disks). Data writes are written completely to both disks. Known as disk mirroring (or disk duplexing if two controllers are used).	Read performance almost twice as fast as a single disk, and fault tolerant. Relatively slow write performance, and uses only 50% of disk capacity.
5	Consists of three or more disks. Data writes are divided into blocks and written across all disks along with a parity stripe for data recovery.	Fast read performance, efficient use of disk space, and fault tolerant. Slow write performance. Uses $1/n$ of disk capacity for parity information where n equals the total number of disks.
10 (1+0)	Consists of four or more disks. Data writes are striped across two or more disks and then mirrored across the same number of disks. Known as mirroring with striping.	Fastest read and write performance and fault tolerant. Uses only 50% of disk capacity.

Rather than placing all secondary data files in a single filegroup, you can create user-defined filegroups into which to place these secondary data files. On a system with multiple filegroups, you can specify the filegroup into which a newly created database object will be placed. This can have performance benefits, but also requires more administrative overhead and performance-tuning expertise. If no filegroup is specified when a database object is created, it is placed in the default filegroup. The default filegroup is the primary filegroup until the default is changed. To change the default filegroup, use the *ALTER DATABASE* Transact-SQL statement.

Note   Changing the default filegroup to a user-defined filegroup can prevent the primary data file from running out of space. When the primary data file runs out of space, it prevents system tables from accepting new information.

Configuring Your SQL Server 2000 Disk Subsystem for Performance, Fault Tolerance, and Recoverability

Configuring your SQL Server 2000 disk subsystem for performance, fault tolerance, and recoverability means achieving the best read and write performance you can afford for the transaction log, the data files, and the tempdb database, while not sacrificing fault tolerance or recoverability.

Note   For performance, use a Small Computer System Interface (SCSI) disk subsystem rather than an Integrated Drive Electronics (IDE) or Enhanced Integrated Drive Electronics (EIDE) subsystem. SCSI controllers are more intelligent, can work multiple channels simultaneously, and are not affected by slower devices on the channel (such as CD-ROMs).

Transaction Log

You should choose your disk subsystem for your transaction log to reflect the fact that the primary function of the transaction log is to provide for recoverability of your data in case one or more of the disks containing your data files should fail. Next, the disk subsystem should reflect the fact that transaction log records are written serially on a continuous basis (sequentially and synchronously), but are only read for backups, to perform transaction rollbacks, and during database recovery when SQL Server 2000 starts. When the transaction log is read for backups, the load can be heavy.

Based on the primary function of the transaction log, the disks containing the transaction log files should not be shared with the data files for the database. Obviously, if your data files and your transaction log files share a common physical disk, you cannot completely recover your data if that disk fails. If your SQL Server 2000 installation contains multiple databases, at a minimum, place the database files from one database on the same physical disk as the transaction log file from another database. This will ensure recoverability of each database if any single disk fails.

The next level in optimizing your transaction log performance is to use dedicated disks for the transaction log files for each database. If you use a disk dedicated to a single transaction log, you can ensure that the disk head remains in place from one write operation to the next. Also read requests will be faster because the data will be laid down sequentially on the disk. Thus, using separate disks for the data files and the transaction log files has a transaction log performance benefit as well as being essential for recoverability.

The next level in optimizing your transaction log performance is to implement a RAID 1 system. This is more expensive (50 percent of your disk space is redundant), but yields significant performance and recoverability benefits. RAID 1 offers almost double the throughput on disk reads (for better backup performance) and minimizes downtime (if one disk fails, the data access shifts to the other). Data writes are somewhat slower, although faster than RAID 5. You can minimize the cost of this solution by minimizing the size of your transaction log (and thereby the size and cost of the disks) and by performing frequent transaction log backups.

Data Files

You should choose your disk subsystem for your data files to reflect the fact that data loss and downtime are generally unacceptable. As discussed in the preceding section, the first step in improving the performance and recoverability of your database is to place the data files and the transaction log files on separate disk subsystems, and to use dedicated disks (if possible) for your data files so that data read and write (I/O) requests are not competing with other I/O requests on those disks.

The next level in optimizing your disk system is to improve I/O performance. Although one large disk can store as much data as a number of small disks, splitting your data among a number of disks results in increased I/O performance (particularly when multiple controllers are used). This increased I/O results from the ability of SQL Server 2000 to perform parallel scans for data using separate operating system threads when the data is spread across multiple disks. There are a number of ways to spread data across multiple disks.

Using multiple data files to spread across multiple disks in a single filegroup is one way to accomplish this. Using RAID to spread a single file (and its data) across multiple disks will also accomplish this, and can achieve superior performance. Using RAID can also provide fault tolerance. If you understand the data access patterns on your system, you can also use multiple filegroups rather than RAID (or in addition to RAID) to place heavily accessed tables and indexes on separate disks to improve I/O performance. However, in most cases, RAID provides most of the benefits of filegroups without the administrative overhead of multiple filegroups. When you have VLDBs, using multiple RAID systems and grouping RAID files in filegroups may be necessary for both performance and database maintenance reasons.

Given the administrative complexity of filegroups, database administrators usually choose RAID for their data files rather than filegroups. RAID 5 is frequently the first choice because of its efficient use of disk space and its fault tolerance. The downside of RAID 5 is relatively poor write performance. RAID 5 is a good choice for systems requiring high read performance and moderate write performance. However, if you need high write performance, choose either RAID 0 or RAID 10.

Note   With RAID 5, if a single drive fails, performance is miserable while the parity stripe is used to reconstruct the lost data (although the system does continue to function while this recovery is occurring).

When you are choosing between RAID 0 and RAID 10, the lower reliability and slower recovery of RAID 0 dictate choosing RAID 10. However, short-term cost factors may make RAID 0 a necessary choice. Although RAID 10 is initially an expensive solution, it provides the performance of RAID 0 and the reliability and recoverability of RAID 1 (the cost of downtime when a drive fails may justify RAID 10).

If you need to use multiple RAID systems, you can choose to place each data file (each RAID system is generally a single data file) in the same filegroup, or you can use multiple filegroups. If you really understand the data access patterns in your database and are very good at performance tuning, you may be able to achieve some performance gain by using different filegroups. In a VLDB environment, using separate filegroups for maintenance reasons may determine how you configure your data files. For example, you may need to back up files or filegroups separately on a VLDB to be able to achieve an effective backup and restore strategy. Backup and restore strategies are covered in Chapter 8.

Tempdb

You should choose your disk subsystem for the tempdb database to reflect the fact that this database is used only for temporary storage for work files (such as intermediate result sets used in complex queries and DBCC operations). Optimizing the tempdb database means enabling it to handle a high volume of reads and writes. Recoverability is not an issue because tempdb is rebuilt each time SQL Server 2000 starts.

You should begin by placing the tempdb data file on its own disk so that it is not competing with other database objects for disk access. Next, consider using a dedicated disk controller for this separate disk. Finally, if tempdb is known to be a bottleneck, use RAID 0. The lack of fault tolerance is irrelevant to tempdb. No data is permanently stored in the tempdb database.

Moving Data and Transaction Log Files

You can detach data and transaction log files from an instance of SQL Server 2000 and reattach them to the same instance or a different instance. Detachment is useful for moving a database to another instance or another server. It is also used to move data and transaction log files to different physical drives. You can use SQL Server Enterprise Manager or Transact-SQL to detach and reattach a database and its associated physical files.

Note   When you move or place data files and transaction log files to an NTFS partition, ensure that the service account used by the SQL Server service has full access to these files.

Detaching and Attaching Databases Using SQL Server Enterprise Manager

To detach a database using SQL Server Enterprise Manager, right-click the database you want to detach, point to All Tasks, and then click Detach Database. See Figure 6.18.

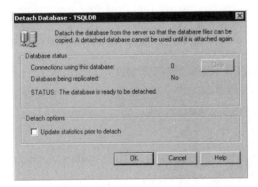

Figure 6.18.   The Detach Database dialog box.

If users are connected to this database, you can click the Clear button to disconnect them and complete the detachment process. You also have the option to update statistics before you detach. Updating statistics before detaching is used when you are moving the database to read-only media (such as a CD-ROM).

After a database has been detached, you can move one or more of the physical files to a new location (such as a dedicated disk or a RAID drive). To reattach a database using SQL Server Enterprise Manager, right-click Databases, point to All Tasks, and then click Attach Database. Figure 6.19 displays the dialog box that appears.

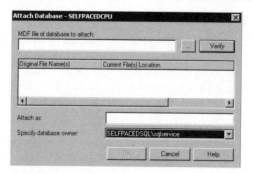

Figure 6.19.   The Attach Database dialog box.

In the Attach Database dialog box, you must enter the complete name and path of the primary data file (the Browse button is available). The primary data file contains the information necessary to find the other files that make up the database. SQL Server 2000 reads this primary file and displays any secondary data files and the transaction log file to attach. If SQL Server 2000 does not find any of these files, it will place a red X in the check box next to that physical file. See Figure 6.20. This will occur whenever you move the secondary or transaction log files to a different location from the primary file. Edit the Current File(s) Location column for each file that has moved. You can also change the database name at this point. Finally, specify the owner of the database being attached and click OK.

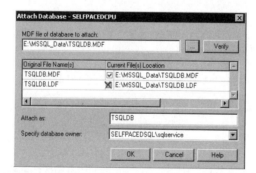

Figure 6.20.   Reattaching a database using SQL Server Enterprise Manager.

Note   If you have more than 16 files to reattach, you must use the Transact-SQL *CREATE DATABASE* statement with the FOR ATTACH clause.

Detaching and Attaching Databases Using Transact-SQL

To detach a database using Transact-SQL, use the *sp_detach_db* system-stored procedure. For example, to detach the TSQLDB database without updating statistics, use the following statement.

```
Sp_detach_db TSQLDB, TRUE
```

To reattach a database using Transact-SQL, use the *sp_attach_db* system-stored procedure. When you use this stored procedure, you can specify up to 16 filenames that are included in the database that you want to attach. The filename list must include at least the primary file, because this file contains the system tables that point to the other files contained in the database. The filename list must also include any files that were moved after the database was detached. For example, to attach the TSQLDB database, use the following statement:

```
sp_attach_db TSQLDB1 ,
    @filename1 =
    'C:\Program Files\Microsoft SQL Server\MSSQL\Data\TSQLDB.mdf'
```

Lesson Summary

The first step in using multiple disks to optimize your SQL Server 2000 production environment is to use separate disks for your transaction log files and your data files. This separation will ensure recoverability in case of a disk failure. Use dedicated disks for all SQL Server 2000 files where possible. Next, use RAID 1 for your transaction log. Use RAID 10 if possible for your data files. Consider using either RAID 0 or RAID 5 if you cannot justify RAID 10 because of financial constraints.

Review

Here are some questions to help you determine whether you have learned enough to move on to the next chapter. If you have difficulty answering these questions, review the material in this chapter before beginning the next chapter. The answers for these questions are located in the Appendix, "Questions and Answers."

1. You want to create a user database containing multiple data files on separate physical disks. You are not experienced at writing Transact-SQL statements. What is the simplest method you can use to create this database?

2. Describe the two methods you can use to change the database recovery model for a database.

3. You created a new database on your system. You used the default properties for the transaction log file. You backed up the new database and the master database. After you performed a bulk load of data into your new database, you notice that the transaction log is quite large. Why did it grow so large and what must you do to reduce the size of the transaction log?

4. You are managing a small database system running on Windows 2000 Server. Although the database is under 1 GB in space, it is very busy (primarily performing writes), and you want to improve its performance. You do not have the budget for a hardware RAID system and are not aware of specific database access patterns. You have already placed the transaction log file on a separate disk from the data file. What is an inexpensive solution?

C H A P T E R   7

Populating a Database

About This Chapter

This chapter prepares you to populate your database from an existing data source. The chapter begins with a discussion of the data transformation, consistency, and validation issues you will encounter when you import data from one or multiple sources into a SQL Server 2000 database. Next, you are introduced to the primary SQL Server 2000 tools used for populating a database. Finally, you learn how and when to use each of these tools.

Before You Begin

To complete this chapter, you must have

- A computer that meets or exceeds the minimum hardware requirements listed in Table 2.1 in the Lesson 1 section of Chapter 2.
- Microsoft Windows 2000 Server running on your computer on an NTFS partition.

- A computer with a NetBIOS name of SelfPacedCPU, configured as a domain controller in the SelfPacedSQL.MSFT domain.

- Installed a default instance and at least one named instance of SQL Server 2000 (see Chapter 2).

Lesson 1: Transferring and Transforming Data

After you have created your user database, you need to populate it with data. Frequently, this consists of importing and transforming existing data from one or more external data sources (such as another database system) to SQL Server 2000. In this lesson, you learn the issues you will face when you choose to import data from another data source. This lesson will also introduce you to the primary tools used to import and transform data, including a brief discussion of the capabilities of each tool. These tools include DTS, Bcp, and the *BULK INSERT* Transact-SQL statement.

After this lesson, you will be able to

- Describe the process of evaluating the quality and consistency of data in an external data source prior to data import
- Understand the types of data transformations that may be necessary when importing data from existing data sources
- Describe the tools provided by SQL Server 2000 for importing data

Estimated lesson time: 15 minutes

Importing Data

Populating your SQL Server 2000 user database frequently consists of the process of importing existing data from external data sources to a newly created destination database. These external data sources include Microsoft or third-party databases, spreadsheets, or text files. Before you can import this data, you must perform the following preliminary tasks to evaluate the external data and determine the steps that will be involved in the import process. These preliminary steps will also help you select the appropriate tool to use.

- Determine the consistency of the existing data within the external data source. The external data source may not have enforced consistency when data was initially input (for example, if the names of states were entered as two-letter abbreviations in some instances and were fully spelled out in other instances).
- Determine whether additional columns must be added. The existing data may be internally consistent but not include necessary columns because these values were assumed (such as values for country or an international telephone area code).
- Determine whether the existing data format should be modified. The existing data may be internally consistent but not be represented in the manner you want to use in the destination database (for example, requiring a change in the date format or the conversion of numerical values to more readable string values, such as 1, 2, and 3 being converted to poor, average, and excellent).

- Determine whether existing data columns should be modified. The existing data may be internally consistent but contain columns that need to be aggregated or separated (such as separating first and last names into separate columns or summarizing daily data into weekly or monthly data).

- Determine whether the import of data will be a one-time task or a task that must be performed periodically. The existing data may need to be migrated from an existing legacy system that will be retired or may need to be extracted from an existing system from which you will extract data on a weekly or monthly basis.

- Determine how to access the existing data. Is the external data source directly accessible, and do you have permission to access the data directly? (If not, the data will have to be exported into a format that SQL Server 2000 can work with, such as a delimited text file.)

DTS Data Transformations

After you have evaluated the data in each external data source, you need to determine how to proceed. Occasionally, changes to data can be made in the external data source, but usually these changes cannot be made in the external data source without either breaking existing applications (for example, adding columns or changing data formats) or consuming too much time (for example, manually enforcing data consistency where none existed previously). These changes can either be made after the data has been imported into SQL Server, using temporary tables and using Transact-SQL statements to scrub and cleanse the data, or can be made during the import process itself. Changes to the data made during the import and export process are referred to as DTS transformations. A DTS transformation occurs when one or more operations or functions are applied against data before that data arrives at the destination. The data at the source is not changed. Transformations make it easy to implement data scrubbing, conversions, and complex data validations during the import and export process.

The type and extent of modifications that must be made will help determine the SQL Server 2000 data transfer tool that you will use, and when you will perform the modifications. Also, whether the data import is a one-time task or a periodic task will frequently determine the tool you will use and how much you automate the necessary transformations. Planning and testing (using data subsets) is essential, particularly for large data sets.

Introducing the Data Transfer Tools

SQL Server 2000 provides a number of tools for importing and exporting data. These tools have differing capabilities to extract subsets of data from an existing data source and to transform data. Table 7.1 briefly describes each of these primary data transfer tools and their capabilities.

Table 7-1.   Data Transfer Tools and Their Functions

Tool	Description
DTS	DTS is a graphical tool used to import, export, and transform data. DTS can work directly with a wide variety of data sources. DTS creates packages that can be scheduled. DTS can also import and export database objects schema (meta data) between SQL Server instances.
Bcp	Bcp is a command-prompt utility used to copy data from a text file to a SQL Server 2000 table or view (or from a SQL Server 2000 table or view to a text file) using ODBC. The transformation capabilities of Bcp are limited and require cryptic format files. Working with Microsoft or third-party databases is a two-step process.
BULK INSERT Transact-SQL statement	*BULK INSERT* is a Transact-SQL command used to copy data from an ASCII text file to a SQL Server 2000 table or view (but not from SQL Server 2000 to a text file) using OLE DB. The *BULK INSERT* statement provides the same functionality of Bcp (and has the same limitations) in a Transact-SQL statement and can be embedded in a DTS package.

Note   There are a number of other methods of moving data between data sources, but they are not normally used to initially populate a database. These additional methods include backup and restore (see Chapters 8 and 9), replication (see Chapter 15), ActiveX scripts, and the *INSERT* and *SELECT INTO* Transact-SQL statements using distributed queries (see Chapter 12).

Lesson Summary

When you are populating a database from existing data stored in an external data source, you must evaluate that data to determine what transformations, if any, must be performed on that data prior to or during importation. You must determine whether the import is a one-time task or will be a periodic task. You must also determine how you will access this data, either directly or through an exported text file. These factors will determine the data transfer tool you use, and when you transform the data.

Lesson 2: Introducing Microsoft Data Transformation Services (DTS)

DTS is a powerful set of graphical tools (and programmable objects) that you can use to import, export, and transform data to and from a wide variety of data sources and destinations. In this lesson, you learn about the components of DTS packages, including connections, tasks, transformations, and workflow. You are also introduced to storage options for DTS packages. Finally, this lesson introduces the DTS tools, including the DTS Import/Export Wizard (Dtswiz.exe), DTS Designer, and the DTS package execution utilities. Subsequent lessons will teach you how to use each of these tools.

After this lesson, you will be able to

- Describe the components of a DTS package
- Describe the data sources to which DTS can establish direct connections
- Describe the type of data transformations that are available
- Describe the DTS workflow options
- Describe the DTS package storage options
- Describe each of the DTS tools

Estimated lesson time: 15 minutes

Understanding a DTS Package

You can create a DTS package to connect to a data source, copy and manage data and database objects, run tasks as jobs from within a package, transform the data, and then store the transformed data and the database objects to the same data source or to a different data destination. You can also notify a user (or process) of the success or failure of the package, including attaching a file to an e-mail message. You define these tasks as discrete steps (known as DTS tasks) and control the execution using precedence constraints (such as performing a certain task if a task succeeds and a different task if the task fails). You create a DTS package in the DTS Import/Export Wizard, in DTS Designer, or programmatically.

DTS Connections

A DTS package must have a valid data source and a valid data destination to which it connects. It can connect to additional data sources during execution (such as lookup tables located on a third data connection). Table 7.2 describes the variety of connections that you can establish during the package creation process.

Table 7-2.   Connection Types

Connection Type	Description
Data source connection	A connection to a standard database (such as Microsoft SQL Server 2000, Microsoft Access 2000, Oracle, dBase, or Paradox), an OLE DB connection to an ODBC data source, a Microsoft Excel 2000 spreadsheet, an HTML source, or any other OLE DB provider. The properties of the data source connection specify the necessary connection parameters.
File connection	A connection to a text file (normally delimited). The properties of the file connection specify the format of the text file. There are multiple formats you can use. For example, the text file format can be either a delimited or a fixed field format.
Data link connection	A connection to an intermediate file (.UDL file) that stores a connection string to create an OLE DB connection that is resolved at run time. The data link connection allows you to encapsulate the connection properties into a separate .UDL data link file. You can then edit the connection string in the data link file (from one data source to another) without changing the SQL Server 2000 DTS package.

DTS Tasks

A DTS package can perform a plethora of tasks, either sequentially or in parallel. Parallel tasks run independently of each other (using separate operating system threads to enhance performance), whereas sequential tasks execute in a defined order based on the success, failure, or completion of predecessor tasks. A DTS task is a discrete unit of work that is part of a data movement and transformation process (such as copying the contents of a text file to a SQL Server 2000 table). DTS tasks that transform data (such as the Parallel Data Pump, the Transform Data, and the Data Driven Query tasks) are based on an architectural component called the DTS data pump. The DTS data pump is an OLE DB service provider that provides the interfaces and the means to import, export, and transform data from an OLE DB data source to an OLE DB destination.

SQL Server 2000 provides a number of DTS tasks that transform data, copy and manage data and meta data, and function as jobs. These tasks are accessed through the DTS Designer tool (except the Parallel Data Pump task, which can only be accessed programmatically). Table 7.3 describes the tasks that are available through DTS Designer (all of which are also accessible programmatically).

DTS can perform column-level transformations on data during the importation process. These transformations can be as simple as changing column names and as complex as your transformation process requires. Using DTS Designer, you can use the Transform Data task or the Data Driven Query task, or you can write an

ActiveX script. Using Visual Basic or Visual C++, you can also write transformations programmatically and use the Parallel Data Pump task. You perform a transformation by mapping a relationship between one or more columns in the data source with one or more columns in the data destination. You then define the transformations you want to occur during importation.

Table 7-3.   Tasks Available through DTS Designer

Category	Task	Description
Tasks that copy and manage data and meta data	Bulk Insert task	Runs the *BULK INSERT* Transact-SQL statement from within a DTS package. This task provides the fastest way to copy information into a table or view, but it does not log error-causing rows. If you need to capture error-causing rows to an exception file, use the Transform Data task instead.
	Execute SQL task	Runs Transact-SQL statements during package execution. You can perform a number of operations with Execute SQL task, which include dropping a table and running stored procedures.
	Copy SQL Server Objects task	Copies SQL Server database objects (meta data) from one SQL Server instance to another. This task can transfer objects from one instance of SQL Server 7.0 to another; from an instance of SQL Server 7.0 to SQL Server 2000; or from one instance of SQL Server 2000 to another instance of SQL Server 2000.
	Transfer Database Objects tasks	A collection of tasks that copy server-wide information (the Copy SQL Server Objects task copies only database-specific information) from one SQL Server instance to another. These tasks include the Transfer Database task, the Transfer Error Messages task, the Transfer Logins task, the Transfer Jobs task, and the Transfer Master Stored Procedures task. These tasks are used by the Copy Database Wizard.
Tasks that transform data	Transform Data task	Copies, transforms, and inserts data from a data source to a data destination. This task is the most basic implementation of the data pump engine in DTS.

Table 7-3.   Tasks Available through DTS Designer

Category	Task	Description
	Data Driven Query task	Selects, customizes, and executes one of several Transact-SQL operations (such as an update or a delete) on a row based on the data in the row. Use this task if the Transform Data task and the Bulk Insert task do not meet the requirements of your application.
Tasks that function as jobs	ActiveX Script task	Runs an ActiveX script. You can use this task to write code to perform functions that are not available in DTS Designer.
	Dynamic Properties task	Retrieves data from an outside source and assigns values retrieved to selected package properties. External sources can be an .INI file, data file, query, global variable, environmental variable, or a constant.
	Execute Package task	Runs other DTS packages as part of a workflow. Do not use this task recursively because it could generate a stack overflow, which could result in MMC shutting down.
	Execute Process task	Runs an executable program or batch file. This task can be used to open any standard application, such as Microsoft Excel, but it is used primarily to run batch files or business applications that work against a data source.
	File Transfer Protocol task	Downloads data from a remote server or an Internet location using FTP. The FTP task and Ftp.exe use the same connection method.
	Send Mail task	Sends an e-mail message as a task. For example, notification can be sent to an administrator about the success or failure of a backup operation. In order to use this task, you need to install a MAPI client on the instance of SQL Server you are running.

Table 7.4 describes the types of transformations that are available.

Table 7-4.   Available Types of Transformations

Transformation Type	Description
Copy Column	Copies data from a single column to a single column (or multiple column to multiple column). By default, allows all possible data type conversions and automatically truncates text (when necessary) without error notification. ActiveX Script uses an ActiveX script to transform (and truncate) data between one or more source and destination columns on a row-by-row basis.
Date Time String	Converts a date or time value in a source column to a different format in the destination column. Both columns must be a string data type.
Lowercase String	Converts string data to lowercase characters and to the destination data type (if necessary) from a source column to the destination column, truncating data as necessary. Both columns must be a string data type.
Uppercase String	Converts string data to uppercase characters and to the destination data type (if necessary) from a source column to the destination column, truncating data as necessary. Both columns must be a string data type.
Middle of String	Extracts a substring of string data from a source column and copies it to a destination column, truncating data if necessary. Can also perform case conversion. Both columns must be a string data type.
Trim String	Removes leading, trailing, and embedded white space from string data in a source column and copies it to a destination column, truncating data if necessary. Can also perform case conversion. Both columns must be a string data type.
Read File	Opens and copies the contents of a file specified in the source column to a destination column. The source column must be a string data type. The destination column must be a string or binary data type.
Write File	Copies the contents of a source column to a file specified in the destination column. The source column must be a string or binary data type.

DTS Package Workflow

DTS uses steps and precedence constraints to order tasks within a DTS package. Steps define the sequence in which tasks within a package execute. In DTS Designer (or programmatically), you use precedence constraints to control this sequence. Precedence constraints sequentially link each task within a package. A task can have multiple precedence constraints. Tasks without precedence constraints operate in parallel. There are three types of precedence constraints, as shown in Table 7.5.

Table 7-5.   Precedence Constraints and Their Functions

Precedence Constraint	Description
Unconditional	If Task 2 is linked to Task 1 by an Unconditional constraint, Task 2 will wait until Task 1 completes and then will execute, regardless of the success or failure of Task 1.
On Success	If Task 3 is linked to Task 2 by an On Success constraint, Task 3 will wait until Task 2 completes, and then will only execute if Task 2 completed successfully.
On Failure	If Task 4 is linked to Task 2 by an On Failure constraint, Task 4 will wait until Task 2 completes and then will only execute if Task 2 failed to complete successfully.

For example, assume Task 1 is a Drop Table task, Task 2 is a Create Table task, Task 3 is a Populate Table task, and Task 4 is a Restore Table task. If the table does not exist, Task 1 will fail and Task 2 will create the table. If the table does exist, Task 1 will drop the table and Task 2 will create the table. Next, if Task 2 creates the table successfully, Task 3 will populate the table. However, if Task 2 fails to create the table successfully, Task 4 will restore the table.

DTS Package Storage

You can store a DTS package to SQL Server 2000, SQL Server 2000 Meta Data Services, a Microsoft Visual Basic file, or a structured storage file. When you save a DTS package, all DTS connections, tasks, transformations, and workflow steps are saved. Table 7.6 describes each of these storage options.

Introducing DTS Tools

You create a DTS package using the DTS Import/Export Wizard, DTS Designer, or programmatically. The DTS Import/Export Wizard is the simplest way to create DTS packages to copy data between data sources, but it limits the complexity of the transformations, the addition of multiple DTS tasks, and the complexity of DTS task workflows. The DTS Import/Export Wizard is available through SQL Server Enterprise Manager and from the Start menu in the Microsoft SQL Server program group. DTS packages created using the DTS Import/Export Wizard can be further customized using DTS Designer, Visual Basic, or Visual C++.

Table 7-6.   DTS Storage Options

Storage Location	Description
SQL Server 2000	Stored as a table in the msdb database on any instance of SQL Server 2000. This is the default save option. Multiple packages and multiple versions can be stored. When you save a package to SQL Server 2000, you have the option of securing the packages with one or more passwords.
Meta Data Services	Stored in the repository database in Meta Data Services on your computer. Allows tracking of columns and tables used in the source and destination, including the lineage (ancestry or original source) of data in a particular row. You can secure a package saved to Meta Data Services by using its own security.
Visual Basic file	Stored in Visual Basic code that you can later open and modify using Visual Basic or Visual C++. You can secure packages saved to a Visual Basic file using a system such as Microsoft Visual SourceSafe.
Structured storage file	Stored in an operating system file. Allows storage and transfer of a DTS package independent of any SQL Server database. Multiple packages and multiple versions can be stored in a single file. When you save a package to a structured storage file, you have the option of securing the packages with one or more passwords.

DTS Designer allows you to modify existing DTS packages or create new DTS packages using graphical objects to help build DTS packages containing complex workflows (such as multiple connections and event-driven logic). DTS Designer is available through the Data Transformation Services container in the SQL Server Enterprise Manager console tree.

You can also create DTS packages using Visual Basic and Visual C++. This method is useful for developers who need to access the DTS object model directly and exert a fine degree of control over package operations. Packages created programmatically can be further customized using DTS Designer. Model templates designed for specific solutions are available for customization (such as data driven queries).

DTS also includes package execution utilities to run and schedule DTS packages from a command prompt. These utilities include the DTS Run (Dtsrunui.exe) utility and the Dtsrun command. The DTS Run utility is an interactive command prompt utility that uses a dialog box to execute a DTS package (and create a Dtsrun batch file), whereas Dtsrun can execute a DTS package from a command prompt using command switches (frequently stored in a batch file).

Lesson Summary

DTS uses packages to connect to and move data between a wide variety of OLE DB data sources. A DTS package can extract data from one or more of these data sources, perform simple or complex transformations on this data, and then store the transformed data to one or more of these data destinations. You can use workflow logic (precedence constraints) within the DTS package. The DTS package itself can be stored in SQL Server 2000, in SQL Server Meta Data Services, as a Visual Basic file, or as a structured storage file. You can create a DTS package using the DTS Import/Export Wizard, DTS Designer, Visual Basic, or Visual C++.

Lesson 3: Transferring and Transforming Data with DTS Graphical Tools

DTS provides two graphical tools that you can use to create DTS packages that transfer and transform data. In this lesson, you will learn to use each of these. First, you will learn to use the DTS Import/Export Wizard to create simple transformations. Then, you will learn to use DTS Designer to create more complex transformations and workflows. You will also learn to save these packages in a variety of formats. Finally, you will learn about extending the functionality of DTS packages.

After this lesson, you will be able to

- Use the DTS Import/Export Wizard to create a DTS package
- Use DTS Designer to create a DTS package
- Save DTS packages to a variety of formats
- Describe additional functionality that can be added to DTS packages

Estimated lesson time: 60 minutes

Using the DTS Import/Export Wizard

The DTS Import/Export Wizard can be started from the Microsoft SQL Server program group on the Start menu and from within SQL Server Enterprise Manager. Within SQL Server Enterprise Manager, you can start this wizard by clicking the Tools menu and then pointing to Wizards, or by right-clicking the Data Transformation Services container in the console tree, pointing to All Tasks, and then clicking either Import Data or Export Data (both bring up the same wizard). The DTS Import/Export Wizard guides you through the steps to import or export data between many different formats.

The first step in this process is selecting the data source in the Choose A Data Source page. The default data source is the Microsoft OLE DB Provider for SQL Server. This data source is used to connect to an instance of SQL Server. Select the data-specific driver for the data storage format from which you want to copy data (such as a text file or an Oracle database) from the Data Source drop-down list. The remaining properties you will define on this page depend upon the data source selected. For example, if your data source is SQL Server, you provide the server name, authentication type, and database. See Figure 7.1.

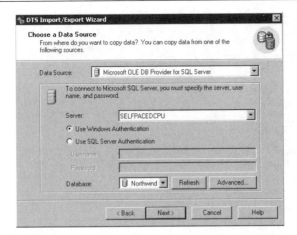

Figure 7.1.   Selecting the data source in the DTS Import/Export Wizard.

If you are using a different data source, other connection information is required. For example, if you are copying data from a text file, you must provide the file-name on the Choose A Data Source page, followed by file format information (including fixed or delimited fields, file type, row and column delimiters, and text qualifiers), which you select on the Select File Format page and the Specify Column Delimiter page. See Figures 7.2, 7.3, and 7.4.

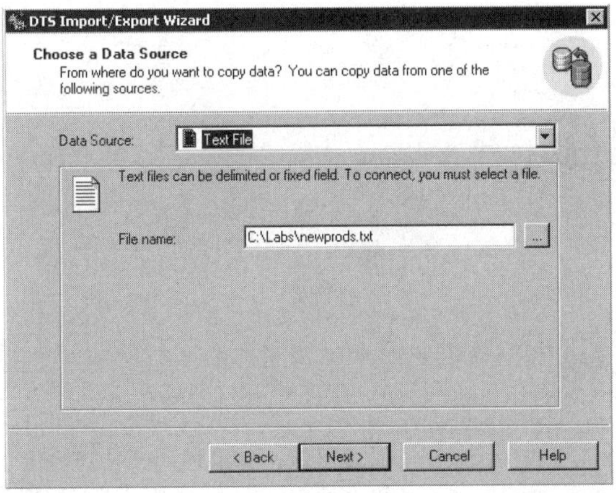

Figure 7.2.   Specifying a text file as the data source.

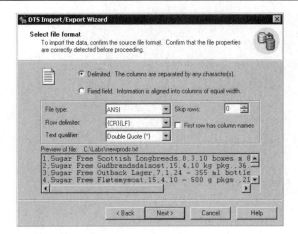

Figure 7.3.   Selecting the file format, field type, and text qualifier.

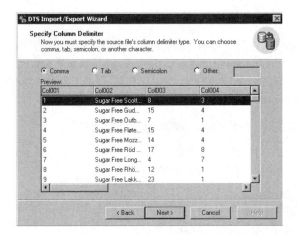

Figure 7.4.   Specifying the column delimiter.

The next step in this process is selecting the data destination in the Choose A Destination page. Again, the default data source is the Microsoft OLE DB Provider for SQL Server, for which you must provide a server name and connection information. You can select from a wide variety of data destinations. Both your data source and your data destination can be products other than SQL Server 2000. See Figure 7.5. For example, you could use DTS to copy data from Oracle to dBase. With SQL Server 2000, you can create a new database on the fly. If you create a new database, the physical location will be the same disk and folder as the master database. The only database properties you can choose in the Create Database dialog box are the name of the database and the sizes of the data file and the transaction log file. See Figure 7.6.

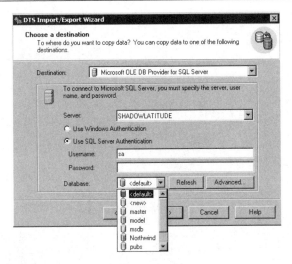

Figure 7.5. Selecting a destination for your data.

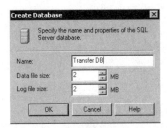

Figure 7.6. Specifying the name and properties of the new database.

After selecting your data source and your data destination, you specify or filter the data you will copy in the Specify Table Copy Or Query page. (This page will not appear if you are creating a new database.) Your choices will vary depending upon the data source and the data destination. If the data source is a database, you can perform a simple copy of data (unfiltered and unordered) by selecting the Copy Table(s) And View(s) From The Source Database option button, or you can perform a more complex copy requiring a Transact-SQL query (selecting only rows matching specified selection criteria and in a certain order) by selecting the Use A Query To Specify The Data To Transfer option button. In addition, if both the data source and destination are SQL Server 7.0 or SQL Server 2000 databases, you can copy database objects (such as stored procedures and logins) by selecting the Copy Objects And Data Between SQL Server Databases option button. See Figure 7.7.

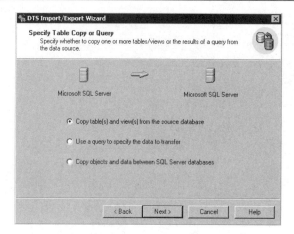

Figure 7.7.   Specifying the type of copy operation.

Copying Entire Tables and Views

If you choose to copy entire tables or views, you then select all or some of the tables or views for copying in the Select Source Tables And Views page. By default, the destination name for each table or view will be the name of the table or view being copied. You can create new table or view names, or select different existing tables or views. See Figure 7.8.

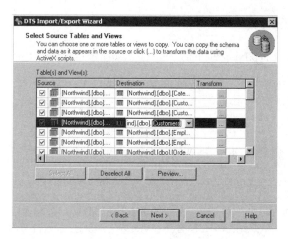

Figure 7.8.   Selecting source tables and views.

If you perform no other action, the contents of each selected table or view will be copied without changes. If the destination table exists, by default, the data being copied will be appended to the existing data. If the destination table does not exist, the table will be created using the specified name. If you want to change these defaults, on the Select Source Tables And Views page, click the ellipsis in the Transform column for each table or view you want to transform. On the Column

Mappings tab of the Column Mappings And Transformations dialog box, you can specify the mappings between source and destination columns, create a new destination table, edit the *CREATE TABLE* Transact-SQL statement (if a new table or view is being created), choose to delete or append rows in the destination table (if an existing table is detected), enable insert identity (if an identity column is detected), and change the data type (if a valid data conversion is available). See Figure 7.9.

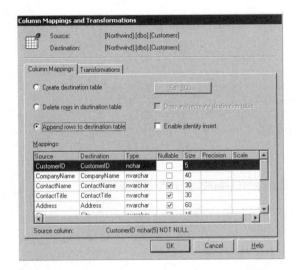

Figure 7.9.   Changing the column mappings and transformations.

You can also specify unique transformations using either VBScript or JScript (VBScript is the default) on the Transformations tab of the Column Mappings And Transformations dialog box. To transform data while it is being copied, edit the script in the test area to customize columns before copying them to the destination. See Figure 7.10. Although you can perform some customized transformations using the DTS Import/Export Wizard, DTS Designer is more appropriate for complex scripting through the use of ActiveX scripting.

Querying to Specify the Data

If you choose to use a query to specify the data to transfer, you can write your own Transact-SQL script in the space provided in the Type SQL Statement page, browse and import an existing script, or click the Query Builder button to graphically create a script using DTS Query Designer. DTS Query Designer is a graphical query-building tool. A Parse button is provided to test the syntax of your script. See Figure 7.11.

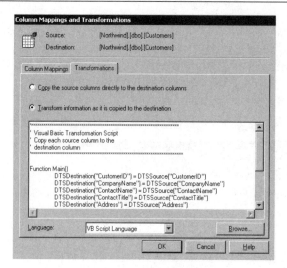

Figure 7.10. Specifying transformation options.

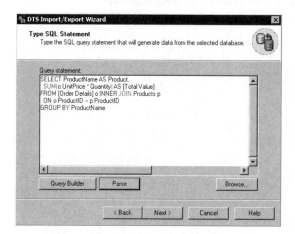

Figure 7.11. Creating a script using the Query Designer.

After you enter your Transact-SQL script and click Next, you can select and then preview your results by clicking the Preview button in the Select Source Tables And Views page (see Figure 7.8) to verify whether the query produces the results you intend. If you perform no other action, the results of the query are copied to a new table called Results. You can modify this name. You can also click the ellipsis in the Transform column in the Select Source Tables and Views page (see Figure 7.8) to modify the column mappings and specify custom transformations in a manner similar to that discussed earlier. See Figure 7.12.

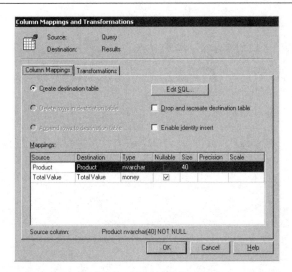

Figure 7.12.   Modifying the column mappings and transformations for your query.

Copying Objects and Data Between SQL Server Databases

If you choose to copy objects and data between SQL Server databases, you can specify which objects you want to transfer between SQL Server instances in the Select Objects To Copy page. You can only copy between SQL Server 7.0 instances or SQL Server 2000 instances or from a SQL Server 7.0 instance to a SQL Server 2000 instance (not from SQL Server 2000 to SQL Server 7.0). By default, destination objects are created for all objects being copied (all objects are copied by default), all corresponding destination objects are dropped before the new ones are created, and all dependent objects are included in the transfer of data. In addition, by default, all data is copied and all existing data on the destination is deleted. See Figure 7.13. You can limit the objects being copied (such as only certain tables or stored procedures, or no indexes).

Saving and Scheduling Packages

The final step in the DTS Import/Export Wizard for any of the types of transformations described so far is to choose to run the package immediately, or to choose to save or to schedule the package on the Save, Schedule, And Replicate Package page. See Figure 7.14. By default, the package will run immediately and will not be saved or scheduled. You can choose to schedule it to run at a later time as a job under the auspices of SQL Server Agent. Jobs and scheduling are covered in Chapter 13. You can also choose to save the package in any of the supported formats. Choosing between these formats is covered in Lesson 4.

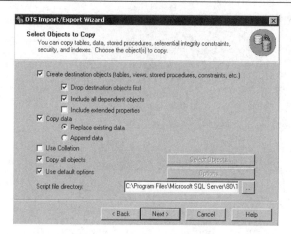

Figure 7.13.   Selecting objects to copy.

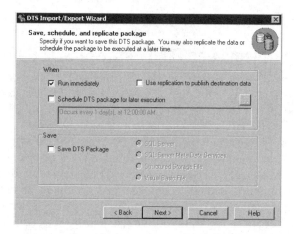

Figure 7.14.   Choosing to save or schedule the package.

Practice: Transferring Tables and Data from the Northwind Database Using the DTS Import/Export Wizard

In this practice you transfer tables and data from the Northwind database to a new database using the DTS Import/Export Wizard. Then, you modify these tables and summarize data in the NorthwindReportData database.

▶ **To transfer tables and data from the Northwind Database using the DTS Import/Export Wizard**

1. Ensure that you are logged on to the SelfPacedSQL.MSFT domain server as Administrator.
2. Click Start, point to Programs, point to Microsoft SQL Server, and then click Import And Export Data.

   The DTS Import/Export Wizard appears.
3. Click Next.

   The Choose A Data Source page appears.
4. In the Data Source drop-down list, verify that the selected data source is Microsoft OLE DB Provider for SQL Server.
5. In the Server drop-down list, select SelfPacedCPU\MyNamedInstance.
6. Verify that the Use Windows Authentication option button is selected.
7. In the Database drop-down list, select Northwind and then click Next.

   The Choose A Destination page appears.
8. In the Destination drop-down list, verify that the selected data destination is Microsoft OLE DB Provider for SQL Server.
9. In the Server drop-down list, select SelfPacedCPU.
10. Verify that the Use Windows Authentication option button is selected.
11. In the Database drop-down list, select <New>.

    The Create Database dialog box appears.
12. In the Name text box, type **NorthwindReportData** and then click OK.

    The Choose A Destination page reappears displaying the new database.
13. Click Next.

    The Specify Table Copy Or Query page appears.
14. Verify that the Copy Table(s) And View(s) From The Source Database option button is selected and then click Next.

    The Select Source Tables And Views page appears.
15. Click the Select All button.

    Notice that the name for each destination table is automatically filled in using the same name as the source table.
16. Click Next.

    The Save, Schedule, And Replicate Package page appears.
17. Verify that the Run Immediately check box is selected.
18. Select the Save DTS Package check box, verify that the SQL Server option button is selected, and then click Next.

    The Save DTS Package page appears.

19. In the Name text box, type **NorthwindTableCopy** and then click Next.

    The Completing The DTS Import/Export Wizard page appears.

20. Click the Finish button.

    The Executing Package dialog box appears displaying the status of the package execution, showing each step. When the package finishes executing, a DTS Import/Export Wizard message box appears stating that 29 tables were successfully copied from Microsoft SQL Server to Microsoft SQL Server.

21. Click OK.

22. In the Executing Package page, briefly review the successfully completed steps and then click the Done button.

23. In the SQL Server Enterprise Manager console tree, expand the default instance and then expand Databases.

    Notice that the NorthwindReportData database appears (you might need to press the F5 key to refresh the console tree).

▶ **To modify tables and summarize data in the NorthwindReportData database using the DTS Import/Export Wizard**

1. Right-click NorthwindReportData, point to All Tasks, and then click Import Data.

   The DTS Import/Export Wizard appears.

2. Click Next.

   The Choose A Data Source page appears.

3. In the Data Source drop-down list, verify that the selected data source is Microsoft OLE DB Provider for SQL Server.

4. In the Server drop-down list, select SelfPacedCPU.

5. Verify that the Use Windows Authentication option button is selected.

6. In the Database drop-down list, select Northwind and then click Next.

   The Choose A Destination page appears.

7. In the Destination drop-down list, verify that the selected data destination is Microsoft OLE DB Provider for SQL Server.

8. In the Server drop-down list, verify that SelfPacedCPU is selected.

9. Verify that the Use Windows Authentication option button is selected.

10. In the Database drop-down list, verify that NorthwindReportData is selected and then click Next.

    The Specify Table Copy Or Query page appears.

11. Select the Use A Query To Specify The Data To Transfer option button and then click Next.

    The Type SQL Statement page appears.

12. Click the Browse button.

    The Open dialog box appears.

13. Using the Look In drop-down list, browse to C:\SelfPacedSQL\CH_7 and open the Query.sql script.

    The contents of the Query.sql script appear in the Query Statement box.

14. Click Next.

    The Select Source Tables And Views page appears.

15. Click the Results cell in the Destination column and type **TotalValue**.

    Make sure you type TotalValue as a single word with no spaces.

16. Click the Preview button.

    The View Data dialog box appears displaying the results of the query.

17. Click OK.

    The Select Source Tables And Views page reappears.

18. Click the ellipsis in the Transform column.

    The Column Mappings And Transformations dialog box appears.

19. Click the Edit SQL button.

    The Create Table SQL Statement dialog box appears.

20. Review the Transact-SQL statement.

    Notice that the TotalValue column allows nulls.

21. Click OK to close the Create Table SQL Statement dialog box.

    The Column Mappings And Transformations dialog box reappears.

22. In the Mappings grid, clear the Nullable check box for the TotalValue row.

23. Click the Edit SQL button to review the Transact-SQL statement.

    The Create Table SQL Statement dialog box appears. Notice that the Total-Value column no longer allows nulls.

24. Click OK to close the Create Table SQL Statement dialog box.

25. Click OK to close the Column Mappings And Transformations dialog box.

    The Select Source Tables And Views page reappears.

26. Click Next.

    The Save, Schedule, And Replicate Package page appears.

27. Verify that the Run Immediately button is selected.

28. Select the Save DTS Package check box.

29. Select the SQL Server Meta Data Services option button, and then click Next.

    The Save DTS Package page appears.

30. In the Name text box, type **NorthwindTableTransform** and then click Next.

    The Completing The DTS Import/Export Wizard page appears.

31. Click the Finish button.

   The Executing Package dialog box appears displaying the status of the package execution, showing each step. When the package finishes executing, a DTS Import/Export Wizard message box appears stating that one table was successfully copied from Microsoft SQL Server to Microsoft SQL Server.

32. Click OK.

33. Briefly review the successfully completed steps in the Executing Package dialog box and then click the Done button.

34. In the SQL Server Enterprise Manager console tree, expand the default instance, expand Databases, expand NorthwindReportData, and then click Tables.

35. In the details pane, right-click TotalValue, point to Open Table, and then click Return All Rows.

   The Data In Table 'TotalValue' In 'NorthwindReportData' On 'SelfPaced-CPU' window appears displaying the contents of this newly created and populated table.

36. Close the Data In Table 'TotalValue' In 'NorthwindReportData' On 'Self-PacedCPU' dialog box.

37. Do not close SQL Server Enterprise Manager.

Using DTS Designer

To create a new package using DTS Designer, in the SQL Server Enterprise Manager console tree, right-click Data Transformation Services and then click New Package. The method of opening an existing package within the Data Transformation Services container depends on how the DTS package was stored. If the DTS package was saved as a structured storage file, right-click Data Transformation Services, and then click Open Package to open the file from disk. If the DTS package was saved to SQL Server, click the Local Packages container in the console tree (in the Data Services container) and then double-click the DTS package in the details pane. If the DTS package was saved to SQL Server Meta Data Services, click the Meta Data Services container in the console tree (in the Data Services container) and then double-click the DTS package in the details pane.

DTS Designer allows you to graphically create connections to data sources and destinations, configure DTS tasks, perform DTS transformations, and specify precedence constraints. You use the drag-and-drop method and you complete the dialog boxes for objects in order to create DTS packages within the design sheet. Figure 7.15 displays the user interface for DTS Designer.

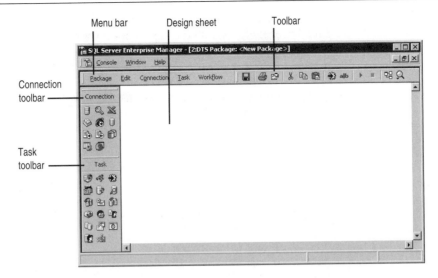

Figure 7.15.   The DTS Designer user interface.

When creating a DTS package using DTS Designer, the first step is to select a data source. You can either drag a data source object from the Connection toolbar to the design sheet or select a data source from the Connection menu item. The Connection Properties dialog box that appears varies based on the data source selected. Complete the dialog box to configure the data source. This dialog box is similar to the dialog box displayed by the DTS Import/Export Wizard. Figure 7.16 displays the dialog box for a connection to SQL Server using the Microsoft OLE DB Provider for SQL Server.

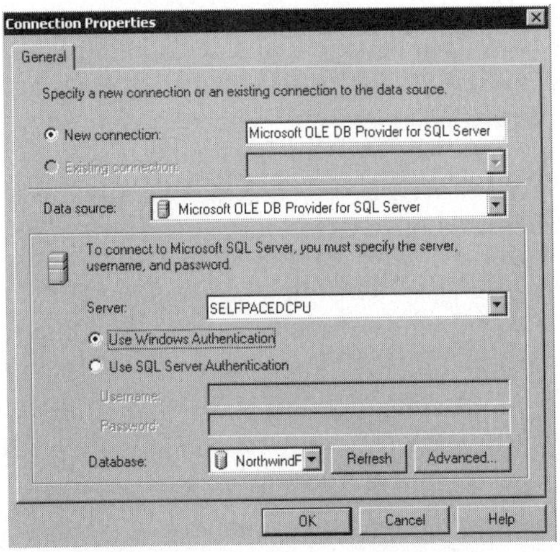

Figure 7.16.   The Connection dialog box.

The next step is to select and configure a data destination in the same manner as described above. Figure 7.17 displays a design sheet consisting of three data sources: two connections to Microsoft OLE DB Provider for SQL Server and one connection to a Text File (Source).

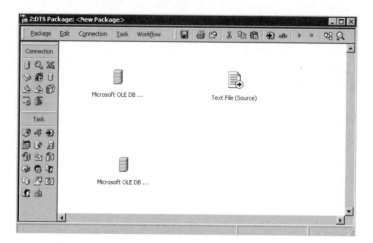

Figure 7.17. Configuring a data destination.

Note A connection to a text file specifies that the text file is either a data source or a data connection.

Next, you need to define the tasks that you want to occur using either the Task menu or the Task toolbar. If you select the Transform Data task, you are prompted to select the data source and the data destination. If you select any other task, a dialog box will appear to prompt you to configure the properties of the task (such as configuring the Execute SQL Task to create a table using an existing data connection). If you select the Transform Data task, a dark gray arrow appears pointing from the data source to the data destination. If you select any other task, it simply appears in the design sheet as an icon. Figure 7.18 displays two Transform Data tasks and an Execute SQL task that creates a table (in addition to three data connections).

To edit and customize a Data Transformation task, double-click the dark gray arrow between the data source and the data destination to open the dialog box for that task. On the Source tab, if the data source is a database, you can filter the data being copied by selecting specific tables or views or by using a Transact-SQL query. Figure 7.19 displays a Transact-SQL query being used to filter the data being imported.

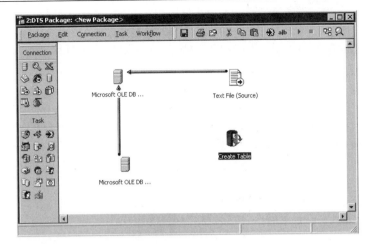

Figure 7.18.   Partial DTS Package without workflow control.

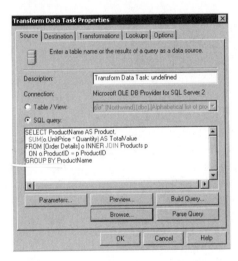

Figure 7.19.   Using a query to filter the imported data.

On the Destination tab, you can define information about the data being imported (such as column definitions). Your choices will vary depending on the data destination. If the data destination is a database, you can create and define a new table or select an existing table for each table being imported.

On the Transformations tab, you can configure custom transformations. By default, the source columns are copied to the destination columns without modification. If you want to modify column data between the data source and the data destination, select the column you want to have modified either in the Name drop-down list or by clicking the arrow between the source and the destination (the arrow between the source and the destination for the selected column will appear bold). Next, click the New button or the Edit button to create a new transformation or modify an existing transformation (double-clicking the black arrow modifies the existing transformation). If you click the New button, you can choose the type of transformation you want from a list of available transformations in the Create New Transformation dialog box. See Figure 7.20.

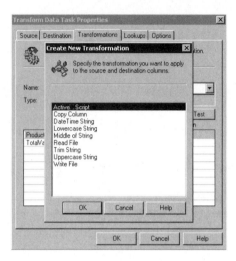

Figure 7.20.   Creating a new transformation.

If you select ActiveX Script from the Create New Transformation dialog box, you can create a new transformation script to perform more complex transformations. See Figure 7.21.

On the Lookups tab, you can define a lookup query. A lookup query requires a data connection to run queries and stored procedures against, in addition to a data source and data destination. Use a lookup query to look up tabular information, perform parallel updates on multiple database systems, validate input before loading, invoke stored procedures in response to input conditions, and use global variable values as query parameters.

On the Options tab, you can define a number of additional properties for the transformation. You can define one or more exception files to be used for recording exception records during package execution. This file can be on either a local drive or a network drive. The file can be written in a SQL Server 7.0 format for backward compatibility. You can split source and destination errors into separate files. You can also define a maximum number of errors allowed before the execution of the package will cease. Finally, you can also define specific execution properties when the destination connection is the Microsoft OLE DB Provider for SQL Server. These properties include specifying high-speed bulk-copy processing, constraint checking during package execution, lock type, batch size, and identity insert properties.

Figure 7.21. Creating a new transformation script.

Once you have configured the Data Transformation task and any other DTS tasks your DTS package will perform, you must configure precedence constraints. In our simple example, we have data from two separate data sources being copied to a data destination. We also have a Create Table task. You use precedence constraints to determine the order of execution of each task. To establish workflow precedence, select two or more tasks in the order the tasks will execute, and then select the type of workflow from the Workflow menu. For example, if the Create Table task must execute before the data copy to the data destination, select the On Success precedence constraint from the Workflow menu. See Figure 7.22.

You could create a Send Mail task and configure an On Failure precedence constraint between the Create Table task and the Send Mail task. This would send an e-mail notification to an administrator if the Create Table task failed. When you are using fully automated and scheduled DTS packages to perform database operations, failure notification is essential.

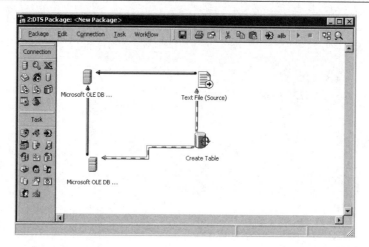

Figure 7.22.   Selecting the On Success precedence constraint.

Practice: Creating a Data Transfer and Transform Package Using DTS Designer

In this practice you create a data transfer and transform package using DTS Designer.

▶ **To create a data transfer and transform package using DTS Designer**

1. Ensure that you are logged on to the SelfPacedSQL.MSFT domain server as Administrator.

2. In the SQL Server Enterprise Manager console tree, expand the Microsoft SQL Servers container, expand the SQL Server Group container, and then expand the default instance.

3. Right-click Data Transformation Services and then click New Package.

   DTS Designer appears.

4. On the Connection menu, click Text File (Source).

   The Connection Properties dialog box appears.

5. In the New Connection text box, type **New Products**.

6. In the File Name text box, type **C:\SelfPacedSQL\CH_7\NewData.txt** and then click OK.

   The Text Files Properties dialog box appears displaying the Select File Format page.

7. Verify that the Delimited Columns Are Separated By Character(s) option button is selected and then click Next.

   The Specify Column Delimiter page appears.

8. Verify that the Comma option button is selected and then click the Finish button.

   The Connection Properties dialog box reappears.

9. Click OK.

   The New Products icon appears on the design sheet.

10. On the Connection menu, click Microsoft OLE DB Provider for SQL Server.

    The Connection Properties dialog box appears.

11. In the New Connection text box, type **Northwind Report Data**.

12. In the Server drop-down list, verify that SelfPacedCPU is selected.

13. In the Database drop-down list, select NorthwindReportData and then click OK.

    The New Products and Northwind Report Data icons both appear on the design sheet.

14. On the Task menu, click Transform Data Task.

    Your mouse pointer changes and displays the words Select Source Connection and has an arrow attached to it.

15. Click the New Products icon.

    Your mouse pointer changes and displays the words Select Destination Connection and has an arrow attached to it.

16. Click the Northwind Report Data icon.

    A dark gray arrow appears pointing from the New Products icon to the Northwind Report Data icon.

17. Double-click the dark gray arrow.

    The Transform Data Task Properties dialog box appears with the Source tab selected.

18. In the Description text box, type **Adding New Products**.

19. Click the Destination tab.

20. Click the Create button to create a new table into which to insert data.

    The Create Destination Table dialog box appears displaying a *CREATE TABLE* statement.

21. Delete the entire *CREATE TABLE* statement.

22. Using Notepad, open the NewProducts.sql file in C:\SelfPacedSQL\CH_7.

23. Copy the contents of this file and paste the contents into the SQL Statement box, and then click OK.

    The Transform Data Task Properties dialog box reappears.

24. Click the Transformations tab.

    Notice the default mappings of source columns to destination columns. In particular, notice that there are more columns in the destination than there are in the source. The reason is that we have added a column entitled TotalValue, which will be an aggregated column from two existing columns. Also notice that columns 8–10 are incorrectly mapped because of the addition of this new column.

25. Right-click the mapping arrow between Col010 and ReorderLevel and then click the Edit button.

The Transformation Options dialog box appears with the General tab selected.

26. Click the Destination Columns tab.

27. In the Selected Columns list, click the < button to remove ReorderLevel.

28. From the Available Columns list, click Discontinued, click the > button and then click OK.

Notice that the mapping has now changed for Col010 to Discontinued.

29. Right-click the mapping arrow between Col009 and UnitsOnOrder and then click the Edit button.

The Transformation Options dialog box appears with the General tab selected.

30. Click the Destination Columns tab.

31. In the Selected Columns list, click the < button to remove UnitsOnOrder.

32. From the Available Columns list, click ReorderLevel, click the > button and then click OK.

Notice that the mapping has now changed for Col009 to ReorderLevel.

33. Right-click the mapping arrow between Col008 and TotalValue and then click the Edit button.

The Transformation Options dialog box appears with the General tab selected.

34. Click the Destination Columns tab.

35. In the Selected Columns list, click the < button to remove TotalValue.

36. From the Available Columns list, click UnitsOnOrder, click the > button and then click OK.

Notice that the mapping has now changed for Col008 to UnitsOnOrder.

37. In the Source column, click Col006, and then press Ctrl and click Col007.

Notice that both Col006 and Col007 are selected.

38. In the Destination column, click TotalValue.

39. Click the New button.

The Create New Transformation dialog box appears.

40. Click ActiveX Script and then click OK.

The Transformation Options dialog box appears with the General tab selected.

41. Click the Properties button.

The ActiveX Script Transformation Properties dialog box appears.

42. Modify the line of code that reads

    `DTSDestination("TotalValue")=DTSSource("Col006")`

    to read

    `DTSDestination("TotalValue")=DTSSource("Col006")*DTSSource("Col007")`

43. Click the Parse button.

    A DTS Designer message box appears stating that the ActiveX script was successfully parsed.

44. Click OK.

45. Click the Test button.

    A testing Transformation dialog box appears to test the Transformation and a Package Execution Results message box appears stating that the package was successfully executed.

46. Click OK.

47. Click the Done button in the Testing Transformation dialog box.

48. Click OK in the ActiveX Script Transformation Properties dialog box.

    The Transformation Options dialog box reappears.

49. Click OK in the Transformation Options dialog box.

    Notice that the mappings now show Col006 and Col007 combined and being mapped to TotalValue.

50. Click OK in the Transform Data Task Properties dialog box.

51. On the Task menu, click Execute SQL Task.

    The Execute SQL Task Properties dialog box appears.

52. In the Description text box, type **Drop Table**.

53. In the Existing Connection drop-down list, click Northwind Report Data.

54. In the SQL Statement box, type **DROP TABLE NewProducts** and then click OK.

    The Drop Table task icon appears on the design sheet.

55. On the Task menu, click Execute SQL Task.

    The Execute SQL Task Properties dialog box appears.

56. In the Description text box, type **Create Table**.

57. In the Existing Connection drop-down list, click Northwind Report Data.

58. Click the Browse button.

    The Select File dialog box appears.

59. Using the Look In drop-down list, browse to C:\SelfPacedSQL\CH_7 and then open the NewProducts.sql script.

    The saved *CREATE TABLE* statement appears in the SQL statement box.

60. Click OK.

The Create Table task icon appears on the design sheet.

61. On the Task menu, click Execute SQL Task.

The Execute SQL Task Properties dialog box appears.

62. In the Description text box, type **Backup Northwind Report Data**.

63. In the Existing Connection drop-down list, click Northwind Report Data.

64. Click the Browse button and then open the BackupNorthwindReportData.sql script in C:\SelfPacedSQL\CH_7.

The saved *BACKUP DATABASE* statement appears in the SQL statement box. Change the drive path in this script if you are not using the C drive for your SQL Server 2000 program and data files.

65. Click OK.

The Backup Northwind Report Data task icon appears on the design sheet.

66. Click the Drop Table task icon and then press Ctrl and click the Create Table task.

Notice that both task icons are selected.

67. On the Workflow menu, click On Completion.

A blue-and-white striped arrow appears between the Drop Table and the Create Table task icons. The Create Table task will execute whenever the Drop Table task completes, regardless of the success of the Drop Table task. If the New-Products table does not exist, the Drop Table task will fail and the Create Table task will create the table.

68. Click the Create Table task icon and then press Ctrl and click the New Products icon.

69. On the Workflow menu, click On Success.

A green-and-white striped arrow appears between the Create Table task and the New Products to Northwind Report Data task icons. The New Products to Northwind Report Data task will only execute when and if the Create Table task creates the NewProducts table.

70. Click the Northwind Report Data icon and then press Ctrl and click the Backup Northwind Report Data icon.

71. On the Workflow menu, click On Success.

A green-and-white striped arrow appears between the New Products to North-wind Report Data task icon and the Backup Northwind Report Data task icon. The Backup Northwind Report Data task will only execute when and if the New Products to Northwind Report Data task completes successfully.

72. On the Package menu, click Save.

The Save DTS Package dialog box appears.

73. In the Package Name text box, type **Lesson 2** and then click OK.

74. On the toolbar, click the Execute button.

    The Executing DTS Package: Lesson 2 dialog box appears displaying the progress of the execution of the DTS package. When the DTS package is complete, a Package Execution Results message box appears stating that the execution of the package was successful.

75. Click OK and then click the Done button.

76. Close DTS Package: Lesson 2 by clicking the Close button for the DTS Designer window.

77. In the SQL Server Enterprise Manager console tree, expand the Microsoft SQL Servers container, expand the SQL Server Group container, expand the default instance, expand Databases, expand NorthwindReportData, and then click Tables.

78. In the details pane, right-click NewProducts, point to Open Table, and then click Return All Rows. You might need to press F5 to refresh the display.

    The Data In Table 'NewProducts' In 'NorthwindReportData' On 'SelfPaced-CPU' dialog box appears. Notice that the new table is populated and the aggregated column, TotalValue, exists.

79. Close the Data In Table 'NewProducts' In 'NorthwindReportData' On 'Self-PacedCPU' window.

80. Do not close SQL Server Enterprise Manager.

Extending DTS Package Functionality

You can extend the capabilities of your DTS packages in a variety of ways. It is beyond the scope of this book to cover all of the ways you can incorporate the plethora and complexity of DTS tasks into DTS packages. However, the following extended functionality deserves specific mention.

Transaction Support

DTS packages support distributed transactions using functions provided by Microsoft Distributed Transaction Coordinator (DTC). To obtain this functionality, DTC must be running on the computer executing the DTS package. Distributed transactions are used to ensure that DTS tasks within a package that occur in parallel are all committed successfully or none are committed. This is particularly useful when a DTS package spans multiple database servers or when multiple DTS packages run under the control of a single DTS package.

Message Queue Task

The Message Queue task allows you to use Message Queuing to send and receive messages between DTS packages. These messages can be text, files, or global variables and their values. Message queuing allows these messages to be sent when the destination DTS package is unavailable (such as when various laptop computers are disconnected). When a destination DTS package becomes available, the originating DTS package continues until complete. Other available options include sending data files to the computer responsible for processing them, distributing files throughout the enterprise, and splitting a large job into several component parts and then parceling them out to different computers in the network.

Note   There are two types of message queuing, transactional and non-transactional. Using transactional message queuing provides assurance that each message is delivered only once.

To use the Message Queue task, you must install Message Queuing server software on your network and Message Queuing client software on the computer running the Message Queue task. For Windows 2000, you install Message Queuing server software on a Windows 2000 domain controller running Active Directory. Thereafter, you can install Message Queuing client software on your computer. For Windows NT, you install MSMQ from the Windows NT 4.0 Option Pack.

Send Mail Task

The Send Mail task allows a DTS package to notify an administrator about its progress (such as the success or failure of a database backup). The Send Mail task can also send attachments, which can consist of dynamically updated files. The Send Mail task requires the installation of Messaging Application Programming Interface (MAPI) on the local computer with a valid user profile for the domain user account used by the SQL Server service.

Programming Templates

SQL Server 2000 also ships with a wide variety of programming samples for Visual C++ and Visual Basic. These samples are located on the SQL Server 2000 compact disk in the \DevTools\Samples\Dts folder in a self-extracting zip file and can be installed during a Custom setup (by default to the C:\Program Files\Microsoft SQL Server\80\Tools\DevTools\Samples\Dts folder).

Lesson Summary

You can use the DTS Import/Export Wizard to copy and transform data and database objects. It is most useful for copying data and database objects between one data source and one data destination with minimal transformations. Use DTS Designer for more complex transformation packages. DTS Designer allows you to create packages to and from multiple data sources and destinations using workflow logic, message queuing, and transaction control. You can also use Visual Basic and Visual C++ to extend the complexity and more finely control the workflow logic of DTS packages.

Lesson 4: Working with DTS Packages

Now that you understand how to create and execute a DTS package, you will learn about storing and securing DTS packages. In addition, you will learn additional methods for executing a saved DTS package, as well as using DTS package logs to troubleshoot problems that occur during the execution of a DTS package. You will also learn about editing DTS packages when data sources and destinations are unavailable. Finally, you will learn about browsing and sharing meta data about DTS packages.

After this lesson, you will be able to

- Understand the different storage options for DTS packages
- Secure a DTS package
- Execute DTS packages from the command prompt
- Edit a DTS package when a data source or destination is unavailable

Estimated lesson time: 15 minutes

Understanding DTS Package Storage Options

As discussed earlier, you can store a DTS package using SQL Server 2000, SQL Server Meta Data Services, a structured storage file, or a Visual Basic file. You use each storage format to accomplish different objectives, based on their capabilities.

SQL Server 2000

Saving a DTS package to SQL Server 2000 allows you to save a DTS package as a binary object in the sysdtspackages table in the msdb database on any SQL Server 2000 instance in your organization. You can keep an inventory of DTS packages in one location on your network. Each version of a DTS package is saved, preserving the development history of a package. This allows you to retrieve and edit any version of a DTS package you choose, not just the most recent version.

When you save a DTS package to SQL Server 2000, you can set both an owner password and a user password. These passwords are used in addition to the Windows Authentication or SQL Server Authentication used to connect to SQL Server 2000. Users with access to the user password can run a DTS package, but cannot open or edit a package. Users must have access to the owner password to open or edit a DTS package. This extra level of security is strongly recommended, particularly on a SQL Server 2000 instance that permits SQL Server Authentication.

Meta Data Services

Saving a DTS package to SQL Server Meta Data Services allows you to track package version, meta data, and data lineage (original data source and transformations) information. You can view version history for packages saved to Meta Data Services in SQL Server Enterprise Manager and can open the version you want. DTS uses the DTS Information Model to store meta data transformation information in Meta Data Services. The DTS Information Model describes the data transformations, how they are grouped, and the types of data accessed. This meta data information can be stored, browsed, and reused.

Saving a DTS package in Meta Data Services allows you to record and track two types of data lineage, row-level and column-level. Row-level data lineage records the source of the data in each row and the transformations that were applied to it. This is useful for providing an audit trail of package execution and row-level transformations. You must specifically enable row-level data lineage by creating a column in each row to contain a lineage identifier. Column-level data lineage provides information regarding the package version and the database tables and columns used. You can browse packages and versions to determine whether any package saved in Meta Data Services uses a particular table or column. This can be particularly useful if a data source is later determined to be of questionable value (such as corrupt or inaccurate data). You enable column-level data lineage by scanning and saving the meta data once a DTS package has been saved to Meta Data Services.

Note   Meta Data Services does not support package-level security.

Structured Storage File

Saving a DTS package to a structured storage file allows you to copy, move, and send a package across the network (such as in a mail message) without storing the package in a database or a repository. Multiple versions and multiple packages can be stored within a single file. Saving to a structured storage file also supports owner and user passwords. You can use the command-prompt DTS package execution utilities to execute a DTS package saved as a structured storage file. A DTS package saved as a structured storage file has a .DTS extension.

Visual Basic File

Saving a DTS package to a Visual Basic file allows the DTS package to be edited using Visual Basic or Visual C++. This allows developers to incorporate DTS packages into Visual Basic programs or used as prototypes to reference the components of the DTS object model. A DTS package saved as a Visual Basic file cannot be reopened and edited with DTS Designer.

Using DTS Package Execution Utilities

DTS provides two command-prompt package execution utilities: the DTS Run utility and the Dtsrun command. Using either of these utilities, a user can execute a DTS package without opening it. If the DTS package was saved using an owner or a user password, you must provide the appropriate password. If the DTS package was saved to a structured file, you must specify the filename. If the DTS package was saved to SQL Server, you must specify connection information to the SQL Server instance containing the DTS package.

DTS Run Utility

The DTS Run Utility is an interactive utility that allows you to connect to a server or specify a file, specify scheduling options, identify and enable an event log, add new global variables and change the properties of existing variables, and create a Dtsrun command with either clear or encrypted arguments for later use. To access the DTS Run utility, execute Dtsrunui from a command prompt.

Dtsrun

The Dtsrun command allows you to run a DTS package from a command prompt using arguments and embed this command in a batch file. For example, to execute the DTS package named MyPackage saved to C:\DTSPackages\DTS1.dts with an owner password of Password, you would type the following command:

```
dtsrun /FC:\DTSPackages\DTS1.dts /NMyPackage /MPassword
```

Note   A DTS package normally executes using the security context of the user executing it. However, if a DTS package is scheduled for execution, it is run in the security context of the owner of the SQL Server Agent job that runs the DTS package. Jobs are covered in Chapter 13.

Using DTS Package Logs and Exception Files

DTS records information about the success or failure of each step in the execution of a package in the DTS package log. This includes start and end times for each step and the length of execution. If a step was not run, this is also recorded. Package logging occurs only when SQL Server 2000 is running on a Windows 2000 server. DTS also uses DTS exception files to save error information about rows of data that were not copied and to save the actual source and destination rows that failed.

Performing Disconnected Edits

You can use DTS Designer to open and edit an existing DTS package. Normally, connectivity to each data source and destination is required to protect against setting invalid properties. However, sometimes those connections are not available.

DTS Designer contains a Disconnected Edit feature that allows you to modify a DTS package when you cannot connect to the original data sources and destinations (such as a DTS package created on a test system for use on a production system in a different site). You can also use this feature to view and modify properties that are not exposed through DTS Designer (such as task names, step names, and connection names).

Note   Disconnected Edit edits properties directly and so should only be used by advanced users when there are no alternate methods of modifying values.

Lesson Summary

DTS packages can be stored in several different ways. Storing a DTS package either in SQL Server 2000 or in a structured storage file allows you to set a user password as well as an owner password. This allows a user to run a DTS package from a command prompt using one of the DTS package execution utilities without being able to view or edit the package. However, storing a DTS package using SQL Server Meta Data Services allows extensive row-level and column-level tracking of data lineage and transformation of meta data information. This is particularly useful when data is being imported and transformed from a wide variety of sources. Finally, DTS Designer provides the Disconnected Edit feature, which allows you to edit a DTS package when the underlying data connections are unavailable.

Lesson 5: Using the Bulk Copy Program (Bcp) and the *BULK INSERT* Transact-SQL Statement

The *BULK INSER*T Transact-SQL statement and the Bcp command-prompt utility are used to import data into SQL Server 2000 from a text file. These methods are designed to efficiently transfer large amounts of data. In this lesson you will learn how to use each of these commands.

After this lesson, you will be able to

- Describe how SQL Server 2000 copies data in bulk using text files
- Describe how to optimize bulk copy operations
- Use the Bcp command-prompt utility to import and export data
- Use the *BULK INSERT* Transact-SQL statement to import data

Estimated lesson time: 30 minutes

Copying Data in Bulk Using Text Files

In addition to using DTS, SQL Server 2000 can import data from text files using the *BULK INSERT* Transact-SQL statement or using the Bcp command-prompt utility. Each is designed to import large quantities of data with minimal transformation during the process at very high speed. The *BULK INSERT* statement is generally faster. The Bcp program has been used for many years (DTS is a recently introduced tool), and veteran database administrators frequently have generated numerous scripts that they use to import data. For this reason, you need to understand Bcp. SQL Server 2000 supports all of those existing Bcp scripts. However, if you need to create new scripts, DTS is much easier to use. It has identical performance because the *BULK INSERT* statement has been encapsulated in the Bulk Insert task and the graphical interface painlessly walks you through the formatting issues.

The text files are generally tab-delimited files (but other delimiters can also be used, such as commas). You must specify the format of this file during the import process. You can specify the format as part of the Bcp command or *BULK INSERT* statement. You can also specify it in a reusable format file. The text files you will use to import from are frequently generated by earlier versions of SQL Server, by other database programs, or by spreadsheets. The data in the text file can be stored in character mode or in binary mode (for SQL Server to SQL Server transfers).

Note   Bcp and the *BULK INSERT* Transact-SQL statement can use the same format file.

Using Bcp

When using Bcp to import data from a data file, you must specify each parameter. The Bcp syntax is quite cryptic and must be entered precisely or the command will fail. Table 7.7 lists the more commonly used parameters. Bcp parameters are case-sensitive.

The following example imports data from the NewData text file to the NewData table on New Database with a column delimiter of a comma, a row delimiter of a new line, using character data, with a batch size of 250, an error size of 50, using the NewData.err error file, connecting using a trusted connection, and specifying a TABLOCK hint:

```
bcp NewDatabase..NewData in C:\SelfPacedSQL\CH_7\NewData.txt -c -t"," -
r\n /e C:\SelfPacedSQL\CH_7\NewData.err -b250 -m50 -T -h "TABLOCK"
```

Note   You must enter the code in the preceding example as a single line without a line break.

Table 7-7.   **Commonly Used Parameters for Bcp**

Argument	Description
Database_name	The database into which the data is being inserted. If not specified, the default database for the specified user is used.
Table_name	The name of the table into which the data is being inserted or from which the data is copied.
"Query"	The query used to filter the data being copied out of SQL Server.
*In	Out*	The direction of the bulk copy operation.
Format	Used to create a format file.
Data_file	The data file used as the source or the destination of the bulk copy operation.
-m	The maximum number of errors that can occur before the bulk copy operation is cancelled. Default is 10.
-f	Specifies the full path of the format file. This parameter is optional.
-e	Specifies the full path of the error file used to record all rows Bcp is unable to transfer to the database. If this option is not used, no error file is created.
-b	Specifies the number of rows per batch of data copied. Each batch is copied to the SQL Server 2000 instance as a single transaction.
-c	Specifies the bulk copy operation using a character data type.
-t	Specifies the field terminator. The default is tab.
-r	Specifies the row terminator. The default is new line.

Table 7-7.   Commonly Used Parameters for Bcp

Argument	Description
-S server_name *[/instance_name]*	Specifies the server name (and instance name if applicable) to which Bcp will connect. Default instance on the local server is the default.
-U	Specifies the login ID.
-P	Specifies the password for the login ID. NULL is the default.
-T	Specifies the use of a trusted connection, using the security credentials of the current user.
-h "hint"	Hints such as TABLOCK, ROWS_PER_BATCH=nn and ORDER ASC I DESC. These hints tell SQL Server how to process the imported data most efficiently.

Practice: Importing Data Using Bcp

In this practice you import data to SQL Server 2000 using the Bcp command-prompt utility.

▶   **To import data using Bcp**

1. Ensure that you are logged on to the SelfPacedSQL.MSFT domain server as Administrator.

2. Click Start, point to Programs, point to Microsoft SQL Server, and then click Query Analyzer.

   SQL Server Analyzer appears displaying the Connect To SQL Server dialog box.

3. In the Connect To SQL Server dialog box, select SelfPacedSQL from the SQL Server combo box, and use Windows authentication.

4. Click OK.

5. On the File menu, click Open.

   The Open Query File dialog box appears.

6. Select NewData.sql in the C:\SelfPacedSQL\CH_7 folder.

   A *CREATE TABLE* statement appears that will create a table called NewData into which you will import data using the Bcp command and bulk copy data.

7. Click the Execute Query button on the toolbar to execute the *NewData.sql* statement.

8. Click Start, point to Programs, point to Accessories, and then click Command Prompt.

   A Command Prompt window appears.

9. Type **bcp** and press ENTER.

   Notice the display of available arguments.

10. Type the following command on a single line:

```
bcp NorthwindReportData..NewData in C:\SelfPacedSQL\CH_7\NewData.txt
-c -t"," -r\n /e C:\SelfPacedSQL\CH_7\NewData.err -b250 -m50 -T -h
"TABLOCK"
```

Note   You must enter the code in the preceding example as a single line without a line break.

11. Press ENTER.

Notice that 1343 rows are copied in batches of 250 rows. The packet size used and the elapsed clock time are also displayed. An empty NewData.err file now appears in the C:\SelfPacedSQL\CH_7 folder.

12. Close the Command Prompt window.

13. In SQL Query Analyzer, click the Clear Window button on the toolbar.

14. In the Query pane, type **SELECT * FROM NewData**.

15. Click the Execute Query button on the toolbar.

Notice that 1343 rows are displayed from the NewData table.

16. Close SQL Query Analyzer.

Using the *BULK INSERT* Transact-SQL Statement

The *BULK INSERT* Transact-SQL statement requires information similar to that required by the Bcp command to perform a bulk copy operation. The following example uses identical information to that used in the preceding Bcp example, except using Transact-SQL.

```
BULK INSERT NewDatabase..NewData
FROM 'C:\SelfPacedSQL\CH_7\NewData.txt'
WITH
(
BATCHSIZE = 250 ,
DATAFILETYPE = 'char' ,
FIELDTERMINATOR = ',' ,
ROWTERMINATOR = '\n',
MAXERRORS = 50 ,
TABLOCK          )
```

Optimizing Bulk Copy Operations

When you perform a bulk copy operation that imports data into SQL Server 2000, the recovery mode of the destination database affects performance. If the database receiving the data is set for full recovery, all row insertions are fully logged. This generates a substantial number of log records during a large bulk copy operation, which can fill up the transaction log and negatively affect performance. For optimum performance during a bulk copy operation, setting the database to bulk-logged recovery is recommended. When you use bulk-logged recovery, the transaction log captures the results of bulk operations, but does not capture row-by-row insertions.

In addition, if you are loading a large amount of data from a single client into an empty table, you should specify the TABLOCK hint (rather than having SQL Server 2000 start with row locks and escalate them to table locks) and use a large batch size using the ROWS_PER_BATCH hint (large batch sizes are generally more efficient than small batch sizes). If the table into which you are importing the data has indexes, it is generally faster to drop all nonclustered indexes and re-create them after the data insertion. If the table has clustered indexes, it is generally faster to order the data in the text file to match the order in the clustered index and specify the ORDER hint.

If the table into which you are importing data is not empty and contains indexes, the decision on whether to drop indexes depends upon the amount of data being inserted compared to the amount of data existing in the table. The greater the percentage of new data, the faster it is to drop all indexes and re-create them after the data is loaded.

Lesson Summary

In addition to DTS, SQL Server 2000 provides the command-prompt utility Bcp and the Transact-SQL *BULK INSERT* statement for importing data from text files. These methods are particularly suited to high-speed insertions of data into a database. Bcp has been used for years as the only method for inserting large amounts of data into SQL Server, and many existing scripts will be in use for many more years. Database administrators must be familiar with Bcp to work with existing scripts (even if the database administrator is not creating any new scripts). The *BULK INSERT* statement can be used from within SQL Query Analyzer, and it is encapsulated within the DTS Bulk Insert task. There are a number of ways to optimize the speed of insertions of large amounts of data using these methods, including using bulk-logged recovery and dropping nonclustered indexes.

Review

Here are some questions to help you determine whether you have learned enough to move on to the next chapter. If you have difficulty answering these questions, review the material in this chapter before beginning the next chapter. The answers for these questions are located in the Appendix, "Questions and Answers."

1. You are analyzing the data in a text file containing data that you want to import into your database. You have determined that the data is internally consistent, but contains fields that are inconsistent with existing data in your database. The text file is representative of data that you will be importing weekly. What is your best solution for achieving the necessary data consistency? You have already determined that you cannot change the original data source.

2. Describe the difference between the On Success precedence constraint and the On Completion precedence constraint.

3. You have created and saved a simple data import and transform package that imports data from the spreadsheets maintained by your salespeople for expense reports. However, you want to add additional functionality to the package, including notifying an administrator after the entire sales staff has uploaded their expense reports. How might you accomplish this?

4. You have created a package that collects completed sales information from several different spreadsheet files used by salespeople in your company. After it collects this information, it inserts the collected information in one of your sales reporting databases. You want to distribute this package to your salespeople to execute regularly as part of their weekly reports. However, you do not want them to be able to open or edit the package. How should you save this package and how should you secure it?

5. You want to import a large amount of data from a text file into a table that contains a clustered and a nonclustered index. The data being inserted exists in the text file in the same order as the clustered index. As part of the process, you first truncate the existing table to replace it with this new data. Should you drop each of the indexes before you insert the new data?

C H A P T E R   8

Developing a Data Restoration Strategy

About This Chapter

One of the primary responsibilities of a database administrator is to secure the information contained in the user databases. This responsibility consists of several different tasks, including designing for fault tolerance, developing a data restoration strategy that anticipates disaster, and securing the data. This chapter covers developing a data restoration strategy, which includes a backup and restore plan. Chapter 9 covers the mechanics of performing backups and restorations. Chapters 10 and 11 cover data security. This chapter prepares you to select the appropriate backup and restore strategy for your database environment. First, you need to understand the issues involved in preparing for disaster. Next, you will learn about the types of database backups that are available to you. Finally, you will learn about how the data restoration process works, and what restoration options are available given the types of database backups and the recovery model you use.

Before You Begin

There are no prerequisites for completing the lessons in this chapter.

Lesson 1: Understanding Data Restoration Issues

In this lesson you will learn about the design goals of a successful data restoration strategy. Next, you will learn about the available types of database backups and restoration options from which you must develop your data restoration strategy. Next, you learn about the system databases that you need to back up (in addition to user databases) to recover successfully from a disk or system failure. Finally, you learn about the components of a successful data restoration plan.

After this lesson, you will be able to

- Describe the goals of a data restoration strategy
- Understand the types of database backups and the restoration options
- Understand the system and user databases that must be backed up
- Develop a successful data restoration plan

Estimated lesson time: 15 minutes

What Are the Goals of a Data Restoration Strategy?

A data restoration strategy must acknowledge that all databases will require data restoration at some point in their life cycle. As a database administrator, you need to minimize how frequently you need to employ data restoration, monitor for problems before they occur, anticipate the full range of possible disasters, increase the speed of restoration when disasters do occur, and quickly verify that the restoration was successful.

Provide Fault Tolerance

You should plan for fault tolerance, where affordable and possible, to keep your SQL Server 2000 installation running in spite of hardware failures. This includes using RAID to provide fault tolerance for your disk subsystem. Beyond your disk subsystem, this also includes protecting your Windows server against failure. Although the full range of these options is beyond the scope of this book, protecting your Windows server should include selecting reliable hardware, using power conditioning and power interruption devices, performing regular system backups, and being prepared for server hardware failures. Hardware failures will occur. You should also consider Windows clustering for high availability. Chapter 16 covers the use of SQL Server 2000 failover clustering using Windows clustering as a high availability solution for your critical 24x7 databases.

Monitor Your Database

You should continually monitor your database to detect problems before they occur. Chapter 14 covers system and database monitoring. In general, this includes using Database Consistency Checker (DBCC) statements to monitor your database for consistency, using SQL Server performance condition alerts to notify you of potential problems (such as transaction log files running out of space), and using SQL Server Agent to automate routine tasks (such as backing up the transaction log regularly).

Plan for All Forms of Failure and Disaster

You should anticipate all forms of possible disasters and develop plans to recover from each. The following is a partial list of some of the disasters that can occur during the life cycle of a database system.

- Loss of a disk containing a data file
- Loss of a disk containing a transaction log
- Loss of the disk containing the system files
- Server failure
- Natural disaster (flood, earthquake, or fire)
- Loss, theft, or destruction of the entire server
- Theft of backup media
- Faulty backup media
- Faulty restoration device
- Inadvertent user error (such as deleting an entire table by accident)
- Malicious employee behavior (such as inserting inaccurate information intentionally)

Determine Acceptable Data Restoration Times

You need to determine the acceptable length of time for data restoration from each type of disaster. The absolute minimum length of time possible will vary depending upon the type of disaster and the size of the database. The acceptable length of time will vary based upon the use of the database. A database being used for Web-based order entry for a large corporation has much stricter data restoration requirements than a decision support database that is updated weekly from an OLTP database. Also, acceptable data restoration time should take into account the fact that the data in the order entry database is much more difficult (if not impossible) to regenerate than the data in the decision support database. For critical databases, consider high-availability solutions such as hot standby servers and failover clustering, covered in Chapter 16. Your knowledge of acceptable data restoration times will help you to make the decisions in your data restoration strategy.

When planning recovery from each type of potential disaster, you need to ask the appropriate questions to plan for all contingencies. For example, if a disk containing a data file fails, ask yourself the questions in the following list (which also suggests some contingencies for which you need to plan).

- What is the true cost of having your database down?
- Is the time required to replace a data disk (assuming you have one on hand) and restore the data from a database backup acceptable?
- Do you need to implement RAID so that a single disk failure does not take your database down?
- How long will the restoration of the data from database backups actually take?
- Will more frequent backups significantly reduce this restoration time?
- What if your tape drive fails during restoration; do you have another tape drive available?

Note   You should periodically test how quickly you can perform a database restoration assuming various types of disasters (such as a natural disaster).

Be Able to Quickly Verify Proper Database Functionality

You must be able to quickly verify that your database is up and functioning properly before you allow users to access the restored database. You can usually accomplish this by using a Transact-SQL script to query the database to determine whether it is working as intended.

What Types of Backups Are Available?

Now that you understand the types of disasters that you need to plan for and the acceptable data restoration time, you can begin to develop a database backup strategy as part of your data restoration plan. First, you need to understand the types of SQL Server 2000 backups that are available to you to protect your data from disk and system failures. Table 8.1 briefly describes the types of backups that you can use in your data restoration plan.

Note   You must use SQL Server 2000 or third-party database backup programs to back up online database files. Microsoft Windows 2000 and Windows NT 4.0 backups cannot back up files that are in use and for this reason cannot back up online SQL Server 2000 database files.

What Types of Data Restorations Are Available?

Table 8.2 briefly describes the types of data restorations that are possible based upon different types of database backups.

Table 8-1.   Types of Backups

Backup Type	Description
Full database backup	Full copy of the database.
Differential database backup	Copy of all modified data pages since the last full database backup.
Filegroup backup	Full copy of all files in a filegroup.
Differential filegroup backup	Copy of all modified data pages since the last full filegroup backup.
File backup	Full copy of a data file.
Differential file backup	Copy of all modified data pages in a data file since the last full file backup.
Transaction log backup	Copies the active portion of the transaction log (which also truncates the log).
Snapshot backup and restore	Full database copy in a very short time (measured in seconds) using third-party hardware and/or software vendors. Can be used with conventional differential and transaction log backups.

Table 8-2.   Types of Data Restorations

Restoration Option	Description
Full database restore	A complete restoration of an entire database using a full database backup, the most recent differential database backup (if any), and all transaction log backups in sequence since the most recent full or differential database backup.
File or filegroup restore with full recovery	A complete restoration of a file or filegroup using a file or filegroup backup, the most recent differential file or filegroup backup (if any), and all transaction log backups in sequence since the most recent file or differential file or filegroup backup.
Recovery to a point in time	A recovery of an entire database to a specified earlier point in time using fully logged transactions in transaction log backups, along with database, file, or filegroup backups.
Recovery to a named transaction	A restoration of an entire database to a specified named mark (such as immediately before or after a specific transaction) using fully logged transactions in transaction log backups, along with database, file, or filegroup backups.

Note   You can also perform a partial restoration of a database to a secondary server to extract needed data. A partial restoration restores only the needed filegroups.

Back Up All Necessary Databases

You need to back up all databases necessary to recover completely from any form of disaster. In addition to the applicable user databases, this includes backing up the appropriate system databases. You must back up the master database regularly using a full database backup (this is the only backup type available for master). The master database contains essential server-wide database objects, such as logins, backup devices, custom system and user error messages, and linked server definitions. You should also back up the msdb database regularly, generally using full database backups (although transaction log backups are sometimes used as well). The msdb database contains SQL Server Agent jobs, the Meta Data Services repository, and the history (and logic) of all database backups performed. Finally, if replication is involved, you must also back up the distribution database. SQL Server 2000 replication is covered in Chapter 15.

Develop and Implement a Data Restoration Plan

After you understand the types of database backups and the restoration options that are available to you, and after you determine the acceptable data restoration times, you need to develop and implement a data restoration plan (which includes a database backup component). Your plan should be in writing and should be reviewed periodically to determine whether the underlying data restoration requirements have changed. The plan should contain a variety of elements, including the following tasks:

- Document each SQL Server 2000 (and SQL Server 6.5 or 7.0) installation, including operating system version, operating system service packs, SQL Server version, SQL Server service packs, data and transaction log file names (and locations), server names, network libraries, collation (character set and sort order for earlier SQL Server versions), and service account name. Store this information in a secure location and keep it current.
- Document what databases are being backed up, how frequently, and using which types of backups. Consider documenting the reasons for the frequency and type of backups. The underlying reasons could change over time.
- Determine what level of automation to implement. Consider implementing regularly scheduled backup jobs and using SQL Server performance condition alerts to back up the transaction log at a certain threshold. Jobs and alerts are covered in Chapter 13.
- Determine who will be responsible for backups and who will verify that the backups actually occur.

- Determine how you will verify the quality of the backups. Consider periodically testing backups by performing restores on a spare server. This is a good practice of your restoration skills, which will be tested when a disaster occurs.

- Determine where to store backup media. Backup media should be secured, and some backup media should be stored offsite (such as in a safe deposit box or with a tape-vault company) to prepare for natural disaster and theft. Consider a fireproof safe onsite where you store several weeks' worth of backups.

- Determine how long to store backup media. Check legal requirements for tax records and similar data.

- Document the backup and the server hardware.

Lesson Summary

Developing a data restoration plan involves determining your organization's acceptable level of database downtime for various types of disasters. Your job as a database administrator is to determine how to use RAID, implement backup and restore strategies, and use standby servers and clustering to achieve this acceptable level of downtime. As part of the backup and restore strategy, you need to determine the frequency and type of database backups to achieve desired speed of data restorations. You need to perform test restorations to verify that this speed can be achieved (and to keep your skills honed). Finally, you need to fully document how each part of this restoration plan will be implemented.

Lesson 2: Understanding the Types of Database Backups

To develop a data restoration plan, you need to understand each of the SQL Server 2000 backup types that are available. In this lesson, you will learn about each database backup type, including what is backed up with each, how they are different, and when to use each type. In Lesson 3 you will learn how to use these different backup types together for various types of data restorations. Once you understand both components, you can develop your data restoration plan.

After this lesson, you will be able to

- Describe the differences between each of the SQL Server 2000 backup types
- Understand when to use each type of backup

Estimated lesson time: 15 minutes

Understanding Full Database Backups

A full database backup is a copy of all data files in a database, including all database activity that occurred while the full database backup was in process. All user data and all database objects, including system tables, indexes, and user-defined tables, are included. A full database backup generally takes more space and more time than any other type of backup. A full database backup is the starting point for a complete database restoration in the event data restoration is required.

You should perform a full database backup after you populate your database with data for the first time. Thereafter, you should perform additional full database backups on a regular basis and after a major population of new data. How frequently you perform a full database backup depends upon the size of your data and how frequently it changes. As a general rule, perform full database backups as frequently as once a day and as infrequently as once a week. If your database is too large to perform a full database backup regularly, you must use file and filegroup backups.

Although SQL Server 2000 backups generally have little impact on database performance, it is still a good idea to schedule full database backups at a time when the database is least busy (such as overnight). However, you must coordinate the timing of a full database backup with scheduled bulk inserts of new data (if any), which are also frequently scheduled to occur overnight.

Understanding Differential Database Backups

A differential database backup is a copy of all changes that have occurred to all data files since the last full database backup, including all database activity that occurred while the differential database backup was in process. This includes all changes to data and database objects. A differential database backup records only the most recent change to a data record if a particular data record has changed more than once since the last full database backup (unlike a transaction log backup, which records each change). A differential database backup takes less time and less space than a full database backup, and is used to reduce database restoration times.

To enhance the speed of differential database backups, SQL Server 2000 tracks all extents that have changed since the last full database backup using a Differential Changed Map (DCM) page. The differential database backup process scans each DCM page to identify (and then back up) all changed extents (each full database backup resets the DCM pages). If the bit for an extent is 0, the extent has not changed since the last full database backup. If the bit is 1, the extent has changed. Through the use of DCM pages, the length of time required to perform a differential backup is proportional to the number of extents modified, not the size of the database.

Note   Because each differential backup records all changes since the last full database backup, only the most recent differential backup is required for restoration of data.

Use differential database backups with medium to large databases in between scheduled full database backups. As the length of time required to perform a full database backup increases, performing differential database backups between each full database backup becomes more useful. Using a recent differential database backup reduces the number of transaction log backups that must be used for a data restoration. Therefore, differential database backups are particularly useful in speeding up data restoration times in medium and large databases where a subset of data changes frequently and results in large transaction log sizes.

Understanding File and Filegroup Backups

A file backup is a copy of a single data file, and a filegroup backup is a copy of each data file in a single filegroup, including all database activity that occurred while the file or filegroup backup was in process. This type of backup takes less time and space than a full database backup. It is used for VLDBs when there is not enough time to back up the entire database in a reasonable amount of time (such as in a 24-hour period). In a VLDB, you can design the database so that certain filegroups contain data that changes frequently and other filegroups contain data that changes infrequently (or perhaps is read-only data). Using this design, you can use a file or filegroup backup to perform frequent backups of the data that changes frequently and perform occasional backups of the infrequently changing data. By splitting the backup into segments, you can perform the necessary backups in the available backup window and achieve acceptable restoration times. With VLDBs, a single file or filegroup can be restored much faster than an entire database.

File and filegroup backups require careful planning so that related data and indexes are backed up (and restored) together. In addition, a full set of transaction log backups is required to restore file and file group backups to a state that is logically consistent with the rest of the database. Finally, you can perform file and filegroup backups in parallel to multiple physical devices to significantly increase backup performance. However, because of the administrative complexity (including the need for sophisticated database design), file and filegroup backups are generally used only for VLDBs.

Understanding Differential File and Differential Filegroup Backups

A differential file backup or a differential filegroup backup is a copy of all changes that have occurred to a file or a filegroup since the last file or filegroup backup, including all database activity that occurred while the differential file or filegroup backup was in process. Differential file and differential filegroup backups are conceptually identical to differential database backups. They take less time and less space than making a complete copy of a file or filegroup, and are used to speed the restore process by reducing the number of transaction log backups that must be applied.

Understanding Transaction Log Backups

A transaction log backup is a sequential record of all transactions recorded in the transaction log since the last transaction log backup. Transaction log backups enable you to recover the database to a specific point in time, such as prior to entering incorrect data. Transaction log backups are only used with the Bulk-Logged Recovery and Full Recovery models. The Simple Recovery model does not use transaction log backups for database restoration and recovery.

When the Bulk-Logged Recovery model is used for bulk-logged operations, changes made by these bulk operations to data files are tracked using a Bulk Changed Map (BCM) page. A transaction log backup scans each BCM page to identify and back up all extents modified by bulk-logged operations since the most recent transaction log backup. This allows bulk-logged operations to be quickly backed up along with the transaction log when bulk-logged recovery is used. However, only the net change of the bulk operation is recorded, not each individual operation. BCM pages are not required when the Full Recovery model is used, because with this recovery model the bulk-logged operation is fully logged in the transaction log.

The length of time required to back up the transaction log will vary significantly depending upon the rate of database transactions, the recovery model used, and the volume of bulk-logged operations. On databases with very high transaction rates and fully logged bulk operations, the size of a transaction log backup can be bigger than a full database backup and require very frequent transaction log backups to regularly truncate the inactive portion of the transaction log.

Note   Because a transaction log backup records only changes since the previous transaction log backup, all transaction log backups are required for restoration of data.

When SQL Server 2000 completes a transaction log backup (unless specified otherwise), it truncates each virtual log file (VLF) that does not contain an active portion of the transaction log. This allows these VLFs to be reused. The active portion of the transaction log includes any portion of the transaction log containing an active transaction or a transaction marked for replication that has not yet replicated. In a production database, you will always be using either the Bulk-Logged Recovery or Full Recovery model and must perform regular transaction log backups to truncate the transaction log. If the transaction log is not regularly truncated, it can fill up. If the transaction log runs out of space, SQL Server 2000 will shut down. You should truncate the transaction log file through regular transaction log backups rather than manually truncating the transaction log file, because truncating it manually breaks the log backup chain. The only time you will back up the transaction log without truncation is when a data file fails and the current active transaction log must be backed up. In this scenario, it cannot be truncated, because the data file is damaged or nonexistent.

How often you need to perform transaction log backups depends upon the rate of transactions, the size of the transaction log file, the type of fault tolerance, and the acceptable data restoration times. It could be as frequent as every 10 or 15 minutes, or it could be only once every two or three hours (or longer if few transactions are occurring). Remember, if a data file disk and a transaction log file disk both fail and no fault tolerance is employed, any data more recent than the most recent transaction log backup must be regenerated using other means, which might not be possible.

Lesson Summary

After you populate a database and before you place it in production, you should make a full database backup. Thereafter, you should perform a full database backup on a regular basis. In addition, you must perform regular transaction log backups to have a record of all changes to the database and to truncate the transaction log so that it can store new transaction log records. In larger databases, use differential database backups between regularly scheduled full database backups to reduce the number of transaction log backups (and the time) that you must use to restore a database. In VLDBs, you must use file and filegroup backups, differential file and differential filegroup backups, and transaction log backups to have an effective data restoration strategy.

Lesson 3: Understanding the Restoration Process

To implement an effective backup and restore strategy, you must understand the SQL Server 2000 restoration process. In this lesson, you learn how SQL Server 2000 performs automatic and manual restorations of data. You will learn about using various types of backups to perform full restorations quickly. You will also learn about partial restoration options that are available with certain types of database backups. Finally, you will review the restoration process given several disaster scenarios.

After this lesson, you will be able to

- Describe the automatic recovery process
- Describe the manual recovery process
- Understand how different types of database backups can increase data restoration speed
- Understand the full and partial data restoration options
- Understand data restoration paths for different disaster scenarios

Estimated lesson time: 15 minutes

Understanding the Recovery Process

SQL Server 2000 has two recovery processes: an automatic process that occurs each time you start SQL Server 2000 and a manual recovery process that you initiate. Understanding the automatic recovery process will help you understand the manual recovery process.

Automatic Recovery Process

The automatic recovery process is designed to ensure that once SQL Server 2000 has started, the data in each database is logically consistent, regardless of how or why SQL Server 2000 was shut down. SQL Server 2000 accomplishes this task by using the transaction log. It reads the active portion of the transaction log for each database and examines all transactions that have occurred since the most recent checkpoint. It identifies all committed transactions and rolls them forward. This means reapplying them to the database. It then identifies all uncommitted transactions and rolls them back. This means ensuring that any uncommitted transactions that were partially written to the database are removed. This process ensures that a logically consistent state exists for each database. The automatic recovery process then issues a checkpoint to mark the transaction log as consistent as of this point.

SQL Server 2000 begins by recovering the master database. The master database contains the information it needs to locate, open, and recover the remaining databases. Next, it recovers the model and msdb databases (and the distribution database if it exists). Next, it recovers each user database. It finishes with clearing and starting the tempdb database. You can examine the restoration process by reviewing the SQL Server error log, a sample of which is shown in Figure 8.1.

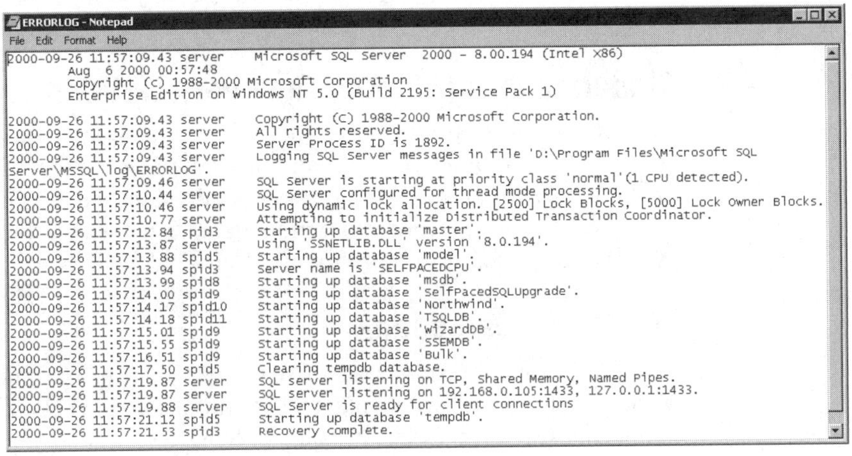

Figure 8.1.   The SQL Server error log.

You cannot control this automatic recovery process directly. However, you can control the maximum amount of time SQL Server 2000 will take to perform the automatic recovery. The default value is 0, which means that SQL Server 2000 will dynamically determine how often it issues a checkpoint. The more frequently checkpoints are issued, the smaller is the portion of the transaction log that must be rolled forward and rolled back. In general, you should rarely need to adjust this value. As with most SQL Server 2000 settings, letting SQL Server 2000 adjust itself dynamically will generally yield the best performance over time.

Manual Recovery Process

The manual recovery process involves applying one or more database backups and then manually recovering them either completely or to a specified point. At the end of the manual recovery process, the database will be logically consistent. The recovery might consist of applying a full database backup, optionally applying the most recent differential database backup, and then applying several transaction log backups. As each database backup is applied, it is marked for no recovery. This means that additional restoration will occur before recovery occurs. After recovery occurs, no further restoration is possible. When the final restoration occurs, it is marked for recovery and SQL Server 2000 rolls forward and rolls back appropriate transactions using the transaction log.

In between the application of each backup, the database is not recovered and is generally not usable. However, you can restore a database to standby (read-only) mode without performing recovery. This allows you to view the state of the data after the application of each backup to identify a point in the transaction log where data restoration should stop (such as the point where a user or application error occurred). Once the point of restoration is identified, recovery must occur to bring the database online in a logically consistent state. After recovery has occurred, no further restoration can occur.

Understanding Manual Recovery Options

All of the database backup types allow you to recover a database, a file, or a file-group to the end of the most recent transaction log backup. In addition, certain types of backups allow you to recover your data to some point earlier in time than the end of the most recent transaction log backup (such as before unwanted data was entered or before certain data was deleted).

Restoring Databases

When you want to restore a database to the end of the most recent transaction log backup, you start with your most recent full database backup. You can restore this full database backup to any instance of SQL Server 2000, not just to the instance from which it was backed up. If you are using differential database backups, you then restore the most recent differential database backup. Finally, in sequence, you then restore each transaction log backup that is more recent than the most recently restored full or differential database backup. As part of the restoration of the final transaction log backup, SQL Server 2000 performs a manual recovery (you must specify this), rolling forward and rolling back outstanding transactions as appropriate. Your database is restored with no data loss.

Note   You can restore SQL Server 7.0 backups to a SQL Server 2000 instance (but not vice versa).

If the most recent full database or differential database backup is damaged or missing, you can still restore using earlier transaction log backups. Thus, if you maintain a complete chain of transaction log backups, you can always recover as long as a single full database backup exists along with all of your transaction log backups. Obviously, applying these additional transaction log backups will take additional time. You perform regular full and differential database backups to reduce the recovery time by requiring the application of fewer transaction log backups. Keeping and securing (and duplicating) a full chain of transaction log backups provides additional fault tolerance in case of damaged or lost backup media.

Restoring Files and Filegroups

When you want to restore a file or a filegroup to the point of the most recent transaction log backup, you start with the most recent backup of the file or filegroup. This recent backup can be either from a file or filegroup backup, or from a full database backup. Restoring a single file from a full database backup takes longer than restoring a file from a file backup. If you are using differential file or filegroup backups, you restore the most recent differential file or filegroup backup. Finally, in sequence, restore each transaction log backup that is more recent than the most recently restored differential file or filegroup backup. As part of the restore of the final transaction log backup, SQL Server 2000 performs a manual recovery (you must specify this), rolling forward and rolling back outstanding transactions as appropriate. Your file or filegroup is restored with no data loss.

Unlike full and differential database backups, file and filegroup backups must have transaction log backups applied to them to make the restored file or filegroup logically consistent with the rest of the database. If you are restoring an entire database using file or filegroup backups, the loss of any single backup media can render the entire database unrecoverable.

Note   Restoring all data files or all filegroups and applying all transaction logs is functionally equivalent to restoring an entire database.

Restoring and Recovering to an Earlier Point in Time

Sometimes you might want to recover to an earlier point in time because of some type of user or application error. You can accomplish this by recovering a database either to a specific point in time within the transaction log or to a named mark within the transaction log.

To recover to a specific point in time, you restore the full database backup and optionally a differential database backup. You then restore the transaction log backups in sequence to the point in time you want to recover to. When you restore the final transaction log that you want to restore, you specify recovery only to a specific point in time within that transaction log backup. Through the use of either the header information of each transaction log backup or the information in the backupset table in the msdb database, you can easily identify the transaction log backup that contains the time to which you want to recover.

Note   *Point-in-time recovery* is recovery of the database. Once you recover to a specific point in time, you cannot recover to a more recent point in time. This means that you cannot use point-in-time recovery to restore a database to standby mode, view that state of the database as of a certain time, and then apply additional transactions.

To recover to a named mark, you must insert marks into the transaction log as part of a transaction. The mark is recorded as a row in the logmarkhistory table in the msdb database. During recovery, you can recover and roll forward to the mark and either include or exclude the mark.

However, recovery to a specific point in time or a named mark is not supported if the final transaction log backup you want to restore contains a bulk-logged transaction that was logged using the Bulk-Logged Recovery model. In addition, you cannot restore a single file or filegroup to a point in time or named mark without restoring the entire database to that particular point.

Recovery from Several Different Disaster Scenarios

Understanding the restoration process from the following disaster scenarios will help you determine backup and restore (and fault tolerance) strategies you will use in your data restoration plan.

User Data Disk Failure

If a disk that contains a data file fails, your restoration path will depend upon whether you have employed RAID for fault tolerance. If you have, you simply replace the disk that failed, reset the RAID configuration, and let RAID rebuild the data. You measure your downtime by the length of time required to replace the disk and reconfigure RAID. If your implementation of RAID supported hot swapping or hot standby, there will be no downtime.

If you have not employed RAID or have employed RAID 0, you must restore your data using database backups. First, you must back up the currently active transaction log using the no truncate option to restore your data completely. Next, you restore the full database backup and optionally the most recent differential backup, specifying no recovery for each restoration. Finally, you restore each necessary transaction log in sequence, specifying no recovery for each restoration until the final transaction log backup. On the final transaction log, restore it specifying recovery. SQL Server 2000 will roll forward and roll back appropriate transactions, and your database will be restored with no data loss.

If your data file and your transaction log file are on the same disk, you can only restore up to your most recent transaction log backup. All other data will have to be regenerated using other means.

User Transaction Log Disk Failure

If a disk that contains a transaction log file fails, no data restoration is needed unless the transaction log file and a data file share the same disk. However, if the transaction log file was not mirrored using RAID 1, you have lost your ability to completely restore your database should a disk containing a data file also fail. In this case, you should immediately back up the entire database using either a full or a differential backup (and make a copy of the backup media). Then, you should replace the failed disk.

Master Database Disk Failure

If a disk containing the master database fails and the master database was not mirrored using RAID 1, you must restore the master database from backup followed by a restoration of each of the necessary system databases. Next, you can either restore each user database from backup or reattach them if their data and transaction log files are intact on other disks.

Lesson Summary

Restoring a database, file, or filegroup from backup requires the database to be recovered to a logically consistent state. SQL Server 2000 uses transaction log backups to perform this task in a manner similar to the way SQL Server 2000 employs automatic recovery each time SQL Server 2000 starts. You can use a full and a differential database backup along with all applicable transaction log files in sequence to completely restore your data from a disk or system failure. For larger databases, you can use file and filegroup backups (and differential file and filegroup backups) along with all applicable transaction log files to completely restore your data from a disk or system failure in a reasonable length of time. You can also recover an entire database to a specific point in time or a named mark in the transaction log provided that the final transaction log backup you want to apply does not contain minimally logged bulk operations.

Review

Here are some questions to help you determine whether you have learned enough to move on to the next chapter. If you have difficulty answering these questions, review the material in this chapter before beginning the next chapter. The answers for these questions are located in the Appendix, "Questions and Answers."

1. You are using RAID 1 for your transaction log and RAID 10 for your database. With this level of fault tolerance, why is it still critical to have a data restoration plan?

2. You are developing your data recovery plan. You have tested the length of time required to perform a full database backup and determined that you can back up the entire database in six hours. You have decided to perform full database backups every night. You have also determined that you need to perform transaction log backups every 15 minutes to minimize the risk of data loss. Should you also use regular differential database backups as part of your data recovery plan?

3. You are responsible for maintaining and restoring, if needed, a decision support database. Several different data sources regularly populate this database using DTS packages. What is the restoration benefit, if any, to using the Full Recovery model for this database given the substantial increase in the number and size of the transaction log backups required?

C H A P T E R   9

Backing Up and Restoring SQL Server

About This Chapter

This chapter prepares you to perform each type of SQL Server 2000 database backup and restore. First, you learn about backup terms, media, and devices. Next, you learn to perform each type of database backup, using SQL Server Enterprise Manager and Transact-SQL. You then learn to restore databases and database files using SQL Server Enterprise Manager and Transact-SQL. Finally, you learn how to restore or rebuild system databases. After you have completed these tasks, you will be ready to apply database security and place your SQL Server 2000 databases into production.

Before You Begin

To complete this chapter, you must have

- A computer that meets or exceeds the minimum hardware requirements listed in Table 2.1, "Hardware Requirements," in the Lesson 1 section of Chapter 2.
- Microsoft Windows 2000 Server running on your computer on an NTFS partition.
- A computer with a NetBIOS name of SelfPacedCPU, configured as a domain controller in the SelfPacedSQL.MSFT domain.

- Installed a default instance and at least one named instance of SQL Server 2000 (see Chapter 2).
- Created the SSEMDB database using the CreateDB.sql script (see Chapter 6).

Lesson 1: Understanding Backup Terms, Media, and Devices

Before you learn to back up your database, you need to become familiar with some terms that are used with SQL Server 2000 backups and restorations. Next, you will learn about the types of backup media on which you can store your backups, including how to choose among them. You will then learn how to create reusable backup devices.

After this lesson, you will be able to

- Understand SQL Server 2000 backup terms
- Select appropriate backup media
- Create backup devices

Estimated lesson time: 15 minutes

Defining Terms

You should become familiar with a variety of terms that are important to understand when performing database backups and restorations. Table 9.1 explains the most important terms.

For example, if two backup devices (such as tape drives) are used to record a backup of a database and the backup set uses three tapes per backup device, there are six tapes in the media set (consisting of three tapes in each media family). A media set can contain multiple backup sets, for example, the appending of one backup set to another backup set on the same tape or set of tapes.

Selecting Backup Media

You can elect to use either disk or tape for your backup media. The SQL Server 2000 backup program supports local tape drives, local disk drives, network disk drives, and named pipes. Named pipes provide an interface for use by third-party backup solutions.

Table 9-1.   Backup Terminologies

Term	Description
Backup	A full or partial copy of a database, transaction log, file, or filegroup forming a backup set. The backup set is recorded on backup media (either tape or disk) using a backup device (a tape drive name or physical filename).
Backup device	The physical file (such as C:\SQLBackups\Full.bak) or specific tape drive (such as \\.\Tape0) that you use to record a backup onto backup media.
Backup file	A file that stores a backup set.
Backup media	The actual physical media (either disk or tape) used to store a backup set using a backup file. Backup media can store multiple backup sets (such as from multiple SQL Server 2000 backups and from Windows 2000 backups).
Backup set	The backup from a single backup operation that resides on backup media. The backup set may reside on a single backup media, a media family, or a media set.
Media family	All media (physical files or tapes) in a media set written by a single backup device for a single backup set.
Media header	Provides information about the contents of the backup media. A media header must be written before a backup set can be recorded on the backup media (this is also called initializing the backup media). Usually, the media header is written one time and remains on the media for the life of the media.
Media set	All media involved in a backup operation. Examples of media sets are: a single tape, a single disk file, one backup device writing a set of tapes, or a set of tapes written by more than one backup device.

Tape

Traditionally, administrators have used tape for database backups because it was cheaper than hard disk space. However, tape drives are relatively slow and have limited capacity. The limitation for SQL Server 2000 backup speed is usually the tape drive itself. You can improve tape backup performance by writing to two tape drives simultaneously. This will effectively cut your backup time in half because the backup is written in parallel to the tape drives. The problem with limited tape capacities for large databases is that if your backup will not fit on a single tape, someone must be there to switch tapes (and insert the correct tape). If not, the backup never completes. Simultaneously writing to multiple tapes helps solve the problem of limited capacity per tape for large databases.

Note   Using a SCSI tape drive attached to the local computer is generally faster than using a remote tape drive using third-party software because you are limited by the speed and contention of the network.

Disk

In the past, disk space was too expensive to use for database backups. However, this is no longer the case. Backup to a local disk is frequently the backup method of choice because it is generally the fastest method. Backup times as fast as eight minutes for a 20-GB database have been reported. If you do back up your data to a local disk, be sure to use a separate physical disk from your data or transaction log files. After being backed up to a local disk, backup files are generally themselves automatically backed up regularly (for example, nightly) to tape to be archived.

For smaller databases, performing a backup to a network drive is also a common scenario. For additional performance in this scenario, administrators sometimes segment the network to minimize or eliminate network contention. You may use the network drive for multiple databases and by multiple SQL Server 2000 installations. This network drive will generally be regularly (and automatically) backed up to tape for archiving. This allows the archiving of backup files to tape from multiple SQL Server 2000 instances to be consolidated to one network location.

Creating Permanent Backup Devices

You can create one or more permanent backup devices that you can use for regular backups, or you can create a new backup file each time you perform a database backup. Generally, you will want to create backup devices that you can reuse, particularly for automation of database backups. Having permanent backup devices allows you to refer to them in backup and restore commands using only a logical name, rather than the complete physical name. Backup devices are recorded in the sysdevices table in the master database. Backup files created on the fly are not recorded in the sysdevices table and thus are not reusable, but rather must be specified each time they are referred to.

SQL Server Enterprise Manager

To create a backup device using SQL Server Enterprise Manager, expand the Management container, right-click Backup, and then click New Backup Device. In the Backup Device Properties – New Device dialog box, specify a logical name for the backup device and define a tape drive name or a filename for the backup device. See Figure 9.1.

To delete a backup device using SQL Server Enterprise Manager, click the Backup container in the console tree (in the Management container) to display a list of all backup devices in the details pane. Right-click the backup device and then click Delete to drop the device.

Note   Backup devices are not specific to any database.

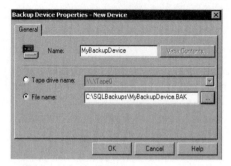

Figure 9.1. Creating a backup device using SQL Server Enterprise Manager.

Transact-SQL

To create a reusable backup device using Transact-SQL, use the *sp_addumpdevice* system stored procedure.

```
Sp_addumpdevice 'disk' , 'FullBackupDevice' , 'E:\SQLBackups\Full.bak'
```

The preceding example creates a disk backup device with a logical name of Full-BackupDevice using a file on the local disk.

```
Sp_addumpdevice 'tape' , 'TLogTapeBackupDevice' , '\\.\Tape0'
```

This example creates a tape backup device with a logical name of TLogTapeBack-upDevice using tape drive 0 (this refers to the first tape drive on the system).

```
Sp_addumpdevice 'disk','TLogBackupDevice' , '\\NetSrv\SQLBak\TLog.bak'
```

The preceding example creates a disk backup device with a logical name of TLog-BackupDevice using a network file referenced using a Universal Naming Convention (UNC) path.

With Transact-SQL, you can create and save a script that creates all of your backup devices at one time. Saving the script is important because you can use it to re-create the backup devices in the master database if you need to (or duplicate this backup device structure on other SQL Server 2000 computers in your enterprise).

To use Transact-SQL to view a list of all devices on your SQL Server instance, use the *sp_helpdevice* system stored procedure. To drop a backup device using Transact-SQL, use the *sp_dropdevice* system stored procedure.

```
Sp_dropdevice 'FullBackupDevice'
```

The preceding example drops the FullBackupDevice backup device, but does not drop the associated physical file.

```
Sp_dropdevice 'FullBackupDevice' , 'DELFILE'
```

The preceding example drops the FullBackupDevice backup device and also drops the associated physical file.

Practice: Creating Backup Devices Using Transact-SQL

In this practice you use a Transact-SQL script to create multiple backup devices using the *sp_addumpdevice* system stored procedure.

▶ **To create backup devices using Transact-SQL**

1. Ensure that you are logged on to the SelfPacedSQL.MSFT domain controller as Administrator.

2. Click Start, point to Programs, point to Microsoft SQL Server, and then click Query Analyzer.

3. In the Connect To SQL Server dialog box, connect to SelfPacedSQL using Windows authentication.

4. Click OK.

5. On the toolbar, click the Load SQL Script button.

   The Open Query File dialog box appears.

6. Open BackupDevices.sql in the C:\SelfPacedSQL\CH_9 folder.

   A Transact-SQL script appears that will create five backup devices using the following logical names: MasterFullBackup, MSDBFullBackup, SSEMDB-FullBackup, SSEMDBDiffBackup, and SSEMDBTLogBackup. The specified physical path does not yet exist. You will create this folder in just a few moments.

7. Click the Execute Query button to execute the BackupDevices.sql statement.

   Notice that the script added five disk devices. SQL Server 2000 does not verify the physical path for a backup device until you are ready to use the backup device.

8. On the toolbar, click the Clear Window button.

9. In the query pane, type **sp_helpdevice** and then click the Execute Query button on the toolbar.

   Notice that the five disk devices appear, along with information regarding the master, model, and tempdb databases.

10. Close SQL Query Analyzer. Do not save any changes.

11. Open Windows Explorer.

12. Create a folder on the C drive called SQLBackups.

13. Close Windows Explorer.

Lesson Summary

Learning backup terminology is important before you start working with backups, backup sets, and media sets. You need to decide which backup media you will use for your backups, tape or disk. Frequently, administrators make backups to disk for performance and then archive them to tape. Once you have determined your backup media, you need to create permanent backup devices that you will use for your backups. Creating reusable backup devices is useful for automating backups, and for referring to backup files in Transact-SQL scripts.

Lesson 2: Backing Up Databases, Files, Filegroups, and Transaction Logs

After determining your backup media and creating backup devices, you are ready to back up your data. In this lesson, you will learn to perform each type of database backup using SQL Server Enterprise Manager and Transact-SQL. You will learn all of the backup options that are available to you when you perform these types of backups using SQL Server Enterprise Manager, and you will learn the equivalent options using Transact-SQL.

After this lesson, you will be able to

- Perform full database backups using SQL Server Enterprise Manager and Transact-SQL
- Perform differential database backups using SQL Server Enterprise Manager and Transact-SQL
- Perform transaction log backups using SQL Server Enterprise Manager and Transact-SQL
- Perform file or filegroup backups using SQL Server Enterprise Manager and Transact-SQL

Estimated lesson time: 60 minutes

Perform Backups Using SQL Server Enterprise Manager

SQL Server Enterprise Manager provides a simple graphical interface to interactively perform database backups. Using SQL Server Enterprise Manager is a good way to begin performing database backups, allowing you to become familiar with backup terms and options. Understanding backup options through SQL Server Enterprise Manager will help you understand the Transact-SQL syntax for backups. You can perform a backup directly with SQL Server Enterprise Manager, or you can use the Create Database Backup Wizard.

Using the Create Database Backup Wizard

The SQL Server Enterprise Manager wizards are available from the Tools menu, and from any taskpad view. Figure 9.2 displays the Select Wizard dialog box, from which you can select a variety of wizards, including the Backup Wizard.

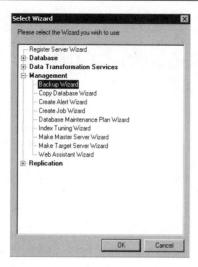

Figure 9.2.   The Select Wizard dialog box.

After you start the Backup Wizard, you select a database to back up in the Create Database To Backup page. You can browse and select any database on the current server. See Figure 9.3.

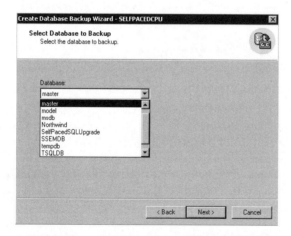

Figure 9.3.   Selecting a database to back up.

After you select the database you want to back up, you must select a name for this backup set in the Type Name And Description For Backup page. Select a descriptive name, such as Northwind Full Backup. You can also provide a description for this backup set. The description is optional, but quite useful when distinguishing between multiple backups. See Figure 9.4.

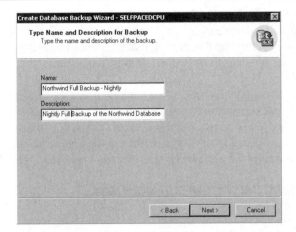

Figure 9.4.   Naming the backup set.

Next, in the Select Type Of Backup page, you select the type of backup you want to perform. Using the Create Database Backup Wizard, you can perform full database, differential database, and transaction log backups (you cannot perform file and filegroup backups). If a particular backup type is grayed out, this means that you cannot perform this type of backup with the database you have chosen. For example, you can only perform a full database backup of the master database, and you cannot perform a transaction log backup of a database that is using the Simple Recovery model. See Figure 9.5.

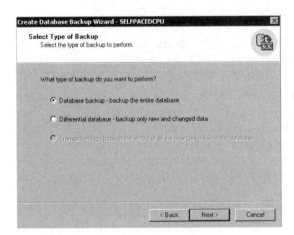

Figure 9.5.   Selecting the type of backup.

Note   You cannot perform a differential database backup of a database until you perform a full database backup of the database.

Next, in the Select Backup Destination And Action page, you select the backup device you want to use for this backup set. You can select a tape, a file, or a previously created backup device. Notice that the default location for a file is the Backup folder for your SQL Server 2000 instance (such as C:\Program Files\Microsoft SQL Server\Mssql\Backup). You can choose to append this backup set to any existing backup sets on the backup media you have selected, or overwrite any existing backup sets on the backup media. You can also choose to have SQL Server 2000 read and verify the integrity of the backup after completing the backup. This does not verify the structure of the data itself, but rather verifies that the backup files have been written and are readable. See Figure 9.6.

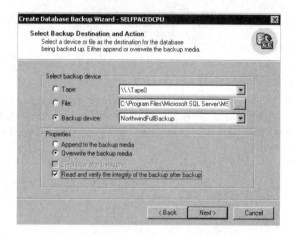

Figure 9.6.   Selecting the backup destination and its properties.

More Info   Performing database consistency checks is covered in Chapter 14.

Next, in the Initialize Media page, if you chose to overwrite the backup media, you can choose to initialize the media (write a media header) by providing a media set name and description. A media set name can be very useful for identifying backup media. For example, if you have a backup tape and you do not know what is on the tape, you can use SQL Server Enterprise Manager or Transact-SQL to retrieve the media header from the tape to help identify its contents (provided that you created a good label in the first place). See Figure 9.7.

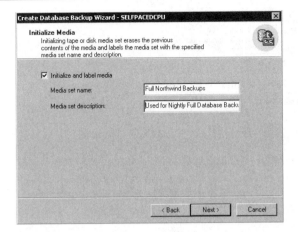

Figure 9.7.   Initializing the backup media.

Next, in the Backup Verification And Scheduling page, unless you have chosen to initialize the backup media and provide a new media set name, you can choose to verify that you are writing to a specified media set and that the backup set expiration date (if any) has passed. You can use this capability to prevent the overwriting of a backup set that has not yet expired or the writing of a backup set to the wrong tape or file. Mistakes such as inserting the wrong tape or clicking the wrong device in the graphical interface are easy to make and can have severe consequences. For example, if you accidentally overwrite a tape storing part of a striped set of backup tapes from a parallel backup or any one of those tapes is damaged, the entire media set is unusable. You can also choose to skip this check of media set names and backup set expiration dates.

Note   SQL Server 2000 only uses the expiration date on the first backup set on the backup media to determine whether the entire backup media can be overwritten.

You have the option to set an expiration date on a backup set when you create it. For example, you may keep one week's worth of backups on disk, each in separate backup devices, and archive these to tape regularly. You could use an expiration date to protect against accidentally overwriting a backup set before the expiration of seven days. Finally, you can also create a job and schedule the backup that you just defined to occur on a regular basis. See Figure 9.8. Jobs and schedules are covered in Chapter 13.

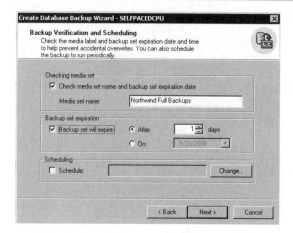

Figure 9.8.   Setting an expiration date and scheduling the backup.

Next, in the Completing The Create Database Backup Wizard page, you are given the opportunity to review the selections you have made before you actually back up the database. You can click the Back button to change any parameter you want to change. Click the Finish button to back up the database. See Figure 9.9.

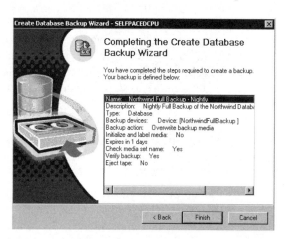

Figure 9.9.   Completing the Create Database Backup Wizard.

Practice: Backing Up the Master Database Using the Create Database Backup Wizard

In this practice you use the Create Database Backup Wizard to back up the master database.

▶ **To back up the master database using the Create Database Backup Wizard**

1. Ensure that you are logged on to the SelfPacedSQL.MSFT domain controller as Administrator.
2. Click Start, point to Programs, point to Microsoft SQL Server, and then click Enterprise Manager.

   SQL Server Enterprise Manager appears displaying the Microsoft SQL Servers and the Event Viewer (Local) console trees in the console root.
3. In the console tree, expand the Microsoft SQL Servers container, expand the SQL Server Group container, and then click the default instance.
4. On the Tools menu, click Wizards.

   The Select Wizard dialog box appears.
5. Expand Management and then double-click Backup Wizard.

   The Welcome To The Create Database Backup Wizard page appears.
6. Click Next.

   The Select Database To Backup page appears.
7. In the Database drop-down list, select master and then click Next.

   The Type Name And Description For Backup page appears.
8. In the Name text box, type **Full master Database Backup #1**.
9. In the Description text box, type **Backup Set #1** and then click Next.

   The Select Type Of Backup page appears. Notice that you can only perform a full database backup of the master database.
10. Click Next.

    The Select Backup Destination And Action page appears.
11. Click the Backup Device option button and then, in the Backup Device drop-down list, select MasterFullBackup.
12. Click the Overwrite The Backup Media option button.
13. Select the Read And Verify The Integrity Of The Backup After Backup check box and then click Next.

    The Initialize Media page appears.
14. Select the Initialize And Label Media check box.
15. In the Media Set Name text box, type **MasterBackups**.

16. In the Media Set Description text box, type **Media for Master Database Backups** and then click Next.

   The Backup Verification And Scheduling page appears.

17. Click Next.

   The Completing The Create Database Backup Wizard page appears. Review the details of the backup you have defined.

18. Click the Finish button.

   The Backup Progress dialog box appears, displaying the progress of the backup of the master database. Next, the Verify Progress dialog box appears, displaying the progress of the verification of the master database backup. When the database backup is complete, a Wizard Complete message box appears.

19. Click OK to close the Wizard Complete message box.

20. Do not close SQL Server Enterprise Manager.

Using SQL Server Enterprise Manager Directly

To create a backup using SQL Server Enterprise Manager directly, you can either click the Databases container and then click Backup Database from the Tools menu, or you can right-click the Databases container (or the container for any specific database), point to All Tasks, and then click Backup Database. You can use SQL Server Enterprise Manager to perform any type of database backup. The General and Options tabs in the SQL Server Backup dialog box allow you to provide the same type of backup information discussed earlier with respect to the Create Database Backup Wizard (such as database, backup set name, type of backup, append or overwrite, and media set name). See Figures 9.10 and 9.11.

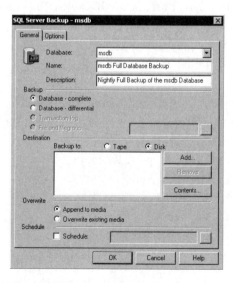

Figure 9.10.   Creating a backup in the General tab.

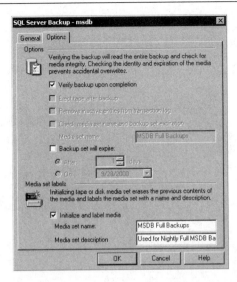

Figure 9.11.   Selecting backup options in the Options tab.

Note   Notice a check box in Figure 9.11 that allows you to choose whether to remove inactive entries from the transaction log. This check box is grayed out if you are not backing up the transaction log. If you are backing up the transaction log, the default is to truncate the transaction log after a backup. Clear the check box to back up the transaction log without truncation (for example, after a disk failure).

In the General tab, if you are performing a file or filegroup backup, click the ellipsis to select the file or filegroup you want to back up. You can select either a single data file or an entire filegroup in the Specify Filegroups And Files dialog box. If you select a filegroup, all files in the group are automatically selected. See Figure 9.12.

After you select the backup media (tape or disk), click the Add button to select a destination for the backup. In the Select Backup Destination dialog box, you can either specify a backup file (if you selected disk), a tape drive (if you selected tape), or an existing backup device. See Figure 9.13.

Note   If you create backup devices using a Transact-SQL statement in SQL Query Analyzer while SQL Server Enterprise Manager is open, you may need to disconnect and reconnect to your SQL Server 2000 instance in SQL Server Enterprise Manager to refresh the connection and access this newly created backup device.

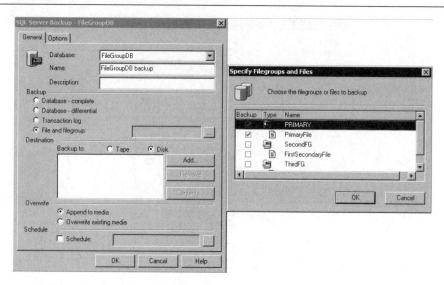

Figure 9.12.   Selecting a file or filegroup.

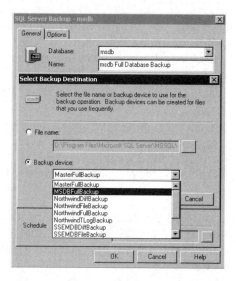

Figure 9.13.   Selecting a backup destination.

After you select a backup device, you can click the Contents button in the General tab to view the contents of the selected backup device (to determine whether you want to overwrite the backup sets on the backup device). If it does contain backup sets, you can view the contents of each backup set in the View Backup Media Contents dialog box. This situation is an example of why using intuitive names and descriptions for your backup sets can be very useful. See Figure 9.14.

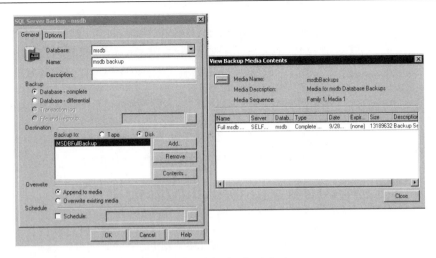

Figure 9.14.   Viewing the contents of the backup device.

Practice: Backing Up the msdb Database Directly Using SQL Server Enterprise Manager

In this practice you use the SQL Server Enterprise Manager directly to back up the msdb database.

▶ **To back up the msdb database directly using SQL Server Enterprise Manager**

1. In the SQL Server Enterprise Manager console tree, expand the Microsoft SQL Servers container, expand the SQL Server Group container, expand the default instance, and then expand Databases.

2. Right-click msdb, point to All Tasks, and then click Backup Database.

   The SQL Server Backup - Msdb dialog box appears with the General tab selected.

3. In the General tab, in the Name text box, type **Full msdb Database Backup #1**.

4. In the Description text box, type **Backup Set #1**.

5. Click the Add button.

   The Select Backup Destination dialog box appears.

6. Click the Backup Device option button.

7. Select MSDBFullBackup from the Backup Device drop-down list, and then click OK.

8. Click the Overwrite Existing Media option button and then click the Options tab.

9. Select the Verify Backup Upon Completion check box.

10. Select the Initialize And Label Media check box.

11. In the Media Set Name text box, type **msdbBackups**.

12. In the Media Set Description text box, type **Media for msdb Database Backups** and then click OK.

    The Backup Progress dialog box appears displaying the progress of the backup of the msdb database. Next, the Verify Progress dialog box appears displaying the progress of the verification of the msdb database backup. When the database backup is complete, a SQL Server Enterprise Manager message box appears.

13. Click OK to close the SQL Server Enterprise Manager message box.

14. Do not close SQL Server Enterprise Manager.

Perform Backups Using Transact-SQL

You can also perform backups using the Transact-SQL BACKUP DATABASE and BACKUP LOG commands. You can view the entire syntax, with all possible options, in SQL Server Books Online. Transact-SQL commands require the same information discussed earlier using SQL Server Enterprise Manager for database backups, but the syntax requires practice and a little patience. In addition, Transact-SQL provides a few additional parameters for additional control of your database backups. Most are for use only with tape devices, but the following options for all backup media are available only by using Transact-SQL.

- You can secure a backup set with a password. You must supply the password to restore the backup.

- You can secure a media set with a password. You must supply the password to restore any backup sets from the media set.

- You can restart an interrupted backup. This is particularly useful for large databases.

Although the BACKUP DATABASE and BACKUP LOG commands are initially intimidating, the following examples will help you become more comfortable with using these commands.

Performing a Full Database Backup

The BACKUP DATABASE command can be very simple or very complex. You can create a backup file on the fly, or use an existing backup device.

```
BACKUP DATABASE Northwind TO DISK = 'C:\SQLBackups\Temp.bak'
```

The preceding example performs a full database backup of the Northwind database to the C:\SQLBackups\Temp.bak file on disk.

```
BACKUP DATABASE Northwind TO NorthwindFullBackup
RESTORE VERIFYONLY FROM NorthwindFullBackup
```

The preceding example performs a full database backup of the Northwind database to the NorthwindFullBackup backup device, and then verifies the backup.

```
BACKUP DATABASE Northwind TO NorthwindFullBackup
WITH FORMAT ,
MEDIANAME = 'NorthwindBackups' ,
MEDIADESCRIPTION = 'Media for Northwind Database Backups' ,
NAME = 'Full Northwind Database Backup #1' ,
DESCRIPTION = 'BackupSet #1' ,
STATS = 25
```

The preceding example performs a full database backup of the Northwind database to the NorthwindFullBackup backup device. It initializes the media, creates the NorthwindBackups media set with a description of Media for Northwind Database Backups, and creates the Full Northwind Database Backup #1 backup set with a description of Backup Set #1. It also reports the progress of the backup in increments of 25 percent.

```
BACKUP DATABASE Northwind TO NWindDevice1, NWindDevice2 WITH MEDIANAME =
   'Media Set for Northwind Database Backups'
```

The preceding example performs a full database backup of the Northwind database to the NwindDevice1 and NwindDevice2 backup devices in parallel. SQL Server 2000 verifies that the media set is labeled Media Set for Northwind Database Backups before it begins writing the backup file to each backup device.

Performing a Differential Database Backup

To perform a differential database backup using the BACKUP DATABASE command, you simply use the WITH DIFFERENTIAL argument with any of the preceding examples (provided you have performed a full database backup first).

```
BACKUP DATABASE Northwind TO NorthwindDiffBackup WITH DIFFERENTIAL
```

The preceding example performs a differential database backup of the Northwind database to the NorthwindDiffBackup backup device.

Performing a File or Filegroup Backup

To perform a file or filegroup backup using the BACKUP DATABASE command, you add the FILE = *logical_filename* or the FILEGROUP = *logical_filegroup_name* argument to the *BACKUP DATABASE* statement.

```
BACKUP DATABASE Northwind FILEGROUP = 'SECOND_FG' TO NorthwindFGBackup
```

The preceding example performs a filegroup backup of the Second_FG filegroup in the Northwind database to the NorthwindFGBackup backup device.

Performing a Transaction Log Backup

Perform a transaction XE "transaction log backups:Transact-SQL" log backup using the BACKUP LOG command, using syntax that is almost identical to that for the BACKUP DATABASE command.

```
BACKUP LOG Northwind TO NorthwindTLogBackup
```

The preceding example performs a transaction log backup of the Northwind database to the NorthwindTLogBackup backup device.

```
BACKUP LOG Northwind TO NorthwindTLogBackup WITH NO_TRUNCATE
```

The preceding example performs a transaction log backup of the Northwind database to the NorthwindTLogBackup backup device, but does not truncate the transaction log (use this command when a disk containing a data file fails).

Practice: Performing Backups Using Transact-SQL

In this practice you use several Transact-SQL scripts to perform a full database backup, a differential database backup, and two transaction log backups of the SSEMDB database.

▶ **To perform backups using Transact-SQL**

1. Ensure that you are logged on to the SelfPacedSQL.MSFT domain controller as Administrator.
2. Click Start, point to Programs, point to Microsoft SQL Server, and then click Query Analyzer.
3. In the Connect To SQL Server dialog box, click OK to connect to SelfPaced-SQL using Windows authentication.
4. On the toolbar, click the Load SQL Script button.

   The Open Query File dialog box appears.
5. Open SSEMDB_Full.sql in the C:\SelfPacedSQL\CH_9 folder.

   A Transact-SQL script appears, which will create the Customer table in the SSEMDB database. It will populate the Customer table with 21 customers from the NewCustomerData1.txt file using a *BULK INSERT* statement. It will then perform a full database backup of the SSEMDB database using the SSEMDB-FullBackup backup device.
6. Press F5 to execute the *SSEMDB_Full.sql* statement.

   In the results pane, notice that the script added 21 customers to this newly created Customer table in the SSEMDB database. Also notice (click the Messages tab) that the SSEMDB database was successfully backed up, including both the data file and a single page from the transaction log file (there was no database activity during the backup).

7. On the toolbar, click the Load SQL Script button.

The Open Query File dialog box appears.

8. Open SSEMDB_TLog1.sql in the C:\SelfPacedSQL\CH_9 folder.

A Transact-SQL script appears, which will add two additional customers to the Customer table using an *INSERT* statement. It will then perform a transaction log backup of the SSEMDB database using the SSEMDBTLogBackup backup device.

9. On the toolbar, click the Execute Query button to execute the *SSEMDB_TLog1.sql* statement.

In the results pane, notice that two new customers (for a new total of 23 customers) were added to the Customer table in the SSEMDB database. Also notice (click the Messages tab) that the SSEMDB transaction log was successfully backed up.

10. On the toolbar, click the Load SQL Script button.

The Open Query File dialog box appears.

11. Open SSEMDB_Diff.sql in the C:\SelfPacedSQL\CH_9 folder.

A Transact-SQL script appears, which will add seven additional customers to the Customer table from the NewCustomerData2.txt file using a *BULK INSERT* statement. It will then perform a differential database backup of the SSEMDB database using the SSEMDBDiffBackup backup device.

12. On the toolbar, click the Execute Query button to execute the *SSEMDB_Diff.sql* statement.

In the results pane, notice that the script added seven new customers (for a new total of 30 customers) to the Customer table in the SSEMDB database. Also notice (click the Messages tab) that the SSEMDB database was successfully backed up, including both the data file and one page from the transaction log file (there was no database activity during the backup).

13. On the toolbar, click the Load SQL Script button.

The Open Query File dialog box appears.

14. Open SSEMDB_TLog2.sql in the C:\SelfPacedSQL\CH_9 folder.

A Transact-SQL script appears, which will add one additional customer to the Customer table using an *INSERT* statement. It will then perform a transaction log backup of the SSEMDB database using the SSEMDBTLogBackup backup device.

15. On the toolbar, click the Execute Query button to execute the *SSEMDB_TLog2.sql* statement.

In the results pane, notice that the script added one new customer (for a new total of 31 customers) to the Customer table in the SSEMDB database. Also notice (click the Messages tab) that the SSEMDB transaction log was successfully backed up.

16. On the toolbar, click the Load SQL Script button.

    The Open Query File dialog box appears.

17. Open SSEMDB_TLog3.sql in the C:\SelfPacedSQL\CH_9 folder.

    A Transact-SQL script appears, which will add one additional customer to the Customer table using an *INSERT* statement. It will then perform another transaction log backup of the SSEMDB database, again using the SSEMDBTLog-Backup backup device.

18. On the toolbar, click the Execute Query button to execute the *SSEMDB_TLog3.sql* statement.

    In the results pane, notice that the script added one new customer (for a new total of 32 customers) to the Customer table in the SSEMDB database. Also notice (click the Messages tab) that the SSEMDB transaction log was successfully backed up.

19. On the toolbar, click the Load SQL Script button.

    The Open Query File dialog box appears.

20. Open SSEMDB_Insert4.sql in the C:\SelfPacedSQL\CH_9 folder.

    A Transact-SQL script appears, which will add one additional customer to the Customer table using an *INSERT* statement. Notice that this insertion is not backed up.

21. On the toolbar, click the Execute Query button to execute the *SSEMDB_Insert4.sql* statement.

    In the results pane, notice that one new customer (for a new total of 33 customers) was added to the Customer table in the SSEMDB database.

22. Do not close SQL Query Analyzer.

Lesson Summary

You can use the SQL Server Enterprise Manager Create Database Backup Wizard to perform full database backups, differential database backups, and transaction log backups. You can also perform backups directly with SQL Server Enterprise Manager. This method allows you to perform any type of database backup. Transact-SQL allows you to fully script each type of database backup. You can specify a number of backup options for both the backup media and the backup set. Working with these properties using SQL Server Enterprise Manager helps you understand the Transact-SQL syntax for specifying the same options.

Lesson 3: Restoring a User Database

Now that you have learned how to perform database backups using SQL Server Enterprise Manager and Transact-SQL, you are ready to use these backups to perform data restorations. In this lesson, you will learn how to view database backups to help determine a restoration sequence. You will learn how to completely restore user databases using SQL Server Enterprise Manager and Transact-SQL. You will also learn how to recover a database to a specified point in time.

After this lesson, you will be able to

- View database and transaction log backup files to determine a restore sequence
- Perform a complete data restoration of a user database using SQL Server Enterprise Manager and Transact-SQL
- Recover a database to a specified point in time using SQL Server Enterprise Manager and Transact-SQL
- Restore a database to standby mode using SQL Server Enterprise Manager and Transact-SQL to determine its state before applying additional backup files

Estimated lesson time: 60 minutes

Determining the Data Restoration Sequence

When you need to perform a data restoration, you must begin by determining the most efficient sequence of backup files to use for accomplishing this task in the shortest time possible. SQL Server Enterprise Manager makes this task easy. Every time you perform any type of backup or restore, SQL Server 2000 records the details of the backup and the restore history in the msdb database. These details include such information as which devices or files the backup is stored on, who performed the backup, and at what time. When you are ready to perform a restoration of a database using SQL Server Enterprise Manager, it uses the information in the msdb system tables to tell you which backup files you need to use to perform the restoration in the quickest time possible. If the msdb database is damaged, you should restore the msdb database from backup before you restore any user databases. This will restore the backup and restore history for all databases on the SQL Server 2000 instance (provided you recently backed up the msdb database).

If you do not have a recent backup of the msdb database or are restoring to another SQL Server 2000 instance, SQL Server 2000 records sufficient information with each backup set to re-create the backup history in the msdb database. You can use SQL Server Enterprise Manager to read each backup file and add the information to the msdb database. SQL Server Enterprise Manager can then use this reconstructed backup history to identify the proper restoration sequence.

Once you have identified the restoration sequence, you need to identify the actual backup media that contains each backup set you want to use. If you labeled them well, this is a simple task. However, occasionally you will need to read the media set name and description to identify the correct backup media and the backup set name and description to identify each backup set on the backup media.

To view the contents of a backup device using SQL Server Enterprise Manager, expand the Management container, click Backup, and then in the details pane, right-click the backup device you want to view and click Properties. In the Backup Device Properties dialog box, the filename or tape drive associated with the backup device will be displayed. Click the View Contents button to display the contents of the backup device in the View Backup Media Contents dialog box. See Figure 9.15.

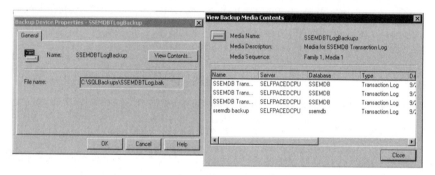

Figure 9.15. Viewing the contents of a backup device using SQL Server Enterprise Manager.

Note   If the backup device does not appear in the Backup container, you will need to re-create the backup history. Re-creating backup history will be covered toward the end of this lesson.

To view the contents of a backup device with Transact-SQL, three commands are available to you to retrieve information regarding the media sets and backup sets. Table 9.2 describes the three commands.

Table 9-2.   Information Retrieval Commands in Transact-SQL

Transact-SQL Command	Description
RESTORE LABELONLY	Retrieves backup media header information, including the media set name and description.
RESTORE HEADERONLY	Retrieves backup set information, including the backup set name and description for every backup set on a particular backup device. This includes internal information regarding LSNs. SQL Server uses this information to determine what backup files it needs to apply and in what order.
RESTORE FILELISTONLY	Retrieves a list of each data and log file backed up within a particular backup set.

Practice: Retrieving Backup Media Information

In this practice you will retrieve backup media information from a backup device using SQL Server Enterprise Manager and Transact-SQL.

▶ **To retrieve backup media information**

1. Ensure that you are logged on to the SelfPacedSQL.MSFT domain controller as Administrator.
2. In the SQL Server Enterprise Manager console tree, expand the default instance, expand the Management container, and then click Backup.

    The backup devices for this SQL Server 2000 instance are displayed in the details pane.
3. In the details pane, right-click SSEMDBTLogBackup and then click Properties.

    The Backup Device Properties – SSEMTLogBackup dialog box appears displaying the filename associated with this backup device.
4. Click the View Contents button.

    The View Backup Media Contents dialog box appears, displaying the contents of the SSEMTLogBackup device. Details regarding three transaction log backup sets appear.
5. Switch to SQL Query Analyzer.
6. On the toolbar, click the Load SQL Script button.

    The Open Query File dialog box appears.
7. Open QueryHeaders.sql in the C:\SelfPacedSQL\CH_9 folder.

    A Transact-SQL script appears, containing five separate queries, which will retrieve information from the SSEMDBTLogBackup backup device.

8. On the toolbar, click the Execute Query button to execute the *QueryHeaders.sql* statement.

   In the results pane, notice five separate result sets. The first result set displays information regarding the media set itself. The second result set displays information regarding each backup set recorded on this backup media. The final three result sets display information regarding each data and transaction log file in each of the three backup sets recorded on this backup media.

9. Compare the information available regarding the backup sets using SQL Server Enterprise Manager and Transact-SQL.

10. Switch to SQL Server Enterprise Manager.

11. Click the Close button to close the View Backup Media Contents dialog box, and then click Cancel to close the Backup Device Properties – SSEMDBTLog-Backup dialog box.

12. Do not close SQL Server Enterprise Manager or SQL Query Analyzer.

Performing Restorations Using SQL Server Enterprise Manager

SQL Server Enterprise Manager provides a simple graphical interface to interactively perform data restorations. You may need to perform a data restoration because a disk containing a data file failed, because an entire SQL Server 2000 installation failed, or because you want to recover data to an earlier point in time.

Note   Before you attempt to restore a backup to a database that is still functioning, be sure to restrict user access to it.

Restoration of an Entire Database from the Failure of a Data Disk

If a disk containing a data file fails, SQL Server Enterprise Manager will display the database containing the damaged data file as suspect (unless you are using RAID). See Figure 9.16.

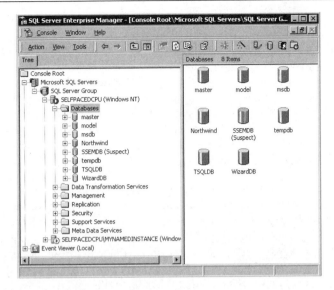

Figure 9.16.   A damaged data file displayed as suspect.

If you discover you have a suspect database, you should immediately back up the transaction log without truncation before you attempt any restoration of your data (otherwise, you will lose all changes since the most recent transaction log backup). Backing up the current transaction log (using the Without Truncation option) allows you to recover up to the point of failure. See Figure 9.17.

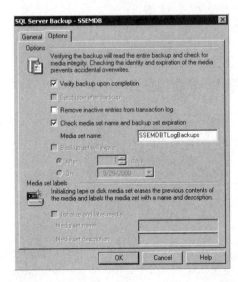

Figure 9.17.   Selecting transaction log backup options.

Next, you should replace the failed disk. If your data is using RAID for fault toler-ance, all that you need to do is to simply add the new drive to the RAID system. If you do not have RAID, you must restore your data to the new disk before your users can access the damaged database. You can either perform a full database res-toration or perform a file or filegroup restoration (see the following section). In either case, to begin the restoration, expand the Databases container, right-click the suspect database in the details pane, point to All Tasks, and then click Restore Database. SQL Server Enterprise Manager will determine the most efficient com-plete database restoration path for this database using the backup information stored in the msdb database. See Figure 9.18.

If one of the backup sets identified by SQL Server Enterprise Manager for use in the restoration of the database is missing in the Restore Database dialog box, you can select other combinations of backup sets to accomplish the data restoration task. SQL Server Enterprise Manager will assist you in selecting a combination of backup sets that you can use to complete the restoration. For example, if you want to start with an earlier full backup than the one selected, click the First Backup To Restore drop-down list and then select an earlier full database backup. SQL Server Enterprise Manager will quickly determine the requisite backup sets given this ear-lier starting point for the data restoration and will display them in the list box at the bottom of the dialog box.

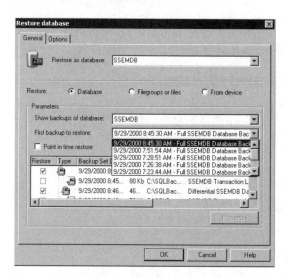

Figure 9.18.   Specifying backup sets to restore.

If you want to view information regarding the content of a particular backup set, select the backup set in the list box at the bottom of the dialog box and then click the Properties button. The properties of the backup set will appear in the Backup Set Properties dialog box, including information you provided when you created the backup set and information recorded by SQL Server 2000 when it performed the backup. See Figure 9.19.

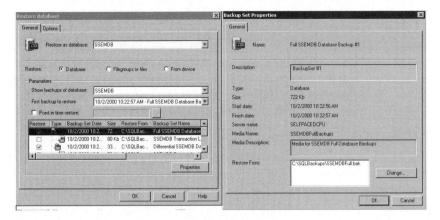

Figure 9.19.   Viewing the properties of a backup set.

If the location of the backup file has moved from the original location recorded in the msdb database, you can click the Change button in the Backup Set Properties dialog box and then specify the new location. For example, you may have originally written the backup file to disk, but it may now be on tape. Or, it may be stored on a network disk in a different location.

After you have determined which backup sets you want to restore, click the Options tab in the Restore Database dialog box to set additional data restoration properties. See Figure 9.20.

Figure 9.20.   Setting additional restoration properties.

In the Options tab under the Restore As column, you can change the physical location of each data file being restored. By default, data files are restored to their original location (overwriting any files with the same names located there). You can also select the recovery completion state. By default, SQL Server 2000 will restore each backup set you selected, and after the last backup has been applied, it will recover the database. This is equivalent to the Transact-SQL recovery option. If you are not applying all of the backups that you want to apply, you must change this setting to allow you to apply additional transaction logs. You have two choices.

- You can choose to leave the database nonoperational but able to restore additional transaction logs. This is equivalent to the Transact-SQL no-recovery option.

- You can choose to leave the database read-only and able to restore additional transaction log files. This is equivalent to the Transact-SQL standby mode option. Selecting the read-only option requires the specification of an undo file that will be created during the restoration. This undo file is created by default in the Backup folder and is named UNDO_*DatabaseName*.DAT. Use a different name to avoid overwriting previous undo files, if necessary. This undo file contains rollback changes that are made to the database to allow you to view the database in a logically consistent state while in standby mode. These consist of incomplete transactions that SQL Server 2000 does not yet know the completion status of. If you choose to apply additional transaction logs, these rolled-back transactions in the undo file will be rolled forward before additional transaction logs are applied.

After you click OK, the selected backup sets are restored, and your database is either recovered or left in a no-recovery state for more transaction logs to be applied.

Restoring a Data File or Filegroup

If you want to perform a file or filegroup restoration rather than a complete database restoration, click the Filegroups Or Files option button in the General tab of the Restore Database dialog box to see a display of all files and filegroups that have been backed up, along with all transaction log files. This includes all data files backed up as part of a full database backup as well as files backed up explicitly as a file or filegroup backup. See Figure 9.21.

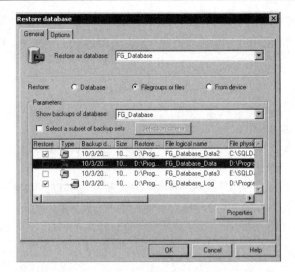

Figure 9.21.   Selecting filegroups or files to restore.

Once you select one or more data files to restore, SQL Server Enterprise Manager selects the transaction log files that must be applied with the data files you selected in order to bring the entire database to a consistent state.

When you click the Select A Subset Of Backup Sets option button, you can use the Selection Criteria button to filter the backup sets based on the data file drive, the date of the backup set, or backup sets of particular files and filegroups only. Remember, to restore a database using a file or filegroup backup, you must restore all transaction log files more recent than the data files you are restoring in order to ensure that your database is in a consistent state. See Figure 9.22.

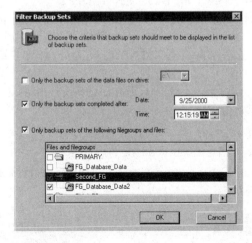

Figure 9.22.   Filtering the criteria for displaying backup sets.

Practice: Performing a Complete Database Restoration

In this practice you will perform a complete database restoration using SQL Server Enterprise Manager.

▶ **To perform a complete database restoration**

1. Ensure that you are logged on to the SelfPacedSQL.MSFT domain controller as Administrator.

2. In the SQL Server Enterprise Manager console tree, right-click your default instance and then click Stop.

   A SQL Server Enterprise Manager dialog box appears asking if you are sure you want to stop the SQL Server Service.

3. Click the Yes button.

   A Service Control Failure dialog box appears asking if you also want to stop the SQL Server Agent service.

4. Click the Yes button.

5. Open Windows Explorer.

6. In the Address window, type **C:\Program Files\Microsoft SQL Server\MSSQL\Data** and then press ENTER on your keyboard.

7. Move the SSEMDB_Data1_Data.mdf file to your desktop.

8. Close Windows Explorer.

9. In the SQL Server Enterprise Manager console tree, expand your default instance.

   After a few moments, notice that SQL Server Enterprise Manager starts the SQL Server service and connects to the default instance.

10. In the console tree, click the Databases container.

    The databases appear in the details pane, with the SSEMDB database marked as suspect (because you moved the data file).

11. In the details pane, right-click SSEMDB, point to All Tasks, and then click Backup Database.

    The SQL Server Backup – SSEMDB dialog box appears.

12. Click the Transaction Log option button.

13. In the Destination group box, click the Add button.

    The Select Backup Destination dialog box appears.

14. Click the Backup Device option button and then select SSEMDBTLogBackup in the Backup Device drop-down list.

15. Click OK.

16. Verify that SSEMDBTLogBackup is the only device listed in the Destination group box.

17. Verify that the Append To Media option button is selected.

18. Click the Options tab.

19. Clear the Remove Inactive Entries From Transaction Log check box and then click OK.

    The Backup Progress dialog box appears displaying the progress of the backup. When the backup has completed, a SQL Server Enterprise Manager message box appears stating the backup operation was a success.

20. Click OK.

21. In the SQL Server Enterprise Manager console tree, right-click SSEMDB, point to All Tasks, and then click Restore Database.

    The Restore Database dialog box appears, displaying the backup sets required to completely restore the SSEMDB database. Notice that SQL Server Enterprise Manager has selected the original full database backup, the differential database backup, and all transaction log backups since the differential database backup (a total of three out of four transaction logs are selected).

22. Click OK to completely restore the SSEMDB database.

    The Restore Progress dialog box appears displaying the progress of the restoration. When the restoration is complete, a SQL Server Enterprise Manager message box appears stating that the restoration of the SSEMDB database was completed successfully.

23. Click OK.

24. In the console tree, expand SSEMDB and then click Tables.

    The tables in the SSEMDB database appear.

25. In the details pane, right-click Customer, point to Open Table, and then click Return All Rows.

    The Data In Table 'Customer' In 'SSEMDB' On 'SelfPacedCPU' window appears displaying the contents of the Customer table after the restoration.

26. Verify that SQL Server Enterprise Manager restored all 33 rows and then close the Data In Table 'Customer' In 'SSEMDB' On 'SelfPacedCPU' window.

27. Do not close SQL Server Enterprise Manager.

Restoring a Database to a Different SQL Server 2000 Instance

You may need to restore a database to a different SQL Server 2000 instance for a variety of reasons. For example, you may want to perform a temporary restoration of a database to an earlier point in time to recover some data accidentally deleted without rolling back your entire production database to that point in time and without taking the entire database down.

When restoring a database to a second SQL Server 2000 instance using SQL Server Enterprise Manager, you must first create the database in SQL Server into which you will restore the database. Generally, you should use the same database name and database file paths as the one you are restoring. If you choose a different name, you will have to select the Force Restore Over Existing Database check box in the Options tab of the Restore Database dialog box when you perform the restoration to the second instance of SQL Server 2000. In addition, if you choose to restore to a different physical path, you will need to adjust the restoration path for the database files.

After you have created the database in the SQL Server instance into which you will restore the database, you must use the information stored with each backup set in the original database to perform the restoration. The reason for this is that the msdb database in this SQL Server 2000 instance has no knowledge of any backups of the database you want to restore. You begin by right-clicking the database in the console tree for the SQL Server 2000 instance that you want to restore, pointing to All Tasks, and then clicking Restore Database. In the General tab of the Restore Database dialog box, click the From Device option button. See Figure 9.23.

Next, you need to click the Select Devices button to select a backup device from which to restore data. However, because this instance has no knowledge of any backup devices for the database being restored, you need to click the type of device (disk or tape), in the Choose Restore Devices dialog box, and then click the Add button to point SQL Server Enterprise Manager toward a backup device from which to read backed up data. See Figure 9.24.

Figure 9.23.   Selecting a device from which to restore.

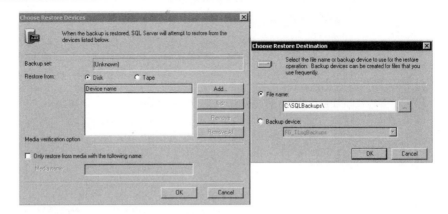

Figure 9.24.   Adding a device from which to read.

After you select a file or tape drive from which to restore data, you can choose among several options. You can view the contents of each backup set on the backup device; you can restore a specified backup set from the backup device and either recover or leave the database able to restore additional transaction logs; or you can choose to read the backup set information from a specified device and add it to the backup history in the msdb database. See Figure 9.25.

Whichever way you choose to proceed, you must work with one backup set at a time. Thus, if you want to read backup set information into the msdb database from a different instance of SQL Server 2000 from three backup devices containing a total of seven backup sets, you will have to read from seven separate backup sets to either perform the restoration or to restore information into the msdb database. In this particular scenario, using Transact-SQL is much quicker than using SQL Server Enterprise Manager.

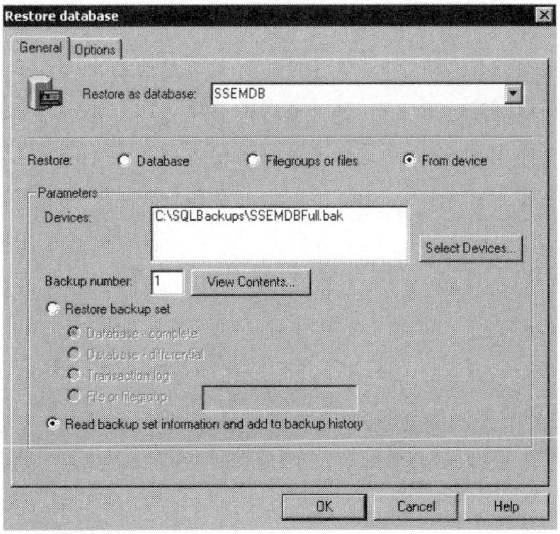

Figure 9.25.   Choosing restore method options.

Recovery of a Database to a Point in Time

If you determine that you need to restore a database to a specified point in time, you may need to restore one or more backup sets and leave the database in no recovery or standby mode between each transaction log restoration. Standby mode allows you to view the condition of the database at the end of each restoration before you apply additional transaction log files. Once you have determined the point in time to which you need to recover, you select the Point In Time Restore check box in the General tab of the Restore Database dialog box, and then choose the date and time at which you need recovery of the database to be halted. See Figure 9.26.

You cannot select a time earlier than the earliest transaction log that you select. In addition, you cannot choose to leave a database nonoperational and able to restore additional transaction logs when you choose point-in-time restore.

Note   Although you can recover to a named mark as well as a specific point in time, you must use Transact-SQL to recover to a named mark.

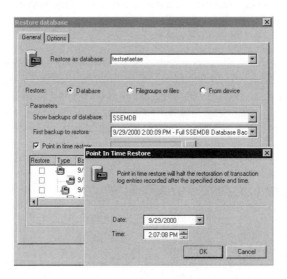

Figure 9.26.   Selecting a point in time for recovery.

Practice: Performing a Database Restoration to a Specified Point in Time

In this practice you will perform a database restoration to a specified point in time using SQL Server Enterprise Manager.

▶ **To perform a database restoration to a specified point in time**

1. Ensure that you are logged on to the SelfPacedSQL.MSFT domain controller as Administrator.

2. In the SQL Server Enterprise Manager console tree, expand your default instance and then expand Databases.

3. In the console tree, right-click SSEMDB, point to All Tasks, and then click Restore Database.

   The Restore Database dialog box appears.

4. In the Parameters group box, clear all backup sets selected by SQL Server Enterprise Manager and then select the Full SSEMDB Database Backup #1 backup set check box. Verify that no other backup sets are selected.

5. Click the Options tab.

6. Click the Leave Database Nonoperational But Able To Restore Additional Transaction Logs option button, and then click OK.

   The Restore Progress dialog box appears displaying the progress of the restoration. When the restoration is complete, a SQL Server Enterprise Manager message box appears stating that the restoration of the SSEMDB database was completed successfully.

7. Click OK.

   In the console tree, notice the SSEMDB database indicates it is loading. You cannot view any database objects in the database.

8. In the console tree, right-click SSEMDB, point to All Tasks, and then click Restore Database.

   Notice that you can perform additional transaction log restorations, but you cannot apply the differential database restoration without restoring the original full database backup.

9. Clear all backup sets selected by SQL Server Enterprise Manager and then select the Full SSEMDB Database Backup #1 backup set check box. Verify that no other backup sets are selected.

10. Click the Options tab.

11. Click the Leave Database Read-Only And Able To Restore Additional Transaction Logs option button, and then click OK.

    The Restore Progress dialog box appears displaying the progress of the restoration. When the restoration is complete, a SQL Server Enterprise Manager message box appears stating that the restoration of the SSEMDB database was completed successfully.

12. Click OK.

    In the console tree, notice that the SSEMDB database now indicates it is read-only.

13. In the console tree, click Tables.

14. In the details pane, right-click Customer, point to Open Table, and then click Return All Rows.

    The Data In Table 'Customer' In 'SSEMDB' On 'SELFPACEDCPU' window appears displaying the contents of the Customer table after the restoration.

    Notice that only 21 rows were restored and then close the Data In Table 'Customer' In 'SSEMDB' On 'SELFPACEDCPU' window.

15. In the console tree, right-click SSEMDB, point to All Tasks, and then click Restore Database.

    Notice that SQL Server Enterprise Manager selects the remaining transaction logs for restoration.

16. Clear all backup sets selected by SQL Server Enterprise Manager and then select the SSEMDB Transaction Log Backup #1 backup set check box. Verify that no other backup sets are selected.

17. Click the Options tab.

18. Click the Leave Database Read-Only And Able To Restore Additional Transaction Logs option button, and then click OK.

    The Restore Progress dialog box appears displaying the progress of the restoration. When the restoration is complete, a SQL Server Enterprise Manager message box appears stating that the restoration of the SSEMDB database was completed successfully.

19. Click OK.

20. In the console tree, click Tables.

21. In the details pane, right-click Customer, point to Open Table, and then click Return All Rows.

    The Data In Table 'Customer' In 'SSEMDB' On 'SELFPACEDCPU' window appears displaying the contents of the Customer table after the restoration.

22. Notice that 23 rows were restored (two additional rows added) and then close the Data In Table 'Customer' In 'SSEMDB' On 'SELFPACEDCPU' window.

23. In the console tree, right-click SSEMDB, point to All Tasks, and then click Restore Database.

    Notice that SQL Server Enterprise Manager selects the remaining transaction logs for restoration.

24. Clear all backup sets selected by SQL Server Enterprise Manager and then select the SSEMDB Transaction Log Backup #2 backup set check box. Verify that no other backup sets are selected.

25. Click the Options tab.

26. Click the Leave Database Read-Only And Able To Restore Additional Transaction Logs option button, and then click OK.

   The Restore Progress dialog box appears displaying the progress of the restoration. When the restoration is complete, a SQL Server Enterprise Manager message box appears stating that the restoration of the SSEMDB database was completed successfully.

27. Click OK.

28. In the console tree, click Tables.

29. In the details pane, right-click Customer, point to Open Table, and then click Return All Rows.

   The Data In Table 'Customer' In 'SSEMDB' On 'SELFPACEDCPU' window appears displaying the contents of the Customer table after the restoration.

30. Notice that 31 rows were restored (8 additional rows added) and then close the Data In Table 'Customer' In 'SSEMDB' On 'SELFPACEDCPU' window.

31. In the console tree, right-click SSEMDB, point to All Tasks, and then click Restore Database.

   Notice that SQL Server Enterprise Manager selects the remaining transaction logs for restoration.

32. Expand the Backup Set Date column so you can view the entire date and time.

33. Select the Point In Time Restore check box.

   The Point in Time Restore dialog box appears.

34. Select a time 15 seconds later than the time of the third transaction log backup and then click OK.

35. Click OK to perform the point-in-time restoration.

   The Restore Progress dialog box appears displaying the progress of the restoration. When the process is finished, a SQL Server Enterprise Manager message box appears stating that the restoration of the SSEMDB database was completed successfully.

36. Click OK.

   Given the small data set we are working with, this practice cannot properly demonstrate this feature. The choice of 15 seconds later is arbitrary and will not show any difference compared to restoring through the end of Transaction Log Backup #3. However, in a production system, it would.

37. In the console tree, click Tables.

38. In the details pane, right-click Customer, point to Open Table, and then click Return All Rows.

   The Data In Table 'Customer' In 'SSEMDB' On 'SelfPacedCPU' window appears displaying the contents of the Customer table after the restoration.

39. Notice that 32 rows were restored, and then close the Data In Table 'Customer' In 'SSEMDB' On 'SelfPacedCPU' window. The thirty-third row was not added.

40. Close SQL Server Enterprise Manager.

Performing Restorations Using Transact-SQL

You can also perform restorations using the Transact-SQL RESTORE DATABASE and RESTORE LOG commands. You can view the entire syntax for each of these commands, with all possible options, in SQL Server Books Online. Transact-SQL commands require the same information discussed earlier with SQL Server Enterprise Manager database restorations, but the syntax requires practice and sometimes patience. In addition, Transact-SQL provides a few additional parameters for additional control of your backup. Most of these parameters are for use only with tape devices, but the following options for all backup media are available only using Transact-SQL.

- You can restrict access to the newly restored database to database administrators as part of the restore process.
- You can move a database to a new location using the MOVE option.
- You can supply a password.
- You can restart an interrupted restore.
- You can recover to a named mark.

Like the BACKUP commands, the RESTORE DATABASE and RESTORE LOG commands are initially intimidating. The following examples will help you learn how to use these commands. Perhaps the most important difference between using SQL Server Enterprise Manager and Transact-SQL is that you must determine and specify the correct backup sets in the correct order, including the specification of the backup set number on the media set.

Restoring a Complete Database

The RESTORE DATABASE and RESTORE LOG commands can be very simple or very complex.

```
RESTORE DATABASE Northwind FROM DISK = 'C:\SQLBackups\Temp.bak'
```

The preceding example restores a full database backup of the Northwind database from the C:\SQLBackups\Temp.bak file on disk.

```
RESTORE DATABASE Northwind FROM NorthwindFullBackup WITH NORECOVERY
RESTORE DATABASE Northwind FROM NorthwindDiffBackup WITH FILE = 2,
NORECOVERY
RESTORE LOG Northwind FROM NorthwindTLogBackup WITH FILE = 4,
NORECOVERY
RESTORE LOG Northwind FROM NorthwindTLogBackup2 WITH FILE = 5
```

The preceding example restores a full database backup of the Northwind database from the NorthwindFullBackup backup device, followed by a restoration of a differential database backup (backup set 2 on the backup device), and then followed by the restoration of two transaction log backups (backup sets 4 and 5 on the backup device). Recovery occurs after the second transaction log is restored.

Restoring a Data File or Filegroup

```
RESTORE DATABASE Northwind FILE = 'Second_Data_File'
FROM File_Backup WITH RESTRICTED_USER, NORECOVERY, STATS = 25
RESTORE LOG Northwind FROM NorthwindTLogBackup WITH FILE = 2
```

The preceding example restores a backup of a secondary data file for the Northwind database from the File_Backup backup device with no recovery and provides notification of the progress of the restoration after each 25 percent completes. The restoration of the transaction log backup follows (backup set 2 on the backup device), and then the database is recovered. After recovery, database access is restricted to database administrators.

Restoration Using the Move Option

```
RESTORE DATABASE Northwind FROM NorthwindFullBackup
WITH NORECOVERY ,
MEDIANAME = 'NorthwindBackups' ,
MEDIAPASSWORD = 'my_password' ,
MOVE = 'Northwind' TO 'D:\SQLDATA\NwindNew.mdf' ,
MOVE = 'NorthwindLog' TO 'E:\SQLLogs\NwindNewLog.ldf' ,
RESTORE LOG Northwind FROM NorthwindTLogBackup
```

The preceding example restores a full database backup of the Northwind database, followed by a restoration of the transaction log. It specifies that the data file is moved to D:\SQLDATA\NwindNew.mdf and that the log file is moved to E:\SQLLogs\NwindNewLog.ldf. Finally, it also specifies that the media set name, NorthwindBackups, must appear on the backup media being restored.

Restoring to Standby Mode

```
RESTORE DATABASE Northwind FROM NorthwindFullBackup WITH NORECOVERY
RESTORE LOG Northwind FROM NorthwindTLogBackup WITH FILE = 4 ,
NORECOVERY
RESTORE LOG Northwind FROM NorthwindTLogBackup WITH FILE = 5 ,
STANDBY = TO 'D:\SQL\UNDO.tmp'
```

The preceding example restores a full database backup of the Northwind database from the NorthwindFullBackup backup device, followed by the restoration of two transaction log backups (backup sets 4 and 5 on the backup device). Recovery to standby mode occurs after the second transaction log is restored.

Restoring to a Specified Point in Time

```
RESTORE DATABASE Northwind FROM NorthwindFullBackup WITH NORECOVERY
RESTORE LOG Northwind FROM NorthwindTLogBackup WITH FILE = 4 ,
NORECOVERY
RESTORE LOG Northwind FROM NorthwindTLogBackup WITH FILE = 5 , RECOVERY,

STOPAT = 'Oct 2, 2000 5:08:32 PM'
```

The preceding example restores a full database backup of the Northwind database from the NorthwindFullBackup backup device, and then followed by the restoration of two transaction log backups (backup sets 4 and 5 on the backup device). Recovery to October 2, 2000 at 5:08:32 P.M. occurs after the second transaction log is restored.

Practice: Performing Restorations Using Transact-SQL

In this practice you use several Transact-SQL scripts to perform a restoration of a full database backup, a differential database backup, and two transaction log backups of the SSEMDB database.

▶ **To perform restorations using Transact-SQL**

1. Ensure that you are logged on to the SelfPacedSQL.MSFT domain controller as Administrator.
2. Switch to SQL Server Query Analyzer.
3. On the SQL Query Analyzer toolbar, click the Load SQL Script button.

   The Open Query File dialog box appears.
4. Open SSEMDB_Restore1.sql in the C:\SelfPacedSQL\CH_9 folder.

   A Transact-SQL script appears, which will restore the SSEMDB full database backup, followed by the SSEMDB differential database backup, and then followed by the restoration of two transaction log backups. The database is left in standby mode using an undo file. The script also contains a *SELECT* statement to display the results of the restoration.
5. On the toolbar, click the Execute Query button to execute the *SSEMDB_Restore1.sql* statement.

   In the results pane, notice that 32 customers were restored. Also notice the restoration of each backup set (click the Messages tab).
6. Open SQL Server Enterprise Manager.
7. In the console tree, expand SQL Server Group, expand your default instance, and then expand Databases.

   Notice that the SSEMDB database is in standby mode (read-only).
8. Switch to SQL Query Analyzer.
9. On the toolbar, click the Load SQL Script button.

The Open Query File dialog box appears.

10. Open SSEMDB_Restore2.sql in the C:\SelfPacedSQL\CH_9 folder.

    A Transact-SQL script appears, which will restore the final transaction log backup file and then perform a recovery of the database. The script also contains a *SELECT* statement to display the results of the restoration.

11. On the toolbar, click the Execute Query button to execute the *SSEMDB_Restore2.sql* statement.

    In the results pane, notice that all 33 customers were restored. Also notice the restoration of each backup set (click the Messages tab).

12. Switch to SQL Server Enterprise Manager.

13. In the console tree, expand your default instance, right-click Databases, and then click Refresh.

    Notice that the SSEMDB database is no longer in standby (read-only) mode.

14. Close both SQL Server Enterprise Manager and SQL Query Analyzer.

Lesson Summary

You can use SQL Server Enterprise Manager or Transact-SQL to perform database restorations. When you use SQL Server Enterprise Manager, you are assisted in restoring backup files in the correct sequence. When you use Transact-SQL, you must determine the sequence on your own. Both SQL Server Enterprise Manager and Transact-SQL provide tools for querying a backup media to determine the contents.

Lesson 4: Restoring and Rebuilding System Databases

If your master database becomes corrupt or if you lose your entire SQL Server 2000 installation, you will need to either restore your master database or rebuild your system databases. In this lesson you will learn how to restore the backup of your master database. You will also learn to rebuild your system databases if they are no longer functioning.

After this lesson, you will be able to

- Restore the master database from backup
- Rebuild the system databases

Estimated lesson time: 15 minutes

Restoring the Master Database

If your master database is functioning but damaged in some fashion (such as the deletion of all logins), you can restore the master database using the most recent full database backup of the master database. Any changes to the master database since the most recent database backup will be lost. You should script database objects when you create them and save the scripts. You should also mirror the system databases using RAID 1 where possible.

To restore the master database, start SQL Server 2000 in single-user mode with the –m option in the Command Prompt window or from the Run dialog box.

```
Sqlservr -m
```

The preceding command starts SQL Server 2000 as an application in a command-prompt window. The text you see when you start SQL Server 2000 as an application is the same text you see in the SQL Server error log. See Figure 9.27.

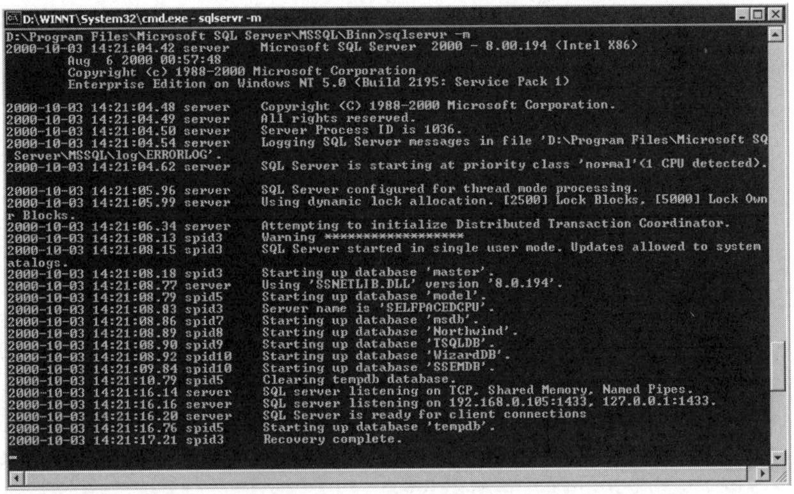

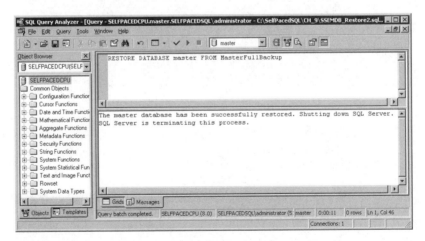

Figure 9.27. Starting SQL Server 2000 as an application in a command-prompt window.

Next, start SQL Query Analyzer and restore your most recent backup of the master database using the same commands you use to restore any user database.

```
RESTORE DATABASE master FROM MasterFullBackup
```

The preceding example restores the master database from the MasterFullBackup backup device. See Figure 9.28.

Figure 9.28. Restoring the master database.

After the restoration of the master database is complete, the SQL Server 2000 application running in single-user mode will stop. You can then restart SQL Server 2000 normally. Assuming that your backup of the master database was current, you are back in business. If not, you will need to re-create database objects and perhaps reattach user databases. You may also need to restore other system databases, depending upon the reason for the restoration of the master database.

Rebuilding the System Databases

If your master database has ceased functioning, you cannot recover quite this easily. In this case, you must rebuild the system databases from scratch (or possibly reinstall SQL Server 2000). To rebuild the system databases, use the Rebuildm.exe utility located in the C:\Program Files\Microsoft SQL Server\80\Tools\Binn folder. When you use the Rebuildm utility, you use the original data files for each of the system databases to rebuild each system database to their original condition in the Rebuild Master dialog box. You must have the original installation files available, either on a local drive or on a network drive. See Figure 9.29.

Note   Remove the Read-only attribute from the original installation files, or the Rebuildm utility will fail.

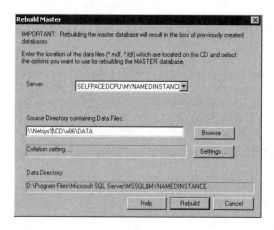

Figure 9.29.   Rebuilding the master database.

Click the Rebuild button to begin the process. You receive a warning in a Rebuild Master dialog box that you are about to rebuild and overwrite all of your system databases. See Figure 9.30.

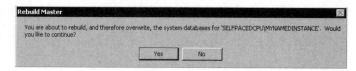

Figure 9.30.   The Rebuild Master warning dialog box.

After the rebuild is complete, you will need to restore your master database in the manner described earlier. Next, restore each system database, particularly the msdb database. If you have customized the model database, restore it. If you are using replication, you will need to restore the distribution database. Replication is covered in Chapter 15. Finally, you may need to restore or reattach any system databases that were affected by the failure of the system databases.

Lesson Summary

If your master database becomes corrupt, you may need to restore or rebuild it. Restoring the master database requires starting SQL Server 2000 in single-user mode. Rebuilding the master database requires rebuilding all system databases using the original installation data files for the system databases. If you must rebuild the system databases, restore these databases from backup to recover to the point of your most recent backups. Any system database activity since your most recent backups will have to be manually regenerated. Finally, reattaching user databases may be required. This is faster than performing a full restore.

Review

Here are some questions to help you determine whether you have learned enough to move on to the next chapter. If you have difficulty answering these questions, review the material in this chapter before beginning the next chapter. The answers for these questions are located in the Appendix, "Questions and Answers."

1. You regularly perform full, differential, and transaction log backups to disk. Are there any other backup tasks that you should perform regularly to protect your database from data loss?

2. You are a new database administrator. You want to create Transact-SQL scripts to automate the backup of your database. However, the syntax is imposing. What are several good methods for familiarizing yourself with the Transact-SQL syntax and the various backup options?

3. What is a major advantage to using SQL Server Enterprise Manager for performing database restorations, rather than Transact-SQL?

4. What is the major difference between performing a restoration of the master database and all other databases?

C H A P T E R   1 0

Managing Access to SQL Server 2000

About This Chapter

Before you place your SQL Server 2000 database into production, you must configure security to permit appropriate access for users and administrators. In this chapter, you will learn how SQL Server 2000 controls access to the server itself. Next, you will learn how SQL Server 2000 controls access to databases, including an introduction to server-wide and database-level permissions. Finally, you will learn to create security accounts (logins) for users using Windows authentication and SQL Server authentication.

Before You Begin

To complete this chapter, you must have

- A computer that meets or exceeds the minimum hardware requirements listed in Table 2.1, "Hardware Requirements," in Lesson 1 of Chapter 2.
- Microsoft Windows 2000 Server running on your computer on an NTFS partition.
- A computer with a NetBIOS name of SelfPacedCPU, configured as a domain controller in the SelfPacedSQL.MSFT domain.
- Installed a default instance and at least one named instance of SQL Server 2000 (see Chapter 2).
- Created the SSEMDB database using the CreateDB.sql script (see Chapter 6).

Lesson 1: Understanding the Authentication Process

Before a user can perform any activities within a database or perform server-wide tasks, SQL Server 2000 must authenticate the user. In this lesson, you will learn about the two authentication mechanisms used by SQL Server 2000 for authentication. You will learn the appropriate use of each mode, including the security implications of allowing SQL Server logins. Finally, you will learn about passing user authentication information between SQL Server 2000 instances for distributed queries and file system access.

After this lesson, you will be able to

- Describe how SQL Server 2000 authenticates users
- Choose between SQL Server 2000 authentication modes
- Change SQL Server 2000 authentication modes
- Enable security account delegation between SQL Server 2000 instances

Estimated lesson time: 15 minutes

Understanding the SQL Server 2000 Authentication Process

Before a user can perform a task or access a database within SQL Server 2000, a database administrator must first create a login granting that user permission to access SQL Server 2000 (and then grant that login permissions within SQL Server 2000). A login is either linked to a specific Windows 2000 (or Windows NT 4.0) user or group, or to a security account created within SQL Server 2000 itself (a SQL Server login). Lesson 3 covers how to create logins using SQL Server 2000 security accounts and Windows 2000 users and groups. Chapter 11 covers granting and managing login permissions within SQL Server 2000.

When a user attempts to access a SQL Server 2000 instance, the user (either directly or through an application) requests a type of authentication and presents identification credentials. The user can request one of two types of authentication, Windows authentication or SQL Server authentication. SQL Server 2000 must verify that the user is a permitted user before allowing access. This means validating the presented credentials for the user.

Windows Authentication

If the user is already authenticated on the Windows domain as a valid Windows user, SQL Server 2000 can be requested to trust this authentication by the operating system and allow the user access to SQL Server 2000 based on those credentials. In this case, the user requesting access presents (this is invisible to the user) either a Kerberos ticket (Windows 2000) or access token (Windows NT 4.0) to SQL Server 2000 as verification of his or her identity. SQL Server 2000 verifies the authenticity of the Kerberos ticket or the access token and then compares the user with the list of Windows users and groups permitted (but not denied) access. Based on this information, SQL Server 2000 then either grants or denies access.

Note   You call a connection using Windows authentication a trusted connection.

SQL Server Authentication

If the user requesting access either has not been authenticated on the Windows domain or wants to connect using a SQL Server 2000 security account, the user can request that SQL Server 2000 directly authenticate the user based upon the submission of a user name and password (if SQL Server 2000 is configured to permit SQL Server authentication). If the user requests SQL Server authentication, SQL Server 2000 compares the user name submitted against the list of SQL Server 2000 security accounts. If SQL Server finds the submitted user name in the sysxlogins table, SQL Server 2000 then encrypts the submitted password and compares it with the encrypted password in this table. Based on this information, SQL Server 2000 then grants or denies access.

Note   The user name and password are submitted to SQL Server 2000 in clear text unless both the client and the server Net-Libraries are using SSL encryption for the entire session.

Comparing Windows Authentication and SQL Server Authentication

Table 10.1 compares the security capabilities of these two types of authentication.

Client Net-Libraries and Authentication

SQL Server 2000 clients use an enabled client Net-Library to communicate with a server Net-Library on a SQL Server 2000 instance. To support the desired network protocol, a matching pair of Net-Libraries must be active on the client and server computers. The TCP/IP Sockets and Named Pipes client Net-Libraries are the default client Net-Libraries for computers running Windows 4.0 or Windows 2000 and are used in that order. In most environments, you will not need to modify client Net-Library settings. However, if a user is having difficulty connecting to a SQL Server 2000 instance, verify the settings for the client Net-Libraries. On the client computer, use the SQL Server Client Network Utility to enable additional or different Net-Libraries, configure custom connection properties for each Net-Library, and specify the order in which the system will attempt to use each enabled Net-Library.

Table 10-1.   Security Capabilities of Windows Authentication Versus SQL Server Authentication

Windows Authentication	SQL Server Authentication
When a user logs into the Windows domain, the user name and password are encrypted before being passed to the Windows domain controller.	The Windows operating system never authenticates the user.
When an authenticated user presents authentication credentials to a SQL Server 2000 instance, the Kerberos ticket or access token submitted is encrypted.	When a user presents authentication credentials to a SQL Server 2000 instance, the user name and password submitted are not encrypted (unless SSL is enabled for the entire session).
Windows 2000 and Windows NT 4.0 support password policies (such as enforcing complex passwords and password expirations).	SQL Server 2000 supports no password policies (passwords can be of any length or complexity, and they never expire).
Windows 2000 and Windows NT 4.0 supports account lockout policies (such as for multiple attempts using an incorrect password).	SQL Server 2000 supports no account lockout policy (a user can try an unlimited number of times until a valid name and password allow access).

You access the SQL Server Client Network Utility from the Microsoft SQL Server program group on the Start menu. See Figure 10.1.

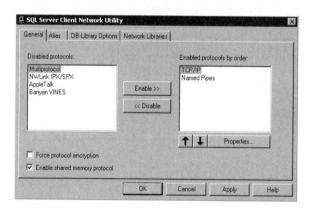

Figure 10.1.   Accessing the SQL Server Client Network Utility.

Note   You can force protocol encryption using SSL. If you select this check box in SQL Server Client Network Utility, the SQL Server 2000 instance you are connecting to must also be using encryption. Use the SQL Server Network Utility to force protocol encryption for the server Net-Libraries.

The Named Pipes and Multiprotocol Net-Libraries require an authenticated connection to the Windows domain before a client can connect to a SQL Server 2000 instance (using either Windows authentication or SQL Server authentication). This means that the user who is requesting authentication must be an authenticated user on the Windows domain. This is not a problem if you are using a Windows client and are logged on to the same domain (or a trusted domain) that contains the SQL Server 2000 computer on which SQL Server 2000 is running. However, if you are attempting to connect to a SQL Server 2000 instance from a computer that has not established a trusted connection to the domain, an attempted connection using either the Named Pipes or the Multiprotocol Net-Libraries will fail (however, TCP/IP sockets will succeed if valid credentials are presented).

Note   The simplest method for establishing an authenticated connection (other than logging on to the domain) is to connect to an existing share within the domain.

Neither the TCP/IP Sockets Net-Library nor any of the other Net-Libraries require prior authentication by the Windows domain. A user (or application) can attempt to connect to an instance of SQL Server 2000 using the TCP/IP network protocol and the TCP/IP Sockets Net-Library from any location provided that communication can be established with the SQL Server 2000 computer. For this reason, understanding how to secure your Windows domain as well as securing your SQL Server 2000 instance is extremely critical to protecting your data.

Selecting a SQL Server 2000 Authentication Mode

During installation, you selected an authentication mode for your SQL Server 2000 instance. The default mode is Windows Authentication Mode. You can also choose to operate a SQL Server 2000 instance in Mixed Mode. Selecting the appropriate authentication mode is critical to securing your SQL Server 2000 installation.

Note   An instance of SQL Server 2000 running on Windows Me or Windows 98 only supports SQL Server authentication because of the limitations of these two operating systems.

Windows Authentication Mode

When SQL Server 2000 is running in Windows Authentication Mode, a user can only connect to a SQL Server 2000 instance using Windows authentication (a trusted connection). This is the default security mode for SQL Server 2000. Windows 2000 (and Windows NT 4.0) provide a variety of methods to secure your Windows environment that are beyond the scope of this book, but are essential to securing your SQL Server 2000 installation. These methods include using account policies, group policies, proxy servers, firewalls, routers, and Internet Protocol Security (IPSec). Using these security mechanisms, requiring a Windows authenticated (trusted) connection provides greater security than using SQL Server 2000 for authentication of users.

Mixed Mode

When SQL Server 2000 is running in Mixed Mode, a user can connect to a SQL Server 2000 instance using either Windows authentication or SQL Server authentication. Using this mode is required for users connecting directly to SQL Server 2000 from Novell NetWare, Apple Macintosh, Banyan Vines, UNIX, and Linux clients. However, using Mixed Mode is inherently less secure than using Windows Authentication Mode, and you should only use it when absolutely necessary.

Switching Authentication Modes

After installation, you must use SQL Server Enterprise Manager to switch authentication modes. In the console tree, right-click the instance and then click Properties. On the Security tab of the SQL Server Properties dialog box, click either the SQL Server And Windows option button or the Windows Only option button to change the authentication mode, and then click OK. See Figure 10.2.

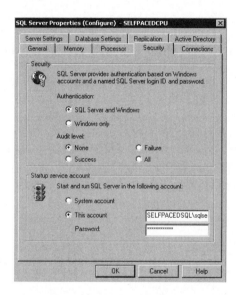

Figure 10.2.   Switching authentication modes.

After you switch modes, you must stop and then restart the SQL Server service for this change to take effect. SQL Server Enterprise Manager will prompt you and ask if you want it to perform this task immediately. See Figure 10.3.

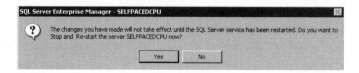

Figure 10.3.   SQL Server Enterprise Manager prompt to stop and restart the SQL Server service.

Note   If the SQL Server Agent service is also running, SQL Server Enterprise Manager will prompt you to stop it as well. However, SQL Server Enterprise Manager will not restart the SQL Server Agent service. You will need to restart it manually.

Practice: Switching SQL Server 2000 Authentication Modes

In this practice, you switch SQL Server 2000 from Windows Authentication Mode to Mixed Mode.

▶   **To switch SQL Server 2000 authentication modes**

1. In the SQL Server Enterprise Manager console tree, expand the Microsoft SQL Servers container and then expand the SQL Server Group container.
2. Right-click the default instance and then click Properties.

    The SQL Server Properties (Configure) – SelfPacedCPU dialog box appears, with the General tab selected.
3. Click the Security tab.
4. Click the SQL Server And Windows option button and then click OK.

    A SQL Server Enterprise Manager – SelfPacedCPU dialog box appears asking if you want to stop and restart the server SelfPacedCPU.
5. Click the Yes button.

    A second SQL Server Enterprise Manager – SelfPacedCPU dialog box may appear asking if you want to stop MSSQLServer and all its dependent services.
6. Click the Yes button.

    After a few moments, the SQL Server service restarts.

Understanding Security Account Delegation

The SQL Server service has the ability to impersonate an authenticated user when accessing resources outside of the SQL Server 2000 instance (such as the file system or another server). This ability ensures that access to these resources is restricted or permitted based on the credentials of the authenticated user, rather than the credentials of the domain user account of the SQL Server service. For the SQL Server service to pass the credentials of a Windows authenticated user to another server, you must enable Windows 2000 security account delegation on both servers.

Security account delegation requires that all servers involved be running Windows 2000, with Kerberos support enabled, and be using the Microsoft Active Directory directory service. Within Active Directory, the user who is attempting to use security account delegation must be trusted for delegation. You select this account option in the user's Properties dialog box, which you access with Active Directory Users And Computers. See Figure 10.4.

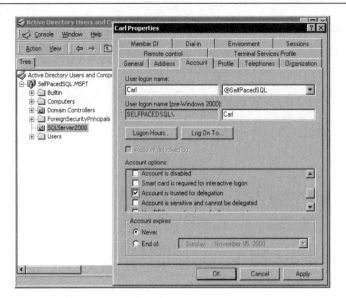

Figure 10.4.   Enabling a computer to be trusted for delegation.

Also, the computer on which the SQL Server 2000 instance is running must be trusted for security account delegation. For a distributed query between two SQL Server 2000 instances on separate computers, each computer must be trusted. You select this option in the computer's Properties dialog box, accessed in Active Directory Users And Computers. See Figure 10.5.

Finally, to use security account delegation, the SQL Server 2000 instance must have a Service Principal Name (SPN). You establish an SPN for a SQL Server 2000 instance with the Setspn utility, which is available in the Windows 2000 Resource Kit. You can assign an SPN in two different ways. You can use the Setspn utility to have a permanent SPN assigned by a Windows 2000 domain administrator to the SQL Server service domain user account based on a port number. Multiple ports and multiple instances require multiple SPNs. To enable delegation, you must use the TCP/IP Net-Library rather than Named Pipes because the SPN targets a specified TCP/IP socket.

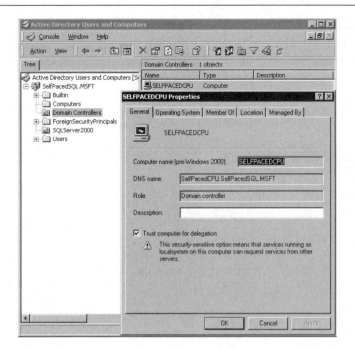

Figure 10.5.   Property settings for trusted computer accounts.

```
Setspn -a MSSQLSvc/SelfPacedCPU.SelfPacedSQL.msft:1433 sqlservice
```

The preceding example adds an SPN on an instance of SQL Server 2000 named SelfPacedCPU.SelfPacedSQL.MSFT that is listening on port 1433 and using the SelfPacedSQL\SQLService domain user account.

You can also have a temporary SPN assigned by running the SQL Server 2000 service under the local system account. When you run the SQL Service service under the local system account, SQL Server will automatically register a temporary SPN at service startup. A temporary SPN expires when the SQL Server service shuts down. If you decide to change from a permanent SPN to a temporary one, you need to delete the previously registered SPN.

```
Setspn -d MSSQLSvc/SelfPacedCPU.SelfPacedSQL.msft:1433 sqlservice
```

The preceding example deletes an SPN on an instance of SQL Server 2000 named SelfPacedCPU.SelfPacedSQL.MSFT that is listening on port 1433 and using the SelfPacedSQL\SQLService domain user account.

Note   If you change the SQL Server service account, you will need to delete any existing SPNs and create new ones.

Lesson Summary

To access SQL Server 2000, a database administrator must either grant access to existing Windows users and groups, or create SQL Server security accounts. A user can specify a connection to SQL Server 2000 either using his or her existing Windows credentials or by specifying a SQL Server login ID and password. The latter method is less secure and is not enabled by default. You must specify Mixed Mode authentication to permit SQL Server logins. Finally, for Windows authentication credentials to be passed between servers, you must enable security account delegation in Windows 2000.

Lesson 2: Understanding the Authorization Process

After SQL Server 2000 has authenticated a user, the user can perform only the administrative tasks and access only the user databases that have been specifically authorized (permitted). In this lesson, you will learn the variety of methods by which an authenticated user receives permissions. First, you will learn about server roles (sometimes referred to as fixed server roles), which grant permissions to perform server-wide tasks. Next, you will be introduced to database-specific permissions, including database owner permissions, database roles, statement permissions, object permissions, and application roles.

After this lesson, you will be able to

- Describe the server roles
- Describe the fixed and user-defined database roles
- Describe database owner permissions
- Describe statement and object permissions

Estimated lesson time: 15 minutes

Understanding Server-Wide Permissions

SQL Server 2000 provides a number of predefined server roles with associated administration permissions. These server roles grant server-wide permissions to perform various tasks and include permissions that you can only grant to users through the use of these server roles. You cannot delete server roles and cannot change their permissions. To grant a user these permissions, you add their login to the server role. With Transact-SQL, you can add a Windows user or group to a server role without first creating a login (SQL Server 2000 will create the login automatically).

Note   Server roles are identical in concept to built-in groups in Windows 2000.

Table 10.2 describes the eight server roles that are available with SQL Server 2000.

Table 10-2.   Server Roles in SQL Server 2000

Server Role	Members of This Server Role Can ...
sysadmin	Perform any task within a SQL Server 2000 instance and within any database. By default, all members of the Windows built-in Administrators group, as well as the sa SQL Server security account, belong to this server role.
serveradmin	Configure SQL Server 2000 using the *sp_configure* system-stored procedure. Can also shut down the SQL Server service. Members of the Windows built-in Server Operators group map well to this server role.
setupadmin	Install and configure linked servers, remote servers, and replication. Can also mark a stored procedure for execution at startup, such as *sp_serveroption*. Members of the Windows built-in Server Operators group map well to this server role.
securityadmin	Perform all security-related operations within SQL Server 2000, including managing *CREATE DATABASE* statement permissions, controlling server logins, and reading the SQL Server error log. Help desk personnel and members of the Windows built-in Server Operators group map well to this server role.
processadmin	Manage processes running in an instance of SQL Server. Can kill user processes, such as runaway queries. Help desk personnel map well to this server role.
dbcreator	Can create, modify, and delete databases. Senior database administrators who are not members of the sysadmin server role map well to this server role.
diskadmin	Can manage disk files and backup devices. Generally only used for backward compatibility with SQL Server 6.x.
bulkadmin	Can execute *BULK INSERT* statements. Allows members of the sysadmin server role to delegate BULK INSERT tasks without granting sysadmin rights. Use carefully because members must also have read access to any data being inserted and INSERT permission on any table into which data will be inserted.

Note   A member of any server role can add other users to that server role.

Understanding Database-Specific Permissions

Access to SQL Server 2000 does not (by itself) grant a user access to any of the databases within SQL Server 2000. In addition, except for membership in the sysadmin role, membership in a server role does not grant any database-specific permissions. Database access rights must be specifically granted by a system administrator or by a member of an administrator role in the database.

Permissions can be granted, denied, or revoked, and include the right to create objects, administer the database, execute certain Transact-SQL statements, insert data to a table, or simply view data within a view. SQL Server 2000 has a number of mechanisms for granting users specific permissions within a database. The various database-specific permissions are described in Table 10.3.

Table 10-3.   Database-Specific Permissions

Permission	Description
Database owner	A user can be specified as the owner of the database, and can perform any activity with respect to the database.
DBO role	All members of the sysadmin server role are automatically members of the dbo role within each database, and can perform any activity with respect to the database.
User	Specified users and groups can be granted user access to a database via their Windows 2000 or SQL Server 2000 security account. A permitted database user is then granted permissions within the database through a database role, the public role, and specific grants of statement and object permissions.
Guest user	An authenticated user who has access to an instance of SQL Server 2000 (but who does not have a user account to access a particular database) can be permitted to access a database as a guest user. The guest account can be granted specific permissions within the database (generally to read certain data). By default, a database does not have a guest user account.
Public role	All users permitted to access a database become members of the public role within each database. The public role can be granted specific permissions (generally permissions needed by all users of the database).
Fixed database role	Permitted users can be added to fixed database roles within a database. Fixed database roles contain predefined rights within a database to perform database-wide activities.
User-defined database role	Permitted users can be added to user-defined database roles within a database. These roles can be created by an administrator and granted specifically delineated rights and permission within the database.
Statement permissions	Permission to execute administrative statements (such as *CREATE PROCEDURE*) can be granted, revoked, or denied to users, groups, and roles.

Table 10-3. Database-Specific Permissions

Permission	Description
Object permissions	Permission to access database objects (such as a table or view) can be granted, revoked, or denied to users, groups, and roles.
Application role	Permission to perform specific activities within a database can be granted to an application, rather than granted to a user. An application connects to a database and activates the application role. Users accessing a database through this connection gain the permissions associated with the application role for the duration of the connection. Permissions assigned to a particular user are irrelevant when the user is accessing the database through an application role.

Fixed Database Roles

Each database contains nine predefined database roles with associated database-wide permissions to perform various tasks. You cannot delete these database roles and cannot change their permissions. To grant a user these permissions within a database, you add the user's database user account to the database role. If these fixed database roles do not grant the combination of rights you need, you can create user-defined database roles with custom rights (generally more restrictive rights).

Table 10.4 describes the nine fixed database roles that are available with SQL Server 2000.

Table 10-4. Fixed Database Roles in SQL Server 2000

Database Role	Members of This Database Role Can ...
db_owner	Perform any task within a SQL Server 2000 database. Members of this role have the same rights as the database owner and the members of the dbo role.
db_accessadmin	Add or remove Windows 2000 or Windows NT 4.0 users and groups and SQL Server users in a database (using the sp_grantdbaccess system stored procedure).
db_securityadmin	Manage all permissions, roles, role membership, and object ownership in a database (using the *GRANT*, *REVOKE*, and *DENY* statements).
db_ddladmin	Add, modify, or drop objects in the database (using the *CREATE*, *ALTER*, and *DROP* statements).
db_backupoperator	Run DBCC commands, issue checkpoints, and back up the database (using the *DBCC*, *CHECKPOINT*, and *BACKUP* Transact-SQL statements).
db_datareader	Read data from any user table or view in the database (you have SELECT permission on all tables and views).

Table 10-4.   Fixed Database Roles in SQL Server 2000

Database Role	Members of This Database Role Can ...
db_datawriter	Modify or delete data from any user table or view in the database (you have *INSERT*, *UPDATE*, and *DELETE* permissions on all tables and views).
db_denydatareader	Not read data from any user table in the database (you do not have SELECT permission on any objects). Can be used with the db_ddladmin role to allow an administrator to create database objects owned by the dbo role, but not be able to read sensitive data contained in those objects.
db_denydatawriter	Not modify or delete data from any user table in the database (you do not have INSERT, UPDATE, and DELETE permissions on any object).

Lesson Summary

In addition to permitting users access to SQL Server 2000, a user must be granted authority to perform actions within SQL Server 2000. Server roles are used to grant different levels of rights to perform server-wide administration functions. Within a database, you can grant users (and groups) database-wide administration rights using database roles. They can also be granted statement and object permissions. User-defined roles can be created with customized rights with respect to statements and objects. Finally, guest user access can be permitted with certain rights and the public role can be used to grant general rights to all authorized users.

Lesson 3: Creating and Managing Logins

Before a user can perform tasks within SQL Server 2000, the user must be granted SQL Server 2000 access through a login and database access through a user account. In this lesson, you will learn to grant access to SQL Server 2000 and its databases using SQL Server Enterprise Manager and Transact-SQL statements. You will also learn to view SQL Server 2000 and database access information using SQL Server Enterprise Manager and Transact-SQL statements.

After this lesson, you will be able to

- Use SQL Server Enterprise Manager to create logins
- Use Transact-SQL statements to create logins
- View the SQL Server 2000 access information
- View database access information

Estimated lesson time: 45 minutes

Granting Access Using SQL Server Enterprise Manager

SQL Server Enterprise Manager provides a simple graphical interface to interactively link an existing Windows 2000 (or Windows NT 4.0) user or group to a login, or to create a SQL Server 2000 login for a SQL Server 2000 security account. You can create a login directly with SQL Server Enterprise Manager, or you can use the Create Login Wizard.

Note   You can only create one login at a time using SQL Server Enterprise Manager.

Using the Create Login Wizard

The SQL Server Enterprise Manager wizards are available from the Tools menu, and are also available from any taskpad view. Figure 10.6 displays the Select Wizard dialog box, from which you can select a variety of wizards, including the Create Login Wizard.

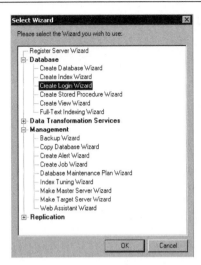

Figure 10.6.   Selecting the Create Login Wizard in the Select Wizard dialog box.

After you start the Create Login Wizard, you are asked to select the authentication mode to use for the login you are creating in the Select Authentication Mode For This Login page. See Figure 10.7.

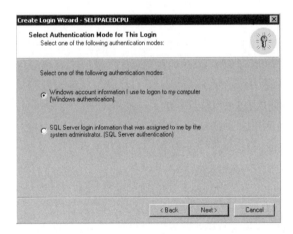

Figure 10.7.   Selecting an authentication mode for the login being created.

If you select Windows authentication, you can link this login ID to an existing Windows 2000 (or Windows NT 4.0) user or group in the Authentication With Windows page. Notice that you can either grant this user or group access to the server, or you can deny them access. See Figure 10.8.

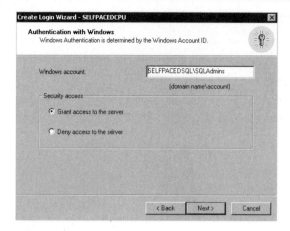

Figure 10.8.   Granting or denying a new login access to the server.

If you select SQL Server authentication, you will create a SQL Server 2000 security account in the Authentication With SQL Server page. You must specify a login name and a password. To deny a SQL Server login, you simply remove the login from the Logins container in SQL Server Enterprise Manager (or the sysxlogins table in the master database). See Figure 10.9.

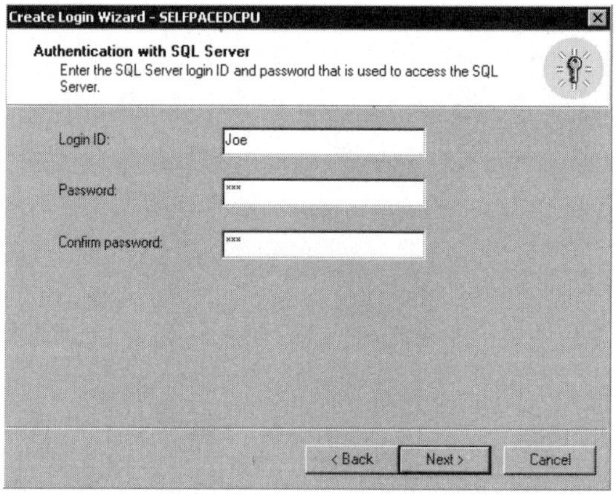

Figure 10.9.   Specifying a login name for a SQL Server 2000 security account.

After you specify the type of login and either link or create the security account, you specify the server role (if any) for this login in the Grant Access To Security Roles page. If the user will not be a server-wide administrator, do not select any server roles. See Figure 10.10.

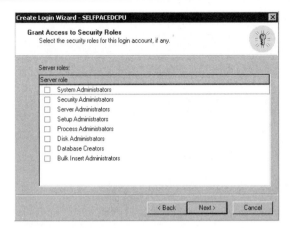

Figure 10.10.   Specifying the server role for the login being created.

Next, you specify the databases (if any) to which this user will have access in the Grant Access To Databases page. Remember that most server roles do not provide database access (other than the sysadmin role). See Figure 10.11.

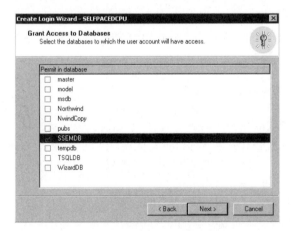

Figure 10.11.   Specifying the databases that the new login may access.

Finally, you are given the opportunity to review the selections you have made before actually creating this new login in the Completing The Create Login Wizard page. You can click the Back button to change any parameter you want to change. Click the Finish button to create the login. See Figure 10.12.

Figure 10.12.   Completing the Create Login Wizard.

Practice: Creating a Login Using the Create Login Wizard

In this practice you use the Create Login Wizard to create a SQL Server login.

▶ **To create a login using the Create Login Wizard**

1. Ensure that you are logged on to the SelfPacedSQL.MSFT domain controller as Administrator.

2. Click Start, point to Programs, point to Microsoft SQL Server, and then click Enterprise Manager.

   SQL Server Enterprise Manager appears displaying the Microsoft SQL Servers and the Event Viewer (Local) console trees in the console root.

3. In the console tree, expand the Microsoft SQL Servers container, expand the SQL Server Group container, and then click the default instance.

4. On the Tools menu, click Wizards.

   The Select Wizard dialog box appears.

5. Expand Database and then double-click Create Login Wizard.

   The Welcome To The Create Login Wizard page appears.

6. Click Next.

   The Select Authentication Mode For This Login page appears.

7. Click the SQL Server Login Information That Was Assigned To Me By The System Administrator (SQL Server Authentication) option button and then click Next.

   The Authentication With SQL Server page appears.

8. In the Login ID text box, type **Joe**.

9. In the Password and Confirm Password text boxes, type **password** and then click Next.

   The Grant Access To Security Roles page appears.

10. Click Next. Do not select any security roles.

    The Grant Access To Databases page appears.

11. Select the SSEMDB check box to permit access to this database only, and then click Next.

    The Completing The Create Login Wizard page appears. Review the details of the login you have defined.

12. Click the Finish button.

    After the login is created, a Wizard Complete! message box appears.

13. Click OK to close the Wizard Complete! message box.

14. In the console tree, expand the Security container, and then click Logins.

    In the details pane, notice that Joe appears as a standard type of login.

15. On the Tools menu, click SQL Query Analyzer.

    SQL Query Analyzer appears. You are connected using Windows authentication.

16. On the File menu, click Connect.

    The Connect To SQL Server dialog box appears.

17. Click the SQL Server Authentication option button.

18. In the Login name text box, type **Joe**.

19. In the Password text box, type **password** and then click OK.

    Notice that you can log on to the default instance of SQL Server 2000 using the SQL Server login Joe. Notice that the title bar indicates that you are connecting as Joe.

20. On the toolbar, select SSEMDB from the database drop-down list.

    Notice that the list contains only those databases to which Joe has access, including system databases. All other databases are hidden.

21. In the query pane, type **SELECT * FROM Customer**.

22. Click the Execute Query button.

    Notice that although Joe has access to the SSEMDB database, Joe does not have SELECT permission on the Customer object. Chapter 11 will cover permissions in more detail.

23. Close SQL Query Analyzer. Do not save any changes.

24. Do not close SQL Server Enterprise Manager.

Using SQL Server Enterprise Manager Directly to Create a Login

To create a login using SQL Server Enterprise Manager directly, right-click Logins in the Security container for the SQL Server 2000 instance, and then click New Login. The General, Server Roles, and Database Access tabs in the SQL Server Login Properties – New Login dialog box allow you to provide the same type of login information discussed in the preceding section with respect to the Create Login Wizard (such as authentication type, server role, and database access). However, they also allow you to configure the login with additional information. When you click the Name ellipsis button in the General tab, an additional SQL Server Login Properties – New Login dialog box appears enabling you to select a Windows domain from a drop-down list, and then browse the names of users and groups in the domain. See Figure 10.13.

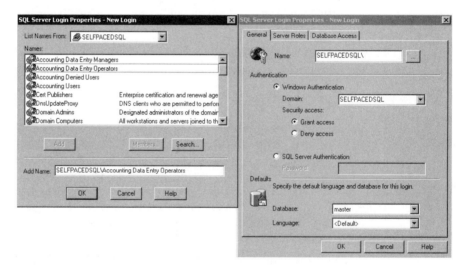

Figure 10.13. Browsing domain user accounts when creating a new login account.

You can also select the default database and language in the General tab. The default database will be the current database when a user logs in. The default for new logins is master, but you will generally change this to a specific user database. The default language will be the default language of the SQL Server 2000 instance, unless specified otherwise (such as Spanish).

Note   You can also deny a Windows 2000 (or Windows NT 4.0) user or group access to SQL Server 2000. This overrides any other access of the user or group (such as through membership in another group that has a different login).

On the Server Roles tab, you select the server role (if any) for this login. A description of each server role is provided in the Description group box for your convenience. See Figure 10.14.

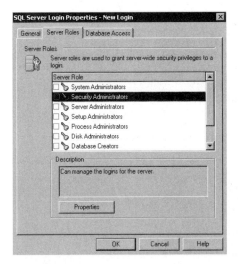

Figure 10.14.   Selecting the server role for the login being created.

If you select a server role and then click the Properties button, you can view a list of all logins that are currently members of that role in the General tab of the Server Role Properties – Sysadmin dialog box. You can also add or remove additional logins to this role from this interface. See Figure 10.15.

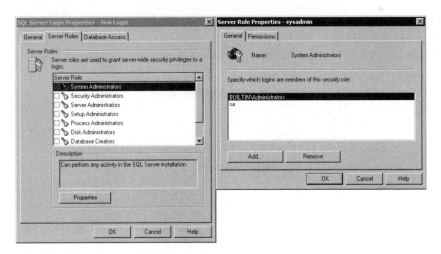

Figure 10.15.   Viewing the logins that are members of a role.

Notice that if the System Administrators server role is selected, you can see that the Windows 2000 built-in Administrator group, and the SQL Server login, sa, are members of the sysadmin server role. If you click the Permissions tab, you can view the permissions granted to the sysadmin server role. See Figure 10.16.

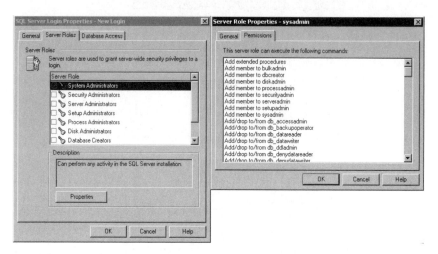

Figure 10.16.   Viewing the permissions of a server role.

On the Database Access tab in the SQL Server Login Properties – New Login dialog box, you can select the databases to which this login will have access, along with the database role to which this login will belong. See Figure 10.17.

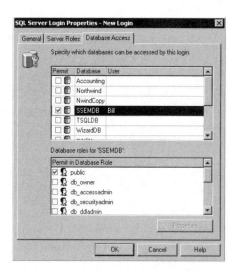

Figure 10.17.   Selecting the databases that the new login may access.

When you select a database, notice that the login is automatically made a member of the public role in each database. You cannot remove a login from the public role.

Practice: Creating a Login Directly Using SQL Server Enterprise Manager

In this practice you use the SQL Server Enterprise Manager directly to create a login for a Windows 2000 user.

▶ **To create a login directly using SQL Server Enterprise Manager**

1. Open Windows Explorer.
2. Double-click Add_AD_Users1.vbs in the C:\SelfPacedSQL\CH_10 folder.

   A Windows Script Host message box appears to tell you that the script has added a single user to the Users container. The Windows Script Host script adds a single user, Bill, to the Users container in the SelfPacedSQL domain with a password of Bill (actually, it will create the user in your current domain).
3. Click OK to close the Windows Script Host message box.
4. Switch to SQL Server Enterprise Manager.
5. In the SQL Server Enterprise Manager console tree, expand the Security container of the default instance.
6. Right-click Logins, and then click New Login.

   The SQL Server Login Properties – New Login dialog box appears, with the General tab selected.
7. To the right of the Name text box, click the ellipsis (…) button.
8. Click Bill in the Names list box for the SelfPacedSQL domain.
9. Click the Add button and then click OK.

   Notice that the Name text box is automatically completed for you.
10. In the Database drop-down list, select SSEMDB.
11. Click the Server Roles tab.
12. Select the Security Administrators check box.
13. Click the Properties button.

    The Server Role Properties – Securityadmin dialog box appears, with the General tab selected.
14. Click the Permissions tab.

    Notice the commands that members of this server role can execute.
15. Click Cancel and then click the Database Access tab.
16. Select the SSEMDB check box.
17. In the Database Roles For 'SSEMDB' list box, select the Db_owner check box and then click OK.

    Notice that SelfPacedSQL\Bill appears in the details pane for the Logins container as a Windows user.
18. Switch to Windows Explorer.

19. Double-click Rights.cmd in the C:\SelfPacedSQL\CH_10 folder.

   A Command Prompt window will open briefly to execute the Rights.cmd batch file. The batch file will grant Windows 2000 users the right to log on locally. This is required to test user access permissions in the rest of this chapter and in Chapter 11.

20. Close Windows Explorer and SQL Server Enterprise Manager, and then log off Windows 2000.

21. Log on to the SelfPacedSQL domain controller with a user name of Bill and a password of password.

22. Click Start, point to Programs, point to Microsoft SQL Server, and then click Query Analyzer.

   The Connect To SQL Server dialog box appears.

23. Click the Windows Authentication option button to connect to SelfPacedSQL using Windows authentication.

24. Click OK.

   SQL Query Analyzer appears. Notice that the title bar indicates that you are connecting as SelfPacedSQL\Bill. Also notice that the current database is SSEMDB.

25. In the query pane, type **SELECT * FROM SSEMDB.dbo.Customer**.

26. Click the Execute Query button.

   Notice that Bill was able to execute this query because Bill is a member of the database owner role in the SSEMDB database.

27. Close SQL Query Analyzer. Do not save any changes.

28. Click Start, point to Programs, point to Microsoft SQL Server, and then click Enterprise Manager.

   SQL Server Enterprise Manager appears displaying the Microsoft SQL Servers container in the console root. Notice that Event Viewer does not appear. Bill has his own profile, and thus can customize his own version of the SQL Server Enterprise Manager console.

29. In the console tree, expand the Microsoft SQL Servers container, expand the SQL Server Group container, expand the default instance container, and then expand Security.

30. Right-click Logins and then click New Login.

   The SQL Server Login Properties – New Login dialog box appears, with the General tab selected.

31. In the Name text box, type **Ana**.

32. Click the SQL Server Authentication option button.

33. In the Password text box, type **password** and then click OK.

   The Confirm Password dialog box appears.

34. In the Confirm New Password text box, type **password** and then click OK.

In the details pane, notice that Ana appears as a standard type of login.

35. In the Security container, right-click Linked Servers.

Notice that Bill is not able to create a linked server. He is able to create a new login because he is a member of the securityadmin server role and he is not able to create a new linked server because he is not a member of the setupadmin server role.

36. Close SQL Server Enterprise Manager and then log off Windows 2000.

37. Log on to Windows 2000 as Administrator with a password of password.

Creating a User-Defined Database Role Using SQL Server Enterprise Manager

To create a user-defined database role using SQL Server Enterprise Manager, expand the Databases container for the SQL Server 2000 instance and then expand the database in which you want to create the new database role. Right-click the Roles container, and then click New Database Role. When the Database Role Properties – New Database Role dialog box appears, click the Add button for a list of members that you can add to this new role. See Figure 10.18.

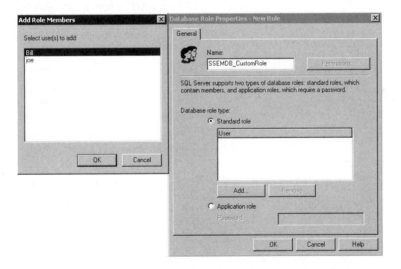

Figure 10.18.   Creating a user-defined database role.

To create a user-defined database role, simply type the name you want to give the new database role in the Name text box. You can add users to the role now, or at a later time by clicking the Add button. Notice also that you can create a standard role or an application role. Application roles are covered in Chapter 11. Finally, notice that the Permissions button is grayed out. You cannot assign permissions to a user-defined database role until after you create it. Assigning permissions to a user-defined database role is covered in Chapter 11.

Granting Access Using Transact-SQL Statements

You can also grant access to SQL Server 2000 and its databases using Transact-SQL system stored procedures. The syntax is relatively simple, and you can create multiple logins in a single script. You can also add logins to server roles and database roles in the same script, as well as create and populate user-defined database roles.

Windows Logins

The system stored procedures shown in Table 10.5 are used to grant, deny, revoke, or modify a login associated with a Windows user or group. Only members of the sysadmin or securityadmin server roles can execute these system stored procedures.

Table 10-5.   System Stored Procedures for Administering User or Group Logins

System Stored Procedure	Description
Sp_grantlogin 'login'	Creates a login for a Windows 2000 (or Windows NT 4.0) user or group.
Sp_revokelogin 'login'	Revokes the login entries from SQL Server for a Windows 2000 (or Windows NT 4.0) user or group. Does not explicitly prevent a revoked user or group from accessing SQL Server 2000, however. For example, if a revoked user is a member of a Windows 2000 or Windows NT 4.0 group that has been granted access to SQL Server 2000, that user can still connect to SQL Server.
Sp_denylogin 'login'	Prevents a Windows 2000 (or Windows NT 4.0) user or members of a Windows group from connecting to SQL Server 2000. Prevents the denied user or group from accessing SQL Server 2000 through another login linked to a Windows user or group.
Sp_defaultdb 'login' , 'database'	Changes the default database for a login.
Sp_defaultlanguage 'login', 'language'	Changes the default language for a login.

```
Sp_grantlogin 'SelfPacedSQL\Bill'
```

The preceding example grants the Windows 2000 user, Bill, in the SelfPacedSQL domain access to SQL Server 2000.

SQL Server Logins

The system stored procedures shown in Table 10.6 are used to grant, revoke, and modify a login associated with a SQL Server security account. Only members of the sysadmin or securityadmin server roles can execute these system stored procedures.

Table 10-6.   System Stored Procedures for Administering Security Account Logins

System Stored Procedure	Description
Sp_addlogin 'login' , *['password' , 'database' , 'language', 'sid', 'encryption_option']*	Creates a new SQL Server login. Password is NULL if not specified. The default database is master if not specified. The default language is the current server language if not specified. By default, the password is encrypted before being stored in the sysxlogins table in the master database.
Sp_droplogin 'login'	Drops a SQL Server login.
Sp_password 'old_password', 'new_password', 'login'	Adds or changes a password for a SQL Server login.
Sp_defaultdb 'login', 'database'	Changes the default database for a login.
Sp_defaultlanguage 'login', 'language'	Changes the default language for a login.

```
Sp_addlogin 'Joe' , 'Joe123' , 'Northwind'
```

The preceding example creates a new SQL Server login, Joe, with a password of Joe123 and a default database of Northwind.

Server Roles

The system stored procedures shown in Table 10.7 are used to add or drop a login to a server role. Only members of the sysadmin server role can add logins to any server role. Members of a server role can add logins to that server role.

Table 10-7.   System Stored Procedures for Adding or Dropping a Login to a Server Role

System Stored Procedure	Description
Sp_ addsrvrolemember 'login' , 'role'	Adds a login as a member of a server role.
Sp_dropsrvrolemember 'login' , 'role'	Drops a login as a member of a server role.

```
Sp_addsrvrolemember 'Joe' , 'securityadmin'
```

The preceding example adds the login Joe to the server role Security Administrator.

Database Access

The system stored procedures shown in Table 10.8 are used to add or drop an existing login or a Windows 2000 user or group as a permitted user in the current database. Unlike using SQL Server Enterprise Manager, you can grant a Windows 2000 (or Windows NT 4.0) group access to a database without first creating an explicit login entry in the sysxlogins table. Only members of the sysadmin server role, and the db_accessadmin and db_owner fixed database roles can execute these system stored procedures.

Table 10-8.   System Stored Procedures for Adding or Dropping Logins, Users, or Groups as Permitted Users

System Stored Procedure	Description
Sp_grantdbaccess 'login' , 'name_in_db'	Adds a login as a user in the current database. Although the user name in the database can be different from the login name, this practice is not recommended (generally too confusing).
Sp_revokedbaccess 'name'	Removes a login as a user in the current database.

```
USE Northwind
EXEC Sp_grantdbaccess 'Joe'
```

The preceding example grants the login Joe access to the current database, using the user name Joe in the Northwind database.

Database Roles

The following system stored procedures are used to change the database owner, add (or drop) a security account to an existing database role, or create (or drop) a user-defined database role (see Table 10.9).

```
Use Northwind
EXEC Sp_addrolemember 'db_securityadmin' , 'SelfPacedSQL\Bill'
```

The preceding example adds the SelfPacedSQL\Bill security account to the db_securityadmin database role in the Northwind database.

Table 10-9.   System Stored Procedures for Changing a Database Owner, Adding or Dropping a Security Account, or Creating a User-Defined Database Role

System Stored Procedure	Description
Sp_changedbowner 'login', remap_alias_flag	Changes the owner of a user database. Only members of the sysadmin server role or the current database owner can change a database owner.
Sp_addrolemember 'role' , 'security_account'	Adds a security account to a database role in the current database. You can add a user-defined database role to a fixed or user-defined database role. Only members of the sysadmin server role and the db_owner and db_security fixed database roles can add members to any database role. Members of a database role can add members to that database role.
Sp_droprolemember 'role' , 'security_account'	Drops a security account from a database role in the current database. Only members of the sysadmin server role and the db_owner and db_security fixed dababase roles can remove members from any database role. Members of a database role can remove members from that database role.

Table 10-9.   System Stored Procedures for Changing a Database Owner, Adding or Dropping a Security Account, or Creating a User-Defined Database Role

System Stored Procedure	Description
Sp_addrole 'role' , 'owner'	Adds a new user-defined database role in the current database. Although you can specify an owner of the role, using the default of dbo is recommended. Members of the sysadmin server role and the db_securityadmin and db_owner fixed database roles can create user-defined database roles.
Sp_droprole 'role'	Drops a user-defined database role in the current database. Members of the sysadmin server role db_securityadmin and the db_owner fixed database roles can create user-defined database roles.

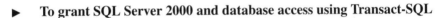

Practice: Granting SQL Server 2000 and Database Access Using Transact-SQL

In this practice you use the Transact-SQL system stored procedures to grant SQL Server 2000 and database access to Windows 2000 users and groups.

▶ **To grant SQL Server 2000 and database access using Transact-SQL**

1. Open Windows Explorer.
2. Double-click Add_AD_Users2.vbs in the C:\SelfPacedSQL\CH_10 folder.
3. A Windows Script Host message box appears to tell you that the process has completed. The Windows Script Host script will add a new Organizational Unit (OU) within Active Directory called SQL Server 2000. Within this new OU, it will add user accounts and three security groups: SQL Server Users, SQL Server Administrators, and Accounting Users. Within the SQL Server Users group, it will add 15 new Windows 2000 users. Within the SQL Server Administrators group, it will add 2 of the 15 Windows 2000 users. Within the Accounting Users group, it will add 3 of the 15 Windows users. Click OK to close the Windows Script Host message box.
4. Click Start, point to Programs, point to Microsoft SQL Server, and then click Query Analyzer.

   The Connect To SQL Server dialog box appears.
5. Click the Windows Authentication option button to connect to SelfPacedSQL using Windows authentication.
6. Click OK.
7. On the toolbar, click the Load SQL Script button.

   The Open Query File dialog box appears.

8. Open SQL_Access.sql in the C:\SelfPacedSQL\CH_10 folder.

   A Transact-SQL script appears, which will create a new database, Accounting, and a new table, Customer. It will populate the Customer table with 21 customers from the NewCustomerData1.txt file using a *BULK INSERT* statement. It will then grant the Windows 2000 group SQL Server Users permission to log in to SQL Server 2000. Next, it will add the Windows 2000 group, SQL Server Administrators, to the sysadmin server role. Next, it will grant access to the Accounting database to the Windows 2000 group, Accounting Users. Finally, it will create a user-defined database role, Data Entry Managers, and add the Windows 2000 user Elba to that role.

9. Click the Execute Query button to execute the SQL_Access.sql statement.

   In the results pane, notice that the Accounting database was created and 21 rows added. The SQL Server Users group was granted login access. The SQL Server Administrators group was added to the sysadmin role. Database access was granted to Accounting Users. The Data Entry Managers database role was created and Elba was added to it.

10. Close SQL Query Analyzer.

Viewing Access Information

As a database administrator, you will need to view your SQL Server 2000 installation to determine the users and groups that have login access, as well as the server roles to which they belong. In addition, you will need to view the databases to which they have access, as well as the database roles to which they belong. You might need to modify access to grant greater or lesser rights as job responsibilities for users change over time. You can view SQL Server 2000 and database access information using SQL Server Enterprise Manager and Transact-SQL system stored procedures.

Using SQL Server Enterprise Manager

When viewing access information using SQL Server Enterprise Manager, start with the Security container for the SQL Server 2000 instance. This container holds a Logins container and a Server Roles container. The Logins container displays all users permitted to access the SQL Server 2000 instance. See Figure 10.19.

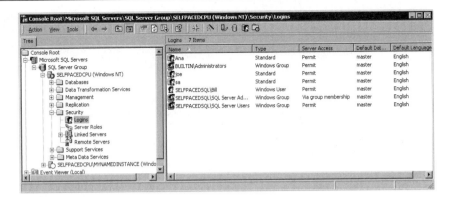

Figure 10.19.   Viewing the logins shown in the Logins container.

Notice both SQL Server logins and Windows 2000 users and groups. Also notice that the SelfPacedSQL\SQL Server Administrators group has access via group membership. This Windows group has login access because it is a member of the sysadmin server role. To delete any login, click the login and then press DELETE on your keyboard. To view or modify the details of any login, including server roles and database access, double-click the login to access the SQL Server Login Properties dialog box. See Figure 10.20.

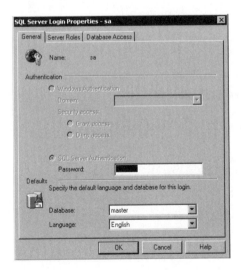

Figure 10.20.   Viewing the details of a login.

Note   A system administrator can change the password of any SQL Server security account.

The Server Roles container displays the server roles. See Figure 10.21.

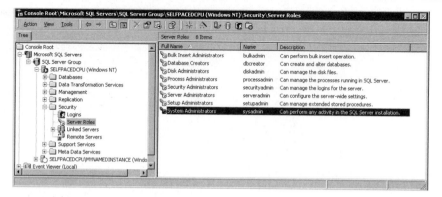

Figure 10.21.   Viewing the server roles.

Double-click any server role to list, add, or remove logins from the server role. See Figure 10.22.

To view database access permissions, you can either view them on a per-user basis or you can view them on a per-database basis. Expand a database container and then click the Users container to view the list of all users permitted to access the database. See Figure 10.23.

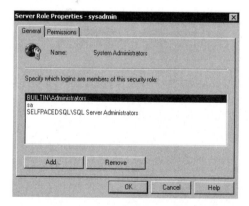

Figure 10.22.   Modifying members of a server role.

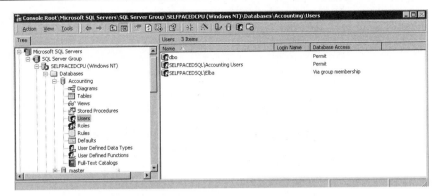

Figure 10.23.   Viewing the list of users who have access to a database.

In Figure 10.23, notice that members of the Windows SelfPacedSQL\Accounting Users group, and the Windows user, SelfPacedSQL\Elba, are permitted to access the Accounting database (in addition to the members of the dbo role). SelfPaced-SQL\Elba has access via group membership. To determine Elba's group membership, double-click SelfPacedSQL\Elba to display the Database User Properties - SelfPacedSQL\Elba dialog box. See Figure 10.24.

In Figure 10.24, notice that Elba has access by virtue of membership in the Data Entry Managers user-defined database role. Click the Permissions button to view Elba's permissions. Select a database role and then click the Properties button to view each role, its members, and the permissions of the role. Permissions are covered in Chapter 11.

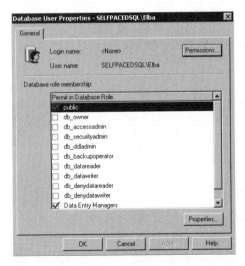

Figure 10.24.   Determining the database role memberships of a user.

To review each database role, click the Roles container in the console tree. See Figure 10.25.

Double-click a database role to list, add, or remove security accounts from the database role. See Figure 10.26.

Using Transact-SQL

You can also view SQL Server 2000 access information using Transact-SQL system stored procedures. The system stored procedures listed in Table 10.10 return information regarding logins, server role members, database access, and database role members. Only members of the sysadmin or securityadmin server roles can execute the *sp_helplogins* system stored procedure. Members of the public role can execute all other system stored procedures in this list.

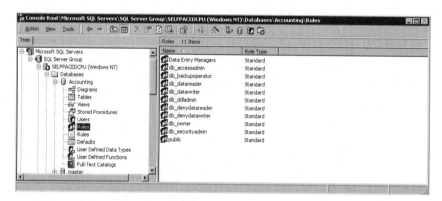

Figure 10.25. Viewing database roles.

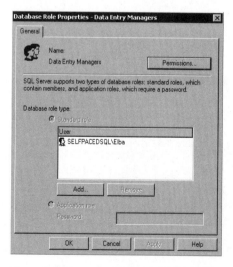

Figure 10.26. Modifying members of a database role.

Note   A Windows user can access SQL Server 2000 through membership in one Windows group and can access a database through membership in another Windows group.

Table 10-10.   System Stored Procedures That Return Access Information

System or Extended Stored Procedure	Description
Sp_helplogins [*'login'*]	Returns information regarding all logins or a specified login, including the databases to which a login has access and database roles of which the login is a member.
Sp_helpsrvrolemember [*'role'*]	Returns information regarding all server roles and their members or all members in a specified server role.
Sp_helpuser [*'security_account'*]	Returns information regarding all users or a specified user in the current database, including all database role memberships.
Sp_helprolemember [*'role'*]	Returns information regarding all database roles or all memberships in a specified database role within the current database.
Sp_helpntgroup [*'name'*]	Returns information regarding all Windows 2000 (or Windows NT 4.0) groups or a specified group within the current database.

Practice: Viewing SQL Server 2000 Access Information

In this practice you use SQL Server Enterprise Manager and Transact-SQL system stored procedures to view SQL Server 2000 access information.

▶ **To view SQL Server 2000 access information**

1. Ensure that you are logged on to the SelfPacedSQL.MSFT domain controller as Administrator.
2. Click Start, point to Programs, point to Microsoft SQL Server, and then click Enterprise Manager.
3. In the console tree, expand the Microsoft SQL Servers container, expand the SQL Server Group container, expand your default instance, expand the Security container, and then click Logins.

   In the details pane, notice the Windows 2000 users and groups, and the SQL Server logins, that have access to SQL Server 2000. Only members of the Self-PacedSQL SQL Server Users group or the SQL Server Administrators group can log in to this SQL Server 2000 instance.

4. In the details pane, double-click SelfPacedSQL\SQL Server Users.

   The SQL Server Login Properties – SelfPacedSQL\SQL Server Users dialog box appears, with the General tab selected.

5. Click the Server Roles tab.

   Notice that this Windows group is not a member of any server role.

6. Click the Database Access tab.

   Notice that this Windows group does not have any database access.

7. Click Cancel.

8. On the Tools menu, click SQL Query Analyzer.

9. On the toolbar, click the Load SQL Script button.

   The Open Query File dialog box appears.

10. Open Logins.sql in the C:\SelfPacedSQL\CH_10 folder.

    A Transact-SQL script appears containing the sp_helplogins system stored procedure.

11. Click the Execute Query button to execute the Logins.sql statement.

    In the results pane, notice two result sets. The first set displays the logins with access to this SQL Server 2000 instance. The second set displays the databases to which each login has access. Notice that neither the SelfPacedSQL\SQL Server Users group nor the SelfPacedSQL\SQL Server Administrators shows any database access.

12. Switch to SQL Server Enterprise Manager.

13. In the details pane, double-click SelfPacedSQL\SQL Server Administrators.

    The SQL Server Login Properties – SelfPacedSQL\SQL Server Administrators dialog box appears. On the General tab, notice that this group has login access through group membership (in the sysadmin server group).

14. Click the Server Roles tab.

    Notice that this Windows group is a member of the System Administrators server role.

15. Click the Database Access tab.

    Notice that this Windows group does not have any database access. No explicit database access is required because a sysadmin has full access by definition.

16. Click Cancel.

17. Switch to SQL Query Analyzer.

18. On the toolbar, click the Load SQL Script button.

19. Open ServerRoleMembers.sql in the C:\SelfPacedSQL\CH_10 folder.

    A Transact-SQL script appears containing the *sp_helpsrvrolemember* system stored procedure, which specifies the sysadmin server role.

20. Click the Execute Query button to execute the *ServerRoleMembers.sql* statement.

    In the results pane, notice that the sysadmin server role contains three members, the two default members and the SelfPacedSQL\SQL Server Administrators group.

21. Switch to SQL Server Enterprise Manager.

22. In the console tree, right-click the Databases container and then click Refresh.

23. In the console tree, expand the Databases container, expand the Accounting database, and then click Users.

    In the details pane, notice that one SelfPacedSQL group and one SelfPacedSQL user can access this database. Also notice that neither this user nor this group has explicit access to this SQL Server 2000 instance. To access this SQL Server 2000 instance, this user and members of this group must belong to the SQL Server Users group. Although we could have granted this user and this group explicit permission to log in to this SQL Server 2000 instance, there are good reasons for this structure. Chapter 11 will cover strategies for using login groups, data access groups, and permissions.

24. In the details pane, double-click SelfPacedSQL\Elba.

    The Database User Properties – SelfPacedSQL\Elba dialog box appears. Notice that Elba is a member of the public role and the Data Entry Managers role. Also notice that no login name exists for this user. She must log in by group membership.

25. Click the Permissions button.

    Notice that Elba has no permissions. In Chapter 11, you will grant permissions to the Data Entry Managers role and the public role.

26. Click Cancel.

27. Click Cancel in the Database User Properties – SelfPacedSQL\Elba dialog box.

28. Switch to SQL Query Analyzer.

29. On the toolbar, click the Load SQL Script button.

    The Open Query File dialog box appears.

30. Open DatabaseAccess.sql in the C:\SelfPacedSQL\CH_10 folder.

    A Transact-SQL script appears containing three system stored procedures that query regarding the Accounting database. The *sp_helpuser* system stored procedure queries regarding the SelfPacedSQL\Accounting Users Windows groups. The *sp_helprolemember* system stored procedure queries regarding the Data Entry Managers user-defined database role. The *sp_helpntgroup* system stored procedure queries regarding all Windows groups with access to the current database.

31. Click the Execute Query button to execute the *DatabaseAccess.sql* statement.

    In the results pane, notice that the SelfPacedSQL\Accounting Users group is a member of the public role in this database. Also notice that SelfPacedSQL\Elba is a member of the Data Entry Managers group. Also notice that the SelfPaced-SQL\Accounting Users group is the only Windows group with database access.

Lesson Summary

You can use SQL Server Enterprise Manager to grant Windows users and groups access to a SQL Server 2000 instance. As part of the same process, you can grant them authorization to perform server-wide tasks, grant them access to specific databases, and add them to database roles. You must perform this process one user at a time. You can use Transact-SQL system stored procedures to perform the same tasks for many users in a single script. You can view SQL Server access and database access rights for users with either SQL Server Enterprise Manager or Transact-SQL.

Review

Here are some questions to help you determine whether you have learned enough to move on to the next chapter. If you have difficulty answering these questions, review the material in this chapter before beginning the next chapter. The answers for these questions are located in the Appendix, "Questions and Answers."

1. You are concerned about keeping the data stored within your SQL Server 2000 installation extremely secure. All of the users who will access this data are Windows 2000 users. Should you permit SQL Server authentication? Why or why not?

2. A member of the help desk staff has complained that although she can log on to SQL Server 2000 and access the Northwind and Pubs databases, she cannot even see the Northwind Reports database. How is this possible?

3. You are creating a new SQL Server 2000 installation. Hundreds of users will require access to several different databases on this SQL Server 2000 instance. Should you use SQL Server Enterprise Manager or Transact-SQL system stored procedures for creating these login and user accounts? Why?

C H A P T E R   1 1

Managing SQL Server Permissions

About This Chapter

After you have provided for user access to SQL Server 2000 and its databases through the use of Microsoft Windows 2000 users and groups, and SQL Server 2000 security accounts where necessary, you must configure permissions for these users. In this chapter, you will learn how to configure database-specific permissions for users, Windows groups, and user-defined database roles. You will also learn how to use application roles. Finally, you will learn some strategies for designing security implementation scenarios combining the use of all these tools.

Before You Begin

To complete this chapter, you must have

- A computer that meets or exceeds the minimum hardware requirements listed in Table 2.1, "Hardware Requirements," in Lesson 1 of Chapter 2.
- Microsoft Windows 2000 Server running on your computer on an NTFS partition.
- A computer with a NetBIOS name of SelfPacedCPU, configured as a domain controller in the SelfPacedSQL.MSFT domain.
- Installed a default instance and at least one named instance of SQL Server 2000 (see Chapter 2).
- Created the SSEMDB database using the CreateDB.sql script (see Chapter 6).
- Completed the practice exercises in Chapter 10.

Lesson 1: Granting Database-Specific Permissions

Regardless of the authentication method by which a user receives access to SQL Server 2000, the user must have permissions to perform any activities within a user database. In the previous chapter you learned how to grant user permissions using server roles and fixed database roles. In this lesson, you learn about the difference between the use of fixed roles and the granting of specific statement and object permissions to users, groups, and user-defined database roles, including how to grant statement and object permissions using SQL Server Enterprise Manager and Transact-SQL statements and system stored procedures.

After this lesson, you will be able to

- Describe each type of database-specific permission
- Grant, revoke, and deny statement permissions
- Grant, revoke, and deny object permissions
- Determine and view effective permissions

Estimated lesson time: 45 minutes

Implementing Permissions

Database users need permission to work with data, execute stored procedures, create database objects, and perform administration tasks. Users acquire full or limited permissions within a database in a variety of ways.

- Membership in the sysadmin server role
- Individual ownership of the database
- Ownership of a database object individually, through a database role, or through a Windows 2000 (or Windows NT 4.0) group
- Membership in a fixed database role
- The granting of specific permissions individually, through a database role, or through a Windows 2000 (or Windows NT 4.0) group
- The inheritance of public role permissions as a permitted database user
- The inheritance of guest user permissions as a user with no permitted database access

Inherited Permissions

The database owner, members of the sysadmin server role, and members of the db_owner fixed database role inherit full permission to perform any activity within a database. In addition, members of a fixed database role inherit broad permissions to perform specific types of tasks. For example, members of the db_securityadmin fixed database role can run *GRANT*, *REVOKE*, or *DENY* statements with respect to all database objects, but they have no permission to execute any *CREATE* or *BACKUP* statement. Likewise, members of the db_ddladmin fixed database role can run any *CREATE* or *BACKUP* statement, but they have no permission to run the *GRANT*, *REVOKE*, or *DENY* statements. Furthermore, members of the db_datareader role can read data from any table or view within the database, and members of the db_datawriter role can write and modify data within all tables and views in the database.

An object owner (you must grant a user the right to create an object) inherits all permissions associated with the object, including the right to grant other users permissions to use the object. Members of the sysadmin server role, the db_ddladmin fixed database role, and the db_securityadmin fixed database role can change ownership of any object in the database (and revoke all permissions on the object).

Permission Actions and Conflicts

The broad scope of permissions contained in server roles and fixed database roles, as well as specifically limited statement and object permissions, can be granted (or denied) to Windows groups and user-defined roles (in addition to individual users). Permissions granted to a group or a role apply to all members of the group or role. The effective permissions of a user that is a member of multiple groups or roles are the cumulative permissions of the roles and groups.

You can also revoke or deny permission to specific roles, groups, or users. As in Windows 2000, the denial of permission takes precedence over all other permissions. For example, if you grant permission to a user to view a table, but that user is a member of a group or role to which you have denied permission, the user is denied permission to view the table.

Note   The grant or denial of permissions to a Windows user or group has no effect when a connection is established using a SQL Server 2000 security account. SQL Server 2000 has no knowledge of that Windows user, only of the SQL Server 2000 security account used and its permissions.

Practice: Creating and Testing Permission Conflicts

In this practice you create a permission conflict and then test it.

▶ **To create and test permission conflicts**

1. Ensure that you are logged on to the SelfPacedSQL.MSFT domain controller as Administrator.

2. Click Start, point to Programs, point to Microsoft SQL Server, and then click Enterprise Manager.

   SQL Server Enterprise Manager appears displaying the Microsoft SQL Servers and the Event Viewer (Local) console trees in the console root.

3. In the console tree, expand the Microsoft SQL Servers container, expand the SQL Server Group container, expand the default instance, expand the Databases Container, expand the SSEMDB database container, and then click Users.

4. In the details pane, double-click Joe.

   The Database User Properties – Joe dialog box appears.

5. In the Database Role Membership group box, select the Db_owner check box and then click the Apply button.

6. Click Start, point to Programs, point to Microsoft SQL Server, and then click Query Analyzer.

   The Connect To SQL Server dialog box appears.

7. Click the SQL Server Authentication option button.

8. In the Login Name text box, type **Joe**.

9. In the Password text box, type **password** and then click OK.

   Notice that you are connected as Joe to the master database.

10. On the toolbar, change the current database to SSEMDB in the database drop-down list.

11. In the query pane, type **SELECT * FROM Customer**.

12. On the toolbar, click the Execute Query button.

    Notice that Joe can view all rows in the Customer table.

13. Switch to SQL Server Enterprise Manager.

14. In the Database Role Membership group box, select the Db_denydatareader check box and then click the Apply button.

    Do not close the Database User Properties – Joe dialog box. You will use this dialog box in the next practice.

15. Switch to SQL Query Analyzer.

16. On the toolbar, click the Execute Query button to re-execute the SELECT *
    FROM Customer query.

    Notice that Joe no longer has permission to view any rows in the Customer
    table. There is a permission conflict, and the DENY permission supersedes all
    grants of permissions.

17. Do not close SQL Server Enterprise Manager or SQL Query Analyzer.

Managing Statement Permissions

Statement permissions are permissions to run particular Transact-SQL statements
that create databases and database objects (such as tables, views, and stored procedures) in that database. Table 11.1 describes the permissions associated with these
statements. Permissions with respect to each of these statements can be granted,
denied, or revoked.

Creating Objects and Chain of Ownership Issues

When a user creates a database object (such as a table or view), the user is the
owner of the object (unless another user, group, or role is specified as the owner).
Allowing a user to own objects can be useful during development of a database, but
it causes problems in production and so you should avoid it for several reasons (as
covered in the rest of this section). It is good practice to have all objects in a production database owned by the dbo role.

When a user references an object in a script, the object can be qualified with the
name of the object owner or it can be unqualified. If the object is unqualified as to
the owner, SQL Server 2000 looks for the object in the database as either owned by
the user executing the script or owned by the dbo role. If it is not found as owned
by either, an error is returned.

```
SELECT * FROM Customer
```

The preceding example will return the data within the Customer table provided that
the table is either owned by the dbo role or owned by the user executing the script.

```
SELECT * FROM Joe.Customer
```

The preceding example will return the data within the Customer table owned by
Joe. If there is another Customer table in the database owned by the dbo role, it will
not be returned. Having multiple tables with the same name and having to specify a
name other than dbo can cause confusion.

In addition, views and stored procedures can be created on tables. When a user
attempts to select information through a view or procedure, SQL Server 2000 must
verify whether the user is permitted to view the data. If the view or procedure is
owned by one user and the underlying table owned by another, SQL Server 2000
must check permissions on each object in the chain. As the chain of ownership

lengthens, this can affect performance. But perhaps more importantly, it can be very confusing for an administrator to trace and debug security issues.

Table 11-1.   Statement Permissions

Transact-SQL Statement	Permission to Execute the Transact-SQL Statement
CREATE DATABASE	Inherited by members of the sysadmin and dbcreator server roles. Although the sysadmin and securityadmin server roles can grant permission directly to security accounts to run this statement, generally the security accounts use the dbcreator server role if the system administrator delegates permission. This permission exists only in the master database.
BACKUP DATABASE BACKUP LOG	Inherited by members of the sysadmin server role and the db_owner and db_backupoperator fixed database roles. Although you can grant permission to run these statements directly to security accounts, generally you will use the db_backupoperator fixed database role.
CREATE TABLE CREATE VIEW CREATE PROCEDURE CREATE DEFAULT CREATE RULE CREATE FUNCTION	Inherited by members of the sysadmin server role and the db_owner and db_ddladmin fixed database roles. Permission to create these objects is sometimes granted directly to programmers (or to a programmers' group or role) during development. By default, objects are owned by the creator of the object (although objects created by members of the sysadmin server role are owned by the dbo role). Members of the db_owner or db_ddladmin fixed database roles can designate the dbo role as the owner of an object they create. In addition, members of the sysadmin server role or the db_owner or db_ddladmin fixed database role can designate any user as the owner of an object they create. However, users who are not members of one of these roles cannot designate another user or the dbo role as the owner of an object they create.
CREATE TRIGGER	Inherited by the table owner on which the trigger is defined, members of the sysadmin server role, and the db_owner and db_ddladmin fixed database roles. These members cannot grant permission to run this statement to other security accounts.

When members of the db_owner and db_ddladmin fixed database roles create a database object, it is good practice to specify the dbo role as the owner of the object. If no owner is specified, ownership will default to the Windows user or SQL Server 2000 login account that created the object.

```
CREATE TABLE Northwind.dbo.CustomerTable
    ( CustID nchar (5) , CustomerName nvarchar (40) )
```

The preceding example shows the creation of a table granting the ownership to the dbo role. Only members of the sysadmin server role and the db_owner or db_ddladmin fixed database roles can successfully execute this statement.

Changing Object Ownership

If a database object exists with an owner other than the dbo role, you might need to change its ownership. A member of the db_owner, db_ddladmin, or db_securityadmin fixed database role, or a member of the sysadmin server role can change the ownership of any object in the database by running the *sp_changeobjectowner* system stored procedure.

```
sp_changeobjectowner 'SelfPacedSQL\Bill.Customer' , 'dbo'
```

The preceding example changes the ownership of the Customer table from Self-PacedSQL\Bill to the dbo role.

Note   Changing the owner of an object removes all existing permissions on the object. If you need to retain the permissions, script out the existing permissions before running the *sp_changeobjectowner* system stored procedure. You can then reapply the permissions by modifying the object owner in the saved script and then running the saved permissions script.

Using SQL Server Enterprise Manager to Grant, Deny, or Revoke Statement Permissions

SQL Server Enterprise Manager provides a simple graphical interface for viewing existing statement permissions and granting, denying, and revoking statement permissions. To view statement permissions within a database, right-click the database and then click Properties. On the Permissions tab in the Properties dialog box, you can view, grant, revoke, or deny permissions. See Figure 11.1.

Notice that each permitted user and user-defined database role is displayed along with the specific statement permissions granted that user or role, if any. A green check means granted, a red X means denied, and a cleared check box means revoked or neutral. Remember that permissions are generally cumulative, but that a DENY permission takes precedence. For example, in this figure the role public has been denied permission to create a table. Therefore, the login Joe will not be able to create a table although he has been specifically granted that permission. However, a denial of statement permissions has no effect on a member of the sysadmin server role (which includes the sa account). Finally, the statement permissions displayed are only those statement permissions directly granted. Statement permissions inherited by a user account by virtue of membership in a server role or a fixed database role are not displayed here.

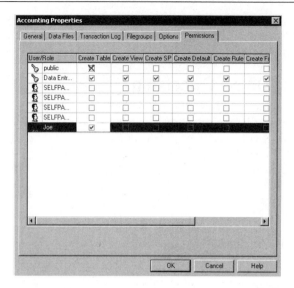

Figure 11.1.   Viewing and changing statement permissions.

Using Transact-SQL to Grant, Deny, or Revoke Statement Permissions

You can use the *GRANT*, *DENY*, and *REVOKE* statements to manage statement permissions using Transact-SQL scripts. These statements can be used to grant, deny, and revoke permission to run specific statements. When these statements are used with the ALL keyword, permissions on all statements and objects are affected.

```
GRANT CREATE TABLE TO Joe, SalesManagers,
[SelfPacedSQL\SQLServerAdmins]
```

The preceding example grants the *CREATE TABLE* statement permission to Joe (a SQL Server login), SalesManagers (a user-defined database role), and SelfPaced-SQL\SQLServerAdmins (a Windows group).

Note   Specify BUILTIN rather than the domain or local computer name when referencing a Windows local built-in group, such as BUILTIN\Backup Operators.

```
DENY CREATE TABLE TO Joe
```

The preceding example denies the *CREATE TABLE* statement permission to Joe. To remove a DENY permission, use the *REVOKE* or the *GRANT* statement.

```
REVOKE ALL FROM Joe
```

The preceding example revokes all grants of permissions to Joe and revokes all denials of permissions to Joe. This includes statement and object permissions.

Viewing Statement Permissions Using Transact-SQL

You can view existing statement permissions within a database using the *sp_helprotect* system stored procedure. All database users have permission to execute this system stored procedure.

```
EXEC sp_helprotect NULL, NULL, NULL, 's'
```

The preceding example lists all statement permissions in the current database.

Practice: Granting and Testing Statement Permissions

In this practice you grant and test statement permissions.

▶   **To grant and test statement permissions**

1. Switch to SQL Query Analyzer.
2. Verify that you are connected as Joe.
3. On the toolbar, click the Load SQL Script button.

    A SQL Query Analyzer dialog box appears asking if you want to save the changes to the previous script.

4. Click the No button.

    The Open Query File dialog box appears.

5. Open CreateTestTable1.sql in the C:\SelfPacedSQL\CH_11 folder.

    A Transact-SQL script appears that will create a new table called TestTable1 and add a single row of data to the newly created table. Notice that ownership of the table is not qualified as to owner. Finally, the script queries the newly created table.

6. On the toolbar, click the Execute Query button.

    Notice that the table is created successfully and one row of data added. Joe can create the table because he is a member of the db_owner role. However, Joe cannot view the data because he is a member of the db_denydatareader fixed database role.

7. Switch to SQL Server Enterprise Manager.

    Notice that the Database User Properties – Joe dialog box is still open from the last practice.

8. In the Database User Properties – Joe dialog box, clear the Db_denydatareader check box and then click the Apply button.

9. Switch to SQL Query Analyzer.

10. In the query pane, highlight SELECT * FROM TestTable1 and then click the Execute Query button on the toolbar.

    Notice that Joe can now execute the query successfully.

11. On the File menu, click Connect.

    The Connect To SQL Server dialog box appears.

12. Click the SQL Server Authentication option button.

13. In the Login Name text box, type **sa** and then click OK.

    Notice that you can connect as sa with no password. In a production environment, you should never enable Mixed Mode authentication and leave the sa password blank.

14. On the toolbar, change the current database to SSEMDB in the database drop-down list.

15. In the query pane, type **SELECT * FROM TestTable1** and then click the Execute Query button on the toolbar.

    Notice that the TestTable1 object is not found when the sa user account does not qualify TestTable1 as to the owner. The reason is that SQL Server 2000 only looks for this object as owned either by the sa user or by the dbo role. Because the table is owned by Joe, it is not found.

16. In the query pane, change the query to read **SELECT * FROM Joe.TestTable1** and then click the Execute Query button on the toolbar.

    Notice that the contents of the TestTable owned by Joe are displayed.

17. Switch to Joe's connection in SQL Query Analyzer.

18. Change the *CREATE TABLE* statement to qualify the owner as the dbo role (the statement should now begin *CREATE TABLE.dbo.TestTable1...*), and then click the Execute Query button on the toolbar.

    Notice that the table is created successfully and one row of data added. However, notice that the data was added to Joe.TestTable1, not to dbo.TestTable1.

19. Switch to SQL Server Enterprise Manager.

20. In the Database User Properties – Joe dialog box, clear the Db_owner check box and then click OK.

21. In the console tree, right-click the SSEMDB database container and then click Properties.

    The SSEMDB Properties dialog box appears, with the General tab selected.

22. Click the Permissions tab.

23. For the user Joe, select the Create Table, Create View, and Create SP check boxes and then click OK.

24. Switch to SQL Query Analyzer.

25. Verify that you are connected as Joe.

26. On the toolbar, click the Load SQL Script button.

    A SQL Query Analyzer dialog box appears asking if you want to save the changes to the previous script.

27. Click the No button.

    The Open Query File dialog box appears.

28. Open CreateTestTable2_Proc2View2.sql in the C:\SelfPacedSQL\CH_11 folder.

    A Transact-SQL script appears that will create a new table called TestTable2, add a single row of data to the newly created table, create a stored procedure that displays three columns from the table, and create a view that displays two columns from the table. Notice that ownership of each object created is not qualified as to owner. Finally, the script queries the newly created table.

29. On the toolbar, click the Execute Query button.

    Notice that the table, procedure, and view are all created successfully. Joe has explicit permission to create tables, stored procedures, and views. Joe can display the contents of the table and the view and execute the stored procedure because he is the owner of these objects.

30. Switch to SQL Server Enterprise Manager.

31. In the console tree, under the SSEMDB container, click the Stored Procedures container.

32. Right-click Stored Procedures and then click Refresh.

    Notice, in the details pane, that Joe is the owner of the TestTable2_Procedure2 stored procedure.

33. Switch to SQL Query Analyzer.

34. Verify that you are connected as Joe.

35. Change the *CREATE TABLE* statement to qualify the owner as the dbo role (the statement should now begin *CREATE TABLE.dbo.TestTable2…*).

36. Highlight the entire *CREATE TABLE* statement (but no other statements in the script), and then click the Execute Query button on the toolbar.

    Notice that Joe cannot create the table specifying the dbo role as the owner. The CREATE TABLE permission does not grant this privilege (unlike membership in the db_owner fixed database role).

37. Switch to the sa connection in SQL Query Analyzer.

38. On the toolbar, click the Load SQL Script button.

    A SQL Query Analyzer dialog box appears asking if you want to save the changes to the previous script.

39. Click the No button.

    The Open Query File dialog box appears.

40. Open TestTable2_ChangeOwner.sql in the C:\SelfPacedSQL\CH_11 folder.

    A Transact-SQL script appears that will change the ownership of TestTable2, TestTable2_Procedure2, and TestTable2View2 to the dbo role. It will then test the ownership change.

41. On the toolbar, click the Execute Query button.

    Notice that the ownership of each of these three database objects is successfully changed.

42. Close all connections in SQL Query Analyzer. Do not save any changes.

43. On the File menu, click Connect.

    The Connect To SQL Server dialog box appears.

44. Click the SQL Server Authentication option button.

45. In the Login Name text box, type **Joe**.

46. In the Password text box, type **password** and then click OK.

    Notice that you are connected as Joe to the master database.

47. On the toolbar, change the current database to SSEMDB in the database drop-down list.

48. In the query pane, type **SELECT * FROM TestTable2** and then click the Execute Query button on the toolbar.

    Notice that Joe cannot view any rows in the TestTable2 table. The dbo role now owns the table. Joe has no SELECT permissions on any objects of which he is not the owner.

49. On the toolbar, click the Clear Window button.

50. In the query pane, type **EXEC sp_helprotect NULL, NULL, NULL, 's'** and then click the Execute Query button on the toolbar.

    Notice that the three statement permissions granted to Joe are displayed. Any permissions granted by virtue of membership in a fixed database role are not displayed.

51. Close all open connections in SQL Query Analyzer, but do not close SQL Query Analyzer.

Managing Object Permissions

Object permissions are permissions to perform actions with respect to tables, views, functions, and stored procedures. Table 11.2 describes the type of object permissions associated with database objects. Permission with respect to each of these statements can be granted, denied, or revoked by members of the sysadmin server role or the db_owner and db_securityadmin fixed database roles (or by a database object owner).

Table 11-2.   Types of Object Permissions Associated with Database Objects

Database Object Permission	Permission on the Database Object
SELECT	Permission to view information in a table, view, column, or certain user-defined functions. Inherited by members of sysadmin server role and the db_owner and db_datareader fixed database roles. Denied to all members of the db_denydatareader fixed database role.
INSERT	Permission to add new data to a table or view. Inherited by members of sysadmin server role and the db_owner and db_datawriter fixed database roles. Denied to all members of the db_denydatawriter fixed database role.
UPDATE	Permission to update data in a table, column, or view. Inherited by members of sysadmin server role and the db_owner and db_datawriter fixed database roles. Denied to all members of the db_denydatawriter fixed database role.
DELETE	Permission to delete data from a table or view. Inherited by members of sysadmin server role and the db_owner and db_datawriter fixed database roles. Denied to all members of the db_denydatawriter fixed database role.
EXECUTE	Permission to run stored procedures and user-defined functions. Inherited by members of sysadmin server role and the db_owner fixed database roles.
REFERENCES	Permission to refer to a table with a FOREIGN KEY constraint without having SELECT permissions on the table. Inherited by members of sysadmin server role and the db_owner and db_datareader fixed database roles. Denied to all members of the db_denydatareader fixed database role.

Notice that you can use the db_datareader and db_denydatareader fixed database roles to grant or deny the SELECT and REFERENCES object permissions with respect to all objects in the database. You can also use the db_datawriter and db_denydatawriter fixed database roles to grant or deny the INSERT, UPDATE, and DELETE object permissions with respect to all objects in the database. To grant the EXECUTE object permission to a user, you generally must specifically grant that permission (to a user, group, or role) because no fixed database role (other than db_owner fixed database role) grants that permission. In addition, if you need to grant or deny object permissions on a subset of the database objects in a database, you must specifically grant or deny those object permissions. You can grant, deny, or revoke them with respect to a user-defined database role, Windows group, SQL Server login, or Windows user.

Finally, a user or role can be denied permission to view or update a table directly, but may be given permissions on the table through a view or a stored procedure.

For example, a view can be created that displays only certain columns or rows in a table. A user can then be permitted to update data through the view (such as certain employee information without seeing all employee information). Or a stored procedure can be created that displays all employee names, but no other information.

Using SQL Server Enterprise Manager

SQL Server Enterprise Manager provides a simple graphical interface for viewing existing object permissions and granting, denying, and revoking object permissions. To view object permissions for a table, view, or stored procedure, right-click the object in the details pane and then click Properties to display the Properties dialog box. Click the Permissions button, which displays the Object Properties dialog box, to view, grant, revoke, or deny permissions. See Figure 11.2.

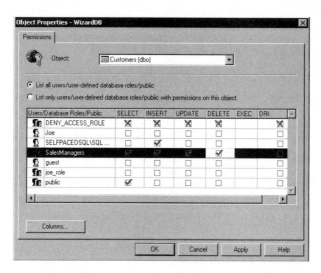

Figure 11.2.   Viewing and changing object permissions.

As in the graphical interface for statement permissions, each permitted user and user-defined database role is displayed along with the specific object permissions granted that user or role. Notice that you can choose to list only the users or roles that actually have permissions on this object. See Figure 11.3.

You can also click a particular user or role and then click the Columns button, which displays the Column Permissions dialog box, to view or control permissions at the column level. For example, you might want to restrict SELECT or UPDATE permissions on a particular column in a table to which you have granted SELECT or UPDATE permissions. See Figure 11.4.

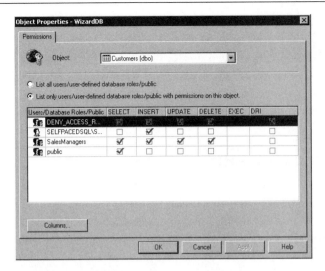

Figure 11.3.   Viewing only users or roles with permissions on the particular object.

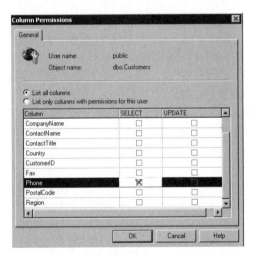

Figure 11.4.   Restricting permissions on a specific column.

In addition, from the Object Properties dialog box for any table, view, or stored procedure, you can change to any other object by clicking that object in the Object drop-down list. See Figure 11.5.

Notice that a stored procedure is now displayed in Figure 11.5. The only permission available for a stored procedure is EXECUTE.

In addition to viewing object permissions from the object perspective, you can also view and manage object permissions from the user or role perspective. In the details pane of Enterprise Manager, right-click a user-defined database role or a permitted user, click Properties, and then click the Permissions button. See Figure 11.6.

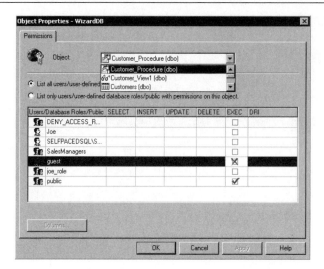

Figure 11.5. Changing the object for which you are viewing permissions.

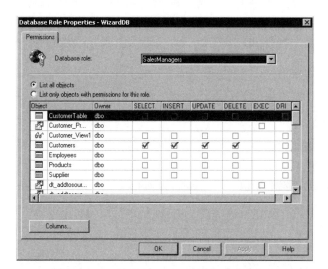

Figure 11.6. Viewing object permissions from the user or role perspective.

In Figure 11.6, notice that you can either list only the objects with permissions for this role or list all objects for which you can configure permissions. This interface eases the task of viewing and configuring permissions from the perspective of a role or a user.

Note After you have configured permissions with SQL Server Enterprise Manager for database objects, you should use the scripting capability of SQL Server Enterprise Manager to generate Transact-SQL scripts to enable you to reconstruct these permissions should the need arise.

Using Transact-SQL to Grant, Deny, or Revoke Object Permissions

You can use the *GRANT*, *DENY*, and *REVOKE* statements to manage object permissions using Transact-SQL scripts.

```
GRANT SELECT ON Customer TO Joe, SalesUsers,
[SelfPacedSQL\SQLServerUsers]
```

The preceding example grants the SELECT object permission on the Customer table to Joe (a SQL Server login), SalesUsers (a user-defined database role), and SelfPacedSQL\SQLServerUsers (a Windows group).

```
DENY INSERT, UPDATE, DELETE TO Joe
```

The preceding example denies the INSERT, UPDATE, and DELETE object permissions to Joe.

When granting object permissions using Transact-SQL statements, you also have the option to use the WITH GRANT OPTION clause. Through the use of this option, you can grant a user, role, or group specified object permissions and also grant that user the right to grant those same permissions to any other permitted user, role, or group in the database.

```
GRANT SELECT ON Customer TO SalesManagers WITH GRANT OPTION
```

The preceding example grants the SELECT object permission on the Customer table to SalesManagers (a user-defined database role). Any member of the Sales-Managers role can grant the SELECT object permission on the Customer table. If the WITH GRANT OPTION clause is granted to a group, a user from this group attempting to grant this permission to another user, group, or role with the *GRANT* statement must use the AS option.

```
GRANT SELECT ON Customer TO Joe AS SalesManagers
```

The preceding example grants the SELECT object permission on the Customer table to Joe. The member of the SalesManagers role executing this *GRANT* statement references his or her membership in the SalesUsers role by using the AS option to validate his or her permission to exercise the GRANT permission.

To revoke the WITH GRANT OPTION clause without revoking the underlying permissions, use the GRANT OPTION FOR clause.

```
REVOKE GRANT OPTION FOR ON Customer FROM Joe AS SalesManagers
```

The preceding example revokes the WITH GRANT OPTION clause from Joe without revoking Joe's permission on the Customer table. To deny or revoke object permissions initially granted using the WITH GRANT OPTION clause, specify the CASCADE clause to also revoke or deny permissions that were granted from the original account.

```
REVOKE GRANT OPTION FOR ON Customer FROM Joe CASCADE AS SalesManagers
```

The preceding example revokes the WITH GRANT OPTION clause from Joe and also revokes all permissions granted by Joe to other users.

Note Use the WITH GRANT OPTION clause with extreme caution. The only future control you have over the security accounts that receive permission is to revoke or deny object permissions after the fact (and possibly after damage has occurred).

Viewing Permissions

You can view existing object permissions within a database using the *sp_helprotect* system stored procedure. All database users have permission to execute this system stored procedure.

```
EXEC sp_helprotect 'Customer'
```

The preceding example lists all object permissions for the Customer table in the current database.

```
EXEC sp_helprotect NULL , 'Joe'
```

The preceding example lists all statement and object permissions that Joe has in the current database.

```
EXEC sp_helprotect NULL , NULL , 'SalesManagers'
```

The preceding example lists all object permissions granted by members of the SalesManagers role in the current database.

Practice: Granting and Testing Object Permissions

In this practice you grant and test object permissions.

▶ **To grant and test object permissions**

1. Switch to SQL Query Analyzer.
2. On the File menu, click Connect.

   The Connect To SQL Server dialog box appears.
3. Click the SQL Server Authentication option button.
4. In the Login Name text box, type **sa** and then click OK.

   Notice that you are connected as sa to the master database.

5. On the toolbar, change the current database to SSEMDB in the database drop-down list.

6. On the toolbar, click the Load SQL Script button.

   The Open Query File dialog box appears.

7. Open View_Proc.sql in the C:\SelfPacedSQL\CH_11 folder.

   A Transact-SQL script appears that will create a new stored procedure called Customer_Procedure, grant EXECUTE permissions on this procedure to the guest group, create a new view called Customer_View1, and grant SELECT permissions on this view to the public group.

8. On the toolbar, click the Execute Query button.

   Notice that the Customer_Procedure was created and EXECUTE permissions were granted to the guest user role. Notice also that the Customer_view was created and SELECT permissions granted to the public role.

9. On the File menu, click Connect.

   The Connect To SQL Server dialog box appears.

10. Click the SQL Server Authentication option button.

11. In the Login Name text box, type **Ana**.

12. In the Password text box, type **password** and then click OK.

    Notice that you are connected as Ana to the master database.

13. On the toolbar, verify that Ana cannot change the current database to SSEMDB in the database drop-down list.

    Ana is not a user in the SSEMDB database.

14. In the query pane, type **EXEC SSEMDB.dbo.Customer_Procedure** and then click the Execute Query button on the toolbar.

    Notice that Ana cannot execute the Customer_Procedure in the SSEMDB database, even though she is not a user in the SSEMDB database and EXECUTE permissions have been granted to the guest user account.

15. Switch to the sa connection in SQL Query Analyzer.

16. On the toolbar, click the Clear Window button.

17. In the query pane, type **sp_helpuser 'guest'** and then click the Execute Query button on the toolbar.

    Notice that there is no guest user account in the SSEMDB database. This is why Ana cannot access the SSEMDB database.

18. On the toolbar, click the Clear Window button.

19. Type **sp_grantdbaccess 'guest'** and then click the Execute Query button on the toolbar.

    Notice that the guest user role has been granted user access to the SSEMDB database.

20. Switch to the Ana connection in SQL Query Analyzer.

21. Re-execute the EXEC SSEMDB.dbo.Customer_Procedure query.

    Notice that Ana is now able to execute the *Customer_Procedure* stored procedure, which displays three of the columns from the Customer table.

22. On a new line, type **SELECT * FROM SSEMDB.dbo.Customer_View1**.

23. Highlight this new query and then click the Execute Query button on the toolbar.

    Notice that Ana is able to select information from Customer_View1. She is a guest user and SELECT permissions have been granted to the public role, of which the guest user is a member.

24. Switch to the sa connection in SQL Query Analyzer.

25. On the toolbar, click the Clear Window button.

26. Type **sp_grantdbaccess 'Ana'** and then click the Execute Query button on the toolbar.

    Notice that Ana has been granted user access to the SSEMDB database.

27. Switch to the Ana connection in SQL Query Analyzer.

28. On the toolbar, click the Execute Query button to re-execute both queries.

    Notice that Ana is no longer able to execute the *Customer_Procedure* stored procedure, although she is able to select from the Customer_View1 view. She is now a user in the SSEMDB database. EXECUTE permissions have only been granted to the guest user account, not to the public role.

29. Switch to SQL Server Enterprise Manager.

30. In the SSEMDB database container, right-click Users and then click Refresh.

31. In the SSEMDB datasbase container, right-click Roles and then click New Database Role.

    The Database Role Properties – New Role dialog box appears.

32. In the Name text box, type **SSEMDB_CustomRole**.

33. Click OK.

    The SSEMDB_CustomRole appears in the details pane.

34. In the details pane, double-click SSEMDB_CustomRole.

    The Database Role Properties – SSEMDB_CustomRole dialog box appears. Notice that no one is currently a member of this user-defined database role.

35. Click the Add button.

    The Add Role Members dialog box appears.

36. Click Ana and then click OK.

    Notice that Ana now appears as a member of the SSEMDB_CustomRole.

37. Click the Apply button.

38. Click the Permissions button.

    The Database Role Properties – SSEMDB dialog box appears. Notice that this role has no current permissions.

39. For the object, Customer_View1, select the Select, Insert, Update, and Delete check boxes.

    Notice that a green check mark appears indicating that this role will be granted SELECT, INSERT, UPDATE, and DELETE permissions on this object.

40. For the object, Customer_View1, select the Select, Insert, Update, and Delete check boxes again.

    Notice that a red X appears indicating that this role will be denied SELECT, INSERT, UPDATE, and DELETE permissions on this object.

41. Click OK.

42. Switch to the Ana connection in SQL Query Analyzer.

43. On the toolbar, click the Execute Query button.

    Notice that Ana can neither execute the stored procedure nor select from the view.

44. Switch to SQL Server Enterprise Manager.

45. In the Database Role Properties - SSEMDB_CustomRole dialog box, click Ana and then click the Remove button.

46. Click OK.

47. In the console tree, click the Stored Procedures container.

48. In the details pane, double-click Customer_Procedure.

    The Stored Procedure Properties – Customer_Procedure dialog box appears.

49. Click the Permissions button.

    The Object Properties – SSEMDB dialog box appears.

50. For the database user, Ana, select the Exec check box and then click OK.

51. In the Stored Procedure Properties – Customer_Procedure dialog box, click OK.

52. Switch to the Ana connection in SQL Query Analyzer.

53. On the toolbar, click the Execute Query button.

    Notice that Ana can execute the stored procedure and select from the view.

54. Switch to SQL Server Enterprise Manager.

55. Click the Tables container.

56. In the details pane, double-click Customer.

    The Table Properties – Customer dialog box appears.

57. Click the Permissions button.

    The Object Properties – SSEMDB dialog box appears.

58. For the user, Ana, click the Select check box twice to deny SELECT permissions on the Customer database object and then click OK.

59. In the Table Properties – Customer dialog box, click OK.

60. Switch to the Ana connection in SQL Query Analyzer.

61. On the toolbar, click the Execute Query button.

    Notice that Ana can still execute the stored procedure and select from the view, although she has been denied direct SELECT permissions on the underlying table.

62. Switch to SQL Server Enterprise Manager.

63. Click the Roles container.

64. In the details pane, double-click SSEMDB_CustomRole.

    The Database Role Properties – SSEMDB_CustomRole dialog box appears.

65. Click the Add button.

    The Add Role Members dialog box appears.

66. Select Ana, and then click OK.

67. Click the Permissions button.

    The Database Role Properties – SSEMDB dialog box appears.

68. For the object Customer_Procedure, click the Exec check box twice to deny EXECUTE permissions and then click OK.

69. Click OK.

70. Switch to the Ana connection in SQL Query Analyzer.

71. On the toolbar, click the Execute Query button.

    Notice that Ana can neither execute the stored procedure nor select from the view.

72. Switch to the sa connection in SQL Query Analyzer.

73. On the toolbar, click the Clear Window button.

74. Type **sp_helprotect 'customer_procedure'** and then click the Execute Query button on the toolbar.

    Notice the object permissions on the customer_procedure database object.

75. On the toolbar, click the Clear Window button.

76. Type **sp_helprotect 'customer_view1'** and then click the Execute Query button on the toolbar.

    Notice the object permissions on the customer_view1 database object.

77. Do not close SQL Server Enterprise Manager or the two connections in SQL Query Analyzer.

Lesson Summary

Statement and object permissions can be specifically granted to, revoked from, or denied to users, Windows groups, and user-defined roles. This capability is used to augment the permissions granted or denied through the use of fixed database roles. Generally, you will use this capability to extend or limit object permissions. However, you generally use fixed database roles (in addition to the sysadmin server role) for statement permissions. You can manage and view permissions using either SQL Server Enterprise Manager or Transact-SQL. The graphical interface makes the task quite simple, and Transact-SQL scripts allow you to apply security to many objects in a single script. When you use SQL Server Enterprise Manager, you should generate scripts to enable you to reconstruct or copy the security structure should the need arise.

Lesson 2: Using Application Roles

In addition to granting access to users and groups and then assigning them permissions, you can create an application role within a database with specific permissions through which users access data in SQL Server 2000. In this lesson, you will learn to create application roles using SQL Server Enterprise Manager and Transact-SQL. You also learn the security implications of using application roles.

After this lesson, you will be able to

- Create application roles
- Activate and use application roles

Estimated lesson time: 30 minutes

Understanding Application Roles

You use an application role to restrict user access to data in SQL Server 2000 through a specific application (such as Microsoft Excel or a custom accounting application). Restricting user access to an application prevents users from executing poorly written queries or attempting to access any sensitive information.

An application role is a database role to which permissions are assigned. An application role contains no members and is inactive by default. You cannot add Windows 2000 or Windows NT 4.0 groups, users, or roles to application roles. An application must submit a password to activate the application role. A password can be hard-coded into an application, or it can be an encrypted key in the registry or in a SQL Server 2000 database.

The permissions of a user accessing SQL Server 2000 through an application role are limited to the permissions granted to the application role. The existing permissions, or the lack of permissions, by the user accessing SQL Server 2000 through an application role are ignored. In addition, an application role is database-specific, meaning that any access beyond the database in which the application role exists is limited to guest user access.

Creating Application Roles

Creating an application role using SQL Server Enterprise Manager is substantially the same as creating a user-defined database role. Within the database in which you are creating the application role, right-click the Roles container and then click New Database Role. In the Database Role Properties – New Role dialog box, enter a name for the new role in the Name text box, click the Application Role option button, and then enter a password into the Password text box. See Figure 11.7.

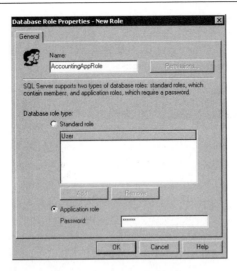

Figure 11.7. Creating an application role.

After creating the application role, configure permissions for the role the same way you configure permissions for a user-defined database role, by clicking the Permissions button. See Figure 11.8.

You can also create an application role using the Transact-SQL *sp_addapprole* system stored procedure.

```
sp_addapprole 'AccountingAppRole' , 'AppPassword'
```

The preceding example creates the AccountingAppRole with a password of App-Password in the current database. You grant permissions to an application role with Transact-SQL using the same *GRANT*, *REVOKE*, and *DENY* statements used to manage user, group, and user-defined database role permissions.

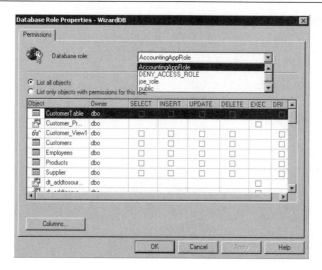

Figure 11.8.   Configuring permissions for the new role.

Activating and Using Application Roles

To activate an application role, use the *sp_setapprole* system stored procedure. Once the application role has been activated, the user (using the application that activated the application role) can perform whatever activities are permitted to the application role.

```
EXEC sp_setapprole 'AccountingAppRole' , {Encrypt N 'AppPassword'} , 'od
bc'
```

The preceding example activates the AccountingAppRole using the AppPassword. It uses the ODBC encryption method before sending the password to SQL Server 2000.

Practice: Creating and Testing Application Roles

In this practice you create and test application roles.

▶   **To create and test application roles**

1. Switch to SQL Server Enterprise Manager.
2. In the console tree, expand the Databases container for the default instance, and then expand the SSEMDB database container.
3. Right-click Roles and then click New Database Role.

    The Database Role Properties – New Role dialog box appears.
4. In the Name text box, type **NewAppRole**.
5. Click the Application Role option button.
6. In the Password text box, type **pass** and then click OK.

7. In the details pane, double-click NewAppRole.

   The Database Role Properties – NewAppRole dialog box appears.

8. Click the Permissions button.

   The Database Role Properties – SSEMDB dialog box appears.

9. For the database object Customer_Procedure, select the Exec check box to grant EXECUTE permissions on this stored procedure.

10. For the database object Customer_View1, select the Select check box to grant SELECT permissions on this view and then click OK.

11. Click OK.

12. Switch to the Ana connection in SQL Query Analyzer.

13. Execute the two queries in the query pane to verify that Ana can neither execute Customer_Procedure nor select from Customer_View1.

14. Do not close this original connection for Ana.

15. On the File menu, click Connect.

    The Connect To SQL Server dialog box appears.

16. Click the SQL Server Authentication option button.

17. In the Login Name text box, type **Ana**.

18. In the Password text box, type **password** and then click OK.

    Notice that you are connected as Ana to the master database.

19. On the toolbar, change the current database to SSEMDB in the database drop-down list.

20. In the query pane, type **EXEC sp_setapprole 'NewAppRole' , 'pass'** and then click the Execute Query button on the toolbar.

    Notice that the NewAppRole has been activated.

21. On the toolbar, click the Clear Window button.

22. In the query pane, type **EXEC customer_procedure** and then click the Execute Query button on the toolbar.

    Notice that Ana can now execute this stored procedure through the application role.

23. On the toolbar, click the Clear Window button.

24. In the query pane, type **SELECT * FROM Customer_View1** and then click the Execute Query button on the toolbar.

    Notice that Ana can now select from this view through the application role.

25. Switch to the original Ana connection in SQL Query Analyzer.

26. Execute the queries.

    Notice that Ana can neither execute the stored procedure nor select from the view. She was able to use the permissions of the application role, but these permissions are valid only for that connection.

27. Close SQL Query Analyzer. This will also deactivate the application role. Do not save any changes.

Lesson Summary

Application roles are useful for limiting user access to specific applications only. You can create an application role and grant it permissions using either SQL Server Enterprise Manager or Transact-SQL. An application then activates the role by using the *sp_setapprole* system stored procedure and passing a password. All rights of users through the application role are limited to the rights of the application role, regardless of the rights of the actual user.

Lesson 3: Designing an Access and Permissions Strategy

Now that you understand the tools available to you for securing your data within SQL Server 2000, you must design an access and permissions strategy that works for your organization. In this lesson, you will learn access and permissions strategies incorporating these tools, and the strengths and weaknesses of each strategy in different environments.

After this lesson, you will be able to

- Understand the different access and permissions strategies available to you
- Evaluate and select an appropriate access and permissions strategy

Estimated lesson time: 15 minutes

Permitting Administrator Access

First, you need to determine which users will need full access to SQL Server 2000. In general, limit the number of users to whom you grant full access. To grant these users full access, you have a number of choices. If these users are currently members of the local Administrators group on the SQL Server 2000 computer (by default, domain administrators are members of the local Administrators group), they already have full access as members of the sysadmin server role. If they are not members of this local group, you can do one of the following:

- Add them individually to the local Administrators group.
- Create a login for each user in SQL Server 2000 using his or her Windows 2000 user account and add this login to the sysadmin server role.
- Create a Windows 2000 global group containing these users and make the SQL Server administrator group a member of the local Administrators group.
- Create a Windows 2000 global group containing these users, create a login for this global group, and add this login to the sysadmin server role.

In general, as the number of Windows 2000 users who will be SQL Server 2000 system administrators increases and as the number of computers running SQL Server 2000 increases, the more useful a dedicated Windows 2000 global security group becomes. Using a Windows group allows you to grant a user administrator access merely by adding him or her to this Windows group.

In addition, you might not want all members of the local Administrators group to have full access to SQL Server 2000. In this case, remove the login for the local

BUILTIN\Administrators group. However, before you remove this login, make sure you have provided alternate administrator access (generally with a dedicated SQL Server Administrator group login).

Using Windows Groups and SQL Server 2000 Server Roles

For users that require administrator access to SQL Server 2000, but for whom you do not want to grant full administrator access, use server roles to grant them the rights they absolutely require. Use combinations of server roles to grant sufficient permissions. Consider using built-in groups and creating Windows groups in which to place users and map these Windows groups to SQL Server 2000 server roles to simplify administration. Remember that adding a user or group to a server role automatically grants them login access to SQL Server 2000. Also remember that you must use BUILTIN rather than the domain or computer name to add a built-in group.

Providing SQL Server 2000 Access

First, enable Mixed Mode authentication only if absolutely necessary. If you must use Mixed Mode authentication, consider enabling SSL encryption for all communication. Create SQL Server 2000 security accounts for each SQL Server login required. Add these SQL Server logins to server roles as required, using the minimum permissions necessary.

Next, grant login access to the Windows users that will need access to SQL Server 2000. Consider creating and granting login access to one Windows 2000 group that will contain all Windows 2000 users requiring access to SQL Server 2000. Also consider creating a second Windows 2000 group that will contain all users that are specifically denied access to SQL Server 2000. Create a login for this Windows 2000 group and specifically deny login access to any members of this group. Using only these two groups will allow you to quickly grant or deny any Windows user access to SQL Server 2000.

Providing Database Access

First, if one user will have responsibility for a particular database, make that user the owner of the database. Next, create user accounts in the database for users that require database access. If you use SQL Server Enterprise Manager, you can only add users who have SQL Server 2000 logins. If you use Transact-SQL, you can add any Windows 2000 user or group. Consider creating Windows groups for each type of user requiring database access with different levels of permissions.

Using Fixed Database Roles for Administrative Access

Add Windows users and groups, and SQL Server logins (if any) to fixed database roles to provide access rights to perform specific tasks. Create Windows groups as appropriate and map these to fixed database roles.

If you plan to use certain fixed database roles in all new databases, consider adding the roles to the model database and then adding the appropriate users. For example, consider creating a Windows group for security operators and then adding that group to the db_securityadmin fixed database role in the model database. Each new database created will then automatically have the db_securityadmin role automatically populated with this Windows group.

Providing Data Access

There are several levels to consider in providing data access. First, determine whether you want to provide guest access to the database. You can create a guest user account in the database and grant the guest user limited rights to view certain tables, views, columns, and stored procedures. You have no way to audit the activities of a specific guest user because the user is not accessing the database through his or her own user account (although you can audit guest user activity). Any rights granted or denied the guest user account have no impact on permitted users.

Next, determine the data access rights that are required by all permitted users in the database. Grant these rights to the public role. This gives you a single place to grant these rights and makes administration easier. All permitted users acquire these rights by default upon connecting to the database.

Next, if certain users or groups require additional access rights to tables, views, stored procedures, and functions, you have a number of options.

- If the users or groups require access to all tables, views, and functions, you can add each of these users or groups to the db_datawriter and/or db_datareader fixed database roles.

- If the users or groups require access to certain tables, views, functions, and stored procedures, you can grant those object permissions individually to each user or group. If there are numerous users or groups who require these permissions, this might not be a good choice.

- If the users or groups require access to certain tables, views, functions, and stored procedures, you can grant those object permissions to a user-defined database role and add each user or group to the role. If you are using SQL Server logins and Windows logins, this allows you to set permissions in a single location, and then simply add and remove users from the role.

- If the users or groups require access to most (but not all) tables, views, and functions, you can add each user or group to the db_datawriter and/or db_datareader fixed database roles and then specifically deny each of these users and groups specific permissions on the restricted objects.

- If the users or groups require access to most (but not all) tables, views, and functions, you can add each user or group to the db_datawriter and/or db_datareader fixed database roles and then place each of these users and groups in a user-defined role and deny specific permissions to this role. Again, if you are using SQL Server logins and Windows logins, this allows you to set permissions in a single location, and then simply add and remove users from the role.

Note   You cannot use the db_datareader and db_datawriter fixed database roles to grant EXECUTE permissions.

Finally, if you need to limit access to tables based on columns, consider using views or stored procedures rather than restricting individual columns. This will generally result in improved performance.

Lesson Summary

SQL Server 2000 provides a myriad of ways to implement security. Choosing the method most appropriate to your environment depends upon fully understanding the options available to you with Windows 2000 (or Windows NT) and SQL Server 2000. In general, choose an access and permissions strategy that enables you to set security in as few places as possible. This will simplify the task of updating and modifying permissions, as well as debugging security problems should they occur.

Review

Here are some questions to help you determine whether you have learned enough to move on to the next chapter. If you have difficulty answering these questions, review the material in this chapter before beginning the next chapter. The answers for these questions are located in the Appendix, "Questions and Answers."

1. You created a Windows 2000 security group for users of the SalesReporting database on your SQL Server 2000 installation and placed the sales managers in this group. You then granted this group access to SQL Server 2000 and the SalesReporting database. In addition, you made this group a member of the db_datawriter and db_datareader fixed database roles. Several members have complained that although they can access the data in each table and view in the database, they are only able to execute certain stored procedures, but not all. To make matters more complicated, one of the members of this group can execute all of the stored procedures without a problem. What are the likely causes of this problem?

2. You need to grant certain users the ability to insert new data into a highly secure database. They also require very limited lookup rights to the data. You are concerned about security for this data. What is the most secure method you can use to allow the users to perform their task?

3. You are designing a security strategy for your SQL Server 2000 installation. You are only allowing access to Windows 2000 users and groups. Is there any advantage to applying permissions to user-defined database groups rather than directly to Windows groups?

C H A P T E R   1 2

Performing Administrative Tasks

About This Chapter

This chapter prepares you to perform a variety of administrative tasks. You will learn about performing configuration, setup, and maintenance tasks related to SQL Server 2000. These tasks include configuring the Microsoft Windows operating system, the SQL Server service, the SQL Server Agent services, and SQL Server Enterprise Manager. You also learn to set up additional features of SQL Server 2000, including SQLAgentMail, SQL Mail, linked servers, and XML support. Finally, you learn about performing periodic maintenance tasks.

Before You Begin

To complete this chapter, you must have

- A computer that meets or exceeds the minimum hardware requirements listed in Table 2.1, "Hardware Requirements," in Lesson 1 of Chapter 2.
- Microsoft Windows 2000 Server running on your computer on an NTFS partition.
- A computer with a NetBIOS name of SelfPacedCPU, configured as a domain controller in the SelfPacedSQL.MSFT domain.
- Installed a default instance and at least one named instance of SQL Server 2000 (see Chapter 2).

Lesson 1: Performing Configuration Tasks

There are a number of tasks you might need to perform to configure the Windows operating system, the SQL Server service, the SQL Server Agent service, and SQL Server Enterprise Manager. In this lesson, you will learn how to set various available configuration options and when the use of each is appropriate. For many environments, little or no configuration is required.

After this lesson, you will be able to

- Verify that Windows 2000 is configured to optimize SQL Server 2000 performance
- Configure properties of the SQL Server service
- Configure properties of the SQL Server Agent service
- Register additional SQL Server instances with SQL Server Enterprise Manager
- Share SQL Server Enterprise Manager registration information

Estimated lesson time: 45 minutes

Configuring Windows 2000 (and Windows NT 4.0)

Optimizing a Windows 2000 (or Windows NT 4.0) server for performance is beyond the scope of this book. However, there are three specific operating system settings that affect SQL Server 2000 that you might need to check or configure.

Maximizing Throughput for Network Operations

During the installation of SQL Server 2000 on any Microsoft Windows 2000 (or Microsoft Windows NT 4.0) server edition, the Setup program automatically configures the operating system (if not already set) to maximize throughput for network applications. This setting optimizes server memory for distributed applications that perform their own memory caching (such as SQL Server 2000).

Changing the default setting is not recommended, and the Full-Text Search feature in SQL Server 2000 requires the default setting. To verify this setting in Windows 2000, open Network And Dial-Up Connections, right-click Local Area Connection, and then click Properties. In the Local Area Connection Properties dialog box, highlight the File And Printer Sharing For Microsoft Networks check box (this check box should already be selected) and then click the Properties button. When the File And Printer Sharing For Microsoft Networks Properties dialog box appears, verify that the Maximize Data Throughput For Network Applications option button is selected. See Figure 12.1.

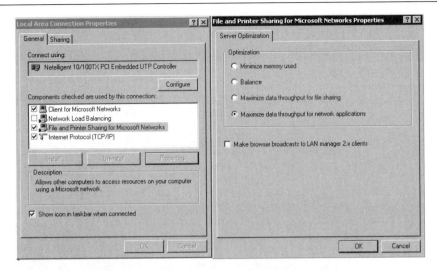

Figure 12.1.   Verifying the Windows 2000 setting for data throughput.

Configuring Server Application Responsiveness

During the installation of SQL Server 2000 on any Windows 2000 (or Windows NT 4.0) server edition, the Setup program automatically configures the operating system (if not already set) to run background and foreground services with equal amounts of processor resources. This setting is optimal for background tasks (such as Windows services).

If you are connecting to your SQL Server 2000 instance from a local client, you can improve the responsiveness of the local client (and all other) foreground applications by optimizing performance for applications. To verify or change this setting, open System in Control Panel, click the Advanced tab in the System Properties dialog box, and then click the Performance Options button. You then make your selections in the Performance Options dialog box. See Figure 12.2.

Configuring Virtual Memory

Although SQL Server 2000 generally is designed to minimize hard disk paging (given sufficient physical memory), Windows 2000 (and Windows NT 4.0) virtual memory size and configuration can affect SQL Server 2000 performance, particularly on a computer hosting a variety of Windows 2000 server applications. In general, consider setting the virtual memory size to 1.5 times the amount of physical memory on the computer. If you are using the Full-Text Search feature, the virtual memory size should be set to three times the amount of physical memory for optimal performance.

In addition, placing paging files on multiple disks generally improves performance. However, avoid placing paging files on disks containing data or transaction log files. To verify or change virtual memory settings, open System in Control Panel, click the Advanced tab, and then click the Performance Options button to display the Performance Options dialog box. In the Virtual Memory group box, click the Change button to display the Virtual Memory dialog box and then either verify or change virtual memory settings. See Figure 12.3.

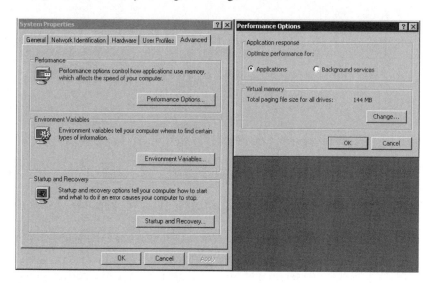

Figure 12.2. Configuring Windows 2000 application responsiveness.

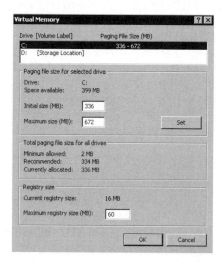

Figure 12.3. Changing Windows 2000 virtual memory settings.

Configuring the SQL Server Service

The SQL Server service is designed to be self-tuning and self-regulating. Although manual tuning of parameters can improve performance in some environments, most SQL Server 2000 installations perform optimally using the default settings.

Configuration options to manually control the behavior of the SQL Server service are available for each of the following:

- Connections
- Database
- Memory
- Processor
- Server

Caution   Tuning these parameters manually can result in a degradation of performance over time rather than an improvement in performance. Use manual tuning with extreme caution, and monitor performance to determine its effect.

You can view or change most configuration settings using SQL Server Enterprise Manager. You can view or change all configuration settings using the *sp_configure* system stored procedure. Executing the *sp_configure* system stored procedure with no parameters displays the current settings for all configuration options. Some options are not visible unless you enable Show Advanced Options. A setting of zero for an option indicates that the SQL Server service is managing the option dynamically. After changing a setting with *sp_configure*, you must either issue the *RECONFIGURE* statement or restart the SQL Server service for the change to take effect (depending upon the change). When changing a setting using SQL Server Enterprise Manager, it will prompt you if you must restart the SQL Server service in order for the setting to take effect.

Note   Each option has a running value and a configured value. If an option has been changed, but not yet activated, the running value and the configured value will differ.

Connections

To change client connection settings using SQL Server Enterprise Manager, right-click the instance name in the console tree, click Properties, and then click the Connections tab in the SQL Server Properties (Configure) dialog box. You can also click SQL Server Configuration Properties from the Tools menu, and then click the Connections tab. See Figure 12.4.

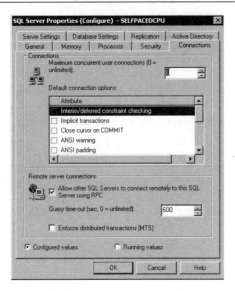

Figure 12.4. Changing client connection settings.

Table 12.1 describes these connection settings using the *sp_configure* option name for each setting. The option in the SQL Server Enterprise Manager interface is more descriptive than the option name.

Table 12-1. Connection Settings

Option Name	Description	When to Use
User connections	Specifies the maximum number of simultaneous user connections, up to the maximum value allowable. The actual number of user connections allowed is dependent upon the version of SQL Server 2000 you are running and upon the limitations of your applications and hardware. Dynamic by default.	To avoid overloading SQL Server 2000 with too many concurrent connections.
User options	Specifies default query-processing options for all client connections. No options are set by default.	To set global query-processing defaults for client connections.
Remote access	Permits or denies access by remote logins via remote stored procedures. Default is to allow remote access.	To secure a local server and prevent remote access.

Table 12-1.   Connection Settings

Option Name	Description	When to Use
Remote proc trans	Enforces the use of distributed transactions using MS DTC to protect server-to-server procedures. Default is not to enforce.	To require an MS DTC distributed transaction to protect Atomicity, Consistency, Isolation, and Durability (ACID) properties of transactions.
Remote query timeout	Specifies the number of seconds before SQL Server 2000 times out when processing a remote query. Default is 600 seconds (10 minutes).	To manage the remote timeout default.

Database

To change database settings using SQL Server Enterprise Manager, right-click the instance name in the console tree, click Properties, and then click the Database Settings tab in the SQL Server Properties (Configure) dialog box. See Figure 12.5.

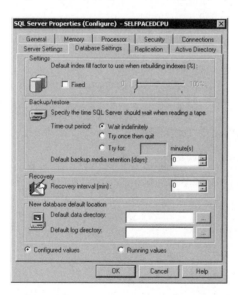

Figure 12.5.   Changing database settings.

Table 12.2 describes these database settings using the *sp_configure* option name for each setting.

The SQL Server Enterprise Manager interface also allows you to specify a new default data and transaction log directory for all new databases in the Database Settings tab of the SQL Server Properties (Configure) dialog box.

Table 12-2.   Database Settings

Option	Description	When to Use
Fill factor	Specifies how full each index page should be when creating a new index using existing data. By default, SQL Server 2000 will fill each clustered and nonclustered index page, leaving only a small amount of space for additional data before a page split must occur.	Set a value to minimize future index page splits. Set at 100% for a read-only table to which new data is not added.
Media retention	Specifies a default length of time to retain each backup. Default is 0.	To set a default media retention value for all backup sets.
Recovery interval	Controls how frequently the checkpoint process runs by specifying a maximum length of time (in minutes) for automatic recovery to complete. Default is dynamic based on number of data modifications and the amount of free space in the transaction log.	To distribute hard disk writes more evenly and avoid spikes of hard disk activity.

Memory

To change memory settings using SQL Server Enterprise Manager, right-click the instance name in the console tree, click Properties, and then click the Memory tab in the SQL Server Properties (Configure) dialog box. See Figure 12.6.

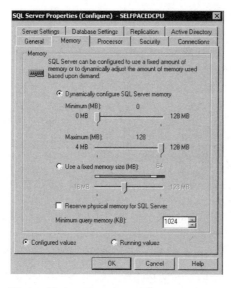

Figure 12.6.   Changing memory settings.

Table 12.3 describes these memory settings using the *sp_configure* option name for each setting.

Table 12-3.   Memory Settings

Option	Description	When to Use
Max server memory	Specifies the maximum amount of memory SQL Server 2000 can use for its buffer pool. Default is dynamic memory allocation.	To limit memory use on a nondedicated computer so other server applications are more responsive.
Min server memory	Guarantees a minimum amount of memory for SQL Server 2000 to use for its buffer pool. Default is dynamic memory allocation.	To guarantee memory use on a non-dedicated computer so SQL Server 2000 is more responsive.
Set working set size	Sets aside a specified amount of physical memory for SQL Server 2000. Used with the max server memory and min server memory settings. Default is zero.	To prevent Windows 2000 from swapping out pages to other server applications (no matter how much they might need memory or how idle SQL Server 2000 is).
Min memory per query	Specifies a minimum amount of memory (in kilobytes) allocated to each query. Default is dynamic.	Increase to improve performance of small to medium queries.

SQL Server 2000 dynamically allocates and deallocates memory within the buffer cache to optimize performance. It bases the amount of memory used on the SQL Server 2000 load and competing memory requirements from other server applications. If all available physical memory is already committed to a server application, it takes processor cycles to reallocate memory between server applications. To ensure that physical memory is immediately available for all server applications running on the Windows computer, you might set a minimum and a maximum server memory value. In this case, SQL Server 2000 will dynamically allocate and deallocate memory between these minimum and maximum values.

Note   Memory required by the SQL Server service for basic operations is not dynamically managed and might cause hard disk paging if insufficient physical memory is available.

On a dedicated SQL Server 2000 computer, setting the minimum and maximum value to the same high value, and setting a working set size equal to that value, might slightly improve performance. With these settings, memory will be allocated to SQL Server 2000 as needed and then remain allocated. It will not be reallocated to other server applications.

Note   If you are running the Full-Text Search feature, you might need to set a maximum memory value so that SQL Server 2000 can reserve sufficient memory for the Microsoft Search service to run optimally. The amount required for the Microsoft Search service depends on the size of tables that contain full-text indexes and the level of full-text query activity.

Processor

To change processor settings using SQL Server Enterprise Manager, right-click the instance name in the console tree, click Properties, and then click the Processor tab in the SQL Server Properties (Configure) dialog box. See Figure 12.7.

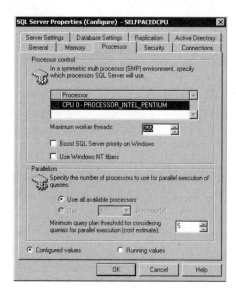

Figure 12.7.   Processor settings.

Table 12.4 describes these processor settings using the *sp_configure* option name for each setting.

Server

To change server settings using SQL Server Enterprise Manager, right-click the instance name in the console tree, click Properties, and then click the Server Settings tab in the SQL Server Properties (Configure) dialog box. See Figure 12.8.

Table 12.5 describes these server settings using the *sp_configure* option name for each setting.

Table 12-4.   Processor Settings

Option	Description	When to Use
Affinity mask	Excludes a processor on a multiprocessor computer from processing SQL Server 2000 threads. Default is equal distribution of SQL Server 2000 processes across all processors.	To exclude SQL Server threads from processors with specific workloads from Windows 2000.
Cost threshold for parallelism	Determines which query plans are considered long or short. Used by SQL Server 2000 to determine when it should create and execute parallel execution plans for queries. Default value is 5.	To force or limit the use of parallel query plans on multiprocessor computers.
Lightweight pooling	Specifies the use of fibers (fiber mode scheduling) within threads, rather than separate threads for each task. Default is thread mode scheduling.	On multiprocessor computers with excessive context switching and a consistently heavy processor load.
Priority boost	Specifies the SQL Server 2000 processor scheduling priority. Default is normal priority (which is 7).	To increase scheduling priority on a dedicated SQL Server 2000 computer with multiple processors.
Max degree of parallelism	Specifies the number of processors used in parallel plan execution. Default is to use all available processors.	To suppress parallel plan generation.
Max worker threads	Specifies the number of worker threads available to SQL Server 2000 processes. Default is 255.	Set to smaller value on systems with low numbers of connections to improve performance.

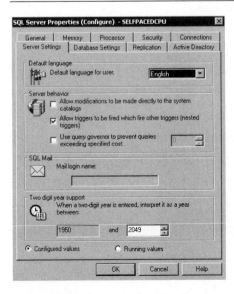

Figure 12.8.   Server settings.

The SQL Server Enterprise Manager interface also allows you to specify a new default language for server messages to users and a mail profile name for a mail session in the Server Settings tab of the SQL Server Properties (Configure) dialog box. Setting up SQLAgentMail and SQL Mail is covered in Lesson 2.

Integration with Active Directory

If your SQL Server 2000 installation is running in a Windows 2000 Microsoft Active Directory environment, you can register your SQL Server 2000 instance in Active Directory. This adds an MS-SQL-SQLServer object as a Service Connection Point (SCP) object in the container for the computer on which the SQL Server 2000 instance is running. An SCP is an Active Directory object that represents services that are available on the network. The MS-SQL-SQLServer object records information about the SQL Server service, such as connection information. Users and applications can search Active Directory for information regarding published SQL Server 2000 instances on the network.

The MSSQLServerADHelper service performs the actual registration task. This service is dynamically started by an instance of SQL Server or the Analysis Manager when needed and then stopped when it has completed its task. This service also verifies that the SQL Server service domain user account has sufficient permissions to update all Active Directory objects for this SQL Server 2000 instance, as well as any databases or replication publications. To register (or unregister) an instance or a database with Active Directory, the SQL Server service domain user account must be a member of either the Windows 2000 or Windows NT 4.0 local Administrators or local Power Users group on the SQL Server 2000 computer.

Table 12-5.   Server Settings

Option	Description	When to Use
Allow updates	Specifies whether direct updates can be made to system tables. When Allow Updates is disabled, updates are not allowed to the system tables, even if a user is assigned the appropriate permissions with the *GRANT* statement. Default is disabled.	Use only with direction from Microsoft Product Support Services.
Nested triggers	Controls whether a trigger can cascade (initiate another trigger). You can nest triggers up to 32 levels. Default is to permit cascading of triggers.	To prevent cascading of triggers.

Table 12-5.   Server Settings

Option	Description	When to Use
Query governor cost limit	Specifies the maximum length of time (in seconds) a query can run. Default is to allow queries to run indefinitely.	To prevent runaway queries.
Two-digit year cutoff	Specifies either the current century or the next century when a two-digit date is used. Default is 2049, meaning that a two-digit date of 49 is interpreted as 2049 and a two-digit date of 50 is interpreted as 1950. Default for OLE Automation objects is 2030.	To provide consistency in date values between SQL Server 2000 and client applications.

You can register (or unregister) an instance using either SQL Server Enterprise Manager or the *sp_ActiveDirectory_SCP* system stored procedure. Using SQL Server Enterprise Manager, right-click the instance name in the console tree, click Properties, and then click the Active Directory tab in the SQL Server Properties (Configure) dialog box. To register an instance of SQL Server 2000, click the Add button. To unregister an instance, click the Remove button. See Figure 12.9.

After registering an instance, you can also register each database using either SQL Server Enterprise Manager or the *sp_ActiveDirectory_Obj* system stored procedure. Using SQL Server Enterprise Manager, right-click the database you want to register, click Properties to display the Properties dialog box, and then click the Options tab. If you have registered the instance with Active Directory, an Active Directory group box will appear in the Options tab. In the Active Directory group box, you select the List This Database In Active Directory check box to enable you to list the database in Active Directory. If the instance is not registered, you will not see the Active Directory group box. See Figure 12.10.

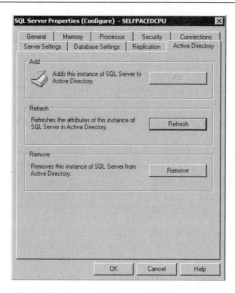

Figure 12.9.   Registering SQL Server in Active Directory.

Figure 12.10.   Registering a database in Active Directory.

Configuring the Service Account

The SQL Server and SQL Server Agent services run under either a domain user account or the local system account. These services must run under a domain user account to perform most server-to-server activities. Although this domain user account does not require any special permissions for most activities, certain SQL

Server 2000 functionality requires the domain user account to have additional permissions, as shown in Table 12.6.

Table 12-6.   Additional Permissions Required for Certain SQL Server 2000 Functionality

Service	Permission	Functionality
SQL Server service	Act as part of the operating system and replace a process-level token.	Run an operating system command for a user who is not a member of the sysadmin server role.
SQL Server service	Member of the local Power Users or local Administrators group.	Publish and manage SQL Server 2000 objects with Active Directory.
SQL Server Agent service	Member of the local Administrators group.	Create operating system and Active Script jobs not belonging to members of the sysadmin server role.
SQL Server Agent service	Member of the local Administrators group.	Configure the SQL Server Agent service to autorestart if it stops unexpectedly.
SQL Server Agent service	Member of the local Administrators group.	Configure the SQL Server Agent service to run jobs when the processor is idle.

If your SQL Server 2000 installation requires the functionality listed in Table 12.6, you must ensure that the domain user account used by the applicable service has sufficient permissions or use the local system account (this account has full local privileges). The details of the functionality mentioned in Table 12.6 are discussed in context in this chapter and in Chapter 13.

Configuring the SQL Server Agent Service

You configure the properties of the SQL Server Agent service using SQL Server Enterprise Manager.

General Properties

To configure the general properties of the SQL Server Agent service, expand the Management container, right-click SQL Server Agent, and then click Properties to display the SQL Server Agent Properties dialog box. See Figure 12.11.

In the General tab, you can configure the location of the error log file, enable the recording of execution trace messages (for troubleshooting), and enable the error file to be written as a non-Unicode file (resulting in a smaller log file size). Recording of execution trace messages can generate large files. You can also configure a recipient on the network to receive net send pop-up message notification of errors recorded by the SQL Server Agent service. Configuring a mail session for the SQL Server Agent service is covered in Lesson 2.

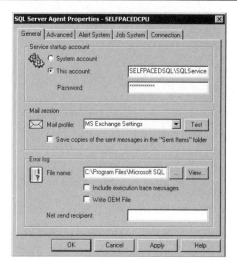

Figure 12.11.   Configuring the general properties of the SQL Server Agent.

Advanced Properties

To configure advanced properties of the SQL Server Agent service, click the Advanced tab in the SQL Server Agent Properties dialog box. See Figure 12.12.

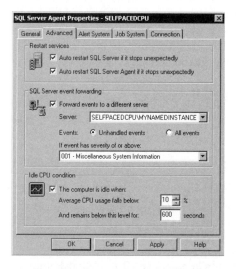

Figure 12.12.   Configuring the advanced properties of the SQL Server Agent.

In the Advanced tab, you can configure the SQL Server Agent service to restart automatically if it stops unexpectedly by selecting the Auto Restart SQL Server Agent If It Stops Unexpectedly check box. This feature requires local administrator rights by the SQL Server Agent service account (either granting them to the domain user account or using the local system account). By default, the SQL Server service is already configured to restart automatically.

In the SQL Server Event Forwarding group box, you can configure the SQL Server Agent service to forward some or all SQL Server events to another server. You can use this feature to enable centralized alert management for a group of servers. Plan carefully, because this generates additional network traffic, generates additional load on the centralized server, and creates a single point of failure. To use this feature, you must use a server that you have registered with SQL Server Enterprise Manager. Configuring alerts is covered in Chapter 13.

In the Idle CPU Condition group box, you can also define when the processor is considered to be idle. In Chapter 13, you learn to create jobs that the SQL Server Agent service runs when the processor is considered to be idle. You define the idle condition by specifying a percentage below which the average processor usage must fall for a defined length of time. This feature requires local administrator rights granted to the SQL Server Agent service account (either granting them to the domain user account or using the local system account).

Connection Properties

You configure the connection properties of the SQL Server Agent service by clicking the Connection tab in the SQL Server Agent Properties dialog box. See Figure 12.13.

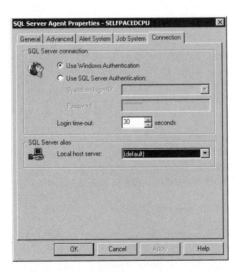

Figure 12.13.   Configuring the connection properties of the SQL Server Agent.

By default, the SQL Server Agent service connects to the local SQL Server 2000 instance using the domain user account specified as the service account. However, in the SQL Server Connection group box, you can specify that all connections to the local instance use a SQL Server login account that is a member of the sysadmin server role. You can also modify the login timeout value from the default of 30 seconds. Finally, if you have configured nondefault client Net-Libraries, you might need to specify a SQL Server alias that you previously created using the Client Network Utility.

Registering SQL Server 2000 Instances with SQL Server Enterprise Manager

Before you can administer and manage SQL Server 2000 (and SQL Server 7.0) instances with SQL Server Enterprise Manager, you must register those instances. When you register an instance, you must specify the server name, instance name (if applicable), the login authentication method, login information if SQL Server authentication is specified, and the logical group within SQL Server Enterprise Manager. You can register instances using the Register SQL Server Wizard or directly with SQL Server Enterprise Manager.

Using the Register SQL Server Wizard

You can select the Register Server Wizard by clicking Wizards from the Tools menu or by right-clicking a server group or registered instance and then clicking New SQL Server Registration. See Figure 12.14.

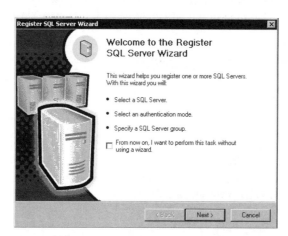

Figure 12.14.   The Register SQL Server Wizard.

You can disable the Register SQL Server Wizard by selecting the From Now On, I Want To Perform This Task Without Using A Wizard check box in the Welcome To The Register SQL Server Wizard page. If you disable the wizard, you must access Register Server Wizard by clicking Wizards from the Tools menu. Click Next to display the Select A SQL Server page. The wizard displays the available instances detected on the network. Select the SQL Server instances you want to register. See Figure 12.15. If an instance is not displayed, you can enter it manually. For example, a server might not be displayed because it is not currently running or because it is not broadcasting its existence.

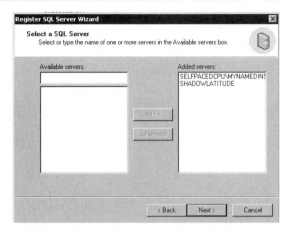

Figure 12.15.   Selecting an instance of SQL Server to be registered.

Click Next to select the authentication mode to connect to each instance in the Select An Authentication Mode page. Notice that you must select the same authentication mode for all instances selected. You can configure custom connection information for specific instances later in the wizard. See Figure 12.16.

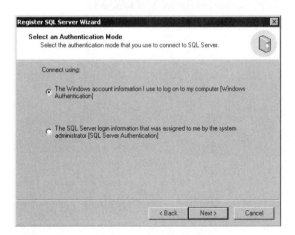

Figure 12.16.   Selecting an authentication mode for servers being registered.

If you select SQL Server authentication, you are prompted for connection information in the Select Connection Option page. You can supply the SQL Server login that will be used each time SQL Server Enterprise Manager connects to any of these instances. You can also configure SQL Server Enterprise Manager to prompt you for a SQL Server login each time it attempts to connect to an instance. This is useful if multiple users are sharing registration information and will be connecting using different SQL Server logins, each with different permissions within an instance. See Figure 12.17.

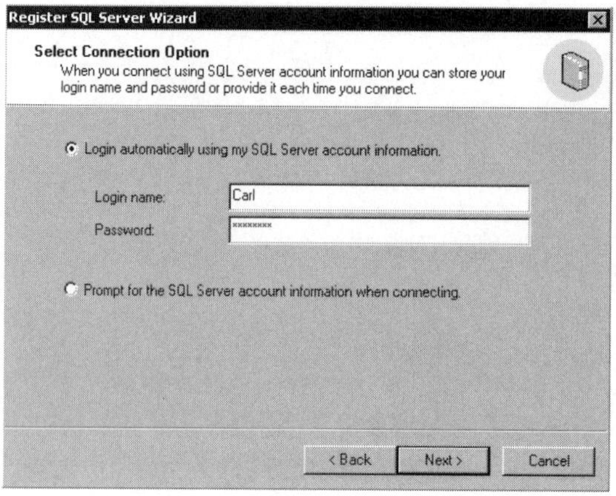

Figure 12.17. Selecting connection options for servers being registered.

Next, in the Select SQL Server Group page, you can choose to add these new instances being registered to an existing SQL Server group within the management console or to a new top-level SQL Server group. See Figure 12.18.

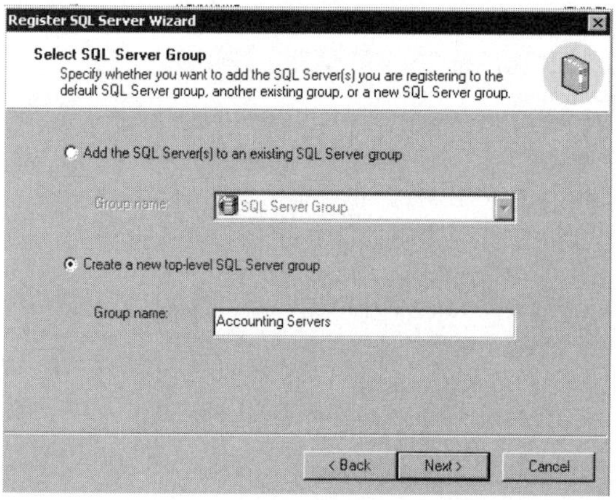

Figure 12.18. Selecting a logical group for servers being registered.

Next, in the Completing The Register SQL Server Wizard page, the Register SQL Server Wizard verifies that it can connect to each instance using the authentication method and credentials specified. See Figure 12.19.

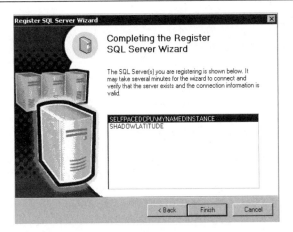

Figure 12.19.   Verifying connections to the servers being registered.

If the wizard is unable to connect to any instance using the registration information provided, you can select the instance that failed and provide custom registration information for that instance. See Figure 12.20.

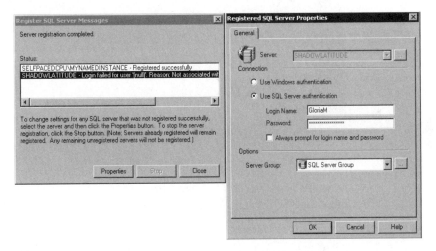

Figure 12.20.   Providing custom registration information for specific instances.

If the connection still fails, you have the option to register the instance without verifying the registration information. This option is useful if the account you want to use has not yet been created or if the instance is not currently running. See Figure 12.21.

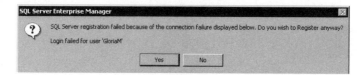

Figure 12.21.   Registering an instance non-verifiable connection information.

Using SQL Server Enterprise Manager

To register instances directly, right-click the SQL Server group or a registered instance, and then click New SQL Server Registration. If you have not previously disabled the Register SQL Server Wizard, in the Welcome To The Register SQL Server Wizard page, select the From Now On, I Want To Perform This Task Without Using A Wizard check box to bypass this wizard. Click Next. See Figure 12.22.

Figure 12.22.   Bypassing the Register SQL Server Wizard.

Next, the Registered SQL Server Properties dialog box appears. You can register individual SQL Server instances by providing the same information discussed in the previous section. See Figure 12.23.

Additionally, you can choose to change the following defaults for a new instance being registered (or for an instance that is already registered):

- Display the SQL Server state (running or not)
- Display system databases and objects
- Automatically start a SQL Server instance (if necessary) when SQL Server Enterprise Manager attempts to connect

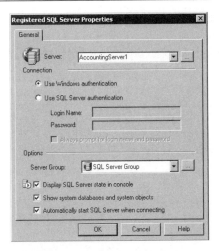

Figure 12.23.   Registration properties for a SQL Server instance.

Sharing Registration Information

By default, registration information within the SQL Server Enterprise Manager management console (as well as customization information) is private to each user. For example, if a system administrator registers 15 separate SQL Server instances, another system administrator logging on to the same computer (using her or his Windows user account) will not see the 15 servers already registered.

However, a system administrator can choose to share this registration information with other system administrators on the same computer or on other computers. This is useful when a number of different system administrators are administering the same instances from a single computer. It is also useful for creating a central registration store when many instances are being administered. This permits administrators to use the same registration configuration regardless of the computer they log in to. To use this capability, the system administrator running SQL Server Enterprise Manager must be a member of the local Administrators group on the computer containing the central store and on the local computer.

To share registration information, click Options from the Tools menu and then, in the SQL Server Enterprise Manager Properties dialog box, clear the Read/Store User Independent check box. See Figure 12.24.

To read registration information from another server that has cleared the Read/Store User Independent check box, click the Read From Remote option button and then, in the Server Name text box, enter the name of the server containing the central store.

Figure 12.24.   Settings for sharing registration information.

Lesson Summary

The SQL Server 2000 Setup program configures the Windows operating system for optimal use by SQL Server 2000 in most environments. However, you should ensure that disks containing data and transaction log files are not also used for virtual memory. The SQL Server service is generally self-tuning. In some environments, manually tuning certain configuration settings might improve performance, but tuning the SQL Server service improperly will negatively affect performance. The service account used by SQL Server and the SQL Server Agent services needs additional rights to perform certain advanced functions. Finally, to enable these advanced functions (such as defining the CPU idle condition), you need to configure advanced properties of the SQL Server Agent service.

Lesson 2: Setting Up Additional Features

SQL Server 2000 can send and receive e-mail, notify pagers, connect with linked servers for distributed queries, and integrate with IIS for XML support. To take advantage of each of these features, you must set up these features. In this lesson, you learn to set up SQLAgentMail and SQL Mail. Next, you learn to set up linked servers for distributed queries and remote stored procedures. You also learn to create ODBC data sources for ODBC clients. Finally, you learn to configure IIS to permit HTTP access to SQL Server 2000.

After this lesson, you will be able to

- Set up SQL Mail and SQLAgentMail
- Set up linked servers
- Create ODBC SQL Server data sources
- Set up a virtual directory in IIS to enable XML access to SQL Server 2000

Estimated lesson time: 45 minutes

Setting Up SQL Mail and SQLAgentMail

SQL Server 2000 can connect with Microsoft Exchange Server, Microsoft Windows Mail, or a Post Office Protocol 3 (POP3) server to send and receive messages using two separate services, SQL Mail and SQLAgentMail. Both services require a MAPI client application (such as Microsoft Outlook) on the local SQL Server 2000 computer and a MAPI messaging profile. A MAPI messaging profile requires the use of a domain user account. Generally, SQL Mail and SQLAgentMail use the same domain user account for administrative convenience.

Using SQL Mail

SQL Mail is the mail service of the SQL Server service. The SQL Server service uses the *xp_sendmail* extended stored procedure to send e-mail from Transact-SQL batches, scripts, stored procedures, and triggers. It establishes a mail session as needed.

```
EXEC xp_sendmail 'Gloria@SelfPacedSQL.msft' ,
@subject = 'Performance Information' ,
@query = 'SELECT * FROM master.dbo.sysperfinfo'
```

The preceding example uses the *xp_sendmail* extended stored procedure to send an e-mail message to Gloria regarding the current SQL Server 2000 performance. This query could be scheduled to run periodically.

The content of an e-mail message can be any of the following:

- A result set from a query
- A message string
- A Transact-SQL statement or batch for execution
- A page for an electronic pager

The SQL Server service uses the *sp_processmail* system stored procedure, or the *xp_findnextmsg*, *xp_readmail*, and *xp_deletemail* extended stored procedures to process e-mail sent to the domain user account used by the SQL Server service. This e-mail typically contains a Transact-SQL statement or batch for execution, with the result set being returned by reply e-mail, including an optional cc: list. For example, an administrator can execute a stored procedure by e-mail that obtains the current status of the server and returns the result set by e-mail to the administrator.

Tip   Create a regularly scheduled job to periodically process e-mail automatically.

Using SQLAgentMail

SQLAgentMail is the mail service of the SQL Server Agent service. The SQL Server Agent service starts a mail session upon startup (if a mail session is configured in SQL Server Enterprise Manager) and sends e-mail and electronic pager notifications to designated users in response to the triggering of an alert or the success or failure of a job. Jobs and alerts are covered in Chapter 13.

Configuring a Messaging (Mail) Profile

Both SQL Mail and SQLAgentMail require the installation of a MAPI client (such as Microsoft Outlook) on the local SQL Server 2000 computer. Next, you must create a messaging profile (also called a mail profile) for the domain user account used by the SQL Server and SQL Server Agent services. You can create the messaging profile by using the MAPI client or the Mail program in Control Panel. If different domain user accounts are used by each service, you must set up a messaging profile for each domain user account. In general, you must log on to Windows 2000 as the domain user to configure the messaging profile for that domain user. If the domain user account is not a local administrator, you might need to give this account permission to log on interactively (locally) so that you can create a messaging profile for this user account. The messaging profile contains the connection information used by the MAPI client to connect to the Microsoft Exchange Server, Microsoft Windows Mail, and/or a POP3 server.

Note   To verify the installation of a valid messaging profile, log on to Windows 2000 with the domain user account used by the SQL Server and SQL Server Agent services. Start the MAPI client and verify that it can send and receive e-mail.

When you create a profile using either the MAPI client or the Mail program in Control Panel, the default messaging profile name in the Profile Name text box for a domain user is MS Exchange Settings. You can use the *xp_get_mapi _default_profile* extended stored procedure to determine the default profile name (if any) for the SQL Server service domain user account. You can use the Mail program in Control Panel to add, review, remove, or change the settings for each messaging profile configured for a domain user account. See Figures 12.25 and 12.26.

Setting Up SQL Mail

After configuring and testing the messaging profile for the SQL Server service domain user account, you are ready to set up SQL Mail. Using SQL Server Enterprise Manager, expand the Support Services container for the instance, right-click SQL Mail, and then click Properties. The SQL Mail Configuration dialog box appears as shown in Figure 12.27.

Select the messaging profile name from the Profile Name drop-down list.

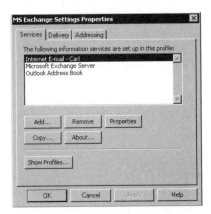

Figure 12.25. Accessing mail settings for messaging profiles.

Figure 12.26. Changing mail settings for messaging profiles.

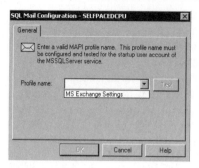

Figure 12.27.   Selecting a messaging profile for SQL Mail.

Note   If the messaging profile does not appear in SQL Server Enterprise Manager, verify that the SQL Server service is using the domain user account for which the messaging profile was created and that the domain user account has full control permissions on the HKEY_LOCAL_MACHINE\SOFTWARE \Clients\Mail registry key.

Click the Test button to verify whether a mail session can be established. See Figure 12.28.

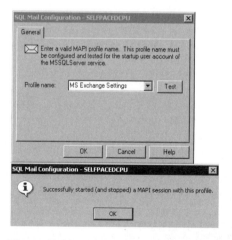

Figure 12.28.   Testing the messaging profile.

You can also set up SQL Mail using the *xp_startmail* system stored procedure.

Setting Up SQLAgentMail

After configuring and testing the messaging profile for the SQL Server Agent service domain user account, you are ready to set up SQLAgentMail. Using SQL Server Enterprise Manager, expand the Management container for the instance, right-click SQL Server Agent, and then click Properties. The SQL Server Agent Properties dialog box appears with the General tab selected, as shown in Figure 12.29.

In the Mail Session group box, select the messaging profile from the Mail Profile drop-down list. Click the Test button to verify whether a mail session can be established. By default, messages sent by the SQL Server Agent service are not saved in the Sent Items folder of the MAPI client. Using SQLAgentMail for jobs and alerts is covered in Chapter 13.

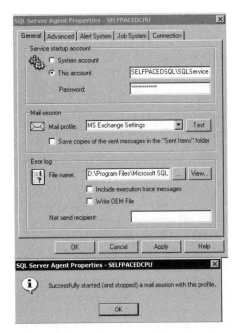

Figure 12.29.   Selecting the messaging profile for the SQLAgentMail.

Setting Up Linked Servers

SQL Server 2000 can connect to linked servers. The primary use of a linked server configuration is the execution of distributed queries, joining information from multiple databases on multiple servers (such as SQL Server 2000, SQL Server 7.0, Oracle, and Access). You can set up a linked server configuration to any OLE DB data source by using SQL Server Enterprise Manager. Although the OLE DB data source is generally another database, it can also be a text file, a spreadsheet, or the results of full-text content searches. See Figure 12.30.

The configuration information specifies the OLE DB data source and the OLE DB provider used to communicate with the remote data source. It also specifies the security context for the connection to the linked server. Although the SQL Server service on the local instance is making the connection, it is making it on behalf of a user with certain permissions. You must configure login mappings between linked servers specifying the security context between each SQL Server instance to ensure that the user can only access information he or she has permission to access.

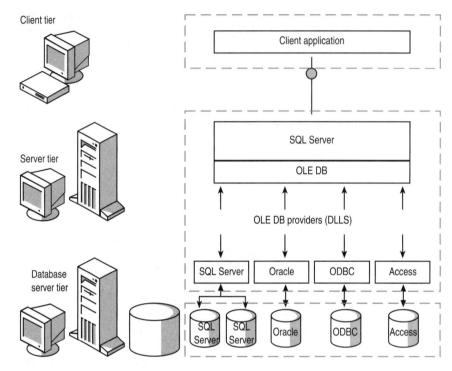

Figure 12.30.   Basics of a linked server configuration.

Note   You can also set up a remote server configuration to another SQL Server instance. However, remote server functionality is provided primarily for backward compatibility. Linked servers provide all the functionality of remote servers, plus additional functionality.

Setting Up Linked Servers Using SQL Server Enterprise Manager

Using SQL Server Enterprise Manager, expand the Security container for the instance, right-click Linked Servers, and then click New Linked Server to display the Linked Server Properties – New Linked Server dialog box. See Figure 12.31.

In the General tab, you enter the name of the linked server in the Linked Server text box. If, in the Server Type group box, you click the SQL Server option button to create a link to a named instance, the name you specify in the Linked Server text box must be the network and instance name of the SQL Server instance. You can select from a list of possible OLE DB providers in the Provider Name drop-down list. These providers manage the access to the specified linked server. Notice that this includes an OLE DB provider for Microsoft Directory Services for querying Active Directory. If you specify any data source other than a SQL Server instance by clicking the Other Data Source option button in the Server Type group box, you must provide additional information specific to that data source (such as product name, data source, and provider string).

Figure 12.31.   Specifying a Provider Name when creating a new linked server.

Next, click the Security tab to map local logins to remote logins. See Figure 12.32.

Figure 12.32.   Mapping local logins to remote logins for a linked server.

On this dialog box, define how local users will connect to the remote data source. You select logins from the local server and define how they will connect to the remote server under Local Server Login To Remote Server Login Mappings. You can choose to have the SQL Server service impersonate the logged-in user or map the logged-in user to a SQL Server login on the remote server. You must provide the password for the remote login account.

Note   For the SQL Server service to impersonate a Windows user between servers, security account delegation must be enabled. See Chapter 10.

Next, determine how the SQL Server service should handle connection attempts made by users with no specific security mapping. You can have the SQL Server service deny all such attempts. You can also have the connection attempt made without a user security context (using the SQL Server service security context), using the login's current security context or using a specified default SQL Server login account.

Finally, in the Server Options tab, you can configure advanced connection parameters (such as a different collation or a specific query timeout value). See Figure 12.33.

Figure 12.33.   Configuring advanced connection parameters for a linked server.

Setting Up Linked Servers Using Transact-SQL

You can also set up a linked server configuration using the *sp_addlinkedserver* system stored procedure.

```
sp_addlinkedserver 'SelfPacedCPU\MyNamedInstance'
```

The preceding example creates a linked server configuration between the current SQL Server 2000 instance and MyNamedInstance on SelfPacedCPU. No security mappings are created. By default, this linked server configuration specifies that all connections use the security context of the logged-in user.

Note   SQL Server 2000 Books Online has excellent examples for connecting to non-SQL Server data sources using the *sp_addlinkedserver* system stored procedure.

Use the *sp_addlinkedsrvlogin* system stored procedure to create or update mappings between logins on the local SQL Server instance and remote logins on the linked server.

```
sp_addlinkedsrvlogin 'SelfPacedCPU\MyNamedInstance' ,
'FALSE' , 'SelfPacedSQL\Bill' , 'sa' , 'sa_password'
```

The preceding example adds a mapping on the local instance between the Windows user Bill in the SelfPacedSQL domain and the sa login on the linked server.

Use the *sp_linkedservers* system stored procedure to obtain a list of linked servers defined for the current instance.

Practice: Setting Up and Testing a Linked Server Configuration

In this practice you use the SQL Server Enterprise Manager to set up a linked server configuration.

▶ **To set up and test a linked server configuration**

1. Ensure that you are logged on to the SelfPacedSQL.MSFT domain controller as Administrator.
2. Click Start, point to Programs, point to Microsoft SQL Server, and then click Enterprise Manager.
3. In the console tree, expand the Microsoft SQL Servers container, expand the SQL Server Group container, expand the default instance, and then expand Security.
4. Right-click Linked Servers and then click New Linked Server.

   The Linked Server Properties – New Linked Server dialog box appears, with the General tab selected.
5. In the Linked Server text box, type **SelfPacedCPU\MyNamedInstance**.
6. Under Server Type, click the SQL Server option button and then click the Security tab.

7. In the For A Login Not Defined In The List Above, Connections Will group box, click the Be Made Using The Login's Current Security Context option button and then click OK.

8. On the Tools menu, click SQL Query Analyzer.

   SQL Query Analyzer appears.

9. In the query pane, type **SELECT * FROM [SelfPacedCPU \MyNamedInstance].Northwind.dbo.Customers** and then click the Execute Query button from the toolbar.

   Notice that the contents of the Customer table are displayed in the results pane.

10. On the File menu, click Connect.

    The Connect To SQL Server dialog box appears.

11. Click the SQL Server Authentication option button.

12. In the Login Name text box, type **Joe**.

13. In the Password text box, type **password** and then click OK.

    SQL Query Analyzer appears.

14. In the query pane, type **SELECT * FROM [SelfPacedCPU \MyNamedInstance].Northwind.dbo.Customers** and then click the Execute Query button from the toolbar.

    Notice that the contents of the Customer table are not displayed in the results pane. There are several reasons why this failed. First, MyNamedInstance does not permit SQL Server logins. Second, Joe does not have a SQL Server login within MyNamedInstance.

15. Switch to SQL Server Enterprise Manager.

16. In the console tree, right-click SelfPacedCPU\MyNamedInstance and then click Properties.

    The SQL Server Properties (Configure) – SelfPacedCPU\MyNamedInstance dialog box appears.

17. Click the Security tab, click the SQL Server And Windows option button, and then click OK.

18. Click the Yes button to restart the SQL Server service.

19. Switch to SQL Query Analyzer.

20. On the toolbar, click the Execute Query button to re-execute the query for the user Joe.

    Notice that the error message has changed. The reason the distributed query failed is that the local login Joe is mapped to a login Joe on MyNamedInstance (which does not yet exist).

21. Switch to SQL Server Enterprise Manager.

22. Expand the SelfPacedCPU\MyNamedInstance container and then expand Security.

23. Right-click Logins and then click New Login.

    The SQL Server Login Properties – New Login dialog box appears.

24. In the Name text box, type **Joe**.

25. Click the SQL Server Authentication option button.

26. In the Password text box, type **password** and then click OK.

    The Confirm Password dialog box appears.

27. In the Confirm New Password text box, type **password** and then click OK.

28. Switch to SQL Query Analyzer.

29. On the toolbar, click the Execute Query button to re-execute the query for the user Joe.

    Notice that the contents of the Customer table are displayed in the results pane. Joe is able to connect to the Northwind database because the guest user account is present in the Northwind database and has SELECT permissions on the Customer table.

30. Switch to SQL Server Enterprise Manager.

31. Expand the SelfPacedCPU container, expand the Security container, and then click Linked Servers.

32. In the details pane, double-click SelfPacedCPU\MyNamedInstance.

    The Linked Server Properties – SelfPacedCPU\MyNamedInstance dialog box appears.

33. Click the Security tab.

34. In the first row under the Local Login column, click the cell's drop-down combo box and then select Ana.

35. In the Remote User cell, type **Joe**.

36. In the Remote Password cell, type **password**.

37. In the second row under the Local Login column, type **Joe** into the cell and then select the Impersonate check box.

38. Under For A Login Not Defined In The List Above, Connections Will, click the Not Be Made option button and then click OK.

    Only Joe and Ana will be permitted to use this linked server configuration.

39. Switch to SQL Query Analyzer.

40. On the toolbar, click the Execute Query button to re-execute the query for the user Joe.

    Notice that the contents of the Customer table are displayed in the results pane.

41. Switch to your administrator connection in SQL Query Analyzer.

42. On the toolbar, click the Execute Query button to re-execute the query.

    Notice that your administrator account can no longer use the linked server connection because no mapping exists.

43. On the File menu, click Connect.

44. The Connect To SQL Server dialog box appears.

45. Click the SQL Server Authentication option button.

46. In the Login Name text box, type **Ana**.

47. In the Password text box, type **password** and then click OK.

    SQL Query Analyzer appears.

48. In the query pane, type **SELECT * FROM [SelfPacedCPU \MyNamedIn-stance].Northwind.dbo.Customers** and then click the Execute Query button on the toolbar.

    Notice that the contents of the Customer table are displayed in the results pane. Ana is using the linked server configuration and accessing data within MyNamedInstance using the permissions granted to Joe.

49. Close SQL Server Enterprise Manager and SQL Query Analyzer. Do not save any changes to queries.

Creating an ODBC SQL Server Data Source

Traditionally, clients connect to a SQL Server 2000 instance using either OLE DB or ODBC. OLE DB clients provide the necessary connection information through the Microsoft OLE DB Provider for SQL Server. ODBC clients can provide the necessary connection information through the use of the Microsoft OLE DB Provider for ODBC, or they can connect to an ODBC SQL Server data source name (DSN) to make a connection.

A DSN is a stored definition recording the ODBC driver, connection information, and driver-specific information. The ODBC Data Source Administrator utility is used to create DSNs. To create a DSN with Windows 2000, open the Data Sources (ODBC) utility from the Administrative Tools folder in Control Panel. See Figure 12.34.

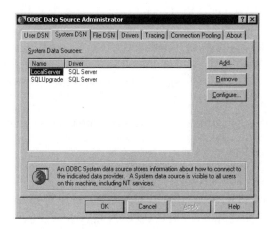

Figure 12.34.   Creating a DSN.

Notice that you can create User DSNs, System DSNs, and File DSNs. User DSNs are specific to the user that created them and local to the computer on which the user created them. System DSNs are available to all login clients and local to the computer on which the user created them. File DSNs are stored in a file. File DSNs can be shared among many users on the network, and need not be a local file on the client computer. After you select the type of DSN (by clicking the appropriate tab) and driver for the new DSN (by clicking the Add button), the Data Source Wizard appears. Figure 12.35 illustrates creating a new ODBC data source using the SQL Server driver.

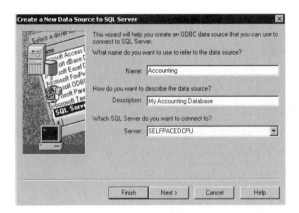

Figure 12.35.   Creating an ODBC data source for a DSN.

In the first page of the wizard, enter a name for the DSN in the Name text box, a description for it in the Description text box, and select the SQL Server instance for which this DSN is storing connection information in the Server drop-down combo box. Next, in the second page, you specify connection information. See Figure 12.36.

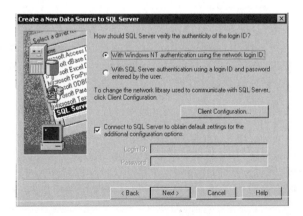

Figure 12.36.   Providing connection information for a DSN.

You can specify that the SQL Server ODBC driver request a trusted connection or use the SQL Server login and password supplied by the user. You can also specify custom client network library parameters for this connection by clicking the Client Configuration button. Next, you can connect to SQL Server to obtain initial settings for the following screens by selecting the Connect To SQL Server To Obtain Default Settings For The Additional Configuration Options check box. Standard defaults are used if you choose not to connect.

Next, in the third page, you can specify a default database by selecting the Change The Default Database To check box or attach a database when this DSN is used by selecting the Attach Database Filename check box. In addition, you can specify ANSI settings for connections using this DSN by selecting the corresponding check box. Finally, if a clustered environment is detected, you can specify use of the failover SQL Server 2000 instance by selecting the Use The Failover SQL Server If The Primary SQL Server Is Not Available check box. See Figure 12.37.

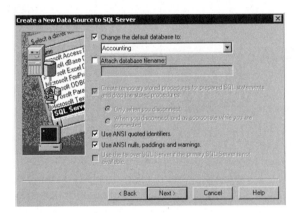

Figure 12.37.   Specifying database settings for a DSN.

Finally, in the fourth page, you can change the language of SQL Server system messages in the corresponding drop-down list, enable encryption, specify character set translation, and choose regional settings by selecting the appropriate check boxes. You can also enable logging of long-running queries (defining what is considered long-running in milliseconds) by selecting the Save Long Running Queries To The Log File check box, and ODBC driver statistics by selecting the Log ODBC Driver Statistics To The Log File check box. See Figure 12.38.

After you have completed the information in the wizard, the ODBC Microsoft SQL Server Setup dialog box appears. You can review your configuration in the information box and test the data source by clicking the Test Data Source button before actually creating the DSN. Figure 12.39 illustrates a successful test for the ODBC data source.

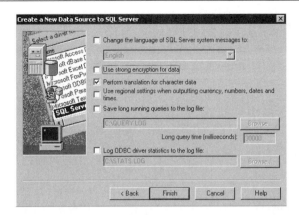

Figure 12.38.   Changing regional, language, and logging settings for a DSN.

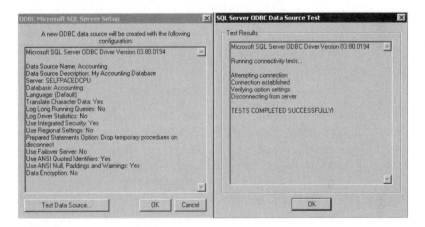

Figure 12.39.   Reviewing and testing a DSN.

Configuring SQL Server XML Support in IIS

One of the most exciting new features of SQL Server 2000 is XML support. You can make a SQL Server 2000 instance an XML-enabled database server. To accomplish this, you configure an IIS virtual directory linked to SQL Server 2000 support. This enables SQL Server 2000 to provide for:

- HTTP access
- XML-Data schemas and XPath queries
- Retrieval and writing of XML data
- The ability to set XML documents as command text and to return result sets as a stream

The details about implementing XML from the programming perspective are beyond the scope of this book. However, the IIS Virtual Directory Management For SQL Server utility makes the task of creating a virtual directory within IIS easy for database administrators. You select this utility by clicking Configure SQL XML Support In IIS in the Microsoft SQL Server program group. Figure 12.40 illustrates the IIS Virtual Directory Management For SQL Server console.

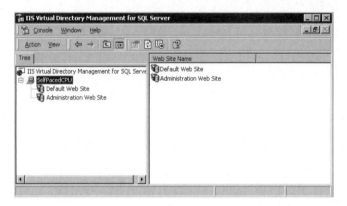

Figure 12.40. IIS Virtual Directory Management for SQL Server console.

In the console tree, expand your server, right-click Default Web Site, point to New, and then click Virtual Directory to begin. The New Virtual Directory Properties dialog box appears. In the General tab, specify a user-friendly name for the virtual directory in the Virtual Directory Name group box. In the Local Path group box, specify a path on the local computer to the files that will be made accessible through this virtual directory. Generally this will be a subfolder under C:\Inetpub and will contain XML queries, templates, and style sheets. See Figure 12.41.

Next, in the Security tab, define the authentication method users will use to obtain access to SQL Server 2000. You can choose to have all users authenticate using either a dedicated SQL Server login or the IIS local user account (for which you can configure permissions). Generally, use this method for guest access with limited permissions. You can also choose to require that each user provide individual authentication (either Windows or SQL Server authentication). See Figure 12.42.

Next, in the SQL Server group box in the Data Source tab, specify the SQL Server 2000 instance whose data is being published through this virtual directory. In addition, you define the default database by browsing the instance to retrieve the database from a list of databases in the Database group box (using the credentials provided on the previous property sheet). See Figure 12.43.

Figure 12.41.   Specifying a name and path for the virtual directory.

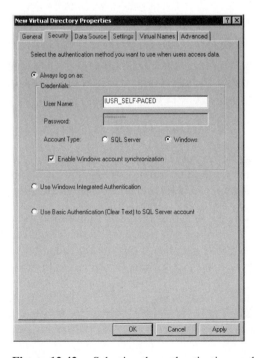

Figure 12.42.   Selecting the authentication method for connecting to the virtual directory.

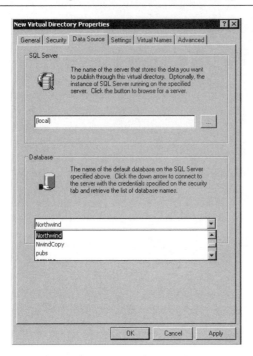

Figure 12.43.   Specifying the server and database published using the virtual directory.

Next, in the Settings tab, specify the type of access to the SQL Server 2000 instance you want to provide by selecting the appropriate check boxes. URL queries allow a user to submit any query, whereas template queries limit the queries that can be submitted through this virtual directory. XPath queries over SQL views allow more control over the structure and appearance of the document returned. XPath queries can be embedded in a URL query or a template. You can also choose to allow user input for values to be passed to a POST query and choose a limit for the size of the user input (in kilobytes). See Figure 12.44.

Next, in the Virtual Names tab, specify any virtual names you want to create by clicking the New button. For example, you might create a virtual name linked to a physical path that contains XML templates or views. See Figure 12.45.

Finally, in the Advanced tab, you can specify a different location for the Sqlisapi.dll in the ISAPI Location group box, provide additional user settings in the Additional User Settings group box, or disable caching in the Caching Options group box. Generally, leave the defaults in place. See Figure 12.46.

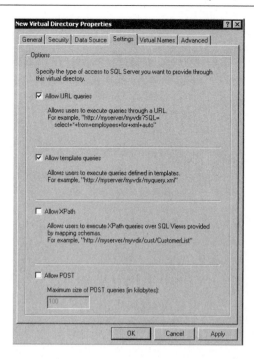

Figure 12.44.   Choosing settings for access to the SQL Server database.

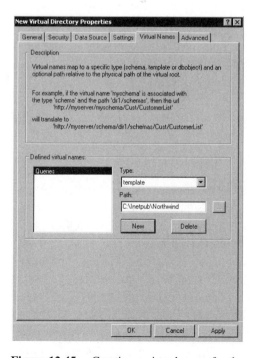

Figure 12.45.   Creating a virtual name for the published data.

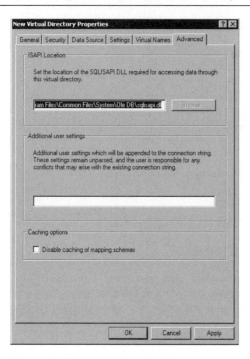

Figure 12.46.   Changing default advanced settings for the virtual directory.

Practice: Creating an IIS Virtual Directory

In this practice you create an IIS virtual directory using the IIS Virtual Directory Management For SQL Server utility.

▶ **To create an IIS virtual directory**

1. Ensure that you are logged on to the SelfPacedSQL.MSFT domain controller as Administrator.

2. Using Windows Explorer, create a new folder called Northwind under C:\Inetpub.

3. Click Start, point to Programs, point to Microsoft SQL Server, and then click Configure SQL XML Support In IIS.

   The IIS Virtual Directory Management For SQL Server console appears, displaying a connection to your server.

4. In the console tree, expand your server, right-click Default Web Site, point to New, and then click Virtual Directory.

   The New Virtual Directory Properties dialog box appears with the General tab selected.

5. In the Virtual Directory Name text box, type **Northwind**.

6. In the Local Path text box, type **C:\InetPub\Northwind**.

7. Click the Security tab.

8. In the User Name text box, type **sa**.

9. Click the Data Source tab.

   A Confirm Password dialog box appears.

10. Click OK to confirm no password for the sa account.

11. In the SQL Server text box, select SelfPacedCPU by clicking the ellipsis button.

12. In the Database text box, select Northwind from the Database drop-down combo box.

13. Click the Settings tab.

14. Select the Allow URL Queries check box and confirm that the Allow Template Queries check box is selected.

15. Click the Virtual Names tab.

16. Click the New button.

    The Virtual Name Configuration dialog box appears.

17. In the Virtual Name text box, type **Queries**.

18. In the Type drop-down list, select Template.

19. In the Path text box, type **C:\Inetpub\Northwind** and then click the Save button.

20. Click OK to create the new virtual directory.

21. Using Notepad, open the XML Query.txt file in the C:\SelfPacedSQL\CH_12 folder.

22. Copy the HTTP query.

23. Open Internet Explorer.

24. Paste the query to the Address drop-down combo box and then click the Go button.

    The contact name and phone number from the Customers table in the Northwind database is displayed.

25. Close Windows Explorer, Notepad, Internet Explorer, and IIS Virtual Directory Management For SQL Server console.

Note   The SQL Server 2000 compact disc contains additional XML queries and exercises. They are located in the DevTools\Samples\Xml folder in a self-extracting ZIP file.

Lesson Summary

Setting up SQL Mail enables the SQL Server service to use e-mail to respond to queries and notify users of the results of Transact-SQL scripts. SQLAgentMail enables the SQL Server Agent service to provide notification regarding alerts and the success or failure of jobs. Setting up linked servers allows users to access data on remote databases without providing connection information each time they connect. ODBC applications may require DSNs, which a database administrator might have to configure. Finally, to create an XML-enabled database server, IIS must be configured with a virtual directory linked to a SQL Server 2000 database and specifying connection parameters and permitted certain XML access types.

Lesson 3: Performing Maintenance Tasks

In addition to configuration and setup tasks, a database administrator must perform a variety of maintenance tasks. In this lesson, you will learn to update distribution statistics, rebuild indexes, and manage full-text indexes. These tasks along with performing backups and performing internal consistency checks are regular maintenance tasks of a database administrator. Backup tasks were covered in Chapter 9 and performing internal consistency checks is covered in Chapter 14.

After this lesson, you will be able to
- Update distribution statistics
- Rebuild indexes
- Maintain full-text indexes

Estimated lesson time: 15 minutes

Updating Distribution Statistics

SQL Server 2000 automatically creates and maintains distribution statistics for all indexes. Distribution statistics describe the selectivity and distribution of key values in each index. The SQL Server 2000 query optimizer uses these statistics to estimate the efficiency of an index in retrieving data in a query. The query optimizer is the component of SQL Server responsible for determining the most efficient method to retrieve data (such as whether to use an index and which index to use). Distribution statistics can also be created and maintained for unindexed columns. They can be created manually using the *CREATE STATISTICS* statement or can be created automatically by the query optimizer.

Although distribution statistics are periodically updated automatically by the SQL Server service, you should refresh them manually whenever significant numbers of changes to keys occur in an index or a significant amount of new data is added to a table. You refresh them manually using the *UPDATE STATISTICS* statement or by displaying the Execution Plan for a query in SQL Query Analyzer (you select Show Execution Plan from the Query menu). Out-of-date and missing statistics are displayed as warnings in the Execution Plan tab in SQL Query Analyzer, which you can respond to by creating or updating distribution statistics. You can also schedule the updating of distribution statistics using the Database Maintenance Plan Wizard, which is covered in Chapter 13.

To verify that the autocreate and autoupdate statistics options are enabled (the default) for a database, right-click the database in SQL Server Enterprise Manager, click Properties, and then click the Options tab. Verify that both of the check boxes are selected.

Maintaining Indexes

Clustered indexes control the order and placement of data stored in the data pages of a table. In a clustered index, the physical order of the rows in a table is the same as the indexed order of the index key values. As new data is entered, SQL Server 2000 might have to reorganize the storage of data to make room for new values in order to maintain the ordering. Nonclustered indexes also have to be reordered when new data requires page splits. When SQL Server 2000 needs to enter data on a page that is full, it allocates a new page and splits the existing data between the new page and the existing page. Page splitting can impair performance during the page split and cause data fragmentation that affects future performance.

To minimize the need for page splits, a fill factor for the index is frequently specified. It can be specified using a server-wide value or on an index-by-index basis. Creating an index using a fill factor leaves pages partially full at the time of index creation. However, a fill factor value has no effect when new data is being entered into tables. When data is added to tables, these partially filled pages become full and page splits begin occurring.

As a database administrator, when page splitting occurs you might need to re-create indexes to reorganize data and re-establish partially filled pages by re-specifying the fill factor. This should only be done when the database is not busy. Creating or modifying a clustered index is time-consuming because during these operations the table's rows are reorganized on disk.

You can rebuild indexes using the Transact-SQL DROP_EXISTING clause of the *CREATE INDEX* statement or the *DBCC DBREINDEX* statement. You can also schedule the rebuilding of indexes using the Database Maintenance Plan Wizard in SQL Server Enterprise Manager.

Maintaining Full-Text Indexes

Full-text indexes are indexes of all character data in one or more tables in a database. The indexes are stored in the file system, but administered through the database. Administration consists of several tasks. The full-text engine is implemented as the Microsoft Search service. At the server level, you can configure the amount of system resources that can be used by the Microsoft Search service to maintain current indexes. At the database level, you enable a database and one or more tables to use the Microsoft Search service. Afterward, you must create (populate) full-text indexes on each full-text enabled table. These full-text indexes are stored in catalogs on the local server.

You can use the Full-Text Indexing Wizard in SQL Server Enterprise Manager to enable full-text indexing for a database, one or more tables, and specified columns within the tables. You can also create a population schedule in the Full-Text Indexing Wizard. To initially populate a full-text index, expand the container for the database containing the full-text catalog and then click the Full-Text Catalogs container. You can right-click Full-Text Catalogs to populate all catalogs, or right-click an individual catalog in the details pane to populate a single catalog.

Note   The design and creation of full-text indexes is generally not the responsibility of the database administrator. However, you might be responsible for rebuilding these indexes and regulating the use of resources by the Microsoft Search service for maintaining these indexes.

After the full-text indexes are populated, you need to determine how to keep them current. To prevent the maintenance of full-text indexes from consuming resources when the database is busy, you can repopulate these indexes manually or on a schedule. You can also configure these indexes to be updated automatically as a background process that runs during periods of low database activity. The three repopulation methods for full-text indexes are shown in Table 12.7.

To perform an update of a full-text index manually, right-click the desired Full-Text Catalog name found in the Full-Text Catalogs container and select either Rebuild Catalog or Start Incremental Population. To enable change tracking, use the *sp_fulltext_table* system stored procedure. To control the amount of resources that may be used by the Microsoft Search service, use the *sp_fulltext_service* system stored procedure.

Lesson Summary

Additional maintenance tasks a database administrator might have to perform include updating distribution statistics, rebuilding indexes, and updating full-text indexes. You can update distribution statistics and rebuild indexes manually, or you can schedule them. You can update full-text indexes manually or on a schedule, or you can configure them to run as low-priority background tasks.

Table 12-7.   Repopulation Methods for Full-Text Indexes

Rebuild Type	Description	When to Use
Full rebuild	A complete rescan of all rows followed by a complete rebuild of the full-text index. Must be performed manually or on a schedule.	Large amounts of data have changed.
Timestamp-based incremental rebuild	A rescan of the rows that have changed since the last full or incremental rebuild. The table that is indexed must contain a timestamp column and this rebuild type only updates changes that also update the timestamp column. Must be performed manually or on a schedule.	Use when a large number, but not a large percentage, of records have changed.
Change tracking	A list of all changes to indexed data is maintained. Generally performed on a schedule or as a background task when processor and memory resources are available.	With scheduled or background process updating.

Review

Here are some questions to help you determine whether you have learned enough to move on to the next chapter. If you have difficulty answering these questions, review the material in this chapter before beginning the next chapter. The answers for these questions are located in the Appendix, "Questions and Answers."

1. You are running a number of server applications on the same computer. You observe that the performance of SQL Server 2000 is initially poor after a period of low activity. What can you do to improve its responsiveness?

2. You want to configure the SQL Server Agent service to send mail to administrators in response to alerts. What is the first task you must perform?

3. You want to enable one of your databases to be queried using XML. What must you do?

C H A P T E R   1 3

Automating Administrative Tasks

About This Chapter

This chapter prepares you to automate a variety of administrative tasks. In this chapter you will learn about defining operators, implementing jobs, and configuring alerts to automate routine tasks and create programmed responses to anticipated events and specified performance conditions. You will also learn to create database maintenance plans. Finally, you will learn to create multiserver jobs.

Before You Begin

To complete this chapter, you must have

- A computer that meets or exceeds the minimum hardware requirements listed in Table 2.1, "Hardware Requirements," in Lesson 1 of Chapter 2.
- Microsoft Windows 2000 Server running on your computer on an NTFS partition.
- A computer with a NetBIOS name of SelfPacedCPU, configured as a domain controller in the SelfPacedSQL.MSFT domain.
- Installed a default instance and at least one named instance of SQL Server 2000 (see Chapter 2).

- Created the SSEMDB database using the CreateDB.sql script (see Chapter 6).
- Created the Customer table in the SSEMDB database using the SSEMDB_Full.sql script (see Chapter 9).

Lesson 1: Defining Operators

The first step toward automating administrative tasks is to define operators to be notified of the success, failure, or completion of an automated task, or on the occurrence of specified events or conditions. In this lesson you will learn to define operators who can be notified by e-mail, pager, or NET SEND notifications. You will also learn how to create a fail-safe operator to be notified in response to an alert when the designated operator for the alert cannot be paged.

After this lesson, you will be able to

- Define operators
- Create a fail-safe operator
- Troubleshoot operator notification problems

Estimated lesson time: 30 minutes

Methods of Notification

SQL Server Agent can be configured to send notifications to operators with respect to jobs, events, and performance conditions. An *operator* is a user or message group that is configured to receive notifications from SQL Server Agent using one of three messaging methods: e-mail, pager, or NET SEND.

E-mail

SQL Server Agent can notify an operator using e-mail provided that SQLAgent-Mail has been configured. As discussed in the previous chapter, SQLAgentMail requires that the SQL Server Agent service use a domain user account. This domain user account must have a MAPI messaging profile on the computer on which SQL Server Agent is running.

Pager

SQL Server Agent can also notify an operator using a pager. Pager notification is implemented using e-mail and third-party paging software. Because pager notification relies on e-mail, SQLAgentMail must be configured in order to enable pager notification.

Note   SQL Server 2000 does not provide any pager software. It relies on you to implement a third-party pager solution. If all operators use the same pager solution, you can provide any special e-mail formatting required for all pager e-mails, including limiting the size of the message (necessary for some pagers), by eliminating the error text. To access this feature in SQL Server Enterprise Manager, expand the Management container for the instance, right-click SQL Server Agent, click Properties, and then click the Alert System tab in the SQL Server Agent Properties dialog box.

NET SEND

SQL Server Agent can also notify an operator via network pop-up using NET SEND. NET SEND is available only with the Windows 2000 and Windows NT 4.0 operating systems. NET SEND uses the Windows Messenger service, which must be running on the recipient computer as well as the sending computer. Messages can be sent to users, computers, or messaging names on the network. A *messaging name* is an alias that a computer will accept messages for and can be created using the NET NAME command-prompt utility.

Fail-Safe Operators

SQL Server Agent can be configured to notify a fail-safe operator in response to an alert if the designated operator cannot be paged or the SQL Server Agent cannot access system tables in the msdb database. Possible reasons for the inability to page an operator include an incorrect pager address or the designated operator being off duty according to the pager's on-duty schedule that you configured when you created a new fail-safe operator. A reason for the inability to access the system tables is disk failure.

Creating Operators

An operator can be an individual, a messaging group, or a computer that can be contacted using one of the three notification methods. You should create a notification plan for all operators, including on-duty schedules and pager addresses. You can create operators using either SQL Server Enterprise Manager or Transact-SQL system stored procedures.

Note   Using e-mail and pager notifications is only as reliable as your messaging infrastructure.

Using SQL Server Enterprise Manager

To create an operator using SQL Server Enterprise Manager, expand the Management container for the instance, expand the SQL Server Agent container, right-click the Operators container, and then click New Operator to display the New Operator Properties dialog box. See Figure 13.1.

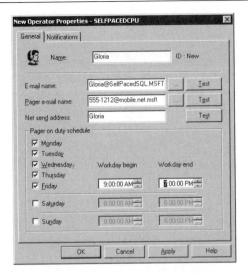

Figure 13.1.   Creating a new operator.

Each operator must have a unique name. In the General tab, you can specify address information for all three types of notifications. You can test the address information (and the underlying infrastructure) by sending a test message. If the message is received by the operator using a particular notification method, the address information for that method is valid and the underlying infrastructure is functioning. You can also specify pager on-duty schedules, including the length and hours of the workday.

Note   Always use fully qualified e-mail addresses to avoid name resolution problems with e-mail aliases. For example, if the display names JohnD and JohnDoe both exist in your e-mail address book, a notification to JohnD cannot be resolved.

You can immediately configure notifications to be sent to this newly created operator by clicking the Notifications tab. See Figure 13.2.

Notice that you can select one or more existing alerts and then designate this new operator to receive notifications with respect to these alerts. You can immediately send e-mail to the operator detailing the newly assigned alert responsibilities. You can also view the most recent statistics on notification attempts for this operator.

Note   Use the Notifications tab for an existing operator to view the alerts and jobs for which the operator is designated to receive notification.

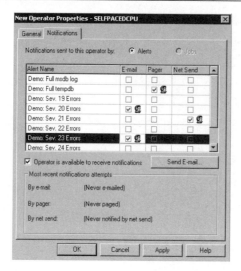

Figure 13.2.   Viewing and configuring operator notifications.

Using Transact-SQL

You can create and update operators using the *sp_add_operator* and *sp_update_operator* system stored procedures. You can view information about currently defined operators using the *sp_help_operator* system stored procedure.

Note   Although you can use Transact-SQL system stored procedures, use of the SQL Server Enterprise Manager graphical interface is recommended. Use the Generate Script feature to archive SQL Server objects created with SQL Server Enterprise Manager.

Creating a Fail-Safe Operator

To create a fail-safe operator using SQL Server Enterprise Manager, expand the Management container for the instance, right-click SQL Server Agent, and then click Properties. In the SQL Server Agent Properties dialog box, click the Alert System tab. See Figure 13.3.

You can select an existing operator as the fail-safe operator from the Operator drop-down list, or you can create one on the fly by selecting New Fail-Safe Operator from the drop-down list. Once you designate an operator as the fail-safe operator, you cannot delete the operator until you designate a different operator or select no fail-safe operator.

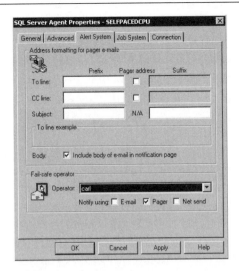

Figure 13.3.   Creating a fail-safe operator.

Practice: Creating Operators and Setting a Fail-Safe Operator

In this practice you use the SQL Server Enterprise Manager to create operators and to set a fail-safe operator. (This practice uses NET SEND because not all readers will have a MAPI client installed. However, if you have a MAPI client installed, you might want to configure SQLAgentMail according to the previous chapter and then create e-mail operators for the practice exercises in this chapter.)

▶ **To create operators and set a fail-safe operator**

1. Ensure that you are logged on to the SelfPacedSQL.MSFT domain controller as Administrator.

2. Click Start, point to Programs, point to Accessories, and then click Command Prompt.

   The Command Prompt window appears.

3. Type **net name failsafe /add**, and then press ENTER.

   The operating system informs you that the message name FailSafe is added successfully.

4. Close the Command Prompt window.

5. Click Start, point to Programs, point to Microsoft SQL Server, and then click Enterprise Manager.

6. In the console tree, expand the Microsoft SQL Servers container, expand the SQL Server Group container, expand the default instance container, expand the Management container, and then expand the SQL Server Agent container.

7. Right-click the Operators container, and then click New Operator.

   The New Operator Properties – SelfPacedCPU dialog box appears.

8. In the Name text box, type **Operator**.

9. In the E-Mail Name text box, type **E-mail** (or use a valid e-mail address).

10. In the Pager E-Mail Name text box, type **Pager** (or use a valid page address).

11. In the Net Send Address text box, type **SelfPacedCPU**, and then click the Test button for this net send address.

    A Test Net Send Address dialog box appears stating that a network pop-up message will be sent to SelfPacedCPU. (The user name, Administrator, is not being used to send messages to this practice because multiple users named Administrator may exist on the network in different domains.)

12. Click OK.

    A Messenger Service message box appears displaying a message from Self-PacedCPU to SelfPacedCPU testing the network pop-up notification.

13. Click OK to close the Messenger Service message box.

14. In the Pager On Duty Schedule group box, configure a pager on-duty schedule such that this operator will be not be on duty when you perform the practice exercises in this chapter.

15. Click OK to close the New Operator Properties – SelfPacedCPU dialog box.

    In the details pane, notice that this operator is now displayed.

16. In the console tree, right-click the SQL Server Agent container, and then click Properties.

    The SQL Server Agent Properties – SelfPacedCPU dialog box appears.

17. Click the Alert System tab.

18. In the Fail-Safe Operator group box, click (New Fail-Safe Operator) from the Operator drop-down list.

    The New Operator Properties – SelfPacedCPU dialog box appears.

19. In the Name text box, type **FailSafe**.

20. In the Net Send Address text box, type **FailSafe**, and then click the Test button for the net send address.

    A Test Net Send Address dialog box appears stating that a network pop-up message will be sent to FailSafe.

21. Click OK.

    A Messenger Service message box appears displaying a message from Self-PacedCPU to FailSafe testing the network pop-up notification.

22. Click OK to close the Messenger Service message box.

23. Click OK to close the New Operator Properties – SelfPacedCPU dialog box.

The SQL Server Agent Properties – SelfPacedCPU dialog box appears displaying FailSafe in the Operator drop-down list as the fail-safe operator to be notified using NET SEND.

24. Click OK.

25. In the console tree, click Operators.

   In the details pane, notice that two operators are now displayed.

26. Leave SQL Server Enterprise Manager running.

Lesson Summary

Creating operators is the first part of automating administrative tasks. Operators can be users, messaging groups, or computers. Operators can be notified using e-mail, pagers, and network pop-up messages. E-mail and pager notifications require the domain user account used by the SQL Server Agent service to be configured to use a MAPI messaging profile for SQLAgentMail. NET SEND messages require the Windows Messenger service, which is available only on the Windows 2000 and Windows NT 4.0 operating systems.

Lesson 2: Creating Jobs

Using SQL Server Agent, you can create and schedule jobs that automate routine administrative tasks. In this lesson, you learn to create simple and complex jobs. You learn to configure permissions for jobs owned by users who are not members of the sysadmin server role. You learn to execute these jobs manually or according to a schedule. You also learn to use operators for notification of the success, failure, or completion of a job. Finally, you learn to review job properties and job execution history.

After this lesson, you will be able to

- Create jobs using single or multiple step jobs
- Create schedules for jobs
- Enable and disable jobs and schedules
- Use operators with jobs for notification of success, failure, or completion
- Troubleshoot job execution problems
- Review jobs and job history

Estimated lesson time: 45 minutes

Implementing Jobs

Database administrators create jobs to perform predictable administrative functions (such as backing up databases or importing data) either according to a schedule or in response to events and conditions. Jobs can be simple operations containing only a single job step or can be extremely complex operations containing many job steps with control of flow logic. SQL Server Agent is responsible for the management and execution of all jobs. SQL Server Agent must be running for jobs to be executed. Jobs can be created on the local server or on one or more target servers in a multiserver administration configuration. Multiserver jobs are covered in Lesson 5 of this chapter.

Types of Job Steps

SQL Server 2000 supports jobs containing operating system commands, CmdExec commands, Transact-SQL statements, Microsoft ActiveX scripts, and replication tasks. Replication jobs are covered in Chapter 15. A single job can contain all of these types of commands, although each job step can contain only a single type of command.

Operating system commands (such as .bat, .cmd, .com, or .exe) must contain the absolute path to the executables, the executable command (including switches and options), and a process exit code. All operating system commands issue an exit code upon completion of execution indicating the success or failure of the command. An exit code of zero indicates that the command completed successfully. Any other exit code indicates a type of command failure. Responses to different types of failures can be programmed into the job logic.

Transact-SQL statements must identify the database in which the statement will execute and provide the statement, function, stored procedure, or extended stored procedure to be executed. A single job step can contain multiple batches of Transact-SQL statements with embedded GO commands. Members of the sysadmin role can write job steps to run on behalf of another database user.

ActiveX scripts must identify the scripting language used by the job step and provide the ActiveX script commands. An ActiveX script can also be compiled and run as a CmdExec executable.

Permissions and Ownership of Jobs

By default, jobs are owned by the creator of the job and operate in the security context of that login, regardless of who executes the job. Members of the sysadmin server role can assign ownership to any valid login. Ownership of a job does not grant the right to execute any particular job step. Permission to execute each Transact-SQL job step is verified by the SQL Server service using permissions granted within SQL Server. By default, permission to execute CmdExec and ActiveX job steps is granted only to jobs owned by members of the sysadmin server role. These job steps run in the security context of the SQL Server Agent service account. Permission to run CmdExec and ActiveX scripting job steps can be granted to users who are not members of the sysadmin fixed server role. These job steps owned by non-sysadmins run in the security context of a specified Windows account called a proxy account and inherit the rights granted to that account. To configure the proxy account in SQL Server Enterprise Manager, expand the Management container in the instance, right-click SQL Server Agent, and then click Properties. In the SQL Server Agent Properties dialog box, click the Job System tab. When you clear the check box in the Non-SysAdmin Job Step Proxy Account group box, the SQL Agent Proxy Account dialog box appears so that you can then configure the proxy account.

Note   SQL Server Agent jobs on Windows Me and Windows 98 always run in the context of the logged-in user.

Multiple Job Steps and Job Responses

A job step either succeeds or fails. On the success of a job step, you can configure the job step to continue to the next step or a specific job step. You can also configure the job step to quit and report success or failure. For example, a job step can succeed in its programmed action and report either success or failure based on the logic of the job. On the failure of a job step, you can also configure a subsequent step or quit the job and report success or failure. See Figure 13.4.

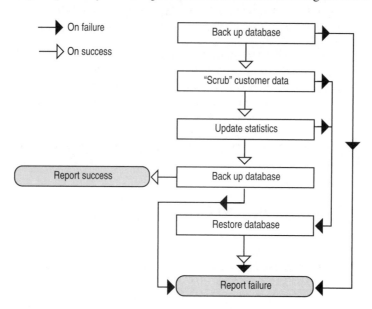

Figure 13.4.   Flow chart showing job step sequence configuration.

Figure 13.4 illustrates the backing up of a database before importing data. If the initial database backup fails, the job quits reporting the failure. If the initial database backup succeeds, the job continues and imports new data to the database using DTS (scrubbing and cleansing the data in the process). If the data import job step succeeds, a statistics update job step executes followed by the execution of another database backup job step (which backs up the database containing the new data). If either the data import job step or the update statistics job step fails, a restore database job step executes and a notification of failure is reported. If the job successfully imports new data, updates the statistics, and then backs up the database, this success is reported. Notice that the restore database job step reports failure to a defined operator regardless of the success or failure of the restore job step. If the restore job step is executed, the job (whose function is to import new data on a regular schedule) has failed. The restore job step succeeds only in restoring the database to its condition prior to the attempted data import. A database administrator must manually determine the cause of the failure at this point.

You must configure operators to be notified of the success, failure, or completion of the job. Without operators being designated to receive notification, the reports of success and failure of the job do not get transmitted to users. By default, failure of a job is automatically logged to the Windows application log, which can be viewed in Event Viewer.

Note   If you want to pass data between job steps, you must use permanent tables, global temporary tables, or operating system files.

Scheduling Jobs

Although you can manually run each job (generally just for testing jobs and job steps), you normally create one or more schedules for a job to fully automate the task. Various types of schedules are available. Jobs can be configured to run continuously (such as certain monitoring jobs), whenever the processor is considered idle (based on your definition), or at recurring intervals (such as hourly, daily, or weekly). Jobs can also be scheduled to run a single time only or in response to a defined alert. Alerts are covered in Lesson 3.

Multiple schedules enable you to have jobs execute on a certain schedule during the workday and on a different schedule in the evening or on weekends. Each schedule can be enabled or disabled. If all schedules are disabled for a particular job, a job can still be executed manually or in response to an alert.

Note   If a job is disabled, it will not execute in response to any alerts or schedules. However, it can still be executed manually. When troubleshooting, verify that the job and all applicable schedules are enabled.

If you configure jobs to execute during periods of low processor utilization, you must first define the CPU idle condition and verify the local administrator permissions of the service account of the SQL Server Agent service. Next, determine how much processor resources each job requires using SQL Profiler and Windows 2000 System Monitor. These monitoring tools are covered in Chapter 14. Define the CPU idle condition to accommodate the processor resources required by all jobs configured with a CPU idle schedule. All such jobs will execute when the CPU idle condition is reached.

Note   SQL Server Agent must be running at the time a job is scheduled in order for the job to execute when scheduled.

Creating Jobs

You can create jobs using the Create Job Wizard or directly by using SQL Server Enterprise Manager. You can also create jobs with Transact-SQL system stored procedures.

Using the Create Job Wizard

You can start the Create Job Wizard from the Wizards list or by clicking Job Scheduling from the Tools menu in SQL Server Enterprise Manager. The Create Job

Wizard is a simple way to begin creating and scheduling jobs. Click Next in the Welcome To The Create Job Wizard page to begin. See Figure 13.5.

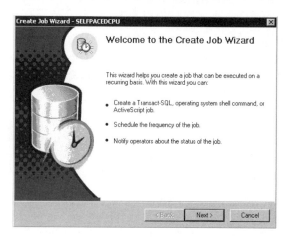

Figure 13.5.   Starting the Create Job Wizard.

In the Select Job Command Type page, you select the type of job you want to create. You can only create single-step jobs using the Create Job Wizard. See Figure 13.6.

You have a choice between three types of commands that the job can execute. If you click the Transact-SQL Command option button and then click Next, the Enter Transact-SQL Statement page appears, which enables you to select the database and enter the statement. You can click the Parse button to parse the Transact-SQL statement to verify that the syntax is valid. See Figure 13.7. You can also open a file containing the statement you want to use.

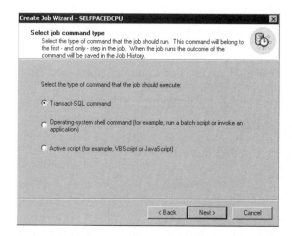

Figure 13.6.   Selecting the type of command for the job to run.

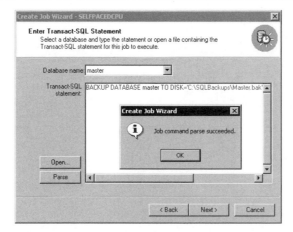

Figure 13.7.   Entering and then parsing a Transact-SQL command.

If you click the Operating-System Shell Command option button and then click Next, the Enter Operating-System Shell Command page appears, which enables you to enter the command for this job to execute. See Figure 13.8.

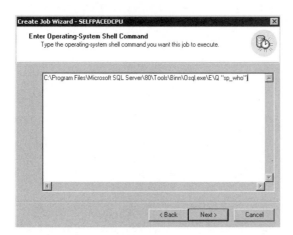

Figure 13.8.   Entering an operating system shell command.

If you click the Active Script option button and then click Next, the Enter Active Script Command page appears, which enables you to enter the Visual Basic script for this job to execute. You can click the Parse button to parse the Visual Basic script to verify that the syntax is valid. See Figure 13.9. You can also open a file containing the script you want to use.

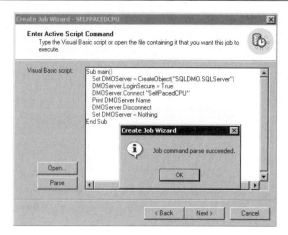

Figure 13.9.   Parsing an Active Script command.

After selecting the type of job and entering the job information, you can specify a job schedule (including running the job immediately) in the Specify Job Schedule page. See Figure 13.10.

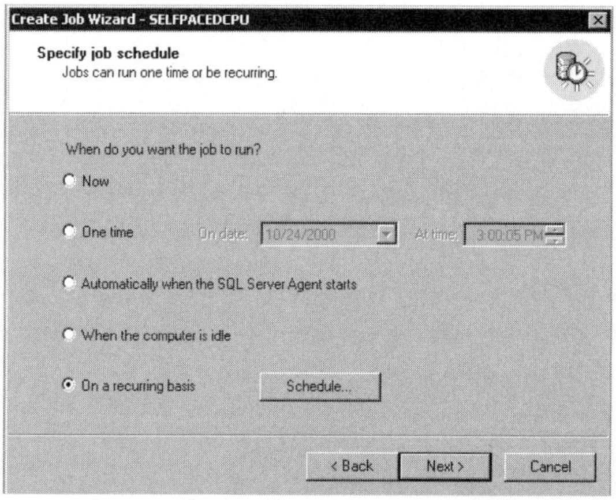

Figure 13.10.   Specifying a job schedule.

If you click the On A Recurring Basis option button, you can click the Schedule button to define this recurring schedule in the Edit Recurring Job Schedule dialog box. You can specify daily, weekly, or monthly and select specific hours, days, or days of the month (such as first Sunday of each month). See Figure 13.11.

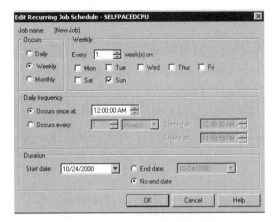

Figure 13.11.   Editing a recurring job schedule.

Next, in the Job Notifications page, you can select an operator to notify via either NET SEND or e-mail. You must select from existing operators. You cannot create a new operator or use pager notification from within the Create Job Wizard. See Figure 13.12.

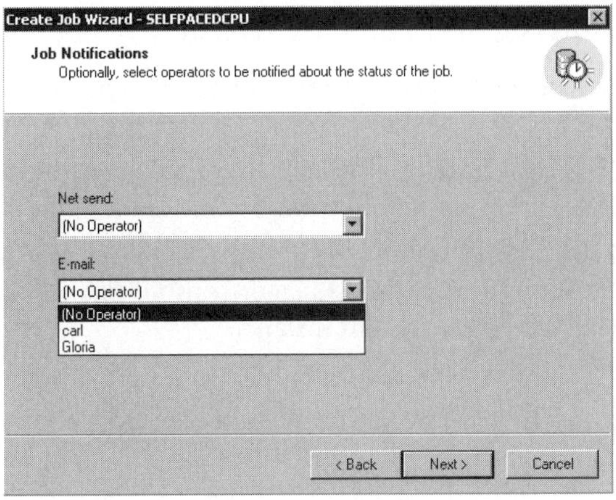

Figure 13.12.   Selecting an operator to notify.

Finally, in the Completing The Create Job Wizard page, you are given the opportunity to specify a name for the new job and to review the selections you have made before you actually create the new job. You can click the Back button to change any parameter you want to change. Click the Finish button to create the job. See Figure 13.13.

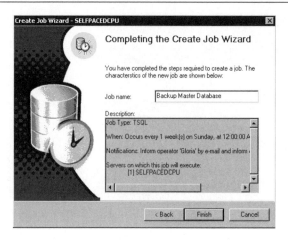

Figure 13.13.   Naming the new job.

Practice: Creating a Job Using the Create Job Wizard

In this practice you use the Create Job Wizard to create a job to back up the master database.

▶ **To create a job using the Create Job Wizard**

1. Ensure that you are logged on to the SelfPacedSQL.MSFT domain controller as Administrator.

   In the SQL Server Enterprise Manager console tree, the Management container and the SQL Server Agent container for the default instance should still be expanded from the previous practice.

2. In the SQL Server Enterprise Manager console tree, click the SQL Server Agent container for the default instance.

3. On the Tools menu, click Job Scheduling.

   The Welcome To The Create Job Wizard page appears.

4. Click Next.

   The Select Job Command Type page appears.

5. Verify that the Transact-SQL Command option button is clicked, and then click Next.

   The Enter Transact-SQL Statement page appears.

6. Verify that master is selected in the Database Name drop-down list, and then type **BACKUP DATABASE master TO DISK = 'C:\SQLBackups\Mas-terDB.bak'** in the Transact-SQL Statement text box. (If you did not create the C:\SQLBackups folder in Chapter 9, you must create it now.)

7. Click the Parse button.

   A Create Job Wizard message box appears stating that the job command parse succeeded.

8. Click OK.

9. Click Next.

   The Specify Job Schedule page appears.

10. Click the On A Recurring Basis option button, and then click the Schedule button.

    The Edit Recurring Job Schedule – SelfPacedCPU dialog box appears.

11. In the Occurs group box, click the Daily option button, and then click OK.

12. Click Next.

    The Job Notifications dialog box appears.

13. In the Net Send drop-down list, click Operator, and then click Next.

    The Completing The Create Job Wizard page appears.

14. In the Job Name text box, type **Backup Master Job**, and then click the Finish button.

    A Create Job Wizard message box appears stating that the job was created successfully.

15. Click OK.

16. In the console tree, click the Jobs container.

17. In the details pane, right-click Backup Master Job, and then click Start Job.

    After a few moments, a Messenger Service message box appears delivering a message to SelfPacedCPU stating that the Backup Master Job succeeded and providing details about the completion of the job.

18. Click OK.

19. In the details pane, right-click Backup Master Job, and then click Refresh Job.

    Notice that the Last Run Status column indicates that the job succeeded and that the Next Run Date is the following day at 12:00:00 AM.

20. Leave SQL Server Enterprise Manager running.

Using SQL Server Enterprise Manager Directly

To create a job using SQL Server Enterprise Manager directly, you can either right-click SQL Server Agent in the Management container, point to New and then click Job, or right-click Jobs in the SQL Server Agent container and then click New Job. The New Job Properties dialog box appears, as illustrated in Figure 13.14.

Figure 13.14.   Specifying properties for a new job.

In the General tab, notice that you can specify the owner of the job (this option will be grayed out if you are not a member of the sysadmin server role). You can also specify a category for the job. The default is uncategorized local. However, if you group jobs into categories, you can locate all jobs in a specified category by clicking the ellipsis next to the Category drop-down list. To save the job, you must supply a name for the job in the Name text box.

Click the Steps tab and then click the New button to display the New Job Step dialog box that you use to create job steps. See Figure 13.15.

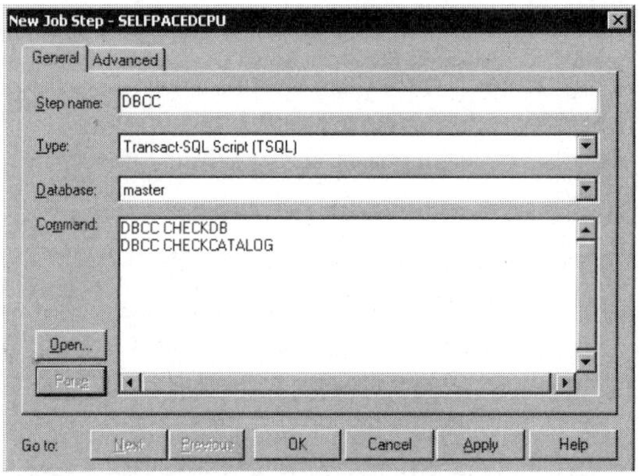

Figure 13.15.   Creating a new job step.

Enter a step name, select the type of job step (the default is Transact-SQL Script), and then enter the appropriate statement, script, or command. A step name is required to continue. Click the Advanced tab to review and set properties of this job step. See Figure 13.16.

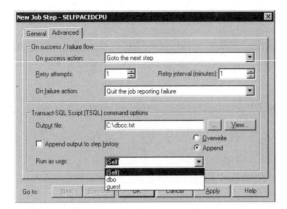

Figure 13.16.   Reviewing properties for a job step.

The default for each job step is to continue to the next step on success and to quit the job on failure and report a failure. If there is no next step, the job quits with success and reports success. You can specify a number of retry attempts (to allow for a connection timeout error, for example) and a time interval between retries. You can also specify an operating system file in which to store the results of a Transact-SQL or CmdExec job step. You can click the View button to view the contents of any existing output file when creating the job step and choose to have the job step append or overwrite the contents of the output file each time the job step runs. You can also choose to have the results of the Transact-SQL script written to the step history along with the report of the success or failure of the job. Finally, you can choose to have this job step run as a user other than the job owner. For example, CmdExec job steps might need different permissions than Transact-SQL statements.

If you have created multiple job steps, you can then review the steps in the Steps tab, edit them, insert new steps, and change the order of steps. See Figure 13.17.

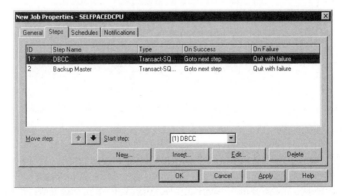

Figure 13.17.   Reviewing and modifying job step order.

You can modify the order of steps and designate a step other than the first step in the list as the starting step (allowing a step to be skipped temporarily without deleting it). The starting step is indicated by the green start flag and also by the step displayed in the Start Step drop-down list. After you complete the job steps, click the Schedules tab to create one or more schedules for the job. See Figure 13.18.

Figure 13.18.   Creating schedules for the job.

Notice that you can also click the New Alert button to define a new alert that executes this job in response to an alert. Alerts are covered in the next lesson. After completing the schedules (and alerts if applicable), click the Notifications tab to designate operators for notifications of the completion, success, and/or failure of a job. See Figure 13.19.

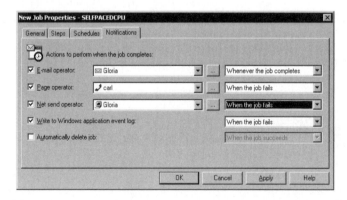

Figure 13.19.   Designating operators for notifications of job status.

Notice that you can select to notify different operators using different mechanisms whenever the job completes, succeeds, or fails. By default, job failures are also written to the Event Viewer application log. You can also choose to have the job automatically deleted after successful completion (such as for a one-time job).

Practice: Creating a Job Using SQL Server Enterprise Manager Directly

In this practice you use the SQL Server Enterprise Manager to create a job directly.

▶ **To create a job using SQL Server Enterprise Manager directly**

1. Ensure that you are logged on to the SelfPacedSQL.MSFT domain controller as Administrator.

   In the SQL Server Enterprise Manager console tree, the Management container and the SQL Server Agent container for the default instance should still be expanded from the previous practice.

2. In the SQL Server Agent container, right-click Jobs, and then click New Job.

   The New Job Properties – SelfPacedCPU dialog box appears. Notice that the default owner for this job is SelfPacedSQL\Administrator.

3. In the Name text box, type **Backup SSEMDB Tlog**, and then click the Steps tab.

4. Click the New button.

   The New Job Step – SelfPacedCPU dialog box appears.

5. In the Step Name text box, type **Backup TLog Step**.

6. Verify that the step type is Transact-SQL Script (TSQL), and then click the Database drop-down list and click SSEMDB.

7. In the Command text box, type **BACKUP LOG SSEMDB TO DISK = 'C:\SQLBackups\SSEMDB.trn'**.

8. Click the Parse button.

   A New Job Step – SelfPacedCPU message box appears stating that the parse succeeded.

9. Click OK to close the message box.

10. Click OK to close the New Job Step – SelfPacedCPU dialog box.

11. Click the Schedules tab.

12. Click the New Schedule button.

    The New Job Schedule – SelfPacedCPU dialog box appears.

13. In the Name text box, type **Workday Schedule**.

14. Click the Change button.

    The Edit Recurring Job Schedule – SelfPacedCPU dialog box appears.

15. In the Occurs group box, click the Daily option button.

16. In the Daily Frequency group box, click the Occurs Every option button.

17. Click OK to close the Edit Recurring Job Schedule – SelfPacedCPU dialog box.

18. Click OK to close the New Job Schedule – SelfPacedCPU dialog box.

19. Click the Notifications tab.

20. Select the Page Operator check box, and then select Operator from the Page Operator drop-down list.

21. Select Whenever The Job Completes from the drop-down list, and then click OK.

    In the details pane for the Jobs container, notice that two jobs appear.

22. In the details pane, right-click Backup SSEMDB Tlog, and then click Start Job.

23. After a few moments, right-click Backup SSEMDB Tlog, and then click Refresh Job.

    Notice that the Last Run Status column will either display Executing or Succeeded. Do not continue until the column indicates that the job succeeded. Click Refresh Job again to update the displayed information, if necessary. Notice that a network pop-up message was not received. You will review job history in the next practice to determine why you did not receive a message.

24. Leave SQL Server Enterprise Manager running.

Using Transact-SQL

You can also create jobs using the *sp_add_job*, *sp_add_jobstep*, *sp_add_jobschedule*, and *sp_update_jobstep* system stored procedures.

Note Although you can use Transact-SQL system stored procedures, use of the SQL Server Enterprise Manager graphical interface is recommended.

Configuring the Proxy Account

If you plan to create jobs containing CmdExec and ActiveX job steps that will be owned by (or executed in the context of) users who are not members of the sysadmin server role, you must configure the proxy account. Right-click SQL Server Agent in the Management container for the instance, and then click Properties. In the SQL Server Agent Properties – SelfPacedCPU dialog box, click the Job System tab. See Figure 13.20.

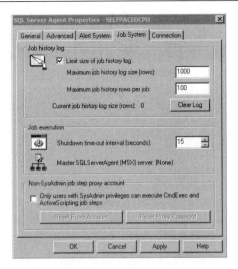

Figure 13.20.   Configuring the proxy account.

Clear the check box in the Non-SysAdmin Job Step Proxy Account group box to allow users without sysadmin privileges to execute CmdExec and ActiveX scripting job steps. You are then prompted, in the SQL Agent Proxy Account dialog box, to provide the name of the proxy account that SQL Server Agent will use to execute these jobs. All CmdExec and ActiveX scripting job steps for non-sysadmins will be executed by SQL Server Agent in the security context of this account. You must provide an existing local or domain user account. Assign this account the permissions you want non-sysadmins to inherit when their jobs are run. If the service account used by the SQL Server service does not have administrator privileges, you must first provide a valid administrator account to access the security account list. See Figure 13.21.

Figure 13.21.   Providing a valid administrator account.

Reviewing Jobs and Job History

The details pane of the Jobs container in SQL Server Enterprise Manager displays information regarding all jobs for the SQL Server 2000 instance. See Figure 13.22.

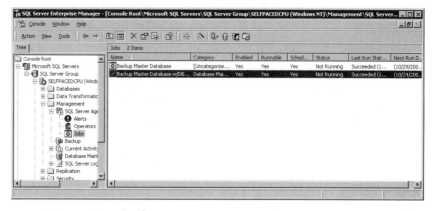

Figure 13.22.   Displaying job information for the current instance of SQL Server 2000.

Information regarding each job is displayed in columns. Click on a column heading to sort the jobs based on that column. Notice the Enabled column. If you are troubleshooting a job that does not run, verify that it is enabled. Information is displayed regarding the status of a job (such as executing or not running), the last time a job ran, and the next time it is scheduled.

> **Note**   Because SQL Server Enterprise Manager is a client application, information displayed must be refreshed to view the most recent information (particularly status, last run, and next run information).

Job Properties

To view or modify the properties of a job, right-click the job, and then click Properties (or double-click the job). Users who are not members of the sysadmin server role can only view or modify jobs they own.

Job History Log

To review the execution history of a job, right-click the job, and then click View Job History. See Figure 13.23.

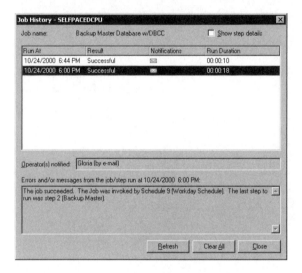

Figure 13.23.   Reviewing the execution history of a job.

Information is displayed regarding each time the job was run, its result, who invoked the job, and operators notified. Select the Show Step Details check box to view the details of each step. Viewing step details displays important information for troubleshooting a job. For example, if a job fails because SQL Server Agent lacked proper permissions, this information will be displayed in the step details. See Figure 13.24.

Figure 13.24.   Viewing details about each step of a job.

You can control the size of the job history log. Right-click the SQL Server Agent container, click Properties, and then click the Job System tab. See Figure 13.25.

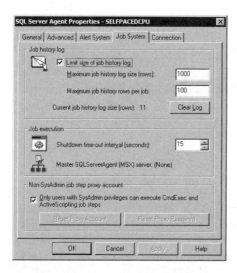

Figure 13.25.   Controlling the history log size.

Notice that the default size of the job history log for each job is 100 rows, and for all jobs combined, the default size is 1000 rows. Notice that you can click the Clear Log button to clear the entire log.

Practice: Reviewing and Modifying a Job and Viewing Job History

In this practice you use the SQL Server Enterprise Manager to view and modify a job and to view job history.

▶ **To review and modify a job and view job history**

1. Ensure that you are logged on to the SelfPacedSQL.MSFT domain controller as Administrator.

   In the SQL Server Enterprise Manager console tree, the Management container and the SQL Server Agent container for the default instance should still be expanded from the previous practice.

2. In the SQL Server Agent container, click Jobs.

3. In the details pane, double-click Backup Master Job.

   The Backup Master Job Properties – SelfPacedCPU dialog box appears.

4. Click the Steps tab.

5. Click the New button.

   The New Job Step – SelfPacedCPU\Backup Master Job dialog box appears.

6. In the Step Name text box, type **DB Consistency Step**.

7. Verify that the step type is Transact-SQL Script (TSQL) and the Database is master.

8. In the Command text box, type **DBCC CHECKDB**.

9. Click OK to close the New Job Step – SelfPacedCPU\Backup Master Job dialog box.

   Notice that two steps now appear. Notice that Step 1 executes first and that the DB Consistency Step will never execute because Step 1 quits with success and with failure. Notice also the green start flag that indicating Step 1 is the starting step. If you attempt to apply or save the job at this point, you will receive a warning stating that the DB Consistency Step will not execute.

10. Click DB Consistency Step in the Start Step drop-down list.

11. Click the Move Step arrow button to move the DB Consistency Step to the first step in the list.

12. Click OK to close the Backup Master Job Properties – SelfPacedCPU dialog box.

13. In the details pane, right-click Backup Master Job, and then click Start Job.

    The Start Job On SelfPacedCPU dialog box appears. Notice that you can choose the step with which to start the job.

14. Verify that the DB Consistency Step is selected, and then click the Start button.

After a few moments, a Messenger Service message box appears delivering a message to SelfPacedCPU stating that the Backup Master Job succeeded and providing details about the completion of the job.

15. Click OK.

16. In the details pane for the Jobs container, right-click Backup Master Job, and then click View Job History.

    The Job History – SelfPacedCPU dialog box appears. Notice that the two jobs appear in the job history log. Also notice, under Errors And/Or Messages From The Job/Step, that the most recently completed job had two steps and that the first time the job ran it only had one step.

17. Select the Show Step Details check box.

    Notice that five lines now appear. In the Step ID column, 0 displays the job outcome information for each time the job ran. Step ID 1 displays information regarding the details of the first step that ran. Step ID 2 displays information regarding the details of the second step that ran.

18. Click Step ID 1 from the most recent run of the job.

    Notice that information from the DBCC CHECKDB statement is displayed under Errors And/Or Messages From The Job/Step.

19. Click Close.

20. In the details pane for the Jobs container, right-click Backup SSEMDB TLog, and then click View Job History.

    The Job History – SelfpacedCPU dialog box appears. Notice the details of the job. In particular, notice that no operators were notified because Operator was not on duty. The fail-safe Operator was not paged because fail-safe operations are used only for alerts (not job outcome notifications).

21. Click Close.

22. Leave SQL Server Enterprise Manager running.

SQL Server Agent Error Log

SQL Server Agent records information, warnings, and errors in the SQL Server Agent error log. SQL Server 2000 maintains up to nine SQL Server Agent error logs. The default name and location for the SQL Server Agent error log is C:\Program Files\Microsoft SQL Server\Mssql\Log\Sqlagent.out. The current error log has a filename extension of .OUT and each archive has an extension number between one and nine (with one being more recent than nine). SQL Server Agent recycles these logs as necessary. To view the error log from within SQL Server Enterprise Manager, right-click the SQL Server Agent container, and then click Display Error Log. Figure 13.26 illustrates the SQL Server Agent Error Log dialog box.

In the Type drop-down list, you can filter errors based on the error type (error, warning, or information) and/or by specific text contained in the error message. In Figure 13.26, notice the last warning message listed in the Contents box for the Sqlagent.out log, which informs you that an idle CPU condition has not yet been defined.

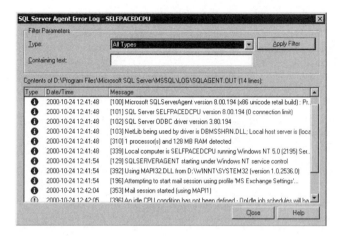

Figure 13.26.   Viewing the error log.

Note   You can use any text editor to view the SQL Server error log.

Transact-SQL

You can also view job properties using the *sp_help_job* and *sp_help_jobstep* system stored procedures. You can view job history using the *sp_help_jobhistory* system stored procedure.

Lesson Summary

Jobs can be created to automate many routine administrative tasks. You can create jobs with multiple job steps using Transact-SQL statements, ActiveX scripts, operating system commands, and replication tasks. Each job step can contain flow logic that specifies actions based on the success or failure of the step. You can configure jobs to notify operators of their success, failure, or completion. You can also create one or more schedules defining when SQL Server Agent will run a job.

Lesson 3: Configuring Alerts

Using SQL Server Agent, you can define alerts and configure responses to alerts. In this lesson, you learn how to create alerts to different types of events, including SQL Server 2000 error messages, user-defined error messages, and performance conditions. You also learn to configure operators to be notified and jobs to be run in response to alerts.

After this lesson, you will be able to

- Define alerts in response to SQL Server events
- Define alerts in response to performance conditions
- Define responses to alerts
- View alerts and alert history

Estimated lesson time: 30 minutes

Defining Alerts

Database administrators define alerts to provide event and performance condition notification and to execute jobs in response to specific SQL Server events or performance conditions. For example, whenever the transaction log becomes 80 percent full, an alert can be configured to fire that executes a job to back up and truncate the transaction log (and to notify an administrator of its success or failure).

SQL Server Agent monitors the Windows application log and compares each SQL Server event logged with the alerts that have been defined. If a match is found, an event alert fires. SQL Server Agent can also monitor specific SQL Server performance object counters and fire a performance condition alert when the value for the counter is less than, equal to, or greater than a defined threshold.

Note   To define alerts, you must be a member of the sysadmin server role.

SQL Server Event Alerts

The sysmessages table in the master database contains system error messages. User-defined event messages can also be added to the sysmessages table using SQL Server Enterprise Manager or the *sp_addmessage* system stored procedure. All user-defined event messages are numbered 50,000 or greater. SQL Server events and messages (errors) have the following attributes:

- **Error number.**   A unique number for each error.
- **Message string.**   Diagnostic information regarding the cause of the error, including the object name.

- **Severity.**   Low numbers indicate information messages and high numbers indicate serious errors.
- **State code.**   Used by Microsoft support engineers to find the source code location for the error.
- **Procedure name.**   The stored procedure name if the error occurred in a stored procedure.
- **Line number.**   The line number of a statement in a stored procedure that caused the error.

SQL Server events and messages (errors) can be written to the application log in a number of ways:

- Any SQL Server error with a severity number of 19 or greater is automatically logged.
- Any SQL Server error can be designated as always logged using the *sp_altermessage* system stored procedure (numerous errors have this designation upon installation).
- An application can force an error to be logged using the *RAISERROR WITH LOG* statement or the *xp_logevent* extended stored procedure.

Note   Make sure to configure the Windows application log to be large enough to hold all SQL Server events without overwriting existing events or running out of space. Also, in order for login events to be logged, Windows auditing must also be enabled.

You define an event alert based on a SQL Server event written to the application log and meeting specified conditions (such as severity level, error number, or containing specified text). SQL Server 2000 includes a number of preconfigured event alerts you can modify and use, or you can create your own.

Performance Conditions

SQL Server 2000 provides objects and counters that are used by Windows 2000 System Monitor (and Windows NT 4.0 Performance Monitor). These same objects and counters can be used by SQL Server Enterprise Manager to define a performance condition alert. To define a performance condition alert, you define the following:

- **Performance object.**   SQL Server object.
- **Counter.**   SQL Server counter.
- **Instance.**   SQL Server instance.
- **Behavior.**   Value of the counter that triggers the alert. Can be equal to, greater than, or less than a specified value.

Note   If performance condition alerts are not viewable within SQL Server Enterprise Manager, verify that the SQL Server service domain user account has full control permissions on the HKEY_LOCAL_MACHINE\SOFTWARE\Microsoft\Windows NT\CurrentVersion\Perflib registry key.

Responses

When an event alert or a performance condition alert fires, one or more operators can be notified using e-mail, pager, or NET SEND. A custom notification message can be added to the alert notification along with the text of the error. A specified job can also be executed in response to the alert.

Configuring Alerts

You can create alerts using the Create Alert Wizard or directly by using SQL Server Enterprise Manager. You can also create alerts with Transact-SQL system stored procedures.

Using the Create Alert Wizard

The SQL Server Enterprise Manager wizards are available from the Tools menu, and are also available from any taskpad view. The Create Alert Wizard is a simple way to create an event alert. Figure 13.27 shows the Welcome To The Create Alert Wizard page.

Figure 13.27.   The Create Alert Wizard welcome screen.

In the Define The Alert page, you can click the For Any Error Of Severity option button to specify that an alert fire if the severity level of the SQL Server event equals or exceeds the severity level you specify in the For Any Error Of Severity drop-down list. See Figure 13.28.

Note   Errors with a severity error below 19 are not automatically logged in the application log.

You can also click the Only If This Error Occurs option button to specify that an alert fire if a specific error occurs. You can browse available error numbers and messages to select the error number by clicking the Only If This Error Occurs ellipsis button. Clicking this button displays the Manage SQL Server Messages dialog box, as illustrated in Figure 13.29.

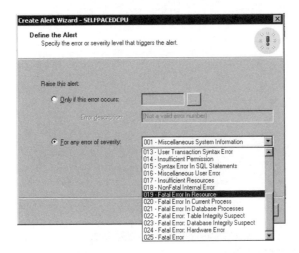

Figure 13.28.   Defining the severity level at which the alert will fire.

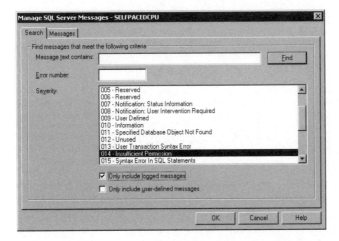

Figure 13.29.   Choosing specific error types for an alert.

Notice that you can search for error messages based on text, error number, and severity level. Notice that you can also limit your search to include only logged messages and/or user-defined messages. After you have defined your search parameters, you click the Find button to begin the search. Figure 13.30 illustrates the results of a search.

Next, in the Specify A Database Or Error Keywords page, you can specify that the event must occur in a particular database or contain specified text. See Figure 13.31.

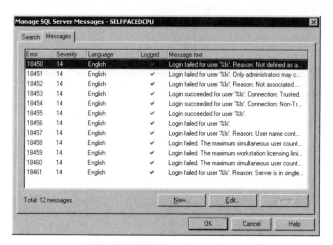

Figure 13.30.   Searching for error messages.

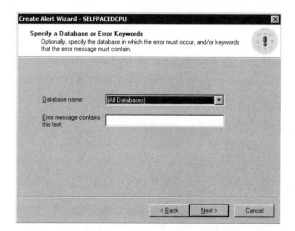

Figure 13.31.   Specifying a particular database or specified text for your search.

Next, in the Define Alert Response page, you specify the response to the alert. You can select from among existing operators and specify the type of notification. You can also select a job to execute, including the option to create a new job on the fly. See Figure 13.32.

Next, in the Define Alert Notification Message page, you can specify the text of the message that will be sent to the operator as part of the alert notification message. You can also choose whether to include the text of the error message in the message to the operator. See Figure 13.33.

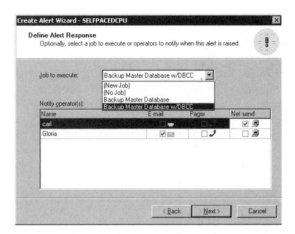

Figure 13.32.   Specifying the response to the alert.

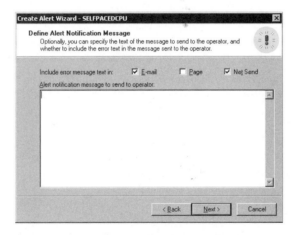

Figure 13.33.   Defining the alert notification message.

Finally, in the Completing The Create Alert Wizard page, you are given the opportunity to specify a name for the alert and to review the selections you have made before you actually create the alert. You can click the Back button to change any parameter you want to change. Click the Finish button to create the alert. See Figure 13.34.

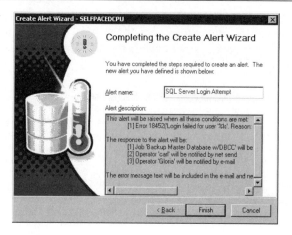

Figure 13.34.   Completing the alert creation process.

Practice: Creating an Event Alert Using the Create Alert Wizard

In this practice you use the Create Alert Wizard to create an event alert.

▶ **To create an event alert using the Create Alert Wizard**

1. Ensure that you are logged on to the SelfPacedSQL.MSFT domain controller as Administrator.

2. In the SQL Server Enterprise Manager console tree, verify that your focus is a container within the default instance.

3. On the Tools menu, click Wizards.

    The Select Wizard dialog box appears.

4. Expand Management, and then double-click Create Alert Wizard.

    The Welcome To The Create Alert Wizard page appears.

5. Click Next.

    The Define The Alert page appears.

6. Click the Only If This Error Occurs option button, and then type **208** in the Only If This Error Occurs text box.

    Notice that the error description for this error indicates an invalid object name.

7. Click Next.

    The Specify A Database Or Error Keywords page appears.

8. In the Database Name drop-down list, click SSEMDB, and then click Next.

    The Define Alert Response page appears.

9. In the Notify Operator grid, select the Net Send check box for Operator, and then click Next.

The Define Alert Notification Message page appears.

10. In the Alert Notification Message To Send To Operator text box, type **The object requested does not exist**, and then click Next.

    The Completing The Create Alert Wizard window appears.

11. In the Alert Name text box, type **SQL Server Invalid Object Alert**, and then click the Finish button.

    A Create Alert Wizard dialog box appears stating that occurrences of error 208 will not invoke this alert because error 208 is not logged by default. The wizard then asks whether you want to have the error always invoke this alert.

12. Click the Yes button to always invoke the alert.

    A Create Alert Wizard message box appears stating that the alert was created successfully.

13. Click OK.

14. In the SQL Server Agent container in the console tree, click Alerts.

    Notice that SQL Server Invalid Object Alert appears in the details pane along with the preconfigured alerts.

15. On the Tools menu, click SQL Query Analyzer.

    SQL Query Analyzer appears with master as the current database.

16. In the query pane, type **SELECT * FROM SSEMDB**, and then click the Execute Query button on the toolbar.

    Notice the invalid object name error message in the results pane.

17. Switch to SQL Server Enterprise Manager.

18. Right-click SQL Server Invalid Object Alert in the details pane, and then click Refresh Alert.

    Review the Count column. Notice that no alert fired.

19. Switch to SQL Query Analyzer.

20. On the toolbar, change the current database to SSEMDB in the database drop-down list, and then click the Execute Query button.

    After a few moments a Messenger Service message box appears displaying information related to this error.

21. Click OK to close the Message Service message box.

22. Switch to SQL Server Enterprise Manager.

23. Right-click SQL Server Invalid Object Alert in the details pane, and then click Refresh Alert.

    Notice that the Count column indicates this alert occurred once and the Last Occurred column displays the date and time that the alert fired.

24. Leave SQL Server Enterprise Manager and SQL Query Analyzer running.

Using SQL Server Enterprise Manager Directly

To create an alert using SQL Server Enterprise Manager directly, you can either right-click SQL Server Agent in the Management container, point to New and then click Alert, or you can right-click Alerts in the SQL Server Agent container and then click New Alert. The New Alert Properties dialog box appears as illustrated in Figure 13.35.

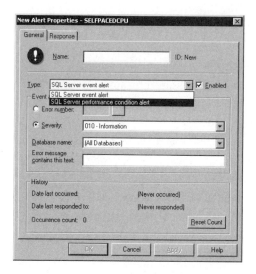

Figure 13.35.   Creating an alert using SQL Server Enterprise Manager directly.

In the General tab, notice that you can select either an event alert or a performance condition alert in the Type drop-down list. The information required to create an event alert is the same as covered earlier in this chapter for the Create Alert Wizard. If you select a performance condition alert, you can define the performance condition that will cause an alert to fire. For example, you can define an alert that will fire whenever the percentage of the transaction log used for the SSEMDB database rises above 80 percent. See Figure 13.36.

Next, click the Response tab to define a response to the alert. When you click the Execute Job check box, you can select from an existing job, or create one on the fly. Click the ellipsis button to view or modify the details of any job for which you have sufficient permissions. You can select operators to notify, create new operators, choose to include the error text in the notification, and provide a message to include in the notification. You can also configure a delay between responses. Use this delay to prevent the firing of multiple alerts from overwhelming your system. For example, if an alert fires and causes a job to execute to resolve the cause of the alert, delay the firing of a second alert until the job has an opportunity to complete its task. See Figure 13.37.

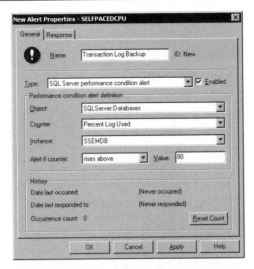

Figure 13.36.   Defining a performance condition alert.

Figure 13.37.   Defining a response to the alert.

User-Defined Error Messages

To add user-defined error messages using SQL Server Enterprise Manager, click
Manage SQL Server Messages on the Tools menu, click the Messages tab, and then
click the New button to display the New SQL Server Message dialog box. In this
dialog box, you select the error number you want to use, define its severity level,
provide the text for the message, specify the language, and specify whether it will
be automatically written to the application log whenever raised. The message string
can contain substitution variables and arguments. See Figure 13.38.

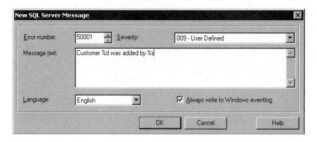

Figure 13.38. Adding user-defined error messages.

You can have a user-defined error message raised when a particular transaction occurs, which can then trigger a defined alert response. For example, a stored procedure can be created that is used to add new customers. Within the stored procedure, a *RAISERROR* statement can raise a user-defined error and pass variables to the error message providing the name of the new customer and the user adding the customer. The defined alert can then notify a database administrator that a new customer was added.

Practice: Creating a Performance Condition Alert Using SQL Server Enterprise Manager Directly

In this practice you create a performance condition alert using use SQL Server Enterprise Manager directly.

▶ **To create a performance condition alert using SQL Server Enterprise Manager directly**

1. Ensure that you are logged on to the SelfPacedSQL.MSFT domain controller as Administrator.
2. In the SQL Server Enterprise Manager console tree, expand the SQL Server Agent container.
3. Right-click Alerts, and then click New Alert.

   The New Alert Properties – SelfPacedCPU dialog box appears, with the General tab selected.
4. In the Name text box, type **SSEMDB TLog Alert**.
5. Click SQL Server Performance Condition Alert in the Type drop-down list.
6. Click SQLServer:Databases in the Object drop-down list.
7. Click Percent Log Used in the Counter drop-down list.
8. Click SSEMDB in the Instance drop-down list.
9. Click Rises Above in the Alert If Counter drop-down list.
10. Type **80** in the Value text box.
11. Click the Response tab.

12. Select the Execute Job check box.

13. Click Backup SSEMDB TLog in the drop-down list.

14. In the Operators To Notify grid, select the Pager check box for Operator.

15. In the Additional Notification Message To Send text box, type **Transaction Log 80% Full**.

16. Verify that the Delay Between Responses spin box is set to one minute, and then click OK.

    In the details pane, notice that the SSEMDB TLog Alert appears.

17. Click Start, point to Programs, point to Administrative Tools, and then click Performance.

    The Performance console appears.

18. On the toolbar, click the Add button.

    The Add Counters dialog box appears.

19. In the Performance Object drop-down list, click SQLServer:Databases.

20. In the Select Counters From List box, click Percent Log Used.

21. In the Select Instances From List box, click SSEMDB.

22. Click the Add button, and then click the Close button.

    A chart displays the Percent Log Used counter for the SSEMDB database.

23. Switch to SQL Query Analyzer.

24. On the toolbar, click the Load SQL Script button.

25. Click the No button if asked to save changes.

    The Open Query File dialog box appears.

26. Open TlogOverflow.sql in the C:\SelfPacedSQL\CH_13 folder.

    A Transact-SQL script appears, which will shrink the transaction log file and then will continually update the ContactName column in the Customer table in the SSEMDB database. Notice that a wait of 10 milliseconds has been specified. This will prevent the transaction log from filling so quickly that the backup job does not have time to finish the backup before the transaction log file automatically grows. Increase this wait time on fast computers and reduce it for slow computers.

27. Click the Execute Query button to execute the TLogOverflow.sql statement.

28. Switch to the Performance console.

    Notice that the transaction log begins to fill up. Several moments after the Percent Log Used counter exceeds 80 percent, a Messenger Service message box appears. Notice the details of the error message. In particular, notice that the network pop-up is delivered to FailSafe. This occurs because Operator, who is designated to receive pager notification when this alert fires, is off duty.

29. Click OK.

After a few more moments, notice that the chart displaying the Percent Log Used counter in the Performance console indicates that the job has executed (the transaction log was truncated).

30. Close the Performance console.
31. Switch to SQL Query Analyzer, and then click the Cancel Query Execution button on the toolbar.
32. Close SQL Query Analyzer.
33. Leave SQL Server Enterprise Manager running.

Using Transact-SQL

You can also define alerts using the *sp_add_alert*, *sp_update_alert*, and *sp_add_notification* system stored procedures. You must be a member of the sysadmin server role to execute these system stored procedures. You can create and manage user-defined error messages using the *sp_addmessage* and *sp_altermessage* system stored procedures. You must be a member of the sysadmin or serveradmin server roles to execute these system stored procedures.

Note   Although you can use Transact-SQL system stored procedures to add alerts, use of the SQL Server Enterprise Manager graphical interface is recommended.

Reviewing Alerts and Alert History

The details pane of the Alerts container in SQL Server Enterprise Manager displays information regarding all alerts for the SQL Server 2000 instance. See Figure 13.39. You must be a member of the sysadmin server role to view alerts.

Information regarding each alert is displayed in columns. Click on a column heading to sort the alerts based on the column. Notice the Enabled column. If you are troubleshooting an alert that does not fire when it should, verify that it is enabled. If an alert is firing too frequently, you might need to disable it before you modify its properties. Information is displayed regarding the last time the alert fired, the notifications that were sent, and how many times the alert has fired since it was last reset.

Note   Because SQL Server Enterprise Manager is a client application, information displayed must be refreshed to view the most recent information (such as last occurred and count information).

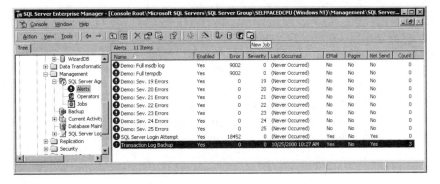

Figure 13.39.   Viewing alert information.

Alert Properties

Right-click an alert, and then click Properties (or double-click the alert) to display the alert's Properties dialog box, where you can view the details on the alert. Click the Reset Count button to reset the counter displaying the number of times the alert has fired.

Transact-SQL

You can also view alert properties using the *sp_help_alert* system stored procedure. You must be a member of the sysadmin server role to execute this system stored procedure.

Lesson Summary

Event alerts can be defined to respond to SQL Server errors that are logged in the Windows application log. Severe errors are always logged in the Event Viewer application log and you can configure any error to be logged. Performance condition alerts can be defined to respond to performance object counter values above, below, or equal to specified values. Responses to alerts can be the execution of a specified job and/or notification of one or more operators.

Lesson 4: Creating a Database Maintenance Plan

SQL Server 2000 provides two separate ways to automate all of the core maintenance tasks a database administrator needs to perform. In this lesson you learn to use the Database Maintenance Plan Wizard to configure the performance of core maintenance tasks at scheduled intervals. You will also be introduced to the Sqlmaint utility, which performs the same functions from a command prompt.

After this lesson, you will be able to

- Create a database maintenance plan using the Database Maintenance Plan Wizard
- Describe the use of the Sqlmaint utility

Estimated lesson time: 15 minutes

Using the Database Maintenance Plan Wizard

The Database Maintenance Plan Wizard allows you to configure the following tasks to execute automatically according to specified schedules.

- Rebuilding indexes using a specified fill factor
- Shrinking a database to a specified size
- Updating distribution statistics
- Performing DBCC consistency checks (covered in Chapter 14)
- Backing up database and transaction log files
- Setting up log shipping (covered in Chapter 16)

To start the Database Maintenance Plan Wizard, from the Tools menu, click Database Maintenance Planner, or in the console tree, right-click Database Maintenance Plans, in the Management container, and then click New Maintenance Plan to display the Welcome To The Database Maintenance Plan Wizard page. See Figure 13.40.

Figure 13.40.   Starting the Database Maintenance Plan Wizard.

Click Next. If this is a master server, the Select Servers page is displayed, where you select one or more target Servers on which this maintenance plan will be carried out. Multiserver jobs are covered in Lesson 5 of this chapter. See Figure 13.41.

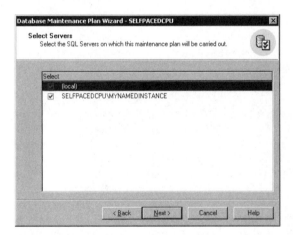

Figure 13.41.   Selecting an instance.

Next, in the Select Databases page, you can select one or more database(s) for which to create a maintenance plan. You can create a single maintenance plan for all databases, or separate plans for specific databases and user and system databases. See Figure 13.42.

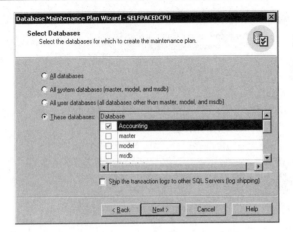

Figure 13.42.   Selecting a database.

After selecting one or more databases, you can include several types of data optimization in this database maintenance plan, which you select in the Update Data Optimization Information page. See Figure 13.43.

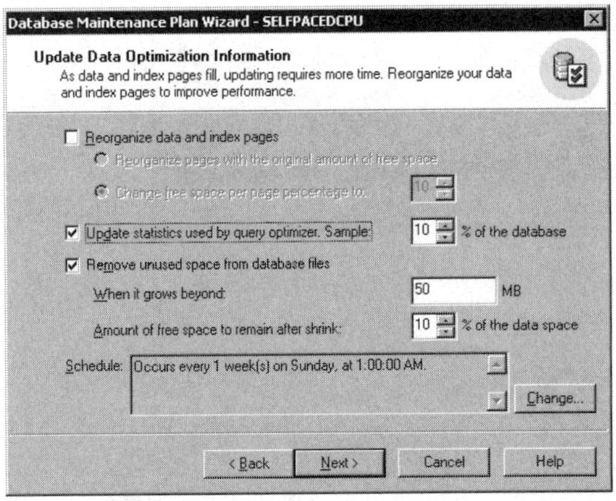

Figure 13.43.   Choosing types of data optimization.

You can choose to have indexes rebuilt or distribution statistics updated. Indexes can be rebuilt using the original fill factor, or you can supply a new fill factor. Statistics can be updated using a sample of 10 percent of the database, or you can supply your own sampling value. SQL Server 2000 generally determines an adequate sample size automatically. The higher the sampling percentage, the more accurate the statistics; however, the higher sampling rates will take more time and use more resources. You can also choose to shrink the database whenever it grows above a certain size and specify the amount of free space that will be left in the data file after the shrink operation. This option is generally used only for small databases sharing hard disk space with other server applications. Finally, you can specify a single schedule for these tasks. Notice that the default is every Sunday at 1:00 A.M.

Next, in the Database Integrity Check page, you can include database integrity checks as part of this database maintenance plan. You can choose to have these checks perform minor repairs and have them performed before backups (recommended). The default schedule for these tasks is every Sunday at 12:00 A.M. See Figure 13.44.

Next, in the Specify The Database Backup Plan page, you can include full database backups as part of this database maintenance plan. Defaults include verifying the integrity of the backup, storing the backup to disk, and performing the backup every Sunday at 2:00 A.M. Notice that this backup takes place after any database optimization and integrity checks have been completed. See Figure 13.45.

Next, in the Specify Backup Disk Directory page, you specify database backup information. For example, if backup to disk is selected, you can use the default location or specify a custom location. You can create subdirectories for each database and choose to remove any backup files older than a specified amount of time. Finally, you can choose the backup file extension. The default is BAK. See Figure 13.46.

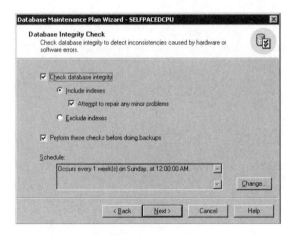

Figure 13.44.   Including database integrity checks.

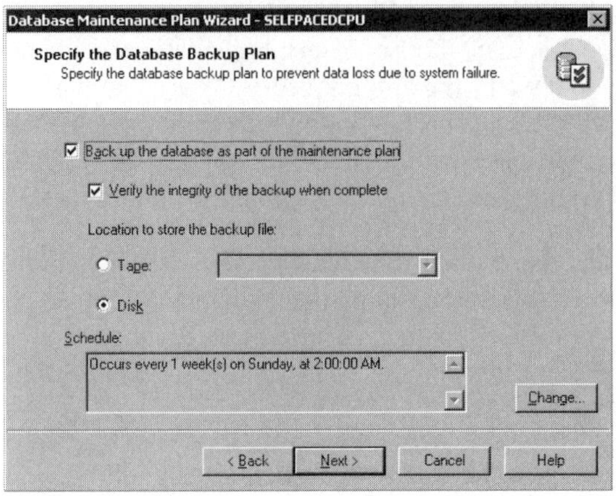

Figure 13.45. Specifying a database backup plan.

Next, in the Specify The Transaction Log Backup Plan page, you can also back up the transaction log file as part of this database maintenance plan. If you include transaction log backups, the defaults include verifying the integrity of the backup, storing the backup to disk, and performing the backups every night (except Sunday) at 12:00 A.M. See Figure 13.47.

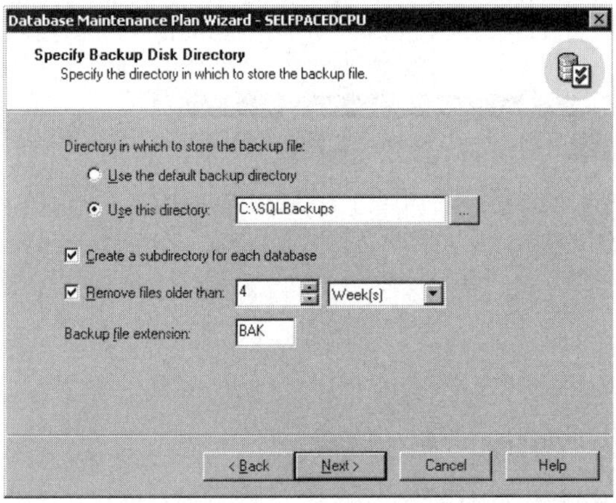

Figure 13.46. Specifying database backup information.

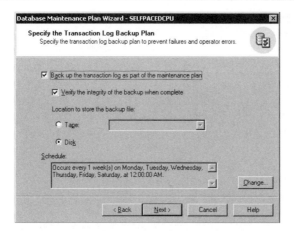

Figure 13.47.   Selecting options for backing up the transaction log file.

Next, in the Specify Transaction Log Backup Disk Directory page, you specify transaction log backup information. For example, if backup to disk is selected, you can use the default location or specify a custom location. You can create subdirectories for each database and choose to remove backup files older than a specified amount of time. Finally, you can choose the backup file extension. The default is TRN. See Figure 13.48.

Next, in the Reports To Generate page, you can specify a file path for a report text file containing details of steps executed by this database maintenance plan, including error information. Each report will add a date to the filename in the form of *MaintenancePlanName_YYYYMMDDHHMM*. You can store the report text file in the default location or specify a custom location. You can choose to remove any report text files older than a specified amount of time and to e-mail each report to a specified operator. See Figure 13.49.

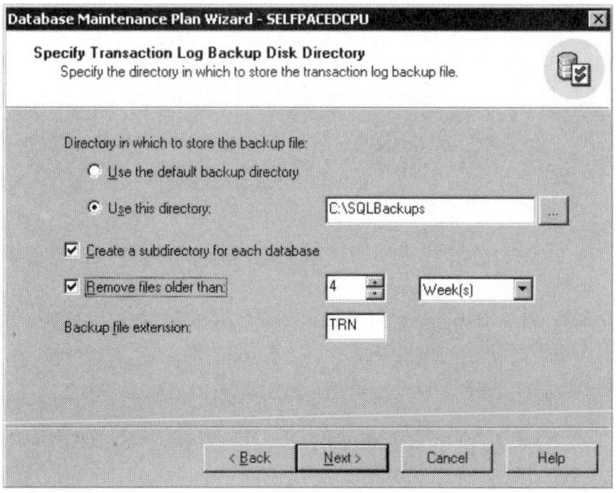

Figure 13.48.   Specifying transaction log backup information.

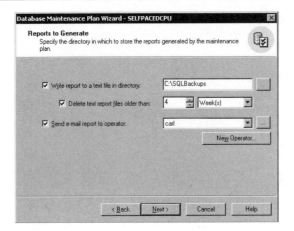

Figure 13.49. Specifying options for reports.

Next, in the Maintenance Plan History page, by default, the history of activity of this database maintenance plan is written to the sysdbmaintplan_history table in the msdb database. After 1000 rows have been filled, by default, older rows are deleted as new rows are added. You can also choose to have all history added to a remote server that functions as a central store for collecting report information. See Figure 13.50.

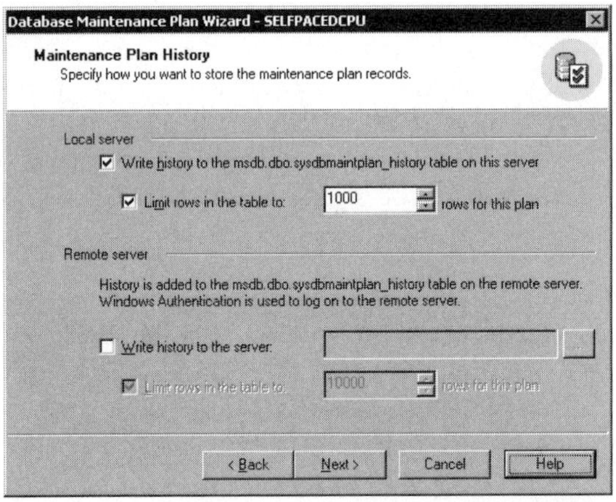

Figure 13.50. Choosing options for maintaining history of the maintenance plan.

Finally, in the Completing The Database Maintenance Plan Wizard, you can provide a name for this plan and review the selections you have made. Click the Back button to review and modify any choices. Click the Finish button to create the plan. See Figure 13.51.

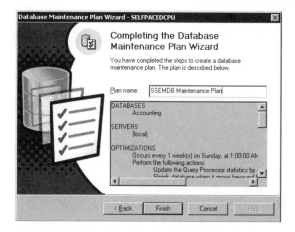

Figure 13.51. Completing the Database Maintenance Plan.

Viewing and Modifying Database Maintenance Plans

After the database maintenance plan has been created, you can view and modify it in one of two ways. First, you can expand the Management container in the instance, expand the SQL Server Agent container, and then click the Jobs container. In the details pane, one or more database maintenance jobs will appear. See Figure 13.52.

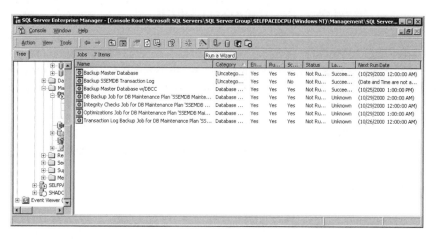

Figure 13.52. Viewing and modifying a plan.

In Figure 13.52, notice four new database maintenance jobs that are part of the SSEMDB Maintenance Plan, including the next run date. You can double-click any job to review the details of the job.

You can also view database maintenance plans by clicking the Database Maintenance Plans container in the console tree. The details pane displays all database maintenance plans. Double-click a plan to view or modify the details of the plan. Right-click the Database Maintenance Plan container or any specific maintenance plan, and then click Maintenance Plan History to view the history of the execution of the entire maintenance plan. See Figure 13.53.

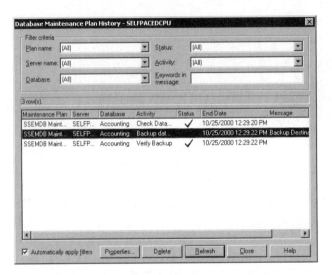

Figure 13.53.   Viewing database maintenance plan history.

Using the Sqlmaint Utility

The Sqlmaint command-prompt utility can also be used to create and execute a database maintenance plan. Generally, you will use the Database Maintenance Plan Wizard to create and modify database maintenance plans because of its ease of use. However, the jobs that are created by the Database Maintenance Plan Wizard actually execute the Sqlmaint utility using specified parameters. In SQL Server Enterprise Manager, expand SQL Server Agent, double-click a maintenance plan job in the Jobs container, click the Steps tab, and then click the Edit button to view the actual Sqlmaint command that is being executed. See Figure 13.54.

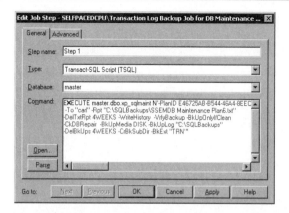

Figure 13.54.   Viewing a specific Sqlmaint command.

To use the Sqlmaint utility, refer to SQL Server Books Online.

Lesson Summary

The Database Maintenance Plan Wizard provides an easy way to automate core maintenance tasks by creating jobs and schedules for these tasks. SQL Server Enterprise Manager also maintains a Database Maintenance Plan History log to view the execution history of all plans in one location. Finally, the Sqlmaint utility is the utility that is run in the background for actually performing these tasks.

Lesson 5: Creating Multiserver Jobs

SQL Server 2000 allows you to automate administrative tasks across multiple SQL Server 2000 instances. In this lesson, you learn to create master servers and target servers. You also learn to create jobs on the master server that propagate to target servers for execution. Finally, you learn to review remote job history from the master server.

After this lesson, you will be able to

- Create master and target servers
- Create jobs for target servers
- Monitor jobs on target servers

Estimated lesson time: 30 minutes

Creating Master and Target Servers

To create multiserver jobs, you must designate a server as a master server and one or more servers as target servers. This allows you to create jobs on a master server, which distributes the jobs to and receives events from target servers. The master server must be a computer running Windows 2000 or Windows NT 4.0. The master server and all target servers must be running in Mixed Authentication Mode. In addition, SQL Server Agent must be running on the master and all target servers. Finally, select a master server that is not a busy production server because target service traffic can cause a performance hit.

To create a master server, right-click the SQL Server Agent container for the instance that will function as the master server, point to Multi Server Administration, and then click Make This A Master. The Welcome To The Make MSX Wizard page appears as shown in Figure 13.55.

Figure 13.55.   The Welcome to the Make MSX Wizard screen.

First, in the Create 'MSXOperator' page, you create an MSXOperator to whom all notifications related to multiserver jobs will be sent. If no MSXOperator is created, multiserver jobs cannot send completion notifications. See Figure 13.56.

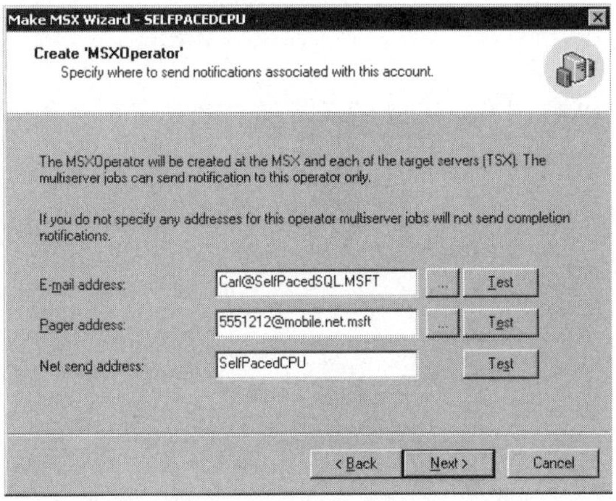

Figure 13.56.   Creating an MSXOperator.

Next, in the Select Servers To Enlist page, select SQL Server instances to enlist as target servers from the list of currently registered servers. You must be a member of the sysadmin server role on each instance you are registering. You cannot enlist an instance that is not registered. The SQL Server and SQL Server Agent services on all target servers (as well as on the master server) must be using domain user accounts for the service account (using the same account for the master and all target servers will ease administration). You can also register servers on the fly. See Figure 13.57.

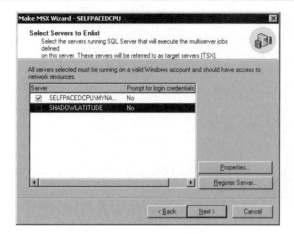

Figure 13.57.   Selecting SQL Server instances to enlist as target servers.

Next, in the Provide Target Server Description page, you can provide a description for each target server. See Figure 13.58.

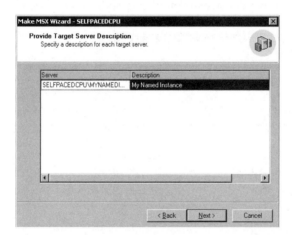

Figure 13.58.   Providing a description for the target servers.

Next, in the Completing The Make MSX Wizard page, click the Finish button to create the MSXOperator and enlist each target server. If the wizard cannot connect to an instance (or if the SQL Server Agent service is not running on the instance), you cannot enlist the instance as a target server. See Figure 13.59.

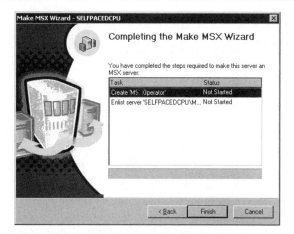

Figure 13.59.   Completing the creation of the MSXOperator.

After the Make MSX Wizard completes, the SQL Server Agent on the master server is designated with an MSX and the SQL Server Agent on each target server is designated with a TSX: *master_server_name*. See Figure 13.60.

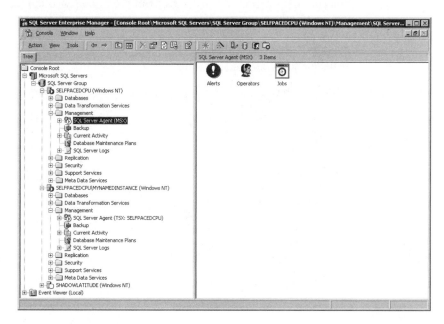

Figure 13.60.   Master and target server designations.

Creating Jobs for Target Servers

You can create jobs on the master server and designate one or more target servers to which these jobs will be distributed. The job definitions are stored on the master server and a copy is retrieved by each target server. Updates to the central copy are periodically distributed to the target servers. These jobs cannot be modified on any target server.

To create a job for target servers, you define the job in the same manner as you did for a local server job in Lesson 2 of this chapter. However, in the General tab, you click the Target Multiple Servers option button and then select one or more target servers by clicking the Change button. The Change Job Target Servers dialog box appears as shown in Figure 13.61.

Note   All database and file system paths used in multiserver jobs must be valid on each target server for the job to succeed on that target server. Establishing a consistent path and naming convention will make multiserver job administration much simpler.

You can then select target servers from the list of enrolled target servers. See Figure 13.62.

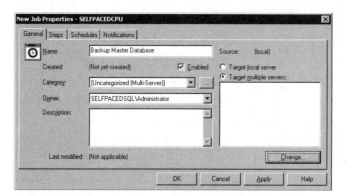

Figure 13.61.   Selecting target servers.

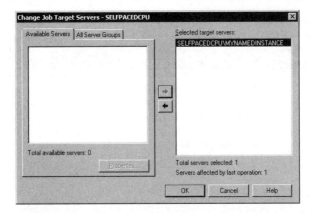

Figure 13.62.   Selecting target servers from the list.

On the master server, all multiserver jobs have their own container. The target servers periodically poll the master server to download new jobs and changes to existing jobs.

Monitoring Jobs on Target Servers

To monitor jobs on target servers, right-click the SQL Server Agent (MSX) container on the master server, point to Multi Server Administration, and then click Manage Target Servers. The Target Servers dialog box appears as shown in Figure 13.63.

In the Target Service Status tab, notice that each target server is listed along with its local time, the last time the target server polled the master server, the number of unread instructions, and the status of each target server (blocked, OK, or offline). You can force a poll by clicking the Force Poll button, defect a target server by clicking the Force Defection button, or post instructions for one or more target servers by clicking the Post Instructions button. Instructions you can post include defecting, setting a polling interval (default is 60 seconds), synchronizing clocks between the master and target servers, and starting a job. The Post Download Instructions dialog box is shown in Figure 13.64.

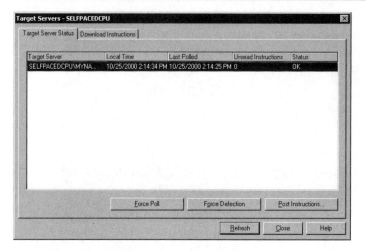

Figure 13.63. Managing target servers.

Figure 13.64. Choosing options for posting instructions.

Click the Download Instructions tab to view details regarding instructions that have been downloaded to one or more target servers. You can also filter displayed instructions based on a particular job by selecting the job name in the Job drop-down list. See Figure 13.65.

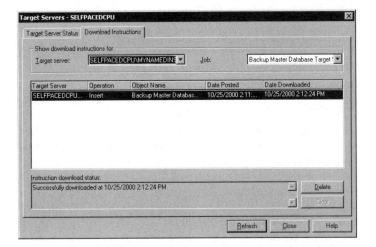

Figure 13.65.   Viewing and filtering instruction details

To view the job status and job history of multiserver jobs, in the details pane for the Multi Server Jobs container, right-click the multiserver job, and then click Job Status. The Multi Server Job Execution Status dialog box appears, as shown in Figure 13.66.

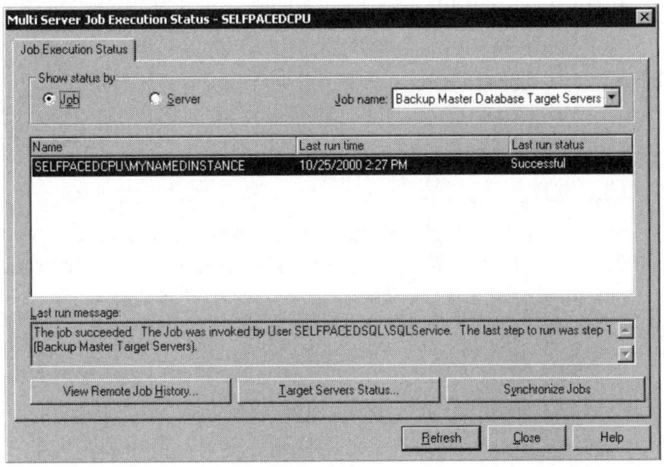

Figure 13.66.   Viewing job status and history.

Notice that you can view status by job or by server to view the last time a job was run and whether it was successful. Click the View Remote Job History button to connect to the remote server and view the history of the job. Click the Target Servers Status button to view the status of a particular server. Click the Synchronize Jobs button to resynchronize all jobs on a particular server or a particular job on all servers.

Practice: Creating a Multiserver Job

In this practice you create a multiserver job.

▶ **To create a multiserver job**

1. Ensure that you are logged on to the SelfPacedSQL.MSFT domain controller as Administrator.

2. In the SQL Server Enterprise Manager console tree, expand the SelfPaced-CPU\MyNamedInstance container, expand the Management container, right-click SQL Server Agent, and then click Start.

3. In the console tree, right-click SQL Server Agent for the default instance, point to Multi Server Administrator, and then click Make This A Master.

   The Welcome To The Make MSX Wizard page appears.

4. Click Next.

   The Create 'MSXOperator' page appears.

5. In the Net Send Address text box, type **SelfPacedCPU**, and then click Next.

   The Select Servers To Enlist page appears.

6. Select the SelfPacedCPU\MyNamedInstance check box, and then click Next.

   The Provide Target Server Description page appears.

7. Enter a description into the Description cell, and then click Next.

   The Completing The Make MSX Wizard page appears.

8. Review the information, and then click the Finish button.

   A Make MSX Wizard message box appears stating that SelfPacedCPU was successfully made an MSX.

9. Click OK.

   In the console tree, notice that the SQL Server Agent for the default instance is designated as an MSX and the SQL Server Agent for the MyNamedInstance is designated as a TSX.

10. In the console tree, expand the SQL Server Agent container for the default instance.

11. Right-click Jobs, and then click New Job.

    The New Job Properties – SelfPacedCPU dialog box appears.

12. In the Name text box, type **Backup All Master Databases**.

13. Click the Target Multiple Servers option button, and then click the Change button.

    The Change Job Target Servers – SelfPacedCPU dialog box appears.

14. Click the right-arrow button to select SelfPacedCPU\MyNamedInstance as a target server for this new job, and then click OK.

15. Click the Steps tab, and then click the New button.

The New Job Step – SelfPacedCPU dialog box appears.

16. In the Step Name text box, type **Backup Master Step**.

17. Verify that the Type drop-down list displays Transact-SQL Script (TSQL) and the Database drop-down list displays master.

18. In the Command text box, type **BACKUP DATABASE master TO DISK='C:\SQLBackups\master.bak'**, and then click OK.

19. Click the Schedules tab, and then click the New Schedule button.

    The New Job Schedule – SelfPacedCPU dialog box appears.

20. In the Name text box, type **Nightly Schedule**.

21. Click the Change button.

    The Edit Recurring Job Schedule – SelfPacedCPU dialog box appears.

22. In the Occurs group box, click the Daily option button, and then click OK to close the Edit Recurring Job Schedule – SelfPacedCPU dialog box.

23. Click OK to close the New Job Schedule – SelfPacedCPU dialog box.

24. Click the Notifications tab.

25. Select the Net Send Operator check box, and then click Whenever The Job Completes in the drop-down list.

26. Click OK to close the New Job Properties – SelfPacedCPU dialog box.

27. In the console tree, expand the Jobs container for the default instance, and then click Multi Server Jobs.

    In the details pane, notice the new multiserver job. After a few moments, the Pending Instructions column will indicate zero. This means that the target server has downloaded the job.

28. In the console tree, expand the SelfPacedCPU\MyNamedInstance container, expand the Management container, expand the SQL Server Agent (TSX: Self-PacedCPU) container, and then click Jobs.

29. If the Backup All Master Databases job is not displayed, right-click the Jobs container, and then click the Refresh button.

30. In the details pane, right-click the Backup All Master Databases job, and then click Properties.

    Notice that you cannot edit a job on a target server.

31. Click the Close button.

32. In the console tree, click the Multi Server Jobs container for the default instance.

33. In the details pane, right-click Backup All Master Databases, point to Start Job, and then click Start On All Targeted Servers.

    Notice that the Pending Instructions column indicates one pending instruction. After several moments, the instruction will be downloaded and a Messenger Service message box appears indicating that the Backup All Master Databases job was run.

34. Click OK.

35. Right-click Backup All Master Databases, and then click Job Status.

    The Multi Server Job Execution Status – SelfPacedCPU dialog box appears displaying information regarding the Backup All Master Databases job and each target server.

36. Click the View Remote Job History button.

    The Job History – SelfPacedCPU\MyNamedInstance dialog box appears. Notice the information displayed from the remote server regarding the job.

37. Click the Close button to close the Job History – SelfPacedCPU\MyNamed-Instance dialog box.

38. Click the Close button to close the Multi Server Job Execution Status – Self-PacedCPU dialog box.

39. Right-click the Backup All Master Databases job, and then click Refresh Job.

    Notice that there are no pending instructions.

40. In the console tree, click the Jobs container for the SelfPacedCPU\MyNamed-Instance container.

41. In the details pane, right-click the Backup All Master Databases job, and then click View Job History.

    The Job History – SelfPacedCPU\MyNamedInstance dialog box appears. Notice that the information displayed is identical to that displayed from the remote server regarding the job.

42. Click the Close button.

43. Close SQL Server Enterprise Manager.

Lesson Summary

You can create jobs that are stored and managed from a central server, called a master server. Target servers can be enlisted, which periodically download these multiserver jobs for execution. The target servers report the status of these jobs to the master server. Using this capability, identical jobs that must be run on multiple servers can be centrally created and managed.

Review

Here are some questions to help you determine whether you have learned enough to move on to the next chapter. If you have difficulty answering these questions, review the material in this chapter before beginning the next chapter. The answers for these questions are located in the Appendix, "Questions and Answers."

1. The database administrator who has been designated as the fail-safe operator is leaving the company. What must you do before you delete this person as an operator?

2. If a job fails to execute when scheduled, what are some troubleshooting steps you can follow?

3. You have defined an alert that backs up the transaction log when it is 90 percent full. However, occasionally the transaction log fills up before the job executes. Why is this occurring and what can be done to solve this problem?

4. You are in charge of managing a small database for your company. This is a part-time responsibility. You are also managing your company's domain controllers, Web site, and e-mail server. You want to automate as many tasks as possible. Where should you start?

5. You want to create a single job that backs up the system databases nightly on every SQL Server instance within your company. You want to ensure that this happens automatically, with notice to you only if there is a problem. Can this be done?

C H A P T E R   1 4

Monitoring SQL Server Performance and Activity

About This Chapter

This chapter prepares you to monitor SQL Server 2000 performance and activity. You will learn about developing a performance monitoring methodology for SQL Server. You will learn about each of the Microsoft tools that are available for monitoring SQL Server 2000, including when the use of each tool is most appropriate. Finally, you will learn how to perform specific monitoring tasks using the most commonly used monitoring tools.

Before You Begin

To complete this chapter, you must have

- A computer that meets or exceeds the minimum hardware requirements listed in Table 2.1, "Hardware Requirements," in Lesson 1 of Chapter 2.
- Microsoft Windows 2000 Server running on your computer on an NTFS partition.
- A computer with a NetBIOS name of SelfPacedCPU, configured as a domain controller in the SelfPacedSQL.MSFT domain.
- Installed a default instance and at least one named instance of SQL Server 2000 (see Chapter 2).
- Created the SSEMDB database using the CreateDB.sql script (see Chapter 6).
- Created the Customer table in the SSEMDB database using the SSEMDB_Full.sql script (see Chapter 9).

Lesson 1: Developing a Performance Monitoring Methodology

Before you begin monitoring SQL Server 2000 performance, you must develop a performance monitoring methodology. In this lesson, you will learn to establish performance-monitoring goals. You will learn what activities and resources are important to monitor. Finally, you will learn how to monitor effectively.

After this lesson, you will be able to

- Establish appropriate and effective monitoring goals
- Determine which activities and resources to monitor
- Develop a long-term monitoring strategy

Estimated lesson time: 15 minutes

Establishing Monitoring Goals

Before you begin monitoring SQL Server 2000 performance, you should determine your monitoring goals. You must decide what performance characteristics to monitor and how to monitor them effectively. The first step in performance monitoring is to understand the fundamental performance goals of any SQL Server installation.

- **User perspective.** To minimize the response time for each query submitted by each user. Response time is defined as the length of time required for the first row of a result set to be returned to the user. This provides visual confirmation that the submitted query is being processed.

- **Server perspective.** To maximize the total server throughput of queries submitted by users. Total server throughput is defined as the total number of queries handled by the server during a given period of time.

Many steps are involved in achieving these performance goals. These steps include providing adequate hardware resources, properly designing the database to avoid excessive blocking, and writing applications that submit efficient queries. As a database administrator, you generally do not have control over all performance factors. However, you do have the monitoring tools to determine and isolate the source of performance problems. Once you understand the source of performance problems, you can determine the best course of action to take to improve query response time and server throughput. For example, if the cause of poor performance is a poorly designed database that is slowed by excessive blocking, throwing more hardware resources at the problem will provide minimal performance benefit. Similarly, if you determine that the problem is either a congested network or an inefficient client application (such as one that generates excessive data roundtrips between the client and server), improving the hardware resources on the server will not resolve the problem.

Identifying Performance Bottlenecks

To improve the performance of your SQL Server 2000 installation, you must first identify the cause of the performance bottleneck. A performance bottleneck is defined as a performance-limiting condition caused by excessive demand on a system resource or database object. A performance bottleneck also causes underutilization of other system resources or database objects. Inadequate hardware resources, such as memory or processor, are common causes of bottlenecks. You can generally solve these problems either by adding additional hardware resources or by moving some of the load to other servers. You can generally detect a hardware resource bottleneck by observing excessive use of one or more hardware resources. Excessive processor use does not necessarily indicate the need for more processor resources. Other factors can also cause excess usage. These include inadequate memory, which causes hard disk paging, or inefficient queries, which can generate excessive processor use.

Low numbers can mean that the system is performing better than expected, but they can also reveal a performance bottleneck. For example, if query response times are low and the hardware resources on your SQL Server 2000 computer are not overworked, you must look beyond hardware resources on the server itself. The problem could be a slow network or congestion preventing queries from reaching SQL Server 2000, inefficient queries, or a poorly designed database. Performance monitoring is the process of identifying performance-limiting factors, so they can be resolved.

Solving one performance bottleneck can reveal another performance bottleneck. For example, if you solve an I/O bottleneck by adding an additional hard disk, you might then find you have a processor bottleneck or a need to further optimize some queries. At some point, the incremental performance gain from solving a bottleneck will not be worth the time or cost. For example, the cost required to improve query response time by 15 percent might not be cost-effective if users consider the current query response time acceptable. However, what is acceptable today can change over time as the number of users increases and the database grows. You might need to optimize queries that were efficient with fewer users and plenty of hardware capacity as database utilization changes.

Determine Trends

When monitoring SQL Server 2000, you must gain an understanding of the normal range of values for various counters. This enables you to detect the onset of problems and take corrective actions before they become critical. You should establish an evolving performance baseline. This involves recording an initial performance baseline using a number of different monitoring tools. This will help you understand how various aspects of your system perform under normal production loads and before any problems arise. You should update this baseline periodically using the same monitoring methods and definitions. Significant changes should be analyzed.

Recording and monitoring the same type of information over time enables the database administrator to recognize values that are far above or far below normal. The cause of abnormal values will generally reveal the onset of a problem that warrants additional investigation. Maintaining an evolving baseline assists the database administrator in determining when additional hardware resources are needed, additional indexes should be created, or frequently run queries need to be optimized. An application or a database design that is efficient for a certain number of users can become inefficient as more users increase competition for server resources. They can also remain efficient, but simply require additional hardware resources to handle the increased load. Regularly monitoring the trends will help you to determine the areas in which you will need to concentrate time and resources.

Note   Using an evolving performance baseline also assists the database administrator in determining peak hours and off-peak hours. This is useful for scheduling maintenance tasks.

Determining Resources and Activities to Monitor

Factors to monitor that affect SQL Server 2000 performance include hardware resources, network traffic, database design, and client applications.

- Hardware resources might be inadequate for the load on the server—for example, insufficient processor resources causing processor queuing.
- Competing server applications on the SQL Server 2000 computer might be using excessive resources—for example, running Microsoft Exchange Server and Microsoft SQL server on the same computer.
- Hardware resource use might be unbalanced—for example, one disk being overused while another disk is underused.
- A hardware resource might be malfunctioning—for example, a disk beginning to fail causing excessive retries.
- General network congestion might occur—causing connection failures and excessive retries.
- Improper use of cursors or ad hoc queries—transferring excessively large amounts of data between client and server, which might only appear as a problem over a slow connection.
- Poor database design—resulting in excessive blocking locks. A blocking lock is a lock on a resource (such as a row or a table) held by a process that prevents another process from accessing the same resource until the first process releases the lock.

- Poorly written applications—resulting in deadlocks. A deadlock occurs when a process holds a lock blocking a second process and the second process holds a lock blocking the first process. When an instance of SQL Server 2000 detects a deadlock (through the use of an algorithm), it will terminate one of the transactions, allowing the other to continue to process.

Isolating the Problem

Determining the source of a problem is generally a process of using one or more monitoring tools to identify the symptoms of the problem. Once you identify the symptoms, you must then perform additional monitoring tasks to obtain more specific information to isolate the source of the problem. In Lesson 2, you will learn about each monitoring tool and its capabilities. In Lesson 3, you learn to perform various monitoring tasks to assist in isolating performance problems with your SQL Server 2000 installation.

Lesson Summary

The goal of performance monitoring is to maintain and improve the overall performance and efficiency of your SQL Server 2000 installation. This consists of improving response times and server throughput. Maintaining an evolving performance baseline enables the database administrator to detect patterns of change before serious problems occur. Solving performance problems involves identifying and isolating performance bottlenecks to determine the areas in which to concentrate resources and most effectively improve performance.

Lesson 2: Choosing Among Monitoring Tools

SQL Server 2000 and Windows 2000 provide a number of tools the database administrator can use to monitor SQL Server performance and activity. In this lesson, you are introduced to each of the tools and its use. The two primary tools are Windows 2000 System Monitor, which is used to monitor overall system resource use, and SQL Profiler, which is used to monitor selected details regarding selected SQL Server events.

After this lesson, you will be able to

- Describe and use each SQL Server 2000 monitoring tool
- Determine the appropriate tools for each monitoring task

Estimated lesson time: 15 minutes

Using System Monitor

Windows 2000 System Monitor (called Performance Monitor in Windows NT 4.0) is used to monitor resource usage on either the local computer or a remote computer. Use System Monitor to detect inadequate resources or resource use levels that warrant additional investigation, such as an excessive number of blocking locks or a significant increase in memory usage. Because System Monitor can impact performance, administrators frequently perform monitoring from a remote computer. If you do run System Monitor from the local computer, you can log the System Monitor data to another disk or computer to reduce impact on performance.

System Monitor is generally used either to view real-time performance data or to record data to disk for later review and analysis. System Monitor includes performance objects, counters, and instances.

- Performance objects generally correspond to hardware resources (such as memory, physical disk, or processor) or Windows services (such as server work queue or print queue).
- Counters are data items regarding aspects of each performance object (such as pages/sec for the memory performance object or writes/sec for the physical disk performance object).
- Instances are multiple performance objects of the same type (such as for multiple processors or hard disks).

System Monitor is extensible, enabling server applications (such as SQL Server 2000) to add performance objects, counters, and instances specific to the particular server application. Table 14.1 describes the performance objects (other than replication performance objects) added to System Monitor by SQL Server 2000 to track activity that is specific to SQL Server.

Table 14-1. Performance Objects for Tracking SQL Server Activity

SQL Server Performance Object	This Counter Measures...	Used to Monitor...
SQL Server: Access Methods	Access to and allocation of logical SQL Server database objects (such as data and index pages).	Index and query efficiency based on types of pages accessed, page splits, and page allocations.
SQL Server: Backup Device	Backup and restore performance information on a per-device basis.	Throughput or progress of backup and restore operations on a per-device basis.
SQL Server: Buffer Manager	Memory buffer use, including free buffer pages and buffer cache hit ratio.	Lack of physical memory, frequency of disk reads, and efficiency of query performance.
SQL Server: Cache Manager	Memory used for caching stored procedures, Transact-SQL statements, and triggers.	Efficiency of plan caching and reuse.
SQL Server: Databases	Database activity, including active transactions, bulk copy throughput, backup and restore throughput, and transaction log activities.	Level of user activity in a database, autogrowth and autoshrink operations, fullness of the transaction log, and performance levels for bulk copy, backup, and restore operations.
SQL Server: General Statistics	General server-wide activity, including user connections and logins.	Overall connection activity.
SQL Server: Latches	Internal SQL Server resource locks (called latches).	Performance bottlenecks based on the number and length of waits for internal resource locks to be granted.
SQL Server: Locks	Individual lock requests made by SQL Server, including number of lock timeouts and number of deadlocks.	Overall number and types of locks. Minimizing locks improves concurrency and performance.
SQL Server: Memory Manager	Overall memory usage, including memory used for connections and locks, available memory, and granted memory.	Overall memory usage for various objects, to determine whether a memory shortage exists.
SQL Server: SQL Statistics	Transact-SQL queries, including T-SQL compilations, T-SQL recompilations, and number of batches received.	Query compilation speed and overall efficiency of the query optimizer. Minimizing compilation time and re-compilation frequency improves performance.
SQL Server: User Settable Object	Custom counters based on stored procedures or Transact-SQL statements.	Custom information, such as product inventory or number of orders.

Using Task Manager

Windows 2000 (and Windows NT 4.0) Task Manager is used to provide a snapshot in real time of the amount of memory and processor resources used by each process and application running on a computer. This snapshot shows the relative server loads of competing server applications on the same computer. It also provides an overview of the total level of memory and processor usage on the computer. You can use this overview to quickly determine whether inadequate hardware resources are a problem.

Note   Task Manager is not available with Windows Me and Windows 98.

Using SQL Profiler

SQL Profiler is a graphical SQL Server 2000 tool used to monitor (trace) selected SQL Server events, and save the information to a table or file with a .TRC filename extension for later analysis. For example, you can monitor slowly executing stored procedures or events immediately preceding deadlocks. You can create traces and then replay them (in real time or step by step) on another computer running SQL Server (a test server) to debug performance and coding problems with Transact-SQL statements or stored procedures.

Note   Certain data columns are required to replay a trace. Use the SQLProfilerTSQL_Replay preconfigured trace template as a starting point for capturing selected data for replay.

A SQL Server event is any action generated within the SQL Server engine. Events include logins, Transact-SQL statements, stored procedures, batches, errors, cursors, and security permission checks. For each event, you can choose to monitor selected information, including computer name, object affected (such as table name), user name, text of the Transact-SQL statement or stored procedure, and time started and stopped. This trace definition information is stored in a template with a .TDF filename extension that defines the information that will be captured into a file or table. The result of this capture of information is called a trace. Using the same definitions over time is useful for detecting performance and usage trends.

You should take care to avoid monitoring too many events, which can affect SQL Server performance. The default maximum size of a trace file is 5 MB. By default, SQL Profiler creates a new trace file when the current trace file reaches the maximum size. The new trace filename is the original .TRC filename with a number appended to it. Limit trace size by limiting the type of events and data collected. Filters such as like and not like, equals and not equals, and greater than or equal and less than or equal should also be used to limit event data (such as by database, application, or user).

Events are grouped into event categories. Within each event category are event classes for capturing data about selected SQL Server events. Table 14.2 describes the event categories that can be monitored.

Table 14-2.   Event Categories That Can Be Monitored with SQL Profiler

Event Category	Event Classes in This Event Category Monitor...	Used to Monitor...
Cursors	Cursor creation, use, and deletion events.	The actual types of cursors being used, which is not necessarily the type specified by the calling application.
Database	Automatic data and transaction log file growth and shrinkage events.	Automatic growth of data and transaction log files, to properly size these files for maximum performance.
Errors and Warnings	Error and warning events, such as stored procedure compilation errors or missing column statistics warnings.	The length of waits for resources, which can indicate contention issues. Also, the efficiency of query optimizer execution plans.
Locks	Lock acquired, canceled, escalated, and released events.	Contention issues based on type and length of locks. Also, deadlocks and timeout events. Can generate large files.
Objects	Object creating, opening, closing, dropping, and deleting events.	Ad hoc creation of objects by applications and users. Can generate particularly large files.
Performance	Query optimizer showplan information and the execution of SQL data manipulation language (DML) operators.	Query execution and query optimizer efficiency by capturing the plan tree, the query plan cost estimates, the query execution statistics, and the query plan tree.
Scans	Tables or indexes scanned.	Types of scans being performed on an object.
Security audit	Audit events.	Logins, logouts, security and permission changes, password changes, and backup and restore events.
Server	Memory change events.	Changes in SQL Server memory usage greater than 1 MB or 5% of the maximum server memory, whichever is greater.
Sessions	Length of time per user connection and amount of SQL Server processor time used by queries submitted using each connection.	Connected users, database activity, and CPU time used, for charging for usage and activity.
Stored procedures	Stored procedure execution information, including cache hits and misses, order of execution, when aged out of cache, and when recompiled.	Memory to determine additional memory needs. Also, use of stored procedures by applications.
Transactions	Transaction execution information.	Types of logging activity by applications. Also, transaction commits and rollbacks, and distributed transactions.

Table 14-2. Event Categories That Can Be Monitored with SQL Profiler (continued)

Event Category	Event Classes in This Event Category Monitor...	Used to Monitor...
TSQL	Execution of SQL Server statements and batch events.	Accuracy of application results compared to expected results during application testing. Also, events that take a long time to run, including the users who submit these queries.
User configurable	Custom events.	User-defined events, such as application progress reports at specified points during application testing.

With SQL Profiler, you can use the preconfigured trace definitions (called templates) either as is or as a basis for custom templates. These templates define the types of event information that SQL Profiler will trace and capture. Table 14.3 describes the preconfigured trace templates that ship with SQL Server 2000.

Note SQL Profiler supports C2-level security auditing for C2-certified systems (C2 is a government-defined security level). To enable C2 Audit Mode, use the *sp_configure* system stored procedure. Refer to the topic "C2 Audit Mode Option" in SQL Server Books Online for further information.

Using SQL Query Analyzer

You can use SQL Query Analyzer to view and analyze the execution plan for a query. You use this plan to determine how efficiently queries are being processed and whether indexes are being used effectively. To view the execution plan for a query, enter the query in the query pane and then click Show Execution Plan on the Query menu. The estimated execution plan displays in the results pane. Refer to the topic "Graphically Displaying the Execution Plan Using SQL Query Analyzer" in SQL Server Books Online for assistance in interpreting the results displayed. The details of analyzing query plans are beyond the scope of this book.

Table 14-3. Preconfigured Trace Templates in SQL Profiler

Template Name	A Trace Using This Definition Captures...
SQLProfilerSP_Counts	The number of stored procedures that run; groups the results by stored procedure name and includes the number of times the procedure has executed.
SQLProfilerStandard	General information regarding SQL batches and stored procedures executed and their connections, in execution order.
SQLProfilerTSQL	Each Transact-SQL statement issued in execution order including the time each statement was issued.

Table 14-3.   Preconfigured Trace Templates in SQL Profiler

Template Name	A Trace Using This Definition Captures...
SQLProfilerTSQL_Duration	Each Transact-SQL statement issued; groups the results by duration (in milliseconds).
SQLProfilerTSQL_Grouped	Each Transact-SQL statement issued; groups the results by user submitting them.
SQLProfilerTSQL_Replay	Details about each Transact-SQL statement issued, in sufficient detail to be used for replay in SQL Query Analyzer. Use this preconfigured template as a starting point for capturing data for replay.
SQLProfilerTSQL_SPs	Details in execution order about each stored procedure that executes, including the Transact-SQL commands within each stored procedure.
SQLProfilerTuning	Duration information and binary data about each stored procedure issued and SQL batch executed. Binary data includes information such as session level settings, type of cursor issued, and lock type.

Using the SQL Server Enterprise Manager Current Activity Window

The SQL Server Enterprise Manager Current Activity window displays a snapshot of information regarding processes, user activity, locks held by processes, and locks held on objects. The current activity window is used to perform ad hoc monitoring to determine blocked and blocking transactions. As a system administrator, you can kill a selected process or send a message to the user who is executing a transaction that is causing a blocking lock or a deadlock. You can also view currently connected users and their last executed statement. Finally, you can view all locks currently in effect on the system based on the database object.

Using Transact-SQL

There are a number of types of Transact-SQL statements that you can issue to monitor SQL Server 2000 activity and performance. These statements can display either current resource information or performance over a period of time.

System Stored Procedures

The system stored procedures you can use to monitor SQL Server 2000 activity and performance are described in Table 14.4.

Table 14-4.   System Stored Procedures for Monitoring Performance

System Stored Procedure	The Procedure Reports...	Used to Monitor...
sp_who	Snapshot of current users and processes, including the currently executing command.	Active users and their processes.
sp_who2	Snapshot of current users and processes with additional columns (also more readable).	Active users and their processes.
sp_lock	Snapshot of current locks.	Blocking locks and deadlocks, and the process causing them.
sp_spaceused	Estimate of current disk space reserved and used by a table or the entire database.	Database or object space usage.
sp_monitor	Statistics, including CPU use, I/O use, and idle time since last execution of *sp_monitor*.	Volume of work performed during period of time.

In addition, all of the functions of SQL Profiler can be executed using stored procedures. These include the *sp_trace_create*, *sp_trace_generateevent*, *sp_trace_setevent*, *sp_trace_setfilter*, and *sp_trace_setstatus* system stored procedures.

DBCC

Transact-SQL provides several types of Database Console Commands (DBCCs) for SQL Server 2000. You use DBCC commands to check physical and logical database consistency, as well as monitor SQL Server. Most inconsistencies detected can also be repaired by specifying the repair option. The DBCC statements most commonly used to check database consistency and monitor performance statistics are described in Table 14.5.

Built-in Functions

Transact-SQL provides a number of built-in functions (also called T-SQL globals) that keep track of specific information regarding SQL Server activity, such as performance statistics about activity since SQL Server was last started. This information is stored in predefined SQL Server counters and accessed using the *SELECT* statement. Table 14.6 describes the most commonly used T-SQL global counters.

Table 14-5.   DBCC Statements Used for Monitoring

DBCC Statement	Statement Activity
DBCC CHECKCATALOG	Verifies that every data type in the syscolumns table also has an entry in the systypes table, and that every table and view in the sysobjects table has at least one column in the syscolumns table.
DBCC CHECKDB	Checks the allocation and structural integrity of all objects in a specified database. Use the repair option to correct minor inconsistencies. Includes the functionality of the *DBCC CHECKALLOC* and *DBCC CHECK-TABLE* statements.
DBCC CHECKCONSTRAINTS	Verifies foreign key and check constraints on a table.
DBCC CHECKFILEGROUP	Performs the same function as *DBCC CHECKDB*, but limited to a single specified filegroup and required tables.
DBCC CONCURRENCYVIOLATION	Checks how many times more than five batches were executed concurrently on the SQL Server 2000 Personal Edition or the SQL Server 2000 Desktop Engine. Performance of the database engine is limited when users execute more than five batches concurrently on these editions.
DBCC DROPCLEANBUFFERS	Removes all clean buffers from the buffer pool. You use this statement to test queries with an empty buffer cache without shutting down and restarting the server.
DBCC OPENTRAN	Displays information regarding the oldest active transaction and oldest distributed and nondistributed replicated transactions within a specified database.
DBCC PROCCACHE	Displays information regarding the contents of the procedure cache, including number of stored procedures in cache, the number currently executing, and the size of the procedure cache.
DBCC SHOWCONTIG	Displays fragmentation information for the data and indexes of a table.
DBCC SHOW_STATISTICS	Displays the current distribution statistics for an index or statistics collection on a table.
DBCC SQLPERF (LOGSPACE)	Displays statistics about transaction log space size and percent used in all databases for a SQL Server instance.
DBCC UPDATEUSAGE	Checks and corrects inaccuracies in space usage reports by the *sp_spaceused* system stored procedure for the sysindexes table.

Table 14-6.   Commonly Used T-SQL Global Counters

Counter	Count Since SQL Server Started
@@CONNECTIONS	Number of connections (including attempted connections)
@@CPU_BUSY	Time in milliseconds that the processor has spent working
@@IDLE	Time in milliseconds that SQL Server has been idle
@@IO_BUSY	Time in milliseconds that SQL Server has spent performing input and output operations
@@PACK_RECEIVED	Number of input packets read from the network

Table 14-6.   Commonly Used T-SQL Global Counters   (continued)

Counter	Count Since SQL Server Started
@@PACK_SENT	Number of output packets written to the network
@@PACKET_ERRORS	Number of network packet errors that have occurred on connections
@@TOTAL_ERRORS	Number of disk read/write errors encountered
@@TOTAL_READ	Number of disk reads (not cache reads)
@@TOTAL_WRITE	Number of disk writes

Trace Flags

Trace flags are an unsupported feature of SQL Server 2000 and might not be supported in future releases. You can use them to temporarily enable specified server characteristics or turn off certain behavior. They leave a record of their activity in the SQL Server error log, and are therefore useful for debugging. They are generally used by developers. However, they are also referenced in Knowledge Base articles. Use *DBCC TRACEON* to enable a specified trace flag. For example, enabling trace flag 3205 disables hardware compression on tape drives. For more information on this topic, refer to Kalen Delaney's book, *Inside Microsoft SQL Server 2000* (Microsoft Press, 2000).

Using SNMP

You can use Simple Network Management Protocol (SNMP) to send management information across different operating system platforms. Management information can include performance statistics and configuration information. SNMP can only monitor the default instance. SQL Server 2000 support for SNMP is enabled automatically on Windows 2000 and Windows NT 4.0 computers supporting SNMP.

Lesson Summary

System Monitor is used to monitor resources used on the local computer or on remote computers by various server processes. Task Manager provides a quick snapshot of per-process usage or overall resource usage. SQL Profiler is used to monitor events and processes that are specific to SQL Server. SQL Query Analyzer is used to display estimated execution plans for query efficiency analysis. The SQL Server Enterprise Manager Current Activity window provides a snapshot of current user and locking activity, and can be used to terminate a process. Transact-SQL system stored procedures and built-in functions can be used to provide snapshots of current activity, or to provide statistics regarding resource usage over a period of time. DBCC statements can be used to check database consistency and monitor SQL Server. SNMP can be used for centralized reporting across various operating systems.

Lesson 3: Performing Monitoring Tasks

Monitoring SQL Server 2000 consists of performing various tasks to monitor levels of resource usage and specific SQL Server events. In this lesson, you will learn to use Windows 2000 System Monitor and Task Manager to monitor memory, I/O, and processor use. You will also monitor the execution of stored procedures and SQL batches using SQL Profiler. Finally, you will monitor locks using the SQL Server Enterprise Manager Current Activity window and system stored procedures.

After this lesson, you will be able to

- Use System Monitor and Task Manager to monitor resource usage
- Use SQL Profiler to monitor stored procedures and Transact-SQL batches
- Use SQL Profiler to monitor user activity
- Use the SQL Server Enterprise Manager Current Activity window and system stored procedures to view blocking locks and deadlocks

Estimated lesson time: 45 minutes

Monitoring Resource Usage

You monitor resource use (memory, I/O, and processor) to determine whether adequate resources exist, and also to determine the relative use of resources by different server processes. It is useful to test resource usage on a computer with minimal load to establish the performance baseline before you place a load on the system.

Task Manager

To monitor resource use with Task Manager, right-click the Windows taskbar and then click Task Manager. You can also press the CTRL+ALT+DEL key combination and then click the Task Manager button in the Windows Security menu. To view resource use on a per-process basis, click the Processes tab in Task Manager. See Figure 14.1.

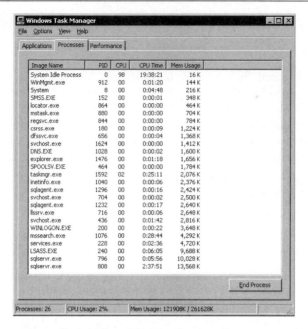

Figure 14.1.   Task Manager (Processes tab).

In the Processes tab, notice the five default columns of information that are displayed. You can sort the information displayed by clicking a column heading. Notice that in Figure 14.1, the columns are ordered based on the amount of memory used for each process. Click Select Columns on the View menu to select additional columns to appear on the Processes page. Figure 14.2 shows the Select Columns dialog box.

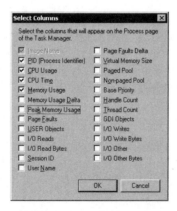

Figure 14.2.   Selecting additional columns within Task Manager.

You can control the frequency with which the information is refreshed (or pause the display) by clicking Update Speed on the View menu in Task Manager. In the Options menu, you can control whether Task Manager always appears on top of other applications on the desktop (this is the default behavior) and also whether Task Manager appears on the Windows taskbar when minimized (default).

Click the Performance tab to view overall resource use on the computer. See Figure 14.3.

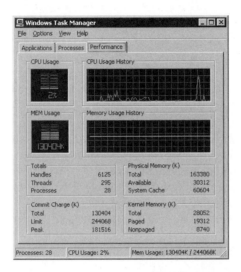

Figure 14.3.   Task Manager (Performance tab).

Notice, in the Totals group box, that you can view processor use, based on handles, threads, and processes. You can also view memory use, based on committed memory (including virtual memory) in the Commit Charge (K) group box, physical memory in the Physical Memory (K) group box, and kernel memory in the Kernel Memory (K) group box. In Figure 14.3, notice that the peak committed memory is higher than the total physical memory on the computer. This indicates that this computer could benefit from additional memory.

Note   When Task Manager is running, the System Tray always displays the overall CPU usage value from Task Manager.

System Monitor

To monitor resource use with System Monitor, click Performance in the Administrative Tools program group. System Monitor is a snap-in within the Performance console. See Figure 14.4.

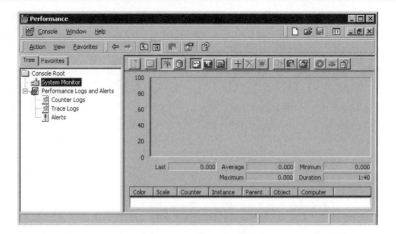

Figure 14.4.   Performance MMC with the System Monitor snap-in.

System Monitor displays the counter values for selected performance objects, counters, and instances. These can be current values, a snapshot of values at a given point in time, or values from a saved Counter Log. To add counters to System Monitor, click the Add button on the toolbar to display the Add Counters dialog box. See Figure 14.5. Notice that you can use counters from the local computer, or you can select a remote computer to monitor.

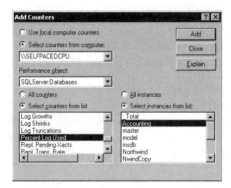

Figure 14.5.   Adding counters to System Monitor.

You can view counter values as a chart, histogram, or report by clicking the corresponding button on the toolbar. See Figures 14.6, 14.7, and 14.8.

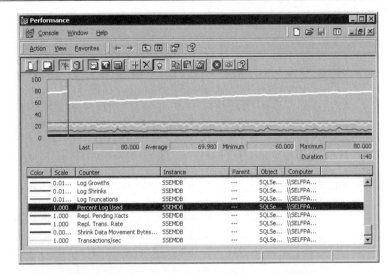

Figure 14.6.   Chart view of System Monitor.

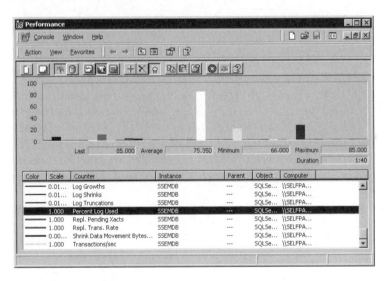

Figure 14.7.   Histogram view of System Monitor.

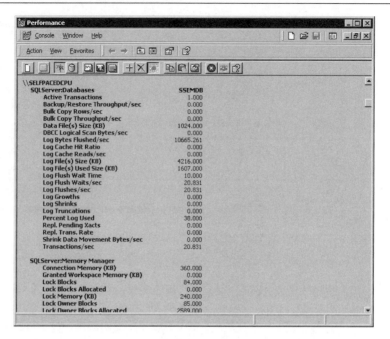

Figure 14.8.   Report view of System Monitor.

Select a counter and then click the Highlight button on the toolbar (or press CTRL+H on your keyboard) to highlight the counter in white in the chart or histogram view. You can only highlight one counter at any given time. Click the Freeze Display button on the toolbar to freeze the counter values at a particular point for further analysis. Click the Properties button on the System Monitor toolbar (not the Performance MMC toolbar) to alter the properties of System Monitor. Properties include update frequency (default is 1 second) and display characteristics.

To create a log for later review, expand Performance Logs And Alerts, right-click Counter Logs, and then click New Log Settings. You will be prompted to enter the name of the new log file in the New Log Settings dialog box, and then the NewLogFile dialog box appears, as shown in Figure 14.9.

You can create a log file definition containing the counters to be logged, the sampling interval, the file size (including enabling file rollover), and a logging schedule.

Memory Objects and Counters

You should monitor your computer to determine whether there is adequate memory on the computer for the processes that are running. Indications of insufficient memory are a lack of available memory and hard disk paging. Multiple counters must be interpreted together. You might also need to determine which processes are using memory and to isolate the memory used by SQL Server. This information is useful for setting minimum and maximum memory values for SQL Server when sharing the computer with other server applications.

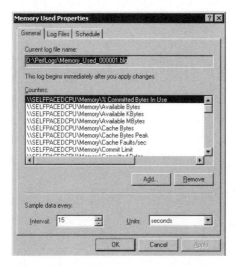

Figure 14.9.   Creating a memory counter log in System Monitor.

Table 14.7 describes the most important memory counters to monitor and provides help in interpreting values received.

Note   You might need to use LogicalDisk counters rather than PhysicalDisk counters if you have multiple logical partitions on a single physical disk. Whereas physical disk counters are enabled by default, logical disk counters are not. Use the Diskperf –yv command to enable logical disk counters (and to reboot the system).

I/O Objects and Counters

Overloaded disk subsystems are one of the most common performance problems with SQL Server installations. I/O-bound disks cause disk queuing and a general degradation of overall system performance. This problem is solved, in most cases, by adding additional disks to RAID or by implementing RAID. However, insufficient memory and inefficient queries can also cause excessive disk I/O. Table 14.8 describes the most important I/O object counters to monitor and provides help on interpreting values received.

Processor Objects and Counters

Inadequate processor resources are also a common performance problem. Additional processors or a faster processor can solve the problem. However, inadequate memory (causing excessive paging and processor use) or inefficient statements (generating excessive processor use) can also be the cause of the performance bottleneck. Table 14.9 describes the most important processor object counters to monitor and provides help on interpreting values received.

Table 14-7.   Memory Object Counters

Object Counter	This Object Counter Reports ...	How to Interpret...
Memory \ Available Mbytes	Megabytes of memory currently available for use.	A low value can indicate a shortage of memory or an application failing to release memory.
Memory \ Pages/sec	Number of pages retrieved from disk or written to free space in the working set on the disk because of hard page faults.	A high value (above 20) can indicate excessive hard disk paging because of a memory shortage.
PhysicalDisk \ Avg. Disk Queue Length	Average number of both read and write requests that were queued.	If an increase in disk queue length is not accompanied by a decrease in memory paging, a memory shortage exists.
Memory \ Page Faults/sec	The overall rate that faulted pages are handled by the processor.	A high value for overall page faults/sec coinciding with a low value for the SQL Server instance indicates that SQL Server is not causing the memory shortage.
Process \ Page Faults/sec for the SQL Server instance	The rate faulted pages occur because of the SQL Server process for a given SQL Server instance.	A high value for overall page faults/sec coinciding with a low value for the SQL Server instance indicates that SQL Server is not causing the memory shortage.
SQL Server: Memory Manager \ Total Server Memory (KB)	Total amount of dynamic memory SQL Server is currently using for its memory buffer.	If this value is consistently close to the total amount of physical memory of the computer (or the configured maximum memory value), more memory might be needed.
Process \ Working Set for the SQL Server instance	Total number of current bytes in the Working Set for the SQL Server instance.	Use this value to determine the maximum memory needed for SQL Server with the current load.
SQL Server: Buffer Manager \ Buffer Cache Hit Ratio	Percentage of pages found in the memory buffer pool without having to incur a read from disk.	This value should generally be above 90%. If not, more memory is generally needed.
SQL Server: Buffer Manager \ Total Pages	Total number of pages in the buffer pool (including data, free, and stolen pages).	A low value can indicate a shortage of memory available for the buffer pool.

Table 14-8.   I/O Object Counters

Object Counter	This Object Counter Reports ...	How to Interpret...
PhysicalDisk \ % Disk Time	Percentage of elapsed time during which the hard disk is busy servicing read or write requests.	A low rate of disk paging coinciding with a high rate of disk usage and disk queuing indicates a disk bottleneck. Can be over 100% if using a RAID device or an intelligent disk controller.
PhysicalDisk \ Avg. Disk Queue Length	Average number of both read and write requests that were queued.	A low rate of disk paging coinciding with a high rate of disk usage and disk queuing indicates a disk bottleneck. A disk queue above 1.5 to 2 times the number of disk spindles indicates a disk bottleneck.
PhysicalDisk \ Current Disk Queue Length	Instantaneous number of both read and write requests that are queued.	Use in conjunction with the PhysicalDisk \ Avg. Disk Queue Length to determine whether a disk bottleneck exists.
PhysicalDisk \ Avg. Disk/sec Write	Average time to write data to disk (disk latency).	A disk latency value above 15 to 20 milliseconds indicates a disk bottleneck.
PhysicalDisk \ Avg. Disk/sec Read	Average time to read data from disk.	A disk latency value above 15 to 20 milliseconds indicates a disk bottleneck.
PhysicalDisk \ Disk Writes/sec	Rate of write operations.	If the rate of disk writes plus disk reads is not close to the capacity of the hard disk and disk latency is high, a faulty disk is likely. If the combined rate is close to the capacity, a disk bottleneck is likely.
PhysicalDisk \ Disk Reads/sec	Rate of read operations.	If the rate of disk writes plus disk reads is not close to the capacity of the hard disk and disk latency is high, a faulty disk is likely. If the combined rate is close to the capacity, a disk bottleneck is likely.

Table 14-9.   Processor Object Counters

Object Counter	This Object Counter Reports ...	How to Interpret...
Processor \ % Processor Time	Percentage of time the processor spent executing non-idle threads.	Rates above 75% generally indicate a processor bottleneck. Systems with values above 60% can generally benefit from more processor power.
System \ Processor Queue Length	Number of threads in the processor queue.	A sustained processor queue above two threads generally indicates a processor bottleneck.

Practice: Monitoring System Resources Using System Monitor and Task Manager

In this practice you use System Monitor and Task Manager to monitor system resource use.

▶ **To monitor system resources using System Monitor and Task Manager**

1. Ensure that you are logged on to the SelfPacedSQL.MSFT domain controller as Administrator.

2. Minimize all running applications.

3. Right-click the Windows taskbar and then click Task Manager.

   Windows Task Manager appears.

4. Click the Performance tab.

   Notice the overall values for process and memory use. In particular, note the delta between Total Physical Memory and both the Total Commit Charge and the Peak Commit Charge. These indicators will tell you if you have an overall memory shortage on your computer.

5. On the Options menu, click Hide When Minimized and then minimize Windows Task Manager.

6. Click Start and then click Run.

7. In the Open drop-down combo box, type **C:\SelfPacedSQL\CH_14 \ Monitor.msc**, and then click OK.

   A preconfigured Performance console appears displaying a number of performance object counters in the Report view. Review the displayed counters.

8. On the toolbar, click the Freeze Display button.

   You will use this frozen display to compare values with a SQL Server load and without a SQL Server load.

9. Click Start and then click Run.

10. In the Open drop-down combo box, type **C:\SelfPacedSQL\CH_14 \ Monitor.msc** and then click OK.

    A second version of the same preconfigured Performance console appears.

11. Right-click the taskbar and then click Tile Windows Vertically.

    The two Performance consoles are displayed side by side.

12. Click Start and then click Run.

13. In the Open drop-down combo box, type **C:\SelfPacedSQL\ CH_14\Load.bat**, and then click OK.

    The OSQL command-prompt utility runs the LoadInLoop.sql command in the Command Prompt window.

14. Minimize the Command Prompt window.

Notice the effect of the load on the performance object counters. Compare the counters between the frozen instance of System Monitor and the unfrozen instance. Notice the load on the disk. Determine whether you have a memory shortage on your computer or the processor needs additional power.

15. Double-click Task Manager in the system tray.

Windows Task Manager appears. Notice the overall values for process and memory use. In particular, notice how the delta between Total Physical Memory and both the Total Commit Charge and the Peak Commit Charge changed. Does your system have a memory shortage?

16. After the OSQL command in the Command Prompt window finishes, notice the reduced load on the computer.

17. Close the Windows Task Manager and both copies of the Performance console.

Monitoring Stored Procedures, Transact SQL Batches, and User Activity

To monitor stored procedures and Transact-SQL batches, click Profiler in the Microsoft SQL Server program group. See Figure 14.10.

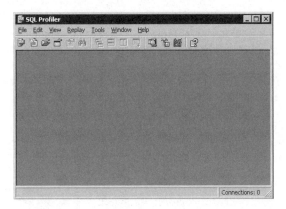

Figure 14.10.   SQL Profiler.

You can create a new trace, create a new template, or open an existing trace file for analysis and replay. To create a new trace, click the New Trace button on the toolbar (or point to New and then click Trace in the File menu) and then, in the Connect To SQL Server dialog box, connect to the SQL Server instance on which you want to trace SQL Server events. The Trace Properties dialog box then appears, as shown in Figure 14.11.

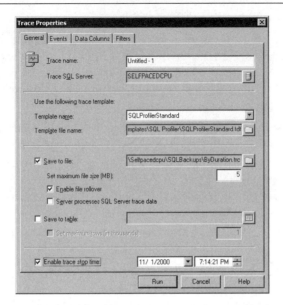

Figure 14.11.   SQL Profiler Trace properties (General tab).

In the General tab, you can create a new trace definition or use one of the preconfigured trace templates. In the Trace Name text box, use a descriptive naming convention for each new trace definition you create. You can choose to save the captured trace information to a file or table, and set a maximum size for the captured data. If you save the captured trace information to a file, notice that the default is to enable file rollover (this creates a new file when the maximum size is reached). You can also enable a stop time for the trace.

In the Events tab, you can choose SQL Server events (event classes) from various categories of events. Certain event classes will already be selected based on the initial template selected. See Figure 14.12.

In the Data Columns tab, you can choose to add (or subtract) to the default data columns to capture the information you want. You will want different types of information for different types of traces. By moving one or more data columns up to the Groups category, you can group the output by that data column. You move data columns up by clicking the Up button. You can also order the data columns in the output, by clicking the Up button or the Down button. See Figure 14.13.

In the Filters tab, you can choose to include or exclude various types of events. Notice that, by default, SQL Profiler events are not captured. See Figure 14.14. You might also want to exclude all events related to the domain user account of the SQL Server service.

Figure 14.12.   SQL Profiler Trace Properties (Events tab).

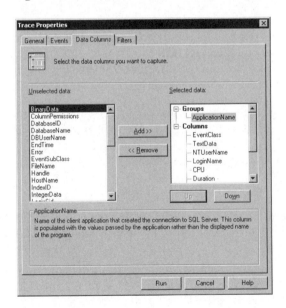

Figure 14.13.   SQL Profiler Trace Properties (Data Columns tab).

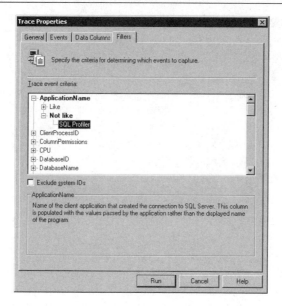

Figure 14.14.   SQL Profiler Trace Properties (Filters tab).

You can also select the Exclude System IDs check box to exclude SQL events referencing system objects. This will generally capture the information you want to analyze and will significantly reduce the size of your trace because system objects that are being accessed can result in 50 to 75 percent of the trace events. Click the Run button to start the trace.

After a trace has been captured, you can search within the trace for specified strings (by clicking the Find String button on the toolbar). You can also choose to save the template for later use or save the data captured for later analysis and comparison by clicking Save As on the File menu.

You should create separate trace templates for different types of traces.

- **Long-running queries.**   Capture all data columns related to the TSQL and Stored Procedure event classes and then group by Duration and filter by length of time.
- **Stored procedure performance.**   Capture all data columns related to the selected Stored Procedure event classes for a specified stored procedure (using the ObjectID event criteria) or for all stored procedures, and then group by ClientProcessID.
- **Cause of a deadlock.**   Capture all data columns related to selected TSQL and Stored Procedure event classes, and group by EventClass. Use the Database ID event criteria to limit to a specified database.
- **Login and logouts.**   Capture the EventClass, EventSubClass, LoginSID, and Login data columns for the Security Audit\Audit Login event class.

■ **Individual user activity.**   Capture all data columns related to the Sessions\ExistingConnection, and TSQL event classes and group by DBUserName.

Practice: Monitoring SQL Batches and Stored Procedures

In this practice you use SQL Profiler to monitor Transact-SQL batches and stored procedures.

▶ **To monitor SQL batches and stored procedures**

1. Ensure that you are logged on to the SelfPacedSQL.MSFT domain controller as Administrator.
2. Click Start, point to Programs, point to Microsoft SQL Server, and then click Profiler.

    SQL Profiler appears.
3. On the toolbar, click the New Trace button.

    The Connect To SQL Server dialog box appears.
4. Make sure that the Windows Authentication option button is selected, and then click OK to connect to the default instance on SelfPacedCPU.

    The Trace Properties dialog box appears.
5. In the Trace Name text box, type **Duration**.
6. In the Template Name drop-down list, click SQLProfilerTSQL_Duration and then click the Events tab.

    Notice that the only event classes being traced are RPC:Completed and SQL:BatchCompleted.
7. Click the Data Columns tab.

    Notice that the data columns selected are being grouped by EventClass and then by Duration.
8. Click the Filters tab.

    Notice that events generated by SQL Profiler are being excluded.
9. Expand DatabaseName and then expand Like.
10. Type **Northwind** in the Like text box.
11. Expand Duration and then expand Greater Than Or Equal.
12. Type **100** in the Greater Than Or Equal text box.
13. Click the Run button.

    Notice that the Duration trace starts.
14. On the toolbar, click the SQL Query Analyzer button.

    The Connect To SQL Server dialog box appears.
15. Make sure that the Windows Authentication option button is selected, and then click OK to connect to the default instance on SelfPacedCPU.

    SQL Query Analyzer appears.

16. On the toolbar, click the Load SQL Script button.

    The Open Query File dialog box appears.

17. Open Duration.sql in the C:\SelfPacedSQL\CH_14 folder.

    A Transact-SQL script appears that performs a variety of *SELECT* statements, which will take differing amounts of time to complete.

18. On the toolbar, click the Execute Query button.

19. Switch to SQL Profiler.

    Notice the *SELECT* statements that appear in the trace.

20. Click the longest-running *SELECT* statement.

    Notice that the Transact-SQL statement executed appears in the lower pane.

21. On the toolbar, click the Properties button.

    The Trace Properties dialog box appears, displaying the trace properties for the Duration trace.

22. Click the Filters tab.

    Notice that the existing filters are displayed. Also notice that you cannot modify a running trace.

23. Click Cancel.

24. On the toolbar, click the Stop Selected Trace button.

25. Close SQL Profiler, but leave the SQL Query Analyzer running.

Monitoring Current Locking and User Activity

To view current locking and user activity in SQL Server Enterprise Manager, expand the Management container for the instance and then expand the Current Activity container. See Figure 14.15.

Notice that there are three containers: Process Info, Locks/Process ID, and Locks/Object. In the console tree, click the Process Info container to view detailed information in the details pane regarding all current connections and processes. See Figures 14.16 and 14.17.

Note To update the information displayed, right-click the Current Activity container and then click Refresh.

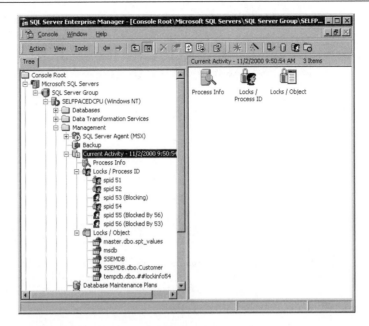

Figure 14.15.   The Current Activity window.

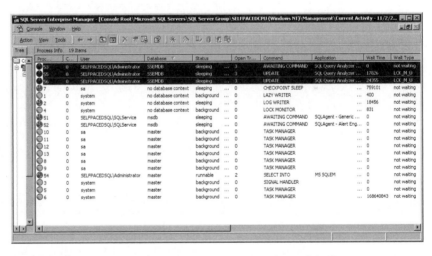

Figure 14.16.   Current Activity window (Process Info—left half).

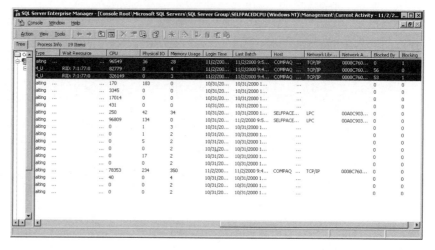

Figure 14.17. Current Activity window (Process Info—right half).

The information available in the Process Info container is described in Table 14.10.

Table 14-10.   Information in the Process Info Container

Column	Description
Process ID	SQL Server Process ID (SPID) of the process.
Context ID	Execution context ID (ECID) of a subthread operating on behalf of the process.
User	User ID of the user who executed the command that initiated the process.
Database	Current database context of the process (certain system processes will have no database context).
Status	Process status (running, sleeping, runnable, or background) of the process.
Open Transactions	Number of open transactions for the process.
Command	SQL Server command currently executing for the process.
Application	Name of the application program being used by the process.
Wait Time	Wait time (in milliseconds), if any, for the process.
Wait Type	A string indicating the current or last wait type for the process.
Wait Resource	Textual representation of a lock resource, such as a row identifier (RID) of the process.
CPU	Cumulative processor time for the process.
Physical IO	Cumulative disk reads and writes for the process.
Memory Usage	Number of pages in the procedure cache that are currently allocated to this process. A negative number indicates pages being freed for another process.

Table 14-10.   Information in the Process Info Container

Column	Description
Login Time	Time a client process logged into the server. For server processes, the time the server started.
Last Batch	Last time a client process executed an *EXECUTE* statement or a remote stored procedure call. For server processes, the time the server started.
Host	Name of the computer that initiated the process.
Network Library	Net-library used by the client to initiate the process.
Network Address	Network address (the Message Authentication Code [MAC] address) for the network interface card (NIC) on the client computer that initiated the process.
Blocked By	SPID of a blocking process for the process.
Blocking	SPID of process being blocked by the process.

The Locks/Process ID container displays each active process. Expand the Locks/Process ID container and then click an active process in the console tree to view the locks held by the process. See Figures 14.18 and 14.19.

Notice that SPID 53 is blocking SPID 56. SPID 53 has been granted an exclusive row lock on the same resource on which SPID 56 is waiting for a lock. For a complete list of the types and modes of locks, refer to the topic "Monitoring with SQL Server Enterprise Manager" in SQL Server Books Online. To view the most recent command issued by the blocking process, right-click the process ID and then click Properties to display the Process Details dialog box. See Figure 14.20.

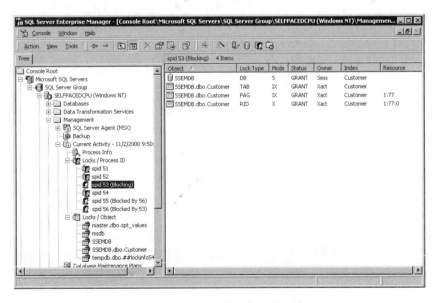

Figure 14.18.   Locks/Process ID information for a blocking process.

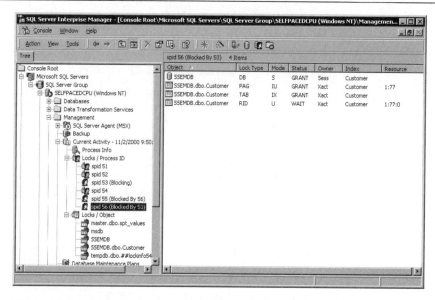

Figure 14.19.   Locks/Process ID information for a blocked process.

Figure 14.20.   Last TSQL command by the blocking process.

In Figure 14.20, notice that the most recent TSQL command batch began a transaction but did not complete the transaction because this open transaction is blocking other processes. To resolve a blocking lock or a deadlock (in the short term), the database administrator can either click the Send Message button to send a message to the user who initiated the blocking process or click the Kill Process button to kill the process directly.

Note   In general, applications should be coded to acquire shared locks rather than exclusive locks when waiting for user input.

The Locks/Object container displays each database object that is locked, from the row and table level up to the database level. See Figure 14.21.

Notice that three processes have locks on the Customer table in the SSEMDB database. Process ID 53 has an exclusive row lock, and process IDs 55 and 56 are waiting to place exclusive row locks on the same row.

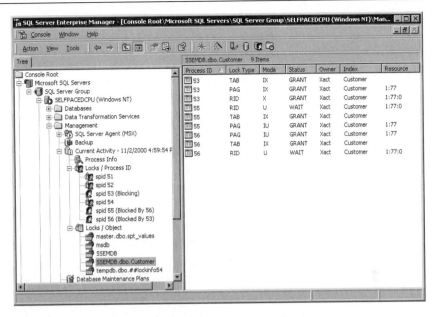

Figure 14.21.   Locks/object information for a locked object.

Practice: Monitoring Blocking Problems Using the Current Activity Window and System Stored Procedures

In this practice you use the SQL Server Enterprise Manager and system stored procedures to monitor blocking problems.

▶ **To monitor blocking problems using the Current Activity window and system stored procedures**

1. Ensure that you are logged on to the SelfPacedSQL.MSFT domain controller as Administrator.

2. Click Start, point to Programs, point to Microsoft SQL Server, and then click Enterprise Manager.

3. Expand the Microsoft SQL Servers container, expand the SQL Server Group container, expand the SelfPacedCPU container, expand the Management container, expand the Current Activity container, and then click Process Info.

    The Process Info details are displayed in the details pane. If you do not see the details, right-click Process Info, point to View, and then click Detail.

4. In the details pane, click the User column to sort the user processes by user name.

    Notice two user processes for SelfPacedSQL\Administrator: one for the existing connection by SQL Server Enterprise Manager to the master database and one for the existing connection by SQL Query Analyzer to the Northwind database. Note the Process ID number for the connection by SQL Query Analyzer.

5. Switch to SQL Query Analyzer.

6. On the toolbar, click the Load SQL Script button.

   The Open Query File dialog box appears.

7. Open BlockLock.sql in the C:\SelfPacedSQL\CH_14 folder.

   A Transact-SQL script appears that will begin a transaction to update the ContactName for a particular CustomerID. It also executes the *sp_lock* system stored procedure.

8. On the toolbar, click the Execute Query button.

   Notice the information returned from the *sp_lock* system stored procedure. In particular, note the locks granted to the SQL Query Analyzer SPID and note in particular the exclusive row lock granted to this process.

9. On the File menu, click Connect.

   The Connect To SQL Server dialog box appears.

10. Make sure that the Windows Authentication option button is selected, and then click OK to connect to the default instance on SelfPacedCPU.

11. On the toolbar, click the Load SQL Script button.

    The Open Query File dialog box appears.

12. Open BlockLock2.sql in the C:\SelfPacedSQL\CH_14 folder.

13. The BlockLock2.sql query appears. This query updates the same customer record, but does not leave the transaction open.

14. On the toolbar, click the Execute Query button.

    Notice that the query does not complete its execution.

15. Switch to SQL Server Enterprise Manager.

16. In the console tree, right-click the Current Activity container and then click Refresh.

17. In the details pane, double-click Locks/Process ID.

    Notice that the first process is blocking the second process.

18. Right-click the blocking process and then click Properties.

    The Process Details dialog box appears displaying the last TSQL command batch executed by the blocking process.

19. Click the Send Message button.

    The Send Message – SelfPacedCPU dialog box appears.

20. In the Message text box, type **Your application is blocking. Please close your open transaction**. Then click the Send button.

    A Send Message message box appears stating that the message was successfully sent and a Messenger Service message box appears containing the message (one message box will appear behind the other message box).

21. Click OK in each of these message boxes to close the message boxes.

22. In the Process Details dialog box, click the Close button.

23. In the console tree, click the process that is blocked.

    In the details pane, notice in the Status column that the lock request for a row lock is waiting.

24. In the console tree, expand the Locks/Object container and then click SSEMDB.dbo.Customer.

    In the details pane, notice the two row locks. The first process was granted an exclusive row lock and the second process is waiting.

25. Switch to SQL Query Analyzer.

    Notice that the second query still has not completed.

26. Switch to the first connection.

27. Highlight ROLLBACK TRAN and then click the Execute Query button on the toolbar.

    Switch to the second query. Notice that it has now executed successfully. Also notice that the second query does not hold any exclusive locks at the end of the transaction.

28. Switch to SQL Server Enterprise Manager.

29. In the console tree, right-click the Current Activity container and then click Refresh.

30. In the details pane, double-click Locks/Process ID.

    Notice that no blocking locks or blocked processes appear.

31. Close SQL Server Enterprise Manager and SQL Query Analyzer.

Lesson Summary

When monitoring SQL Server performance and activity, determine the monitoring task and then select the appropriate tool. Rather than monitoring for everything all at once, perform specific and limited monitoring tasks. Repeat these same tasks over time to establish your evolving baseline. Use the SQL Server Enterprise Manager Current Activity window to manage deadlocks and to view current blocking locks.

Review

Here are some questions to help you determine whether you have learned enough to move on to the next chapter. If you have difficulty answering these questions, review the material in this chapter before beginning the next chapter. The answers for these questions are located in the Appendix, "Questions and Answers."

1. You have recently been hired as the new database administrator for a medium-sized database. You have been tasked with improving the performance of the database, although no specific problems are apparent. Where should you start?

2. You want to be able to quickly view overall levels of resource use on a computer running SQL Server to determine whether resources are adequate. What is the most appropriate tool for the task?

3. You have been viewing current server activity through SQL Server Enterprise Manager. You have noticed a number of blocking locks. What steps should you take to determine whether this is a serious problem?

C H A P T E R   1 5

Using SQL Server Replication

About This Chapter

This chapter prepares you to use SQL Server replication. You will learn about the types of replication that are available and physical replication topologies used to implement them. You will learn about the planning issues involved in setting up replication to perform efficiently and securely. You will learn to use SQL Server Enterprise Manager to implement replication, create publications, and configure Subscribers. Finally, you will learn to monitor replication and configure properties of Distributors and replication agents.

Before You Begin

To complete this chapter, you must have

- A computer that meets or exceeds the minimum hardware requirements listed in Table 2.1, "Hardware Requirements," in the Lesson 1 section of Chapter 2.
- Microsoft Windows 2000 Server running on your computer on an NTFS partition.
- A computer with a NetBIOS name of SelfPacedCPU configured as a domain controller in the SelfPacedSQL.MSFT domain.
- Installed a default instance and at least one named instance of SQL Server 2000 (see Chapter 2).

Lesson 1: Introducing Replication

SQL Server 2000 has several different replication solutions to enable you to distribute data and stored procedures between servers in your environment. In this lesson, you will learn about uses for replication and the terminology used in replication. Next, you will learn about each type of replication. You will also learn about physical replication topologies. Finally, you will learn about the different tools available for implementing a replication solution.

After this lesson, you will be able to

- Understand the replication terminology
- Describe how each type of replication functions
- Select among physical replication topologies
- Choose replication implementation tools

Estimated lesson time: 15 minutes

Describing Replication

Replication is the process of automatically distributing copies of data and database objects among SQL Server instances, and keeping the distributed information synchronized.

Reasons to Replicate Information

There are many reasons to replicate data and stored procedures among servers. These include

- **Reducing network traffic between separate physical locations.** Rather than requiring users in the New York office of a company to query data on a server in London across a link with limited bandwidth, the data could be replicated to a server in New York (at a time when the bandwidth was not heavily used) and accessed locally.
- **Separating OLTP operations from decision support functions.** Rather than having decision support personnel query a busy OLTP server, the data could be replicated to a dedicated decision support server for querying.
- **Combining data from multiple locations.** Data can be entered into a local SQL Server instance at each of several regional offices of a company and then replicated to the national (or international) office and merged automatically.
- **Data redundancy.** Data can be replicated to a standby server, which can be used for decision support queries, and provide a copy of data in the event of a server failure.

- **Scaling out.**   Data that you make available over the Internet can be replicated to various servers in different geographic regions for load balancing.
- **Supporting mobile users.**   Data can be replicated to laptop computers, which can be updated offline. When the mobile users reconnect to the network, changed data can be replicated to and synchronized with a centralized database.

Types of Replication

SQL Server 2000 supports three types of replication: snapshot, transactional, and merge. Snapshot replication is the periodic replication of an entire set of data as of a specific moment in time from a local server to remote servers. You would typically use this type of replication in databases where the amount of data to be replicated is small and the source data is static. You can grant remote servers a limited capability to update the replicated data. Transactional replication is the replication of an initial snapshot of data to remote servers plus the replication of individual transactions occurring at the local server that incrementally modify data contained in the initial snapshot. These replicated transactions are applied to the replicated data at each remote server to keep the data on the remote server synchronized with the data on the local server. You use this type of replication when you must keep the data current on the remote servers. You can grant remote servers a limited capability to update the replicated data. Merge replication is the replication of an initial snapshot of data to remote servers plus the replication of changes that occur at any remote server back to the local server for synchronization, conflict resolution, and re-replication to remote servers. You use merge replication when numerous changes are made to the same data, or when remote offline computers need to operate autonomously, such as in the case of a mobile user.

Replication Terminology

SQL Server replication uses terminology from the publishing industry to represent the components of replication. The server that is replicating stored information to other servers is called the Publisher. The information being replicated consists of one or more publications. Each publication is a logical collection of information from a single database consisting of one or more articles. An article can be one or more of the following:

- Part or all of a table (can be filtered by columns and/or rows)
- A stored procedure or view definition
- The execution of a stored procedure
- A view
- An indexed view
- A user-defined function

Each Publisher uses a Distributor to assist in the replication process. The Distributor stores the distribution database, history information, and metadata. The exact role of the Distributor varies with the type of replication. The Distributor used by a Publisher can be either local (the same SQL Server instance) or remote (a separate SQL Server instance).

Servers that receive replicated information are called Subscribers. Subscribers receive selected publications (called a subscription) from one or more Publishers. Depending upon the type of replication being implemented, Subscribers may be permitted to modify replicated information and replicate the changed information back to the Publisher. Subscribers can be specifically authorized or can be anonymous (such as for Internet publications). With large publications, the use of anonymous subscriptions can improve performance.

The replication process is automated through the use of replication agents. A replication agent is generally a SQL Server Agent job configured by an administrator to perform specified tasks on a specified schedule. By default, replication agents run in the security context of the SQL Server Agent domain user account on Windows 2000 and Windows NT 4.0. They run in the security context of the logged-in user on Windows Me and Windows 98. There are a number of replication agents for different replication tasks. Each agent is configured to run according to a specified schedule. Different types of replication use one or more of these agents.

- **Snapshot Agent.**   Creates an initial snapshot of each publication being replicated, including schema information. All types of replication use this agent. You can have one Snapshot Agent per publication.

- **Distribution Agent.**   Moves snapshot information and incremental changes from the Distributor to Subscribers. Snapshot and transactional replication use this agent. By default, all subscriptions to a publication share one distribution agent (called a shared agent). However, you can configure each subscription to have its own distribution agent (called an independent agent).

- **Log Reader Agent.**   Moves transactions marked for replication from the transaction log on the Publisher to the Distributor. Transactional replication uses this agent. Each database that you mark for transactional replication will have one Log Reader Agent that runs on the Distributor and connects to the Publisher.

- **Queue Reader Agent.**   Applies changes made by offline Subscribers to a Publication. Snapshot and transactional replication use this agent if queued updating is enabled. This agent runs on the Distributor and only one instance of this agent exists to service all Publishers and publications for a given Distributor.

- **Merge Agent.**   Moves snapshot information from the Distributor to Subscribers. It also moves and reconciles changes to replicated data between the Publisher and Subscribers. This agent also deactivates subscriptions whose data has not been updated within a maximum publication retention period (14 days by default). Merge replication uses this agent. Each subscription to a merge publication has its own merge agent that synchronizes data between the Publisher and the Subscriber.

- **Agent History Clean Up Agent.**   Removes agent history from the distribution database and is used to manage the size of the distribution database. All types of replication use this agent. This agent runs every 10 minutes by default.

- **Distribution Clean Up Agent.**   Removes replicated transactions from the distribution database, and deactivates inactive Subscribers whose data has not been updated within a specified maximum distribution retention period (72 hours by default). If anonymous subscriptions are permitted, replicated transactions are not removed until the maximum retention period expires. Snapshot and transactional replication use this agent. This agent runs every 10 minutes by default.

- **Expired Subscription Clean Up Agent.**   Detects and removes expired subscriptions. All types of replication use this agent. This agent runs once a day by default.

- **Reinitialize Subscriptions Having Data Validation Failures Agent.**   Reinitializes all subscriptions having data validation failures. This agent is run manually by default.

- **Replication Agents Checkup Agent.**   Detects replication agents that are inactive and logs this information to the Windows application log. This agent runs every 10 minutes by default.

Note   The Snapshot Agent, Distribution Agent, and Merge Agent can be embedded into applications using ActiveX controls.

Understanding the Types of Replication

To implement replication, you must understand how each type of replication functions. Each type of replication provides a replication solution with a different set of tradeoffs.

Snapshot Replication

With snapshot replication, the Snapshot Agent periodically (according to a specified schedule) copies all data marked for replication from the Publisher to a snapshot folder on the Distributor. The Distribution Agent periodically copies all the data in the snapshot folder to each Subscriber and updates the entire publication at the Subscriber with the updated snapshot information. The Snapshot Agent runs on the Distributor, and the Distribution Agent can run either on the Distributor or on each Subscriber. Both agents record history and error information to the distribution database. Figure 15.1 illustrates the snapshot replication process.

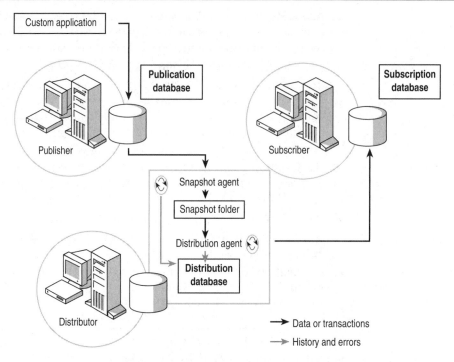

Figure 15.1.   The snapshot replication process.

Snapshot replication is most appropriate for data that does not change rapidly, for small publications that can be refreshed in their entirety without overwhelming the network, and for information that does not need to be completely current all the time (such as historical sales information).

With snapshot replication, you can elect to permit Subscribers to update replicated information using the Immediate Updating and/or Queued Updating options. These Updatable Subscription options are useful for occasional changes by Subscribers. If changes are frequent, use merge replication instead. Also, with the Updatable Subscription options, updates are part of a transaction. This means that the entire update either propagates or is rolled back if a conflict occurs. With merge replication, conflicts are resolved on a row-by-row basis.

If the Immediate Updating option is used, a two-phase commit (2PC) transaction is automatically initiated by the Subscriber with the Publisher whenever a Subscriber attempts to update replicated data. A 2PC transaction consists of a prepare phase and a commit phase under the control of the MS DTC service on the Subscriber, which serves as the transaction manager. During the prepare phase, the transaction manager coordinates with the SQL Server service on the Publisher and on the Subscriber, each acting as a resource manager, to ensure that the transaction can occur successfully in both databases. During the commit phase, if the transaction manager receives successful prepare notifications from each resource manager, the commit command is sent to each resource manager, and the transaction commits at the Publisher and the Subscriber. If a conflict exists on the Publisher (because of a conflicting update not yet replicated to the Subscriber), the transaction initiated by the Subscriber fails. The 2PC transaction ensures that no conflicts occur because the Publisher detects all conflicts before a transaction is committed.

If the Queued Updating option is used, changes made by a Subscriber are placed in a queue and periodically updated to the Publisher. Modifications can be made without an active network connection to the Publisher. The queued changes are applied at the Publisher when network connectivity is restored. Either the queue can be in a SQL Server database, or you can elect to use Microsoft Message Queuing if you are running Windows 2000. See "Queued Updating Components" in Books Online for more information on installing and using Microsoft Message Queuing. Because updates do not happen in real time, conflicts can occur if another Subscriber or the Publisher has changed the same data. Conflicts are resolved using a conflict resolution policy defined when the publication is created.

If you enable both options, Queued Updating functions as a failover in case Immediate Updating fails (such as due to a network failure). This is useful if the Publisher and updating Subscribers are normally connected, but you want to ensure that Subscribers can make updates in the event that network connectivity is lost.

Transactional Replication

With transactional replication, the Snapshot Agent copies an initial snapshot of data marked for replication and copies it from the Publisher to a snapshot folder on the Distributor. The Distribution Agent applies this initial snapshot to each Subscriber. The Log Reader Agent monitors changes to data marked for replication and captures each transaction log change into the distribution database on the Distributor. The Distribution Agent applies each change to each Subscriber in the original order of execution. If a stored procedure is used to update a large number of rows, the stored procedure can be replicated rather than each modified row. All three of these replication agents record history and error information to the distribution database. Figure 15.2 illustrates the transactional replication process.

The Distribution Agent can be scheduled to run continuously for minimum latency between the Publisher and Subscribers, or can be set to run on a specified schedule. Subscribers with a network connection to the Distributor can receive changes in near real time. After all Subscribers receive replicated transactions, the Distribution Clean Up Agent removes the transactions from the distribution database. If a Subscriber does not receive replicated transactions before the expiration of a specified retention period (72 hours by default), the replicated transaction is deleted and the subscription deactivated. This prevents the distribution database from becoming too large. A deactivated subscription can be reactivated and a new snapshot applied to bring the Subscriber current.

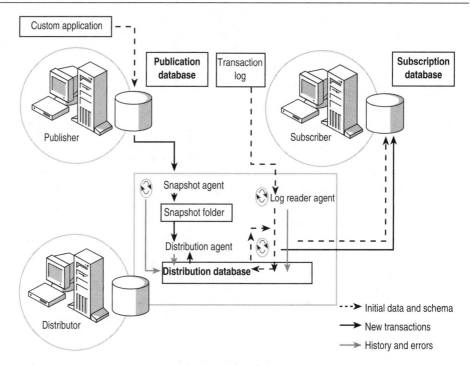

Figure 15.2.   Transactional replication process.

Transactional replication can also be configured to support Updatable Subscriptions using the Immediate Updating and/or Queued Updating options discussed in the preceding section for snapshot replication.

Merge Replication

With merge replication, the Snapshot Agent copies an initial snapshot of data marked for replication from the Publisher to a snapshot folder on the Distributor. The Merge Agent applies this initial snapshot to each Subscriber. The Merge Agent also monitors and merges changes to replicated data occurring at the Publisher and at each Subscriber. If a merged change results in a conflict at the Publisher, the Merge Agent resolves the conflict using a resolution method specified by the administrator. You can choose among a variety of conflict resolvers or create a custom resolver. Both agents record history and error information to the distribution database (this is the only function of the distribution database with merge replication). Figure 15.3 illustrates the merge replication process.

The Merge Agent relies on a unique column existing for each row in a table that is being replicated in order to identify the row across multiple copies of the table on multiple servers and to track conflicts between rows. If a unique column does not exist, the Snapshot Agent adds one when the publication is created. The Snapshot Agent also creates triggers on the Publisher when the publication is created. These triggers monitor replicated rows and record changes in merge system tables. The Merge Agent creates identical triggers on each Subscriber when the initial snapshot is applied.

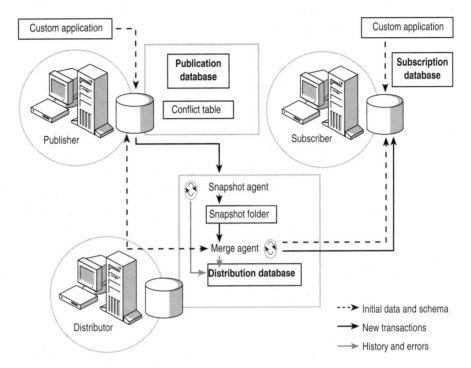

Figure 15.3.   Merge replication process.

The Merge Agent can be scheduled to run continuously for minimum latency between the Publisher and Subscribers, or can be set to run on a specified schedule. Subscribers with a network connection to the Publisher can receive changes in near real time. If a Subscriber does not receive replicated transactions before the expiration of a specified retention period (14 days by default), the subscription is deactivated. A deactivated subscription can be reactivated and a new snapshot applied to bring the Subscriber current.

Selecting a Physical Replication Model

There are a number of physical replication models that you can implement with your replication solution. If you are using snapshot or transactional replication, you will frequently use a remote Distributor. This Distributor may provide replication services to multiple Publishers and multiple Subscribers. If the amount of data being replicated is small, the Distributor and the Publisher frequently reside on the same computer.

If you are replicating over a link with a limited bandwidth or an expensive communications link to multiple Subscribers, you can publish to a remote Subscriber that republishes to other Subscribers on its side of the link. This remote Subscriber is called a Republisher or a Publishing Subscriber.

With merge replication, a central Subscriber is frequently used to merge information from multiple regional Publishers to a central location. This model requires horizontal partitioning of data to avoid conflicts and generally uses a column to identify regional data. This central Subscriber model can also be used with snapshot and transactional replication. In addition, because merge replication makes limited use of the distribution database, the Publisher and the Distributor frequently reside on the same computer.

Choosing Replication Implementation Tools

SQL Server Enterprise Manager is the primary tool used to implement and monitor replication. A Replication container serves as a central location to organize and administer publications and subscriptions. Replication Monitor, which is a node within the Replication container, is used to view and manage replication agents. Replication Monitor also includes the ability to set alerts on replication events.

In addition, you can implement, monitor, and administer replication using a number of other methods.

- **ActiveX Controls.**   Used within custom applications written using Visual Basic or Visual C++. ActiveX controls enable you to control Snapshot Agent, Merge Agent, and Distribution Agent activity programmatically. For example, an application can have a Synchronize button that you can click to activate the Merge Agent to merge and synchronize data on demand.
- **SQL-DMO.**   Used to create custom applications to configure, implement, or maintain a replication environment.
- **Replication Distributor Interface.**   Provides the ability to replicate data from heterogeneous data sources (such as Access or Oracle).
- **Stored Procedures.**   Used primarily to script replication on multiple servers, based on a replication configuration initially configured using SQL Server Enterprise Manager.
- **Windows Synchronization Manager.**   This utility is available with Windows 2000 in the Accessories program group and, with any computer using Internet Explorer 5.0, on the Tools menu. It is a centralized location for managing and synchronizing SQL Server publications and other applications (such as Web pages and e-mail).
- **Active Directory Services.**   You can publish replication objects to Active Directory, permitting users to discover and subscribe to publications (if permitted).

Lesson Summary

You can use replication to distribute data to multiple locations and automatically keep the data synchronized between all replication locations. There are three basic types of replication used to implement a replication solution: snapshot, transactional, and merge. Replication is automated through the use of replication agents performing tasks according to specified schedules. SQL Server Enterprise Manager is the primary tool used to implement, monitor, and administer replication solutions. ActiveX controls are also frequently embedded into custom applications to manage replication.

Lesson 2: Planning for Replication

Replication requires planning for a variety of issues, some of which will be covered in this lesson. In this lesson you will learn about planning replication security. You will also learn about filtering data for performance and security. Finally, you will learn about options for storing and applying the initial snapshot.

After this lesson, you will be able to

- Plan replication security
- Understand data filtering options
- Choose among initial snapshot options

Estimated lesson time: 15 minutes

Planning for Replication Security

Replication security is implemented at a number of levels. First, only members of the sysadmin server role can create and administer Distributors, Publishers, and Subscribers. This includes enabling a database for replication. At the database level, only a member of the sysadmin server role or the db_owner fixed database role in the database being published can create and configure publications and subscriptions. Only members of the sysadmin server role or the replmonitor fixed database role in the distribution database can view replication activity.

When a remote Distributor is used, security can be configured for connections between the Publisher and the Distributor. The connection uses the distributor_admin SQL Server login account (Mixed Mode Authentication must be used). At the remote Distributor, the Publisher can be configured as trusted (no password required) or nontrusted (requiring a password). Using a nontrusted configuration is recommended.

Note   The only ways you should change the distributor_admin password are: using the Distributor tab in Publisher And Distributor Properties in Enterprise Manager or using the *sp_changedistributor_password* system-stored procedure.

By default on Windows 2000 and Windows NT 4.0, the snapshot folder used for replication is located at C:\Program Files\Microsoft SQL Server\Mssql\Repldata on the Distributor and uses the hidden administrative share (for example, \\Self-PacedCPU\C$\Program Files\Microsoft SQL Server\Mssql\Repldata). On Windows Me and Windows 98, the same path is used but no share is created. Each Snapshot Agent must have full control access to this folder. Each Distribution Agent and Merge Agent must have read access to the snapshot folder location. By default on Windows 2000 and Windows NT 4.0, these agents run in the security context of the SQL Server Agent domain user account. Replication agents can only access this administrative share if the domain user account is a member of the local Administrators group on the Distributor. If the domain user account is not a member of the local Administrators group on the Distributor or if Windows Me and Windows 98 computers are involved in replication, you should create a share for the snapshot folder and grant necessary permissions to the share to the domain user accounts under which these replication agents will run.

Each publication contains a publication access list (PAL) containing the logins permitted to access the publication. By default, the logins included on the PAL for a new publication are members of the sysadmin server role (this includes the SQL Server Agent domain user account) and the login of the user creating the publication (such as a member of the db_owner role). In complex replication environments, you might need to add additional users to the PAL.

The following permissions are required in order for replication to function properly.

- The Snapshot Agent must be able to connect to the publication database on the Publisher and the distribution database on the Distributor (in addition to the snapshot folder discussed in the section "Transactional Replication").

- The Log Reader Agent must be able to connect to the publication database on the Publisher and the distribution database on the Distributor.

- The Distribution Agent must be able to connect to the distribution database on the Distributor and the subscription database on the Subscriber (in addition to the snapshot folder discussed in the section "Transactional Replication").

- The Merge Agent must be able to connect to the distribution database on the Distributor, the publication database on the Publisher, and the subscription database on the Subscriber (in addition to the snapshot folder discussed in the section "Transactional Replication").

Filtering Published Data

Filtering published data is used for security purposes and to enhance performance. Filtering allows you to limit published data horizontally (only specified rows) or vertically (only specified columns). For example, columns containing sensitive information or large image data can be eliminated from replication. Also, rows containing information not related to a particular sales region can be eliminated. Filters can be static or dynamic.

Static filters limit rows or columns for a publication, and all Subscribers receive the same data (unless transformable subscriptions are used). All types of replication can use static filters. To create different partitions of data for different Subscribers using static filters, either separate publications must be created or transformable subscriptions must be used. Horizontal filtering can significantly affect the performance of transactional replication because every row must be evaluated in the publication database transaction log.

Dynamic filters are used to provide different partitions of data to different Subscribers based on SQL Server functions (such as user name or host name). Join filters are used to maintain referential integrity between two tables involved in replication (such as a primary key/foreign key relationship). Dynamic and join filters are available only for merge replication. When you are using dynamic filters, dynamic snapshots can also be used to create custom snapshots for each type of Subscriber. This can significantly improve the performance when applying the initial snapshot, but does require additional space for the snapshot folder and additional time to create the initial snapshot.

Transformable subscriptions with a custom filter can be used with snapshot and transactional replication to dynamically create partitions of data for individual Subscribers. Transformable subscriptions use the capabilities of DTS to customize and transform data being replicated based on the needs of individual Subscribers. However, updatable subscriptions are incompatible with transformable subscriptions.

Choosing Initial Snapshot Options

By default, initial snapshot files are copied to the Repldata folder on the Distributor. However, you can choose to store the snapshot files in an alternate location, such as a network drive or on a compact disc, instead of or in addition to the default location. Snapshot files saved to an alternate location can be compressed (using the Microsoft CAB file format) to fit onto removable media or to speed transmission over a slow network connection. Compressing snapshot files takes additional time.

By default, either the Distribution Agent or the Merge Agent applies the snapshot to the subscription database. For large publications, applying the initial snapshot manually from compact disc or other storage device (such as tape) might be faster than sending the file over the network.

Finally, because snapshot files can consume substantial hard disk space, you can choose not to maintain snapshot files. Snapshot files are automatically retained if you specify that the snapshot be retained or if you enable the publication for anonymous subscriptions. If you choose neither of these options, SQL Server will delete the snapshot after all Subscribers have applied the initial snapshot. If a new Subscriber attempts to synchronize, the Subscriber will either have to wait until the next time a snapshot is generated automatically or an administrator will have to manually start the Snapshot Agent.

Lesson Summary

Only members of the sysadmin server role can configure the overall replication topology. Members of the sysadmin server role and the db_owner fixed database role in a database can create and configure publications and subscriptions. The Snapshot Agent must have full control permissions and the Distribution Agent and the Merge Agents must have read permissions to the snapshot folder (unless the initial snapshot is applied manually). In addition, the appropriate permissions must be granted to the replication agents on the publication, distribution, and subscription databases. In addition, published data is frequently filtered horizontally and vertically to improve performance and customize data based on individual Subscriber needs. In addition to static filters, dynamic filters and transformable subscriptions are used to filter data based on custom needs. Finally, the initial snapshot can be copied to an alternate location (such as a compact disk) and compacted using the Microsoft CAB file format.

Lesson 3: Implementing Replication

Replication is generally implemented using SQL Server Enterprise Manager wizards. In this lesson, you learn to configure the properties of a Distributor and a Publisher. You also learn to implement snapshot, transactional, and merge replication. Finally, you learn to configure push, pull, and anonymous subscriptions.

After this lesson, you will be able to

- Configure the properties of a Distributor
- Configure the properties of a Publisher
- Configure snapshot replication
- Configure transactional replication
- Configure merge replication
- Configure push, pull, and anonymous subscriptions

Estimated lesson time: 45 minutes

Configuring Distributor and Publisher Properties

You can configure the properties of a Distributor and a Publisher using the Configure Publishing And Distribution Wizard. You can also configure the properties of a Distributor and a Publisher as part of the process of creating a publication using the Create And Manage Publications Wizard. You can start the Configure Publishing And Distribution Wizard from the Tools menu by clicking Wizards, expanding the Replication container in the Select Wizard dialog box, and then double-clicking Configure Publishing And Distribution Wizard, or by right-clicking the Replication container and then clicking Configure Publishing, Subscribers, And Distribution. The Welcome To The Configure Publishing And Distribution Wizard page appears, as shown in Figure 15.4.

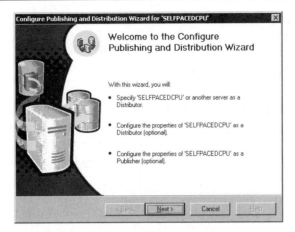

Figure 15.4. Starting the Configure Publishing And Distribution Wizard.

Click Next to either configure the local server as a Distributor or select an existing Distributor for this Publisher. The Select Distributor page appears, as shown in Figure 15.5.

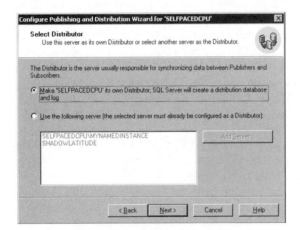

Figure 15.5. Selecting a Distributor.

The default is to use the local server as the Distributor, creating the distribution database and transaction log file. If you select a remote server, that server must already be configured as a Distributor. In addition, you must register the remote server with SQL Server Enterprise Manager before you can select it as the Distributor. Finally, you must have permission to use the remote Distributor.

Next, if you choose to use the local server as the Distributor, the Specify Snapshot Folder page appears where you can specify the location of the snapshot folder. The default location for the snapshot folder on the default instance is C:\Program Files\Microsoft SQL Server\Mssql\ReplData. See Figure 15.6.

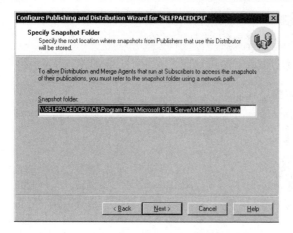

Figure 15.6.   Specifying a snapshot folder.

Notice in the Snapshot Folder text box that the default folder is using the C$ administrative share. The Snapshot Agent must have full control access to this folder, and the Distribution Agents and the Merge Agents must have read access. To use a dedicated share at a specified location, you can create the share through Windows Explorer or by clicking the Snapshot Folder ellipsis button. When the Browse For Folder dialog box appears, right-click the Repldata folder (or any other specified folder) and then click Properties. In the Repldata Properties dialog box, click the Sharing tab. Select the Share This Folder option button and then click the Permissions button. In the Permissions For Repldata dialog box, remove Everyone and then add the SQL Server Agent service domain user account, granting Full Control permissions. In Figure 15.7, a Repldata share is created.

In Figure 15.7, notice that the Repldata share is created and the SQL Server Agent domain user account granted Full Control permissions through the share. If additional users (such as Windows Me and Windows 98 users involved in merge replication) must access this snapshot folder, they can be granted read access to permit them to download the snapshot files.

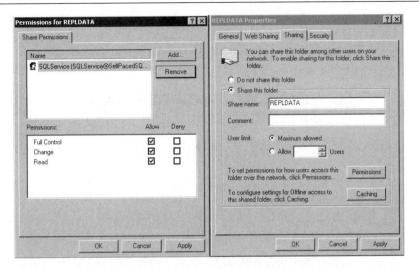

Figure 15.7.   Creating a share for the snapshot folder and assigning permissions.

Next, in the Customize The Configuration page, you are given the opportunity to customize the properties of the Distributor or accept the defaults. See Figure 15.8.

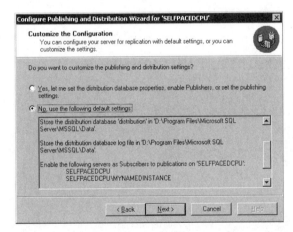

Figure 15.8.   Choosing the default settings for the Distributor.

Elect to customize settings if you need to change the default location for the distribution database and transaction log, enable additional Publishers to use this Distributor (only the local server is enabled by default), enable publication databases, or to change enabled Subscribers (all registered instances are enabled by default). Using RAID 1, RAID 10, or a dedicated drive for the distribution database and for the transaction log is recommended for most production environments.

If you elect to customize Distributor properties, the Provide Distribution Database Information page appears. In this page, you can modify the distribution database name, the location for the database file, and the location for the transaction log file. See Figure 15.9.

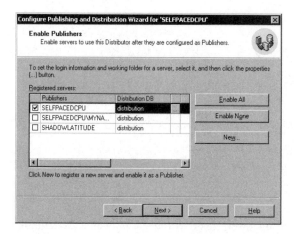

Figure 15.9.   Modifying distribution database properties.

Notice that you must choose a local path for the distribution database. Next, in the Enable Publishers page, you can enable additional Publishers. See Figure 15.10.

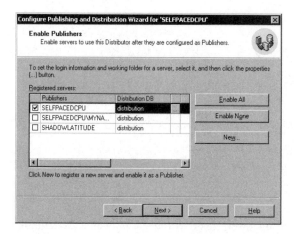

Figure 15.10.   Enabling additional Publishers to use a Distributor.

A Publisher cannot use a Distributor unless the Publisher is enabled on that Distributor. By default, only the current instance on the local server is enabled. Click a Publisher's ellipsis button in the Registered Servers grid to view Publisher properties for that Publisher. See Figure 15.11.

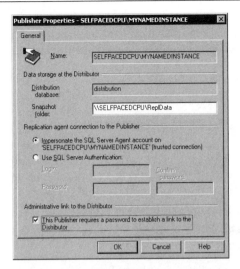

Figure 15.11.   Configuring Publisher properties.

Each Publisher can use a different snapshot folder. You can specify a SQL Server login account rather than the SQL Server Agent service domain user account for all replication agents. Finally, if the Publisher and the Distributor are on separate computers, you can require a password for the link between the two (recommended).

Next, in the Enable Publication Databases page, you can enable specific databases for replication. See Figure 15.12.

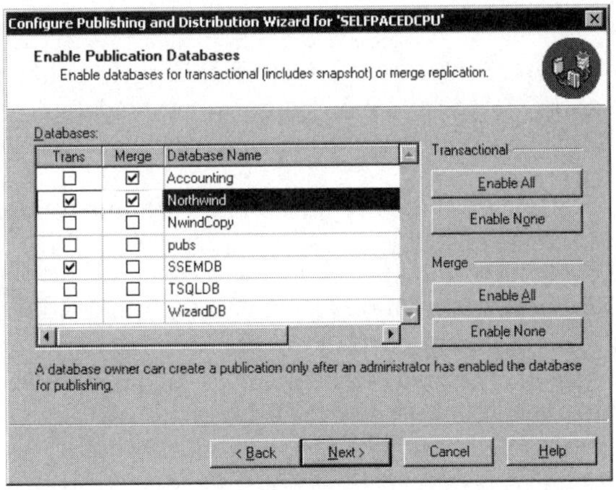

Figure 15.12.   Enabling databases for replication.

A member of the sysadmin server role can also enable a database for replication at the time a publication is created. However, if a member of the db_owner fixed database role in a database will be creating the publications, a member of the sysadmin server role must first enable the database for replication. In the Trans column of the

Databases grid, click the appropriate Trans check box to enable a database for snapshot or transactional replication. In the Merge column, click the appropriate Merge check box to enable a database for merge replication.

Next, in the Enable Subscribers page, you can enable specified servers to subscribe to publications from this Publisher. See Figure 15.13.

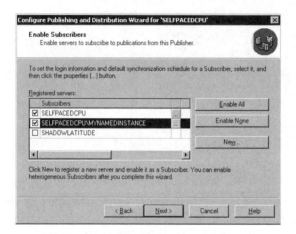

Figure 15.13.   Enabling Subscribers.

All registered servers are enabled by default. Click the ellipsis button to display the Subscriber Properties dialog box. You use the General tab of this dialog box to configure Subscriber login information and a default synchronization schedule for a Subscriber. See Figure 15.14.

Similar to other replication agents, a replication agent connecting to a Subscriber uses the SQL Server Agent domain user account by default. You can elect to use a SQL Server login account.

Click the Schedules tab to modify the default schedule for each Distribution and Merge Agent. See Figure 15.15.

Notice that each new Distribution Agent is set to run continuously by default and that each new Merge Agent is set to run hourly by default. You can change these defaults. You can also override these default schedules for each new agent when configuring new subscriptions.

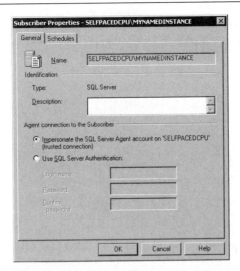

Figure 15.14.   General Subscriber properties.

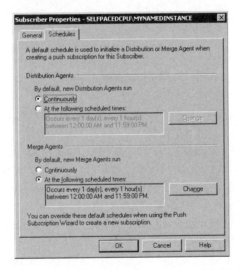

Figure 15.15.   Default schedules for all Distribution Agents and Merge Agents.

Finally, in the Completing The Configure Publishing And Distribution Wizard page, you can review all of your choices before the distribution database is created and the Distributor and Publisher configured. See Figure 15.16.

After the Configure Publishing And Distribution Wizard completes, a SQL Server Enterprise Manager message box appears to notify you that Replication Monitor has been added to the console tree. Using Replication Monitor is covered in Lesson 4 of this chapter.

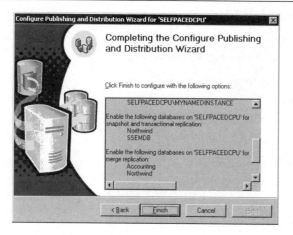

Figure 15.16.   Final review of Distributor and Publisher properties.

Practice: Configuring a Distributor

In this practice you create and configure a Distributor using the Configure Publishing And Distribution Wizard in the SQL Server Enterprise Manager.

► **To configure a Distributor**

1. Ensure that you are logged on to the SelfPacedSQL.MSFT domain controller as Administrator.
2. Click Start, point to Programs, point to Microsoft SQL Server, and then click Enterprise Manager.

   SQL Server Enterprise Manager appears displaying the Microsoft SQL Servers and the Event Viewer (Local) console trees in the console root.
3. In the console tree, expand the Microsoft SQL Servers container, expand the SQL Server Group container, and then expand the default instance.
4. Right-click the Replication container and then click Configure Publishing, Subscribers, And Distribution.

   The Welcome To The Configure Publishing And Distribution Wizard page appears.
5. Click Next.

   The Select Distributor page appears.
6. Verify that SelfPacedCPU is selected to be its own Distributor and then click Next.

   The Specify Snapshot Folder page appears.
7. Click the ellipsis next to the Snapshot Folder text box.

   The Browse For Folder dialog box appears with the Repldata folder selected.
8. Right-click the Repldata folder and then click Sharing.

   The Repldata Properties dialog box appears.

9. Click the Share This Folder option button.

10. Click the Permissions button.

    The Permissions For Repldata dialog box appears.

11. Click the Remove button to remove Everyone from the Name list box, and then click the Add button.

    The Select Users, Computers, Or Groups dialog box appears.

12. In the Name list box, double-click SQLService and then click OK. In the Permissions group box, select the Full Control check box.

13. Click OK to close the Permissions For Repldata dialog box.

14. Click OK to close the Repldata Properties dialog box.

15. Click OK to close the Browse For Folder dialog box.

16. In the Snapshot Folder text box, type **\\SelfPacedCPU\Repldata** (replacing the default entry that uses the C$ hidden administrative share), and then click Next.

    A SQL Server Enterprise Manager dialog box appears stating that the \\SelfpacedCPU\Repldata path cannot be verified and asking whether you want to use it anyway.

17. Click the Yes button.

    The Customize The Configuration page appears.

18. Verify that the No, Use The Following Default Settings option button is selected, review the Distributor properties, and then click Next.

    The Completing The Configure Publishing And Distribution Wizard page appears.

19. Click the Finish button to configure SelfPacedCPU as a Distributor.

    A SQL Server Enterprise Manager dialog box appears to show the progress of the Distributor configuration.

20. When a SQL Server Enterprise Manager message box appears stating that the SelfPacedCPU was successfully enabled as the Distributor, click OK.

    A SQL Server Enterprise Manager dialog box appears stating that Replication Monitor has been added to the console tree.

21. Click the Close button. Leave SQL Server Enterprise Manager running.

Creating a Publication

To create your first publication, use the Create Publication Wizard. You can start this wizard from the Tools menu by clicking Wizards, expanding the Replication container in the Select Wizard dialog box, and then double-clicking Create Publication Wizard. Alternatively, you can right-click the Publications container in the console tree (in the Replication container) and then click New Publication. The Welcome To The Create Publication Wizard page appears as shown in Figure 15.17.

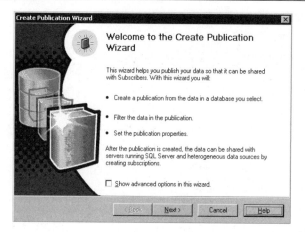

Figure 15.17.   Starting the Create Publication Wizard.

Notice that you can select the Show Advanced Options In This Wizard check box. Showing advanced options allows the enabling of updatable and transformable subscriptions.

Next, in the Choose Publication Database page, select the database containing the data and objects to publish. See Figure 15.18.

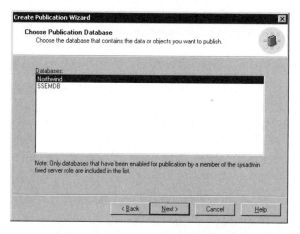

Figure 15.18.   Select the publication database.

If a member of the sysadmin server role runs the Create Publication Wizard, all user databases are displayed and any database selected is automatically enabled for replication. If a member of the db_owner fixed database role in a database runs the Create Publication Wizard, the only databases that will appear are databases that have previously been enabled for replication and with respect to which they are db_owners.

Next, in the Select Publication Type page, you select the type of publication. See Figure 15.19.

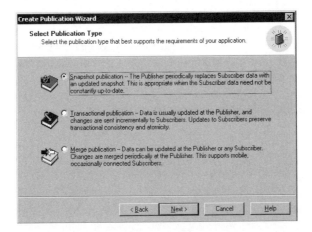

Figure 15.19.   Select the type of publication.

You can select the Snapshot Publication, Transactional Publication, or Merge Publication option button.

Creating a Snapshot Publication

If you select the Snapshot Publication option button and you opted to view advanced options, the Updatable Subscriptions page appears. In this page, you can enable the immediate updating and/or the queued updating options. See Figure 15.20.

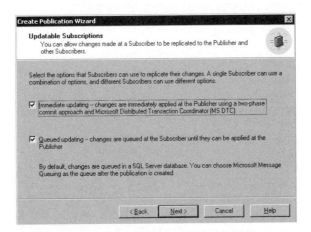

Figure 15.20.   Enabling updatable subscriptions.

Notice that if you selected queued updating, changes are queued in a SQL Server database by default. If you want to use Microsoft Message Queuing, you enable this after the publication is created.

If you do not enable updatable subscriptions, the Transform Published Data page appears, and you can choose to permit transformable subscriptions. See Figure 15.21. This is an advanced option that will not appear unless you select the Show Advanced Options In This Wizard check box (see Figure 15.17).

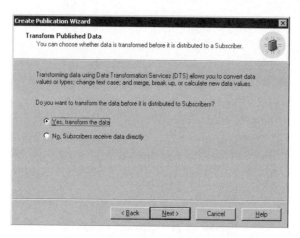

Figure 15.21.   Permitting transformable subscriptions.

Next, in the Specify Subscriber Types page, you must specify the types of Subscribers that will subscribe to this publication. See Figure 15.22.

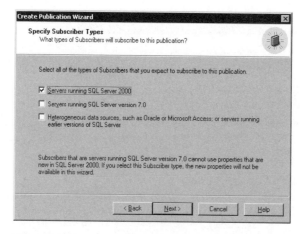

Figure 15.22.   Specifying the type of Subscriber.

If you specify that a publication will be supporting subscriptions from SQL Server 7.0 and heterogeneous data sources, options that are incompatible with these types of Subscribers will not be displayed in the wizard. For example, replicating views to SQL Server 7.0 Subscribers is not supported.

Note   If you specify SQL Server 2000 Subscribers, but do not enable any of the new features, SQL Server 7.0 or heterogeneous data sources will still be able to subscribe to the publication.

Next, in the Specify Articles page, specify the articles that will be published as part of this publication. See Figure 15.23.

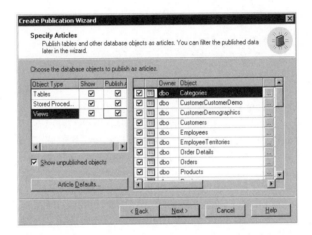

Figure 15.23.   Specifying articles for publication.

You can select among tables, stored procedures, and views. You might not see all three types of objects, depending upon choices you made earlier. For example, if you permit transformable subscriptions, you can only publish tables. With respect to published tables, stored procedures, or views, click the Article Defaults button to globally set properties or the ellipsis button for each object to configure properties specifically for the article. By default, replicated articles have the same name in the subscription database as in the publication database. In addition, if a database object with the same name exists in the subscription database, by default it is dropped and re-created. You can also choose to replicate additional objects (such as user triggers) or not replicate indexes (they are replicated by default). For example, click the Article Defaults button to display the Default Article Type dialog box, double-click Table Articles to display the Default Table Article Properties dialog box, and then click the Snapshot tab to modify default table article properties. Figure 15.24 shows the Default Table Article Properties dialog box with the Snapshot tab selected.

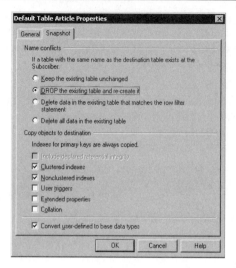

Figure 15.24. Modifying default table article properties.

Next, in the Article Issues box, depending upon the articles you choose to publish and the type of subscriptions permitted, you might receive a message regarding issues involving uniqueidentifier, timestamp, and IDENTITY columns. There are specific types of issues for each column type depending upon the replication type and design of the published database. Refer to the topic "Article Issues" in Books Online for more information regarding these issues. You might also receive a message regarding tables, objects, and views referencing objects not included in the publication. If a database object references other database objects, you must publish each of these database objects or create them manually at the Subscriber. Figure 15.25 displays an Article Issues page.

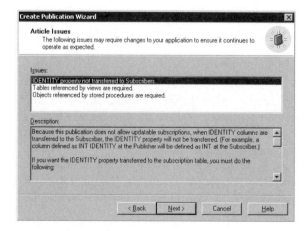

Figure 15.25. Article issues.

In Figure 15.25, notice that an IDENTITY column is being replicated. By default, the value of the column will be replicated, but not the IDENTITY property of the column.

Next, in the Select Publication Name And Description page, select a descriptive name for the publication, describe the publication, and choose whether to list the publication in Active Directory. The option to list the publication in the Active Directory will be grayed out if the SQL Server instance has not been listed in the Active Directory database. See Figure 15.26.

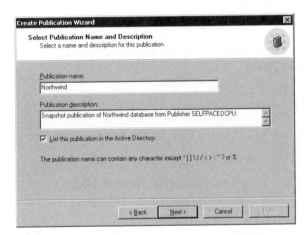

Figure 15.26.   Naming the publication and listing it in Active Directory.

Next, in the Customize The Properties Of The Publication page, you can elect to customize the publication by defining data filters, enabling anonymous subscriptions, and configuring a custom schedule for the Snapshot Agent. See Figure 15.27. By default, the Snapshot Agent runs immediately after the publication is created and weekly thereafter.

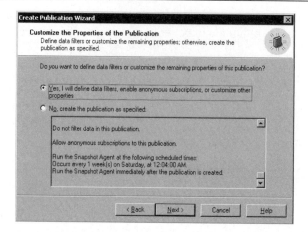

Figure 15.27.   Choosing to customize the publication properties.

If you elect to customize the publication, the Filter Data page appears. You can choose to filter the articles in the publication vertically and/or horizontally. See Figure 15.28.

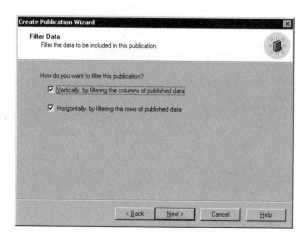

Figure 15.28.   Choosing to filter data.

If you chose to filter vertically, the Filter Table Columns page appears. You can elect to exclude specific columns from any published table. See Figure 15.29.

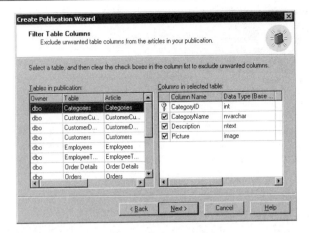

Figure 15.29.   Filtering table columns.

By default, all columns are published. To exclude a column, select an article and then clear the check box for the column.

If you chose to filter horizontally, the Filter Table Rows page appears. See Figure 15.30. You can elect to limit rows by selecting the article and then clicking the ellipsis button to display the Specify Filter dialog box. See Figure 15.31. By default, all rows are published.

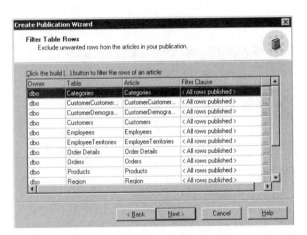

Figure 15.30.   Filtering table rows.

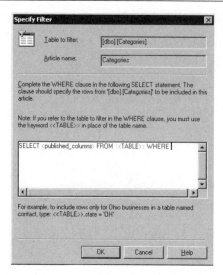

Figure 15.31.   Specifying a row filter.

In the Specify Filter dialog box, to filter published rows for a selected article, complete the WHERE clause. Next, in the Allow Anonymous Subscriptions page, you can choose to permit anonymous subscriptions. See Figure 15.32. This is an advanced option that will not appear unless you select the Show Advanced Options In This Wizard check box (see Figure 15.17). This option is used primarily for Internet publishing or for publications to a large number of Subscribers.

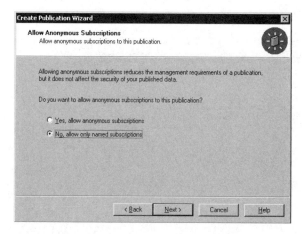

Figure 15.32.   Allowing anonymous subscriptions.

If you choose to filter the publication vertically and horizontally, both the Filter Table Columns page and the Filter Table Rows page will appear. Next, in the Set Snapshot Agent Schedule page, you can accept the default schedule or click the Change button to modify the schedule. By default, the Snapshot Agent generally runs nightly (weekly is the default setting for publications that support anonymous subscriptions). Also, there is an option to create the first snapshot immediately if anonymous Subscribers are supported. Otherwise, you generally create the initial snapshot when you create the first subscription. See Figure 15.33.

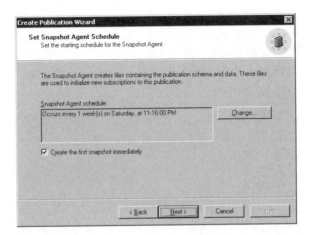

Figure 15.33.   Setting the Snapshot Agent schedule.

Finally, in the Completing The Create Publication Wizard page, review the publication options and then click the Finish button. See Figure 15.34.

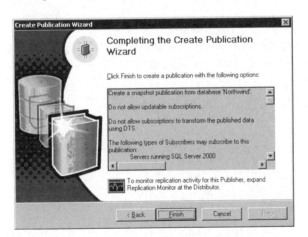

Figure 15.34.   Completing the Create Publication Wizard.

Creating a Transactional Publication

Creating a transactional publication is substantially the same as creating a snapshot publication.

Practice: Creating a Transactional Publication

In this practice you create a transactional publication using the Create Publication Wizard in the SQL Server Enterprise Manager.

▶ **To create a transactional publication**

1. In the SQL Server Enterprise Manager console tree, expand the Replication container for the default instance.

2. Right-click the Publications container and then click New Publication.

    The Welcome To The Create Publication Wizard page appears.

3. Select the Show Advanced Options In This Wizard check box and then click Next.

    The Choose Publication Database page appears.

4. In the Databases list box, click Pubs and then click Next.

    The Select Publication Type page appears.

5. Click the option button labeled Transactional Publication – Data Is Usually Updated At The Publisher, And Changes Are Sent Incrementally To Subscribers. Updates To Subscribers Preserve Transactional Consistency And Atomicity, and then click Next.

    The Updatable Subscriptions page appears.

6. Select both the Immediate Updating – Changes Are Immediately Applied At The Publisher Using A Two-Phase Commit Approach And Microsoft Distributed Transaction Coordinator (MS DTC) check box and the Queued Updating – Changes Are Queued At The Subscriber Until They Can Be Applied At The Publisher check box, and then click Next.

    The Specify Subscriber Types page appears.

7. Verify that only the Servers Running SQL Server 2000 check box is selected and then click Next.

    The Specify Articles page appears.

8. Locate the Tables cell in the Object Type column, and then select the corresponding Publish All check box.

9. Locate the Stored Procedures cell in the Object Type column, and then select the corresponding Publish All check box.

    Notice that tables without primary keys will not be published.

10. Click Next.

    The Article Issues page appears.

11. Click Next.

    The Select Publication Name And Description page appears.

12. In the Publication Name text box, type **PubsSales** and then click Next.

    The Customize The Properties Of The Publication page appears.

13. Verify that the No, Create The Publication As Specified option button is selected, review the publication properties, and then click Next.

    The Completing The Create Publication Wizard page appears.

14. Click the Finish button to create the publication.

    Notice that a SQL Server Enterprise Manager dialog box appears to show the progress of the publication being created.

15. When a second SQL Server Enterprise Manager dialog box appears stating that the publication was successfully created, click the Close button.

16. Do not close SQL Server Enterprise Manager.

Configuring Merge Replication

When you select the merge publication option in the Select Publication Type page of the Create Publication Wizard (see Figure 15.19), the Specify Subscriber Types page appears. In addition to the types of Subscribers supported by other publication types, you can also choose to support Subscribers with devices running SQL Server CE. See Figure 15.35.

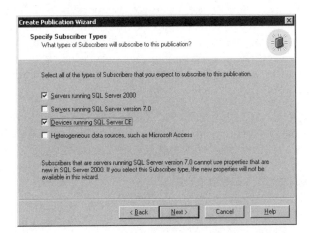

Figure 15.35.   Specifying Subscribers using SQL Server CE devices.

Note   If you choose to support devices running Windows CE, anonymous subscriptions are enabled and cannot be disabled.

In the Specify Articles page (see Figure 15.23), you can customize conflict resolution settings for a merge publication. Click the Article Defaults button to display the Default Article Type dialog box, and then click Table Articles to display the Default Table Article Properties dialog box. See Figure 15.36.

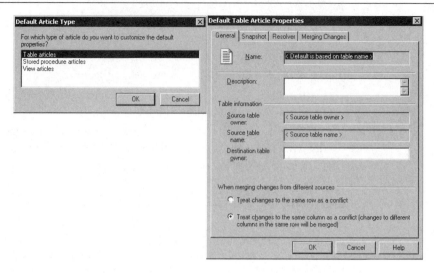

Figure 15.36. Defining what constitutes a conflict.

By default, in the General tab, when you are merging changes from multiple sources, changes must be made to the same column to be considered a conflict. You can change this default to specify that changes to any column in a given row be considered a conflict. For example, if one Subscriber changes the phone number for a supplier and another Subscriber changes the contact name for the supplier, by default this is not considered a conflict.

Click the Resolver tab to permit Subscribers to interactively resolve conflicts during on-demand synchronizations. Subscribers cannot use Windows Synchronization Manager unless this check box is selected. See Figure 15.37.

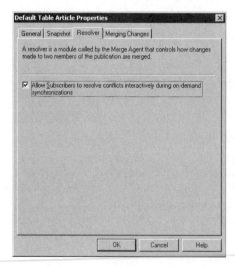

Figure 15.37. Permitting interactive conflict resolution.

In the Merging Changes tab, you can choose to add an additional layer of permissions. See Figure 15.38.

You can require that the Merge Agent security account have permissions to perform INSERT, UPDATE, and DELETE commands, in addition to the permissions required to access the publication database. This is used to limit the types of changes a Subscriber can make. This permission information is stored in the snapshot. If these permissions are changed after the initial snapshot is created, a new snapshot must be created. In addition, by default, multicolumn updates in the same row are made in a single *UPDATE* statement.

In addition to changing the default merge conflict properties, you can change the conflict resolution properties for each article by clicking the ellipsis button next to the article in the Specify Articles page and then clicking the Resolver tab when the Table Article Properties dialog box appears. See Figure 15.39.

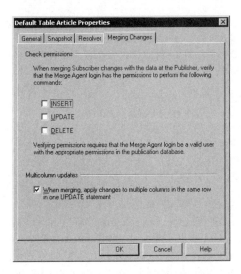

Figure 15.38.   Requiring additional permissions for the Merge Agent.

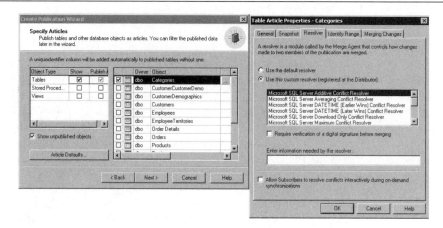

Figure 15.39.   Specifying a custom resolver for an article.

By default, conflicts are resolved based on a priority weighting system. With this default resolver, all Subscribers have equal priority (although you can grant different Subscribers different priorities), and the first change to synchronize takes precedence in the event of a conflict.

Instead of the default resolver, you can select either one of the custom resolvers that ship with SQL Server 2000 or create your own using stored procedures or COM objects. The custom resolvers provided with SQL Server 2000 can resolve conflicts in a number of different ways, including the earliest change, most recent change, highest value, lowest value, or averaging. See the topic "Microsoft Resolver Descriptions" in Books Online for a full description of each custom resolver.

In addition, in the Identity Range tab, for any article containing an IDENTITY column, you can choose to have SQL Server automatically assign a range of values for each Subscriber. This allows each Subscriber to add new rows using the IDENTITY property and still ensure that no duplicate values occur. See Figure 15.40.

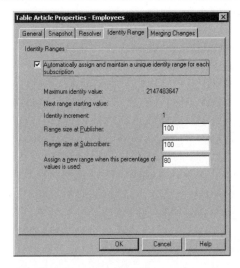

Figure 15.40.   Defining identity ranges for Subscribers.

The next two pages, the Article Issues page and the Select Publication Name and Description page, are substantially identical to the equivalent pages for a Snapshot or a Transaction Replication publication. See Figures 15.25 and 15.26.

In the Filter Data page, if you choose to customize the properties of the publication, you can filter the publication vertically and/or horizontally. See Figure 15.41.

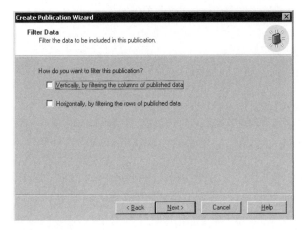

Figure 15.41.   Choosing to filter a publication vertically and/or horizontally.

If you chose to filter data vertically, the Filter Table Columns page appears. See Figure 15.28. If you choose to filter data horizontally, merge replication permits you to choose between dynamic and static filters on the Enable Dynamic Filters page. See Figure 15.42.

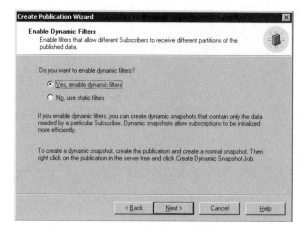

Figure 15.42.   Choosing dynamic filters.

Next, in the Generate Filters Automatically page, you can choose to generate either static or dynamic horizontal filters automatically. See Figure 15.43.

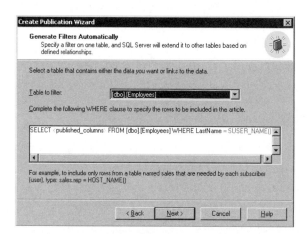

Figure 15.43.   Generating filters automatically.

Using this capability, you specify a table containing a column of the characteristics on which you want to filter. For example, in Figure 15.43, the initial filter is based on the LastName column in the Employees table and the name of the logged-in user. Next, in the Filter Table Rows page, SQL Server uses this initial filter to create suggested filters (using join filters) for related tables to limit data being replicated based on the user name. See Figure 15.44.

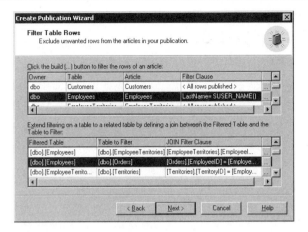

Figure 15.44.   Automatically generated filters.

Next, in the Validate Subscriber Information page, by default SQL Server validates Subscriber information used in the dynamic filter automatically each time the Merge Agent reconnects. This page appears only if you have enabled dynamic filters. See Figure 15.45.

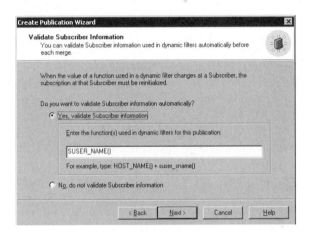

Figure 15.45.   Validating dynamic filter information automatically.

This is used to ensure that information is partitioned consistently with each merge. Based on the filtering function used in Figure 15.45, if a Subscriber logs in using a different user name and attempts to synchronize, the synchronization would fail. Generally this is the desired behavior.

Next, in the Optimize Synchronization page, you can choose to improve synchronization performance by storing additional information at the Publisher. See Figure 15.46.

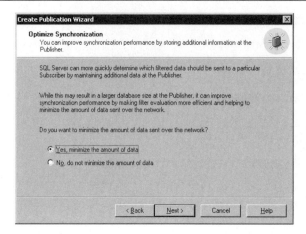

Figure 15.46. Optimizing the synchronization performance setting.

Click the Yes, Minimize The Amount Of Data option button to choose to optimize synchronization during merge replication. This minimizes network traffic when determining whether a change at the Publisher is within the partition of data that needs to be merged with a Subscriber. This is very useful for synchronization over slow network links, but does require additional storage space at the Publisher.

The next two pages, the Allow Anonymous Subscriptions page and the Set Snapshot Agent Schedule page, are substantially identical to the equivalent pages for a Snapshot or a Transaction Replication publication (see Figures 15.32 and 15.33). The Allow Anonymous Subscriptions page is an advanced option that will not appear unless you select the Show Advanced Options In This Wizard check box (see Figure 15.17). On the Set Snapshot Agent Schedule page, by default, the initial snapshot is run immediately for merge publications. Finally, the Completing The Create Publication Wizard appears (see Figure 15.34).

Note If you enable dynamic filters, you can create dynamic snapshots after creating the normal snapshot by right-clicking the publication and then clicking Create Dynamic Snapshot Job.

Practice: Creating a Merge Publication

In this practice you create a merge publication using the Create Publication Wizard in the SQL Server Enterprise Manager.

▶ **To create a merge publication**

1. In the SQL Server Enterprise Manager console tree, expand the Replication container for the default instance.

2. Right-click the Publications container and then click New Publication.

   The Welcome To The Create Publication Wizard page appears.

3. Select the Show Advanced Options In This Wizard check box and then click Next.

   The Choose Publication Database page appears.

4. In the Databases list box, click Northwind and then click Next.

   The Select Publication Type page appears.

5. Click the option button labeled Merge Publication – Data Can Be Updated At The Publisher Or Any Subscriber. Changes Are Merged Periodically At The Publisher. This Supports Mobile, Occasionally Connected Subscribers, and then click Next.

   The Specify Subscriber Types page appears.

6. Verify that only the Servers Running SQL Server 2000 check box is selected and then click Next.

   The Specify Articles page appears.

7. Click the Article Defaults button.

   The Default Article Type dialog box appears.

8. Verify Table Articles is selected and then click OK.

   The Default Table Article Properties dialog box appears.

9. Click the Resolver tab.

10. Select the Allow Subscribers To Resolve Conflicts Interactively During On-Demand Synchronization check box, and then click OK.

    The Specify Articles dialog box reappears.

11. Locate the Tables cell in the Object Type column, and then select the corresponding Publish All check box.

12. Click Next.

    The Article Issues page appears.

13. Click Next.

    The Select Publication Name And Description page appears.

14. In the Publication Name text box, type **NorthwindSales** and then click Next.

    The Customize The Properties Of The Publication page appears.

15. Click the Yes, I Will Define Data Filters, Enable Anonymous Subscriptions, Or Customize Other Properties option button and then click Next.

    The Filter Data page appears.

16. Select the Horizontally, By Filtering The Rows Of Published Data check box and then click Next.

    The Enable Dynamic Filters page appears.

17. Verify that the No, Use Static Filters option button is selected and then click Next.

    The Generate Filters Automatically page appears.

18. To create a user-defined function to use for the filter, click Start, point to Programs, point to Microsoft SQL Server, and then click Query Analyzer.

    The Connect To SQL Server dialog box appears.

19. Ensure that the Windows Authentication option button is selected, and then click OK to connect to the default instance on SelfPacedCPU.

    On the toolbar, click the Load SQL Script button.

    The Open Query File dialog box appears.

20. Open the UDF.sql file in C:\SelfPacedSQL\CH_15.

    The script creates a user-defined function to return rows based on the week number.

21. On the toolbar, click the Execute Query button.

22. After the script executes successfully, close Query Analyzer to return to the Create Publication Wizard.

23. In the Table To Filter drop-down list, click [dbo].[Orders].

24. In the text box, complete the WHERE clause in the *SELECT* statement by typing **dbo.udf_wknum(orderdate) between 1 and 12** and then click Next.

    A SQL Server Enterprise Manager dialog box appears to display the progress of the filters being generated for the publication. When the filters have been created, the Filter Table Rows page appears.

25. Click Next.

    The Optimize Synchronization page appears.

26. Click the Yes, Minimize The Amount Of Data option button and then click Next.

    The Allow Anonymous Subscriptions page appears.

27. Verify that the No, Allow Only Named Subscriptions option button is selected and then click Next.

    The Set Snapshot Agent Schedule page appears.

28. Verify that the Create The First Snapshot Immediately check box is selected and then click Next.

    The Completing The Create Publication Wizard page appears.

29. Review the properties of the publication and then click the Finish button to create the publication.

    Notice that a SQL Server Enterprise Manager dialog box appears to display the progress of the publication being created.

30. When a second SQL Server Enterprise Manager dialog box appears stating that the publication was successfully created, click the Close button.

31. Do not close SQL Server Enterprise Manager.

Configuring Push Subscriptions

Once you have created a publication, you can configure push subscriptions on the Publisher using the Push Subscription Wizard. A *push subscription* is a subscription that is initiated and configured centrally from the Publisher. You can start this wizard from the Tools menu by clicking Wizards, expanding the Replication container in the Select Wizard dialog box, and then double-clicking Create Push Subscription Wizard, or by right-clicking a publication and then clicking Push New Subscription. The Welcome To The Push Subscription Wizard page appears, illustrated in Figure 15.47.

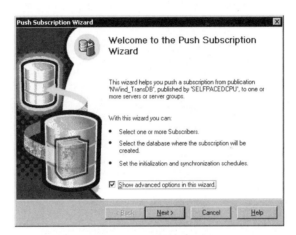

Figure 15.47.   Starting the Push Subscription Wizard.

Notice that you can select the Show Advanced Options In This Wizard check box. Showing advanced options allows the updatable subscription options to be set and the configuring of the applicable replication agent to run at the Subscriber rather than the Distributor.

Next, in the Choose Subscribers page, select the Subscribers to whom you want to push this publication. See Figure 15.48. You select one or more Subscribers. A Subscriber must be enabled. If a member of the sysadmin server role runs the Push Subscription Wizard, a registered instance can be enabled on the fly. If a member of the db_owner role in a database runs the Push Subscription Wizard, no additional Subscribers can be enabled.

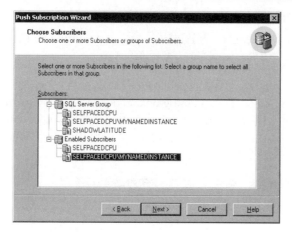

Figure 15.48.   Choosing Subscribers.

Next, in the Choose Destination Database page, specify a destination database for the publication. See Figure 15.49.

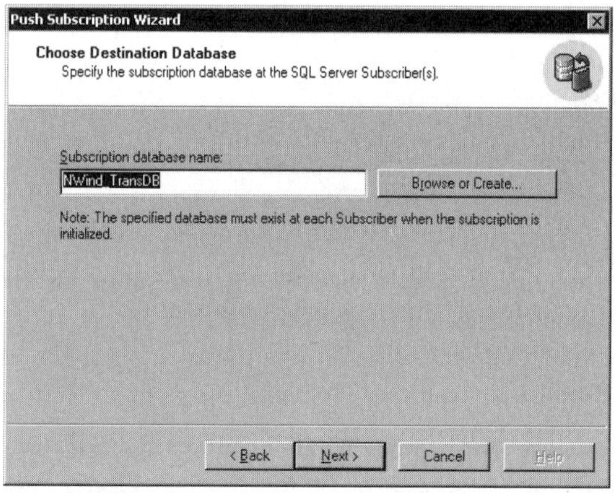

Figure 15.49.   Choosing a destination database.

By default the name of the destination database (also called the subscription database) is the same as the publication database. The destination database must exist at each Subscriber prior to initialization. Click the Browse Or Create button to either verify or create the subscription database.

Next, depending upon the type of publication, specify the location for the Distribution Agent in the Set Distribution Agent Location page (see Figure 15.50) or the Merge Agent in the Set Merge Agent Location page (see Figure 15.51). By default, this agent runs at the Distributor, using the server resources of the Distributor. However, you can elect to have this agent run at the Subscriber, using the server resources of the Subscriber (provided the Subscriber is running Windows 2000 or

Windows NT 4.0). This is an advanced option that will not appear unless you select the Show Advanced Options In This Wizard check box (see Figure 15.47).

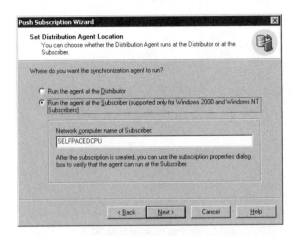

Figure 15.50. Setting the Distribution Agent location.

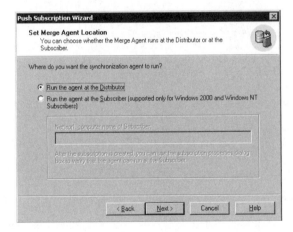

Figure 15.51. Setting the Merge Agent location.

Next, specify the Schedule for the Distribution Schedule Agent in the Set Distribution Agent Schedule page (see Figure 15.52) or the Merge Agent in the Set Merge Agent Schedule page. See Figure 15.53.

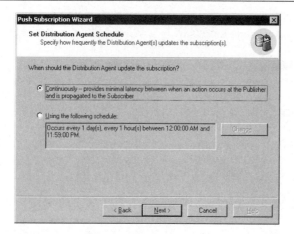

Figure 15.52.   Setting the Distribution Agent schedule.

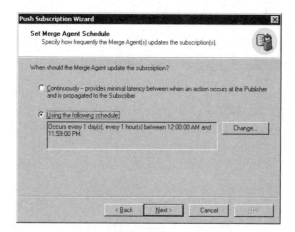

Figure 15.53.   Setting the Merge Agent schedule.

Notice that the default schedule for Distribution Agents is continuous and the default schedule for Merge Agents is hourly.

Next, in the Initialize Subscription page, specify whether and when to initialize the subscription. Figure 15.54 illustrates specifying initialization by the Distribution Agent and Figure 15.55 illustrates specifying initialization by the Merge Agent.

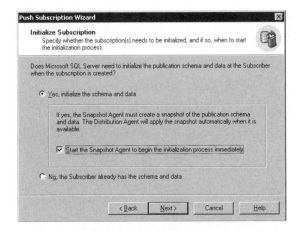

Figure 15.54.   Specifying initialization by the Distribution Agent.

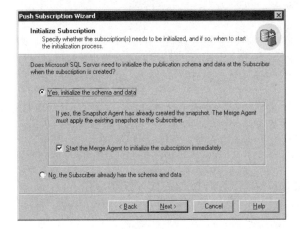

Figure 15.55.   Specifying initialization by the Merge Agent.

You can choose to have the Snapshot Agent create the snapshot immediately (if it has not already done so) and then initialize the subscription (rather than wait for the next scheduled run of the Snapshot Agent) by clicking the Yes, Initialize The Schema And Data option button and then selecting the Start The Snapshot Agent To Begin The Initialization Process Immediately check box. This check box will not appear if the snapshot files have not already been created. Remember, the snapshot files must be created before the Distribution Agent or Merge Agent can initialize the subscription. If you have applied the snapshot files manually (using a compact disc or other removable media), specify that the Subscriber already has the schema and data by clicking the No, The Subscriber Already Has The Schema And Data option button.

Next, in the Updatable Subscriptions page, if you are configuring a subscription for a snapshot or transactional publication supporting one of the updatable subscriptions options, you can specify the type of updatable subscriptions. The available options on this page will vary depending on the type of updatable subscriptions enabled in the publication. See Figure 15.56.

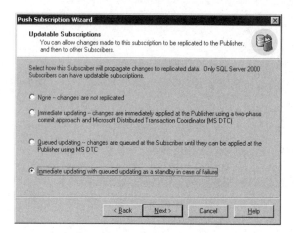

Figure 15.56.   Specifying the type of updatable subscriptions.

Next, in the Specify DTS Package page, if you are configuring a subscription for a snapshot or transactional publication using transformable subscriptions, you must specify a DTS package to use with the subscription. Notice that the DTS package can be located at either the Distributor or the Subscriber. See Figure 15.57.

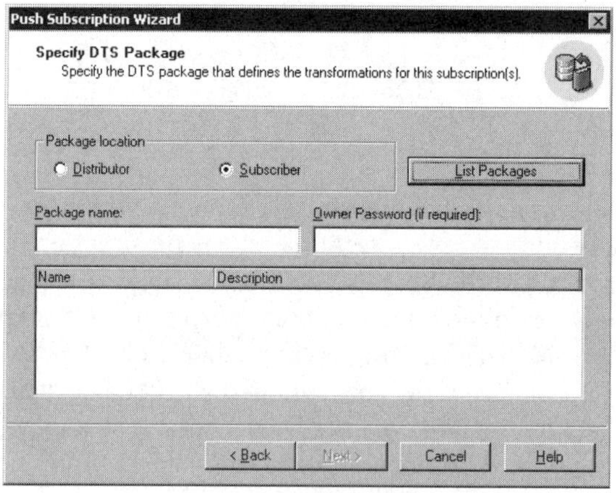

Figure 15.57.   Specifying the DTS package.

Next, in the Set Subscription Priority page, if you are configuring a subscription for a merge publication, specify the subscription priority. See Figure 15.58.

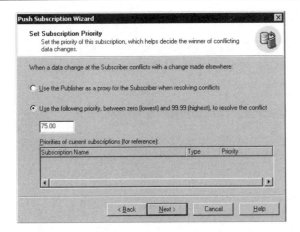

Figure 15.58.   Setting the subscription priority for conflict resolution.

The Use The Publisher As A Proxy For The Subscriber When Resolving Conflicts option button is selected by default. This default subscription priority assigns zero priority to all Subscribers. The Publisher merges changes made by a Subscriber and, in effect, assumes authorship of these changes (acting as a proxy for the Subscriber). A subscription without an assigned priority is called a local subscription. However, you can assign a priority to a subscription by clicking the Use The Following Priority Between Zero (Lowest) And 99.99 (Highest), To Resolve The Conflict option button. A subscription with an assigned priority is called a global subscription. In this case, changes made by the Subscriber are merged with data at the Publisher and the priority of the Subscriber making the change is stored in the metadata for the change. This assures that a change made by a higher priority Subscriber is not overwritten by a change by a lower priority Subscriber.

Next, in the Start Required Services page, SQL Server Agent verifies that the required services are running on the Distributor (see Figure 15.59). The SQL Server Agent service is always required. The MSDTC service is required for updatable subscriptions (unless Microsoft Message Queuing has been enabled). If a required service is not running, by default SQL Server Agent will start the service when the wizard finishes. Clear the check box if you want to start it manually.

Finally, in the Completing The Push Subscription Wizard page, review the subscription options and then click the Finish button to create the push subscription. See Figure 15.60.

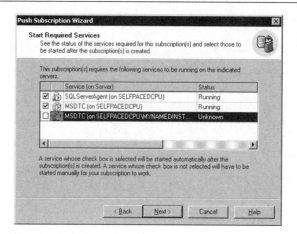

Figure 15.59.   Starting required services.

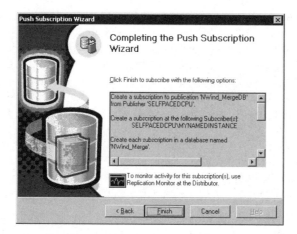

Figure 15.60.   Completing the Push Subscription Wizard.

Practice: Creating a Push Subscription

In this practice you create a push subscription using the Create Push Subscription Wizard in the SQL Server Enterprise Manager.

▶ **To create a push subscription**

1. In the SQL Server Enterprise Manager console tree, expand the Replication container for the default instance and then expand the Publications container.

2. Right-click PubsSales:pubs and then click Push New Subscription.

   The Welcome To The Push Subscription Wizard page appears.

3. Select the Show Advanced Options In This Wizard check box and then click Next.

   The Choose Subscribers page appears.

4. In the Subscribers list box, click SelfPacedCPU\MyNamedInstance and then click Next.

   The Choose Destination Database page appears.

5. Click the Browse Or Create button.

   The Browse Databases On SelfPacedCPU\MyNamedInstance dialog box appears.

6. Click the Create New button.

   The Database Properties dialog box appears.

7. In the Name text box, type **PubsPush** and then click OK.

8. In the Browse Databases On SelfPacedCPU\MyNamedInstance dialog box, verify that PubsPush is selected and then click OK.

9. In the Choose Destination Database page, click Next.

   The Set Distribution Agent Location page appears.

10. Verify that the Run The Agent At The Distributor option button is selected and then click Next.

    The Set Distribution Agent Schedule page appears.

11. Verify that the Continuously – Provides Minimal Latency Between When An Action Occurs At The Publisher And Is Propagated To The Subscriber option button is selected and then click Next.

    The Initialize Subscription page appears.

12. Verify that the Yes, Initialize The Schema And Data option button is selected.

13. Select the Start The Snapshot Agent To Begin The Initialization Process Immediately check box and then click Next.

    The Updatable Subscriptions page appears.

14. Click the Immediate Updating With Queued Updating As A Standby In Case Of Failure option button, and then click Next.

    The Start Required Services page appears. Notice that the SQL Server Agent service on SelfPacedCPU is required along with the MS DTC service on both instances of SQL Server.

15. In the grid, verify that the check box for each listed service is selected and then click Next.

    The Completing The Push Subscription Wizard page appears.

16. Review the properties of the push subscription and then click the Finish button.

    Notice that a SQL Server Enterprise Manager dialog box appears to show the progress of the push subscription being created.

17. When the push subscription is completed successfully, a second SQL Server Enterprise Manager dialog box appears. Click the Close button.

18. Do not close SQL Server Enterprise Manager.

Configuring a Pull Subscription

To configure a pull subscription using SQL Server Enterprise Manager, it must be run from a Subscriber using the Pull Subscription Wizard. A pull subscription is initiated by the Subscriber, based on a schedule set at the Subscriber, and replicated data is pulled from the Publisher using the resources of the Subscriber. In the case of a merge publication, a pull subscription pushes data back to the Publisher. You can start this wizard from the Tools menu by clicking Wizards, expanding Replication in the Select Wizard dialog box, and then double-clicking Create Pull Subscription Wizard, or by right-clicking Subscriptions and then clicking New Pull Subscription. Figure 15.61 shows the Welcome To The Pull Subscription Wizard page.

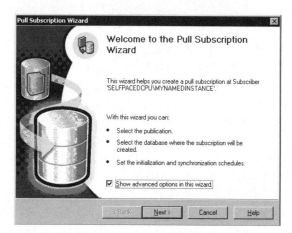

Figure 15.61.   Starting the Pull Subscription Wizard.

Notice that you can select the Show Advanced Options In This Wizard check box. Showing advanced options allows the updatable subscription options to be set.

Next, in the Look For Publications page, you can search for publications from servers registered with SQL Server Enterprise Manager, or you can search the Active Directory database for publications listed with Active Directory by Publishers running SQL Server 2000. See Figure 15.62.

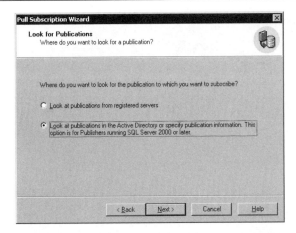

Figure 15.62.   Selecting where to look for a publication.

If you choose to look at publications in the Active Directory database, you can enter the publication information in the Specify Publication page without having to register the server with SQL Server Enterprise Manager. This is useful if you do not have sufficient permission to register the Publisher, but know the necessary publication information and have permission to subscribe to the publication. See Figure 15.63. If you do not know the necessary publication information and want to search for a publication, click the Browse button. In the Find SQL Server Publications dialog box, you can search for SQL Server publications based on the publication name or using advanced search criteria. See Figure 15.64.

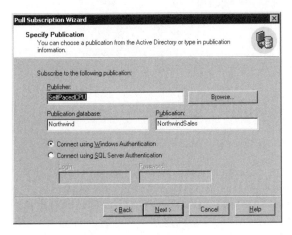

Figure 15.63.   Using Active Directory to subscribe to a publication.

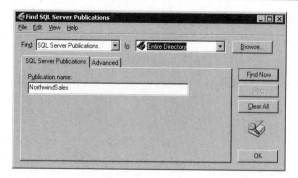

Figure 15.64.   Specifying in Active Directory for a publication.

If you choose to search for publications registered with SQL Server Enterprise Manager, in the Choose Publication page, select the publication to which you want to subscribe. See Figure 15.65. This page displays publications that are accessible (using the PAL for each publication) based on the login used to connect to the SQL Server instance by SQL Server Enterprise Manager and those that allow anonymous subscriptions.

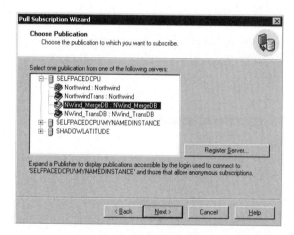

Figure 15.65.   Searching registered servers for a publication.

After selecting a publication in the Choose Destination Database page (and being authenticated based on the PAL), select the database on the destination server in which to create the subscription. Select an existing database from the list box or create a new database by clicking the New button. See Figure 15.66.

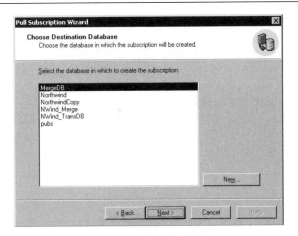

Figure 15.66.   Choosing a destination database.

Next, if you have selected a publication permitting anonymous subscriptions, you can elect to make the subscription anonymous in the Allow Anonymous Subscription page. If a subscription is anonymous, no information about the Subscriber is retained by the Publisher. See Figure 15.67.

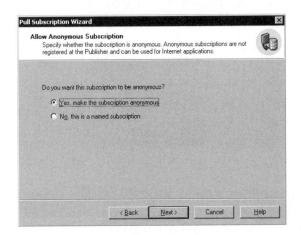

Figure 15.67.   Making a subscription anonymous.

If you have selected a publication that is permitted to have updatable subscriptions, you can choose the type of updatable subscriptions in the Updatable Subscriptions page. See Figure 15.68. If you select one of the 2PC types, in the Specify Updating Subscription Login page, specify the login to be used by the Subscriber to connect to the Publisher. Choices are using a predefined linked server (or remote server) login or a SQL Server login. See Figure 15.69.

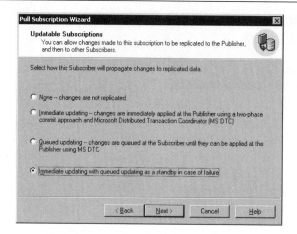

Figure 15.68.   Setting updatable subscription type.

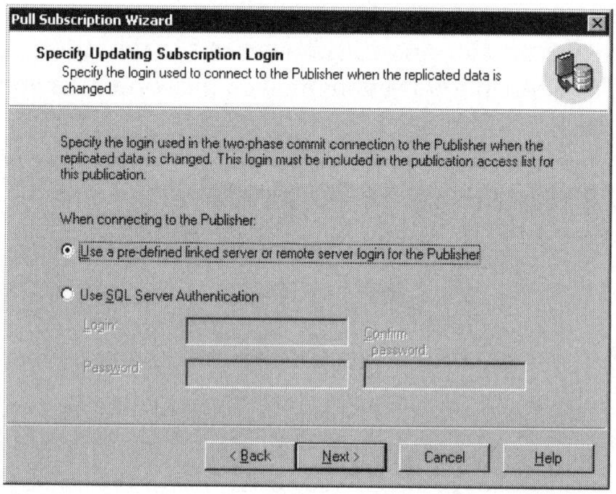

Figure 15.69.   Specifying an updating subscription login.

Next, in the Initialize Subscription page, you can choose to initialize the subscription immediately or specify that the Subscriber already has the snapshot files. This option is identical to a push subscription (see Figures 15.54 and 15.55). Next, in the Snapshot Delivery page, specify how to access the snapshot files. See Figure 15.70.

You can use the default snapshot location for the publication or an alternate location (such as a compact disc or an FTP address). The replication agent created with this subscription (either a Distribution Agent or a Merge Agent) must have read access to the snapshot files.

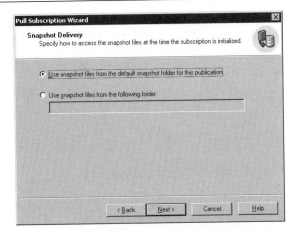

Figure 15.70. Specify the location to access the snapshot files.

Next, specify a schedule for the replication agent (either the Merge Agent in the Set Merge Agent Schedule page or the Distribution Agent in the Set Distribution Agent Schedule page). Options include continuous, according to a set schedule, or on demand only. The On Demand Only option allows a pull Subscriber to use SQL Server Enterprise Manager or the Windows Synchronization Manager to synchronize the subscription. Figure 15.71 illustrates the Set Merge Agent Schedule page.

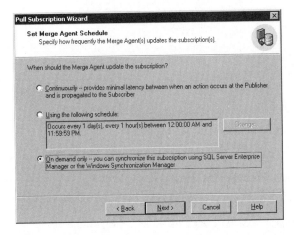

Figure 15.71. Specifying an agent schedule.

Note To configure an on-demand pull subscription, the domain user account used by the SQL Server Agent service must have full control permissions on the following registry key: HKLM\Software\Microsoft\Microsoft SQL Server\80\Replication\Subscriptions.

Next, if a merge publication is subscribed to, the Set Subscription Priority Page appears. This is the same as with a push subscription. See Figure 15.58.

Next, in the Start Required Services page, the necessary services for this subscription are displayed. If the On Demand Only option was selected in the Set Merge Agent Schedule page, the Start Required Services page will not appear. The SQL Server Agent service will always be one of the options. If a 2PC type of updatable subscription is selected, the MS DTC service will also be selected. See Figure 15.72.

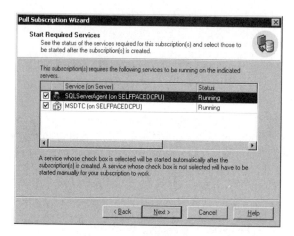

Figure 15.72.   Starting required services.

Finally, in the Completing The Pull Subscription Wizard page, review the subscription options selected and then click the Finish button to create the pull subscription.

Practice: Creating a Pull Subscription

In this practice you create a pull subscription using the Create Pull Subscription Wizard in the SQL Server Enterprise Manager.

▶ **To create a pull subscription**

1. Click the Start button, and the click Run.
2. In the Open box, type **Regedt32** and then click OK.

   The Registry Editor appears.
3. Expand HKEY_LOCAL_MACHINE, expand Software, expand Microsoft, expand Microsoft SQL Server, expand 80, expand Replication, and then click Subscriptions.
4. On the Security menu, click Permissions.

   The Permissions For Subscriptions dialog box appears.
5. Click the Add button.

   The Select Users, Computers Or Groups dialog box appears.

6. Double-click SQLService and then click OK.

   The SQLService domain user account is added to the Name list box.

7. In the Name list box, click SQLService, and then in the Permissions group box, select the Full Control check box.

8. Click OK to close the Permissions for Subscriptions dialog box.

9. Close Registry Editor.

10. In the SQL Server Enterprise Manager console tree, expand the SelfPaced-CPU\MyNamedInstance container and then expand the Replication container for MyNamedInstance.

11. Right-click the Subscriptions container and then click New Pull Subscription.

    The Welcome To The Pull Subscription Wizard page appears.

12. Select the Show Advanced Options In This Wizard check box and then click Next.

    The Look For Publications page appears.

13. Verify that the Look At Publications From Registered Servers option button is selected, and then click Next.

    The Choose Publication page appears.

14. Expand SelfPacedCPU, click NorthwindSales: Northwind, and then click Next.

    The Choose Destination Database page appears.

15. Click the New button.

    The Database Properties dialog box appears.

16. In the Name text box, type **NWindPull** and then click OK.

    The NWindPull database is created using default parameters.

17. In the Choose Destination Database page, verify that NWindPull is selected and then click Next.

    The Initialize Subscription page appears.

18. Verify that the Yes, Initialize The Schema And Data option button is selected.

19. Select the Start The Merge Agent To Initialize The Subscription Immediately check box and then click Next.

    The Snapshot Delivery page appears.

20. Verify that the Use Snapshot Files From The Default Snapshot Folder For This Publication option button is selected and then click Next.

    The Set Merge Agent Schedule page appears.

21. Click the On Demand Only – You Can Synchronize This Subscription Using SQL Server Enterprise Manager Or The Windows Synchronization Manager and then click Next.

    The Set Subscription Priority page appears.

22. Verify that the Use The Publisher As A Proxy For The Subscriber When Resolving Conflicts option button is selected and then click Next.

    The Completing The Pull Subscription Wizard page appears.

23. Review the properties of the pull subscription and then click the Finish button.

    Notice that a SQL Server Enterprise Manager dialog box appears to display the progress of the pull subscription being created.

24. When the pull subscription is completed successfully, click OK.

25. Do not close SQL Server Enterprise Manager.

Lesson Summary

The first step in implementing a replication solution is to define a Distributor and enable Publishers, databases, and Subscribers. You can use the Configure Publishing And Distribution Wizard for this task. Use the Create Publication Wizard to create snapshot, transactional, and merge publications. Configure Subscribers using the Push Subscription Wizard or the Pull Subscription Wizard.

Lesson 4: Monitoring and Administering Replication

After you have implemented a replication solution, you need to monitor and administer replication. In this lesson, you will learn to use Replication Monitor to view the status of replication agents and their tasks. You will also learn to review and modify the properties of the Distributor, publications, subscriptions, and replication agents.

After this lesson, you will be able to

- Monitor replication tasks with Replication Monitor
- Configure replication alerts
- Review and modify Distributor properties
- Review and modify publication properties
- Review and modify replication agent properties
- Review and modify subscription properties

Estimated lesson time: 30 minutes

Monitoring with Replication Monitor

Replication Monitor shows up as a container in the SQL Server Enterprise Manager console tree for a SQL Server instance that is enabled as a Distributor when you are either a member of the sysadmin fixed server role, or a member of the replmonitor role in the distribution database. It displays a list of all Publishers using the Distributor, the status of all publications, and the status of all replication agents. It can be used to set up and monitor replication alerts. It can also be used to stop and start replication agents, and reinitialize subscriptions. Finally, you can also configure Replication Monitor as a top-level node in Enterprise Manager to monitor and administer multiple Distributors (by right-clicking Microsoft SQL Servers in the console tree and then clicking Show Replication Monitor Group).

To open Replication Monitor for a Distributor, connect to the Distributor (by expanding a SQL Server instance enabled as a Distributor) and expand the Replication Monitor container in the Enterprise Manager console tree. When you first expand Replication Monitor, a SQL Server Enterprise Manager dialog box will appear informing you that by default Replication Monitor is not automatically refreshed (to save Distributor resources). See Figure 15.73.

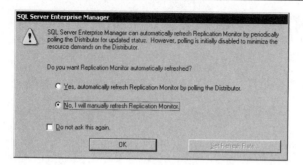

Figure 15.73.   Configuring Replication Monitor refresh properties.

During testing, you might want to select the Yes, Automatically Refresh Replication Monitor By Polling The Distributor option button to have Replication Monitor automatically refresh. If you choose automatic refresh, you can click the Set Refresh Rate button to choose a refresh rate (the default is 10 seconds). However, during production, you should select the No, I Will Manually Refresh Replication Monitor option button to save Distributor resources.

Publications

After you open Replication Monitor, you can view the status of various replication components. See Figure 15.74. Notice that each Publisher authorized to use this Distributor is displayed. In the details pane, the status of the Snapshot Agent for the selected publication is displayed along with each replication agent for the publication. Only the last action is displayed in the details pane. To view the history of any replication agent for a publication, right-click the replication agent and then select Agent History as illustrated in Figure 15.75. This displays the Agent History dialog box.

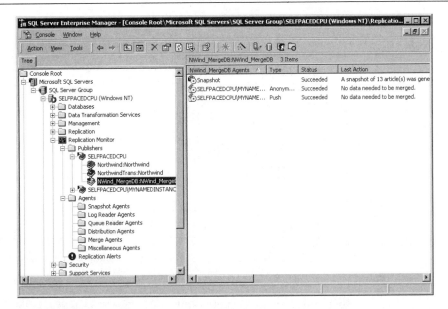

Figure 15.74.   Using Replication Monitor.

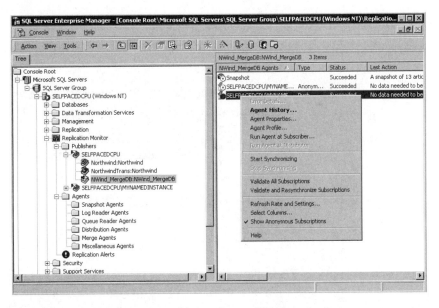

Figure 15.75.   Displaying agent history for a publication.

Agents

You can also view replication information based on the type of agent rather than based on the publication. Expand the Agents container in Replication Monitor and select a type of replication agent. For example, click the Snapshot Agents container to view the status of all Snapshot Agents. See Figure 15.76.

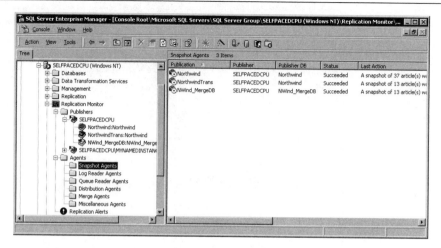

Figure 15.76.   Displaying the status of all Snapshot Agents.

In this figure, notice that each Snapshot Agent has successfully generated a snapshot. If a publication is not replicating successfully, check the status of the Snapshot Agent to verify that the initial snapshot has been created.

Alerts

You can also configure Replication Alerts by selecting an alert within the Replication Alerts container. See Figure 15.77.

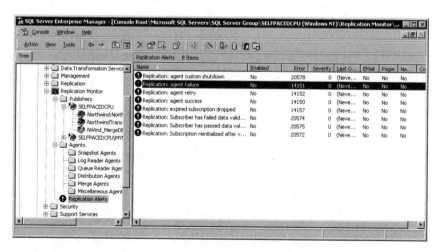

Figure 15.77.   Configuring replication alerts.

SQL Server 2000 ships with eight preconfigured replication alerts. To use one of these alerts, you must enable the alert and configure operators to be notified. You do this by right-clicking an alert in the Replication Alerts container, clicking Properties, and then enabling the alert and configuring operators in the Replication Alert Properties dialog box.

Practice: Monitoring Replication

In this practice you monitor publications and subscriptions using SQL Server Enterprise Manager.

▶ **To monitor replication**

1. In the SQL Server Enterprise Manager console tree, expand the Replication Monitor container.

   A SQL Server Enterprise Manager dialog box appears.

2. Click the Yes, Automatically Refresh Replication Monitor By Polling The Distributor option button and then click OK.

3. Expand the Agents container and then click the Snapshot Agents container.

4. In the details pane, verify that a snapshot was created for each publication by viewing the Status column.

5. In the details pane, right-click NorthwindSales and then click Agent History.

   The Snapshot Agent History dialog box appears.

6. Click the Session Details button.

   The Latest History Of Snapshot Agent dialog box appears. In the list box, notice the steps taken to create the snapshot files.

7. Click the Close button.

8. In the Snapshot Agent History dialog box, click the Agent Profile button.

   The Snapshot Agent Profiles dialog box appears.

9. Click the View Details button.

   The Replication Agent Profile Details dialog box appears. Notice the parameters for the Snapshot Agent.

10. Click the Close button.

11. In the Snapshot Agent Profiles dialog box, click OK.

12. In the console tree, in the Replication Monitor container, expand Publishers, expand SelfPacedCPU, and then click PubSales: pubs.

    In the details pane, notice the status of each replication agent. Only the Snapshot Agent has run because there are no replicated or queued transactions.

13. On the Tools menu, click SQL Query Analyzer.

14. On the toolbar, click the Load SQL Script button.

    The Open Query File dialog box appears.

15. Open PubsUpdate.sql in the C:\SelfPacedSQL\CH_15 folder.

    The script contains an *UPDATE* statement that updates the last name of the author, Johnson White, to Johnson Black.

16. On the toolbar, click the Execute Query button.

17. Switch to SQL Server Enterprise Manager.

18. In the details pane, observe the Log Reader Agent and the Distribution Agent (named SelfPacedCPU\MyNamedInstance:PubsPush). After about 10 seconds, each of these agents will run and update the PubsPush database on SelfPaced-CPU\MyNamedInstance. Each agent will indicate that one transaction with two commands was delivered. After about 10 more seconds, these agents will indicate that no replicated transactions are currently available.

19. Do not close SQL Server Enterprise Manager or SQL Query Analyzer.

Reviewing and Modifying Distributor Properties

To review and modify Distributor properties, right-click Replication Monitor in the console tree and then click Distributor Properties. Figure 15.78 shows the Publisher And Distributor Properties dialog box.

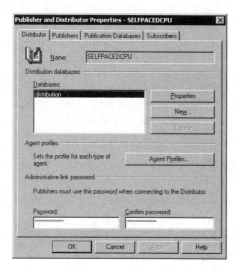

Figure 15.78. Viewing and modifying Distributor properties.

In the Distributor tab, you can configure properties of the Distributor, including the replication agent profiles for all new agents (more on agent profiles on the next page). You can also enable or disable Publishers in the Publishers tab, publication databases in the Publication Databases tab, and Subscribers in the Subscribers tab. To configure transaction and history retention periods, click the Properties button in the Distributor tab. Figure 15.79 shows the Distribution Database Properties dialog box.

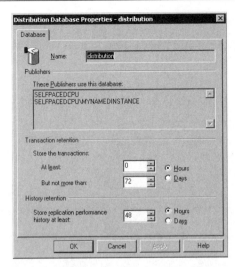

Figure 15.79.   Viewing and modifying retention periods.

Notice that the default maximum retention period for transactions is 72 hours and the default maximum retention period for replication performance history is 48 hours. These settings help determine the size of the distribution database. For example, if a Subscriber to a transactional publication fails to retrieve replicated transactions on schedule, they will remain in the distribution database for 72 hours by default. The distribution database must have sufficient hard disk space to store this volume of replicated transactions. After the expiration of this maximum retention period, a Subscriber will have to reinitialize the subscription. This requires a current snapshot and will cause a performance hit.

Reviewing and Modifying Publication Properties

To view and modify the properties of a publication, you can select the publication either in Replication Monitor or from the Publications container for the published database. Right-click the selected publication and then click Properties. If the publication has existing subscriptions, you will receive a warning stating that many properties cannot be modified. The SQL Server Enterprise Manager message box is shown in Figure 15.80. Although you can modify some properties, you will need to drop all subscriptions to modify many properties of a subscription. Click OK to close the SQL Server Enterprise Manager message box.

The Publication Properties dialog box appears, with the General tab selected. Each publication has many properties that can be viewed and modified. See Figure 15.81.

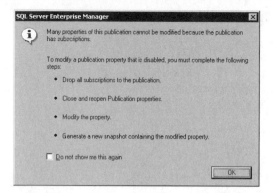

Figure 15.80. Modifying a publication with existing subscriptions notice.

Figure 15.81. Reviewing and modifying publication properties.

In the General tab, notice that the default subscription expiration period for a subscription to a merge publication is 14 days. For some environments, you might want to configure subscriptions to never expire.

Reviewing and Modifying Replication Agent Profile

Each replication agent has a profile that defines the parameters used by the agent to perform its task. This includes values such as timeout values and Bcp batch size parameters. A set of default replication agent profiles is defined for each type of replication agent when a Distributor is configured and can be modified as a property of the Distributor. To modify the profile for an existing replication agent, in the Agents container, right-click the replication agent and then click Agent Profiles. The Distribution Agent Profiles dialog box appears, shown in Figure 15.82.

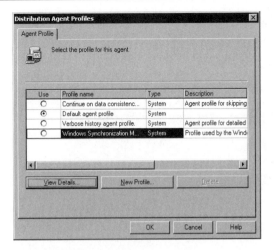

Figure 15.82.   Reviewing and modifying replication agent profile details.

The agent profile for a Distribution Agent is displayed in Figure 15.82. Notice that the default agent profile is being used, and that three other profiles are available for this agent. One profile specifies that the agent will continue despite data consistency errors. By default, an agent will cease data synchronization if data consistency errors are detected. In some environments you might want to override this default. You can also configure the agent profile to perform verbose history logging for troubleshooting purposes or configure the agent profile for use with Windows Synchronization Manager using a smaller batch size. To view the details of a profile, click the View Details button. The Replication Agent Profile Details dialog box appears, shown in Figure 15.83.

Figure 15.83.   Reviewing and modifying agent profile details.

Notice the types of parameters that can be set or modified. Each replication agent has different default settings and different available alternate profiles. You can also create a new profile for an agent.

Reviewing and Modifying Subscription Properties

To review or modify subscription properties of a publication, right-click the publication in the Publications container, click Properties, and then click the Subscriptions tab in the Publication Properties dialog box. Each current subscription of the publication is displayed. See Figure 15.84.

Figure 15.84.   Reviewing subscriptions.

To view the properties of a subscription, click the subscription in the Subscription container, and then click Properties. The Subscription Properties dialog box appears, as shown in Figure 15.85.

Click the Synchronization tab to view or modify the location at which the agent will run. On Windows 2000 and Windows NT 4.0 Subscribers, you can have the agent run at the Subscriber to reduce the load on the Distributor. See Figure 15.86.

You can review the status of a subscription from the Subscriber side by expanding the Replication folder in the console tree of Enterprise Manager and then clicking Subscriptions. See Figure 15.87.

Figure 15.85.   Reviewing general properties of a subscription.

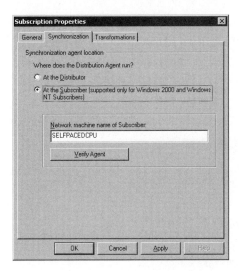

Figure 15.86.   Specifying the replication agent location.

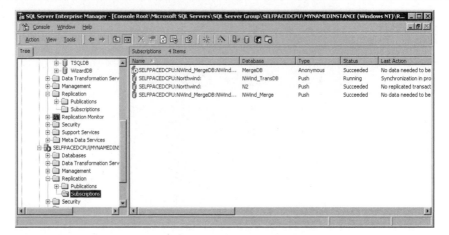

Figure 15.87. Viewing subscription status on a Subscriber.

Each subscription is displayed in the details pane along with the current status of the subscription.

Viewing and Resolving Merge Replication Conflicts

To view and resolve a merge replication conflict at the Distributor, right-click the merge publication in the Replication container of Enterprise Manager and then click View Conflicts. The Microsoft Replication Conflict Viewer dialog box appears, shown in Figure 15.88.

Figure 15.88. Viewing replication conflicts.

If any tables have conflicts, they will be displayed. Click the View button to resolve any conflicts. See Figure 15.89.

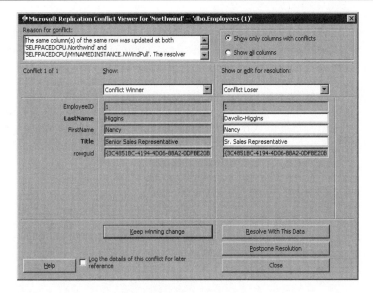

Figure 15.89.   Microsoft Replication Conflict Viewer.

Notice that you can resolve the conflict by selecting the winner as selected by SQL Server, you can select the loser, or you can edit the conflicting information. You can also choose to postpone resolution or log the details for later reference.

Using Windows Synchronization Manager

To use Windows Synchronization Manager on a Subscriber, click Start, point to Programs, point to Accessories, and then click Synchronize. The Items To Synchronize dialog box appears, illustrated in Figure 15.90.

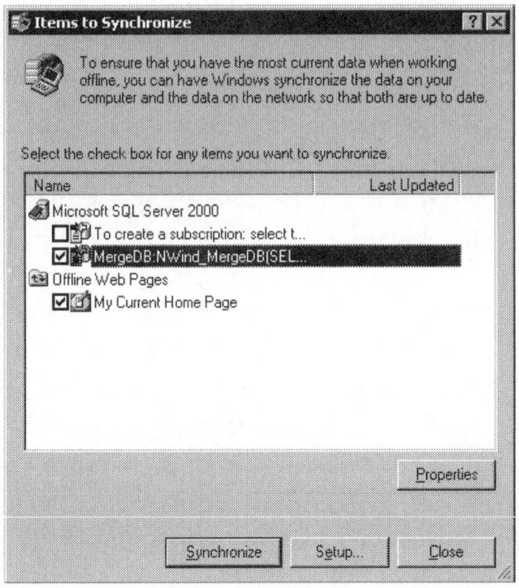

Figure 15.90.   Windows Synchronization Manager.

Notice that various items can be synchronized using Windows Synchronization Manager. Select a subscription to a publication, and then click the Synchronize button to immediately synchronize each item containing a check mark in its check box. If interactive conflict resolution is enabled for a publication, you will be prompted to resolve any conflicts that occur during synchronization. Click the Setup button to display the Synchronization Settings dialog box and to configure synchronization settings for each item. Items can be synchronized on logon and logoff, when the processor is idle, or according to a schedule. See Figure 15.91.

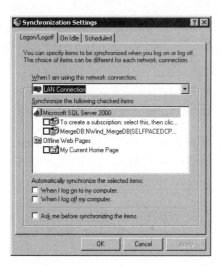

Figure 15.91.   Synchronization settings.

Select a subscription to a publication, and then click the Properties button to configure properties of the subscription. The SQL Server Subscription Properties page appears with the General tab selected (see Figure 15.92). You can synchronize with the current default Publisher or select a different Publisher with which to synchronize. This is useful if your default Publisher is temporarily offline or if a network link is temporarily down. You can also select this other Publisher as the new default Publisher by clicking the Make This Publisher The Default Synchronization Partner check box. You also reinitialize or remove the subscription by clicking either the Reinitialize Subscription button or the Remove Subscription button.

Click the Subscriber tab to modify the login account that a given push subscription uses to connect to this Subscriber (see Figure 15.93). Click the Publisher tab to modify the login account that a given pull subscription uses to connect to the Publisher (see Figure 15.94). Click the Distributor tab to modify the login account that a given pull subscription uses to connect to the Distributor (see Figure 15.95). You can either select the current login account for the user activating Synchronization Manager, or you can specify a SQL Server login account (see Figure 15.95).

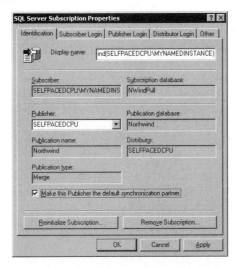

Figure 15.92.   Specifying a default Publisher in the General tab of the Subscription properties page.

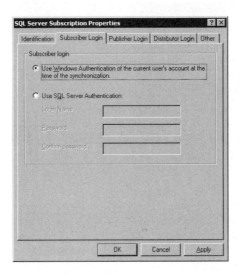

Figure 15.93.   Subscriber login properties.

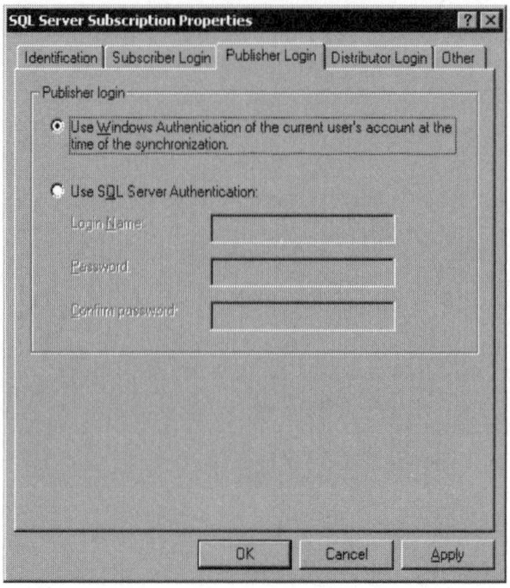

Figure 15.94.   Publisher login properties.

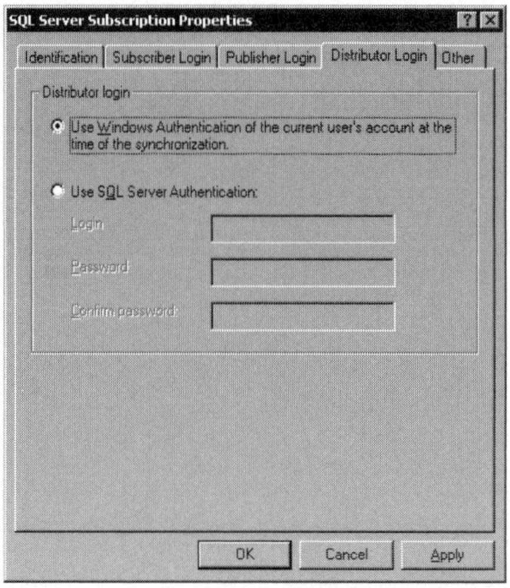

Figure 15.95.   Distributor login properties.

Click the Other tab to enable automatic or interactive conflict resolution. You can also configure login and query timeout settings. This can be useful for slow links. The defaults are 15 seconds for logins and 30 seconds for queries (see Figure 15.96).

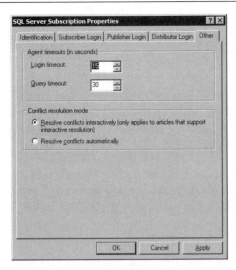

Figure 15.96.   Configuring automatic or interactive conflict resolution.

Practice: Resolving Conflicts Interactively Using Windows Synchronization Manager

In this practice you resolve conflicts interactively using Windows Synchronization Manager.

▶ **To resolve conflicts interactively using Windows Synchronization Manager**

1. Switch to SQL Query Analyzer.
2. On the toolbar, click the Load SQL Script button.

   The Open Query File dialog box appears.
3. Open NorthwindUpdate.sql in the C:\SelfPacedSQL\CH_15 folder.

   This script updates Employee ID 1, changing the last name and title.
4. On the toolbar, click the Execute Query button.
5. On the File menu, click Connect.

   The Connect To SQL Server dialog box appears.
6. Click the SQL Server ellipsis button to select an instance of SQL Server.

   The Select Server dialog box appears.
7. Click SelfPacedCPU\MyNamedInstance and then click OK.
8. Verify that the Windows Authentication option button is selected, and then click OK.
9. On the toolbar, click the Load SQL Script button.

   The Open Query File dialog box appears.

10. Open NwindPullUpdate.sql in the C:\SelfPacedSQL\CH_15 folder.

    This script updates Employee ID 1, changing the last name and title. Notice that the last name and title for this employee are different from the script in step 3.

11. On the toolbar, click the Execute Query button.

12. To synchronize using Windows Synchronization Manager, click Start, point to Programs, point to Accessories, and then click Synchronize.

13. Click NwindPull: NorthwindSales and then click the Properties button.

    The SQL Server Subscription Properties dialog box appears.

14. Click the Other tab.

15. Click the Resolve Conflicts Interactively (Only Applies To Articles That Support Interactive Resolution) option button and then click OK.

    A Microsoft SQL Server 2000 dialog box appears asking if you are sure you want to change the conflict resolution mode.

16. Click the Yes button.

17. Clear the My Current Home Page check box, verify that only the NwindPull: NorthwindSales check box is selected, and then click the Synchronize button.

    The Synchronizing dialog box appears. After a few moments, the Microsoft Replication Conflict Viewer for 'Northwind' – '[dbo].[Employees]' dialog box appears. Notice that you can use pull-down menus to view the data at the Publisher and at the Subscriber.

18. Click the Resolve With This Data option button.

    The Synchronization process completes.

19. In SQL Query Analyzer, in the connection to MyNamedInstance, click the Clear Window button on the toolbar.

20. In the query pane, type **SELECT * FROM Employees WHERE EmployeeID = 1** and then click the Execute Query button on the toolbar.

    Notice that the resolved data has been replicated to MyNamedInstance.

21. Close SQL Server Enterprise Manager and SQL Query Analyzer.

Lesson Summary

Use Replication Monitor to monitor all aspects of replication. You can monitor using a publication focus or an agent focus. From within Replication Monitor, you can view the status of any publication or agent. You can start or stop an agent, or view its history. You can view the details of a publication. Although you can modify some details of a publication that has existing publications, to modify all details you must drop all existing subscriptions. You can also review and resolve replication conflicts for a merge publication using Microsoft Replication Conflict Viewer. Finally, you can use Windows Synchronization Manager to interactively control synchronization on a Subscriber, if that publication option is enabled.

Review

Here are some questions to help you determine whether you have learned enough to move on to the next chapter. If you have difficulty answering these questions, review the material in this chapter before beginning the next chapter. The answers for these questions are located in the Appendix, "Questions and Answers."

1. You have a number of users in Brazil that need to access data for the purpose of sales analysis. The data is stored in a centralized database in New York. They have been accessing the database in New York over a 56K dedicated link that is also supporting a variety of other interoffice traffic. You want to implement a replication solution between your New York office and your Brazil office. What type of replication would you implement and what additional information do you need to know?

2. You have implemented a merge replication solution. Each Subscriber running on Windows 2000 and Windows NT 4.0 is able to initialize the subscription and replicate data successfully with the Publisher. However, your Windows Me and Windows 98 Subscribers are unable to successfully replicate with the Publisher. What is a likely source of this problem? How would you solve this problem?

3. You are planning to implement a merge replication solution. What is the benefit of using a dedicated Distributor?

4. You have implemented transactional replication. You have been monitoring the size of the distribution database on the Distributor and notice that its size seems to be larger than anticipated. What might be the cause of this? What Distributor setting could you modify to affect its size?

C H A P T E R   1 6

Maintaining High Availability

About This Chapter

In previous chapters, you learned about maintaining the availability of your SQL Server databases by using RAID for storage of data and transaction log files; performing full, differential, and transaction log backups; and implementing replication. In environments that require the assurance of higher availability, such as Web-based solutions and 24x7 operations, additional methods for maintaining high availability are frequently implemented. In this chapter, you will learn about the function of standby servers and you will learn how to automate the maintenance of standby servers by using log shipping. Finally, you will be introduced to the use of SQL Server failover clusters.

Before You Begin

To complete this chapter, you must have

- A computer that meets or exceeds the minimum hardware requirements listed in Table 2.1, "Hardware Requirements," in Lesson 1 of Chapter 2.
- Microsoft Windows 2000 Server running on your computer on an NTFS partition.
- A computer with a NetBIOS name of SelfPacedCPU configured as a domain controller in the SelfPacedSQL.MSFT domain.
- Installed a default instance and at least one named instance of SQL Server 2000 (see Chapter 2).
- Failover clusters to achieve automatic failover to another server node in the event of server failure.

Lesson 1: Using Standby Servers

A standby server can be maintained to take the place of the primary production server, if needed. In this lesson, you will learn about setting up and maintaining a standby server. This includes learning how to automate the maintenance of a standby server. You will also learn how to bring a standby server online, and how to bring the primary server back online.

After this lesson, you will be able to

- Set up a standby server
- Automate log shipping
- Monitor log shipping
- Bring a standby server online
- Bring a primary server back online

Estimated lesson time: 45 minutes

Using a Standby Server

A standby server is a secondary SQL Server installation that is kept up-to-date with a primary SQL Server installation through the application of transaction log backup files. By using standby servers, a database administrator can minimize the length of time that users are unable to access one or more production database(s) in case of server failure or the need for server maintenance. The databases on a standby server can also be used as reporting servers to offload reporting and analysis tasks.

A standby server must maintain an exact copy of one or more production databases on the primary server. This is initially accomplished through the use of a full database backup on the primary server that is restored to the standby server using either the NORECOVERY or the STANDBY restoration options. Using one of these two options leaves the standby database in recovery mode, so that additional transaction logs can be applied to it.

Next, to maintain an exact copy on the standby server, regular transaction log backups are performed on the primary server and applied to the standby server (again leaving the standby server in recovery mode). The frequency with which transaction log backups are performed on the primary server and applied to the standby server determines the amount of work (and length of time) required to bring the standby server up-to-date and online in the event the standby server must be promoted.

To promote the standby server to become the new primary server, all unapplied transaction log backup files must be applied to the standby server. In addition, the active portion of the transaction log on the primary server must be backed up and applied to the standby server. This final restoration is performed using the RECOVERY option. Users can then use the database on the standby server, which contains all data from the primary server exactly as it was prior to its failure (other than uncommitted transactions, which are permanently lost).

Note   Using RAID for transaction log files is critical for ensuring that the active portion of the transaction log is available for backup and application to the standby server.

The active portion of the transaction log on the primary server can be backed up using the NORECOVERY backup option. This option leaves the primary database in recovery mode. When the primary server is ready to be brought back online, the transaction logs from the standby server (for the period that users were using the standby server as the primary server) can be applied to the primary server. This avoids the necessity of applying a complete database backup and all applicable transaction logs to restore the primary server. The result is a significant decrease in the time required to bring the primary server back online.

When the standby server is brought online for use in place of the primary server, either the standby server must be renamed using the name of the primary server or user processes must know to connect to the standby server (using the name of a standby server) rather than the primary server. All uncommitted transactions must be restarted. Uncommitted transactions cannot be maintained between the primary server and the standby server.

Note   Use the SQL Server Setup program to rename a SQL Server 2000 installation after renaming the server using Windows 2000 or Windows NT 4.0.

User logins must be created on the standby server prior to bringing the standby server online as the new primary server. This is generally accomplished using one of the following methods.

- User logins from the primary server can be scripted and these scripts used to create the necessary logins on the standby server when needed.
- The DTS Transfer Logins Task in DTS Designer can be used within a job to automate the process of backing up, copying, and restoring the contents of the sysxlogins system table from the primary server to the standby server.

If the standby server is only providing services to a single production server, you might want to create the logins on the standby server when the standby server is created. However, if the standby server is providing services to multiple databases from multiple instances of SQL Server, generally you will not create logins on the standby server until it is brought online as the primary server for a particular database.

Automating Log Shipping

You can automate the process of maintaining a standby server by creating backup, copy, and restore jobs that are periodically executed by SQL Server Agent on the primary server and on the standby server. This automated process is called log shipping. You can also designate a third server to monitor the execution of the log shipping jobs on the primary server and on the standby server; the third server is frequently used to monitor other pairs of log shipping servers as well.

Note   The log shipping feature is available only in the Enterprise, Enterprise Evaluation, and Developer Editions of SQL Server 2000.

You can create these jobs using the Database Maintenance Plan Wizard in SQL Server Enterprise Manager. You must be a member of the sysadmin server role to run the Database Maintenance Plan Wizard. To start the Database Maintenance Plan Wizard, click Database Maintenance Planner on the Tools menu, or right-click the Database Maintenance Plan container (in the Management container) and then click New Maintenance Plan. (The use of most of the Database Maintenance Plan Wizard features was covered in Chapter 13.)

In the Select Servers page, select the primary server. See Figure 16.1.

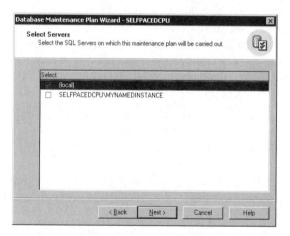

Figure 16.1.   Selecting a primary server for log shipping.

Next, in the Select Databases page, select the database for which you want to configure log shipping, and specify log shipping by selecting the Ship The Transaction Logs To Other SQL Servers (Log Shipping) check box. You can select only one database at a time. See Figure 16.2.

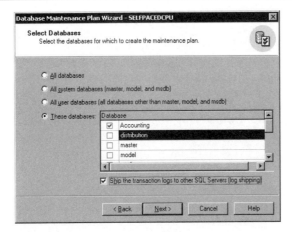

Figure 16.2.   Selecting a database for log shipping.

Next, advance to the Specify the Database Backup Plan and clear the Back Up The Database As Part Of The Maintenance Plan check box. See Figure 16.3.

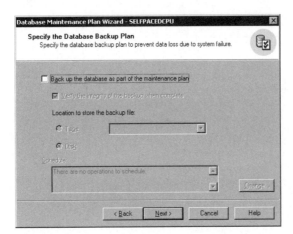

Figure 16.3.   Clearing the full database backup check box.

Note   You do not need to perform a full database backup as part of a log shipping database maintenance plan, although you will need to either perform an initial full backup or use an existing full backup.

Next, in the Specify Transaction Log Backup Disk Directory page, specify the directory into which the transaction log backup files will be stored. Make sure this location has sufficient space to hold the shipped logs, or log shipping will fail. See Figure 16.4.

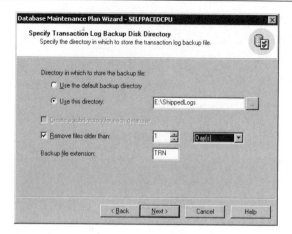

Figure 16.4.   Selecting a storage location for transaction log backups.

Next, in the Specify The Transaction Log Share page, specify the network share for the storage location for the transaction log backup files. See Figure 16.5.

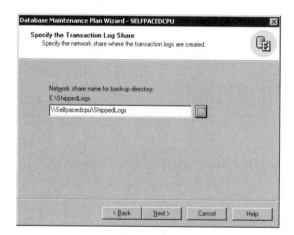

Figure 16.5.   Specifying the network share for the transaction log backup files.

You must create this network share for the directory in which the transaction log backup files are stored. The domain user account used by the SQL Server Agent service on the primary server must have read and write access to this network share, and the domain user account used by the SQL Server Agent service on the standby server must have read access to this network share.

Next, in the Specify The Log Shipping Destinations page, click the Add button to display the Add Destination Database dialog box, where you specify the standby server and configure its properties. The standby server is called the destination server in the wizard. In addition to using log shipping to create and maintain standby servers, you can also use log shipping to create read-only copies of one or more production server databases rather than using replication. Figure 16.6 illustrates the Specify The Log Shipping Destinations page after a log shipping destination has been specified.

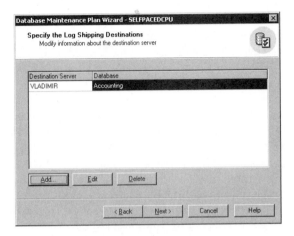

Figure 16.6. Specifying the standby server.

In the Add Destination Database dialog box, there are a number of properties you can configure for the destination database. See Figure 16.7.

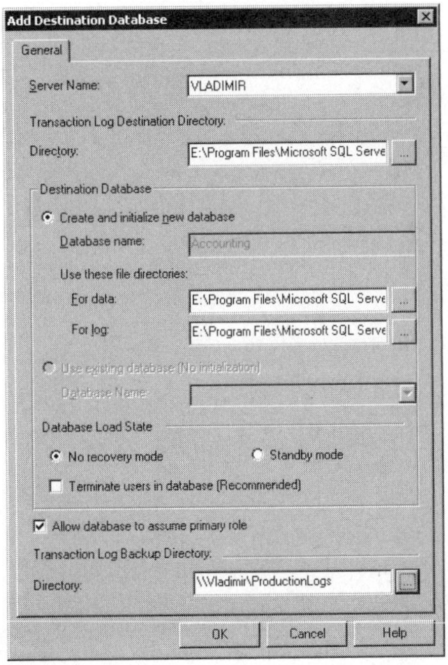

Figure 16.7. Specifying the properties of the destination database.

In the Destination Database group box, you can choose to specify a different database name for the destination database. This is useful for creating a destination read-only database for reporting purposes. If you want the destination database to be viewable for read-only queries, you must select the Standby Mode option button in the Database Load State group box. The default is the No Recovery Mode option button. If you choose to update and overwrite an existing database (rather than creating a new database), you should select the Terminate Users In Database (Recommended) check box to automatically terminate all users in the existing database. If you want to use the destination database as a standby server that may need to assume the role of the primary server, you must select the Allow Database To Assume Primary Role check box to specify that it can assume the primary role if necessary. When you select this check box, you must specify the directory, in the Directory text box, for storing transaction log backups during the period the standby server is functioning as the primary server.

Next, in the Initialize The Destination Databases page, you specify the backup file containing a full database backup to be used to initialize the destination database on the standby server (see Figure 16.8).

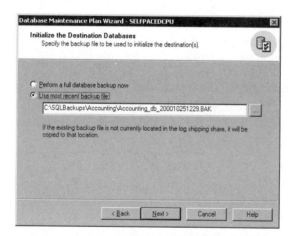

Figure 16.8.   Specifying the backup file for initialization.

You can choose to perform a full backup immediately by selecting the Perform A Full Database Backup Now option button, or you can select the Use Most Recent Backup File option button to specify an existing recent backup file. If you specify a recent backup file, you must include the path and filename of the existing backup file in the Use Most Recent Backup File text box. This backup file will be placed in the log shipping share so that it is available to the standby server for initialization of the destination database.

Next, in the Log Shipping Schedules page, specify the log shipping schedule. See Figure 16.9.

In the Backup Schedule group box, the default frequency for backing up the transaction log on the primary server is 15 minutes. Click the Change button to display the Edit Recurring Job Schedule dialog box to modify this frequency. Next, in the Copy/Load Frequency spin box, specify the frequency with which the transaction log backup files are copied to the standby server and restored (the default is 15 minutes). In the Load Delay spin box, you can specify a delay between the copy and the load (restore) of the transaction log backup files (the default is no delay). Finally, in the File Retention Period spin box, you can specify the length of time the transaction log backup files are retained on the log shipping share (the default is 24 hours). If the standby server is unable to copy these files before the retention period expires, the destination database on the standby server will have to be reinitialized. The frequency of the transaction log backups and the length of the file retention period will affect the amount of disk space that the transaction log backup files will require.

Next, in the Log Shipping Thresholds page, specify the log shipping alert thresholds. See Figure 16.10.

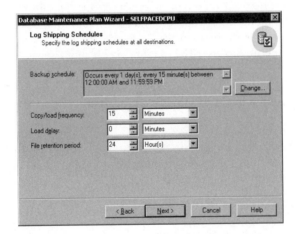

Figure 16.9.   Specifying the log shipping schedule.

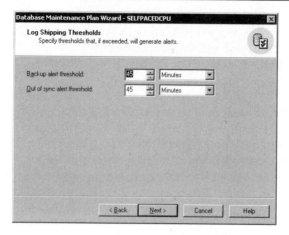

Figure 16.10.   Specifying the log shipping alert thresholds.

The Backup Alert Threshold alert defines the maximum length of time between transaction log backups on the primary server (the default is 45 minutes or three times the interval between transaction log backups). If the defined length of time is exceeded, an alert will fire to notify an administrator of a problem with the automated log shipping process. The Out Of Sync Alert Threshold alert defines the maximum length of time between the most recent transaction log backup on the primary server and the restore of the transaction log backup to the standby server (the default is 45 minutes or three times the interval between transaction log restores).

Next, in the Specify The Log Shipping Monitor Server Information page, specify a log shipping monitor for monitoring log shipping jobs on the primary server and the standby server. See Figure 16.11.

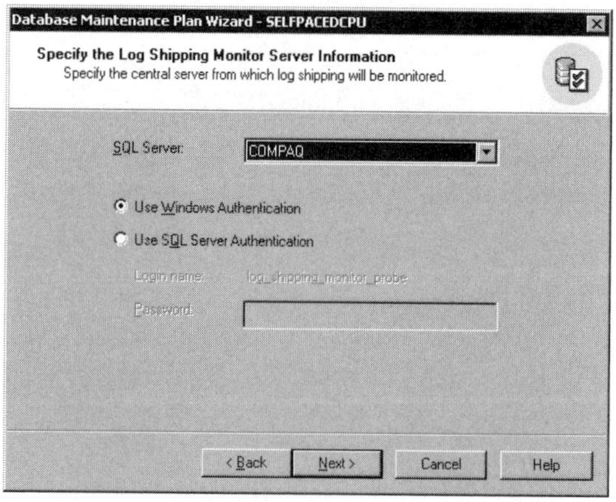

Figure 16.11.   Specifying a central monitoring server.

This should generally be a server other than the primary or the standby server. The monitoring server can provide monitoring services to multiple log shipping pairs of servers. You must specify the authentication mode the SQL Server Agent service will use to connect to the monitoring server. Select either Windows authentication or SQL Server authentication. If SQL Server authentication is selected, you must use the SQL Server login account, log_shipping_monitor_probe.

The next two pages, the Reports To Generate page and the Maintenance Plan History page, were covered in Chapter 13. See Figures 13.49 and 13.50.

When you are finished configuring your maintenance plan, the Database Maintenance Plan Wizard Summary page appears. See Figure 16.12. Verify that the plan information is correct, and then click Next. Finally, click the Finish button in the Completing The Database Maintenance Plan Wizard page, as shown in Figure 16.13.

After the Database Maintenance Plan Wizard completes its task, the database selected for log shipping is restored in recovery mode (using either the NORE-COVERY or STANDBY options) on the standby server. See Figure 16.14.

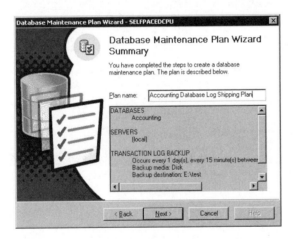

Figure 16.12. Database Maintenance Plan Summary page.

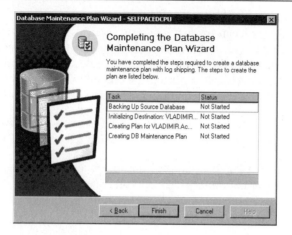

Figure 16.13.   Completing the Database Maintenance Plan Wizard page.

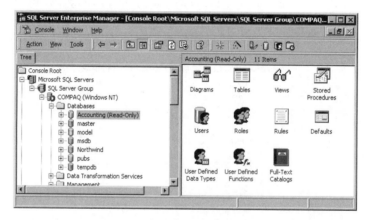

Figure 16.14.   Standby server with database in standby mode.

Practice: Creating a Standby Server

In this practice you use the Database Maintenance Planner Wizard in SQL Server Enterprise Manager to automate log shipping.

▶   **To create a standby server**

1. Ensure that you are logged on to the SelfPacedSQL.MSFT domain controller as Administrator.

2. Click Start, point to Programs, point to Microsoft SQL Server, and then click Enterprise Manager.

3. In the console tree, expand the Microsoft SQL Servers container, expand the SQL Server Group container, expand the default instance container, and then expand the Databases container.

4. Right-click Databases, point to All Tasks, and then click Attach Database.

   The Attach Database – SelfPacedCPU dialog box appears.

5. Click the ellipsis button to browse for the MDF file.

   The Browse for Existing File – SelfPacedCPU dialog box appears.

6. Click LogShipDB.mdf in C:\SelfPacedSQL\CH_16 and then click OK.

   Notice that the LogShipDB database is about to be attached.

7. In the Specify Database Owner drop-down box, click Sa.

8. Click OK to attach the LogShipDB database.

   A SQL Server Enterprise Manager message box appears to inform you that attachment of the database has completed successfully.

9. Click OK.

   Notice that the LogShipDB database appears in the list of databases.

10. Right-click the LogShipDB container, point to All Tasks, and then click Maintenance Plan.

    The Welcome To The Database Maintenance Plan Wizard page appears.

11. Click Next.

    The Select Servers page appears.

12. Select the (Local) check box and then click Next.

    The Select Databases page appears with the LogShipDB check box selected.

13. Select the Ship The Transaction Logs To Other SQL Servers (Log Shipping) check box and then click Next.

    The Update Data Optimization Information page appears.

14. Click Next.

    The Database Integrity Check page appears.

15. Click Next.

    The Specify The Database Backup Plan page appears.

16. Clear the Back Up The Database As Part Of The Maintenance Plan check box and then click Next.

    The Specify Transaction Log Backup Disk Directory page appears.

17. Verify that the Use The Default Backup Directory option button is selected.

18. Select the Remove Files Older Than check box and then click 1 in the spin box and Hour(s) in the drop-down list.

19. Click Next.

    The Specify The Transaction Log Share page appears.

20. Open Windows Explorer and browse to C:\Program Files\Microsoft SQL Server\Mssql.

21. Right-click Backup and then click Sharing.

    The Backup Properties dialog box appears.

22. Click the Share This Folder option button, change the share name to **ProductionBackup** in the Share Name drop-down combo box, and then click OK.

23. Browse to C:\Program Files\Microsoft SQL Server\Mssql \$MyNamedInstance.

24. Right-click Backup and then click Sharing.

    The Backup Properties dialog box appears.

25. Click the Share This Folder option button, change the name to **StandbyBackup** in the Share Name drop-down combo box, and then click OK.

26. Close Windows Explorer.

27. Switch to the Database Maintenance Plan Wizard.

28. In the Network Share Name For Backup Directory text box, type **\\SelfPacedCPU\ProductionBackup** and then click Next.

    The wizard verifies that the specified share exists, and the Specify The Log Shipping Destinations page appears.

29. Click the Add button.

    The Add Destination Database dialog box appears.

30. In the Server Name drop-down list, click SelfPacedCPU\MyNamedInstance.

31. In the Database Load State group box, click the Standby Mode option button and then select the Terminate Users In Database (Recommended) check box.

32. Select the Allow Database To Assume Primary Role check box.

33. In the Directory text box, type **\\SelfPacedCPU\StandbyBackup** and then click OK.

    The wizard verifies that the specified share exists and the Specify The Log Shipping Destinations page reappears displaying the destination server and database.

34. Click Next.

    The Initialize The Destination Databases page appears.

35. Verify that the Perform A Full Database Backup Now option button is selected and then click Next.

    The Log Shipping Schedules page appears.

36. Click the Change button to modify the backup schedule.

    The Edit Recurring Job Schedule dialog box appears. Note that there are two spin boxes, one for changing the number and one for specifying the increment of time.

37. In the Daily Frequency group box, change the Occurs Every spin box from 15 to 1 (minute) and then click OK.

    The Log Shipping Schedules page reappears.

38. Change the Copy/Load Frequency spin box from 15 (minutes) to 1.

39. Change the File Retention Period spin box from 24 (hours) to 1 (hour(s)).

40. Click Next.

The Log Shipping Thresholds page appears. Notice that the Backup Alert Threshold is set to 5 minutes and the Out Of Sync Alert Threshold is set to 3 minutes.

41. Click Next.

The Specify The Log Shipping Monitor Server Information page appears.

42. In the SQL Server drop-down list, verify that SelfPacedCPU is displayed and then click Next.

The Reports To Generate page appears.

43. Click Next.

The Maintenance Plan History page appears.

44. Click Next.

The Database Maintenance Plan Wizard Summary page appears.

45. In the Plan Name text box, type **Log Shipping** and then click Next.

The Completing The Database Maintenance Plan Wizard page appears.

46. Click the Finish button.

Notice the progress of the steps the wizard is performing.

47. Click OK to acknowledge a Database Maintenance Plan Wizard message box informing you that the maintenance plan was created successfully.

48. In the console tree, expand the SelfPacedCPU\MyNamedInstance container and then expand the Databases container.

49. Click the Databases container and then, on the toolbar, click the Refresh button.

In the Databases container for the SelfPacedCPU\MyNamedInstance, notice that the LogShipDB database container appears containing a read-only copy of the LogShipDB database. If it does not appear, right-click the Databases container and then click Refresh.

50. Leave SQL Server Enterprise Manager running.

Monitoring Log Shipping

To monitor the status of log shipping on the monitor server, expand the Management container of that server and then click Log Shipping Monitor (if you have just configured log shipping, right-click the Management container and then click Refresh). The status of all log shipping servers is displayed in the details pane. See Figure 16.15.

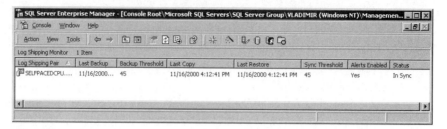

Figure 16.15. Log shipping monitor.

The log shipping monitor displays the date and time of the most recent transaction log backup on the primary server in the Last Backup column, the most recent copy of the transaction log backup file to the network share in the Last Copy column, the most recent restore of the transaction log backup file to the standby server in the Last Restore column, and the synchronization status in the Status column. Click the Show/Hide Console Tree/Favorites button on the toolbar to display only the details pane.

To view the backup history for the primary server, right-click the log shipping pair and then click View Backup History to display the Database Maintenance Plan History dialog box. See Figure 16.16.

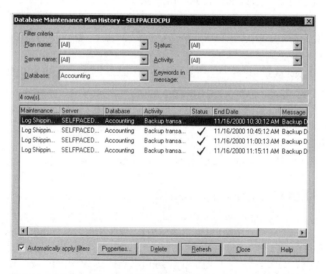

Figure 16.16. Viewing the backup history for the primary server from the monitor server.

To view the copy and restore history for the standby server, right-click the log shipping pair and then click View Copy/Restore History to display the Secondary Server Log Shipping History dialog box. See Figure 16.17.

To modify the properties of log shipping, right-click the log shipping pair and then click Properties to display the Log Shipping Pair Properties dialog box. Log shipping information is displayed on this page, including the last backup file, the last file copied, the last file loaded, and the times and deltas for each. See Figure 16.18.

Click the Source tab to modify alert properties for the primary server (see Figure 16.19). Click the View Backup Schedule button to view the backup schedule.

Click the Destination tab to modify the alert properties for the standby server (see Figure 16.20). Click the View Copy Schedule button to view how often database copies are made, or click the View Load Schedule button to view how often the database is restored.

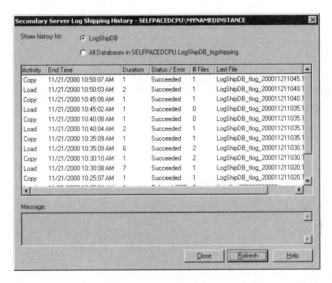

Figure 16.17.   Viewing the copy/restore history for the standby server from the monitor server.

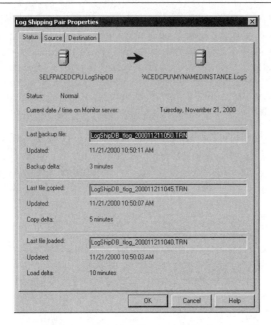

Figure 16.18. Viewing log shipping pair properties.

Figure 16.19. Viewing the Source tab of log shipping pair properties.

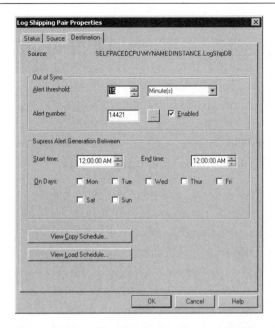

Figure 16.20. Viewing the Destination tab of log shipping pair properties.

Practice: Monitoring Log Shipping

In this practice you use the Log Shipping Monitor in SQL Server Enterprise Manager to monitor log shipping.

▶ **To monitor log shipping**

1. Ensure that you are logged on to the SelfPacedSQL.MSFT domain controller as Administrator.
2. In the SQL Server Enterprise Manager console tree, expand the Management container in the default instance.
3. Click the Management container and then, on the toolbar, click the Refresh button.
4. In the Management container, click Log Shipping Monitor.

   The current status of the log shipping pair is displayed in the details pane.
5. On the toolbar, click the Show/Hide Console Tree/Favorites button.

   Notice that the window now displays only the contents of the details pane (for easier viewing of all columns).
6. Right-click the log shipping pair and then click View Backup History.

   The Database Maintenance Plan History – SelfPacedCPU dialog box appears displaying the history of the Log Shipping maintenance plan. Notice that the transaction log is being backed up every minute and each successful job has a blue check mark in the status column.
7. Click the Close button.

8. Right-click the log shipping pair and then click View Copy/Restore History.

    The Secondary Server Log Shipping History – SelfPacedCPU\MyNamedInstance dialog box appears. Notice that the copy job and the load job occur every minute. The load job restores all transaction log backup files that have been copied, and then the copy job connects to the primary server and copies any new transaction log backup files to the standby server.

9. Click the Close button.

10. Right-click the log shipping pair and then click Properties.

    The Log Shipping Pair Properties dialog box appears. Notice that Load Delta indicates that the synchronization delay between the primary database and the standby database is one minute (it will be two minutes on some slower computers).

11. Click OK to close the Log Shipping Pair Properties dialog box.

12. On the Tools menu, click SQL Query Analyzer.

    SQL Query Analyzer appears displaying a connection to the SelfPacedCPU default instance.

13. On the toolbar, click the Load SQL Script button.

    The Open Query File dialog box appears.

14. Open LogShipChangeData.sql in the C:\SelfPacedSQL\CH_16 folder.

    Notice that this script changes the ContactTitle field for one of the customers in the LogShipDB database.

15. On the toolbar, click the Execute Query button to execute the query.

    Notice that the ContactTitle field for CustomerID ANATR is changed.

16. Leave SQL Query Analyzer and SQL Server Enterprise Manager running.

Bringing a Standby Server Online

To bring a standby server online, you must run the following system stored procedures in order.

1. Run *sp_change_primary_role* on the primary server. Use the @db_name argument to specify the appropriate database. Use the @backup_log argument to specify a backup of the current transaction log and the @terminate argument to specify a roll back of all incomplete transactions. You can specify the recovery state of the database after the completion of the stored procedure: RECOVERY, NO RECOVERY, or STANDBY (default is RECOVERY) with the @final_state argument. Finally, you can specify the access level of the database after the completion of the stored procedure: MULTI_USER, RESTRICTED_USER, or SINGLE_USER (default is MULTI_USER) with the @access_level argument.

2. Run *sp_change_secondary_role* on the standby server. Use the @db_name to specify the appropriate database. Use the @db_name argument to specify the

application of pending transaction log backup files to the standby database. Use the @db_name argument to convert the standby database to a primary database. You can specify the recovery state of the database after the completion of the stored procedure: RECOVERY, NO RECOVERY, or STANDBY (default is RECOVERY) with the @final_state argument. Finally, you can specify the access level of the database after the completion of the stored procedure: MULTI_USER, RESTRICTED_USER, or SINGLE_USER (default is MULTI_USER) with the @access_level argument.

Note   If the secondary server (the standby server) has a job running against this database at the same time the system stored procedure is run, you will receive a Transact-SQL error indicating that exclusive access to the database to restore the transaction log files could not be obtained. Either rerun the system stored procedure or complete the restore using SQL Server Enterprise Manager.

3. Run *sp_change_monitor_role* on the log shipping monitor server. This system stored procedure updates the monitor server to reflect the changed log shipping roles, using the @primary_server argument to designate the primary server being replaced, the @secondary_server argument to designate the standby server being converted to a primary server, the @database argument to designate the standby database being converted to a primary database, and the @new_source argument to specify the network share the new primary server will use for storing its transaction log backup files.

In addition, you must verify that the new primary server contains all required logins. You can use a saved Transact-SQL script, or if you used the DTS Transfer Logins Task to create a Bcp output file containing these logins, you can use the *sp_resolve_logins* system stored procedure to input these logins from the Bcp output file.

After completion of these steps, the standby server is ready to function as the new primary server. The former primary server is no longer part of a shipping pair. You must add the original primary server or another server as a standby server to re-establish a shipping pair. To bring the original primary server back online, repeat the three-step process just described.

Practice: Bringing a Standby Server Online as the Primary Server

In this practice you use stored procedures to bring a standby server online as the primary server and deactivate the primary server and its log shipping jobs.

▶ **To bring a standby server online as the primary server**

1. Ensure that you are logged on to the SelfPacedSQL.MSFT domain controller as Administrator.

2. In SQL Query Analyzer, verify that you are connected to the default instance of SQL Server on SelfPacedCPU and then click the Load SQL Script button on the toolbar.

   The Open Query File dialog box appears.

3. Open DemotePrimary.sql in the C:\SelfPacedSQL\CH_16 folder.

   This script runs the *sp_change_primary_role* system stored procedure, which backs up the current transaction log for the LogShipDB database and sets the database to read-only.

4. On the toolbar, click the Execute Query button to execute the DemotePrimary.sql script.

   The script executes and displays a message regarding the backup of the current transaction log.

Note   If you get an access denied permissions error, the SQL Server Agent service does not have sufficient permissions. Either verify all required permissions, or make the SQLService account a member of the local Administrators group (and restart all services), and then rerun this lab from the beginning.

---

5. Switch to SQL Server Enterprise Manager.

6. On the toolbar, click the Show/Hide Console Tree/Favorites button to show the console tree (if necessary).

7. Expand the SelfPacedCPU\MyNamedInstance container, expand the Management container, expand the SQL Server Agent container, click the Jobs container, and then click Local Server Jobs.

   The current jobs are displayed in the details pane.

8. In the details pane, right-click the Log Shipping Copy For SelfPacedCPU LogShipDB_Logshipping job and then click Disable Job.

9. In the details pane, right-click the Log Shipping Restore For SelfPacedCPU LogShipDB_Logshipping job and then click Disable Job.

10. Switch to SQL Query Analyzer.

11. On the File menu, click Connect.

    The Connect To SQL Server dialog box appears.

12. In the SQL Server drop-down list, select SelfPacedCPU\MyNamedInstance, verify that the Windows Authentication option button is selected, and then click OK.

13. On the toolbar, click the Load SQL Script button.

    The Open Query File dialog box appears.

14. Open PromoteSecondary.sql in the C:\SelfPacedSQL\CH_16 folder.

    This script runs the sp_change_secondary_role system stored procedure, which copies the current transaction log from the primary server and restores it to the LogShipDB database on the standby server. It also restores the database to multiuser mode and removes the read-only setting.

15. On the toolbar, click the Execute Query button to execute the PromoteSecondary.sql script.

    Notice that the script copies the current transaction log (and any other logs it has not previously copied) and applies it to the database on the standby server. It deletes the copy and load jobs that were running on the former standby server and enables the transaction log backup job on the new primary server. If the second result set indicates that exclusive control of the database could not be obtained to perform the restore task, rerun the system stored procedure.

16. Switch to the SQL query pane containing the connection to the default instance.

17. On the toolbar, click the Load SQL Script button.

    The Open Query File dialog box appears.

18. Open UpdateMonitorServer.sql in the C:\SelfPacedSQL\CH_16 folder.

    This script runs the *sp_change_monitor_role* system stored procedure, updating the monitor server regarding the change in the role of the primary and standby server. It also specifies the storage location for the transaction log backup files being created on the new primary (former standby) server.

19. On the toolbar, click the Execute Query button to execute the UpdateMonitorServer.sql script.

20. Switch to the SQL query pane containing the connection to SelfPaced-CPU\MyNamedInstance.

21. On the toolbar, click the Clear Window button.

22. In the query pane, **type SELECT * FROM LogShipDB.dbo.Customers WHERE CustomerID = 'ANATR'** and then click the Execute Query button on the toolbar.

    Notice that the ContactTitle change was captured in the transaction log and applied to the new primary server before it was restored.

23. On the toolbar, click the Clear Window button.

24. In the query pane, type **UPDATE LogShipDB.dbo.Customers SET ContactTitle = 'Owner' WHERE CustomerID = 'ANATR'** and then click the Execute Query button on the toolbar.

    Notice that the query executes successfully. The new primary database is functioning successfully. If you receive an error stating that BEGIN TRANSACTION could not run because the database is read-only, you are connected to the default instance rather than to the named instance.

25. Close SQL Server Enterprise Manager and SQL Query Analyzer.

Lesson Summary

Using a standby server enables the database administrator to quickly bring a server online in case of a server failure or to perform necessary maintenance on a primary server. Log shipping automates this process using jobs and alerts administered by SQL Server Agent service on the primary server and on the standby server. A monitoring server is used to monitor log shipping pairs of servers. Bringing a standby server online as the primary server requires the execution of three system stored procedures. In addition, the database administrator must ensure that the new primary server has the necessary logins for the databases being promoted. This can be accomplished using the DTS Transfer Logins Task or using Transact-SQL scripts.

Lesson 2: Using Failover Clustering

SQL Server 2000 failover clustering can be used to provide almost instantaneous availability of a secondary node in a failover cluster configuration in case the primary node fails for any reason. Failover clustering provides a higher level of availability than the use of standby servers. In this lesson, you will be introduced to the Microsoft Cluster Service (MSCS). You will learn about the use of active/active and active/passive failover clusters. You will also learn how to create and configure a SQL Server virtual server on a failover cluster. Finally, you will learn about maintaining a failover cluster.

After this lesson, you will be able to

- Install SQL Server on multiple nodes in a failover cluster
- Describe types of failover clusters
- Maintain a failover cluster
- Recover from a cluster node failure

Estimated lesson time: 15 minutes

Introducing MSCS

MSCS is a service of Windows 2000 and Windows NT 4.0 that is used to form server clusters (also called failover clusters). A server cluster is a group of independent computer systems working together as a single system and sharing a common storage system (generally a RAID system). Each computer frequently has identical hardware. Windows 2000 Data Center supports up to four nodes (each server in a cluster is called a node). Windows 2000 Advanced Server and Windows NT 4.0 Enterprise Edition support two nodes. Applications run on a server cluster, rather than on a specific node in the server cluster. The MSCS clustering software monitors each node and ensures that an application running on the server cluster continues to run regardless of the failure of an individual node. See Figure 16.21.

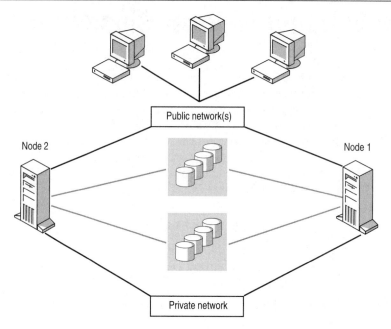

Figure 16.21. Failover cluster.

Note   Installing and administering a server cluster on Windows 2000 or Windows NT 4.0 is beyond the scope of this book.

Creating a Virtual Server on a Server Cluster

SQL Server 2000 runs as a virtual server across two or more nodes in the server cluster. To install SQL Server 2000 on an existing server cluster, run the SQL Server Setup program on one of the nodes in the server cluster. The Setup program automatically detects the presence of the server cluster. Select the Virtual Server option button in the Computer Name page to define a virtual server and install the executable files on each node in the server cluster (for example, to C:\Program Files\Microsoft SQL Server on each node). This enables each node to run SQL Server executable programs if necessary. The data files (for system and user databases) for the virtual server can only be installed in the shared RAID system. This enables the data files to be available to any node.

During setup, you define a virtual server name and assign an IP address to the virtual server. A virtual server can use multiple IP addresses to support multiple subnets that provide redundancy in the event of a network adapter or router failure. SQL Server clients connect to this virtual server, rather than to any individual node. By default, the virtual server runs on the node on which you are installing SQL Server, although you can select another node as the primary node. One or more secondary nodes in the server cluster function as the failover nodes, ready to pick up the load of the primary node in the event of failure.

A node in a server cluster can be either active or passive. You can create up to 16 instances of SQL Server 2000 in a server cluster. Each instance can run on any node in the server cluster. You must plan to have sufficient hardware resources (memory and processor) in each failover node to provide services in the event a primary node fails. There are several ways to accomplish this.

- **Active/passive clusters.** In an active/passive cluster, one node serves exclusively as the failover node for another node. In the event of failure of the primary (active) node, the failover (passive) node has sufficient hardware resources to handle the load of the primary node with no degradation in throughput or performance. Using an active/passive configuration is generally required for mission-critical applications. However, in an active/passive cluster, the passive node in the server cluster is essentially unused unless the primary node fails.

- **Active/active clusters.** In an active/active cluster, each node serves as the primary node for a virtual server as well as the failover node for another virtual server. In the event of failure of one of the nodes, the remaining node (or nodes) must handle the load of both virtual servers. This generally means some degradation of service for both virtual servers until the failed node is repaired. You must plan to leave sufficient headroom on each active node to provide adequate service to all services running on the failover node in the event of a node failure. The use of an active/active cluster is a more cost-effective use of computer hardware when all nodes are functioning properly.

Planning Issues

There are a number of installation and configuration considerations you must be aware of when running SQL Server 2000 in a clustered environment.

- If you plan to use MS DTC in a clustered environment, you must run the Cluster Wizard on each node before you install SQL Server 2000. This enables MS DTC to run in clustered mode.

- If you have configured a minimum server memory setting for a node, you must ensure that the failover node has sufficient memory capacity to provide this minimum memory in the event of a failover event. Generally, you should allow SQL Server to dynamically allocate memory in a server cluster.

- If you are using AWE on one node, all nodes should have the same amount of AWE. In addition, ensure that the total value of the max server memory setting for all instances is less than the lowest amount of physical memory available on any of the nodes in the failover cluster.

- Ensure that the recovery interval is set to zero to allow SQL Server to set the recovery interval. This setting affects the length of time SQL Server will take to fail over to a failover node.

- Service account passwords for each SQL Server service must be identical on all nodes. If you change a password using SQL Server Enterprise Manager, it will change the password on all nodes automatically.
- If you use an internal disk controller, disable caching. To optimize performance, use an external disk controller that is certified for database use.
- On Windows NT 4.0, the domain user account used by the SQL Server and SQL Server Agent services must be a member of the local Administrators group on each node in the server cluster.
- If you are using replication, use the shared disk system for the snapshot files so they remain always available in the event of a node failure.

Disaster Recovery

In the event the primary node used by a virtual server fails, a secondary node takes over. A recovery of the database occurs automatically, and the failover node takes over and handles all user connections (user connections do not need to be reestablished). User processes are oblivious to the change, other than a minor wait for the failover to complete.

To recover, run the Setup program to remove the failed node from the configuration. This takes approximately one minute. Next, repair or replace the failed node. Finally, rerun the Setup program and add the rebuilt node. The Setup program takes care of the rest of the process. The active node does not have to be stopped during this process, so users can continue working.

Lesson Summary

Failover clustering provides the highest level of availability for SQL Server 2000 installations. Failover clustering is based on MSCS and is available only on Windows 2000 Data Center, Windows 2000 Advanced Server, and Windows NT 4.0 Enterprise Edition. When the SQL Server Setup program detects a server cluster, you can choose to install a virtual server, selecting one of the nodes in the server cluster as the primary node. If this node fails, the virtual server will automatically fail over to a secondary node. The secondary node can either be inactive or function as the primary node for another virtual server.

Review

Here are some questions to help you determine whether you have learned the content of this chapter. If you have difficulty answering the questions, review the material in this chapter. The answers for these questions are located in the Appendix, "Questions and Answers."

1. You are the database administrator for a number of SQL Server installations that generally must be available 24 x 7. What are the major failover differences between the use of standby servers with log shipping and the use of failover clustering?

2. You are administering 10 production servers. You are planning to implement log shipping to provide for a quick restore of each production server in the case of a system failure. What is the minimum number of computers you can use to accomplish this task? What is the minimum number of computers you would recommend be used?

Preparation for MCP Exam 70-228

Installing and Configuring SQL Server 2000

Installing Microsoft SQL Server 2000 requires a well thought-out plan and overall implementation. The choices you make during installation have a direct effect on the operations of the server. For example, the method you select to install SQL Server, how you plan to upgrade existing SQL servers, and how many instances you install on a single server are all choices you need to make no matter what version of SQL Server you install. However, there are some choices that only those administrators deploying the Enterprise edition of SQL Server need to consider. In this domain, we review issues you need to be aware of when installing SQL Server, particularly focusing on those issues that you face when deploying SQL Server 2000 Enterprise edition.

Tested Skills and Suggested Practices

The skills that you need to successfully master the Installing and Configuring SQL Server 2000 objective domain on the *Installing, Configuring, and Administering Microsoft SQL Server 2000 Enterprise Edition* exam include:

- **Installing SQL Server 2000.**

  - Practice 1: Use the SQL Server Books Online to identify the hardware requirements for installing SQL Server 2000 Enterprise edition and compare them to the server on which you are installing SQL Server 2000.

  - Practice 2: Identify the differences in features between the various editions of SQL Server 2000 and why one particular version is chosen over another.

  - Practice 3: Install SQL Server 2000 Enterprise edition and specify it as the default instance. Specify the path for the data files to be stored on a different drive from where program files are stored.

  - Practice 4: Install a named instance of SQL Server 2000 Enterprise edition, and set the collation to LATIN1_GENERAL_CI_AI.

- Practice 5: Use the SQL Server Books Online to identify the hardware require-ments for creating a SQL Server cluster and compare those requirements to your setup.

- **Upgrading to SQL Server 2000.**

  - Practice 1: Use the SQL Server Books Online to identify the prerequisites for upgrading to SQL Server 2000.

  - Practice 2: Use the SQL Server Books Online to identify the rules for running multiple versions of SQL Server on the same computer. Install a named instance of SQL Server 2000 on a server running a default instance of SQL Server 2000.

  - Practice 3: Use the SQL Server Books Online to identify the options available under the Copy Database Wizard and the SQL Server Upgrade Wizard.

  - Practice 4: Use the SQL Server Books Online to identify the backward compat-ibility issues between SQL Server 2000 and SQL Server 7.0 as well as between SQL Server 6.5 and SQL Server 7.0.

- **Configuring a linked server.**

  - Practice 1: Use the SQL Server Books Online to identify the benefits of creating a linked server versus a remote server.

  - Practice 2: Create a linked server to a SQL server or a file data source, such as a Microsoft Access database file or Excel spreadsheet, using Enterprise Manager.

  - Practice 3: Use the SQL Server Books Online to determine the parameters for the sp_addlinkedserver command. Use this command to create a linked server to a SQL server or a file data source.

  - Practice 4: Use the SQL Server Books Online to identify the requirements for linking to SQL Server while it is running different collation types.

- **Configuring SQL Mail and SQLAgentMail.**

  - Practice 1: Set up SQL Server Services to use a domain user account for startup. Configure a mail profile for the domain user account. (Note that even if you do not have an actual mail server running, you should still be able to create a sam-ple mail profile for testing purposes.)

  - Practice 2: Configure SQL Mail to use the mail profile you created. Configure SQL Mail to start automatically when SQL Server starts.

  - Practice 3: Configure SQLAgentMail to use the mail profile you created.

  - Practice 4: Use the SQL Server Books Online to identify the stored procedures used by SQL Mail to process incoming messages.

- **Granting permissions to execute stored procedures.**

  - Practice 1: As a database owner of the Northwind database, create a simple stored procedure that selects the first and last names from the Employees table. Now create a new SQL logon that has public access to the Northwind database. From the Query Analyzer, connect as the new SQL user and try to execute the stored procedure.

  - Practice 2: Grant your new user execute permission for the stored procedure you created in Practice 1. Execute the stored procedure from the Query Analyzer as the new user.

  - Practice 3: Grant the public role execute permission for your stored procedure and remove execute permission from your new user. Execute the stored procedure from the Query Analyzer as the new user.

  - Practice 4: With the public role having execute permission, deny execute permission to your new user. Execute the stored procedure from the Query Analyzer as the new user.

- **Configuring network libraries.**

  - Practice 1: Use the SQL Server Books Online to identify the network libraries available under Windows 2000 Server.

  - Practice 2: Configure a client workstation to connect to the SQL Server 2000 machine using the Multiprotocol library.

  - Practice 3: Change the TCP/IP socket value on the SQL Server, and configure a client to connect using newly assigned port values.

- **Troubleshooting failed installations.**

  - Practice 1: Find the most recent SQL Server error log and open it using Notepad. Note the types of messages logged and their formats.

  - Practice 2: Access the SQL Server error logs using Enterprise Manager.

  - Practice 3: Open the Windows NT or 2000 Event Viewer and view the Application log. Note the types of messages logged and their formats.

  - Practice 4: Run the SQLDIAG.EXE program and review the SQLDIAG.TXT output file.

  - Practice 5: Find the SQLSTP.LOG file and open it using Notepad. Note the types of messages logged and their formats.

  - Practice 6: Access the Microsoft Online Troubleshooters at *http://support.microsoft.com/support/sql/tshooter.asp*. Follow one of the troubleshooters through the step-by-step process of diagnosing a problem.

Further Reading

This section lists supplemental readings by objective. We recommend that you study these sources thoroughly before taking exam 70-228.

Objective 1.1

Microsoft SQL Server 2000 product documentation. To access Books Online, click the Start button, point to Programs, then Microsoft SQL Server, and then select Books Online. Select the Contents tab and expand Installing SQL Server. This volume contains articles on most aspects of installing SQL Server. The overview has the hardware and software requirements document and there are thorough explanations of named instances and the advanced installation options.

Microsoft Corporation. *Microsoft SQL Server 2000 Administrator's Companion*. Redmond, Washington: Microsoft Press, 2000. Chapters 4 through 12 discuss the planning and installation of SQL Server 2000.

Objective 1.2

Microsoft SQL Server 2000 product documentation. To access Books Online, click the Start button, point to Programs, then Microsoft SQL Server, and then select Books Online. Select the Contents tab and expand Installing SQL Server. Then expand the topic Upgrading to SQL Server 2000: Overview. This contains the requirements document and instructional documents for upgrading from SQL Server 7.0. There are also sections on using the Copy Database Wizard and Upgrade Wizard.

In Part 1 of this book, Chapter 4, "Upgrading to SQL Server 2000," Lesson 3 covers the process of upgrading a SQL Server involved in replication. Microsoft Corporation.

Objective 1.3

Microsoft SQL Server 2000 product documentation. To access Books Online, click the Start button, point to Programs, then Microsoft SQL Server, and then select Books Online. Select the Contents tab and expand Administering SQL Server. Then expand Managing Servers, and then Configuring Linked Servers. This covers security and OLE DB providers.

Objective 1.4

Microsoft SQL Server 2000 product documentation. To access Books Online, click the Start button, point to Programs, then Microsoft SQL Server, and then select Books Online. Select the Contents tab and expand Administering SQL Server, then Managing Servers, and then SQL Mail. This section details information about the configuration of SQL Mail and mail profiles as well as using the SQL Mail stored procedures.

Objective 1.5

Microsoft SQL Server 2000 product documentation. To access Books Online, click the Start button, point to Programs, then Microsoft SQL Server, and then select Books Online. Select the Contents tab and expand Administering SQL Server, then Managing Servers, and then Configuring Network Connections. This section discusses network protocols and using the SQL Server 2000 Network Utilities.

Objective 1.6

Microsoft Corporation. SQL Server Troubleshooters. Access this site at *http://support.microsoft.com/support/sql/tshooter.asp*. The troubleshooter is a tool that lets you tell it your problem by selecting a series of statements that describe the symptoms and then it gives you possible solutions.

Microsoft Corporation. TechNet. Access this site at *http://www.microsoft.com/technet*. Microsoft TechNet is an excellent resource for finding solutions to common problems.

Microsoft SQL Server 2000 product documentation. To access Books Online, click the Start button, point to Programs, then Microsoft SQL Server, and then select Books Online. Select the Contents tab and expand Troubleshooting. This volume covers many aspects of troubleshooting SQL Server issues, including how to view the error logs and a description of error messages.

OBJECTIVE 1.1

Install SQL Server 2000.

The method of installation you select for deploying Microsoft SQL Server 2000 depends upon your organization's deployment plan for SQL. If SQL Server is deployed within an Enterprise network, be sure to leverage all of the setup options provided in SQL Server 2000, such as **unattended installation**, to make the deployment process effortless.

In this objective, we review the information you need to know to successfully install SQL Server 2000. We also review the installation features and illustrate how certain choices made during the install can affect the deployment of the server.

When you install SQL Server 2000, you can either install the server manually or as an unattended installation. Choose an unattended installation if you want to perform several installations of SQL Server with identical configurations on different computers. The core requirement for an unattended installation is a setup file. The setup file contains all the instructions SQL Server requires to configure the server as you specify. There are three types of setup files that you can use with unattended installations:

- **SETUP.ISS**

- **sample setup files**

- **specialized setup files**

When installing SQL Server 2000, you can choose to select a domain account, a local user account, or a built-in system account to run the **SQL Services**. **SQL Server Service** and **SQLServiceAgent** are the two services that comprise SQL Server. The role that SQL Server plays in your environment determines the type of account you select. If its role consists of communicating with other SQL servers on the network, you need to specify a domain account because network privileges are required when communicating from one SQL server to another. For a domain account, Microsoft recommends that the account be a member of the Administrators local group for that SQL Server computer.

If SQL Server does not require any form of collaboration with other SQL servers and you will not be running services, such as **SQL Mail**, specifying a local user account or local system account will suffice. Configuring SQL Services to start by using a local system account has an administrative advantage: you are not required to create and manage a local user or domain account.

With the release of SQL Server 2000, administrators are able to install multiple instances of SQL Server onto a single server. When you install SQL Server 2000, you can choose to install it as the default instance or as a named instance. A named instance must be referenced as Server\Instance Name. For example, if you install SQL Server 2000 onto a server named Marketing and create an instance SQL1, you reference it as Marketing\SQL1. An instance name cannot be longer than 16 characters, and you cannot use SQL Server reserved names or sysnames. SQL Server does not limit the number of instances you can install on a single server, but your server's hardware limitations will.

You also need to consider file locations during the installation process. Do not simply select the default file locations without understanding the effects they will have on server performance and growth issues including capacity planning.

SQL Server 2000 requires at least two operating system files to store database objects and data. Every database starts with a **primary data file**, which holds data as well as pointers to other files in the database. The second required file is the **transaction log**, which holds information to recover the database. An optional third type of operating system file that is used to store data or spread data across multiple disk drives is a **secondary data file**.

If your organization relies heavily on the services and data of SQL Server, waiting for a tape to restore can critically affect your success. Organizations that require continuous uptime should implement Microsoft Cluster Services (MSCS), which does not require the use of backup files and decreases the lag time between switching servers.

To create a SQL Server 2000 clustered environment with MSCS, you need to run either Windows 2000 Advanced Server or Windows 2000 DataCenter Server. Running Windows 2000 Advanced Server enables you to create a two-node cluster, whereas DataCenter Server supports a four-node cluster. A node is any server that is part of the clustered environment. The machines that make up the cluster must also be running a copy of SQL Server 2000 Enterprise edition because it's the only version of SQL Server 2000 that supports clustering.

Objective 1.1 Questions

70-228.01.01.001

Your organization has just completed the development of a new e-commerce Web site that uses SQL Server 2000. The nature of the application requires the server to run around the clock. You choose to deploy SQL Server in a failover cluster. Which operating system must you install SQL Server 2000 on if you want to configure a failover cluster? (Choose all that apply.)

A. Windows 2000 Server

B. Windows 2000 Advanced Server

C. Windows NT 4.0 Server

D. Windows NT 4.0 Enterprise edition

70-228.01.01.002

Your organization is ready to roll out a new accounting application. The data for the application must be stored on SQL Server 2000. Due to the size of the data, you need to deploy six SQL Server 2000 machines, each configured with the exact same network and database settings.

You want to accomplish the following goals:

- Ease the process of installing SQL Server 2000 multiple times

- Ensure that SQL Server Services uses a domain user account

- Install SQL Server 2000 as a named instance on each of the six servers

You create a specialized setup file using the Record Unattended .iss file option in Microsoft SQL Server Setup. The only changes you make to the specialized setup file are to specify the domain user account to be used for the SQL Server and SQLServerAgent Services.

Which results does your installation achieve? (Choose all that apply.)

A. You have eased the install process on multiple machines.

B. The SQL Server and SQLServerAgent Services use a domain account to start up.

C. SQL Server 2000 is installed as a named instance on each of the servers.

D. The solution does not achieve any of the required results.

70-228.01.01.003

You are installing SQL Server 2000 to a server named Finance_SQL, which is located in the Finance department. It is a member of the Seattle NT 4.0 domain. Finance_SQL must interact with two other SQL servers named Marketing_SQL and Accounting_SQL. Both Marketing_SQL and Accounting_SQL are members of the Seattle domain. Which Windows user account should you assign SQL Server 2000 and SQL Server Agent Services to run as?

A. Local administrator account for the Finance_SQL computer

B. Local system account

C. The sa account for the Finance_SQL server

D. Domain user account

70-228.01.01.004

Your organization is in the process of expanding support for its e-commerce to customers in Germany, France, and Spain. When users log on to the site, they can select the language in which they want to view the site. Data from all of the language-specific sites will be entered into a single database stored on a SQL Server 2000 server. You want the SQL server to be configured with the fastest sorting order. When installing SQL Server, which collation type should you specify?

A. Latin1_General_BIN

B. Latin1_General_CI_AS

C. Latin1_General_CI

D. Latin1_General_CI_AS_KS

70-228.01.01.005

You are configuring two SQL servers that will be part of a SQL Server Federation. The servers are running Windows 2000 Advanced Server, and they have identical drive layouts consisting of two physical 18 GB drives formatted using the Windows NT file system (NTFS). The partitioning is as follows: drive C is 4 GB and contains Windows 2000, drive D is 14 GB, and drive E is 18 GB. The servers also have a fibre channel storage device attached to them with 36 GB of usable disk space. MSCS has been configured on the servers. You need to install SQL Server 2000 on both nodes. Where should you specify that the program files and data files be installed to ensure optimal performance and reliability?

A. Both program files and data files should be installed to the shared storage device.

B. Program files should be installed to a shared storage device, and data files should be installed on drive E.

C. Data files should be installed on a shared storage device, and program files should be installed on drive D.

D. Program files should be installed to the quorum disk, and data files should be installed to the shared storage device.

Objective 1.1 Answers

70-228.01.01.001

► **Correct Answers: B and D**

A. **Incorrect:** See explanation for answer B.

B. **Correct:** SQL Server 2000 Enterprise edition enables you to install and configure a failover cluster. Failover clustering is used to provide high availability by configuring each instance of SQL Server failover to a node in the cluster. Windows 2000 Advanced Server and Windows NT 4.0 Enterprise edition both support MSCS; therefore, they also support SQL Server failover clustering. Using either Windows 2000 Advanced Server or Windows NT 4.0 Enterprise edition, you can create a two-node cluster. However, Windows 2000 DataCenter Server supports up to a four-node cluster.

C. **Incorrect:** See explanation for answer B.

D. **Correct:** See explanation for answer B.

70-228.01.01.002

► **Correct Answers: A and B**

A. **Correct:** When you choose to run an unattended installation of SQL Server 2000, you can specify three distinct sources for the unattended install. The first source is the SQL Server 2000 CD, where sample unattended installation files are provided. These sample files include scripts that install only typical installations of SQL Server or the client tools. The second source of instructions for the unattended install is the SETUP.ISS file, which is written to when you execute an installation of SQL Server 2000 using the Setup screens. However, if you need to specify a domain user account or do not wish to run through an install simply to create a SETUP.ISS file, you can use the Record Unattended .iss file option in Microsoft SQL Server Setup.

B. **Correct:** By specifying the domain user account you want the services to use during the creation of the specialized setup file, you ensure that the services start up using the domain account.

C. **Incorrect:** Unless specified in the specialized setup file, SQL Server 2000 installs all installations as a default install. You must specify in the file that Setup install SQL Server 2000 as a named instance.

D. **Incorrect:** Two of the three requirements are achieved: you can use the setup file to install similarly configured SQL Server 2000 installations, and the domain user account is used to start up the SQL Server Services.

70-228.01.01.003

▶ **Correct Answers: D**

A. **Incorrect:** The local administrator account for the Finance_SQL computer does not have network privileges and is unable to communicate with other SQL servers on the network.

B. **Incorrect:** The local system account does not have network access under Windows NT 4.0 and Windows 2000. It is also restricted from interacting with other SQL servers on the network. Therefore, it cannot take part in publishing, distributing, or subscribing to information from other SQL servers.

C. **Incorrect:** The sa account is a SQL Server account and not a Windows domain account. The sa account has full permissions to configure and maintain the SQL Server, but it cannot start the SQL Server Services.

D. **Correct:** As long as the domain user account has a certain set of permissions, it enables the SQL Services to start and allows interaction with other SQL servers.

70-228.01.01.004

▶ **Correct Answers: A**

A. **Correct:** When you install SQL Server 2000, it's important that you know which languages the database is expected to support. Changing the collation type of a database is not a simple procedure; it requires that you reinstall SQL Server. After selecting the correct collation type, you should also be aware of the sorting parameters. How the database sorts has a direct effect upon the performance of the database. In this case, Latin1_General_BIN indicates the Binary sorting order. Binary is the fastest sorting order and is case sensitive.

B. **Incorrect:** A language type ending with CI_AS indicates Case Insensitive and Accent Sensitive sorting.

C. **Incorrect:** In this case, there are fewer sorting parameters than option B, but Case Insensitive is still slower than Binary sorting.

D. **Incorrect:** The number of sorting parameters specified for this collation type makes it the slowest of the four choices. KS indicates Kana Sensitive. Kana Sensitive instructs SQL to distinguish between the two types of Kana characters, which are found only in the Japanese language. Select Kana Sensitive sorting only when it is relevant.

70-228.01.01.005

▶ **Correct Answers: C**

A. **Incorrect:** Program files for SQL Server should always be stored on the local drive of the server. Even though a SQL server may be configured to operate as a node in a cluster, the server is capable of running multiple instances of SQL Server that are not virtual servers. Therefore, if a failure were to occur with the clustered instance, clients could continue to attach to other instances of SQL Server running on the server.

B. **Incorrect:** See explanation for answer A.

C. **Correct:** When a node in a cluster fails, MSCS will failover automatically to the second node. Clients will continue to attach to the SQL server through the virtual server and gain access to their data as the failover node now has control of the storage device and SQL Server data. If the data files were stored on the local drive for the primary node, the failover would still occur, but no data would be available to the clients.

D. **Incorrect:** Program files should not be stored on the quorum disk. The quorum disk stores files critical to the server's failover or recovery. Installing the program files to the quorum disk may require that you change access permissions to the disk, inhibiting MSCS from reading the disk when required.

O B J E C T I V E   1 . 2

Upgrade to SQL Server 2000.

With the introduction of named and default **instances**, SQL Server 2000 can accommodate earlier versions of Microsoft SQL Server already installed on your computer. The SQL Server 2000 Setup detects versions of SQL Server 7.0 or SQL Server 2000 currently installed and provides the appropriate options.

If SQL Server 7.0 is detected during the SQL Server 2000 setup process, you have the option to upgrade the SQL Server 7.0 databases and overwrite all SQL Server 7.0 program files. The SQL Server 2000 setup process also allows you to upgrade to a different edition of SQL Server to gain added features.

Alternatively, you can perform an online database upgrade of SQL Server 7.0 databases to SQL Server 2000 database format using the **Copy Database Wizard**. With this option, you can move or copy a database from SQL Server 7.0 to an instance of SQL Server 2000 with no server downtime. Another advantage of this method is that you can select specific databases to upgrade, leaving other databases in their SQL Server 7.0 format. If both versions of SQL Server must run on the same computer at the same time, then SQL Server 7.0 must remain the default instance, and the database to be upgraded must be upgraded to a named instance of SQL Server 2000. If the upgrade is to occur on a remote computer, then the SQL Server 7.0 database can be upgraded to either a default or a named instance of SQL Server 2000 on the remote computer.

Upgrades from SQL Server 6.5 to SQL Server 2000 are accomplished via the **SQL Server Upgrade Wizard**. Upon completion of the SQL Server Upgrade Wizard, SQL Server 2000 is the active version, but it is possible to switch between versions using the Microsoft SQL Server Switch program or the **vswitch** command.

SQL servers involved in replication pose a logistical problem for upgrading. Although it is possible to replicate between different versions of SQL Server, you are limited to the functionality of the earliest version used. In general, SQL servers involved in replication should be upgraded in the following order: the **Distributor**, the **Publisher**, and then the **Subscribers**.

SQL Server 2000 is backward compatible with SQL Server 7.0, and upgraded databases should function the same. SQL Server 6.5 databases that are upgraded to SQL

Server 2000 may share the same compatibility issues that exist in upgrading to SQL Server 7.0. Most compatibility issues center around applications that were written using Transact-SQL (T-SQL) statements to directly access system catalogs or configuration settings that no longer exist or directly rely on the physical layout of database segments, whose structure has changed to use files and **filegroups**.

To answer the questions in this objective, you should be familiar with the available upgrade options from SQL Server 7.0 to SQL Server 2000 as well as from SQL Server 6.5 to SQL Server 2000. You should know the rules for running multiple versions of SQL Server on the same computer as well as the prerequisites for upgrading to SQL Server 2000. You should also be able to determine the appropriate situations in which to use the Copy Database Wizard instead of a full SQL Server 7.0 to SQL Server 2000 version upgrade.

Objective 1.2 Questions

70-228.01.02.001

You are planning to upgrade a SQL Server 6.5 database to SQL Server 2000 on a single computer. Which of the following steps are required prior to running the SQL Server Upgrade Wizard? (Choose all that apply.)

A. Upgrade the SQL Server 6.5 database to SQL Server 7.0 format.

B. Install an instance of SQL Server 2000.

C. Ensure that Service Pack 3 has been applied to SQL Server 6.5.

D. Ensure that you have available disk space equal to at least 1.5 times the size of the SQL Server 6.5 database that you are upgrading.

70-228.01.02.002

You are planning to upgrade an accounting database running on SQL Server 7.0 to SQL Server 2000. The accounting database is the only database on the server. The database is full-text enabled and participates in replication.

Upon completion of the upgrade, you must meet the following requirements:

- The database must be running on the default instance of SQL Server 2000.

- Full-text must be enabled.

- The database must be optimized for good query performance.

- The database must continue to participate in replication.

You choose to perform an online upgrade of the database using the Copy Database Wizard. You install a default instance of SQL Server 2000 to a remote computer. You run the Copy Database Wizard to upgrade the SQL Server 7.0 database to SQL Server 2000 running on the remote computer. When the upgrade completes, you run sp_updatestats to update statistics on the tables in the accounting database.

Which requirement or requirements are met? (Choose all that apply.)

A. The database is running on the default instance of SQL Server 2000.

B. Full-text is enabled.

C. The database has been optimized for good query performance.

D. The database continues to participate in replication.

70-228.01.02.003

Which of the following are advantages of using the Copy Database Wizard to upgrade a SQL Server 7.0 database to SQL Server 2000? (Choose all that apply.)

A. You can selectively choose which databases you want to upgrade.

B. A database having the same name on both source and destination servers can be moved or copied.

C. The upgrade process can be scheduled to run at a specific time.

D. The SQL Server 7.0 database can remain in read/write mode during the upgrade operation.

70-228.01.02.004

You have SQL Server 6.5 installed on the same computer as SQL Server 7.0. SQL Server 7.0 is the active version. You install a named instance of SQL Server 2000. Which of the following statements are true? (Choose all that apply.)

A. Using the vswitch command, you can switch between SQL Server 6.5 and the named instance of SQL Server 2000.

B. Using the vswitch command, you can switch between SQL Server 7.0 and the named instance of SQL Server 2000.

C. Using the vswitch command, you can switch between SQL Server 7.0 and SQL Server 6.5.

D. SQL Server 7.0 and the named instance of SQL Server 2000 can run at the same time.

70-228.01.02.005

You are upgrading from SQL Server 6.5 to SQL Server 2000. Which of the following objects will not transfer as part of the upgrade?

A. Replication settings

B. Full-text settings

C. SQL Executive scheduled tasks

D. Logon information

Objective 1.2 Answers

70-228.01.02.001

▶ **Correct Answers: B and D**

A. **Incorrect:** SQL Server 2000 Upgrade Wizard can directly upgrade SQL Server 6.5 databases. There is no reason to upgrade to SQL Server 7.0, and then upgrade to SQL Server 2000.

B. **Correct:** In order to run the SQL Server Upgrade Wizard, you must have an instance of SQL Server 2000 already installed.

C. **Incorrect:** When the upgrade from SQL Server 6.5 to SQL Server 2000 occurs on the same computer, Service Pack 5 or later must be applied.

D. **Correct:** Free disk space in the amount of at least 1.5 times the size of the SQL Server 6.5 database that you are upgrading must be available for the upgrade to be successful.

70-228.01.02.002

▶ **Correct Answers: A and C**

A. **Correct:** The SQL Server 7.0 database was upgraded to the default instance of SQL Server 2000 on a remote computer.

B. **Incorrect:** The SQL Server 7.0 to SQL Server 2000 upgrade process marks the database as full-text disabled. Full-text catalogs must be repopulated after an upgrade.

C. **Correct:** Running sp_updatestats after the upgrade to SQL Server 2000 is recommended for good query performance.

D. **Incorrect:** The Copy Database Wizard cannot be used for databases involved in replication. A regular server upgrade is required.

70-228.01.02.003

▶ **Correct Answers: A and C**

A. **Correct:** The Copy Database Wizard allows you to move or copy one or more databases, leaving other SQL Server 7.0 databases intact.

B. **Incorrect:** You must resolve any duplicate database names between source and destination servers prior to upgrading the databases. The database selection screen will note that the source database already exists on the destination server.

C. **Correct:** The actual move or copy operation is performed through a series of Data Transformation Services (DTS) packages, which can be scheduled to run at a specific time.

D. **Incorrect:** In order to prevent any chance of data corruption, the SQL Server 7.0 database must be in read-only mode during the upgrade.

70-228.01.02.004

▶ **Correct Answers: C and D**

A. **Incorrect:** In order to be able to switch between SQL Server 6.5 and SQL Server 2000 using the vswitch command, SQL Server 7.0 needs to be upgraded to the default instance of SQL Server 2000. You can then switch between SQL Server 6.5 and the default instance of SQL Server 2000.

B. **Incorrect:** By installing a named instance of SQL Server 2000 and leaving the existing installation of SQL Server 7.0 intact, you can run both versions of SQL Server at the same time without using the vswitch command.

C. **Correct:** In this configuration, you can switch between SQL Server 7.0 and SQL Server 6.5 using the vswitch command.

D. **Correct:** By installing a named instance of SQL Server 2000 and leaving the existing installation of SQL Server 7.0 intact, you can run both versions of SQL Server at the same time without using the vswitch command.

70-228.01.02.005

▶ **Correct Answers: B**

A. **Incorrect:** Articles, subscriptions, publications, and any distribution databases are transferred and upgraded as part of the version upgrade.

B. **Correct:** SQL 6.5 did not have the option for full-text indexing. However, even in a SQL Server 7.0 to SQL Server 2000 upgrade, the full-text catalogs need to be rebuilt.

C. **Incorrect:** All tasks scheduled by SQL Executive are transferred and upgraded as part of the version upgrade.

D. **Incorrect:** Logon and remote logon information is transferred as part of the version upgrade.

Create a linked server.

Linked servers is a feature that was introduced with the release of SQL Server 7.0. Primarily, linked servers enable your SQL server to communicate with and access data located on other database servers including non-Microsoft SQL servers. SQL Server can do this through the use of OLE DB, an API that enables universal data access.

Prior to SQL Server 7.0, servers had to use the **remote server** feature of SQL Server to communicate with each other. There were a few limitations with the remote server feature including the type of servers you could communicate with and the set up and management of remote servers. For example, you could not configure an Oracle server to remotely connect to a SQL Server 6.5 machine. Also, both the local and remote servers needed to be configured with user information.

Linked servers enhance remote communications by enabling SQL Server to communicate with a greater number of data sources. It also allows you to load balance your SQL Server environment through the use of **distributed queries** and **distributed transactions**.

Distributed queries enable you to access data from multiple heterogeneous data sources. Using a single query, you can access tables and views located on the same computer or a different computer no matter which data source is servicing the query. Distributed transactions are transactions that involve the use of two or more data sources. For example, you can write a transaction that updates databases located on two different SQL servers. Both distributed queries and transactions require the use of linked servers.

There are two methods for creating a linked server. You can create a linked server by using a stored procedure or by using SQL Server Enterprise Manager. In either case, the steps are straightforward. However, you need to understand the various setup and configuration options available to you when creating a linked server. These configuration options include the data source you are linking to, the **collation** type, and the security settings for user logon mappings. The ability to create a linked server definition is dependent upon the privileges defined for the user creating the link. Only users who are assigned the fixed server roles of sysadmin or setupadmin are permitted to create a linked server.

In the case of T-SQL, you can utilize the sp_addlinkedserver or sp_dropserver system-stored procedures, and you can add or delete a linked server definition. Once you have created a linked server definition, there are issues with managing the actual link. We explore these in Objective 4.4.

Objective 1.3 Questions

70-228.01.03.001

A finance application your company wants to deploy must be able to run distributed queries against multiple SQL servers. You need to grant appropriate permissions to a user, so that the user can create and manage the linked servers. Which fixed server role should you assign the user? (Choose all that apply.)

A. setupadmin

B. securityadmin

C. sysadmin

D. ddladmin

70-228.01.03.002

Your company just completed a merger with an organization based in Japan. You are responsible for integrating the two organizations' database resources, so that data can be extracted from a single application no matter where the data is stored. Both organizations have deployed SQL Server 2000. You decide to implement linked servers and distributed queries. The default collation for the servers in Japan is set to JAPANESE_CI_AI. The default collation for the local SQL Server instance is set to LATIN_GENERAL_CI_AI_KS. The column's collation for the data on the Japanese server is set to JAPANESE_BINARY. The local server's linked server option, Use Remote Collation, equals ON, and the collation name is set to LATIN1_GENERAL_BIN. Which collation will SQL Server use for each column?

A. LATIN_GENERAL_CI_AI_KS

B. LATIN1_GENERAL_BIN

C. JAPANESE_CI_AI

D. JAPANESE_BINARY

70-228.01.03.003

Users are complaining about the response time when they execute queries against the Reports database, which is configured to run on the SQL Server 2000 server named Accounting1. You look into the problem further and find that the hardware configuration for the server is not capable of handling the user load. You decide to partition the database across a second SQL server for the purposes of load balancing. Partitioning requires that you create a linked server. Accounting2 is running SQL Server 2000. The password for the sa account is Microsoft99, and the Reports database has been configured on the server.

Which one of the following T-SQL statements allows you to create a link to the server named Accounting2?

A. `EXEC sp_addlinkedserver 'ACCOUNTING2','SQL Server', 'MSDAORA', '' , '' , 'REPORTS'`

B. `EXEC sp_addlinkedserver 'ACCOUNTING2','SQLOLEDB', 'SQL Server', '' , '' , 'REPORTS'`

C. `EXEC sp_addlinkedserver 'ACCOUNTING2','SQL Server', 'SQLOLEDB', '' , '' , 'REPORTS'`

D. `EXEC sp_addlinkedserver 'ACCOUNTING2','SQL Server', 'SQLOLEDB', '' , '' , `
   `'DRIVER={SQL Server};SERVER=ACCOUNTING2;UID= sa;PWD=Microsoft99; ', 'REPORTS'`

70-228.01.03.004

Users in the Accounting department need to access a SQL server named Purchasing in order to run queries against the database named Reports. To help ease administration, you decide to create a link to the Purchasing SQL server and map all local logons to the linked server using the Windows NT domain user JACK and the password jack007. The username is defined in the Windows NT domain EASTCOAST. Which of the following T-SQL commands enables you to create this link with the required options?

A. `EXEC sp_addlinkedserver 'PURCHASING', 'SQL Server', 'SQLOLEDB', '' , '' , 'REPORTS'`
   `GO`
   `EXEC sp_addlinkedsrvlogin 'PURCHASING', 'true'`

B. `EXEC sp_addlinkedserver 'PURCHASING', 'SQL Server', 'SQLOLEDB', '' , '' , 'REPORTS'`
   `GO`
   `EXEC sp_addlinkedsrvlogin 'PURCHASING', 'false', NULL, NULL, NULL`

C. `EXEC sp_addlinkedserver 'PURCHASING', 'SQL Server', 'SQLOLEDB', '' , '' , 'REPORTS'`
   `GO`
   `EXEC sp_addlinkedsrvlogin 'PURCHASING', 'false', 'EASTCOAST\JACK', 'JACK', 'jack007'`

D. `EXEC sp_addlinkedserver 'PURCHASING', 'SQL Server', 'Microsoft.Jet.OLEDB.4.0', '' , `
   `'' , 'REPORTS'`
   `GO`
   `EXEC sp_addlinkedsrvlogin 'PURCHASING', 'false', 'EASTCOAST\JACK', 'JACK', 'jack007'`

Objective 1.3 Answers

70-228.01.03.001

▶ **Correct Answers: A and C**

　A. **Correct:** The setupadmin (setup administrator) fixed server role permits users to add/remove linked servers. It also allows users to execute certain stored procedures, such as sp_serveroption.

B. **Incorrect:** The securityadmin (security administrator) fixed server role permits users to manage SQL Server logons. Users assigned this role cannot manage linked servers.

C. **Correct:** The sysadmin fixed server role permits users to perform any activity in SQL Server including managing linked servers.

D. **Incorrect:** The ddladmin fixed db role grants a user the role of Data Definition Language (DDL) administrator. DDL SQL statements are used to define, create, and manage all of the objects in a SQL database. CREATE VIEW, CREATE TABLE, and DROP TABLE are all examples of DDL statements.

70-228.01.03.002

▶ **Correct Answers: C**

A. **Incorrect:** See explanation for answer C.

B. **Incorrect:** See explanation for answer C.

C. **Correct:** SQL Server 2000 has the capability to support multiple collations. Under SQL Server 7.0, serverwide collation was the only collation supported. When you create a link to another server, SQL Server 2000 uses certain parameters to determine the collation it uses for each column. The collation chosen is dependent on the type of linked server (SQL Server or other), whether or not the collation name has been set, and whether the Use Remote Collation option has been set to ON or OFF. In this case the Use Remote Collation is ON so the local server will use the collation of the server in Japan.

D. **Incorrect:** See explanation for answer C.

70-228.01.03.003

▶ **Correct Answers: C**

A. **Incorrect:** The provider name is incorrect, MSDAORA should be used only when connecting to an Oracle server. For SQL servers, you can choose to leave the provider_name blank and the default value SQLOLEDB will be used, or you can specify SQLOLEDB. Other provider_name parameter values include MSDASQL when specifying an open database connectivity (ODBC) data source and Microsoft.Jet.OLEDB.4.0 to specify a Microsoft Access database file or a Microsoft Excel spreadsheet.

B. **Incorrect:** The statement will fail as the provider_name and product_name are in the wrong order. The provider_name parameter (SQLOLEDB) must come after the product_name (SQL Server).

C. **Correct:** A link to the Accounting2 server will be created, specifying Reports as the database name. The syntax for the sp_addlinkedserver statement is as follows:

```
sp_addlinkedserver [ @server = ] 'server'
[ , [@srvproduct = ] 'product_name' ]
[ , [@provider = ] 'provider_name' ]
[ , [@datasrc = ] 'data_source' ]
```

```
[ , [@location = ] 'location' ]
[ , [@provstr = ] 'provider_string' ]
[ , [@catalog = ] 'catalog' ]
```

D. **Incorrect:** When creating a link to a SQL server, you have the option of specifying the actual server name using SQLOLEDB as the provider_name parameter value, or you can choose to use an ODBC connection string. If an ODBC connection string is used, the provider_name parameter value must be set to MSDASQL.

70-228.01.03.004

▶ **Correct Answers: C**

A. **Incorrect:** This command allows you to create a link to the Purchasing database; however, it connects all local logons to the linked server using the user's own credentials.

B. **Incorrect:** Again, this command allows you to create a link to the Purchasing server, but no username or password has been specified, and therefore all mappings to the linked server will fail.

C. **Correct:** The statement maps Jack's domain username to the remote server Purchasing using his Windows NT domain name and password. All users will use the mapping to access the Reports database on the Purchasing SQL server.

D. **Incorrect:** The code to create the mapping is correct; however, the provider_name parameter value is incorrect. Microsoft.Jet.OLEDB.4.0 should only be used when connecting to an Excel spreadsheet or an Access database file.

O B J E C T I V E   1 . 4

Configure SQL Mail and SQLAgentMail.

SQL Server 2000 provides two **Messaging Application Programming Interface (MAPI)** compliant services that allow you to configure SQL Server to generate e-mail messages triggered by alerts or events. The MSSQLServer Service processes mail for the mail session referred to as SQL Mail. SQL Mail uses a number of stored procedures to manipulate e-mail, process queries received by e-mail, and reply to e-mail messages.

The SQLAgentMail Service operates independently of SQL Mail and processes mail exclusively for SQL Server Agent events. SQLAgentMail can be configured to send e-mail messages when an alert is triggered or when a scheduled task succeeds or fails.

Both SQL Mail and SQLAgentMail require mail profiles. Mail profiles are specific to the Windows NT or 2000 domain user account that is activated when a user logs on. SQL Mail uses the same domain user account used to start an instance of SQL Server. In order to use SQL Mail, a mail profile must be created for this account. SQL Mail and SQLAgentMail can share the same domain user account and the same mail profile, share the same domain user account but have different mail profiles, or use different domain user accounts with different mail profiles.

Once mail profiles are created for SQL Mail and SQLAgentMail, the services can be configured. The SQL Mail Service can be set to start automatically when SQL Server starts, or it can be started manually under the Support Services folder in SQL Enterprise Manager. The service may also be started and stopped using the stored procedures **xp_startmail** and **xp_stopmail**. A new SQLAgentMail session is started each time the SQLServerAgent Service is started.

SQL Mail can be used to process e-mail manually or automatically. To set up automated processing, you must create a regularly scheduled job that uses the stored procedure **sp_processmail** to find, read, respond to, and delete messages. Manually processing e-mail messages requires the use of the following stored procedures: **xp_findnextmsg** to retrieve the message ID, **xp_readmail** to read the message or attachment, **xp_deletemail** to delete the message, and **xp_sendmail** to send a message.

To answer the questions in this objective, you should understand the steps required to configure SQL Mail and SQLAgentMail. You should be familiar with creating mail profiles and know which service accounts require profiles. You should also understand the function of each of the extended stored procedures used by SQL Mail and the permissions needed to execute them.

Objective 1.4 Questions

70-228.01.04.001

You are configuring SQL Mail and SQLAgentMail for SQL Server 2000 on a Windows NT 4.0 server that is part of a domain. The SQL Server Service is assigned a domain user account named SQLService-Account as the service startup account. The SQL Server Agent Service is assigned a local system account as the service startup account. A second server in the domain is running Microsoft Exchange.

You must meet the following requirements:

- E-mail can be sent from both SQL Mail and SQLAgentMail.

- SQL Mail must use a different mailbox than SQLAgentMail.

- SQL Mail must be started automatically when SQL Server starts.

- SQL Mail must be processed on an automated basis.

You log on to the computer running SQL Server using the domain username SQLServiceAccount and the correct password. You configure a new mail profile named SQLServiceAccount1 to connect to the Exchange server for the mailbox SQLServiceAccount. You create a second profile named SQLService-Account2 to connect to the Exchange server for the mailbox SQLServiceAccount. You open the Outlook client and successfully test sending and receiving e-mail for both profiles. Using Enterprise Manager, you expand the server view, select Support Services, right-click SQL Mail, and select Properties. In Profile Name, you select the SQLServiceAccount1 profile. You select Test and receive a message that SQL Mail has started and stopped successfully. You right-click SQL Mail again and select Properties. In Profile Name, you select the SQLServiceAccount2 profile. You select Test and receive a message that SQL Mail has started and stopped successfully. You create a scheduled job that runs xp_startmail, sp_processmail, and xp_stopmail every hour.

Which requirement or requirements are met? (Choose all that apply.)

A. E-mail can be sent from both SQL Mail and SQLAgentMail.

B. SQL Mail uses a different mailbox than SQLAgentMail.

C. SQL Mail starts automatically when SQL Server starts.

D. SQL Mail processes mail on an automated basis.

70-228.01.04.002

Which of the following are required for SQL Mail to function? (Choose all that apply.)

A. A mail server that is MAPI compliant

B. A Windows NT or 2000 domain user account separate from the account used to start the SQLAgent-Mail Service

C. A post office connection

D. A mail profile created for the same domain user account that is used to start SQL Server

70-228.01.04.003

Which of the following extended stored procedures are directly used by the stored procedure sp_processmail to handle incoming mail messages? (Choose all that apply.)

A. xp_startmail

B. xp_findnextmsg

C. xp_deletemail

D. xp_stopmail

70-228.01.04.004

You have an e-commerce application running on SQL Server 2000. You want SQL Server to send an e-mail message to a user letting her know when a new order has been received in the Orders table. Both SQL Mail and SQLAgentMail are enabled on the server. Which of the following accomplishes this task?

A. Create an alert for the event. SQLAgentMail will send an e-mail whenever the alert is triggered.

B. Create a trigger on the Orders table for insert that executes sp_processmail.

C. Create a trigger on the Orders table for insert that executes xp_sendmail.

D. Create a recurring scheduled task that uses the stored procedure sp_processmail.

70-228.01.04.005

Which of the following procedures can be executed only by members of the sysadmin fixed server role or db_owner fixed database role?

A. xp_startmail

B. sp_processmail

C. xp_sendmail

D. xp_deletemail

Objective 1.4 Answers

70-228.01.04.001

▶ **Correct Answers: B and D**

A. **Incorrect:** Mail can be sent only from SQL Mail. The SQLAgentMail Service is set up to use a local system account. In order to send e-mail, the SQLAgentMail Service needs to be set up to use a properly configured domain user account. Once the SQLAgentMail Service is assigned a domain user account, a mail profile can be created, and the SQLAgentMail Service can be configured to use the mail profile.

B. **Correct:** SQL Mail is configured to use the SQLServiceAccount, which has a mailbox and mail profile created. In this scenario, two mail profiles were created for the same domain user account. SQLAgentMail has no mailbox at this point because it is set to use a local system account. To continue to satisfy this requirement, the SQLAgentMail Service would either need to be configured to use the SQLServiceAccount with a mail profile attached to a different mailbox or be assigned a domain user account that is different from the SQL Mail account with a mail profile configured for that account.

C. **Incorrect:** In order to start SQL Mail automatically, you need to select Autostart SQL Mail when SQL Server starts. This option is accessible by selecting the Support Services folder, right-clicking on SQL Mail, and selecting Properties. The option is not enabled by default.

D. **Correct:** The scheduled task accomplishes the task of starting, processing, and stopping the SQL Mail Service on an hourly basis without operator intervention.

70-228.01.04.002

▶ **Correct Answers: A, C, and D**

A. **Correct:** SQL Mail establishes an extended MAPI connection with a mail host and uses stored procedures to process mail.

B. **Incorrect:** SQL Mail and SQLAgentMail can be configured to use the same domain user account. Different domain user accounts may be used, but this is not required.

C. **Correct:** SQL Mail must establish a connection with a post office. Post office connections can be established through Microsoft Exchange Server, Windows NT Mail, a POP3 server, or any MAPI-enabled e-mail system.

D. **Correct:** SQL Mail requires the use of a domain user account to start the service. This account must have a mail profile configured and assigned to SQL Mail during configuration of the service.

70-228.01.04.003

▶ **Correct Answers: B and C**

A. **Incorrect:** The stored procedure xp_startmail simply starts a SQL Mail client session. It is not used directly by sp_processmail.

B. **Correct:** The stored procedure xp_findnextmsg returns the message ID for output and is used with sp_processmail to process mail.

C. **Correct:** The stored procedure xp_deletemail deletes messages from the SQL Mail inbox and is used by sp_processmail to process mail.

D. **Incorrect:** The stored procedure xp_stopmail simply stops a SQL Mail client session. It is not used directly by sp_processmail.

70-228.01.04.004

▶ **Correct Answers: C**

A. **Incorrect:** Alerts are generated for error messages or events that are abnormal and should be investigated. The insert of a record into the orders table is not an event that will trigger an alert.

B. **Incorrect:** The stored procedure sp_processmail is used to process incoming messages. The requirement in this scenario is to send a new mail message.

C. **Correct:** You can use xp_sendmail to send a message to a specified recipient from a trigger. The trigger occurs when a record is inserted into the orders table.

D. **Incorrect:** The stored procedure sp_processmail is used to process incoming messages. The requirement in this scenario is to send a new mail message.

70-228.01.04.005

▶ **Correct Answers: B**

A. **Incorrect:** Execute permissions for xp_startmail default to members of the sysadmin fixed server role, but can be granted to other users.

B. **Correct:** Only members of the sysadmin fixed server role or db_owner fixed database role can execute this procedure.

C. **Incorrect:** Execute permissions for xp_sendmail default to members of the sysadmin fixed server role, but can be granted to other users.

D. **Incorrect:** Execute permissions for xp_deletemail default to members of the sysadmin fixed server role, but can be granted to other users.

OBJECTIVE 1.5

Configure network libraries.

Network libraries are a set of dynamic link libraries (DLLs) that enable SQL Server to communicate over a variety of protocols. Essentially, the network libraries separate the networking functions of SQL Server from its database services. The DLLs conduct the network operations needed to communicate with other clients and other servers using **interprocess communication (IPC)** mechanisms. For example, if you configure SQL Server to use the TCP/IP set of network libraries, it uses Windows sockets as its IPC mechanism.

SQL Server 2000 supports seven types of network libraries: **Named Pipes**, TCP/IP Sockets, Multiprotocol, NWLink IPX/SPX, AppleTalk ADSP, and Banyan VINES. When you first install SQL Server, the server is configured to support all of the libraries. However, it is important to note that if the server is not running a particular protocol, it is not able to support communications using that library. For example, if a server is not running TCP/IP, clients trying to connect over TCP/IP will not be able to do so.

Not all SQL Server 2000 clients support each of the network libraries. Windows 95 and 98 machines do not support Named Pipes. SQL Server must be running either TCP/IP or IPX/SPX to communicate successfully with Windows 95/98 client machines.

If you are running TCP/IP, SQL Server is configured to listen for any SQL-specific communication on port 1433. If you change the port number from the default value of 1433, you must ensure that the ports on your client machines are also changed; otherwise they will continue to attempt a connection over port 1433.

If SQL Server is running in a true heterogenous environment, where clients are connecting over various protocols, setting the server to support the Multiprotocol Net Library is beneficial. The Multiprotocol Net Library forces SQL Server to switch between the various protocols until it finds one that the client is attempting to use to connect to the server. The server supports only the protocols that it is configured to run. For example, if an IPX/SPX client attempts to connect to a SQL server configured to run the Multiprotocol Net Library and the server is only configured with TCP/IP, communication will fail. The Multiprotocol Net Library is the only library that can support encryption for both user password authentication and data. Clients cannot connect to SQL Server 2000 running named instances.

Even though SQL Server is configured to support all of the network libraries, you have to activate the SQL Server Net Library for the protocol you need to support. For example, you need to activate support for NWLink IPX/SPX as SQL Server does not listen on that protocol. The network library configuration for a server can be changed by running the SQL Server Network Utility. For SQL Server 2000 clients, you must use the Client Network Utility.

Objective 1.5 Questions

70-228.01.05.001

You have deployed a SQL Server 2000 server configured to use Named Pipes and the IPX/SPX protocol. Your environment consists of a mixture of Windows 2000 Professional, Windows NT 4.0 Workstation, and Windows 98 client machines. Both Windows 2000 Professional and Windows NT 4.0 Workstation can successfully connect to the SQL server; however, Windows 98 machines cannot. All of the client machines are configured with the TCP/IP protocol. What could be causing the problem for the Windows 98 machines?

A. ODBC is not configured correctly on the Windows 98 machines.

B. Windows 98 does not support Named Pipes.

C. Windows 98 supports TCP/IP only when connecting to SQL Server.

D. The TCP/IP socket number is incorrectly specified under Client Configuration.

70-228.01.05.002

You have Windows 2000 and NetWare running in your environment. The servers are configured to run IPX/SPX as the only protocol. The Accounting department has a legacy UNIX server it connects to and is therefore configured to use TCP/IP. How should you configure the SQL Server 2000 machine to enable connectivity from both Windows 2000 and NetWare to clients' machines in Accounting?

A. Configure the server to use TCP/IP.

B. Configure the server to use Multiprotocol.

C. Configure the server to use Named Pipes.

D. None of the above.

70-228.01.05.003

The Accounting department produces end of quarter reports for the various departments and management groups within the organization. Because of the sensitivity of the material, the senior management team has requested that its reports be stored on a separate database and access be restricted to the server. The senior management team consists of five department heads. You must configure the network settings for the SQL Server.

You want to accomplish the following goals:

■ Restrict clients from connecting to the default TCP/IP port of SQL Server

■ Enable encryption of the data sent between the client and SQL Server

■ Restrict the number of connections to the server to five connections

You configure the SQL server to run the TCP/IP protocol. You then configure the network library setting of the SQL server to use Multiprotocol. You set the TCP/IP socket to 1435, changing it from the default port of 1433. Which goals do you achieve? (Choose all that apply.)

A. Users can no longer connect to the SQL server without knowing the TCP/IP port value.

B. Users' logons will be encrypted.

C. The SQL server can support only five connections at a time.

D. None of the goals are accomplished.

70-228.01.05.004

The current configuration for your SQL Server environment consists of a mixture of SQL Server 6.5 and 2000 machines. You have been given the go-ahead to begin upgrading to SQL Server 2000. You decide to first upgrade the client utilities running on client machines from SQL Server 6.5 to SQL Server 2000. However, you now have clients calling into the Help Desk complaining that they can no longer log on to the SQL servers. Further investigation reveals that the servers having this problem are SQL Server 6.5 machines. The SQL 6.5 servers are configured to run Integrated Security (Windows Authentication in SQL Server 7.0/2000). SQL Server 2000 servers are running in Windows authentication mode and a Windows 2000 server is providing name resolution. Clients are running Windows NT Workstation and the SQL Server 2000 client utilities. TCP/IP is the only protocol configured on the users' machines. What could be the reason that users can log on to SQL Server 2000 machines, but not SQL 6.5 servers?

A. Clients running SQL Server 2000 client utilities cannot log on to SQL Server 6.5 machines running Integrated Security.

B. SQL Server requires that WINS be running for client server name resolution.

C. SQL Server 6.5 servers do not support Windows Authentication connections over TCP/IP.

D. The TCP/IP Net Library on the SQL Server 6.5 machine must be upgraded to SQL Server 2000.

Objective 1.5 Answers

70-228.01.05.001

► **Correct Answers: B**

A. **Incorrect:** See explanation for answer B.

B. **Correct:** Windows NT and 2000 are the only client machines that connect to a SQL server using Named Pipes alone. Because SQL Server is configured to support only Named Pipes, clients will not be able to connect unless they also support communication over Named Pipes. When communicating with SQL Server, Windows 95 and 98 clients must utilize one of the other supported protocols, such as IPX/ SPX or TCP/IP. In this case, the Windows 98 machines cannot connect to the SQL server using IPX/ SPX because they aren't running the protocol locally. Even in the case of a server configured to support the Multiprotocol Net Library, unless TCP/IP is configured to run on the server, clients are not able to connect. The Multiprotocol library detects the protocol the client is attempting to connect with, and then communicates with it using that protocol, but the SQL server must be running that protocol to support communication.

C. **Incorrect:** See explanation for answer B.

D. **Incorrect:** See explanation for answer B.

70-228.01.05.002

▶ **Correct Answers: D**

A. **Incorrect:** See explanation for answer D.

B. **Incorrect:** See explanation for answer D.

C. **Incorrect:** See explanation for answer D.

D. **Correct:** The SQL server must be configured to run the IPX/SPX and TCP/IP protocols.

70-228.01.05.003

▶ **Correct Answers: A and B**

A. **Correct:** After changing the TCP/IP port, clients need to know the network port value. By default, SQL Server uses port 1433 for the TCP/IP network library, and all SQL Server clients are configured to connect to the SQL server using that port. Changing the port increases the difficulty for unauthorized clients to connect to the TCP/IP server.

B. **Correct:** The Multiprotocol Net Library encrypts user password authentication and any data sent to the SQL server. It is also capable of supporting the secured sockets layer (SSL) by configuring the setting using the Server Network Utility. Encryption using the Multiprotocol Net Library is not supported for Windows 98 clients.

C. **Incorrect:** Administrators can restrict the number of connections made through a particular network library using the Server Network Utility. For example, setting the connections to five for the TCP/IP network library restricts the number of connections to the server via TCP/IP to five clients. If you want to restrict the overall number of connections, you can do so by changing the user connections parameter using the sp_configure stored procedure.

D. **Incorrect:** Two of the goals are accomplished, users are restricted to connecting to the SQL server using the default TCP/IP port settings, and logons to the SQL server are encrypted.

70-228.01.05.004

▶ **Correct Answers: C**

A. **Incorrect:** See explanation for answer C.

B. **Incorrect:** See explanation for answer C.

C. **Correct:** SQL Server 6.5 requires that clients communicate over Named Pipes or the Multiprotocol Net Library if Windows Authentication is used. If you have SQL Server 2000 clients connecting to a SQL Server 6.5 server running Integrated Security, your clients cannot use the TCP/IP Net Library as the sole means of communication. You must configure the client to use either Named Pipes or the Multiprotocol Net Library.

D. **Incorrect:** See explanation for answer C.

O B J E C T I V E   1 . 6

Troubleshoot failed installations.

After verifying that you have met the minimum hardware and software requirements to install a particular edition of SQL Server 2000, your installation fails or you experience problems starting SQL Server after the installation. The first place to start troubleshooting is with the SQL Server error log. The error log is started when SQL Server is started, and the log is closed when the SQL Server Service is stopped. The past six logs are kept and follow the naming convention of ERRORLOG.1 through ERRORLOG.6, with ERRORLOG.6 being the oldest log file. Each time a new log file is started, the numbers are simply rotated. You can view the error logs using any ASCII editor. If you can connect to your SQL server, you can also view the log files from within Enterprise Manager by expanding the Management Folder under the appropriate server. The SQL Server error log records informational messages, warning messages, and error messages as well as the date and time an event occurred.

The Microsoft **Windows NT and Windows 2000 Application logs** record events from SQL Server and SQL Server Agent and log other events occurring within the Windows NT and 2000 operating system. Symbols are used to denote the type of message generated in the log. Double-click on a message to view the details.

SQL Server 2000 also ships with the **SQLDIAG.EXE** program.

Knowing where Setup fails can help you determine potential problems. The setup process consists of three phases. The first phase sets up options for your SQL Server installation, the second phase performs the physical file copy, and the third phase runs **CNFGSVR.EXE** to configure SQL Server. The third phase is the most significant in that it is the phase during which SQL Server and the SQL Agent Services are added. SQL Server is started in single-user mode, and the initial installation scripts are run. Any errors encountered during these phases are written to the **SQLSTP.LOG** file.

Microsoft also provides **Online Troubleshooters** to help diagnose any problems that may occur with an installation of SQL Server. Online Troubleshooters are Web-based guides that walk you through the steps necessary to diagnose and resolve many common problems.

Objective 1.6 Questions

70-228.01.06.001

You are having problems installing SQL Server Enterprise edition. You verify that you have met the minimum software and hardware requirements. The installation begins, but appears to stop after Setup copies files from the installation location to your hard drive. Your first step is to check the SQL Server error log. No messages are reported. What should your next step be?

A. Run the SQLDIAG.EXE program and review the SQLDIAG.TXT file.

B. View the SQLSTP.LOG file.

C. View the Windows NT or 2000 System log.

D. Use the Microsoft Online Troubleshooters.

70-228.01.06.002

The SQL Server error log records which type of messages? (Choose all that apply.)

A. Informational messages

B. Success Audit messages

C. Failure Audit messages

D. Error messages

70-228.01.06.003

Which of the following log files used in troubleshooting allow you to filter by event type (e.g., filter by Warning)?

A. SQLSTP.LOG

B. Windows NT or 2000 Application log

C. SQL Server error log

D. SQLDIAG.TXT

70-228.01.06.004

When SQL Server is started from the command line, events are logged to which of the following? (Choose all that apply.)

A. The Windows NT or Windows 2000 Application log

B. The SQL Server error log

C. The screen (monitor)

D. SQLSTP.LOG

70-228.01.06.005

Your SQL Server installation appears to have completed successfully, but the SQL Server Services will not load. You want to view the SQL Server error log. The log can be viewed from which of the following? (Choose all that apply.)

A. The Microsoft Notepad application

B. The command-line utility Edit

C. Enterprise Manager

D. The output file generated by running SQLDIAG.EXE

Objective 1.6 Answers

70-228.01.06.001

▶ **Correct Answers: B**

A. **Incorrect:** This utility captures the SQL Server error logs into one file. Because the SQL Server error log did not contain any error messages, this will not help you.

B. **Correct:** This log file reports problems encountered during set up and can help pinpoint where Setup failed. Because it appears that the installation completed the second phase of file copy, it is likely that the installation failed during the third phase of running CNFGSVR.EXE. The SQLSTP.LOG file should contain the exact process that was running at the time of failure.

C. **Incorrect:** Although this is a good place to look, it should not be the next step. The System log does not track application events, so you will not find any SQL Server error messages.

D. **Incorrect:** Although the Troubleshooters are useful, using them would not be the next step, especially because you have no error message to start with.

70-228.01.06.002

▶ **Correct Answers: A and D**

A. **Correct:** The SQL Server error log records messages about the general state of the SQL Server application.

B. **Incorrect:** This message type is used by the Windows NT or 2000 Security log to track successful audited security access attempts.

C. **Incorrect:** This message type is used by the Windows NT or 2000 Security log to track failed audited security access attempts.

D. **Correct:** The SQL Server error log records messages that indicate a significant problem that most likely requires operator intervention.

70-228.01.06.003

▶ **Correct Answers: B**

A. **Incorrect:** The SQLSTP.LOG file is viewed through an ASCII editor and has no filtering capability.

B. **Correct:** When the Application log is viewed through the Windows NT or 2000 Event Viewer, you can filter events by Warning, Error, Information, Success Audit, and Failure Audit.

C. **Incorrect:** The SQL Server error log allows you to sort messages by date, source, or message, but not filter by type of message.

D. **Incorrect:** The SQLDIAG.TXT file is viewed through an ASCII editor and has no filtering capability.

70-228.01.06.004

▶ **Correct Answers: B and C**

A. **Incorrect:** Only if SQL Server is started as a service under Windows NT or 2000 will the events be logged to the Application log.

B. **Correct:** Events are automatically logged to the SQL Server error log no matter which method is employed to start SQL Server.

C. **Correct:** The screen is the default output device, so errors display on screen as they occur. Output can be redirected from the command line to a printer or file.

D. **Incorrect:** The SQLSTP.LOG file is written to only during the installation of SQL Server.

70-228.01.06.005

▶ **Correct Answers: A, B, and D**

A. **Correct:** Any ASCII editor can read the SQL Server error log file.

B. **Correct:** Any ASCII editor can read the SQL Server error log file.

C. **Incorrect:** Because the SQL Server Services will not start, you will be unable to use Enterprise Manager to view the error log file.

D. **Correct:** This utility captures all of the SQL Server error logs into one file named SQLDIAG.TXT.

OBJECTIVE DOMAIN   2

Creating SQL Server 2000 Databases

Creating databases in a Microsoft SQL Server 2000 environment requires an understanding of the business functions the database is modeling as well as the database concepts and features used to characterize those business functions. Before creating a database, it is important to have a good logical design of your business requirements and a good physical design that takes advantage of hardware resources and software configuration options. Whether the database application is complex, such as a database that is part of a federated server environment, or simple, such as a name and address database, the most substantial performance gains come from a well-designed database. However, performance can still be a concern even after a database has been created. You should be familiar with the various database level options that can affect performance. You should also know the commands used to set these database options, how to determine which options are currently set, and what the defaults are for each option.

SQL Server 2000 databases consist of many components, including tables, indexes, views, stored procedures, triggers, alerts, user-defined data types, and full-text indexes. Understanding these components ensures that your database will meet your business requirements and perform well. For example, defining appropriate indexes on tables dramatically improves query performance, and creating views on joined tables can help secure sensitive data. You should understand how to create and manage database objects in simple and complex environments.

When working with SQL Server 2000 databases, you should also be able to create new databases, attach and detach databases, add or delete data or transaction log files, create filegroups and assign files to them, change the default filegroup, rename a database, and change the database owner.

Tested Skills and Suggested Practices

The skills that you need to successfully master the Creating SQL Server 2000 Databases objective domain on the *Installing, Configuring, and Administering Microsoft SQL Server 2000 Enterprise Edition* exam include:

- **Configuring database options.**

  - Practice 1: Using the Query Analyzer, issue the following command against the Northwind database: `SELECT DATABASEPROPERTEX ('Northwind', 'ISAUTO-CLOSE')`. Determine the current state for IsAutoUpdateStatistics, IsAutoCreate-Statistics, Recovery, and Updateability.

  - Practice 2: Using the Query Analyzer, issue the following command against the Northwind database: `ALTER DATABASE Northwind SET AUTO_CLOSE ON`.

  - Practice 3: Use Enterprise Manager to check the status of the AUTO_CLOSE option of the Northwind database, and set it to OFF.

  - Practice 4: Create a new user and assign the user the fixed database role of db_owner for the Northwind database. Log on as the user and attempt to change a database option through Enterprise Manager on the Northwind database. Attempt to change a database option on the Model database.

- **Attaching databases.**

  - Practice 1: Add or delete data from the Northwind database. For example, you can add an employee to the Employees table. Stop your SQL Server Service and copy the NORTHWND.MDF and NORTHWND.LDF to a new folder. Restart the SQL Server Service and delete the Northwind sample database from the default instance of your SQL Server machine. Using the Transact-SQL (T-SQL) sp_attach_db command, point to the copies of the .mdf and .ldf files for the Northwind database you just deleted, and re-create the database on the same machine. Check to see if the changes you made are still intact.

  - Practice 2: Detach the Northwind database using the sp_detach_db T-SQL command. This time use Enterprise Manager to reattach the database.

- **Creating and altering databases.**

  - Practice 1: Using Enterprise Manager, create a Grades database with a primary data file of 4 MB. Allow the database to autogrow, but restrict the growth to 8 MB. If possible, create the transaction log file on a separate physical disk drive. Set the log size to be 2 MB, but allow it to autogrow with a restricted growth of 4 MB.

- Practice 2: Create a user-defined filegroup. Create a secondary data file of 2 MB (allow it to autogrow, but do not restrict the growth) and assign it to the new filegroup. Make the user-defined filegroup the default filegroup.

- Practice 3: Using T-SQL commands, rename the database from Grades to Students.

- Practice 4: Using Enterprise Manager, delete the Students database.

- **Creating and managing objects.**

  - Practice 1: Using the Northwind database, issue T-SQL commands to create a view that restricts users from seeing the address, city, and phone number for all employees. Assign the view to a user in the database using Enterprise Manager.

  - Practice 2: Repeat the previous exercise using Enterprise Manager to create the view.

  - Practice 3: Create a table and name it Salary Information. Add an Employee Name and Salary column to the table. Create a column in the Employee table and name it Salary. Create a trigger that updates the Salary table with the employee's name and salary each time you insert data into the Salary column of the Employee table.

Further Reading

This section lists supplemental readings by objective. We recommend that you study these sources thoroughly before taking exam 70-228.

Objective 2.1

Microsoft SQL Server 2000 product documentation. To access Books Online, click the Start button, point to Programs, then Microsoft SQL Server, and then select Books Online. Select the Contents tab and expand Optimizing Database Performance. This topic contains subsections detailing database design, query tuning, and optimizing server performance.

"Microsoft SQL Server 7.0 Performance Tuning Guide." (This article can be downloaded for free at *http:// msdn.microsoft.com/library /techart/msdn_sql7perftune.htm.*) This document discusses database performance monitoring and tuning.

Howe, D. R. *Data Analysis for Data Base Design* 2d ed. New York, New York: Routledge, Chapman, and Hall, 1989. Review Chapter 8. This book provides an introduction to entity-relationship modeling, which is useful for validating a logical database design.

Objective 2.2

Microsoft SQL Server 2000 product documentation. To access Books Online, click the Start button, point to Programs, then Microsoft SQL Server, and then select Books Online. Select the Contents tab and expand Creating and Maintaining Databases, then Databases, and then Modifying a Database. This section details how to modify a database. It also includes the subtopic "Attaching and Detaching a Database," which covers moving the database files.

Microsoft SQL Server 2000 product documentation. To access Books Online, click the Start button, point to Programs, then Microsoft SQL Server, and then select Books Online. Select the Index tab. Find sp_attach_db, sp_detach_db, and sp_attach_single_file_db. This will provide links to the "Transact-SQL Reference" volume. The syntax and arguments for each stored procedure are detailed, and there are usage examples and links to related stored procedures.

Objective 2.3

Microsoft SQL Server 2000 product documentation. To access Books Online, click the Start button, point to Programs, then Microsoft SQL Server, and then select Books Online. Select the Contents tab and expand Creating and Maintaining Databases, then Databases, and then select Creating a Database. This article details how to create a database and contains a link to the CREATE DATABASE command in the "Transact-SQL Reference" volume.

Microsoft Corporation. *Microsoft SQL Server 2000 Administrator's Companion*. Redmond, Washington: Microsoft Press, 2000. Chapter 9, "Creating Databases," contains a complete discussion on creating databases in SQL Server 2000.

Objective 2.4

Microsoft SQL Server 2000 product documentation. To access Books Online, click the Start button, point to Programs, then Microsoft SQL Server, and then select Books Online. Select the Contents tab and expand Creating and Maintaining Databases and the Indexes. This topic covers how to design and create the different types of indexes found in SQL Server 2000. You should also look at the topic "Views" for information on creating different types of views.

Microsoft Corporation. *Microsoft SQL Server 2000 Administrator's Companion*. Redmond, Washington: Microsoft Press, 2000. Chapters 15, 16, 17, 18, and 22 are discussions on creating and using most of the available objects in SQL Server 2000.

OBJECTIVE 2.1

Configure database options for performance.

Some database-level options affect database performance. These options can be set by the system administrator; database owner; and members of the sysadmin fixed server roles, dbcreator fixed server roles, and db_owner fixed database roles. Database options are unique to each database and can be set by using sp_dboption or the SET clause of the ALTER DATABASE statement. In some instances, the database options can be set directly through Enterprise Manager.

Setting the **AUTO_CLOSE** database option to ON shuts down the database when the last user exits and all running processes are complete. The database automatically reopens when a user accesses the database. The AUTO_CLOSE option allows the database files to function as regular files for copy and backup, which is useful in the Desktop edition of SQL Server 2000. It is not suggested that you set this option on systems in which you expect repeat or continual access to the database because the overhead of shutting down and reopening a database is prohibitive. The default setting for this option is OFF.

Setting the **AUTO_CREATE_STATISTICS** and **AUTO_UPDATE_STATISTICS** to ON improves query performance. As a result, when the query optimizer is determining how to process a query, it is provided with accurate information about the data in the database tables. Both options are set to ON by default.

Setting the database recovery option to **BULK_LOGGED** or **SIMPLE** can improve performance because logging is minimal in BULK_LOGGED mode and nonexistent in the case of SIMPLE recovery. However, in exchange for the performance gain, you lose the ability to fully recover a database. The default recovery option for all editions, except the Desktop edition, is **FULL**.

If you have a database that is only used for querying data, setting the **READ_ONLY** database state option improves query performance because no locking needs to take place.

Objective 2.1 Questions

70-228.02.01.001

Your company's e-commerce site needs to update its SQL Server 2000 Inventory database from an external data source. A few million records need to be loaded and indexed.

You must accomplish the following goals:

- Maximize database performance during the load

- Ensure the transaction log does not become full during the load

- Maintain a level of log recoverability during the load

- Ensure that the database is fully recoverable after the load

You start by doing a full backup of the Inventory database. Then, using Enterprise Manager, you right-click on the Inventory database, select Properties, click on the Options tab, and set the recovery model to SIMPLE. You start the load and index operation. Upon completion of the load, you use Enterprise Manager to set the recovery model back to FULL. Which of the following goals have been met? (Choose all that apply.)

A. You have maximized performance during the load.

B. You have ensured that the transaction log does not fill up during the load.

C. You have maintained a level of log recoverability during the load.

D. You have ensured that the database is fully recoverable after the load.

70-228.02.01.002

You have just migrated a SQL Server Desktop edition database named People to SQL Server 2000 Enterprise edition. You want to make sure that the People database is not set to AUTO_CLOSE when there are no users connected to the database. Which of the following commands accomplish this? (Choose all that apply.)

A. Run the stored procedure `EXEC sp_configure 'People', 'AUTOCLOSE'`.

B. Using Enterprise Manager, right-click on the People database, select Properties, choose the Options tab, and note whether the AUTO_CLOSE option is selected.

C. Run the T-SQL command `SELECT DATABASEPROPERTYEX ('People', 'IsAutoClose')`.

D. Run the stored procedure `EXEC sp_dboption 'People', 'AUTOCLOSE'`.

70-228.02.01.003

You need to change the State option for the Sales database from READ_ONLY to READ_WRITE. You are logged onto the SQL Server as a user named RGM who is not the owner of the Sales database. Being a member of which of the following server or database roles still allows user RGM to make the change? (Choose all that apply.)

A. dbcreator fixed server role

B. serveradmin fixed server role

C. db_accessadmin fixed database role for the Sales database

D. db_owner fixed database role for the Sales database

70-228.02.01.004

Your company will be installing a new application that needs to reference a preexisting SQL Server 2000 database named Repository.

You must meet the following requirements:

- No data should be able to be entered or updated in the Repository database.

- Statistics do not need to be automatically created or updated on the Repository database.

- Any newly created databases should, by default, not create statistics.

- Any changes made should take effect immediately without requiring a restart of the SQL Server Services.

You set the database state option on the Repository database to READ_ONLY. You set the AUTO_UPDATE_STATISTICS database option to OFF for the Repository database. You set the AUTO_CREATE_STATISTICS database option to OFF in the MASTER database to change the default for any newly created databases. You issue a checkpoint in the Repository database for the changes to take effect. Which of the following requirements are met? (Choose all that apply.)

A. Data cannot be entered or updated in the Repository database.

B. Statistics will not be automatically created or updated on the Repository database.

C. Newly created databases will, by default, not create statistics.

D. Changes made should take effect immediately.

Objective 2.1 Answers

70-228.02.01.001

▶ **Correct Answers: A, B, and D**

A. **Correct:** By setting the database option for recovery to SIMPLE, no transactions are being logged, which improves performance during bulk copy and index operations.

B. **Correct:** When the recovery model is set to SIMPLE, no logging occurs. Therefore, there is no concern for the transaction logs becoming full.

C. **Incorrect:** The SIMPLE recovery model does not provide for transaction logging, so recovery is limited to the last good full (or incremental) backup. The preferable recovery model for this scenario is BULK_LOGGED, which minimally logs bulk copy operations, thereby maximizing performance during a bulk load and minimizing log space while still providing a level of transaction log recovery. Under BULK_LOGGED, recovery can occur to the end of a transaction log backup but not to a point in time, as is possible with the FULL recovery model.

D. **Correct:** This requirement is met by setting the recovery model back to FULL after the load is complete.

70-228.02.01.002

▶ **Correct Answers: B, C, and D**

A. **Incorrect:** This is not a valid command. The stored procedure sp_configure is used to set serverwide options, not database-level options.

B. **Correct:** Enterprise Manager can be used to select/deselect this database option.

C. **Correct:** This query returns the status of the AUTO_CLOSE database option. A status of 0 indicates the option is set to OFF, whereas a status of 1 indicates the option is set to ON.

D. **Correct:** This stored procedure is supported for backward compatibility. Microsoft recommends using an ALTER DATABASE command or the Enterprise Manger to set database options, but currently sp_dboption can still be used to check or change the status of a database option.

70-228.02.01.003

▶ **Correct Answers: A and D**

A. **Correct:** Members of the dbcreator fixed server role can create, alter, and drop databases.

B. **Incorrect:** Members of the serveradmin fixed server role can set serverwide configuration options and shut down the server, but they do not have permission to modify database level options.

C. **Incorrect:** Members of the db_accessadmin fixed database role can add or remove user IDs within the database.

D. **Correct:** Members of the db_owner fixed database role have all permissions within the database.

70-228.02.01.004

▶ **Correct Answers: A and D**

A. **Correct:** Setting the State option in the Repository database to READ_ONLY ensures that no data can be modified. An added benefit of this option is that query performance should be improved because no locks need to occur on the database.

B. **Incorrect:** Setting the AUTO_UPDATE_STATISTICS database option to OFF stops the statistics from being automatically updated, but not from being automatically created. To meet this requirement you would also need to set the AUTO_CREATE_STATISTICS database option to OFF.

C. **Incorrect:** The AUTO_CREATE_STATISTICS database option should have been set to OFF in the Model database, not the Master. New databases are created based on settings in the Model database. Modification of any settings or options in the Master database is not suggested.

D. **Correct:** Issuing the checkpoint in the Repository database is unnecessary because a checkpoint is automatically issued after a database option change. Nonetheless, the changes made will take effect immediately without requiring the SQL Server Services to be restarted.

Attach and detach databases.

SQL Server administrators will find instances when they must either re-create or move a database from one SQL server to another. Using the **sp_attach_db** command along with the **sp_detach_db** command can be a convenient and easy way to complete this task.

To move a database from Server1 to Server2, an administrator must first run the sp_detach_db command on Server1. Running sp_detach_db removes the database from that server. However, it leaves the database data files and log files intact. To attach the database to Server2, an administrator simply copies the database files to Server2 and runs the sp_attach_db command.

T-SQL is just one method of attaching and detaching a database. Using Enterprise Manager, administrators can also remove or add a database very easily. In fact, many may find that Enterprise Manager is more user-friendly because of its graphical user interface and the way it deals with multiple database files.

Administrators must be aware of some limitations when using the sp_attach_db command. Only members of the sysadmin and dbcreator fixed server roles can execute this procedure. Also, you cannot specify more than 16 files as part of the command.

Objective 2.2 Questions

70-228.02.02.001

You work for a software company that uses SQL Server 2000 for the client/server software application it sells. The quality assurance (QA) group needs to test this software by creating a real-world environment. This environment consists of SQL Server 2000 machines configured with the actual database clients the servers will be interacting with. As part of the testing phase, each tester will create a copy of the database on his or her SQL Server machine. Which fixed server or database role must a user be assigned in order to successfully create a copy of the database on the user's local machine using the sp_attach_db command? (Choose all that apply.)

A. diskadmin

B. sysadmin

C. serveradmin

D. dbcreator

70-228.02.02.002

The SQL server named ACCOUNTING1 in your company's accounting department has just suffered a hard disk failure. You can no longer access the database because the data was stored on the drive that failed. Your company's disaster recovery plan consists of stopping the SQL server and backing up the .mdf and .ldf files for the server to a backup tape every night. There are a total of 19 data files for the database stored on ACCOUNTING1. Which of the following methods should you use to attach the files to a replacement server you have configured with SQL Server 2000?

A. Use the sp_attach_db stored procedure.

B. Run sp_attach_single_file_db 19 times, each time specifying a different data file.

C. Use the CREATE DATABASE with the FOR ATTACH clause.

D. SQL Server 2000 only supports restoring a database with data files greater than 16 by using the RESTORE DATABASE command.

70-228.02.02.003

Your organization has just completed a merger with another company. Both organizations have deployed SQL Server 2000 machines. You decide to consolidate all of your company's databases onto a single SQL server named MAIN. You first want to test what the final configuration for the SQL server will be like, so you plan on creating a copy of each of the databases on the SQL server named MAIN.

You want to accomplish the following goals:

- You want to use the sp_attach_db command to create the databases on the new server.

- Users must be able to access the databases on all of the SQL servers.

- All of the databases must be re-created on the MAIN SQL server.

You run sp_detach_db on each of the SQL servers that have databases needing to be consolidated onto MAIN. You then move the data files to MAIN and run the sp_attach_db command. Which of the following does your solution achieve? (Choose all that apply.)

A. You can use the sp_attach_db command to create the databases on MAIN.

B. Users will be able to continue accessing data on each of the SQL servers.

C. You can access MAIN and see all of the databases that existed across all of the other SQL servers.

D. None of the goals were achieved.

70-228.02.02.004

You are using the sp_attach_db command to create a new database. The value for the @dbname parameter should meet which of the following criteria?

A. The database name you specify should be the same as the database to which the data files belong.

B. The database name cannot be greater than 16 characters.

C. The database name cannot contain decimals.

D. The name must be unique.

Objective 2.2 Answers

70-228.02.02.001

▶ **Correct Answers: B and D**

A. **Incorrect:** The diskadmin fixed server role grants the user permission to maintain the files associated with a database.

B. **Correct:** Users assigned the dbcreator and sysadmin fixed server role have the appropriate permissions to run the sp_attach_db command.

C. **Incorrect:** The serveradmin fixed server role only has permissions to alter SQL Server settings, such as memory allocation, network settings, or restricting the number of connections to the server. It does not enable a user to run the sp_attach_db command.

D. **Correct:** See explanation for answer B.

70-228.02.02.002

► **Correct Answers: C**

A. **Incorrect:** You cannot specify more than 16 file names at a time when using the sp_attach_db command to attach database files to the current server.

B. **Incorrect:** The sp_attach_single_file_db command should only be used when attaching a file to a database that has a single data file on the current server.

C. **Correct:** Due to the limitation with sp_attach_db, you must use the CREATE DATABASE with the FOR ATTACH clause when you are attaching more than 16 data files. Microsoft recommends you use the sp_attach_db command system-stored procedure instead of using CREATE DATABASE FOR ATTACH. However, in this case, the sp_attach_db will not work due to the file number limitations.

D. **Incorrect:** See explanation for answer C.

70-228.02.02.003

► **Correct Answers: A and C**

A. **Correct:** The sp_attach_db command allows you to create the databases on MAIN.

B. **Incorrect:** By running the sp_detach_db command on each SQL server, you remove the database from the SQL server. Additionally, moving the data files instead of executing a file copy makes for a longer process before you can re-create each of the SQL server databases.

C. **Correct:** After moving the data files to MAIN and running the sp_attach_db command, SQL Server creates each of the databases as they were previously on the other SQL machines.

D. **Incorrect:** Two of the goals were achieved: you can create the databases using the sp_attach_db command, and MAIN will have copies of the databases existing on it.

70-228.02.02.004

► **Correct Answers: D**

A. **Incorrect:** See explanation for answer D.

B. **Incorrect:** See explanation for answer D.

C. **Incorrect:** See explanation for answer D.

D. **Correct:** Other than rules you must follow when creating a database, the database name you specify must be unique for that SQL server. If you are running the command to replace an existing server with the same name, you must first detach the database or delete it from the server.

OBJECTIVE 2.3

Create and alter databases.

To ensure optimal performance, you should understand how to design the components that make up a database before actually creating a database. Modifying the design of a database that has been put into production can be very time consuming. A significant amount of time should be spent planning the logical and physical layout of components including tables and indexes.

SQL Server 2000 databases utilize a set of operating system files to store data and objects. Every database starts with a **primary data file**, which holds data as well as pointers to other files in the database. A second required file is the **transaction log**, which holds information to recover the database. An optional third type of operating system file is a **secondary data file**, which stores data or spreads data across multiple disk drives.

SQL Server 2000 allows database objects to be assigned to **filegroups** for allocation, performance, and administration purposes. Every database starts with a default **primary filegroup**, which contains the primary data file. New objects that are created in the database are assigned to the default filegroup. You can also create **user-defined filegroups** and assign database objects to them. A user-defined filegroup may be set as the default filegroup. As a result, newly created objects are assigned to the user-defined filegroup, thereby isolating a database's system tables to the primary filegroup.

When creating a database, you need to specify the files and filegroups used to store the database as well as provide a database name, owner, and size. Database names must follow the rules used for **identifiers**. The default owner of a database is the user who creates the database. Upon database creation, it is recommended that you set a maximum database size to avoid running out of server disk space. You can create databases by using T-SQL commands, through Enterprise Manager, or by using the **Create Database Wizard**.

Changes to an existing database can be made through T-SQL commands or Enterprise Manager. Changes might include expanding or shrinking a database, adding or deleting data or transaction log files, creating filegroups, or setting database options.

Objective 2.3 Questions

70-228.02.03.001

You are creating a database for the accounting department. You are confident that your logical database design is correct. You want to maximize performance when implementing the physical design. Which of the following is the best option for data placement if you want to maximize performance on a single server with multiple physical drives?

A. Create the transaction log in the primary filegroup.

B. Create files or filegroups on as many different physical disks as possible.

C. Place frequently accessed tables and clustered indexes belonging to those tables on different filegroups spread across as many different physical disks as possible.

D. Place different tables used in the same join queries in the same filegroup.

70-228.02.03.002

You are creating a SQL Server 2000 database named Finance on a server with four physical disk drives, each with 1 GB of available disk space.

You want to accomplish the following goals:

- Isolate system objects and tables from user objects

- Utilize data placement for transaction log recovery and performance

- Avoid the risk of the data and log files running out of space

- Ensure that the database does not fill up any of the physical disk drives

You create the Finance database with a primary data file of 300 MB and a transaction log of 100 MB on the first physical disk (disk 1). You set the primary data file and log file to grow automatically. You create a second filegroup and set it as the default filegroup. You create a second data file on physical disk 2 and assign it to the second filegroup. You set the second data file to grow automatically and restrict the growth to 700 MB. Which of the goals have you accomplished? (Choose all that apply.)

A. You have isolated system objects and tables from user objects.

B. You have utilized data placement for transaction log recovery and performance.

C. You have avoided the risk of the data and log files running out of space.

D. You have ensured that the database will not fill up any of the physical disk drives.

70-228.02.03.003

Using Enterprise Manager, you check the properties of the Orders database and notice that the AUTO_SHRINK option is not set. You would like to manually remove unused pages from an Orders database. Which of the following statements is true in regards to shrinking a database? (Choose all that apply.)

A. You cannot shrink an entire database to be smaller than its original size.

B. You cannot shrink individual database files to be smaller than their initial size.

C. It is possible to shrink a transaction log file.

D. It is possible to shrink a database while a database backup is running.

70-228.02.03.004

Your company is planning a Catalog database that it wants to distribute on CD-ROM to its customers. You create the database using sp_create_removable. The database is populated with information on all of your company's products. The president asks you to create a CD-ROM for distribution. You run sp_certify_removable. Everything is configured properly, and you copy the database files to the CD-ROM. Users within your company start calling because they can no longer access the database. Why?

A. The stored procedure sp_certify_removable detaches the database for copying to CD-ROM and removes the database from the server.

B. The stored procedure sp_certify_removable leaves the database in a READ_ONLY state. You must change the database state option to READ_WRITE for the users to gain access to the database.

C. The stored procedure sp_certify_removable leaves the database offline. You must put the database back online before users can gain access to the database.

D. The stored procedure sp_certify_removable makes the database accessible only from the CD-ROM. You must make the database accessible to your users via CD-ROM.

70-228.02.03.005

You have to rename the Accounting database. Which of the following steps are recommended prior to performing a rename? (Choose all that apply.)

A. Set the database to single-user mode.

B. Make sure no one is accessing the database.

C. Make sure the new database name follows the rules for identifiers.

D. Make sure the user you log on as to perform the rename is a member of the fixed database role db_owner.

70-228.02.03.006

Which of the following statements are true regarding a SQL Server 2000 data file? (Choose all that apply.)

A. A data file can be a member of only one filegroup.

B. A data file is the smallest unit of recovery.

C. A data file can be part of a log file.

D. A data file can be used by more than one database.

Objective 2.3 Answers

70-228.02.03.001

▶ **Correct Answers: B**

A. **Incorrect:** Transaction logs are separate files that cannot be part of any filegroup.

B. **Correct:** Spreading data files across as many different physical disks as possible improves I/O performance because multiple disk heads would be reading data at the same time.

C. **Incorrect:** You can only place nonclustered indexes on a different filegroup than the base table. Placing nonclustered indexes on different filegroups spread across as many different physical disks as possible would improve performance because multiple disk heads would be reading data at the same time.

D. **Incorrect:** The opposite is true. Performance would be improved if the tables used in the same join query were placed in different filegroups spread across as many different physical disks as possible because multiple disk heads would be reading data at the same time.

70-228.02.03.002

▶ **Correct Answers: A and C**

A. **Correct:** By creating a user-defined filegroup and making it the default filegroup, any new objects created will automatically be assigned to the user-defined filegroup, thereby isolating all of the system tables to the primary filegroup.

B. **Incorrect:** Placing the transaction log file on the same physical disk as the primary data file does not utilize the physical disks for log recovery or performance. Creating the transaction log on a separate physical disk would provide better recovery in the event physical disk 1 became damaged, and it would provide better performance because parallel read/writes could occur.

C. **Correct:** By setting the autogrow feature for the primary data file, the secondary data file, and the transaction log, you have avoided the risk of the data and log files running out of space.

D. **Incorrect:** You have restricted growth on the second data file but not on the primary or transaction log files. Space on physical disk 1 could be exhausted if the transaction log grows beyond 600 MB.

70-228.02.03.003

▶ **Correct Answers: A and C**

A. **Correct:** Whatever size the database was originally created with is the smallest size to which the entire database can be shrunk. For example, if a database was originally created with a size of 50 MB and grew to 100 MB, assuming all data is deleted, the smallest size the database can be shrunk to is 50 MB.

B. **Incorrect:** Using DBCC SHRINKFILE, it is possible to shrink individual database files to be smaller than their initial size.

C. **Correct:** Transaction log files can be shrunk, but never to a size less than the virtual log file. For example, a transaction log file of 250 MB may be made up of five 50 MB virtual logs. Shrinking the transaction log file may delete all of the unused virtual logs, but will leave one 50 MB log file.

D. **Incorrect:** It is not possible to shrink a database while a backup is running, nor is it possible to back up a database while it is being shrunk.

70-228.02.03.004

▶ **Correct Answers: C**

A. **Incorrect:** The stored procedure sp_certify_removable does not detach or remove the database from the originating SQL server. The database is left intact, but is placed offline.

B. **Incorrect:** The stored procedure sp_certify_removable places the database offline, not to a READ_ONLY state.

C. **Correct:** The database is placed offline so that users cannot make modifications to the database during the copy to a CD-ROM. You must remember to manually place the database back online after the copy is complete.

D. **Incorrect:** The stored procedure sp_certify_removable simply checks that the database is correctly configured for distribution on removable media, and if so, places the database offline. Once placed back online, users can continue to access the database as before.

70-228.02.03.005

▶ **Correct Answers: A, B, and C**

A. **Correct:** This is a recommended step. The database should be set to single-user mode prior to a rename to ensure that no one is able to access the database during the rename.

B. **Correct:** It is recommended that no one access the database during a rename.

C. **Correct:** This is required. The new database name must meet the rules for identifiers.

D. **Incorrect:** Only members of the fixed server roles sysadmin and dbcreator can rename a database. The fixed database role of db_owner does not provide the necessary permissions to rename a database.

70-228.02.03.006

▶ **Correct Answers: A and B**

A. **Correct:** Data files cannot span filegroups.

B. **Correct:** Individual data files can be restored. You can accomplish table level restores by creating a user-defined filegroup, creating a secondary data file, and assigning an individual table to the user-defined filegroup.

C. **Incorrect:** Log files cannot share space with data files.

D. **Incorrect:** Files and filegroups that contain objects belonging to one database cannot be shared by another database.

OBJECTIVE 2.4

Create and manage objects.

Within a SQL Server database, there are numerous objects an administrator must create and manage. These objects can be administered through T-SQL commands or Enterprise Manager. In this objective, the questions focus on how to create and manage objects, such as **distributed views**, which you will encounter when deploying SQL Server 2000 as a federated database.

Objects within SQL Server 2000 include:

- **Tables** Without tables, storing data in a database would be impossible. Tables are the components that make up a database. A basic table consists of columns that have been assigned certain data types.

- **Views** Views have multiple purposes but are mainly designed to restrict the data a user can access. For example, if you have sensitive data in a few columns of a table, you can create a view, and then assign permissions to that view for a user or a group of users. By restricting full access to the table, users are only capable of seeing the information that the view is designed to present. Views are also useful when you need to present data from multiple tables. By creating joins from multiple tables, you can present data to a user as though it is coming from a single table. You can create a view using Enterprise Manager or the CREATE VIEW T-SQL command.

- **Triggers** SQL Server administrators have multiple methods of restricting or enforcing the type of data that can be entered into a database. These methods include CHECK constraints, rules, defaults, and triggers. Triggers are a special class of stored procedures that execute after an event, such as an UPDATE, DELETE, or INSERT to a table or view. Triggers are more flexible than other data-restricting methods because they can reference other tables in the database. This enables the administrator to enforce the business rules for an organization, which can be applied throughout an entire database. You can create triggers by using the CREATE TRIGGER T-SQL command or by using Enterprise Manager.

- **Alerts** Alerts are launched when a certain SQL Server error message is raised or a SQL Server Performance threshold is reached. Alerts can notify an administrator when the system goes down or when there is the potential for the system to go down. For example, an alert can be created using the sp_add_alert stored procedure to notify the administrator when the number of SQL Server connections reaches its maximum. You can also create alerts using Enterprise Manager.

- **Indexes** Indexes increase the efficiency of data lookups and enforce the uniqueness of data rows. There are three types of indexes: **clustered**, **nonclustered**, and **unique**. Clustered indexes require that data stored in a table is physically sorted and stored according to an index key defined for that table. You can only have one clustered index per table. Database tables for which nonclustered indexes are defined do not require the data to be sorted or stored according to a physical order. A table can have up to 249 nonclustered indexes. Unique indexes restrict the key values of a table from being duplicated. Indexes are created using the CREATE INDEX T-SQL command or Enterprise Manager. You can create an index while creating a table or after the fact.

- **User-defined data types** Use user-defined data types with multiple tables within a database that require the same type of data be stored in a column in each table. By creating a user-defined data type, you decrease the amount of administration a single database requires because you do not have to continuously create a custom data type for each new table you create. For example, you would create a user-defined data type if you were creating an employee database where the employee ID is used in each of the tables of the database. A user-defined data type called EMPLOY-EEID could be created, which specifies the number of characters or numbers that an employee's ID could potentially have. All user-defined data types are defined from SQL Server 2000 data types. Use the sp_addtype system-stored procedure or Enterprise Manager to create user-defined data types.

When deploying SQL Server 2000 within a federated server environment, objects you create, such as tables and views, require additional planning and configuration before you can create them. A federated server environment consists of member servers in which each member server stores member tables and distributed views. Essentially, the data that is stored on a single database is partitioned across member servers for performance and scalability purposes. To successfully answer some of the questions you will encounter on the exam, you should familiarize yourself with the concepts behind federated servers and the objects of federated servers, such as distributed views and member tables.

Objective 2.4 Questions

70-228.02.04.001

Over the past month, traffic to your company's e-commerce site has doubled. Performance of the Web site has in turn suffered. You have tuned your SQL Server 2000 machine, but it has not resulted in significant improvements. You decide to implement a federation of SQL servers in an attempt to balance the load across multiple SQL servers rather than a single server. You want to create a distributed partitioned view called Distributed_View1. Which of the following is required so that a distributed view is created?

A. The name of the view must begin with Distributed.

B. The view must contain the UNION ALL clause.

C. You must use the CHECK OPTION clause within the view.

D. An ORDER BY clause has to be included in the view.

70-228.02.04.002

You are designing the database architecture for your company's data warehousing solution. The database itself needs to hold approximately 28 terabytes (TB) of information. You also expect users to run queries that will tax the server's processors. As the uptime and response of the database is critical to business operations, you decide to create a federation of databases to hold the data.

You want to accomplish the following goals:

- You want to create member tables on each of the member servers. Each table must hold a set range of data.

- You want to restrict users from seeing the data in the Salary column of the HR table.

- You want to allow only currency values to be entered into the Payment column of the Vendor table.

You create member servers and member tables on each server. You restrict the data range on each member table by using a CHECK constraint to enforce the data range on each table. You create a view named No_Salary on the Human Resources table restricting users from seeing salary information. Finally, you create a rule to enforce values being entered into the Payment column of the Vendor table to be of the money data type. Which results does your solution achieve? (Choose all that apply.)

A. The CHECK constraint value that is part of the CREATE TABLE syntax ensures that none of the values for the member tables overlap.

B. Only users not assigned the No_Salary view can view salary information.

C. Data entry clerks hired to enter data into the Vendor table cannot make the mistake of entering non-currency values.

D. None of the goals were achieved.

70-228.02.04.003

By default, SQL Server only creates an entry in the Windows NT or 2000 Application Event log for those sysmessages that are of severity 19 or higher. Which stored procedure can you use so that an alert is generated for those sysmessages with a severity lower than 19?

A. sp_altermessage

B. xp_logevent

C. sp_add_alert

D. sp_add_notification

70-228.02.04.004

You are designing a SQL Server 2000 database that will store customer purchase history. You want information in the Marketing table updated each time a customer makes a purchase. What type of object could you create to achieve this?

A. alert

B. view

C. trigger

D. index

70-228.02.04.005

Users are complaining about the lag time when they run a particular query against the Sales database. After analyzing the query, you find that the data being requested is the sales figures for each client. Clients are listed in the table by client name and number. What type of object could you create to decrease the query execution time?

A. alert

B. view

C. identifier

D. index

70-228.02.04.006

The Human Resources database contains a table that lists each employee's information including employee first name, employee last name, social security number, salary, address, and employee ID. There are a total of 55,000 employees listed in the table. The Human Resources department is preparing a mailing to those employees that live in the state of Washington and needs a list containing the employees' name and address. Because temporary employees will be doing the mailing, Human Resources wants to restrict the workers from seeing sensitive employee information, such as salaries and social security numbers.

You want to accomplish the following goals:

- Decrease the execution time for the query

- Restrict users from seeing the data in the Salary column of the Human Resources table

- Store data in the table so that the employees are listed in alphabetical order

You create a view that restricts users from seeing the Salary, Social Security Number, and Employee ID columns. You then create a clustered index view on the State column in the Employees table. Which of the following goals does your solution accomplish? (Choose all that apply.)

A. Query execution time is decreased as an index is created for the data stored in the Employees table.

B. Users are restricted from seeing employee sensitive data.

C. Data will be stored in alphabetical order.

D. None of the goals are accomplished.

Objective 2.4 Answers

70-228.02.04.001

▶ **Correct Answers: B**

A. **Incorrect:** Distributed partitioned views must follow the same naming conventions as other views defined in SQL Server 2000. It is not required that the name contain or start with the word Distributed.

B. **Correct:** A distributed partitioned view consists of tables that reside on more than one SQL server. These tables are referred to as member tables. By using the UNION ALL clause, the view can combine the information from all of the member tables within a single view. Therefore, when a user or application references the view, the data location is transparent.

C. **Incorrect:** The CHECK OPTION confirms that data being inserted or updated through a view conforms to the criteria for displaying data set by the view. For example, if a view restricts a user from seeing the salary of those employees earning more than $100,000, a user could not enter the salary value for an employee earning greater than $100,000.

D. **Incorrect:** The ORDER BY clause enables you to sort the results from a query by one or more columns. It is not required for a distributed partitioned view.

70-228.02.04.002

▶ **Correct Answers: B and C**

A. **Incorrect:** The CHECK constraint only ensures that the values you enter for the column ranges are enforced. It cannot verify that the values do not overlap with those configured in the other tables.

B. **Correct:** Views can be used not only to assist users in seeing data more easily, but they can also be used to restrict users from seeing secure data.

C. **Correct:** Rules enforce the type of values that can be entered into a table. Rules only apply to data yet to be entered into the table; existing data is not affected by the rule.

D. **Incorrect:** Two of the goals were achieved. You can restrict users viewing confidential data in the Human Resources table, and only certain types of data can be entered into the Vendor table.

70-228.02.04.003

▶ **Correct Answers: A**

A. **Correct:** The stored procedure sp_altermessage can force SQL Server to record event messages for those sysmessages that have a severity lower than 19.

B. **Incorrect:** The xp_logevent procedure creates a log entry of user-defined messages in the SQL Server log file and the Microsoft Windows NT or 2000 Event Viewer.

C. **Incorrect:** The stored procedure sp_add_alert enables you to create an alert that is triggered when a particular threshold has been reached. For example, if the disk drive where you store data files for SQL Server reaches capacity, an alert can be created that sends a message to the administrator (as long as a notification has been created). The stored procedure sp_add_alert creates an alert only for sysmessages that are logged, which means severity 19 or higher unless modified by sp_altermessage.

D. **Incorrect:** The stored procedure sp_add_notification enables you to create a notification after a particular SQL Server alert has been generated.

70-228.02.04.004

▶ **Correct Answers: C**

A. **Incorrect:** See explanation for answer C.

B. **Incorrect:** See explanation for answer C.

C. **Correct:** A trigger is a stored procedure that executes automatically after a particular action, such as INSERT or UPDATE, has been performed on a table. For example, a trigger that updates a second table can be written to execute after an insert has been made to the first table.

D. **Incorrect:** See explanation for answer C.

70-228.02.04.005

▶ **Correct Answers: D**

A. **Incorrect:** See explanation for answer D.

B. **Incorrect:** See explanation for answer D.

C. **Incorrect:** See explanation for answer D.

D. **Correct:** Indexes are created on a table to help decrease the actual execution time for a query by removing the need for full table scans to locate the row or rows of data the query is requesting.

70-228.02.04.006

▶ **Correct Answers: A, B, and C**

A. **Correct:** Indexes decrease overall query execution time as SQL Server has more efficient methods of searching through the data in a table.

B. **Correct:** Views are a useful method of restricting the data a user can see in a table.

C. **Correct:** Clustered indexes store data in a table according to a physical order determined by the index. Because a clustered index stores data in such a manner, you can only have one clustered index per table.

D. **Incorrect:** All three of the goals are accomplished.

OBJECTIVE DOMAIN 3

Managing, Monitoring, and Troubleshooting SQL Server 2000 Databases

The Managing, Monitoring, and Troubleshooting SQL Server 2000 Databases domain examines the tasks administrators will face on a day-to-day basis. These tasks include:

- Creating a database and ensuring that the database performs well

  When creating a database, administrators must take into consideration certain SQL Server configuration settings, such as database and log file location. These settings will ultimately affect the performance of the database.

- Altering the database schema after it has been created

  The schema design for the database is possibly the most important stage in planning the deployment of the database. Poor schema design not only affects the performance and scalability of the database, but it also governs how SQL Server interacts with it. Understanding how to successfully alter the schema plays an important role in the day-to-day administration of any database.

- Utilizing built-in tools for administrating SQL Server 2000

  To accomplish tasks such as creating, altering, and managing a database, administrators must be aware of every available tool. With a better knowledge of these tools and how they work, administrators can more easily accomplish their tasks.

- Performing database and table integrity checks to avoid future problems with database reliability

Constantly checking on the status of a database's integrity is tantamount to the successful operation of a database. For example, a corrupt index that goes unnoticed will have a direct effect on the performance of the database.

- Executing procedures to ensure quick and reliable data recovery

Understanding the most efficient method of recovering lost or corrupted data allows an administrator to get downed systems up and running quickly.

Tested Skills and Suggested Practices

The skills that you need to successfully master the Managing, Monitoring, and Troubleshooting SQL Server 2000 Databases objective domain on the *Installing, Configuring, and Administering Microsoft SQL Server 2000 Enterprise Edition* exam include:

- **Optimizing database performance.**

  - Practice 1: Using Transact-SQL (T-SQL) commands, configure the Max Worker Threads value to be 128 for the default instance of SQL Server.

  - Practice 2: Create a stored procedure that queries data from several tables within the Northwind database. Execute the stored procedure within a loop so that you can monitor it using the SQL Server 2000 Profiler utility. Configure the Profiler to monitor for table scans, locks, and other objects that could hinder the queries' performance.

  - Practice 3: Execute the stored procedure you used in Practice 2. Run it through a loop again, but this time monitor SQL Server's performance using Performance Monitor. You should monitor the server for processor and memory utilization along with SQL Server specific performance objects, such as the number of lock requests.

- **Optimizing data storage.**

  - Practice 1: Using Enterprise Manager, create a new filegroup in the Northwind database. Then create a new file (preferably on a separate disk drive), and assign it to the new filegroup.

  - Practice 2: Assign an existing table to a new filegroup. Right-click on the Customers table, select Design Table, right-click on any column, and select Properties. From the Tables tab, select Table Filegroup, and select the new filegroup created in Practice 1 from the drop-down list.

  - Practice 3: Assign an existing index to a new filegroup. Right-click on the Customers table, select Design Table, right-click on any column, and select Properties. From the Index/Keys tab, select the index box and the index you want to move. In the Index Filegroup, select the new filegroup created in Practice 1.

- **Modifying the database schema.**

  - Practice 1: Using the Northwind database, change the presentation format of the OrderDate column located in the Orders table. Change the date to the European format in which the day comes before the month.

  - Practice 2: Alter the table so that it displays the time along with the date. Have the time also show the number of milliseconds.

- **Performing disaster recovery operations.**

  - Practice 1: Set the Northwind database to BULK_LOGGED recovery using the T-SQL command `ALTER DATABASE NORTHWIND SET RECOVERY BULK_LOGGED`. Using Enterprise Manager, view the database Options tab found under Properties for the Northwind database. Verify that the database is set to the BULK_LOGGED recovery model. Set it to FULL using Enterprise Manager.

  - Practice 2: Using Enterprise Manager, back up the Northwind database to a file named C:\NORTHWIND.BAK. Select Overwrite Existing Media. Issue the same command using the T-SQL command `BACKUP DATABASE NORTHWIND TO DISK = 'C:\NORTHWIND.BAK' WITH INIT`.

  - Practice 3: Back up the Northwind database transaction log using the T-SQL command `BACKUP LOG NORTHWIND TO DISK = 'C:\NORTHWINDLOG.BAK' WITH INIT`.

  - Practice 4: Using Enterprise Manager, restore the Northwind database and transaction log from Practices 2 and 3.

- **Performing integrity checks.**

  - Practice 1: Using T-SQL commands, run an integrity check on the Northwind database. Specify the NOINDEX argument when executing the DBCC command.

  - Practice 2: Create a scheduled job that will run an integrity check on the Employees table located in the Northwind database.

  - Practice 3: Execute the appropriate DBCC statement to monitor fragmentation of data and indexes within the Northwind database.

- **Troubleshooting transactions and locking by using SQL Profiler, SQL Server Enterprise Manager, or T-SQL.**

  - Practice 1: Using the Query Analyzer, connect to SQL Server and use the Northwind database to issue `SELECT * FROM ORDERS`. Use the Current Activity window in Enterprise Manager to find the system process ID (SPID) that issued the command, and review the information tracked.

- Practice 2: Using the Query Analyzer, run sp_who. Find the SPID that issued the command, and review the information tracked. Compare it to the information tracked in Practice 1.

- Practice 3: Using the SQL Profiler, create a new trace. Track Security Audit events of Audit Login and Audit Logout. Add data columns for LoginName and StartTime. Filter where LoginName is Like sa. Start the trace. Use the Query Analyzer to connect and disconnect as user sa, and view the results of the trace.

- Practice 4: Using the Query Analyzer, run sp_lock. Review the types of locks reported.

Further Reading

This section lists supplemental readings by objective. We recommend that you study these sources thoroughly before taking exam 70-228.

Objective 3.1

Microsoft SQL Server 2000 product documentation. To access Books Online, click the Start button, point to Programs, then Microsoft SQL Server, and then select Books Online. Choose the Contents tab, expand Optimizing Database Performance, and select "Optimizing Database Performance Overview." This article provides links to other topics that cover performance tuning and database performance.

Part 1; Self-Paced Training for Microsoft SQL Server 2000 System Administration. Chapter 14, "Monitoring SQL Server Performance and Activity," covers the topic of detecting and resolving performance issues with SQL Server and databases created on the server. Chapter 12, "Performing Administrative Tasks," also covers configuration parameters that you alter to optimize database performance.

Objective 3.2

Microsoft SQL Server 2000 product documentation. To access Books Online, click the Start button, point to Programs, then Microsoft SQL Server, and then select Books Online. Choose the Contents tab and expand Optimizing Database Performance, then Database Design, then Physical Database Design, and then Data Placement Using Filegroups. This volume contains articles on placing tables and indexes on filegroups.

Microsoft SQL Server 2000 product documentation. To access Books Online, click the Start button, point to Programs, then Microsoft SQL Server, and then select Books Online. Choose the Contents tab and expand Optimizing Database Performance, then Database Design, then Physical Database Design, and then RAID. This volume covers the use of RAID systems with SQL Server 2000.

Part 1; Self-Paced Training for Microsoft SQL Server 2000 System Administration. Chapter 6, "Creating and Configuring User Databases," Lesson 4 discusses the use of multiple disks and RAID systems.

Objective 3.3

Microsoft SQL Server 2000 product documentation. To access Books Online, click the Start button, point to Programs, then Microsoft SQL Server, and then select Books Online. Choose the Contents tab, expand Transact-SQL Reference, and then select "ALTER DATABASE." Also expand Replication, then Implementing Replication, and then select "Schema Changes on Publication Databases." These articles cover modifying the database schema.

Microsoft Corporation. *Microsoft SQL Server 2000 Administrator's Companion*. Redmond, Washington: Microsoft Press, 2000. Chapter 15, "Managing Tables Using Transact-SQL and Enterprise Manager," details altering schemas using the Enterprise Manager and using T-SQL.

Objective 3.4

Microsoft SQL Server 2000 product documentation. To access Books Online, click the Start button, point to Programs, then Microsoft SQL Server, and then select Books Online. Choose the Contents tab and expand Administering SQL Server, and then Backing Up and Restoring Databases. This volume contains sections that cover disaster recovery.

Part 1; Self-Paced Training for Microsoft SQL Server 2000 System Administration. Chapter 8, "Developing a Data Restoration Strategy," Lesson 3 deals with selecting and designing a backup and restore strategy.

Objective 3.5

Microsoft SQL Server 2000 product documentation. To access Books Online, click the Start button, point to Programs, then Microsoft SQL Server, and then select Books Online. Choose the Contents tab and expand Using SQL Server Tools, then Database Maintenance Plan Wizard Help. This topic describes how to use the Database Maintenance Plan wizard with an article on database integrity checks.

Microsoft SQL Server 2000 product documentation. To access Books Online, click the Start button, point to Programs, then Microsoft SQL Server, and then select Books Online. Choose the Contents tab and expand SQL Server Architecture, and then Administration Architecture, and then select "Data Integrity Validation." This article discusses the use of DBCC and its features in SQL Server 2000.

Objective 3.6

Microsoft SQL Server 2000 product documentation. To access Books Online, click the Start button, point to Programs, then Microsoft SQL Server, and then select Books Online. Choose the Contents tab and expand Administering SQL Server, then Monitoring Server Performance and Activity, and then select "Monitoring with SQL Profiler." This article covers the use of SQL Profiler for such actions as troubleshooting transactions and debugging T-SQL statements.

Part 1; Self-Paced Training for Microsoft SQL Server 2000 System Administration. Review Chapter 14, "Monitoring SQL Server Performance and Activity," Lesson 3 for a full discussion of all of the monitoring options available with SQL Server 2000.

OBJECTIVE 3.1

Optimize database performance.

Both the SQL Server configuration and the database design affect database performance. In fact, most database performance issues are the result of poor planning and design when creating a database.

One of the first steps to successfully tune your database is to pinpoint the cause of the performance bottleneck. Is it the server or is it the database design? Running performance tools, such as Windows 2000 Performance Monitor, and monitoring for SQL specific counters is one method you can use to help determine causes for poor database performance. However, unless you know how to interpret this data, you will be unable to diagnose the cause of the problem. For example, you monitor your SQL server and notice high CPU utilization. Without further investigation as well as an understanding of what the server is doing at that time, you do not have a solid path to follow to help diagnose the issue.

Another useful tool for monitoring database performance is the SQL Server 2000 Profiler application. Profiler enables you to record database activity, which you can then analyze with built-in tools, such as the Index Tuning Wizard. Configure the Profiler to record all database and server activity, such as the stored procedures being executed on the server, or specific activities, such as T-SQL transactions. When used in conjunction, Performance Monitor and SQL Server 2000 Profiler can help you quickly pinpoint many SQL Server specific bottlenecks.

One such bottleneck can be the cause of a high number of table scans. **Table scans** occur when SQL Server searches through all of the rows in a table to find the requested data rather than searching a single row. By searching all of the rows, the server inefficiently uses memory and CPU time. Table scans indicate poorly indexed tables within a database. By creating an index, such as a clustered index, you supply the server with a specified row that it can use to efficiently search for data in the table.

Creating indexes in the appropriate places is part of good database design. Other design features include optimizing queries, denormalizing the database to simplify complex processes, and identifying and optimizing the larger tables within the database. For example, if you are running a report against a large table, you might consider creating a column or columns within that table that will help propagate data, and therefore help to retrieve data faster for that report.

The type of storage system the database resides on can also affect its performance, particularly if the database is large (more than a gigabyte). To help increase the performance of a database, consider placing data files for the database on the fastest drives within the server. Additionally, you should create the data files so they reside on a RAID device. For example, RAID 5 enables SQL Server to read from the drives almost 50 percent faster than if they were on a non-RAID device. RAID devices also have the advantage of offering redundancy when storing data.

SQL Server settings also have a major effect on database performance. Before changing any of these settings, be sure you thoroughly understand what effects they will have, not only on SQL Server, but also on other applications that could be running on the server. For example, some administrators will change the **Max Worker Threads** value without considering its effects on the server. Max Worker Threads determines the number of worker threads allocated for SQL Server. The more threads you have, the more system resources are required to create and maintain the threads. Because worker threads can be costly, you should only specify the amount of threads that makes sense. By default, the Max Worker Threads value under SQL Server 2000 is set to 255. When determining the number of worker threads required for SQL Server, be aware of the number of concurrent users your server will need to host at any given time. The worker thread value is pooled, so in case the number of connections to the SQL server goes beyond the Max Worker Thread value, SQL Server will begin to share the threads across connections.

There are other performance issues that are not covered in this overview. Refer to the "Further Reading" section to learn about other sources of information.

Objective 3.1 Questions

70-228.03.01.001

Administrators in the HR department are complaining about the time it takes to retrieve a list of retired employees from the database. After looking into the situation, you do not find any significant problems with the query they are running that could cause a large lag time in returning the results. You run SQL Server Profiler and find that when the query is executed, a larger number of table scans appear in the trace. Which of the following is the best method to reduce query execution time in this case?

A. Increase the amount of memory in the server.

B. Create or reindex tables in the database.

C. Increase the number of CPUs in the server.

D. Configure the SQL server to use Windows NT Fibers.

70-228.03.01.002

You are creating a SQL Server database on a server configured with a RAID array controller. The server has a total of five 18 GB drives installed.

You want to accomplish the following goals:

- Recover the data even after a single drive failure.

- Allow for growth of the database beyond 18 GB.

- Configure the drives so that SQL Server performs optimally.

You create a RAID 5 disk array and store the database and transaction log files on the logical drive. You specify all five drives to be part of the array.

Which of the following does your solution achieve? (Choose all that apply.)

A. If a drive were to fail, users could continue to access SQL Server data.

B. Disk drive capacity will not be an issue when the database grows beyond 18 GB.

C. Creating a RAID 5 array increases the read performance of the server.

D. None of the goals are achieved.

70-228.03.01.003

Your SQL 2000 server has 512 users created in the Logins directory. You have been monitoring the system for usage and have noticed that there are never more than 281 users connected to the server at a single time. Realizing this, you want to ensure that server resources are being allocated correctly. A coworker suggests that you look into changing the Max Worker Thread setting, which is currently set to 512. What value should you change it to?

A. Change it to 128.

B. Change it to 300.

C. Leave it at 512.

D. Change it to 256.

70-228.03.01.004

You recently deployed a Web-based application that stores data on a SQL Server 2000 machine. The application is accessible to users both internal and external to your organization. Even though the site has only been up and running for a week, complaints are coming in regarding the response time of the application, specifically when users must retrieve a list containing available vendors. You gather performance monitoring data for the site and find that the Processor Queue Length for the CPUs on the SQL server are extremely high. What should you do to resolve the problem?

A. Increase the number of processors in the machine.

B. Increase the amount of RAM.

C. Insert a faster SCSI board.

D. Increase the size of the temp database.

70-228.03.01.005

You have a SQL Server 2000 machine that is extremely slow when accessed. You run some basic Performance Monitor sessions and find that a deadlock is occurring in the Marketing database that's configured on the server.

You want to accomplish the following goals:

- Find the cause of the deadlock that is occurring.

- Monitor the database for excessive table scans.

- Apply the optimal indexes to the database for maximum performance.

You run the SQL Profiler application and save the trace file. While running the Profiler, you configure the Profiler to use the following counters: Stored Procedures/RPC:Starting, TSQL/SQL:BatchStarting, Locks/Lock:Deadlock, and Locks/Lock:Deadlock Chain. After the trace is complete, you run the Index Tuning Wizard and create the indexes it recommends for the database.

Which of the following does your solution achieve? (Choose all that apply.)

A. You can find the cause of the deadlock.

B. Indexes are applied optimally to the database.

C. SQL Server Profiler displays table scans that are occurring.

D. None of the goals are accomplished.

Objective 3.1 Answers

70-228.03.01.001

▶ **Correct Answers: B**

A. **Incorrect:** Increasing the amount of memory would be a possible resolution if SQL Server were showing signs of increased memory usage during query execution. In this case, there are a large amount of table scans, which indicates a poorly designed database schema.

B. **Correct:** High table scans are a sign of a poorly indexed table. When SQL Server has to search for data in a table that is not indexed, it must do so by searching through each row of the table; therefore, it ends up scanning the entire table.

C. **Incorrect:** Increasing the number of CPUs may help increase the response time of the server, but it is an inefficient method of resolving the problem.

D. **Incorrect:** Selecting to use Windows NT Fibers enables the Windows 2000 operating system to avoid the transition between the user mode of the application and the kernel mode of the thread. This transition can be a costly operation. By reducing this transition, a server can be more efficient. However, in the case of high table scans, the problem must be addressed at the schema level for the database.

70-228.03.01.002

▶ **Correct Answers: A, B, and C**

A. **Correct:** Level 5 RAID stripes data and parity information across the set of disk drives making up the drive array. In case a single drive were to fail, information stored on the array would still be accessible because of the parity information written to the drives.

B. **Correct:** By creating a disk array, you create a single logical drive. The size of this logical drive is approximately the sum of all of the drives within the array less approximately 20 percent used for overhead when creating the array.

C. **Correct:** Striping data with parity increases read performance compared to other RAID levels, such as disk mirroring.

D. **Incorrect:** All three goals are achieved.

70-228.03.01.003

▶ **Correct Answers: B**

A. **Incorrect:** See the explanation for answer B.

B. **Correct:** For each client connection to SQL Server, an operating system thread is created, which can be extremely costly to system resources. To improve overall system performance, SQL Server implements thread pooling: one thread handles each user connection. However, if the number of worker threads is less than the number of user connections, SQL Server pools the worker threads, reducing the number of threads that need to be created. You must specify a Max Worker Thread value that is capable of supporting the expected users to the system. Creating a large thread value forces more system resources to be used.

C. **Incorrect:** See the explanation for answer B.

D. **Incorrect:** See the explanation for answer B.

70-228.03.01.004

▶ **Correct Answers: A**

A. **Correct:** The Processor Queue Length counter denotes the number of threads waiting for processor time. If the queue is large, you must increase the number of processors in the server, replace the processors with faster ones, optimize the queries, or improve the indexes.

B. **Incorrect:** See the explanation for answer A.

C. **Incorrect:** See the explanation for answer A.

D. **Incorrect:** See the explanation for answer A.

70-228.03.01.005

▶ **Correct Answers: A and B**

A. **Correct:** SQL Server Profiler is an excellent tool for monitoring SQL Server activity. Unlike Windows 2000's Performance Monitor, SQL Server Profiler enables you to monitor detailed SQL Server transactions including monitoring for deadlocks and their causes. By specifying the Profiler to monitor for specific counters, you can better determine the cause of the deadlock.

B. **Correct:** The Index Tuning Wizard analyzes the trace file and recommends indexes that should be created.

C. **Incorrect:** You must configure SQL Server Profiler to monitor for table scans.

D. **Incorrect:** Two of the goals are accomplished.

Optimize data storage.

Although SQL Server 2000 is designed to store large amounts of data and support large numbers of users, it benefits both large and small companies by providing them with easy-to-use data storage options. Optimizing data storage requires early planning of your organization's storage needs as well as an understanding of how SQL Server utilizes I/O subsystems and the placement of database objects on disks to maximize performance.

Hardware and software implementations of RAID can directly affect the performance of SQL Server. Hardware disk arrays provide better performance than those implemented through the operating system's software because I/O functions are handled directly through the controller.

Various levels of RAID configurations designate differences in performance, redundancy, storage capacity, and cost. With RAID 0, data is striped in a fixed order across all disks in the array. Read/write operations can be performed independently and simultaneously, thereby improving performance. RAID 0 provides no fault tolerance, so if one disk in the array fails, data that is striped across all other disks becomes unavailable. RAID 5 also stripes data across a disk array but writes parity information in such a way that data and parity data are always on different disks. RAID 5 offers lower performance than RAID 0; however, it has higher reliability because a single disk can fail and all data remains accessible.

The placement of database objects within a database can also improve performance. You can create database objects, such as tables and indexes, on specific filegroups within a database, and you can create these filegroups on specific disks. By partitioning tables and indexes correctly, you can improve query performance and process queries in parallel.

Objective 3.2 Questions

70-228.03.02.001

You are building a SQL server with five physical disks. You want to achieve the best performance possible, but you also want to achieve a high level of redundancy. Which RAID level best meets your requirements?

A. Level 10 (1 + 0)

B. Level 1

C. Level 5

D. Level 0

70-228.03.02.002

Which of the following data storage options use disk striping to spread data across multiple disks in order to achieve better performance? (Choose all that apply.)

A. Creating database files on multiple physical disks and assigning filegroups to each file

B. RAID 3

C. Hardware-based disk duplexing

D. Software-based disk mirroring

70-228.03.02.003

Placing SQL Server data files on which of the following will provide the best performance benefits when reading data? (Choose all that apply.)

A. A Windows NT volume formatted using NTFS with a 64-KB extent size

B. A Windows NT volume formatted using FAT

C. A Windows NT compressed drive

D. A Windows NT disk mirror

70-228.03.02.004

Assuming you are planning your data storage requirements for optimal performance, which of the following is the best option for improving performance?

A. Create the transaction log in the primary filegroup.

B. Create files or filegroups on as many different physical disks as possible.

C. Place frequently accessed tables and clustered indexes belonging to those tables on different filegroups spread across as many different physical disks as possible.

D. Place different tables used in the same join queries in the same filegroup.

70-228.03.02.005

What is the primary advantage of a software-based implementation of RAID 5 versus a hardware-based implementation?

A. Performance

B. Redundancy

C. Ease of installation

D. Cost

Objective 3.2 Answers

70-228.03.02.001

▶ **Correct Answers: C**

A. **Incorrect:** This RAID level is not possible with five disks. Because each disk drive requires a mirrored disk, RAID 10 always requires an even number of disks. RAID 10 requires a minimum of four disks. If a sixth disk were available, this configuration would provide the best combination of performance and fault tolerance of any RAID level. Three disks would be used to configure a striped array with parity, which would then be mirrored to an identical set of striped disks.

B. **Incorrect:** RAID 1 uses disk mirroring to provide redundancy. All data written to the primary disk is also written to the mirror disk. RAID 1 provides improved read performance; however, write performance is less than that achieved by RAID 5. Because each disk drive requires a mirrored disk, RAID 1 always requires an even number of disks.

C. **Correct:** By ensuring that data and parity data are always written to separate disks, RAID 5 achieves a high level of fault tolerance because a failed disk does not affect data retrieval. Optimal read/write performance is achieved because data is spread across multiple disks and can be accessed in parallel.

D. **Incorrect:** RAID 0 offers the same performance benefits as RAID 5, but it does not offer any redundancy.

70-228.03.02.002

▶ **Correct Answers: A and B**

A. **Correct:** SQL Server uses proportional fill to evenly distribute data across all of the files and all of the disks.

B. **Correct:** RAID 3 employs disk striping to improve performance.

C. **Incorrect:** Hardware-based disk duplexing does not use disk striping technology to spread data across multiple disks. Disk duplexing is a form of disk mirroring that also provides protection against disk controller failure.

D. **Incorrect:** Disk mirroring does not stripe data across multiple drives. Instead it provides a mirror of the data on another drive.

70-228.03.02.003

▶ **Correct Answers: A and D**

A. **Correct:** SQL Server performance can be improved when databases are created on NTFS volumes with a 64-KB extent size.

B. **Incorrect:** Performance is not improved by the FAT file system. Databases stored on volumes formatted using NTFS with a 64-KB extent size will have improved performance over those stored on volumes formatted using the FAT file system.

C. **Incorrect:** SQL Server data and transaction log files should never be placed on compressed drives.

D. **Correct:** Windows NT disk mirroring will improve data reads.

70-228.03.02.004

▶ **Correct Answers: B**

A. **Incorrect:** Transaction logs are separate files that cannot be part of a filegroup.

B. **Correct:** Spreading data files across as many different physical disks as possible is beneficial because I/O performance is improved due to multiple disk heads reading data at the same time.

C. **Incorrect:** The only type of index that can be placed in a filegroup not containing its base table is a nonclustered index. Placing nonclustered indexes on different filegroups spread across as many different physical disks as possible improves performance because it allows multiple disk heads to read data simultaneously.

D. **Incorrect:** Performance would be improved if the tables used in the same join query were placed in different filegroups spread across as many different physical disks as possible because it allows multiple disk heads to read data simultaneously.

70-228.03.02.005

▶ **Correct Answers: D**

A. **Incorrect:** Hardware-based RAID 5 offers better performance because no processor cycles are required.

B. **Incorrect:** Both implementations offer the same level of redundancy.

C. **Incorrect:** Both implementations are comparable in terms of ease of installation.

D. **Correct:** Because it is built into the operating system, software-based RAID 5 does not require any additional cost for specialized hardware.

O B J E C T I V E   3 . 3

Modify the database schema.

As discussed in the previous objective, the design of a database affects overall performance of the database. Keeping that in mind, this objective discusses ways to edit the schema not only for the purposes of improving performance, but also for managing users' needs and requirements.

There are two major methods used to edit an existing database schema: SQL Server 2000 Enterprise Manager and SQL Server 2000 Query Analyzer. By utilizing the schema manipulation tools within Enterprise Manager, administrators can easily add, delete, or modify tables from databases. They can also get more specific by modifying views, triggers, indexes, and relationships attributed to the table.

Many tasks that administrators perform when modifying the schema are repetitive. For that reason, most administrators turn to T-SQL. Creating T-SQL statements enables administrators to have greater control over their modifications. It also allows them to easily complete tasks that may require executing repeated steps, for example, selecting columns from a table according to a predetermined search query and then deleting those columns from the table.

When manipulating schema, keep in mind that specific restrictions may prevent you from changing certain information. These restrictions could be in the form of security restrictions or may be some constraint enforced by SQL Server logic. For example, edits to the schema of a database that is published to Subscriber servers will not be applied unless the schema was changed using Enterprise Manager or replication-stored procedures.

T-SQL has a set of commands that you can use to edit the schema. As previously mentioned, these commands will fail if they do not pass security or other requirements. Some of the commands that you should become familiar with include:

- **ALTER TABLE** Execute the ALTER TABLE command before manipulating an existing table. You must execute the ALTER command when adding or dropping columns and constraints, or disabling or enabling constraints and triggers.

- **ALTER VIEW** Use the ALTER VIEW command to change previously created views. Also use it to modify indexed views.

- **ALTER TRIGGER** Use the ALTER TRIGGER command to modify previously created triggers.

Objective 3.3 Questions

70-228.03.03.001

All customer information is stored on a SQL server named Sales. The Contracts table, which is part of the Sales database, stores customer contract information, such as the start and end date of each contract and any specific discounts specified in the contract. The Contracts table has a column named Titles, which contains the title of each contract. Because of some changes in the way contracts are written, you must delete the Titles column. However, SQL Server is not allowing you to do so. You have been assigned the role of system administrator and dbo for that table. Which of the following represents the best explanation for why you can't delete the column?

A. There is not enough room on the temp database.

B. The column must be null before you can delete it.

C. A rule has been bound to the column.

D. The column contains a default value.

70-228.03.03.002

The sales office in Chicago publishes data to the West Coast sales office in Los Angeles. The marketing group in Chicago has given you a list of vendors who are no longer associated with your organization, so you must change some of the tables in the database. Using T-SQL commands, you execute a series of ALTER TABLE commands on the required tables. The next morning you receive an e-mail from the marketing group informing you that the Los Angeles office can still view vendor information that was supposed to be deleted. You run a query on the Chicago database and find that the information is correct. What could be the reason for the incorrect information at the Los Angeles office?

A. When servers are involved in a Publisher/Subscriber relationship, you must manually update any schema changes to a database on both the Publisher and Subscriber.

B. You need to create a Distributor as part of the replication so that schema changes are successfully carried over to the Subscriber server.

C. Schema changes cannot be overwritten on a Subscriber server unless the subscriber's database is first dropped.

D. You cannot edit the schema of a database involved in replication using an ALTER TABLE statement.

70-228.03.03.003

You want to create a table within the Patient_Records table. You also want to enable full-text indexing for the table. Which tools can you use to do so? (Choose all that apply.)

A. Database Designer

B. Table Designer

C. SQL Server Enterprise Manager

D. SQL Server Query Analyzer

70-228.03.03.004

A user in the Marketing department is having trouble updating the Distributors table in the Marketing database. Which of the following stored procedures can you execute to display a list of permissions for that table?

A. sp_table_privileges

B. sp_srvrolepermission

C. sp_grantdbaccess

D. sp_table_privileges_ex

Objective 3.3 Answers

70-228.03.03.001

▶ **Correct Answers: C**

A. **Incorrect:** The size of the temp database does not affect your ability to delete a single column from a table.

B. **Incorrect:** A column can be deleted even if it contains data. Situations that prevent a column from being deleted include the column being involved in replication or having an index defined on the column.

C. **Correct:** A column that has a rule bound to it cannot be deleted. The rule must be dropped first, and as long as other constraints, such as indexes, primary keys, or foreign keys, are not associated with the column, the column can be deleted.

D. **Incorrect:** See the explanation for answer C.

70-228.03.03.002

▶ **Correct Answers: D**

    A. **Incorrect:** See the explanation for answer D.

    B. **Incorrect:** See the explanation for answer D.

    C. **Incorrect:** See the explanation for answer D.

    D. **Correct:** You can only edit a database's schema on a Publisher and have it replicate successfully to the Subscriber if the changes are done through the replication publication properties of Enterprise Manager or by using replication-stored procedures.

70-228.03.03.003

▶ **Correct Answers: C and D**

    A. **Incorrect:** You cannot use Database Designer to create a full-text index.

    B. **Incorrect:** You cannot use Table Designer to create a full-text index.

    C. **Correct:** You can right-click on a table in Enterprise Manager and choose to enable Full-Text Indexing.

    D. **Correct:** You can execute the sp_fulltext_table command to mark or unmark a table for full-text indexing.

70-228.03.03.004

▶ **Correct Answers: A**

    A. **Correct:** INSERT, UPDATE, DELETE, and SELECT permissions are just some of the permissions returned by the sp_table_privileges stored procedure.

    B. **Incorrect:** Executing sp_srvrolepermission returns the list of fixed server roles.

    C. **Incorrect:** You can add a security account in the current database for Microsoft SQL Server using sp_grantdbaccess.

    D. **Incorrect:** The stored procedure sp_table_privileges_ex is used to return privilege information for tables located on a linked server.

OBJECTIVE 3.4

Perform disaster recovery operations.

The recovery model you select for a database dictates backup and recovery procedures. Objective 2.1 discusses SIMPLE, FULL, and BULK_LOGGED recovery models in relation to database performance. However, database performance is just one factor to consider when analyzing recovery requirements. Selecting the appropriate recovery model for a database and creating a disaster recovery strategy requires an understanding of the availability requirements and the acceptable level of exposure to data loss within your environment.

All of the recovery models can utilize **database backups**, which capture an exact duplicate of the data in the database, and **differential database backups**, which capture only the data that has changed since the last database backup. You can create database backups and differential database backups by using the **BACKUP DATABASE** T-SQL command or by using Enterprise Manager.

The recovery models differ in their ability to use transaction logs to recover a database up to the point of failure. The SIMPLE recovery model does not use transaction logging, so recovery is only available to the point of the last good database or differential backup. The BULK_LOGGED recovery model minimally logs bulk copy operations, so it provides recovery to the end of a transaction log backup when the log backup contains bulk changes. Therefore, it is possible that you may need to manually redo any transactions occurring after the last transaction log backup. Under the FULL recovery model, all transactions are logged and recovery is available to the point of failure or to a specific point in time. You can create transaction log backups via the **BACKUP LOG** T-SQL command or through Enterprise Manager.

Restore database and differential backups by using the **RESTORE DATABASE** T-SQL command or through Enterprise Manager. Restore transaction logs by using the **RESTORE LOG** T-SQL command or through Enterprise Manager.

You can switch the recovery model for a database to meet the technical and business needs of an organization. For example, during bulk load operations, it may be wise to switch the recovery model to BULK_LOGGED for increased performance, and then switch it back to FULL for superior recovery when the load operation is complete.

Objective 3.4 Questions

70-228.03.04.001

Your company currently backs up its SQL Server 2000 master database once a week. You suspect that this needs to be increased based on the activity occurring. Which of the following operations will update the master database, thereby requiring a backup? (Choose all that apply.)

A. Changing a database configuration option

B. Deleting a filegroup from a database

C. Creating a new user database

D. Changing security for a user on a user database

70-228.03.04.002

You have a 10 GB database named Litigation running on SQL Server 2000 for your company's Legal department. A large case is underway, and the database is used around the clock from Monday through Friday. The database is set up for SIMPLE recovery. A database backup occurs every Sunday evening at 11:00 P.M.

You must meet the following goals:

- Estimate the amount of space required for a database backup.

- Increase the frequency of backups throughout the week.

- Minimize the time required to perform backups that occur during the week.

- Maximize database performance and still be able to restore up to the last database backup.

You issue the sp_helpdb command on the Litigation database to determine the amount of space a database backup requires. You schedule database backups to occur Mondays, Wednesdays, and Fridays. You switch the database to the FULL recovery model.

Which of the goals have you accomplished?

A. You have estimated the space required for a database backup.

B. You have increased the frequency of backups throughout the week.

C. You have minimized the time required to perform backups during the week.

D. You have maximized database performance and are still able to restore up to the last database backup.

70-228.03.04.003

Your company's SQL Server 2000 Accounting database experienced a critical failure and needs to be restored. The database uses the FULL recovery model with database backups occurring nightly at 11:00 P.M. Transaction log backups occur daily at 10:00 A.M. and 2:00 P.M. The critical failure occurred at 8:00 P.M. You expect to be able to recover up to the point of failure. You create a backup of the currently active transaction log. Which of the following must be done before this transaction log can be applied?

A. Restore the 11:00 P.M. database backup from the previous night, and issue the T-SQL command
   `RESTORE DATABASE ACCOUNTING WITH RECOVERY` to recover the database.

B. Restore the 11:00 P.M. database backup from the previous night, and apply the 10:00 A.M. and 2:00 P.M. transaction logs created since the database backup.

C. Stop and restart the SQL Server Service.

D. Issue a checkpoint in the database prior to restoring the final transaction log.

70-228.03.04.004

Your company is planning the rollout of a very large, mission-critical intranet database. The database has two filegroups: a primary filegroup and a secondary filegroup named Contacts, which isolates a single table. The company policy requires point of failure recovery. Due to its large size, the database takes a long time to back up, and it is not feasible to do more than one database backup each night. The SQL Server 2000 machine has several physical disk drives (assigned to drive letters F:, G:, and H:) that are dedicated for backup purposes.

You must design the backup strategy to accomplish the following:

■ Maximize the speed of the nightly database backup.

■ Enable the Contacts filegroup to be restored independently of the primary filegroup.

■ Minimize the amount of time it takes to recover the database to a point of failure following a database restore.

■ Select the most appropriate recovery model.

You run the system-stored procedure sp_spaceused and determine that the nightly database backup will fit on any of the three physical disks dedicated for backup. Your plan is to back up the database to a backup device you create on drive F:. You plan to implement differential backups at hourly intervals and transaction log backups every 15 minutes to devices you create on drive G:. You plan to set the database recovery model to SIMPLE.

Which of the following requirements are met? (Choose all that apply.)

A. You have maximized the speed of the nightly database backup.

B. The Contacts filegroup can be restored independently of the primary filegroup.

C. Following a database restore, you have minimized the time it would take to recover a database to the point of failure.

D. You have set the database to the appropriate recovery model.

70-228.03.04.005

The Human Resources director contacts you to restore the department's SQL Server 2000 Personnel database. One of the users has accidentally processed benefit statements for the wrong group of employees. The processing took place at 11:00 A.M. on Friday, October 13, 2000. The director would like the database restored to the condition it was in at 10:30 A.M. and will figure out what transactions need to be reposted from that time. The last database backup, PERS_FULL, was at 11:00 P.M. the previous night. The last transaction log backup, PERS_LOG1, was at 10:00 A.M. that morning. You back up the currently active transaction log to PERS_LOG2. Which of the following commands would you use to perform the restore?

A.
```
RESTORE DATABASE PERSONNEL FROM PERS_FULL WITH NORECOVERY
GO
RESTORE LOG PERSONNEL FROM PERS_LOG1 WITH NORECOVERY
GO
RESTORE LOG PERSONNEL FROM PERS_LOG2 WITH RECOVERY, AFTER = 'OCT 13, 2000 10:30 AM'
GO
```

B.
```
RESTORE DATABASE PERSONNEL FROM PERS_FULL WITH NORECOVERY
GO
RESTORE LOG PERSONNEL FROM PERS_LOG2 WITH RECOVERY
GO
```

C.
```
RESTORE DATABASE PERSONNEL FROM PERS_FULL WITH NORECOVERY
GO
RESTORE LOG PERSONNEL FROM PERS_LOG2 WITH RECOVERY, STOPAT = 'OCT 13, 2000 10:30 AM'
GO
```

D.
```
RESTORE DATABASE PERSONNEL FROM PERS_FULL WITH NORECOVERY
GO
RESTORE LOG PERSONNEL FROM PERS_LOG1 WITH NORECOVERY
GO
RESTORE LOG PERSONNEL FROM PERS_LOG2 WITH RECOVERY, STOPAT = 'OCT 13, 2000 10:30 AM'
GO
```

Objective 3.4 Answers

70-228.03.04.001

▶ **Correct Answers: A and C**

A. **Correct:** Database configuration options as well as serverwide settings will update the master database.

B. **Incorrect:** This operation does not affect the master database.

C. **Correct:** Creating a new user database will update the master database.

D. **Incorrect:** This operation does not affect the master database.

70-228.03.04.002

▶ **Correct Answers: B**

A. **Incorrect:** The sp_helpdb command shows you the total size of the database including unused space. The sp_spaceused system-stored procedure provides the size of only the data that is used in a database, which is a good estimate of the size of the database backup.

B. **Correct:** You have increased the number of backups by scheduling backups to occur on Mondays, Wednesdays, and Fridays.

C. **Incorrect:** Database backups take more time than differential database backups. To minimize the required time, differential database backups should be scheduled during the week with a database backup occurring on Sunday.

D. **Incorrect:** By switching the database recovery model to FULL, you have added additional database overhead for transaction logging. If the recovery requirement is to be able to restore to the last database backup, the SIMPLE recovery model is adequate and provides better database performance because there is no transaction logging.

70-228.03.04.003

▶ **Correct Answers: B**

A. **Incorrect:** If you recover the database without first applying the transaction log backups, you cannot restore past that point without restarting the entire restore operation, starting with the database backup. All transaction logs should be applied before the database is recovered.

B. **Correct:** This is the correct sequence of events. Once all preceding transaction logs have been applied to the restored database, the final transaction log can be restored.

C. **Incorrect:** This is not a step used in recovery.

D. **Incorrect:** This is not a step used in recovery.

70-228.03.04.004

▶ **Correct Answers: B and C**

A. **Incorrect:** To increase the speed of the nightly backups, you should create multiple backup devices on the three physical drives. SQL Server 2000 can use parallel I/O to increase the speed of backup and restore operations because each backup device can be written to or read from at the same time.

B. **Correct:** Database backups allow for individual files and filegroups to be restored. There is also a separate file backup operation that can capture just the database files that you are interested in backing up. Note that files and filegroups must be restored in conjunction with transaction logs to ensure the integrity of the database.

C. **Correct:** By implementing differential and transaction log backups, you have reduced the time it takes to recover a database to the point of failure because only the transaction log backups created since the last differential backup need to be applied. If differential backups were not implemented, every transaction log would need to be applied to the restored database to recover to the point of failure, which would take much longer.

D. **Incorrect:** SIMPLE recovery does not allow for transaction logging. In order to accomplish point of failure recovery, the database should be set to use the FULL recovery model.

70-228.03.04.005

▶ **Correct Answers: D**

A. **Incorrect:** The first two steps are correct. You need to restore the database as well as the transaction log from 10:00 A.M. The syntax is wrong in the final command. AFTER is not a valid clause. The AFTER clause is used in conjunction with the STOPATMARK or STOPBEFOREMARK clause when recovering a database to a mark in a log file.

B. **Incorrect:** The first step is correct. However, the 10:00 A.M. transaction log has not been applied, and the second command would restore the entire PERS_LOG2 transaction log and would not recover to a specific point in time.

C. **Incorrect:** The 10:00 A.M. transaction log restore is missing from this solution. The second step should be RESTORE LOG PERSONNEL FROM PERS_LOG1 WITH NORECOVERY.

D. **Correct:** This solution would correctly restore the database, apply the 10:00 A.M. transaction log, and then recover the most current transaction log up to the point of 10:30 A.M., which is prior to the user error occurring.

OBJECTIVE 3.5

Perform integrity checks.

Integrity checks are imperative to the upkeep of any database that is critical to the day-to-day operations of a business. You can perform database integrity checks by using built-in **Database Consistency Checker (DBCC)** utilities, which are included with SQL Server 2000. These utilities perform the same function as the check disk utilities under the Windows operating systems. Basically, as users continuously access data, corruption of that data will inevitably occur over a period of time. By scheduling integrity checks on a regular basis, you can avoid permanent data destruction before it occurs.

Like many of the administrative tasks that you execute in SQL Server 2000, you can launch an integrity check using SQL Server Enterprise Manager or by executing T-SQL commands. Before you can actually run an integrity check on a database, all users must be disconnected from that specific database.

Using Enterprise Manager, you launch an integrity check via the **Database Mainte-nance Plan Wizard**. The wizard enables you to schedule and launch many of the day-to-day administrative tasks you normally perform when running Microsoft SQL Server. The following options are available to you when executing an integrity check using the Maintenance Plan Wizard:

- Check database integrity. Without selecting this option, the Include indexes, Attempt to repair any minor problems, Exclude indexes, and Perform these checks before doing backups options will not be available. This prevents the administrator from having the wizard run any integrity checks on the database.

- Include indexes. This option forces each data and index page of a database to be checked. Selecting this option offers a more thorough integrity check, thereby increasing its duration.

- Attempt to repair any minor problems. This option is only available if the Include Indexes check box has been selected. By selecting the Attempt to repair any minor problems option, SQL Server automatically corrects easily correctable problems.

- Exclude indexes. Selecting this option decreases the duration of the integrity check. However, corrupt indexes are usually the reason that integrity checks on a database fail. If you do not select this option, you will not know whether the database is truly consistent.

- Perform these tests before doing backups. If you continually back up a database with potential problems that have not been corrected by running an integrity check or by some other means, you may face a catastrophe when you need to recover data from the backup source. Selecting this option assures you that the data being backed up has passed the integrity check according to your specified parameters.

Executing DBCC commands via T-SQL statements allows you greater flexibility. For example, using the DBCC CHECKTABLE command, you can run an integrity check on the data, index, text, ntext, and image pages for the specified table or indexed view. Other DBCC commands that you can execute using T-SQL include:

- **DBCC CHECKALLOC**

- **DBCC CHECKCONSTRAINTS**

- **DBCC NEWALLOC**

- **DBCC CHECKDB**

The following commands are used to correct known problems with specific objects of a database.

- **DBCC DBREINDEX**

- **DBCC INDEXDEFRAG**

Objective 3.5 Questions

70-228.03.05.001

The database storing data from a recent marketing survey conducted by your company is showing signs of possible corruption. You want to run an integrity check on the tables in the database. Which of the following must be done before you can run the integrity check?

A. Users must close the data entry program they are using to input survey results.

B. The database must be in single-user mode.

C. Permissions for the data files must be set to Full Control for Everyone.

D. You must run an integrity check of the database filegroups.

70-228.03.05.002

You want to monitor fragmentation of data and indexes for a specified table using T-SQL. Which DBCC statement should you execute to do this?

A. SHOWCONTIG

B. CHECKALLOC

C. SQLPERF

D. SHOW_STATISTICS

70-228.03.05.003

A SQL Server severity error appears stating that the integrity of an index in a table is corrupted.

You want to accomplish the following goals:

- Confirm the integrity of other objects in the database.

- Determine if the problem is being caused by a disk error or cache.

- Ensure that the index works correctly.

You run DBCC CHECKDB to determine if other objects, such as tables, in the database are also corrupted. You then reboot the server to clear the cache and check the status of the index. After rebooting, you still find a problem with the index. You then delete the index, and re-create it.

Which of the following goals are accomplished? (Choose all that apply.)

A. You are able to determine if any other object in the database is corrupt.

B. By rebooting the server, you can determine whether cache is causing the problem.

C. Re-creating the index ensures that the index will work correctly.

D. None of the goals are accomplished.

70-228.03.05.004

You're hosting your Web site's data on a SQL Server 2000 machine. As part of your daily maintenance tasks, you back up the database and run an integrity check on the database. You want to keep the downtime for the system to a minimum. Which of the following should you do to increase the speed of the DBCC checks?

A. Run the Index Tuning Wizard before running the integrity check.

B. Move the temp table to a faster disk, such as a RAID device.

C. Increase the size of the master database.

D. Increase the size of the database's transaction log.

Objective 3.5 Answers

70-228.03.05.001

▶ **Correct Answers: B**

A. **Incorrect:** In order to run an integrity check on a database, the database must be in single-user mode. Closing client/server applications does not guarantee that the database is in single-user mode.

B. **Correct:** Before running an integrity check, the database must be in single-user mode.

C. **Incorrect:** Permissions for the database files should never have to be changed for any SQL server task, such as running an integrity check.

D. **Incorrect:** You do not have to run an integrity check of the filegroups independent of or before an integrity check of the tables.

70-228.03.05.002

▶ **Correct Answers: A**

A. **Correct:** The DBCC statement SHOWCONTIG displays the fragmentation information for the data and indexes of the specified table.

B. **Incorrect:** The DBCC statement CHECKALLOC checks the allocation and use of all pages in the specified database.

C. **Incorrect:** The DBCC statement SQLPERF provides statistics about the use of transaction log space in all databases.

D. **Incorrect:** The DBCC statement SHOW_STATISTICS displays the current distribution statistics for the specified target on the specified table.

70-228.03.05.003

▶ **Correct Answers: A, B, and C**

A. **Correct:** Running the DBCC CHECKDB command will check the integrity of all objects within a database.

B. **Correct:** Rebooting the server and checking the status of the index allows you to determine if the server's cache is the cause of the problem. Rebooting the server forces the cache for the system to clear along with any corrupt data that may be present.

C. **Correct:** If cache is not the cause of the problem, you have to re-create the index.

D. **Incorrect:** All of the goals are accomplished.

70-228.03.05.004

▶ **Correct Answers: B**

A. **Incorrect:** A well-indexed database does nothing to increase the speed of the DBCC check against the database.

B. **Correct:** The DBCC operation utilizes the tempdb for spooling, particularly when dealing with a large database. If transactions to and from the tempdb are faster, it also helps DBCC operations to proceed faster.

C. **Incorrect:** See the explanation for answer B.

D. **Incorrect:** See the explanation for answer B.

Troubleshoot transactions and locking by using SQL Profiler, SQL Server Enterprise Manager, or Transact-SQL.

You can monitor SQL Server 2000 transactions by using a number of built-in tools including **SQL Server Profiler**, the **Current Activity window** available within Enterprise Manager, T-SQL statements, SQL and Windows NT or 2000 server error logs, and Windows NT or 2000 Performance Monitor.

SQL Server Profiler is a graphical tool that captures information about events. You can use it to save a sequence of events to a file, which you can later replay step-by-step to determine where a problem is occurring. You can set SQL Server Profiler to monitor only the events you want to view. Use SQL Server Profiler to monitor performance, debug T-SQL statements and stored procedures, troubleshoot poorly performing queries, and review security auditing events. Start SQL Server Profiler from within Enterprise Manager or from the SQL Server Profiler icon within the Microsoft SQL Server program group.

You can use the Current Activity window within Enterprise Manager as a monitoring tool to view currently blocked or blocking transactions. You can also view current user connections, the status of commands that active users are running, and any locked objects. System administrators can terminate processes from within this tool.

You can also use T-SQL commands to view and troubleshoot transactions. Use **DBCC OPENTRAN** to determine if an open transaction exists within a log. Use **DBCC INPUTBUFFER** to display the last statement sent from a client to the SQL server. To view general statistics about SQL Server activity, use **sp_monitor**. Use **sp_lock** to show current object locks, and **sp_who** to show current users and processes.

Windows NT Performance Monitor or Windows 2000 System Monitor allows you to view SQL Server objects and performance counters in conjunction with other objects, such as memory, cache, threads, and other processes. This information, as well as the SQL Server and Windows NT or 2000 error logs, can assist in troubleshooting events occurring with SQL Server 2000.

Objective 3.6 Questions

70-228.03.06.001

Which of the following tools allows you to see a list of currently connected users and the processes they are running on an instance of SQL Server? (Choose all that apply.)

A. sp_who

B. The Current Activity window in Enterprise Manager

C. sp_monitor

D. Windows NT Performance Monitor/Windows 2000 System Monitor

70-228.03.06.002

The transaction log file for your company's Medical Records database is set to autogrow. You suspect that there has been a significant increase in the number of transactions posted to the database, and you would like to evaluate whether the autogrow percentage increment should be increased. Which of the following SQL Profiler event categories would you use to monitor the frequency of growth of the transaction log file?

A. Object event category

B. Database event category

C. Performance event category

D. Transactions event category

70-228.03.06.003

Your company has implemented a new policy, which requires auditing SQL Server logons.

You must implement the new policy and accomplish the following:

- Track who has logged on to SQL Server.

- Track who has logged out of SQL Server.

- Do not track logon or logout of the sa user account.

- Track the time selected events begin.

You create a new trace in SQL Profiler, and you select the Security Audit event class and include the Audit Login event. You include data columns for EventClass, LoginName, StartTime, and SPID. Then you create a filter on TargetLoginName specifying Not Like sa.

Which of the following does your solution achieve? (Choose all that apply.)

A. You are tracking who has logged on to SQL Server.

B. You are tracking who has logged out of SQL Server.

C. You are not tracking logon or logout events for the sa user account.

D. You are tracking the time selected events begin.

70-228.03.06.004

You are diagnosing a problem reported by a user logged on to SQL Server as JAQ. You would like to display the last SQL statement sent from JAQ's machine to SQL Server. Which of the following would accomplish this task?

A. Display the Current Activity window in Enterprise Manager. Find the appropriate logon name, and view the Command column.

B. Run DBCC OPENTRAN ('JAQ').

C. Run DBCC INPUTBUFFER ('JAQ').

D. Run EXEC sp_who 'JAQ' to determine the SPID of the user, and then run DBCC INPUTBUFFER (XYZ), where XYZ is the SPID.

70-228.03.06.005

Users report that performance seems slow when using SQL Server 2000 running on a Windows 2000 server. You suspect there is a link between the performance of SQL Server and the operating system. In order to monitor disk activity, you run System Monitor and add Physical Disk counters for %Disk Time and Avg Disk Queue Length. You also want to isolate the I/O generated by SQL Server. Which of the following SQL Server counters would you add to System Monitor to assist in this task?

A. SQL Server Databases counter: Transaction/sec

B. SQL Server Buffer Manager counter: Page Reads/sec

C. SQL Server Locks counter: Number of Deadlocks/sec

D. SQL Server General Statistics counter: Logouts/sec

Objective 3.6 Answers

70-228.03.06.001

▶ **Correct Answers: A and B**

A. **Correct:** The sp_who stored procedure displays a list of current users and processes that they are running.

B. **Correct:** The Current Activity window displays currently connected users and the processes that they are running.

C. **Incorrect:** The sp_monitor stored procedure displays statistics about how busy the SQL Server is. Statistics reported include the number of seconds the server's CPU has been busy performing SQL Server tasks, the number of seconds SQL Server has spent performing I/O operations, and the number of packets read and written by SQL Server. The sp_monitor stored procedure displays current values for these functions as well as how much the values have changed since the last time the procedure was run.

D. **Incorrect:** The Performance Monitor in Windows NT or the System Monitor in Windows 2000 allow you to see the performance statistics and activity of SQL Server, but do not display details, such as a list of users and the processes they are running.

70-228.03.06.002

▶ **Correct Answers: B**

A. **Incorrect:** The Object event category monitors when an object is opened, created, deleted, or used.

B. **Correct:** The Database event category monitors when a data or log file automatically grows or shrinks.

C. **Incorrect:** The Performance event category monitors the execution of SQL data manipulation language operations.

D. **Incorrect:** The Transactions event category monitors the status of transactions including the types of transactions being logged and when transactions are committed or rolled back.

70-228.03.06.003

▶ **Correct Answers: A and D**

A. **Correct:** By including the Audit Login event, you are tracking every time a user logs on to SQL Server.

B. **Incorrect:** The solution does not include tracking the Audit Logout event. This event would need to be included in order to view logouts.

C. **Incorrect:** The filter specified in this solution is the correct filter criteria, but it is being applied to the wrong data column. The appropriate data column is LoginName.

D. **Correct:** By including the data column for StartTime, you are tracking the time an event begins.

70-228.03.06.004

▶ **Correct Answers: D**

A. **Incorrect:** The Current Activity window's command column shows you the current command being executed for a user. This column does not show you the last SQL statement sent from the client.

B. **Incorrect:** DBCC OPENTRAN displays information about the oldest active transaction within a database.

C. **Incorrect:** The DBCC INPUTBUFFER is the correct command to show the last SQL statement sent from a client, but the argument passed is incorrect. The valid argument for this command is the SPID.

D. **Correct:** The stored procedure sp_who provides the appropriate SPID, which is then used as the argument for the DBCC INPUTBUFFER command. The DBCC INPUTBUFFER command shows you the last SQL statement sent from the client machine.

70-228.03.06.005

▶ **Correct Answers: B**

A. **Incorrect:** This counter shows the number of transactions started for the database per second.

B. **Correct:** This counter shows the number of physical database page reads that are issued per second. This in conjunction with the Page Writes/sec counter shows I/O generated by SQL Server.

C. **Incorrect:** This counter shows the number of lock requests per second that resulted in a deadlock.

D. **Incorrect:** This counter shows the total number of logout operations started per second.

Extracting and Transforming Data with SQL Server 2000

In order to make informed business decisions, corporations must have access to relevant data. Often, data is stored in many different systems on many different platforms. SQL Server 2000 provides tools to help centralize and transform data from dissimilar systems and makes data easily accessible.

With added support for XML and the Internet, SQL Server 2000 databases can be accessed from the URL of a browser, and XML data can be read from and written back to SQL Server databases. Data can be imported using built-in SQL Server tools or popular programming languages. SQL Server wizards provide step-by-step guides for simple data imports and sophisticated tools to handle complex data transformations.

When data from disparate systems are merged, data conversion may be needed. SQL Server has built-in capabilities to manage most data type conversions without user input, and it provides functions to handle explicit data conversions when necessary. By using replication strategies, you can make data accessible to remote locations. Replication can also provide fault tolerance to ensure critical data is always available.

Tested Skills and Suggested Practices

The skills that you need to successfully master the Extracting and Transforming Data with SQL Server 2000 objective domain on the *Installing, Configuring, and Administering Microsoft SQL Server 2000 Enterprise Edition* exam include:

- **Setting up IIS virtual directories to support XML.**

  - Practice 1: Run the IIS Virtual Directory Management for SQL Server Utility. Set up a virtual directory for the Northwind database. Configure only the option to allow URL queries.

- Practice 2: Run a URL query against the Northwind database (for example, `HTTP:// MYWEBSERVER/MYVIRTUALDIRECTORY/?SQL=SELECT * FROM ORDERS FOR XML AUTO&ROOT=ROOT`).

- Practice 3: Modify the virtual directory properties to allow for template queries. Create a template query named MYQUERY.XML to select first and last names from the Employees table in the Northwind database (for example, `<ROOT XMLNS:SQL="URN:SCHEMAS-MICROSOFT-COM:XML-SQL"><SQL:QUERY>SELECT FIRSTNAME, LASTNAME FROM EMPLOYEES FOR XML AUTO</SQL:QUERY></ ROOT>`). Run the template query from a URL (for example, *http://mywebserver /myvirtualdirectory/template/myquery.xml*).

- **Importing and exporting data.**

  - Practice 1: Using SQL Server Enterprise Manager and the Data Transformation Services, import an existing database from another SQL Server 2000 server. Existing users and database roles should also be copied over.

  - Practice 2: Using the bcp command utility, export the Northwind's Employees table to a text file. Using command options, specify the file to be exported as comma delimited.

  - Practice 3: Repeat practice 1, but this time import the data after creating a DTS task through the DTS Designer.

- **Developing and managing DTS packages.**

  - Practice 1: Run the DTS Import/Export Wizard to create a package to connect to an Access data source (or other data source), and copy tables from the Access database to the Northwind database. Select Transform and review the options available. Save the package to SQL Server.

  - Practice 2: Edit the saved package in DTS Designer. Add an Execute SQL Task to drop the table created (DROP TABLE XYZ) and associate it with the connection to the SQL server. Right-click on the Execute SQL Task and select Execute Step to ensure the table gets dropped.

  - Practice 3: Select the package, select the Save As option, and assign an owner and user password. Attempt to run the package.

- **Managing linked servers.**

  - Practice 1: Create a linked server that points to a SQL Server 2000 machine. On the remote machine, create a user that has dbo privileges to the Northwind database.

  - Practice 2: Using the sp_addlinkedserverlogin stored procedure, map a logon to the new username you created.

    ▪ Practice 3: Create a distributed query that updates information to the Customers table of the Northwind database.

▪ **Converting data types.**

    ▪ Practice 1: Use the stored procedure sp_addtype, to add a data type named telephone as varchar (12), not null.

    ▪ Practice 2: Using the SQL Query Analyzer, convert the current date to the style of 1 (for example, `SELECT CONVERT(CHAR(12), GETDATE (), 1)`).

    ▪ Practice 3: Using the SQL Query Analyzer and the Northwind database, convert the money data type to decimal (for example, `SELECT CAST (FREIGHT AS DEC-IMAL (10,5)) FROM ORDERS`).

▪ **Configuring, maintaining, and troubleshooting replication services.**

    ▪ Practice 1: Install SQL Server 2000 on a second server. Using Enterprise Manager, create a Snapshot replication job that copies the Northwind's database from SQL server 1 to SQL server 2.

    ▪ Practice 2: Alter information in the Northwind's database, and create a Transactional replication job that copies the database from SQL server 1 to SQL server 2.

    ▪ Practice 3: Create a Merge replication job that copies altered data from SQL server 2 to SQL server 1.

Further Reading

This section lists supplemental readings by objective. We recommend that you study these sources thoroughly before taking exam 70-228.

Objective 4.1

Microsoft SQL Server 2000 product documentation. To access Books Online, click the Start button, point to Programs, then Microsoft SQL Server, and then select Books Online. Select the Contents tab and expand XML and Internet Support. This volume contains an overview of the XML and Internet support within SQL Server 2000. It also details how to implement XML templates and XPath queries.

Ozu, Nicola, et al. *Beginning XML*. Birmingham, England: Wrox Press Ltd., 2000. This book is an excellent source for understanding the basics of XML and XPath.

Objective 4.2

Microsoft SQL Server 2000 product documentation. To access Books Online, click the Start button, point to Programs, then Microsoft SQL Server, and then select Books Online. Select the Contents tab and expand Data Import/Export Architecture. This volume provides a good overview and contains related links to additional information for each of the topics.

Part 1: Self-Paced Training for Microsoft SQL Server 2000 System Administration. Chapter 7, "Populating a Database," Lesson 1 covers the topic of transferring and transforming data.

Objective 4.3

Microsoft SQL Server 2000 product documentation. To access Books Online, click the Start button, point to Programs, then Microsoft SQL Server, and then select Books Online. Select the Contents tab and expand Data Transformation Services. This volume contains information about the tools available for DTS and how to create, manage, and execute DTS packages. Start with the DTS overview and follow the links to the related topics.

Chaffin, Mark, et al. *Professional SQL Server 2000 DTS (Data Transformation Services)*. Birmingham, England: Wrox Press Ltd., 2000. This book provides an in-depth look at DTS in SQL Server 2000 and includes descriptions of how to use all the new features.

Objective 4.4

Microsoft SQL Server 2000 product documentation. To access Books Online, click the Start button, point to Programs, then Microsoft SQL Server, and then select Books Online. Select the Search tab and type "**managing" near "linked servers"**. This query will return several articles that cover managing linked servers.

Part 1: Self-Paced Training for Microsoft SQL Server 2000 System Administration. Chapter 12, "Performing Administrative Tasks," discusses the configuration of linked servers.

Microsoft Corporation. *The Microsoft SQL Server 2000 Administrator's Companion*. Redmond, Washington: Microsoft Press, 2000. Chapters 26, 27, and 28 cover configuration, management, and tuning of Snapshot, Transactional, and Merge replication.

Objective 4.5

Microsoft SQL Server 2000 product documentation. To access Books Online, click the Start button, point to Programs, then Microsoft SQL Server, and then select Books Online. Select the Contents tab and expand Accessing and Changing Relational Data, Transact-SQL Syntax Elements, and Using Data Types. The "Data Type Conversion" article in this volume provides an overview of the implicit and explicit conversions as well as the functions contained in SQL Server 2000.

Objective 4.6

Microsoft SQL Server 2000 product documentation. To access Books Online, click the Start button, point to Programs, then Microsoft SQL Server, and then select Books Online. Select the Contents tab and expand Replication. This volume contains information on Snapshot replication, Transactional replication, and Merge replication.

Part 1: Self-Paced Training for Microsoft SQL Server 2000 System Administration. Chapter 15, "Using SQL Server Replication," Lesson 2 discusses planning replication. You should also review Lesson 3, which covers the actual implementation of replication.

Set up Internet Information Services (IIS) virtual directories to support XML.

SQL Server 2000 can be accessed via **HTTP**. This allows you to enter queries directly into a **URL**, retrieve and write **XML** data, and execute **XPath** queries. You must first set up a virtual directory using the **IIS Virtual Directory Management for SQL Server Utility** to allow access to SQL Server databases via HTTP.

The utility can be accessed through the Microsoft SQL Server program group and can run under Windows NT with IIS 4.0 or higher and Microsoft Management Console 1.2. It can also run under Windows 2000 with the Administrative Tools pack installed. Prior to running the utility, create a physical directory for each database for which you want to enable HTTP access. The directory is normally created within the wwwroot directory of the Web server that hosts the Web site you will be accessing. This directory is associated with the virtual directory created by the utility. In addition, you should create subdirectories within this directory. The subdirectories are associated with virtual names for template files and schema files.

Template files are valid XML documents that contain one or more SQL statements and are used to avoid writing lengthy SQL statements directly to the URL. Template files referenced on the URL line must be stored in the template subdirectory. When specifying an XPath query against an **XDR schema,** the XDR schema file must be stored in the schema subdirectory. When accessing database objects directly from the URL, such as tables and views, the virtual name for the dbobject type must be specified.

When running the IIS Virtual Directory Management for SQL Server Utility, you also need to specify SQL Server logon information, the name of the database to be accessed, and the options to be made available via HTTP. For example, you could allow only template queries from the URL to control the data to which you want users to have access.

Objective 4.1 Questions

70-228.04.01.001

You want to provide HTTP access to a set of query templates in a Contacts database on SQL Server 2000. These templates were developed to display names and addresses for various groups.

You want to accomplish the following:

- Be able to access the BUSINESS.XML template file from the URL

- Be able to access the PERSONAL.XML template file from the URL

- Allow XPath queries

- Enhance security by preventing users from executing queries via the URL

You create a subdirectory called C:\Inetpub\Wwwroot\Contacts. You create a subdirectory under Contacts named Template, and copy the BUSINESS.XML template file to this directory. You create a subdirectory under Template named Personal, and copy the PERSONAL.XML template file to this directory. Using the IIS Virtual Directory Management for SQL Server Utility, you create a virtual directory associated with the Contacts directory. You create the correct data source and supply the correct logon information to your database. On the Settings tab, you clear the Allow URL queries check box. On the Virtual Names tab, you create a new virtual name for template type and specify the path to the Template directory. You do not create virtual names for schema or dbobject types.

Which of the following goals have been met? (Choose all that apply.)

A. You are able to access the BUSINESS.XML file from the URL.

B. You are able to access the PERSONAL.XML file from the URL.

C. Allow XPath queries.

D. Enhance security by preventing users from executing queries via the URL.

70-228.04.01.002

You are running the IIS Virtual Directory Management for SQL Server Utility on a Windows NT 4.0 server. Which of the following components must first be installed? (Choose all that apply.)

A. IIS 4.0 or higher

B. IIS 3.0 or higher

C. Microsoft Management Console (MMC) 1.2 or higher

D. Service Pack 5 (SP5) for Windows NT

70-228.04.01.003

You want to be able to access the Orders table in your database directly from the URL. To accomplish this, which virtual name must you configure when setting up the IIS Virtual Directory Management for SQL Server Utility?

A. Template

B. dbobject

C. Schema

D. No virtual name is required to access tables directly from the URL.

70-228.04.01.004

To specify SQL queries directly in the URL, which of the following options are you required to configure?

A. Select the Allow XPath check box in the Settings tab in the IIS Virtual Directory Management for SQL Server Utility.

B. Define a virtual name of dbobject type in the IIS Virtual Directory Management for SQL Server Utility.

C. Define a virtual name of schema type in the IIS Virtual Directory Management for SQL Server Utility.

D. Select the Allow URL queries check box in the Settings tab in the IIS Virtual Directory Management for SQL Server Utility.

70-228.04.01.005

Which of the following characters have special meaning in the URL line and must be indicated by their hexadecimal value if used to execute a SQL query from the URL or specify a template file from the URL? (Choose all that apply.)

A. ?

B. @

C. *

D. #

Objective 4.1 Answers

70-228.04.01.001

► **Correct Answers: A, B, and D**

A. **Correct:** In order to access the template, it must be stored in the directory associated with the virtual name of template type or one of its subdirectories. You accomplished this by creating the virtual name of template type, specifying the path to the Template subdirectory of the virtual directory, and copying the BUSINESS.XML file to this directory.

B. **Correct:** This goal is accomplished because the PERSONAL.XML file exists in a subdirectory of the directory associated with the virtual name of template type.

C. **Incorrect:** This is an option on the Settings tab that was not set and is not set by default. In addition, the virtual name of schema type should have been created and associated with a schema directory.

D. **Correct:** This option was set correctly on the Settings tab within the utility.

70-228.04.01.002

► **Correct Answers: A and C**

A. **Correct:** IIS 4.0 or higher is required to run the utility.

B. **Incorrect:** IIS 4.0 or higher is required to run the utility.

C. **Correct:** MMC 1.2 or higher is required to run the utility.

D. **Incorrect:** SP5 for Windows NT is not required to run the utility. In order to run IIS 4.0, Windows NT requires SP4 or higher.

70-228.04.01.003

► **Correct Answers: B**

A. **Incorrect:** The virtual name of template type must be created in the utility in order to access template files from the URL line.

B. **Correct:** The virtual name of dbobject type is specified in the URL when accessing database objects, such as tables and views, directly from the URL.

C. **Incorrect:** The virtual name of schema type is needed to run XPath queries against an annotated XDR schema.

D. **Incorrect:** The virtual name of dbobject type is required.

70-228.04.01.004

▶ **Correct Answers: D**

    A. **Incorrect:** This is only required to run XPath queries.

    B. **Incorrect:** This is only required if you want to directly access a database object from the URL.

    C. **Incorrect:** This is only required if you want to use XPath queries.

    D. **Correct:** This is required to submit SQL statements directly through the URL.

70-228.04.01.005

▶ **Correct Answers: A and D**

    A. **Correct:** The ? separates the URL and its parameters. You must use the hexadecimal value %F3 instead.

    B. **Incorrect:** This is not considered a special character in the URL line.

    C. **Incorrect:** This is not considered a special character in the URL line.

    D. **Correct:** The # indicates a bookmark. You must use the hexadecimal value %23 instead.

OBJECTIVE 4.2

Import and export data.

There are several methods of importing and exporting data from SQL Server 2000. You can use applications such as the **bulk copy utility (bcp)**. You can also write programs to import and export data by using popular development languages, such as C++ and Visual Basic, to take advantage of existing APIs, which enable you to interact with SQL Server.

The method you select to execute a data transfer between SQL Server and a source or destination server depends on your needs. For instance, the bcp command prompt utility is mostly used to import or export data stored in a text file, such as a comma delimited file. The **Data Transformation Services (DTS)** is also an excellent tool for importing or exporting data because it's stored in the database, eliminating the need for specially created text files.

Another method of transforming data is the **BULK INSERT** statement. This statement is used primarily to import data from a data file to an instance of SQL Server using T-SQL.

The SELECT and INSERT T-SQL commands can also be used for data transformation tasks. However, because of the nature of the commands, you are limited to only importing data. These commands do not perform as well as the BULK INSERT statement or the bcp command-line utility.

In some cases, administrators may find it easier to provide remote access to data rather than create complex data transformation tasks. Distributed queries provide access to heterogeneous data. As a result, SQL Server users do not have to concern themselves with having the proper drivers or connection strings configured on their local machines. Administrators can create linked servers to machines running applications such as Sybase, Oracle, or SQL Server 2000, and users are not required to change any local configurations on their machines. Because distributed queries utilize OLE DB providers, users are able to connect to a wide variety of data sources through a single T-SQL statement, and then import or export data from an instance of SQL Server.

Importing and exporting data using the SQL Server replication services is yet another method of transferring data. You can set up **Publisher**, **Distributor**, and **Subscriber** servers. Replication services only allow you to import or export data between servers running versions of Microsoft SQL Server. They are not useful for interacting with heterogenous environments.

Objective 4.2 Questions

70-228.04.02.001

Your company recently merged with a former competitor and now you must make customer information available to the senior management team. Currently, the other company's information resides on an Oracle database server, whereas you have configured a SQL Server 2000 machine named Sales to store all of your company's client information. You decide to import information from the Oracle database into SQL Server 2000 using the bcp command utility. How should you configure the Sales database server located on SQL Server 2000 to help increase the performance of the bcp utility?

A. Set the database option select into/bulkcopy to false for the Sales database.

B. Set the database option select into/bulkcopy to true for the Sales database.

C. Set the database option select into/bulkcopy to false for the Sales database server.

D. Set the database option select into/bulkcopy to true for the Sales database server.

70-228.04.02.002

Information from a legacy database was exported to an Access database file. You now need to move the information to a SQL Server 2000 database. You decide to create a DTS package that can be executed at the SQL server. Which of the following allows you to create a DTS package and execute the package?

A. dtsrun utility

B. DTS Designer

C. DTS Run utility for Windows

D. bcp command

70-228.04.02.003

The district sales manager for your regional office requests a report detailing the quarterly sales for three sales offices located in Hamburg, London, and Madrid. After speaking with the database administrators in each office, you find out that both Hamburg and London store their information on an Oracle database, whereas Madrid stores information on an Access database. You also find out that each of the databases has a single table that contains sales information for each of the past three years.

You want to accomplish the following goals:

- Import data from all three sales offices into a database residing on a SQL Server 2000 machine

- Use a single task to import information from all three databases

- Import information for the current year's third quarter

You create a distributed query that imports information from each of the three offices.

Which of the following does your solution achieve? (Choose all that apply.)

A. Information from Oracle and Access databases can be imported into SQL Server 2000.

B. All of the information can be imported using a single query.

C. Only data from the third quarter will be imported.

D. None of the goals are accomplished.

70-228.04.02.004

You have a central database that stores sales and inventory information for each warehouse for your company's e-commerce site. This information must be exported to the local SQL Server 2000 for each warehouse. Because the information you are exporting is large in size, which of the following mapping methods will help increase performance of the data transformation task?

A. One-to-one column mapping

B. Many-to-many mapping

C. N-to-n column mapping

D. Many-to-one mapping

70-228.04.02.005

Which of the following arguments would you use in the bcp command line to specify the collation type you would like to import data in as?

A. –N

B. –a

C. –w

D. –C

Objective 4.2 Answers

70-228.04.02.001

▶ **Correct Answers: B**

A. **Incorrect:** See the explanation for answer B.

B. **Correct:** This enables nonlogged operations, increasing the speed with which data is imported.

C. **Incorrect:** See the explanation for answer B.

D. **Incorrect:** See the explanation for answer B.

70-228.04.02.002

▶ **Correct Answers: B**

A. **Incorrect:** The dtsrun utility can only execute DTS packages that were previously created.

B. **Correct:** You can use the DTS Designer to both create and execute DTS packages.

C. **Incorrect:** The DTS Run utility for Windows is a graphical user interface that offers the same commands and options as the dtsrun utility.

D. **Incorrect:** Even though you can import or export data, you cannot create a DTS package using the bcp command-line utility.

70-228.04.02.003

▶ **Correct Answers: A, B, and C**

A. **Correct:** Distributed queries use Microsoft's OLE DB provider, which enables SQL Server to connect to and exchange data with heterogenous databases.

B. **Correct:** Because a distributed query is written as any other T-SQL query, all of the databases to be imported can be specified in a single query. You must ensure that the correct OLE DB providers are specified in the query statement.

C. **Correct:** Distributed queries allow you to reference SELECT, INSERT, DELETE, and UPDATE statements when importing data from external sources. You can specify a SELECT and INSERT for only third-quarter data in the query statement.

D. **Incorrect:** All three goals are accomplished.

70-228.04.02.004

▶ **Correct Answers: B**

A. **Incorrect:** See the explanation for answer B.

B. **Correct:** To increase performance when importing large amounts of information or information that requires numerous transformations and complex scripting code, use many-to-many mappings whenever possible. This allows you to avoid mapping a separate transformation function for each column. Also, the script engine is not invoked for each transformation.

C. **Incorrect:** See the explanation for answer B.

D. **Incorrect:** See the explanation for answer B.

70-228.04.02.005

▶ **Correct Answers: D**

A. **Incorrect:** The –N argument specifies the Unicode native data format you want to use.

B. **Incorrect:** The –a argument specifies the packet size you want use during the import or export of data.

C. **Incorrect:** The –w argument specifies the Unicode character data format to be used during import or export.

D. **Correct:** The –C argument allows you to specify the code page for the collation type you would like to import the data in as.

Develop and manage Data Transformation Services (DTS) packages.

A Data Transformation Services (DTS) package is a collection of DTS tasks, data transformations, connections, and workflow used to transform and centralize data from various sources. DTS provides organizations with the ability to create complex, custom data groupings from data stored in dissimilar systems. DTS packages are built, executed, and managed using a set of tools available in SQL Server 2000.

Before copying or transforming data through DTS, a valid connection must be established between the source and destination data. Valid data sources include fixed or delimited text files; standard databases such as Access, Paradox, dBase, SQL Server, and Oracle; and OLE DB connections to ODBC data sources. You can configure connections through the **DTS Import/Export Wizard** or the **DTS Designer**, or you can use programming languages.

DTS tasks define the individual steps to be performed in a package. DTS tasks can include dropping and re-creating database objects, executing queries, sending messages, launching external programs, and transforming data. You can add tasks to a package through the DTS Designer or by using programming languages.

You can establish mappings between source and destination columns by using **DTS Transformations**. For example, data type conversions can occur between source and destination columns, strings can be trimmed, and substrings can be extracted from a source column and placed in a destination column. By using DTS Transformations, you can also read and write to data files specified by source columns.

DTS Workflow determines the order in which tasks are executed in a DTS package. Each task is represented by a step. You can execute steps in parallel, or you can define conditional branches based on the success or failure of a particular task.

You can schedule the DTS packages for execution through the Schedule Package option of the DTS node in Enterprise Manager or through SQL Server Agent using the **dtsrun** command-line utility.

Objective 4.3 Questions

70-228.04.03.001

Your company is a reseller of computer equipment. Your supplier provides you with a database in dBase III format that contains a Products table listing information about the products you resell. The file is updated and sent via FTP to a location on your server every Friday—new products are added, old products are removed, and prices are updated. The table contains a column for ProductName, UnitPrice, and Description. You are developing a SQL Server database driven e-commerce application to allow your customers to purchase products online.

You want to accomplish the following:

- Import the data from the dBase Products table to a SQL Server database Products table in the ABC database.

- Schedule the database import to occur automatically every Saturday.

- Add a 10 percent markup to the UnitPrice column during the data import.

- Add a new text column named Image when the SQL Server Products table is created. This column must be available for a weekly update from an external query you are writing within your application.

You run the DTS Import/Export Wizard and select dBase III as your data source. You supply the path and file name to the file that is sent to you by your supplier. You select the ABC database on your SQL server as the destination. You choose "Copy tables from the source database," select the Products table, and click Transform. You choose the options to "Create destination table" and "Drop and re-create destination table." You click the Transformations tab and select "Transform information as it is copied to the destination." In the VB Script language, you find `DTSDestination('UnitPrice') = DTSSource('UnitPrice')` and change it to read `DTSDestination('UnitPrice') = (DTSSource('UnitPrice') * 1.10)`. You schedule the package to occur weekly on Saturday, and then save the DTS package to SQL Server. You execute the package and receive no errors. You find the newly created Products table in the ABC database, select design, and add a text column named Image. You save the table. Which of the following goals have you met? (Choose all that apply.)

A. You have imported data from the dBase III Products table to the Products table in the ABC database on SQL Server.

B. You have scheduled the database import to occur automatically every Saturday.

C. During the data import, you have added a 10 percent markup to the UnitPrice column.

D. You have added a column for Image to the Products table on the ABC SQL Server database, which is available for the weekly update from an external query written within your application.

70-228.04.03.002

You have a DTS package named EOMCLOSE, which contains four versions. The package was saved to a SQL Server named Accounting with an owner password of ACCT.

You must meet the following goals:

- Execute the package through a batch file with no user input required.

- Write the status of the package execution to the server's Application log.

- Execute the package using a trusted connection.

- Execute the most recent version of the package, supplying the appropriate password.

You create an EOMCLOSE.BAT file containing the following command line: DTSRUN.EXE /S Accounting /N EOMCLOSE /P ACCT /E /L True. You run the batch file.

Which of the goals have you accomplished? (Choose all that apply.)

A. You have executed the package through a batch file with no user input.

B. The status of the package execution is written to the server's Application log.

C. The package executes using a trusted connection.

D. You have executed the most recent version of the package, specifying the appropriate password.

70-228.04.03.003

You have a DTS package that transfers employee information from an Access database to SQL Server. The package is failing about one-quarter of the way through the Employee table transformation. You suspect bad data in the source table. Which of the following should be used to isolate the row where the error may be occurring?

A. Package log

B. Exception file

C. Error file

D. Windows NT or 2000 Application log

70-228.04.03.004

You have created a simple package using the DTS Import/Export Wizard to copy the Orders table from an Access database to a SQL Server database named Inventory. The Orders table has two columns, OrderID and CustomerID, both integer data types. When viewed through DTS Designer, you see Connection 1, which is the Access connection, and Connection 2, which is the SQL Server connection. A Transform Data Task indicated by a gray arrow joins the two connections and transfers the two columns of data from the Access Orders table to the SQL Server Orders table.

You want to modify the package to meet the following requirements:

- Add a task to drop the Orders table from the SQL Server Inventory database.

- Add a task to create the Orders table in the SQL Server Inventory database.

- The existing Transform Data Task should run only if the Orders table is successfully created.

- The package should be saved with the ability for a user to run the package through Enterprise Manager but not edit the package.

Using DTS Designer, you modify the package to add a SQL task with the SQL statement DROP TABLE [inventory].[dbo].[orders], using existing Connection 2. You add another SQL task with the SQL statement CREATE TABLE [inventory].[dbo].[orders] ([OrderID] int NOT NULL, [customer] int NOT NULL), using existing Connection 1. You select the Drop Table and Create Table icons so that both tasks are highlighted and add an On Completion Workflow event. You select the Create Table icon and the Connection 1 icon so that both icons are highlighted and add an On Success Workflow event. You select the Save As option from the Packages menu, provide a name for the package, set an owner password of ORDERRUN, and save the package to SQL Server.

Which of the following requirements have been met? (Choose all that apply.)

A. You have added a task to drop the Orders table from the SQL Server Inventory database.

B. You have added a task to create the Orders table in the SQL Server Inventory database.

C. The existing Transform Data Task will run only if the Orders table is successfully created.

D. You have saved the package so that a user can run the package through Enterprise Manager but not edit the package.

70-228.04.03.005

A SQL Server Services database contains an EOM table, which has a CloseDate column and one row. A month-end process updates the CloseDate with the date the month was closed. Employees enter time into a TimeEntry table containing columns for DateWorked, Name, Hours, and Description.

You want to create a DTS package to accomplish the following goals:

- Select all records in the TimeEntry table up to and including the date the month was closed.

- Retrieve the date the month was closed from the CloseDate table during package execution.

- Store the records from the selected time entry records in a single global variable.

- Be able to access the records from the selected time entry records as a disconnected ADO recordset.

You create a DTS package with a connection to the SQL Server Services database. You add an Execute SQL task with a description of GetDate, containing the SQL statement SELECT CLOSEDATE FROM EOM.

You create a global variable vDateClosed as type date and value of 1/1/2000. You create a global variable vOutput as type string and no value. You set the Execute SQL task to output Row Value for CloseDate to the global variable vCloseDate. You add another Execute SQL task with a description of GetRecords, containing the SQL statement `SELECT * FROM TIMEENTRY WHERE DATEWORKED >= ?`. You set this Execute SQL task to output the rowset to the global variable vOutput.

Which of the following goals have been met? (Choose all that apply.)

A. All the records in the TimeEntry table up to and including the date the month was closed are selected.

B. The date the month was closed is retrieved from the CloseDate table during package execution.

C. The recordset from the selected time entry records is stored in a global variable.

D. The recordset from the selected time entry records is accessible as a disconnected ADO recordset.

70-228.04.03.006

Which of the following DTS tasks allows for the use of parameterized queries? (Choose all that apply.)

A. Execute SQL task

B. Data Driven Query task

C. Transform Data task

D. Copy SQL Server Objects task

Objective 4.3 Answers

70-228.04.03.001

▶ **Correct Answers: A, B, and C**

A. **Correct:** dBase III is a valid data source and SQL Server is a valid destination database.

B. **Correct:** The package was scheduled directly from the DTS Import/Export Wizard. The package could have also been scheduled using the SQL Server Agent and the dtsrun command-line utility.

C. **Correct:** Using the Transformation option and editing the VB Script language accomplishes the goal of marking up the UnitPrice during the data import.

D. **Incorrect:** Although you have successfully added the Image column to the Products table, the column will not be available for the weekly update from within your application. When you created the package, you selected "Drop and re-create the destination tables." This means that your Products table on the ABC SQL Server database will be dropped and re-created based on the Products table from dBase III, which does not contain an Image column. For the column to be available after each import, it should be created during the import. To do this, select the Edit SQL button on the Column Mappings and Transformations screen within the DTS Import/Export Wizard. You can add a column to be created in the Create Table statement.

70-228.04.03.002

▶ **Correct Answers: A and C**

A. **Correct:** The dtsrun utility allows you to pass command-line switches to execute packages without any user input. The dtsrunui utility allows you to prompt the user for input. In this case, the dtsrun command does not have the appropriate switches, so it will return an error. However, it is the correct command to use when you want to execute a package through a batch file with no user input.

B. **Incorrect:** The /W True switch would be the correct switch to use. The /L switch specified in this example is used to designate the name of the package log file.

C. **Correct:** The /E switch indicates that a trusted connection should be attempted. Alternatively, a /U and /P switch could be designated for SQL Server logon.

D. **Incorrect:** The most recent version of the package would be executed because the /V switch was not used to specify a different version. However, the switch used in this example is not correct. The correct switch is /M. The /P switch is used to designate the SQL Server logon password.

70-228.04.03.003

▶ **Correct Answers: B**

A. **Incorrect:** During execution, a package writes information to the package log about all steps in the package. If the step succeeds, the start/stop times are recorded and the step execution time noted. If a step fails, the log lists the step and notes that the step was not executed. The log does not show row-level errors.

B. **Correct:** Exception files record information about failed rows. Exception files can be used by tasks that transform data to detect row-level errors.

C. **Incorrect:** The error file contains a list of the steps executed and their results as well as a list of the steps not executed. This file does not show row-level errors.

D. **Incorrect:** This file shows the execution status of the package.

70-228.04.03.004

▶ **Correct Answers: A and C**

A. **Correct:** Adding a SQL task with the Drop Table SQL statement using Connection 2 accomplishes this requirement.

B. **Incorrect:** Adding a SQL task with the Create Table SQL statement is correct, but it is performed against Connection 1, which is incorrect. This task needs to be performed using Connection 2, the SQL Server connection.

C. **Correct:** By adding the On Success Workflow event between the Create Table icon and the Connection 1 icon, you have set a precedence constraint enforcing the successful completion of the Create Table task before the Transform Data Task can begin.

D. **Incorrect:** You have only added an owner password. If known, this password would allow a user to run and edit the package. For the user to just be able to run a package, you should set a user password when you save the package.

70-228.04.03.005

▶ **Correct Answers: B, C, and D**

A. **Incorrect:** The question mark acts as a placeholder for an input parameter in the GetRecords Execute SQL task. However, the GetRecords task did not define an input parameter. The global variable vCloseDate should have been defined for parameter 1 in this task. The records would then have been selected correctly.

B. **Correct:** The GetDate Execute SQL task correctly queries the CloseDate table and stores the output in the global variable vCloseDate.

C. **Correct:** The GetRecords task is set to output the rowset to the global variable vOutput.

D. **Correct:** Saving the recordset as a global variable allows the recordset to be manipulated as a disconnected ADO recordset. All ADO methods and properties can be used on the recordset.

70-228.04.03.006

▶ **Correct Answers: A, B, and C**

A. **Correct:** The Execute SQL task allows you to write a parameterized query where the value in the SQL statement is filled in at runtime by using a question mark as a parameter placeholder.

B. **Correct:** The Data Driven Query task can execute different parameterized SQL statements for each row source.

C. **Correct:** The Transform Data task allows you to write a parameterized query where the value in the SQL statement is filled in at runtime by using a question mark as a parameter placeholder.

D. **Incorrect:** The Copy SQL Server Objects task does not allow for the use of parameterized queries.

OBJECTIVE 4.4

Manage linked servers.

Once a linked server is created, there are certain configuration and management choices that you may need to make. The configuration settings you change depend on the information you are attempting to access from the linked server. These changes can be implemented either through SQL Server 2000 Enterprise Manager or T-SQL statements. In this objective, we review possible configuration changes that you could make to a linked server.

Using Enterprise Manager or the sp_serveroption T-SQL command, you can set server options that will affect remote or linked servers. These options include:

- Collation compatible. Evaluates comparisons on character columns. If this option is set to true, SQL Server will not evaluate comparisons on character columns locally. Only set this option to true if you are certain that the remote server's data source has the same character set and sort order as the local machine you are configuring.

- Collation name. Indicates the collation name if you have specified that the remote server's collation type should be used. Enter the collation name under this parameter.

- Connect timeout. Indicates the time period before a connection attempt to a linked server fails.

- Data access. Enables or disables a linked server for distributed query access.

- dist. Indicates whether or not the server is a Distributor.

- dpub. Indicates whether the server is a remote Publisher to the Distributor.

- Lazy schema validation. Enforces whether a check is run against the schema before the actual query is executed. If you anticipate a database schema changing for remote servers, use this option. A schema that has changed may cause distributed queries to fail.

- pub. Indicates whether the server will be a Publisher.

- Query timeout. Indicates the query timeout period. If you are running large queries, you may want to increase the timeout period; otherwise the system may time out before the query finishes executing.

- rpc. Allows you to enable rpc to the remote server.

- rpc out. Allows you to enable rpc from the remote server.

- Sub. Allows you to configure the server as a Subscriber.

- System. Used only for internal use.

- Use remote collation. Allows you to use the collation type of the remote server.

Other than configuring existing linked server objects, you will also need to set permissions to the linked server. By accessing the Security folder, and then selecting the Linked Server icon, you can set the permissions to the linked server. You can also execute the sp_addlinkedlogin stored procedure.

Objective 4.4 Questions

70-228.04.04.001

As part of your data warehousing solution, you have created several distributed queries to heterogenous database servers in your environment. Your disaster recovery plan calls for linked server information to be re-created in the shortest period of time. Which database do you need to back up in order to recover linked server information?

A. The remote server's master database

B. The local server's master database

C. The local database to which information is being imported

D. The source database from which information is being exported

70-228.04.04.002

You are running a set of distributed queries to generate sales reports for your Los Angeles sales office. The distributed query links to the SQL server in Spokane and the SQL server running in Seattle. You try generating a report by executing a distributed query and find that the query fails. You e-mail the database administrator in Spokane and ask why this might be happening. You find out that the schema has been changed on the server in Spokane. What do you need to do to correct the problem so that it does not occur again?

A. Set the lazy schema validation option for linked servers to true.

B. Re-establish the link with the remote server in Los Angeles.

C. Set the lazy schema validation option for linked servers to false.

D. Increase the connection timeout option value.

70-228.04.04.003

Because your company develops software for non-English-speaking countries, developers and testers are required to change the collation type for databases to which they may be linking. Which of the following stored procedures can they execute to do this?

A. sp_addlinkedserver

B. sp_configure

C. sp_dboption

D. sp_serveroption

70-228.04.04.004

You are having trouble updating the column of a table on a linked server. Which stored procedure can you execute to view privilege information for the column?

A. sp_column_privileges_ex

B. sp_table_privileges

C. sp_column_privileges

D. sp_table_privileges_ex

Objective 4.4 Answers

70-228.04.04.001

▶ **Correct Answers: B**

A. **Incorrect:** See the explanation for answer B.

B. **Correct:** In addition to other system information, the master database stores data pertaining to linked servers, remote logons, distributed queries, and remote procedure calls.

C. **Incorrect:** See the explanation for answer B.

D. **Incorrect:** See the explanation for answer B.

70-228.04.04.002

▶ **Correct Answers: C**

A. **Incorrect:** If the lazy schema validation option is set to true, schemas on remote tables will not be verified until actual execution of the query. In some cases, this may cause the query to fail if the schema has been changed between the time the query is compiled and executed.

B. **Incorrect:** This will correct the problem but only temporarily. If the administrator in Los Angeles decides to change the schema once more, you will face the same problem.

C. **Correct:** This forces the schema to be validated before the query is executed. Therefore, even if the schema on the remote server is changed, the query will still execute successfully.

D. **Incorrect:** This value determines the timeout value that SQL Server uses when trying to connect to a linked server.

70-228.04.04.003

▶ **Correct Answers: D**

A. **Incorrect:** This stored procedure adds a linked server, but you cannot use it to specify the collation type to use for the server.

B. **Incorrect:** This stored procedure displays the current global configuration for the server. The command can also be used to change the global settings, but collation type is not one of those settings.

C. **Incorrect:** This stored procedure allows you to view or change the options for a specific database.

D. **Correct:** This stored procedure enables you to set the collation type for a remote or linked server by using the collation name option of the command.

70-228.04.04.004

▶ **Correct Answers: A**

A. **Correct:** This stored procedure displays privilege information about a column defined on a table on a linked server.

B. **Incorrect:** This stored procedure displays privilege information about the specific table in the current database.

C. **Incorrect:** This stored procedure displays privilege information about the specified column in the current database.

D. **Incorrect:** This stored procedure displays privilege information about the specified table on a linked server.

OBJECTIVE 4.5

Convert data types.

Every SQL Server object that stores data has an associated **data type**, which defines the type of data the object can store. Such objects include columns, variables, expressions, and parameters used in stored procedures. All data stored within these objects must conform to a set of system data types supplied by SQL Server 2000. Common examples of system-supplied data types include **int**, **decimal**, **money**, **datetime**, **char**, **text**, **image**, and **binary**.

You can also create user-defined data types based on system data types. User-defined data types are useful in situations in which you want to store the same data type with the same length and null attribute across multiple tables or databases. To create user-defined data types, you can use Enterprise Manager or the **sp_addtype** stored procedure. By creating the data type in the model database, you can make user-defined data types available to all newly created databases.

When objects of different data types are combined, moved, or compared, data type conversion may need to occur. SQL Server 2000 supports implicit and explicit data type conversions. Implicit conversions are handled directly through SQL Server and are hidden to the user. Explicit conversions use the **CAST** or **CONVERT** functions. Not all data type conversions are possible. For example, an implicit conversion of nchar to binary is not supported, but an explicit conversion between the data types is possible. Neither conversion method supports nchar to image data type conversion.

All data types have a length attribute, which is the number of characters for character data types and the number of bytes used to store a number for numeric data types. Numeric data types define two additional attributes of an object: precision and scale. The **precision** attribute defines the number of digits the number can contain. The **scale** attribute defines the number of digits that can be stored to the right of the decimal point. When working with numeric data types, SQL Server views each combination of precision and scale as a different data type. When two expressions have data types of different length, precision and scale are combined; the length, precision, and scale of the result is determined by the length, precision, and scale of the input expression. Data type precedence rules and collation precedence rules come into play when combining different data types and data types that have different collations.

Objective 4.5 Questions

70-228.04.05.001

On which of the following data type conversions will an implicit conversion occur?

A. datetime to numeric

B. char to numeric

C. money to char

D. ntext to varchar

70-228.04.05.002

Expression A has a data type of varchar. Expression A is combined by an operator with Expression B. Which of the following could Expression A be combined with and still yield a resulting data type of varchar? (Choose all that apply.)

A. Expression B having a data type of char

B. Expression B having a data type of binary

C. Expression B having a data type of decimal

D. Expression B having a data type of money

70-228.04.05.003

You are attempting to convert an expression from data type int to data type char. Which of the following results do you expect?

A. This is an unsupported data type conversion.

B. The result will be truncated.

C. The result will display an *, indicating that the result length is too short to display.

D. The result will display an E, indicating that an error is being returned because the result length is too short to display.

70-228.04.05.004

Which of the following data type conversions are not possible? (Choose all that apply.)

A. char to varchar

B. money to char

C. datetime to text

D. image to text

70-228.04.05.005

If Expression A, having a data type of decimal and a value of 25.55, is multiplied by Expression B, having a data type of decimal and a value of 1.257, what are the precision and scale values of the result?

A. Precision of 4 and scale of 5

B. Precision of 2 and scale of 3

C. Precision of 10 and scale of 5

D. Precision of 9 and scale of 5

Objective 4.5 Answers

70-228.04.05.001

▶ **Correct Answers: B**

A. **Incorrect:** This conversion is explicit, requiring the use of the CAST or CONVERT function.

B. **Correct:** This conversion is implicit.

C. **Incorrect:** This conversion is explicit, requiring the use of the CAST or CONVERT function.

D. **Incorrect:** This conversion is explicit, requiring the use of the CAST or CONVERT function.

70-228.04.05.002

▶ **Correct Answers: A and B**

A. **Correct:** When expressions with different data types are combined, the data type with lower precedence is converted to the data type with higher precedence. Char has a lower data type precedence than varchar, so the resulting data type would remain varchar.

B. **Correct:** Binary has a lower data type precedence than varchar, so the resulting data type would remain varchar.

C. **Incorrect:** Decimal has a higher data type precedence than varchar, so the resulting data type would be converted to decimal.

D. **Incorrect:** Money has a higher data type precedence than varchar, so the resulting data type would be converted to money.

70-228.04.05.003

▶ **Correct Answers: C**

A. **Incorrect:** This data type conversion is an implicit conversion.

B. **Incorrect:** Some conversions to data type char are truncated, such as text to char. Int to char data type conversions are not truncated.

C. **Correct:** When converting from int, smallint, or tinyint to char or varchar, the result will display an *, indicating that the result length is too short to display.

D. **Incorrect:** Some conversions to data type char will display an error, such as data type money to data type char. Int to char data type conversions do not display an E.

70-228.04.05.004

▶ **Correct Answers: C and D**

A. **Incorrect:** This data type conversion is implicit.

B. **Incorrect:** This data type conversion can be explicitly defined using the CAST or CONVERT function.

C. **Correct:** This data type conversion is not possible.

D. **Correct:** This data type conversion is not possible.

70-228.04.05.005

▶ **Correct Answers: D**

A. **Incorrect:** See the explanation for answer D.

B. **Incorrect:** See the explanation for answer D.

C. **Incorrect:** See the explanation for answer D.

D. **Correct:** Precision is the number of digits in a number. Scale is the number of digits to the right of the decimal point in a number. The result precision of two expressions of data type decimal is calculated using the formula $p1 + p2 + 1$, where $p1$ and $p2$ are the precision of expression 1 and expression 2, respectively. The result scale of two expressions of data type decimal is calculated using the formula $s1 + s2$, where $s1$ and $s2$ are the scale of expression 1 and expression 2, respectively. In this example, expression 1 has a precision of 4 and a scale of 2, and expression 2 has a precision of 4 and a scale of 3. Using the formula, precision equals $4 + 4 + 1$, or 9. Scale equals $2 + 3$, or 5.

Configure, maintain, and troubleshoot replication services.

Microsoft SQL Server primarily implements three types of data replication models: **Merge replication**, **Snapshot replication**, and **Transactional replication**. The replication topology you select can consist of one or a combination of all three topology methods.

Replication can be configured using SQL Server 2000 Enterprise Manager or T-SQL stored procedures. The method you select for replication depends upon the requirements you must meet for data replication. For example, financial institutions require real-time replication of data, whereas educational institutions may only require nightly updates using Snapshot replication.

A typical replication topology consists of a Publisher, a Distributor, and a Subscriber server. Data that must be replicated to the Subscriber server is stored on the Publisher server. After receiving the data from the Publisher, the Distributor then copies the data to the Subscriber. By implementing a Distributor, you prevent the Publisher from being overwhelmed with replication requests.

When deciding upon the type of replication to implement, administrators should consider the following:

- Merge replication. Merge replication enables Subscriber servers to work independently of each other. This can help reduce the amount of traffic being sent back and forth during the workday. Instead, data can be synchronized once during off-peak hours.

- Snapshot replication. Snapshot replication is extremely useful in copying data or database objects to a specified Subscriber server or servers in its entirety if you are dealing with a small amount of data. If the data set you are dealing with is large in size and requires constant updates, Snapshot replication is not the best method to use for replicating that information.

- Transactional replication. Transactional replication should be used when data you are copying over is large in size and has frequent updates. This method of replication eliminates the need to bulk copy the data between servers, which degrades server and network performance.

You should also be aware of hardware requirements when servers are taking part in any form of replication. Depending upon their role, servers will require additional CPU processing, memory, or disk I/O capacity when replicating SQL Server data.

Objective 4.6 Questions

70-228.04.06.001

You are upgrading your environment from SQL Server 7.0 to SQL Server 2000. In which order should you upgrade the servers that take part in the data replication?

A. Subscriber, Distributor, and then Publisher

B. Distributor, Publisher, and then Subscriber

C. Publisher, Distributor, and then Subscriber

D. Replication order does not matter

70-228.04.06.002

Customer sales information from your company's e-commerce site is stored on a single SQL Server 2000 machine. This information must be replicated to SQL Server 2000 machines located at multiple customer support sites. Customer service agents query the database to view the product purchased by the customer and whether or not they have a support contract. Which replication model should you implement so that the SQL servers in the customer support department have the most recent sales information?

A. Merge replication

B. Snapshot replication

C. Snapshot and Merge replication

D. Transactional replication

70-228.04.06.003

Replication has been configured between a Publisher and three Subscriber servers. A replication task between the Publisher and one of the Subscribers is failing. Which tool can you use to view the history of the Merge Agent?

A. Windows 2000 Performance Monitor

B. SQL Server Replication Monitor

C. SQL Server Profiler

D. Windows 2000 Event Viewer

70-228.04.06.004

You attempt to replicate information from a Distributor server to a Subscriber server, but the job fails while the query is still executing. Which of the following parameters should you reconfigure to resolve the problem?

A. Increase the QueryTimeOut

B. Decrease the PollingInterval

C. Increase the MaxBcpThreads

D. Decrease the HistoryVerboseLevel

70-228.04.06.005

Your organization has decided to expand its sales force by opening 15 additional regional sales offices. This requires that you deploy a SQL Server at each office to store critical sales and marketing information. You need to properly size the Publisher, Distributor, and Subscriber servers. If the data you are replicating is large in size (over 2 GB) and you have over 25 Subscriber servers, which server resource will this have an immediate effect upon?

A. CPU of the Subscriber servers

B. Memory in the distribution database

C. Memory in the Subscriber servers

D. Disk controller in the Distributor

70-228.04.06.006

Your company has recently purchased a point of sales application for cash registers in its department stores. The back-end database for the point of sale application is SQL Server 2000.

You want to accomplish the following goals:

- Allow each cash register the capability of displaying transactions completed at other department stores.

- Allow managers at the store's headquarters to view sales information from each store.

- Configure the replication task so that data is copied in the fastest possible way.

You create a Transactional replication job between each SQL server in each department store and the main SQL server residing at headquarters. You then create a second Transactional replication that copies updated data to each of the department store databases. You also create a Snapshot replication to copy data between the primary SQL server and the secondary SQL server at each department store.

Which of the following goals do you accomplish? (Choose all that apply.)

A. Each cashier can view transactions that have occurred at other department stores.

B. Managers at headquarters can view the sales data for each department store using the local SQL server.

C. Replication between the primary and secondary server will occur faster using Snapshot replication.

D. All three goals are accomplished.

Objective 4.6 Answers

70-228.04.06.001

▶ **Correct Answers: C**

A. **Incorrect:** See the explanation for answer C.

B. **Incorrect:** See the explanation for answer C.

C. **Correct:** SQL Server 2000 can send data to SQL Server 7.0 servers, but SQL Server 2000 will not accept SQL Server 7.0 data to be imported.

D. **Incorrect:** See the explanation for answer C.

70-228.04.06.002

▶ **Correct Answers: D**

A. **Incorrect:** The Merge replication model involves merging information from Subscriber servers, and then updating the Publisher database with this information, which then pushes out the merged information to the Subscribers. This is not a feasible solution for this particular problem. The customer support department requires continuous sales information updates so that they know exactly what the customer has purchased. Merging information back to the Publisher would take additional time and would delay the support servers from receiving updated sales information.

B. **Incorrect:** Snapshot replication takes an image of the data and replicates it to the Subscriber servers. This is an inefficient method of keeping the Subscriber servers continuously updated because it requires snapshots to be taken every time the database is altered. Compared to Transactional replication, snapshots can be resource and time intensive.

C. **Incorrect:** By implementing both types of replication, it is possible that the Publisher database will be overwritten.

D. **Correct:** Transactional replication involves first synchronizing all of the Subscriber databases with the Publisher. Then, as information is modified at the Publisher, it is immediately sent out to the Subscribers, populating the database with the most up-to-date information.

70-228.04.06.003

▶ **Correct Answers: B**

A. **Incorrect:** Performance Monitor enables you to monitor the activity not only of the Windows 2000 Server operating system, but also applications including SQL Server 2000. However, it does not allow you to view a detailed history of the Merge Agent.

B. **Correct:** The Replication Monitor logs detailed information regarding replication jobs executing on the server. You can view the history of the replication agents including the Merge Agent from the Replication Monitor.

C. **Incorrect:** The Profiler enables you to monitor detailed SQL Server activity, such as the stored procedures being executed on the server. However, the Profiler does not log any replication event history.

D. **Incorrect:** System and application events, such as certain SQL Server event history, are written to the Windows 2000 Event logs. You use the Event Viewer to view these various logs.

70-228.04.06.004

▶ **Correct Answers: A**

A. **Correct:** The QueryTimeOut specifies the number of seconds allowed for a query to complete executing. If you are attempting to execute a fairly complex query, one that will take a longer period of time, consider increasing the QueryTimeOut value to avoid failed replication jobs.

B. **Incorrect:** The PollingInterval specifies the number of seconds the distribution database is queried for replicated transactions.

C. **Incorrect:** The MaxBcpThreads value controls the number of bulk copy operations that you can execute at a given time. It does not have any effect on the queries executing between servers.

D. **Incorrect:** The HistoryVerboseLevel value enables you to specify the amount of history logged for a distribution job.

70-228.04.06.005

▶ **Correct Answers: B**

A. **Incorrect:** See the explanation for answer B.

B. **Correct:** If the Distributor server is supporting replication to a large number of Subscriber servers, you can enhance the overall performance of the replication task by increasing the amount of memory in the Distributor server.

C. **Incorrect:** See the explanation for answer B.

D. **Incorrect:** See the explanation for answer B.

70-228.04.06.006

▶ **Correct Answers: A and B**

A. **Correct:** By configuring a Transactional replication job, you ensure that data from other department stores will be replicated to the local department store in real time.

B. **Correct:** The SQL server at headquarters will be updated with sales information from each department store, enabling reports to be run against the server without having to query local servers in each department store.

C. **Incorrect:** A better method of replication between the servers is Transactional replication. As a transaction occurs on the primary server, the secondary server can be updated. A Snapshot replication involves copying all of the data and objects from the primary server to the secondary server, overwriting data that might have changed very little from the night before.

D. **Incorrect:** Only two of the goals are accomplished.

OBJECTIVE DOMAIN 5

Managing and Monitoring SQL Server 2000 Security

Security is extremely important to the successful rollout of an application. This is particularly true when deploying a database that is accessible to the public through some Internet-based application. Administrators must also be prudent when deploying a database in-house because it typically stores company-sensitive data.

Due to the flexibility of Microsoft SQL Server 2000, there are several ways an administrator can accomplish a task. However, depending on the situation, one method may be more efficient than another, or a particular method may implement a more restrictive security than was originally intended. In this domain, we review the various methods and tools available to a SQL Server administrator for planning, designing, and implementing database security.

Tested Skills and Suggested Practices

The skills that you need to successfully master the Managing and Monitoring SQL Server 2000 Security objective domain on the *Installing, Configuring, and Administering Microsoft SQL Server 2000 Enterprise Edition* exam include:

- **Configuring mixed security modes or Windows Authentication.**

    - Practice 1: Using only T-SQL statements, view the current security mode for a SQL Server installation.

    - Practice 2: After noting the system administrator (sa) password, change a SQL Server security mode from Windows Authentication to Mixed Mode. Log on to SQL Server with a SQL Server userID and password.

- Practice 3: Change the authentication for the server back to Windows Authentication.

- **Creating and managing logons.**

  - Practice 1: Use the stored procedure sp_grantlogin to allow an existing Windows NT or 2000 user to connect to SQL Server, and then connect to SQL Server as that user.

  - Practice 2: Use the stored procedure sp_addlogin to create a new SQL Server logon with a password, and then connect to SQL Server using the new logon.

  - Practice 3: Use Enterprise Manager to change the password and default database for the SQL Server logon created in Practice 2.

- **Creating and managing database users.**

  - Practice 1: Using Enterprise Manager and T-SQL statements, create a user in the Northwind database with database owner (dbo) privileges.

  - Practice 2: Using the newly created dbo account, create a second SQL Server database account and grant the user access to the Northwind database. Execute the appropriate stored procedure to restrict the user from logging on to the server and accessing the database.

- **Creating and managing security roles.**

  - Practice 1: Use the stored procedure sp_addsrvrolemember to add a Windows NT or 2000 user to the sysadmin fixed server role.

  - Practice 2: Use Enterprise Manager to add a Windows NT or 2000 user to the fixed database role db_owner in the Northwind database.

  - Practice 3: Use the stored procedure sp_helprole to view the roles in the Northwind database.

  - Practice 4: Use the stored procedure sp_helpuser to view information about the dbo user.

- **Enforcing and managing security using stored procedures, triggers, views, and user-defined functions.**

  - Practice 1: Create a view that restricts a user from viewing the home telephone numbers of the employees listed in the Employees table of the Northwind database.

  - Practice 2: Create a trigger within the Orders table of the Northwind database that ensures a user with the EmployeeID of 7 does not enter a freight amount greater than 1500.

- **Setting permissions on databases.**

  - Practice 1: Use Enterprise Manager to grant SELECT access to the Company Name and Address columns of the Customers table in the Northwind database for an existing database user.

  - Practice 2: Use the T-SQL command DENY to remove all access to the Orders table in the Northwind database for the public role.

  - Practice 3: Use the T-SQL command REVOKE to revoke the denied SELECT permission in Practice 2 from the Orders table in the Northwind database for the public role.

- **Managing security audits.**

  - Practice 1: Configure SQL Server to utilize the Windows Event log so that it audits failed SQL Server logon attempts. Then try to access SQL Server using an invalid userID. View the log to see the event generated.

  - Practice 2: Repeat Practice 1, but this time view the failed attempt using SQL Server Profiler.

Further Reading

This section lists supplemental readings by objective. We recommend that you study these sources thoroughly before taking exam 70-228.

Objective 5.1

Microsoft SQL Server 2000 product documentation. To access Books Online, click the Start button, point to Programs, then Microsoft SQL Server, and then select Books Online. Choose the Contents tab and expand Administering SQL Server, then Managing Security, and then Security Levels. This volume contains the article "Authentication Modes," which fully describes Windows Authentication and SQL Server Authentication. It also contains links to articles on how to set up the available authentication modes.

Part 1: Self-Paced Training for Microsoft SQL Server 2000 System Administration. Chapter 10, "Managing Access to SQL Server 2000," Lesson 1 reviews the authentication process for both mixed security mode and Windows Authentication.

Objective 5.2

Microsoft SQL Server 2000 product documentation. To access Books Online, click the Start button, point to Programs, then Microsoft SQL Server, and then select Books Online. Choose the Contents tab and expand Administering SQL Server, then Managing Security, and then Creating Security Accounts. This volume covers adding and managing both Windows and SQL Server logons. It also contains articles on security rules and some of the fixed roles found in SQL Server 2000.

Part 1: Self-Paced Training for Microsoft SQL Server 2000 System Administration. Chapter 10, "Managing Access to SQL Server 2000," covers authentication and security accounts. Lesson 3 of the training kit specifically covers creating and adding users to SQL Server.

Objective 5.3

Microsoft SQL Server 2000 product documentation. To access Books Online, click the Start button, point to Programs, then Microsoft SQL Server, and then select Books Online. Choose the Contents tab and expand Administering SQL Server, then Managing Security, and then Managing Security Accounts. The articles "Viewing Database Users" and "Removing a SQL Server Database Role" contain information on the administrative tasks for managing database users and roles.

Part 1: Self-Paced Training for Microsoft SQL Server 2000 System Administration. Chapter 10, "Managing Access to SQL Server 2000," Lesson 3 covers the topic of adding and creating users to SQL Server.

Objective 5.4

Microsoft SQL Server 2000 product documentation. To access Books Online, click the Start button, point to Programs, then Microsoft SQL Server, and then select Books Online. Choose the Contents tab and expand SQL Server Architecture, then Database Architecture, then Logical Database Components, and then Logins, Users, Roles, and Groups. This topic contains the article "Roles," which discusses the fixed server and database roles found in SQL Server 2000.

Part 1: Self-Paced Training for Microsoft SQL Server 2000 System Administration. Chapter 11, "Managing SQL Server Permissions," Lesson 1 covers server and database roles.

Objective 5.5

Microsoft SQL Server 2000 product documentation. To access Books Online, click the Start button, point to Programs, then Microsoft SQL Server, and then select Books Online. Choose the Contents tab and expand Creating and Maintaining Databases. The article "Enforcing Business Rules with Triggers" discusses how to use triggers as a constraint mechanism and what their value is over the CHECK constraint.

Microsoft SQL Server 2000 product documentation. To access Books Online, click the Start button, point to Programs, then Microsoft SQL Server, and then select Books Online. Choose the Contents tab and expand Administering SQL Server, then Managing Security, then Managing Permissions, and then Using Ownership Chains. In this volume the article "Using Views as Security Mechanisms" details the type of security you can achieve with views.

Objective 5.6

Microsoft SQL Server 2000 product documentation. To access Books Online, click the Start button, point to Programs, then Microsoft SQL Server, and then select Books Online. Choose the Contents tab and expand Administering SQL Server, then Managing Security, and then Managing Permissions. This topic contains articles on all aspects of permissions in SQL Server 2000.

Part 1: Self-Paced Training for Microsoft SQL Server 2000 System Administration. Chapter 11, "Managing SQL Server Permissions," covers managing permissions.

Objective 5.7

Microsoft SQL Server 2000 product documentation. To access Books Online, click the Start button, point to Programs, then Microsoft SQL Server, and then select Books Online. Choose the Contents tab and expand Administering SQL Server, then Managing Security. The article "Auditing SQL Server Activity" describes using the SQL Profiler for auditing SQL Server, and the article "Using Audit Logs" contains information on how to set up your audit log files.

Part 1: Self-Paced Training for Microsoft SQL Server 2000 System Administration. Chapter 14, "Monitoring SQL Server Performance and Activity," reviews auditing SQL Server activity.

OBJECTIVE 5.1

Configure mixed security modes or Windows Authentication.

SQL Server 2000 provides administrators with the option of running the server in two security modes: **Windows Authentication** or **Mixed Mode**. Windows Authentication requires that the SQL server be part of a Windows domain (Windows NT or 2000). Mixed Mode offers flexibility in assigning users SQL Server logons and having users authenticated against these logons. In Mixed Mode, users can also log on using Windows user accounts and be authenticated against a domain.

Windows Authentication has specific benefits over Mixed Mode, which can help form your security strategy. Some of these benefits include:

- Secure validation. Integration with the Windows domain ensures secure validation when authenticating to a Microsoft SQL Server machine.

- Audit account activity. Administrators can implement more detailed auditing of user activity.

- Password encryption. User passwords are encrypted, preventing an individual from viewing passwords through network sniffers or analyzers.

- Account lockout. By locking out a user's Windows domain account, SQL Server administrators can prevent a user from gaining access to the SQL server.

- Tight integration with Windows NT 4.0/2000. For Windows users, SQL Server administrators can easily grant or disable access to a SQL server and a SQL Server database. In addition, the SQL Server administrator can assign users to a Windows domain group and grant access to the entire group rather than individual users, decreasing administrative overhead.

- Trusted connection. The SQL Server 2000 client software requests a Windows trusted connection to SQL Server 2000 when a connection is attempted. Windows does not open a trusted connection unless the client has logged on successfully using a valid Windows account.

Administrators have the ability to switch modes by using SQL Server Enterprise Manager or by executing a system stored procedure.

Objective 5.1 Questions

70-228.05.01.001

You are installing SQL Server 2000 on a Windows 2000 Advanced Server machine. Before creating any databases, you want to set the security mode for the SQL server. Which of the following tools or commands will enable you to do so? (Choose all that apply.)

A. SQL Server Enterprise Manager

B. The sp_serverproperty stored procedure

C. The Server Roles option under the Security folder

D. The Users option for each database

70-228.05.01.002

A Windows 2000 Professional workstation, which is a member of the Seattle Windows 2000 Domain, is configured to execute an Interactive SQL (ISQL) command on a nightly basis. The ISQL command will transpose data from a SQL Server database and FTP the data to a server in the Vancouver sales office. You must be able to execute an ISQL job running on the workstation without exposing security information for the SQL server. How should you configure the SQL server to enable this?

A. Use SQL Server Authentication.

B. Make the SQL Server Service a member of the domain administrators.

C. Make the SQL Server Service a member of the local administrators group for the workstation.

D. Configure SQL Server 2000 to use Windows Authentication mode.

70-228.05.01.003

Which of the following is not a unique feature of Windows Authentication?

A. Encrypts a user's password

B. Allows Windows 98 machines running SQL Server to run Windows Authentication

C. Audits users' logons

D. Disables a user's logon after failed attempts

70-228.05.01.004

When you installed SQL Server 2000, you configured the server to run under Windows Authentication mode. The machine on which you installed SQL Server belongs to the ENGINEERING Windows 2000 domain. By default, who will have administrative privileges to the SQL server?

A. The user you installed SQL Server under

B. Any member of the Windows 2000 Power Users group

C. Any user in the Windows 2000 domain with the username of sa

D. The logon account you specify to start the SQL Server Services

Objective 5.1 Answers

70-228.05.01.001

▶ **Correct Answers: A and B**

A. **Correct:** You can run the server under only Windows Authentication mode, or under Windows Authentication and SQL Server Authentication modes. You can modify a server's security mode through the registration properties for the server under Enterprise Manager.

B. **Correct:** The sp_serverproperty stored procedure enables you to set and configure several SQL Server settings including the authentication mode for the server.

C. **Incorrect:** You can create, delete, or modify server roles, but you cannot alter the authentication mode for the server.

D. **Incorrect:** You can add, delete, and modify users' accounts associated with a database, but you cannot alter the authentication mode for the server.

70-228.05.01.002

▶ **Correct Answers: D**

A. **Incorrect:** See the explanation for answer D.

B. **Incorrect:** See the explanation for answer D.

C. **Incorrect:** See the explanation for answer D.

D. **Correct:** If the U or P options under ISQL are not specified, ISQL will use the Windows Authentication mode. Therefore, if the workstation is a member of a domain, you do not have to specify SQL Server username/password information as part of the ISQL command.

70-228.05.01.003

▶ **Correct Answers: B**

A. **Incorrect:** Windows Authentication is able to encrypt a user's password. SQL Server sends the password clear text, which can be a security breach.

B. **Correct:** You cannot configure SQL Server to run under Windows Authentication mode if it is installed on a Windows 95, Windows 98, or Windows Me machine.

C. **Incorrect:** You can log who accesses the SQL server to the Windows Security Event log.

D. **Incorrect:** The value you specify for a user's Windows account for failed logons is the number of attempts a user will have to log on before being locked out.

70-228.05.01.004

▶ **Correct Answers: A**

A. **Correct:** By default, SQL Server will grant administrative access to that particular instance of SQL Server 2000 to any built-in administrators for the server and the user logon you installed SQL Server under.

B. **Incorrect:** Only domain administrators, administrators of the local server, or the user logon you installed SQL Server under will have admin privileges of the machine.

C. **Incorrect:** See the explanation for answer A.

D. **Incorrect:** Even though you can configure the SQL Server Services to start up using an administrative account, it is not necessary. If you specify a user with no administrative privileges on the domain or the local server, the user will not have admin privileges of the SQL server even if he or she can start the services.

Create and manage logons.

You must establish a logon account in order to gain access to SQL Server. Depending on the configuration of SQL Server's security authentication mode, SQL Server 2000 logon accounts can be created independently of Windows NT and 2000 logon accounts or mapped directly to them. Using Windows Authentication, the logon account is created in Windows NT or 2000 and is then granted access to connect within SQL Server. Using Mixed Mode Authentication, the logon account is created within SQL Server.

For ease of administration when using Windows Authentication, consider granting permission to Windows NT and 2000 local and global groups rather than to individual users. You can explicitly deny logon access to a Windows group or individual user as well. The stored procedures **sp_grantlogin** and **sp_denylogin** are used to allow or deny access to a Windows NT and 2000 user or group. You can also use Enterprise Manager to control SQL Server access to Windows users and groups.

In Mixed Mode Authentication, SQL Server logons can be added and removed by using Enterprise Manager or by using **sp_addlogin** and **sp_droplogin**. By default, an sa SQL Server logon account is created when SQL Server is installed. This account is assigned the sysadmin fixed server role and cannot be changed.

Once you create or map a SQL Server logon account to an existing Windows NT or 2000 user or group, you must create a corresponding account in each database the account needs to access. This is accomplished through Enterprise Manager or by using the stored procedure **sp_grantdbaccess**. You can log on to a database without a SQL Server logon account existing in the database only if the database contains a **guest** user account. A guest account exists in master and tempdb databases, but does not exist by default in newly created databases.

The **Create Login Wizard** simplifies the account creation process by combining the steps to create or map a logon account, assign server roles, and grant access to databases.

Objective 5.2 Questions

70-228.05.02.001

Your Windows NT SQL Server, BETA, contains the local group Personnel with members Joe and Steve. The server is a member of the domain ALPHA, which contains a global group Contractors with members Frank and Jane. The SQL server also has a built-in local Administrators group.

You want to accomplish the following goals:

- Joe and Steve must be able to access SQL Server.

- Frank must be able to access SQL Server.

- Members of the built-in local Administrators group must be able to access SQL Server.

- Jane should not be allowed access to SQL Server.

You add the global group Contractors to the local group Personnel through Windows NT. You run the stored procedure EXEC sp_grantlogin 'BETA\Personnel'. You run the stored procedure EXEC sp_grantlogin 'BETA\Administrators'. You run the stored procedure EXEC sp_denylogin 'ALPHA\Jane'.

Which of the following goals have been met? (Choose all that apply.)

A. Joe and Steve can access SQL Server.

B. Frank can access SQL Server.

C. Members of the built-in local Administrators group can access SQL Server.

D. Jane cannot access SQL Server.

70-228.05.02.002

The Windows NT user FINANCE\Angela is a member of the FINANCE\Managers and FINANCE\Sales-reps Windows NT groups. As a user, FINANCE\Angela has not been granted any access to SQL Server or to any databases. However, the FINANCE\Salesreps group has been granted permission to connect to SQL Server, and the FINANCE\Managers group has been granted access to the Regions database. User FINANCE\Angela creates a Contacts table in the Regions database. FINANCE\Angela is later removed from the FINANCE\Managers group. Which of the following statements are correct? (Choose all that apply.)

A. User FINANCE\Angela can access the Regions database.

B. User FINANCE\Angela can only access the Contacts table in the Regions database.

C. User FINANCE\Angela can access any database to which the FINANCE\Salesreps Windows NT group has been granted access.

D. User FINANCE\Angela can log on to SQL Server.

70-228.05.02.003

Your company is running several instances of SQL Server 2000 on different computers. You are interested in setting up Security Account Delegation so that the authentication credentials originally supplied by a client are retained when the client connects to other instances of SQL Server within the environment. Which of the following are required to set up Security Account Delegation? (Choose all that apply.)

A. You must use Named Pipes.

B. The servers must be running Windows NT.

C. Kerberos support must be enabled.

D. You must use Active Directory.

70-228.05.02.004

User SALES\AdamJ is moving to a different position within the company. The SQL Server to which he connects is configured for Mixed Mode Authentication. The user connects to SQL Server through Windows Authentication, and the SALES\AdamJ account exists only in the Marketing database. The user creates and owns the table SALES\AdamJ.Contacts. The user is not a member of any Windows NT groups that have been assigned access to SQL Server.

You want to accomplish the following goals:

- Transfer ownership of the SALES\AdamJ.Contacts table to SALES\SarahD.

- Remove all permissions defined for SALES\AdamJ in the Marketing database.

- Remove the user from the Marketing database.

- Allow the user to connect to the Marketing database as guest.

You connect to the Marketing database as a member of the sysadmin fixed server role. You run the stored procedure EXEC sp_grantdbaccess 'guest' to create the guest account in the Marketing database. You run the stored procedure EXEC sp_changeobjectowner 'SALES\AdamJ.Contacts', 'SALES\SarahD' to transfer the view owned by user AdamJ to user SarahD. You run the stored procedure EXEC sp_revokedbacess 'SALES\AdamJ' to remove the user account from the database. You run the stored procedure EXEC sp_revokelogin 'SALES\AdamJ' to remove the user from SQL Server.

Which of the following goals have you achieved? (Choose all that apply.)

A. You have transferred ownership of the SALES\AdamJ.Contacts view to SALES\SarahD.

B. You have removed all permissions defined for SALES\AdamJ in the Marketing database.

C. You have removed the user SALES\AdamJ from the Marketing database.

D. You have allowed the user to connect to the Marketing database as guest.

70-228.05.02.005

Your SQL server is configured to use Windows Authentication. You want to allow the Windows 2000 domain user CORP\Jennifer access to SQL Server. Which of the following commands would accomplish this?

A. `EXEC sp_createlogin 'CORP\Jennifer'`

B. `EXEC sp_addlogin 'CORP\Jennifer'`

C. `EXEC sp_grantlogin 'CORP\Jennifer'`

D. `EXEC sp_grantdbaccess 'CORP\Jennifer'`

Objective 5.2 Answers

70-228.05.02.001

▶ **Correct Answers: A, B, and D**

A. **Correct:** Joe and Steve are members of the local Personnel group, which was granted logon access to SQL Server.

B. **Correct:** Frank is a member of the global group Contractors, which was added to the local group Personnel, which was granted logon access to SQL Server.

C. **Incorrect:** To grant logon access to a built-in local group, BUILTIN should be specified instead of the domain or computer name. The correct command is:

```
EXEC sp_grantlogin 'BUILTIN\Administrators'
```

D. **Correct:** Even though Jane is a member of the global group Contractors, which was added to the local group Personnel, which was granted logon access to SQL Server, Jane cannot access SQL Server because she was explicitly denied access.

70-228.05.02.002

▶ **Correct Answers: C and D**

A. **Incorrect:** User FINANCE\Angela has been removed from the FINANCE\Managers group, which is where permission to the database is granted.

B. **Incorrect:** User FINANCE\Angela has been removed from the FINANCE\Managers group, which is where permission to the database is granted. Because FINANCE\Angela created a table, an entry in the Sysusers table is created for FINANCE\Angela. This designates her as the owner of the table, but no entry is placed in the Sysxlogins table granting her access to the database.

C. **Correct:** Even though user FINANCE\Angela may not have explicit access to any database, she may gain permission through membership in the FINANCE\Salesreps group.

D. **Correct:** User FINANCE\Angela can log on to SQL Server because the FINANCE\Salesreps Windows NT group has been granted permission to connect to SQL Server, and FINANCE\Angela is a member of the group.

70-228.05.02.003

▶ **Correct Answers: C and D**

A. **Incorrect:** Named Pipes cannot be used because enabling delegation requires that a Service Principal Name (SPN) be assigned to the service account of the SQL Server Service at a particular TCP/IP socket. Therefore, TCP/IP must be used.

B. **Incorrect:** Security Account Delegation is only available if the servers to which you want to connect are running Windows 2000.

C. **Correct:** Security Account Delegation is only available if the servers to which you want to connect have Kerberos support enabled.

D. **Correct:** You must be using Active Directory for Security Account Delegation to work.

70-228.05.02.004

▶ **Correct Answers: A, B, and C**

A. **Correct:** The stored procedure sp_changeobjectowner changes the owner of an object, such as a table or stored procedure. Because the user owns objects within the database, this step is necessary before removing the user from the database.

B. **Correct:** The stored procedure sp_revokedbaccess automatically removes all permissions defined for the user.

C. **Correct:** The stored procedure sp_revokedbaccess removes the user account from the database, preventing the user from accessing the database under that security account.

D. **Incorrect:** Running the stored procedure sp_grantdbaccess correctly sets up the database to allow for guest access. However, by running the stored procedure sp_revokelogin to remove the user from SQL Server, you are preventing the user from accessing the database as guest. A guest logon to a database occurs when a database has a guest account and the user attempting access has a valid logon to access SQL Server.

70-228.05.02.005

▶ **Correct Answers: C**

A. **Incorrect:** This is not a valid stored procedure.

B. **Incorrect:** The stored procedure sp_addlogin creates a SQL Server logon that allows a user to connect to an instance of SQL Server using SQL Server Authentication.

C. **Correct:** The stored procedure sp_grantlogin allows a Windows NT or Windows 2000 user or group to connect to SQL Server using Windows Authentication.

D. **Incorrect:** The stored procedure sp_grantdbaccess is used to add a security account to the current database for a SQL Server logon or a Windows NT/2000 user or group. The account must first exist on the SQL server.

OBJECTIVE 5.3

Create and manage database users.

Only after a user has been assigned access to SQL Server through a logon account can the user be created within a database. Database access can be assigned to:

- A user or group account that is a member of a Windows domain. (SQL Server must be configured to support Windows Authentication.)

- A SQL Server logon account

- A **guest account**

- A **dbo** account

A logon account must have an assigned database user account or use of the default database user accounts. A database user account can be assigned to Windows domain users, Windows domain groups, or SQL Server logons. You can assign a database user account to a logon by using SQL Server Enterprise Manager from either the Security folder or the Database folder. Access can also be granted using the **sp_grantdbaccess** stored procedure. Only database owners and database access administrators can assign a database user account to a logon.

When a database is created, special user accounts called guest and dbo are created inside the database. The guest account allows a user to log on to a database without a user account that has permissions on the database. A user logon assumes the identity of the guest user when a guest user account is created for the database and the user logon has access to SQL Server but does not have access to the database. Permissions can be applied to the guest account, and the guest user can be deleted and added to all databases except the master and tempdb databases.

Only members of the sysadmin fixed server role, which includes the sa logon account, are mapped to the dbo account. Objects created by members of the sysadmin fixed server role are automatically owned by the dbo account, not the user's account. The dbo account cannot be removed from a database.

Objective 5.3 Questions

70-228.05.03.001

A new employee in the Marketing department needs dbo access to the Marketing database running on the SQL server MK1. Which stored procedure enables you to create this user account in the database?

A. sp_grantdbaccess

B. sp_grantlogin

C. sp_addrole

D. sp_addlogin

70-228.05.03.002

An employee who was recently hired in the Marketing department is now transferring to Human Resources. You want to delete the employee's user account from the Marketing database. Which stored procedure would you use?

A. sp_changeobjectowner

B. sp_change_user_login

C. sp_denylogin

D. sp_revokedbaccess

70-228.05.03.003

You have been asked to enable access to the Human Resources database for Jack, who is a member of the Human Resources group defined in your Windows 2000 domain. If Jack's account has not been added to the Human Resources database on the SQL Server 2000 machine, under what circumstances will his account log on as the guest user account? (Choose all that apply.)

A. If the Human Resources Windows 2000 domain group has a guest member account.

B. If the Human Resources database contains a guest user account.

C. If Jack has permissions to access the SQL Server but not the Human Resources database.

D. Jack does not have permissions to access the SQL Server or the Human Resources database.

70-228.05.03.004

You have just completed installing SQL Server 2000 and are ready to create a new database. Which user is automatically assigned dbo privileges to the newly created database?

A. The user creating the database

B. The user account assigned to start and stop the SQL Server Services

C. Any user assigned dbo permissions to the master database

D. Any user assigned the role of serveradmin

70-228.05.03.005

You are running SQL Server 2000 in a Windows 2000 domain.

You want to accomplish the following goals:

- Grant access to the Engineering database for all of the members in the Windows 2000 Engineering group in the most efficient way.

- User authentication must be encrypted.

- You must be able to revoke SQL Server access for individual users accessing the SQL Server.

You configure the SQL server to support SQL Server and Windows Authentication. You then grant database access permission to each user in the Windows 2000 Engineering group.

Which of the following does your solution achieve? (Choose all that apply.)

A. Users are created and administered in the most efficient manner.

B. User authentication will be encrypted.

C. You can revoke an individual user from accessing the SQL Server.

D. All of the goals are achieved.

Objective 5.3 Answers

70-228.05.03.001

▶ **Correct Answers: A**

A. **Correct:** Executing sp_grantdbaccess with the appropriate command options allows you to grant a user database access and dbo permissions to the database.

B. **Incorrect:** This stored procedure grants an existing Windows NT or 2000 domain user or group permissions to connect to SQL Server using Windows Authentication.

C. **Incorrect:** The stored procedure sp_addrole creates a SQL Server role in the current database; it does not allow you to add a user to the database.

D. **Incorrect:** This stored procedure creates a SQL Server logon, but it does not allow you to grant a user permissions to a database. To assign permissions to a user for a particular database, you must use the sp_grantdbaccess stored procedure.

70-228.05.03.002

▶ **Correct Answers: D**

A. **Incorrect:** This stored procedure changes the owner for a particular object within a database; it does not remove the user from the database.

B. **Incorrect:** You would execute this procedure if you want to change a user's logon credentials, but it does not remove the user's account from the database.

C. **Incorrect:** Executing sp_denylogin prevents the user from logging on, but it does not remove the user's account from the database.

D. **Correct:** Just as you grant permissions for a user to access a database, you have to revoke those permissions to deny access. Therefore, you need to execute the sp_revokedbaccess stored procedure.

70-228.05.03.003

▶ **Correct Answers: B and C**

A. **Incorrect:** See the explanation for answer B.

B. **Correct:** If Jack has not been granted explicit access to the Human Resources database, but his account can access the SQL Server, he can still gain access if the Human Resources database has a guest user account created. His permissions to the database will be limited to what the guest account has been granted.

C. **Correct:** See the explanation for answer B.

D. **Incorrect:** See the explanation for answer B.

70-228.05.03.004

▶ **Correct Answers: A**

A. **Correct:** By default, the only person assigned dbo permissions of a newly created SQL Server database is the person who created the database.

B. **Incorrect:** See the explanation for answer A.

C. **Incorrect:** See the explanation for answer A.

D. **Incorrect:** The serveradmin role only allows a user to alter the configuration of the SQL Server. The user does not have any database privileges.

70-228.05.03.005

▶ **Correct Answers: B and C**

A. **Incorrect:** It would be better to assign the entire Windows 2000 group permission rather than assigning each member of the group permission.

B. **Correct:** If Windows Authentication is configured, logon information will be encrypted.

C. **Correct:** You can revoke a user's access to the SQL Server by denying him or her access to log on to the domain.

D. **Incorrect:** Only two of the goals are achieved.

OBJECTIVE 5.4

Create and manage security roles.

Roles are used to simplify security administration. Roles can contain SQL Server logons and Windows NT or 2000 users and groups. They can also contain other roles, which allow permissions to be set hierarchically and to be applied to many users at once. Several types of roles exist within SQL Server: **fixed server roles**, **fixed database roles**, **user-defined database roles**, and the **public role**.

Fixed server and fixed database roles define sets of permissions that can only be assigned to user accounts by adding users to the fixed roles. Fixed server roles exist at the server level. Members must have a SQL Server or Windows NT or 2000 logon account to be added to the role. The highest level fixed server role is **sysadmin**, which allows members to perform any activity in SQL Server. The built-in Administrators group in Windows NT or 2000 is assigned the sysadmin fixed server role by default. The seven other fixed server roles are subsets of the sysadmin role: **serveradmin**, **setupadmin**, **securityadmin**, **processadmin**, **dbcreator**, **diskadmin**, and **bulkadmin**.

Fixed database roles are defined at the database level and exist in each database. The highest level fixed database role is **db_owner**, which allows members to perform any activity within the database. The eight other fixed database roles are subsets of the db_owner role: **db_accessadmin**, **db_datareader**, **db_datawriter**, **db_ddladmin**, **db_securityadmin**, **db_backupoperator**, **db_denydatareader**, and **db_denydatawriter**.

You can create user-defined database roles to define a set of permissions for SQL Server authenticated logons or for a group of users who do not have a corresponding Windows NT or 2000 group. Database roles exist only in the database in which they are created. Users can belong to more than one database role, and more than one database role can be active at any one time for a given user. When a user is a member of more than one role, permissions are cumulative with the exception of the DENY permission. If one role grants access and another denies access, the DENY permission will be applied because deny access is more restrictive and takes precedence.

The public role is a special role that exists in every database and cannot be deleted. Every user is automatically made a member of the public role, which defines the default permissions for users in the database.

Objective 5.4 Questions

70-228.05.04.001

The user-defined role Salesrep has been denied access to the Commission column in the Sales table of the Corp database. User Lauren needs access to read all data in all user tables in the Corp database but should also be restricted from viewing the Commission column. Which of the following role assignments will accomplish this? (Choose all that apply.)

A. Add the fixed database role db_datareader to the user-defined database Salesrep, and make Lauren a member of the Salesrep role.

B. Add the user-defined database role Salesrep to the fixed database role db_datareader, and make Lauren a member of the Salesrep role.

C. Create a circular role by adding the db_datareader role to the Salesrep role, and then add the Salesrep role to the db_datareader role.

D. Make Lauren a member of the user-defined database role Salesrep and a member of the fixed database role db_datareader.

70-228.05.04.002

Your company has the following security requirements:

- Maya must be able to manage all aspects of SQL Server.

- Jose is responsible for database backups and maintenance, but he should not be able to see data or create databases.

- Sonia must be able to create tables and databases.

- The Windows NT group CORPORATE\hr and Ramine, the president, need access to view the Emp_ID and Salary columns of the Payroll table in the Employee database.

Maya is assigned the fixed server role of sysadmin. Jose is assigned the fixed database role of db_backupoperator. Sonia is assigned the fixed database role of db_owner in the Employee database. Access to the Payroll table in the Employee database is revoked for the public role. A new HRSal role is created with SELECT permission on Emp_ID and Salary to the Payroll table in the Employee database. The Windows NT group CORPORATE\hr and the user Ramine are added as members of the role. In all other databases, the public role grants SELECT access to all tables. Which of the requirements have been accomplished? (Choose all that apply.)

A. Maya can manage all aspects of SQL Server.

B. Jose can perform backups and maintenance of databases, but he cannot see data or create databases.

C. Sonia can create tables and databases.

D. The Windows NT group CORPORATE\hr and the user Ramine can view the Emp_ID and Salary columns in the Employee database.

70-228.05.04.003

Members belonging to which of the following roles can add members to fixed database roles? (Choose all that apply.)

A. db_owner

B. db_securityadmin

C. sysadmin

D. securityadmin

70-228.05.04.004

You want to view a list of the members belonging to the db_owner role. Which of the following would accomplish this? (Choose all that apply.)

A. EXEC sp_helpsrvrolemember 'db_owner'

B. EXEC sp_helprole 'db_owner'

C. EXEC sp_helpuser 'db_owner'

D. EXEC sp_helpgroup 'db_owner'

70-228.05.04.005

Which of the following commands would allow SQL Server user Gayle to view all data from all user tables in the current database?

A. EXEC sp_addrolemember 'db_datareader', 'Gayle'

B. EXEC sp_addsrvrolemember 'db_owner', 'Gayle'

C. EXEC sp_addrolemember 'db_ddladmin', 'Gayle'

D. EXEC sp_addsrvrolemember 'db_accessadmin', 'Gayle'

70-228.05.04.006

You are administering a SQL Server 2000 machine and you need to implement security for the Sales database.

You want to accomplish the following goals:

■   Restrict access to the Sales database only to those users running the SALES_ENTRY application.

■   Grant access to five users in the Windows NT Marketing group to the Sales database.

■   Overwrite existing permissions to the Sales database for these five users with those granted by the application.

You grant access to the SQL server for the Windows NT Marketing group with SELECT, UPDATE, and DELETE permissions to the Sales database. You then create an application role for the SALES_ENTRY application and use the sp_setapprole system stored procedure to activate the application role.

Which of the following does your solution achieve? (Choose all that apply.)

A.   Users are restricted to only those permissions granted in the application role.

B.   All of the users in the Windows NT Marketing group have access to the Sales database.

C.   Only those users running the SALES_ENTRY application have access to the Sales database.

D.   None of the goals are achieved.

Objective 5.4 Answers

70-228.05.04.001

▶ **Correct Answers: B and D**

A.   **Incorrect:** Fixed database roles cannot be added to user-defined roles.

B.   **Correct:** User-defined database roles can be added to fixed database roles. Once Lauren is a member of the Salesrep role, which is a member of the db_datareader role, Lauren will inherit the permissions granted to the db_datareader role. Because deny permissions take precedence, Lauren will not be able to view the Commissions column in the Sales table of the Corp database.

C.   **Incorrect:** You cannot create circular roles. If the Salesrep role is a member of the db_datareader role, then the db_datareader role cannot be a member of Salesrep role. In this case, db_datareader cannot be a member of the Salesrep role because you cannot add a fixed database role to a user-defined database role.

D. **Correct:** When a user belongs to more than one role, permissions are cumulative with the exception of the deny permission, which takes precedence. In this scenario, Lauren has access to read all data in all user tables through her membership in the db_datareader role. However, she will still be restricted from viewing the Commission columns in the Sales table because this permission has been denied through her membership in the Salesrep role.

70-228.05.04.002

▶ **Correct Answers: A and D**

A. **Correct:** The fixed server role sysadmin allows full access to SQL Server.

B. **Incorrect:** By assigning Jose the fixed database role db_backupoperator, Jose is able to back up and perform maintenance, but he has not been denied access to view data. Access to view data is provided through the public role.

C. **Incorrect:** The fixed database role of db_owner allows Sonia to create tables within the Employee database, but not within other databases. Assigning Sonia to the fixed server role dbcreator would allow her to create databases within SQL Server.

D. **Correct:** The HRSal role assigns the appropriate rights to the Payroll table in the Employee database, and both the group and the user are added to the role.

70-228.05.04.003

▶ **Correct Answers: A and C**

A. **Correct:** Members of the fixed database role db_owner can add members to fixed database roles.

B. **Incorrect:** Members of the fixed database role db_securityadmin can only add members to user-defined database roles, not to fixed database roles.

C. **Correct:** Members of the sysadmin fixed server role sysadmin have complete control within SQL Server.

D. **Incorrect:** Members of the fixed server role securityadmin can manage server logons, such as changing passwords and setting default databases.

70-228.05.04.004

▶ **Correct Answers: C and D**

A. **Incorrect:** The stored procedure sp_helpsrvrolemember is used to view a list of members belonging to a fixed server role. The db_owner role is a fixed database role.

B. **Incorrect:** The stored procedure sp_helprole returns information about roles in the current database, but it does not display a list of users belonging to the role.

C. **Correct:** The stored procedure sp_helpuser displays information on users and roles in the current database. If no security account is specified as an argument, the stored procedure will return all users and roles.

D. **Correct:** Executing the stored procedure sp_helpgroup for a database role is equivalent to executing sp_helpuser for a database role.

70-228.05.04.005

▶ **Correct Answers: A**

A. **Correct:** The stored procedure sp_addrolemember is the correct command to add users to roles. The fixed database role db_datareader allows view access to all data in all user tables in a database.

B. **Incorrect:** The stored procedure sp_addsrvrolemember is used to add users to fixed server roles, such as sysadmin. In addition, members of the db_owner role have all permissions in the database. Assigning Gayle to the db_owner role would not be appropriate if the only access Gayle needs is view access.

C. **Incorrect:** Executing this command would assign Gayle to the fixed database role of db_ddladmin, which allows members to add, modify, or drop objects within a database.

D. **Incorrect:** The stored procedure sp_addsrvrolemember is used to add users to fixed server roles. The fixed database role db_accessadmin allows members to add or remove Windows NT or 2000 users or groups and SQL Server users from a database.

70-228.05.04.006

▶ **Correct Answers: A, B, and C**

A. **Correct:** By assigning the application role to the users and providing them with the appropriate information to activate the role, they can access the Sales database with restricted permissions.

B. **Correct:** See the explanation for answer A.

C. **Correct:** See the explanation for answer A.

D. **Incorrect:** All of the goals are achieved.

Enforce and manage security by using stored procedures, triggers, views, and user-defined functions.

Views, triggers, stored procedures, and user-defined functions can be utilized not only to control what data is viewed but also to secure objects and data within a database.

To utilize a trigger for security purposes, the trigger must be created within the correct tables. Triggers can be configured to execute a set of T-SQL statements when an UPDATE, DELETE, or INSERT is issued against a table or view. The text within the trigger determines its usefulness as well as the ability of the trigger to enforce the required security.

By granting or denying EXECUTE permissions to SQL Server stored procedures, users can be restricted from accessing or modifying data within the database. Views enable administrators to restrict the parts of the database's data a user or a group of users can actually see.

Security through stored procedures, views, triggers, and user-defined functions can be used in conjunction with other security features of SQL Server 2000, such as fixed database roles. Administrators can implement these features and their functionality according to the type and extent of security they want to apply to a particular database.

Objective 5.5 Questions

70-228.05.05.001

You are deploying a new Human Resources application that stores employee information. The application uses SQL Server 2000 as its data source. Once the application is rolled out to the Human Resources department, temporary personnel will begin entering employee information, which requires that they be able to view employee data residing in the old SQL Server database named HR1. The table they need to view contains personal information of all employees, such as address, start date, manager, and salary information. You do not want the temporary personnel to be able to view anyone's salary information because that will be entered by the Human Resources administrator. What can you do to prevent the temporary personnel from viewing this sensitive data?

A. Create a trigger that e-mails the Human Resources administrator any time salary data has been viewed.

B. Delete salary information from the table.

C. Create an application role that prevents users from using SQL Server Query Analyzer, and therefore prevents the user from executing the SELECT * FROM command.

D. Create a view that allows users to view everything but salary information. The temporary personnel should then be assigned to a SQL Server role that has access to the view.

70-228.05.05.002

You have developed an application that requires users to log on to the application before gaining access to data. Before allowing a user to update information in the Contacts table, you want to verify that the user has appropriate rights to do so. Verification involves selecting information from a table containing security rights to each table in the database for a particular user. Which of the following is the most efficient verification method?

A. trigger

B. stored procedure

C. view

D. user-defined function

70-228.05.05.003

Tyler has CREATE TABLE permissions in the Sales databases. Tyler creates a table named Customers in the Sales database, and then Selena creates a stored procedure that selects information on that table. Bethany is now given EXECUTE permissions on that stored procedure, but she is not given SELECT permissions on the Customers table. What happens when Bethany tries to execute the stored procedure?

A. All valid rows from the SELECT statement in the stored procedure are returned to Bethany.

B. Bethany receives an error message that she does not have valid permissions.

C. Bethany receives an error message that she cannot execute the stored procedure.

D. The stored procedure executes, but no rows are returned.

Objective 5.5 Answers

70-228.05.05.001

▶ **Correct Answers: D**

A. **Incorrect:** This would not prevent the temporary personnel from viewing the data, it would only let the HR administrator know that it had happened.

B. **Incorrect:** This will prevent the Human Resources administrator from viewing and entering the information into the new Human Resources application.

C. **Incorrect:** Someone familiar with SQL Server client tools can still use SQL Server Enterprise Manager to view table contents.

D. **Correct:** The view can be designed so that the temporary personnel can only see information you want them see. By assigning them to a role, you ensure that all of the temporary personnel are restricted to viewing only the data you want them to see.

70-228.05.05.002

▶ **Correct Answers: A**

A. **Correct:** A trigger would be the most efficient way to verify user security rights in this case. Triggers can be configured to launch at the point when an event, such as an INSERT or DELETE, takes place. Using a trigger eliminates the need to write additional code within a stored procedure to check for a particular event or status.

B. **Incorrect:** Before executing a stored procedure to verify security rights, you need a method to call the stored procedure. The only way to do this is by using a trigger.

C. **Incorrect:** A view can only control the data a user can see. Views by themselves cannot prevent a user from updating data to a table.

D. **Incorrect:** User-defined functions comprised of T-SQL statements could be used to verify security rights. However, similar to a single stored procedure, the function would need to be launched as soon as a user attempted to insert data into the Contacts table.

70-228.05.05.003

▶ **Correct Answers: B**

A. **Incorrect:** See the explanation for answer B.

B. **Correct:** The ownership chain is not the same for the stored procedure and the table; therefore, the rows are not returned.

C. **Incorrect:** See the explanation for answer B.

D. **Incorrect:** See the explanation for answer B.

OBJECTIVE 5.6

Set permissions in a database.

Permissions granted to Windows NT or 2000 users and groups, SQL Server users, and SQL Server database roles determine the type of activity that can be performed within the database. Permissions are database dependent and can only be set for objects that exist within the current database. There are three classes of permissions: **object permissions**, **statement permissions**, and **implied permissions**.

Object permissions define how users work with data and execute procedures. Permissions that can be set on objects include SELECT, INSERT, UPDATE, DELETE, and EXECUTE. To provide column-level security, a column list is supplied by the SELECT and UPDATE permissions. EXECUTE is the only object permission that can be granted on a stored procedure.

Statement permissions deal with creating a database or an item in a database and are applied to the statement itself, not to a specific object in the database. Statement permissions include BACKUP DATABASE, BACKUP LOG, CREATE DATABASE, CREATE DEFAULT, CREATE FUNCTION, CREATE PROCEDURE, CREATE RULE, CREATE TABLE, and CREATE VIEW.

Implied permissions are indirectly granted to a member of a fixed server role or a database object owner. For example, database object owners can perform any activity on any object they own because they have implied permissions on objects they create.

Permissions can be granted, denied, or revoked by using T-SQL statements or Enterprise Manager. Statement and object permissions can be granted using the T-SQL command **GRANT**. The DENY permission allows you to limit permissions by removing previously granted permissions of a user, group, or role and preventing the user, group, or role from inheriting permissions through its group or role memberships. The T-SQL command **DENY** is used to deny object and statement permissions. The REVOKE permission allows you to revoke a permission that has been previously granted or denied. Revoking a granted permission is different than denying a granted permission: a revoked permission does not prevent the user, group, or role from inheriting the granted permission from a higher level. The T-SQL command REVOKE is used to revoke a previously granted or denied permission.

Objective 5.6 Questions

70-228.05.06.001

When setting object permissions on a table using the GRANT T-SQL command, which of the following permissions accept a column list as an argument? (Choose all that apply.)

A. INSERT

B. SELECT

C. DELETE

D. UPDATE

70-228.05.06.002

SQL Server user Miguel is leaving the XYZ Company. Management is requesting a list of permissions that have been granted by Miguel in the Revenue database. Assuming the Revenue database is the current database, which of the following commands would you execute to provide management with the information requested?

A. `EXEC sp_helprotect NULL, 'Miguel'`

B. `EXEC sp_helprotect NULL, NULL, 'Miguel'`

C. `EXEC sp_helprotect NULL, NULL, 'Miguel', 'o'`

D. `EXEC sp_helprotect 'Miguel'`

70-228.05.06.003

User Melissa is a member of the Paralegal role, which has been denied SELECT, UPDATE, and DELETE access to the Partners table in the Attorney database. The Paralegal role has been granted SELECT and UPDATE access to the Associates table in the database, but has been denied DELETE access to the table. User Melissa was explicitly granted UPDATE access and denied DELETE access to the Associates table in the database.

You must meet the following objectives:

- Melissa needs to select information from the Partners table.

- Melissa needs to select information from the Associates table.

- Melissa should not be allowed to update information in the Associates table.

- Melissa needs to delete information from the Associates table.

You create a view of the Partners table. You explicitly grant SELECT permission to the Partners view for the Melissa user account. You revoke the UPDATE and DELETE permission from the Associates table for the Melissa user account. You revoke the denied DELETE access to the Associates table for the Paralegal role. Which of the following objectives are met? (Choose all that apply.)

A. Melissa can select information from the Partners view.

B. Melissa can select information from the Associates table.

C. Melissa cannot update information in the Associates table.

D. Melissa can delete information from the Associates table.

70-228.05.06.004

Members of certain fixed server roles have implied permissions to execute T-SQL statements. Which fixed server roles do not have permissions to execute any T-SQL statements? (Choose all that apply.)

A. diskadmin

B. setupadmin

C. processadmin

D. bulkadmin

Objective 5.6 Answers

70-228.05.06.001

▶ **Correct Answers: B and D**

A. **Incorrect:** The INSERT permission affects an entire row in a database table and can therefore not accept a column list as an argument when being granted, denied, or revoked.

B. **Correct:** The SELECT permission can be selectively applied to columns in a table and can therefore accept a column list as an argument when being granted, denied, or revoked.

C. **Incorrect:** The DELETE permission affects an entire row in a database table and can therefore not accept a column list as an argument when being granted, denied, or revoked.

D. **Correct:** The UPDATE permission can be selectively applied to columns in a table and can therefore accept a column list as an argument when being granted, denied, or revoked.

70-228.05.06.002

▶ **Correct Answers: B**

A. **Incorrect:** The arguments supplied are not correct. This command would provide a list of permissions that have been granted to Miguel, not those that Miguel has granted. See the explanation for answer B for additional information on arguments for the stored procedure sp_helprotect.

B. **Correct:** The stored procedure sp_helpprotect provides information about user permissions for object or statement permissions. The first two arguments have NULL placeholders. The first argument is used when you want to specify the name of an object or statement. The second argument is used when you want to specify the name of a security account to which permissions have been granted. The third argument is used to specify the security account of the user who granted permissions. A fourth argument is used when you want to specify the type of permission, such as object permission or statement permission.

C. **Incorrect:** This command would provide a list of permissions granted by Miguel, but it would only include object permissions and not statement permissions. See the explanation for answer B for additional information on arguments for the stored procedure sp_helprotect.

D. **Incorrect:** This command would provide a list of permissions granted to an object named Miguel, and it would not return any records unless there was an object in the database, such as a table or view, named Miguel. See the explanation for answer B for additional information on arguments for the stored procedure sp_helprotect.

70-228.05.06.003

▶ **Correct Answers: B and D**

A. **Incorrect:** Explicitly granting SELECT access to the Melissa user account will not allow Melissa to select information from the Partners view because access has been denied to the Paralegal role. The DENY permission takes precedence.

B. **Correct:** The Paralegal role was granted SELECT access to the Associates table, and the Melissa user account was not explicitly denied SELECT access.

C. **Incorrect:** UPDATE permission was revoked from the Melissa user account. However, because the Paralegal role was granted UPDATE access to the Associates table, the permission is inherited from Melissa's membership in the Paralegal role. A revoked permission does not stop inheritance from a higher level.

D. **Correct:** The denied DELETE permission was revoked from the Melissa user account and from the Paralegal role.

70-228.05.06.004

► **Correct Answers: A and B**

A. **Correct:** Members of the fixed server role diskadmin do not have permissions to execute any T-SQL statements, only certain stored procedures.

B. **Correct:** Members of the fixed server role setupadmin do not have permissions to execute any T-SQL statements, only certain stored procedures.

C. **Incorrect:** Members of the fixed server role processadmin have implied permissions to issue the T-SQL KILL statement to end an active SQL Server process.

D. **Incorrect:** Members of the fixed server role bulkadmin have implied permissions to issue the T-SQL BULK INSERT statement.

OBJECTIVE 5.7

Manage security auditing.

Microsoft SQL Server 2000 provides administrators with applications that can be used to monitor and detect activity that could possibly compromise the security of a SQL Server database. This capability is crucial to the successful implementation of any security plan.

The **SQL Server Profiler** application not only monitors SQL Server transactions, but it can also be configured to monitor specific user events including:

- The origin of a specific event (for example, the computer name of the workstation sending the request)

- The actual text of the SQL statement being passed

- The name of the user who caused the event to occur

- The date and time of the event

- The success or failure of the event

- The object being accessed

Using the preceding information along with additional security events captured by the Profiler, an administrator can view exactly what a user is doing or attempting to do.

When configuring the Profiler to audit an event, administrators should keep in mind the effect the audit will have on the overall performance of the server. The more events you choose to audit, the greater the performance degradation of the system.

You can also use **Microsoft Windows Application log** to view SQL Server activity. SQL Server can be configured to write new events to specific logs including the Security log. Administrators can use the Security log to view failed logon attempts.

Objective 5.7 Questions

70-228.05.07.001

The administrator for a SQL Server 2000 server wants to view audit information for the SQL Server. Which of the following tools or log files will not provide the administrator with this information?

A. SQL Profiler

B. Windows 2000 Security log

C. SQLSTP.LOG file

D. error log file

70-228.05.07.002

Your SQL Server is crashing. As part of your debugging process, you start the server in minimal configuration using the –f option of SQLSEVR.EXE..How will auditing be affected for the SQL Server?

A. Only users logging on with Windows accounts will be audited.

B. Only users authenticated with SQL Server logons will be audited.

C. Auditing will not run.

D. Only DBCC events will be audited.

70-228.05.07.003

You want to change the auditing configuration for SQL Server 2000 in the Marketing department. Which of the following methods would you use to accomplish this?

A. xp_loginconfig

B. SQL Server Enterprise Manager

C. xp_logininfo

D. xp_msver

70-228.05.07.004

You must assign a user in the Engineering group to enable or modify events to be audited with the ENGI-NEERING SQL Server. To which fixed server role would you assign this person to allow this ability?

A. sysadmin

B. serveradmin

C. processadmin

D. bulkadmin

Objective 5.7 Answers

70-228.05.07.001

▶ **Correct Answers: C**

A. **Incorrect:** The SQL Profiler utility enables administrators to track and record SQL Server activity including logon attempts and access to SQL Server objects and statements.

B. **Incorrect:** SQL Server can be configured to store audit information in the Event Viewer Security log.

C. **Correct:** The SQLSTP.LOG file stores information regarding SQL Server installations performed on that server; no audit information is recorded to the log file.

D. **Incorrect:** The error log file stores error information related to SQL Server activity.

70-228.05.07.002

▶ **Correct Answers: C**

A. **Incorrect:** See the explanation for answer C.

B. **Incorrect:** See the explanation for answer C.

C. **Correct:** The –f option starts SQL Server with a minimal configuration; this will prevent auditing from occurring for the SQL Server.

D. **Incorrect:** See the explanation for answer C.

70-228.05.07.003

▶ **Correct Answers: B**

A. **Incorrect:** You can view the security configuration for a server including auditing information, but you cannot modify or set any auditing.

B. **Correct:** Enterprise Manager allows you to view, modify, and set the auditing configuration for a SQL server.

C. **Incorrect:** You can only view detailed information for a particular account that has access to the SQL server.

D. **Incorrect:** The stored procedure xp_msver returns the Microsoft SQL Server version information.

70-228.05.07.004

▶ **Correct Answers: A**

A. **Correct:** Only members of the sysadmin role can edit, create, or delete an event to be audited.

B. **Incorrect:** Members of the serveradmin role can change SQL Server configurations, but they cannot audit properties.

C. **Incorrect:** Users in the processadmin fixed server role can monitor and kill SQL Server processes.

D. **Incorrect:** Users assigned the fixed server role of bulkadmin can execute BULK INSERT statements into the database.

OBJECTIVE DOMAIN 6

Managing, Monitoring, and Troubleshooting SQL Server 2000

You can automate SQL Server administrative tasks that occur regularly and that can be administered through programming languages by using jobs, alerts, and operators. For example, you can create jobs to back up all SQL Server databases and schedule them to run on a recurring basis. On completion or failure of a job, an operator can be e-mailed or paged. SQL Server Agent is responsible for coordinating and carrying out these tasks.

Using various tools, including Windows NT Performance Monitor and Windows 2000 System Monitor, you can review the performance of SQL Server. Monitoring allows you to gather baseline information about your current configuration. As changes to a database are made, monitoring can help determine whether the servers and database applications are working efficiently, and if the current configuration will be able to handle additional users or an increase in server workload.

Bottlenecks on system resources are bound to occur. Monitoring of disk I/O activity, CPU usage, and memory usage can help determine where bottlenecks exist. For example, a CPU that is constantly reporting 100 percent utilization may indicate the need for an upgrade to a faster CPU or the addition of multiple processors.

Tested Skills and Suggested Practices

The skills that you need to successfully master the Managing, Monitoring, and Troubleshooting SQL Server 2000 objective domain on the *Installing, Configuring, and Administering Microsoft SQL Server 2000 Enterprise Edition* exam include:

- **Creating, managing, and troubleshooting SQL Server Agent jobs.**

- Practice 1: Use Enterprise Manager to create a new job with one job step to back up the Northwind database.

- Practice 2: Use the stored procedure sp_add_jobschedule to execute the job created in Practice 1 every day at 11:00 P.M.

- Practice 3: Manually execute the job created in Practice 1 and view the job history.

- **Configuring alerts and operators by using SQL Server Agent.**

  - Practice 1: Create a new operator and configure the operator to receive alert notification through Net Send.

  - Practice 2: Create an alert that notifies the newly created operator when the number of users connected to SQL Server exceeds 10.

  - Practice 3: Generate activity on the SQL Server that will cause the alert to be sent to the operator.

- **Optimizing hardware resource usage.**

  - Practice 1: Run Performance Monitor or System Monitor to monitor disk activity. Use the counters for Physical Disk: %Disk Time and Physical Disk: Avg. Disk Queue Length to detect bottlenecks within the disk subsystem.

  - Practice 2: Run Performance Monitor or System Monitor to monitor CPU usage. Use the Processor: % Processor counter to monitor the amount of time the CPU spends processing a nonidle thread.

  - Practice 3: Run Performance Monitor or System Monitor to monitor memory usage. Use the SQL Server: Memory Manager: Total Server Memory to determine the total amount of dynamic memory the server is currently using.

- **Optimizing and troubleshooting SQL Server system activity.**

  - Practice 1: Launch SQL Profiler and create a trace that monitors activity occurring on the SQL server.

  - Practice 2: Create several queries that will retrieve data from several tables in the Northwind database. You should run the queries within a loop, thus creating continuous requests to the server. Using the Profiler, monitor the system for the query with the highest duration time.

  - Practice 3: Using Windows Performance Monitor, monitor the SQL Server machine for processor utilization while the queries are running.

Further Reading

This section lists supplemental readings by objective. We recommend that you study these sources thoroughly before taking exam 70-228.

Objective 6.1

Microsoft SQL Server 2000 product documentation. To access Books Online, click the Start button, point to Programs, then Microsoft SQL Server, and then select Books Online. Select the Contents tab and expand Administering SQL Server, then Automating Administrative Tasks, and then Implementing Jobs. This volume contains the articles "Creating Jobs" and "Creating Job Steps." These articles discuss ways to create jobs and job steps and include links to examples using both T-SQL and Enterprise Manager.

Part 1: Self-Paced Training for Microsoft SQL Server 2000 System Administration. Chapter 13, "Automating Administrative Tasks," Lesson 2 reviews creating and managing SQL Server Agent jobs.

Objective 6.2

Microsoft SQL Server 2000 product documentation. To access Books Online, click the Start button, point to Programs, then Microsoft SQL Server, and then select Books Online. Select the Contents tab and expand Administering SQL Server, then Automating Administrative Tasks, and then Responding to Events. This volume contains articles on defining, modifying, and viewing operators, alerts, and events.

Part 1: Self-Paced Training for Microsoft SQL Server 2000 System Administration. Chapter 13, "Automating Administrative Tasks," Lesson 1 covers the methods through which operators can be notified, and Lesson 3 reviews the events to which SQL Server can alert administrators.

Objective 6.3

Microsoft SQL Server 2000 product documentation. To access Books Online, click the Start button, point to Programs, then Microsoft SQL Server, and then select Books Online. Select the Contents tab and expand Administering SQL Server, then Monitoring Server Performance and Activity, and then Monitoring with System Monitor. This volume contains articles on the different resources that can be monitored by System Monitor and a subsection "Using SQL Server Objects" that details the individual SQL Server Objects and their counters.

Part 1: Self-Paced Training for Microsoft SQL Server 2000 System Administration. Chapter 14, "Monitoring SQL Server Performance and Activity,"" Lesson 2 reviews detecting performance bottlenecks.

Objective 6.4

Microsoft SQL Server 2000 product documentation. To access Books Online, click the Start button, point to Programs, then Microsoft SQL Server, and then select Books Online. Select the Contents tab and expand Administering SQL Server, then Monitoring Server Performance and Activity, and then Evaluating Performance. This topic contains articles on establishing a performance baseline, identifying bottlenecks, and determining user activity. Also, select the volume "Monitoring with SQL Profiler" for detailed information on the SQL Profiler tool.

Part 1: Self-Paced Training for Microsoft SQL Server 2000 System Administration. Chapter 14, "Monitoring SQL Server Performance and Activity," Lesson 3 reviews the various tools available to monitor SQL Server Performance.

Create, manage, and troubleshoot SQL Server Agent jobs.

SQL Server Agent jobs automate administrative tasks and specify run times at recurring intervals or in response to alerts. Jobs consist of one or more job steps, which include operating system commands, T-SQL statements, Microsoft **ActiveX scripts**, or replication tasks, performed in order of execution by SQL Server Agent. Job execution order is determined by what the job owner specifies as the action to be taken when an individual job step succeeds or fails.

To execute a job, there must be at least one job step. You can create jobs and job steps through Enterprise Manager or by executing the stored procedures **sp_add_job** and **sp_add_jobstep**. You can also organize jobs into job categories to make management easier. Only the owner of a job or members of the fixed server role sysadmin can start or stop a job, modify a job, or assign ownership of a job to another user. You can reassign ownership through Enterprise Manager, or members of the sysadmin role can execute the stored procedure **sp_manage_jobs_by_login**.

When creating job steps that include operating system commands, you must specify the **CmdExec** command as well as the full path to all executables. Job steps that include T-SQL commands must specify the database in which to execute the job. Job steps that execute ActiveX scripts must specify the language in which the ActiveX script is written, such as Microsoft Visual Basic Script or Microsoft JScript. Replication job steps can execute the Distribution agent, the Log Reader agent, the Merge agent, the Queue Reader agent, or the Snapshot agent. Replication jobs are automatically created when you create a publication using replication.

You can schedule jobs to run by using Enterprise Manager or by executing the stored procedure **sp_add_jobschedule**. In addition to scheduling jobs based on a time, you can define jobs to run when SQL Server Agent starts or when CPU resources are at a level you have defined as idle. You can view jobs and job history through Enterprise Manager or by executing **sp_help_job** or **sp_help_jobhistory**. The SQL Server Agent error log records error and warning messages, which can be used to troubleshoot specific job problems.

If you are managing two or more servers running multiple instances of SQL Server and want to use multiserver administration, you must designate at least one master server and at least one target server. A master server stores the central copy of a job definition and distributes the jobs to target servers. Target servers periodically connect to a master server to update their list of jobs to be performed and to report the status of jobs they have executed.

Objective 6.1 Questions

70-228.06.01.001

In which of the following circumstances can SQL Server Agent jobs be set to run? (Choose all that apply.)

A. When SQL Server Agent starts.

B. When CPU utilization is at a level you have defined as idle.

C. You can manually set a job to start, even if the job is already running through a scheduled job.

D. You set a job to run once at a specified date and time.

70-228.06.01.002

In a multiserver administration environment, you execute the stored procedure sp_add_jobstep to add a new step to an existing job on a master server. To ensure that all target servers have the most current job definitions, which of the following commands should you run?

A. sp_update_job

B. sp_post_msx_operation

C. sp_help_job

D. It is not necessary to run a command to update target servers. The stored procedure sp_add_jobstep posts the required changes to the download list automatically.

70-228.06.01.003

Mary is responsible for automating the backup of the Real_Estate database.

She wants to accomplish the following goals:

- Create a new category to organize administrative jobs related to the Real_Estate database.

- Create a job to back up the Real_Estate database.

- Assign the backup job to the category created for the Real_Estate database.

- Send failed events for the backup job to the Windows Application log.

Mary issues the following commands:

```
USE msdb
EXEC sp_add_category 'JOB', 'LOCAL', 'Real Estate Admin'
EXEC sp_add_job @job_name='Real Estate Backup', @category_name='Real Estate Admin',
@notify_level_netsend=1
EXEC sp_add_jobstep @job_name='Real Estate Backup', @step_name='Backup',
@sub-system='TSQL', @command='BACKUP DATABASE [REAL_ESTATE] to [REBACKUP]'
```

Which of the following goals have been met? (Choose all that apply.)

A. A new category was created to organize administrative jobs related to the Real_Estate database.

B. A job was created to back up the Real_Estate database.

C. The backup job was assigned to the category for administration of the Real_Estate database.

D. Failed events for the backup job are sent to the Windows Application log.

70-228.06.01.004

Which database does SQL Server use to store job definitions?

A. Jobs are stored in the msdb database.

B. Jobs are stored in the master database.

C. Jobs are stored in the specific database for which the job was designed to run.

D. Jobs are stored as operating system files and are not part of any database.

70-228.06.01.005

Using a nonsysadmin logon account, Ron creates and schedules a SQL Server Agent job in which one of the steps issues a CmdExec command to run a batch file to stop and start various services. Which of the following is required for Ron to successfully run the job he created?

A. Ron needs to be a member of the sysadmin fixed server role.

B. SQL Server Agent must be configured to allow nonsysadmin logon accounts permission to run CmdExec job steps.

C. Ron needs to be a member of the serveradmin fixed server role.

D. Ron can run the job successfully without any additional configuration or rights.

Objective 6.1 Answers

70-228.06.01.001

▶ **Correct Answers: A, B, and D**

   A. **Correct:** You can set a job to start automatically when SQL Server Agent starts.

   B. **Correct:** You can set a job to start when CPU usage becomes idle. Enterprise Manager is used to set CPU idle time and duration. An idle CPU condition is specified by the percentage that the average CPU usage must remain below and the duration in seconds before the computer is considered idle.

   C. **Incorrect:** You can run a job manually, but only one instance of a job can be running at a time. SQL Server Agent will refuse the request to run a job that is already running.

   D. **Correct:** You can set a job to start at a specific date and time or on a recurring schedule.

70-228.06.01.002

▶ **Correct Answers: B**

   A. **Incorrect:** The stored procedure sp_update_job is used to change the attributes of a job, such as the name, assigned category, or notification method.

   B. **Correct:** The stored procedure sp_post_msx_operation will post the changes to the download list so that target servers can download the updated job. Posting changes to the download list manually is only necessary if the job modifications are made by using sp_add_jobstep, sp_update_jobstep, sp_add_jobschedule, sp_update_jobschedule, or sp_delete_jobschedule. The stored procedures sp_update_job and sp_delete_job automatically post changes to the download list, so running the sp_post_msx_operation is not necessary when running these stored procedures.

   C. **Incorrect:** The stored procedure sp_help_job returns information about defined jobs including job name, job type, owner, and job status.

   D. **Incorrect:** The stored procedure sp_add_jobstep does not post changes to the download list automatically. The only stored procedures that post changes to the download list automatically are sp_update_job and sp_delete_job.

70-228.06.01.003

▶ **Correct Answers: A, B, and C**

   A. **Correct:** The stored procedure sp_add_category is used to add a category of jobs, alerts, and operators to SQL Server.

   B. **Correct:** The stored procedure sp_add_job is used to create a new job, and the stored procedure sp_add_jobstep is used to add an operation to the job.

C. **Correct:** The stored procedure sp_add_job accepts the argument @category_name, which specifies to which category the job should be assigned.

D. **Incorrect:** The argument @notify_level_netsend is used to send a network message upon the completion of a job. The value of 1 indicates to send the message on success. In order to place an entry in the Windows Application log upon a failure, the stored procedure sp_add_job needs the argument @notify_level_eventlog with a value of 2.

70-228.06.01.004

▶ ## Correct Answers: A

A. **Correct:** Jobs are stored in the msdb database. When the SQL Server Agent service starts, it queries the system tables in the msdb database to determine which jobs to enable.

B. **Incorrect:** Jobs are stored in the msdb database, not the master database.

C. **Incorrect:** Though certain job steps may be specific to a database, jobs are not database dependent and are not stored in specific databases.

D. **Incorrect:** Jobs are stored in the system tables of the msdb database.

70-228.06.01.005

▶ ## Correct Answers: B

A. **Incorrect:** Being a member of the sysadmin fixed server role would allow Ron to run the job successfully, but it is not required in order to run CmdExec job steps. SQL Server needs to be configured to allow nonsysadmin logon accounts permission to run CmdExec job steps.

B. **Correct:** Configuring SQL Server Agent to allow nonsysadmin accounts permission to run CmdExec and ActiveScripting job steps is done through SQL Server Agent properties within Enterprise Manager.

C. **Incorrect:** The serveradmin fixed server role allows server-wide configuration options to be set. This would not allow Ron to run the job successfully.

D. **Incorrect:** Unless SQL Server is configured to allow nonsysadmin logon accounts permission to run CmdExec job steps, Ron cannot run the job successfully.

OBJECTIVE 6.2

Configure alerts and operators by using SQL Server Agent.

An important management feature of Microsoft SQL Server 2000 is its ability to alert administrators when a specific task or event occurs. Tasks include the completion of database backup and restoration jobs, the completion of an integrity check, and the completion of a custom command. Events that an administrator can be alerted to are usually severity 19 or higher **sysmessages** errors, any **RAISERROR** statement invoked by using the WITH LOG syntax, or any application logged using **xp_logevent**.

To create an alert in Microsoft SQL Server 2000, in Enterprise Manager, select the SQL server on which you want to create the alert, open the Management folder, and right-click on SQL Server Agent. Choose New and then Alert. When you create an alert using Enterprise Manager, you are also able to define how to notify the user of the alert. Using T-SQL, you can execute the **sp_add_alert** system stored procedure to create an alert. After creating the alert, execute the **sp_add_notification** to create a notification for the alert. To execute either the sp_add_alert or sp_add_notification, you must be a member of the **sysadmin** fixed server role.

After specifying the task or event for the alert, you must specify the recipient of the alert notification. SQL Server 2000 assigns users, known as operators, to receive alert notification. Alerts can notify an operator of an event by using three methods:

- **e-mail notification**   An operator is sent an e-mail notification of the alert. The SQL Server must be configured with a MAPI-1 compliant e-mail client for this to take place.

- **pager notification**   Microsoft SQL Server sends out pager notification by generating an e-mail addressed to the pager. You must have third-party pager-to-e-mail software and/or hardware configured on the SQL Server.

- **net send notification**   To use net send notifications, you must be running Windows NT 4.0 or Windows 2000. Net send notifications are only useful if you know the user will be logged on to his or her machine. Noncritical notifications should be sent using the net send method.

When adding an operator to the SQL Server, you can use Enterprise Manager or the **sp_add_operator** system stored procedure. To execute the sp_add_operator stored procedure, you must be a member of the sysadmin fixed server role. Under specific circumstances, SQL Server Agent may not be able to successfully send pager notifications to the defined operators of the SQL Server. In this case, the SQL Server Agent then proceeds to notify the **fail-safe operator**, which the SQL Server administrator defines. Once defined as the fail-safe operator, the user cannot be deleted unless another user is specified.

Objective 6.2 Questions

70-228.06.02.001

Jessica is the database administrator for an e-commerce-based application. The database is portioned across four SQL Server 2000 machines.

Jessica wants to accomplish the following goals:

- Specify her own SQL Server account as the operator for the master SQL Server Agent.

- Be notified by an alert if any one of the processors on any of the SQL servers records 90 percent utilization for 30 seconds or higher.

- Be notified by an alert sending an e-mail to her Internet e-mail account.

Jessica executes the sp_add_operator system stored procedure to add herself as an operator for the master SQL Server Agent. She installs and configures a MAPI-1 compliant e-mail client on each of the servers. She then creates the alert using the sp_add_alert stored procedure.

Which of the following goals are accomplished?

A. Jessica is added as an operator who is capable of sending out alerts regarding both the local and remote SQL servers.

B. Jessica will be notified if the processor in any of the remote SQL servers goes beyond 90 percent utilization.

C. If a processor on the local machine goes beyond the established threshold, Jessica will be notified by e-mail.

D. None of the goals is achieved.

70-228.06.02.002

You are adding three SQL Server 2000 machines to handle the increased seasonal load on your organization's e-commerce Web site. You have configured several operators and alerts on the SQL Server named SQL1. Which of the following methods can you use to duplicate alert and operator information from SQL1 to the three new SQL servers?

A. Generate a SQL script of all of the operators and alerts created on the SQL1.

B. Copy the Sysobjects table from SQL1 to each of the three new SQL servers.

C. Copy the Sqlagent_info table from SQL1 to each of the three new SQL servers.

D. Copy the Sysalerts table from SQL1 to each of the three new SQL servers.

70-228.06.02.003

You have created an alert on a SQL Server 2000 machine that will notify you by e-mail if the available memory falls below 200 MB and stays below 200 MB for over 10 seconds. What may happen if the memory utilization falls below 200 MB and stays that way for 15 seconds?

A. You will receive an e-mail alert every five seconds.

B. You may not receive notification of the low memory availability.

C. You will not be notified by e-mail; however, an entry will be written to the Windows Event log for the server.

D. You will always be notified of the alert.

70-228.06.02.004

Alison, Dylan, and Jordan are administrators of a Microsoft SQL Server 2000 machine. All three are defined as operators on the server, and each is configured to be alerted by the SQL Server Agent via a pager if an alert is generated. Under what circumstance will the fail-safe operator be notified of an alert?

A. If one of the three operators is deleted

B. If the SQL Server Agent cannot access the Sysoperators system table in the msdb database

C. If the SQL Server Agent service is not running

D. If the SQL Server Agent cannot access the Sysnotifications system table in the msdb database

Objective 6.2 Answers

70-228.06.02.001

▶ **Correct Answers: C**

A. **Incorrect:** Running the sp_add_operator only creates an operator for that local server. If you want SQL Server Agent to notify you of activity taking place on remote servers, you must also execute sp_add_targetsvrgrp_member and sp_msx_enlist along with the sp_add_operator stored procedures.

B. **Incorrect:** Because the operator was not configured correctly, Jessica cannot be notified of activity occurring on a remote server.

C. **Correct:** Because a MAPI-1 compliant e-mail client was configured on the server, SQL Server 2000 will be able to send e-mail alerts to designated users successfully.

D. **Incorrect:** One of the goals is achieved.

70-228.06.02.002

▶ **Correct Answers: A**

A. **Correct:** By right-clicking the Operators object in the Management folder of SQL Server Enterprise Manager, administrators can choose to generate SQL scripts to create one or all of the operators and alerts that have been defined.

B. **Incorrect:** The Sysobjects table contains one row for each object created in the database. Objects include constraints, logs, rules, stored procedures, and default objects.

C. **Incorrect:** The Sqlagent_info table does not contain information regarding operators created on that local SQL server.

D. **Incorrect:** This will only create alerts that are corrupted.

70-228.06.02.003

▶ **Correct Answers: B**

A. **Incorrect:** See the explanation for answer B.

B. **Correct:** Unless a performance counter maintains a value for at least 20 seconds, the SQL Server Agent may fail to see a counter cross the specified threshold. For you to be alerted each time the memory falls below 200 MB for over 10 seconds, the memory availability counter would need to maintain its value for 20 seconds each time.

C. **Incorrect:** See the explanation for answer B.

D. **Incorrect:** See the explanation for answer B.

70-228.06.02.004

▶ **Correct Answers: D**

A. **Incorrect:** See the explanation for answer D.

B. **Incorrect:** See the explanation for answer D.

C. **Incorrect:** If the SQL Server Agent service is not running, the server will fail to monitor for specified alerts, and operators will not be notified.

D. **Correct:** The fail-safe operator is notified of an alert under two circumstances: the operator responsible for the alert could not be paged, and the SQL Server Agent could not gain access to the Sysnotifications table.

OBJECTIVE 6.3

Optimize hardware resource usage.

SQL Server provides objects and counters that are used by Windows NT Performance Monitor and Windows 2000 System Monitor to measure the performance of hardware resources including processor utilization, disk I/O activity, and memory usage. You should use these tools to set thresholds on counters and configure system alerts when performance exceeds thresholds.

Bottlenecks in memory can occur when SQL Server does not have enough physical memory to store frequently accessed data in cache. The SQL Server **Memory Manager object** provides counters to monitor memory usage. For example, the counter **Target Server Memory** reports the total amount of dynamic memory the server can use, whereas the counter **Total Server Memory** reports the total amount of dynamic memory the server is currently using.

The **Buffer Manager object** provides counters to report database page reads and writes and monitors physical disk I/O activity. For example, the counter **Buffer Cache Hit Ratio** reports the percentage of database pages found in cache without having to read from a disk. The goal is to have a consistently high ratio because it is much faster to read from cache than from a disk. Increasing the amount of memory available to SQL Server can increase the buffer cache hit ratio. **Page Reads/sec** and **Page Writes/sec** are two Buffer Manager object counters that measure the number of physical database page reads and writes per second. If increasing the cache does not decrease the number of physical page reads and writes, then you should consider changing indexes, optimizing queries, or modifying the database design.

Examine processor utilization periodically to identify potential bottlenecks. Processor bottlenecks can occur from the type of work SQL Server performs. For example, queries requiring a large number of calculations may cause processor utilization to reach 100 percent. Consistently high processor utilization may affect other applications running on the same server, perhaps creating the need for a dedicated SQL Server or adding additional processors. You can use the processor counter **% User Time** to measure the amount of time the processor spends executing user processes, such as SQL Server tasks.

Objective 6.3 Questions

70-228.06.03.001

System Monitor is consistently reporting over 90 percent for the counter Physical Disk: %Disk Time, indicating a bottleneck within the disk subsystem. Which of the following counters would you use to isolate the amount of disk activity being generated by SQL Server components?

A.   SQL Server Memory Manager counter SQL Cache Memory

B.   SQL Server Cache Manager counter Cache Use Counts/sec

C.   SQL Server Buffer Manager counters Page Reads/sec and Page Writes/sec

D.   SQL Server Database counter Transactions/sec

70-228.06.03.002

Which of the following SQL Server objects contains the SQL Cache Memory counter?

A.   Memory Manager object

B.   Buffer Manager object

C.   Cache Manager object

D.   Database object

70-228.06.03.003

The counters Physical Disk: Current Disk Queue Length and %Disk are both consistently high on a SQL server configured with a hardware implementation of RAID 5. Which of the following might help to eliminate this type of bottleneck? (Choose all that apply.)

A.   Use faster disk drives.

B.   Add additional disks to the RAID.

C.   Add additional memory.

D.   Add an additional processor.

70-228.06.03.004

SQL Server is configured so that memory is not allocated dynamically. The min server memory and max server memory options have both been set to 128 MB. While running System Monitor, you notice that the Process: Working Set counter for SQL Server is consistently below the amount of memory SQL Server is configured to use. What does this indicate?

A. This indicates that SQL Server is not configured with enough memory.

B. This indicates that SQL Server memory is optimally configured.

C. This indicates that SQL Server is configured to use more memory than it needs.

D. This indicates that the set working set size option was configured so that Windows 2000 does not swap out SQL Server pages.

Objective 6.3 Answers

70-228.06.03.001

► **Correct Answers: C**

A. **Incorrect:** This counter displays the total amount of dynamic memory the server is using for the dynamic SQL cache.

B. **Incorrect:** This counter displays the number of times each type of cache object has been used.

C. **Correct:** These counters show the disk activity being generated by SQL Server by displaying the total number of physical page reads and writes per second across all SQL Server databases.

D. **Incorrect:** This counter displays the number of transactions started for a database per second.

70-228.06.03.002

► **Correct Answers: A**

A. **Correct:** The Memory Manager object provides counters to monitor overall server memory usage.

B. **Incorrect:** The Buffer Manager object provides counters to monitor the physical I/O activity for SQL Server database reads and writes as well as how SQL Server uses memory to store data pages and the procedure cache.

C. **Incorrect:** The Cache Manager object provides counters to monitor how SQL Server uses memory to store objects including stored procedures, triggers, and T-SQL statements.

D. **Incorrect:** The Database object provides counters to monitor backup and restore throughput, transaction log activities, and bulk-copy operations.

70-228.06.03.003

▶ **Correct Answers: A and B**

A. **Correct:** Consistently high values for both Current Disk Queue Length and %Disk counters indicate a bottleneck with the disk subsystem. Increasing the speed of the disk drives should help alleviate the bottleneck.

B. **Correct:** Adding additional disks to the RAID would help spread data across more disks, thereby improving read/write performance.

C. **Incorrect:** Because the bottleneck is related to the disk subsystem, it is unlikely that adding additional memory will resolve the bottleneck.

D. **Incorrect:** Because the bottleneck is related to the disk subsystem and the RAID is implemented at the hardware level, thereby not utilizing the CPU as would a software-based RAID, it is unlikely that adding an additional processor will resolve the bottleneck.

70-228.06.03.004

▶ **Correct Answers: C**

A. **Incorrect:** See the explanation for answer C

B. **Incorrect:** See the explanation for answer C.

C. **Correct:** The Working Set counter shows the amount of memory being used by the SQL Server process. The counter is consistently showing that the SQL Server process is using less memory than what the min server memory option is set to, which indicates that the SQL server is configured to use more memory than it needs.

D. **Incorrect:** The set working set size option is used to reserve physical memory space for SQL Server equal to the server memory setting, which in this case is 128 MB for both min and max server memory options. By setting this option, Windows 2000 will not swap out SQL Server pages to other processes, even if SQL Server is idle. The fact that the Working Set counter was reporting a value below the min server memory option indicates that the set working set size option was not configured.

Optimize and troubleshoot SQL Server system activity.

After putting a SQL server into production, you may start to notice system degradation. This degradation can be produced by an unexpected load placed on the server, poor database design, or server settings that need to be reconfigured. When attempting to address issues with SQL Server system activity, administrators need to pinpoint the cause of the problem in order to correct it.

Two applications can help administrators quickly and accurately pinpoint problems with SQL Server system activity: **SQL Server Profiler** and **Windows Performance Monitor**. These specific applications allow administrators to monitor system activity and view what may be the cause of the issue they are trying to track down. For example, if clients are complaining about the response time of an application, the SQL Server administrator can launch the Profiler to view what is happening while a client is using the application. The administrator may find that there is a specific query that is taking an extremely long time to complete. Using this information, the administrator can then tune the query using other tools, such as Query Analyzer.

Although the Profiler relates detailed information for the type of activity occurring on the server, administrators can use Performance Monitor to view what effect this activity has on server resources. For example, an administrator may notice that a query with a long execution duration is causing SQL Server deadlocks to occur when the query is being executed, thus causing the prolonged wait time for query execution.

Understanding how to track down a problem is tantamount to the success an administrator will have in resolving the cause of a problem. Both SQL Server Profiler and Windows Performance Monitor have specific counters that help track down the most common system problems that occur on a SQL server.

Counters in Windows Performance Monitor that help diagnose SQL Server issues include:

- Processor: % Processor Time. Amount of time a specific processor spends processing a nonidle thread.

- System: Processor Queue Length. Number of threads waiting for processor time. A high processor queue length along with high processor utilization can indicate the need to upgrade or add processors.

- Processor: % Privileged Time. Percentage of time the CPU spends executing Windows kernel commands. A consistently high value for the counter in conjunction with the Physical Disk counters is a good indication that the SQL server could be I/O bound. One possible remedy would be to upgrade the disk subsystem, increasing the disk I/O rate.

- Memory: Available Bytes. Number of bytes of memory currently available for use by processes. Administrators can also choose to monitor the memory in kilobytes and megabytes. Monitoring this counter over time can be helpful when determining whether or not memory leaks exist in the system.

- Memory: Pages/sec. Number of pages that were retrieved from disk due to the hard page faults or written to disk to free space in the Working Set due to the page faults. A high rate may indicate excessive paging.

- Process: Page Faults/sec. Number of page faults for the SQL Server process instance. Monitoring this counter can help eliminate SQL Server as the cause of the excessive paging or another process running on the server.

Event and event classes that you can trace using the SQL Profiler include:

- Stored Procedures/SP:Starting. Indicates when the stored procedure being called has started.

- Stored Procedures/SP:Completed. Indicates when the stored procedure being executed has completed.

- Stored Procedure/SP:CacheMiss. If a stored procedure is not found in the procedure cache, a CacheMiss is recorded in the trace.

- Locks/Lock:Deadlock. An extremely useful event/event class when attempting to diagnose deadlocks occurring on the SQL server.

- Locks/Lock:Deadlock Chain. The actual events leading up to the deadlock are indicated in this field of the trace file.

Objective 6.4 Questions

70-228.06.04.001

Users are complaining about the performance of a client/server application you have deployed in-house. The biggest complaint is regarding the time it takes to retrieve the list of hardware manufacturers. You look at the schema to see whether or not an index is created for the table where hardware manufacturers are listed, and you find a clustered index has been created. You then monitor SQL Server activity using Windows 2000 Performance Monitor. You find that the processor queue length is constantly at three, and the average processor utilization for both processors is below 50 percent. What is the most efficient step to take to decrease processor queue length?

A. Add an additional processor to the server.

B. Monitor the system for SQL Server locking.

C. Increase the number of worker threads.

D. Increase the memory in the machine.

70-228.06.04.002

You work for a software company that has developed a client/server application to be used as a patient billing application within a hospital. A large hospital that has deployed the application is complaining that the response time for the SQL server seems to degrade as the day goes on. You decide to trace memory utilization on the machine. Which Windows 2000 Performance Monitor counter will provide information for memory utilization?

A. Context Switches/sec

B. Batch Requests/sec

C. Interrupts/sec

D. Buffer Cache Hit Ratio

70-228.06.04.003

You are fine-tuning a SQL Server 2000 database. Along with using Windows 2000 Performance Monitor, you are also using SQL Server Profiler. One issue you have noticed with the application accessing the database is the amount of time it takes to log on to the application. After talking with the developers, you discover that there are several queries being executed during the logon procedure. Using SQL Server Profiler, what counters can you monitor to find long-running SQL statements?

A. TSQL/RPC:BatchStarting and TSQL/RPC:Starting

B. TSQL/SQL:BatchCompleted and TSQL/RPC:Completed

C. TSQL/SQL:BatchCompleted and TSQL/RPC:Starting

D. TSQL/RPC:Starting and TSQL/RPC:Completed

70-228.06.04.004

Julian is the SQL Server administrator for a law firm that is storing its documentation on the database server. Recently, the law firm archived an additional 100,000 documents onto the server for a new project. This has caused an additional load to be placed on the SQL server, and now performance is suffering. Julian launches Windows 2000 Performance Monitor and monitors a number of counters. In doing so, he notices a high number of latch requests per second. What is this an indication of?

A. High processor utilization

B. Low network bandwidth

C. Insufficient available memory

D. Low Max Worker Thread value

70-228.06.04.005

You are monitoring your SQL Server 2000 server in an attempt to determine which queries are taking the most time to execute. You create a trace using SQL Server Profiler on the local server. How can you prevent the trace from monitoring SQL Server Query Analyzer?

A. Remove SQL Query Analyzer from the selected events you want to trace.

B. Remove the Application Name column from the data columns you want to capture.

C. Edit the General tab in the Trace Properties window.

D. Edit the Filters tab in the Trace Properties window.

Objective 6.4 Answers

70-228.06.04.001

▶ **Correct Answers: B**

A. **Incorrect:** If the processor utilization of the processors is below 50 percent and the processor queue length remains high, the problem will not be most effectively corrected by adding additional processors. An optimal system's processors should be running high, and the processor queue length should be zero or at times no higher than two.

B. **Correct:** Object locking with SQL Server can cause blocking. Therefore, if a process cannot execute because an object is locked, the processor queue length will remain high.

C. **Incorrect:** If processor utilization were above 80 percent, it would be possible that SQL is running out of threads to help process workload. However, because the utilization of the processors remains low, it is a good indication that there is a problem elsewhere.

D. **Incorrect:** A high processor queue length is usually an indication that a processor bottleneck exists and that you need additional processors in the server.

70-228.06.04.002

▶ **Correct Answers: D**

A. **Incorrect:** Context Switches/sec indicates the number of times per second the system has to change from executing one thread to executing another. Administrators may find that by enabling fibre-based scheduling in SQL Server, the number of context switches per second will drop.

B. **Incorrect:** Batch Requests/sec indicates the number of SQL batch requests that are being received by the SQL server.

C. **Incorrect:** Interrupts/sec indicates the number of hardware interrupts received by and processed by the SQL server's processor.

D. **Correct:** Buffer Cache Hit Ratio shows you the number of data pages that SQL Server requested that were already present in memory. This counter should remain above 80 percent. If the counter falls below 80 percent, your system may require additional memory.

70-228.06.04.003

▶ **Correct Answers: B**

A. **Incorrect:** See the explanation for answer B.

B. **Correct:** The TSQL/SQL:BatchCompleted counter tells you how long the execution of the SQL batch took to complete. The TSQL/RPC:Completed counter lets you know when the remote procedure call has been completed.

C. **Incorrect:** See the explanation for answer B.

D. **Incorrect:** It is necessary to know how long the actual SQL batch took to complete; simply monitoring the remote procedure calls will not be sufficient.

70-228.06.04.004

▶ **Correct Answers: C**

A. **Incorrect:** See the explanation for answer C.

B. **Incorrect:** See the explanation for answer C.

C. **Correct:** A high number of latch requests per second is an indication that the server is running low on memory, or the server's I/O capacity needs to be increased.

D. **Incorrect:** See the explanation for answer C.

70-228.06.04.005

▶ **Correct Answers: D**

A. **Incorrect:** SQL Server Query Analyzer cannot be removed from the selected events you want to trace on the Events tab in the Trace Properties window.

B. **Incorrect:** Removing the Application Name column from the data columns you want to capture will cause all application names from that data to be removed.

C. **Incorrect:** The General tab in the Trace Properties window does not allow you to include or exclude a trace event criteria, such as SQL Query Analyzer, from the trace.

D. **Correct:** The Filters tab in the Trace Properties window allows you to include or exclude the application name for the application that created the event.

A P P E N D I X

Questions and Answers

The following questions and answers are for Part 1 of this book.

Chapter 1: Overview of SQL Server 2000

Page 31

1. You are planning to deploy SQL Server 2000 to support Internet-based sales of your products. You need this installation to handle a large volume of transactions and to be available 24 x 7. Which edition of SQL Server 2000 should you choose?

   You should choose the Enterprise Edition because you need all of the high performance and fault-tolerant features of the Enterprise Edition.

2. You want to allow users to query SQL Server 2000 using their Internet browser via the Internet. What components of SQL Server 2000 are required?

   First of all, you need the SQL Server service. Next, you need to configure IIS to access SQL Server 2000 using some of the client communication components. The specific client communication components will depend on your specific configuration.

3. The SQL Server 2000 database environment has a physical design component and a logical design component. As a database administrator, one of your tasks is to optimize the performance of SQL Server 2000. With which type of database design do you have the most ability to affect performance?

   As the database administrator, you have the most ability to affect performance by optimizing the physical database component, including choice of hardware and placement of data and log files.

4. You have an existing server application that uses SQL Server 2000 running on Microsoft Windows 2000 servers. You have clients who access this server application using Windows 95 and Windows 98 client applications. You want to extend this server application to clients using an existing Novell network. What type of authentication decisions must you make?

   You must decide whether the clients who will access SQL Server 2000 from the Novell network will be authenticated by the Windows operating

system prior to attempting to access SQL Server 2000. If they will not be authenticated by the Windows operating system, you must configure SQL Server 2000 to use Mixed Mode authentication and provide each user with a SQL Server login.

Chapter 2: Installing SQL Server 2000

Page 71

1. You have decided to install SQL Server 2000 on a test computer to evaluate the new features available. You have a Pentium III 400-MHz laptop with 96 MB of memory. Will this laptop be sufficient for testing the new features of SQL Server 2000?

   Probably, but additional information is needed. The processor is fast enough for all editions and all Windows operating systems editions. However, the question does not tell us how much hard drive space is available on the laptop. Assuming enough space can be made available, this laptop could be used to install the Personal edition on any Windows operating system. This laptop does not have enough memory to properly test any SQL Server 2000 edition on any Windows 2000 Server edition. It does have sufficient memory to test any SQL Server 2000 edition on any Microsoft Windows NT 4.0 Server edition.

2. You are installing SQL Server 2000. You want it to be able to use your Microsoft Exchange Server to notify you when jobs succeed or fail. What type of account should you use for the SQL Server and SQL Server Agent services?

   You should use a domain user account for the SQL Server and SQL Server Agent services. A domain user account is required for access to Microsoft Exchange Server.

3. You are installing SQL Server 2000. You have a mixed network of computers including Windows NT servers and Novell servers. Your network supports both TCP/IP and NWLink IPX/SPX. Should you perform a typical or a Custom setup?

   If you want to configure support for NWLink IPX/SPX during setup, you must perform a Custom setup. The option to configure SQL Server 2000 to listen on NWLink IPX/SPX is not available when a Typical setup is performed. However, because all network libraries are installed during all types of setups, you can also use the Server Network Utility to configure NWLink IPX/SPX after SQL Server 2000 is installed. Finally, because your network supports TCP/IP as well as NWLink IPX/SPX, support for

TCP/IP might be sufficient for your needs without configuring NWLink IPX/SPX in SQL Server 2000.

4. You are installing SQL Server 2000. You have heard that SQL Server 2000 allows you to install SQL Server 2000 side by side with SQL Server 7.0. If you install SQL Server 2000 as a named instance, what issues should you be aware of?

Installing a named instance of SQL Server 2000 on the same computer as an installation of SQL Server 7.0 will replace all of the SQL Server 7.0 client tools and utilities with the SQL Server 2000 versions of these tools and utilities. It will also install the SQL Server 2000 version of Books Online in place of the SQL Server 7.0 Books Online. However, it will leave your SQL Server 7.0 databases intact and functioning using the SQL Server 7.0 database engine.

5. You are installing SQL Server 2000. You plan to install identical configurations on multiple computers to test the configuration's performance on different hardware platforms. You do not want to click your way through the SQL Server 2000 interactive Setup program each time you install SQL Server 2000. What should you do?

You should use the capability of the SQL Server 2000 Setup program to record an unattended .ISS file for you to use to perform unattended installations. This allows you to perform identical installations on multiple computers without having to interactively navigate your way through the SQL Server 2000 Setup program screens each time you install SQL Server 2000.

6. You have installed SQL Server 2000 on a test computer for evaluation. You had a problem initially starting the SQL Server service due to a logon failure. You solved the problem. You want to review the SQL Server error log related to the failure to start the SQL Server service. Can you do this, and if so, how?

You can use SQL Server Enterprise Manager or any text editor to review the current error log or any of the previous six error logs.

Chapter 3: Preparing to Use SQL Server 2000

Page 105

1. You have installed SQL Server 2000 on a test computer for evaluation. Gloria, another database administrator at your company, logged on to the SQL Server 2000 computer and attempted to review the new files that were added. She reports that she cannot view all of the files that were installed. Why might this be happening? Is there a problem?

The SQL Server 2000 Setup program locks down certain folders within the NTFS file system to prevent unauthorized tampering. Only the service account used by the SQL Server and SQL Server Agent services and members of the local Administrators group can access the unique program and data files for each instance. The reason Gloria cannot view all of the new files that were added is most likely because she is not a member of the local

Administrators group on the computer upon which SQL Server was installed. This is not a problem. This is by design. If Gloria will be administering this SQL Server 2000 installation, she might need to be added to the local Administrators group. However, she does not have to be a member of the local Administrators group to administer this SQL Server installation. Chapters 10 and 11 cover security in detail.

2. You have installed SQL Server 2000 on a test computer for evaluation. During installation, you used the local system account as the service account for the SQL Server and SQL Server Agent services. You have decided you need to configure and use a dedicated domain user account for these services. How should you change the service account for these services?

   You should use SQL Server Enterprise Manager to change the service account for both the SQL Server and the SQL Server Agent services. This will set the appropriate access permissions in the NTFS file system and the Windows registry for this dedicated domain user account. It will also update the Microsoft Search service with respect to the use of this domain user account by the SQL Server service.

3. You have installed SQL Server 2000 on a test computer for evaluation. You want to verify that you can connect to SQL Server 2000 and begin configuring objects in SQL Server 2000. What tool would you start with and why?

   You would probably begin with SQL Server Enterprise Manager. Although you could use Osql or SQL Query Analyzer to test connectivity, SQL Server Enterprise Manager is the primary tool for administering SQL Server 2000 objects.

Chapter 4: Upgrading to SQL Server 2000

Page 133

1. You are planning to upgrade your SQL Server 7.0 installation running on Windows NT 4.0 Server to SQL Server 2000. You want to test SQL Server 2000 on the same computer on which you currently have SQL Server 7.0 installed, and you need to keep the SQL Server 7.0 installation available for users. What issues do you need to consider?

   The first issue you need to consider is whether you need to upgrade the hardware or software to support SQL Server 2000. Windows NT 4.0 must be running Service Pack 5. Next, you must install SQL Server 2000 as a named instance. When you do this, you need to be aware that the Setup program will upgrade the SQL Server 7.0 client tools to SQL Server 2000 client tools. This includes SQL Server Enterprise Manager and SQL

Query Analyzer. Finally, you must have sufficient hard drive space for the named instance of SQL Server 2000.

2. You have recently performed a version upgrade of SQL Server 7.0 to SQL Server 2000. Although overall performance has improved, full-text searches are not working. Why might this be?

   During the version upgrade, full-text catalogs were disabled. You need to repopulate the full-text catalogs manually. Maintaining full-text catalogs is covered in Chapter 12.

3. You have decided that you cannot afford the downtime associated with a version upgrade of your SQL Server 7.0 installation and have decided to perform an online database upgrade of your production databases. What settings and objects will you have to re-create manually?

   You will have to re-create any server settings and SQL Server Agent jobs and alerts. Also, you cannot upgrade any databases involved in replication.

4. You have been testing SQL Server 2000 on the same computer on which you have been running your SQL Server 6.5 installation. You decide to upgrade your SQL Server 6.5 installation. However, you cannot locate the SQL Server Upgrade Wizard. It is not located on the Start menu and you cannot find it on your hard drive. Why?

   The SQL Server Upgrade Wizard is only installed when you install an instance of SQL Server 2000 as the default instance. The reason for this is that you can only upgrade to the default instance. If the wizard does not appear, you probably installed SQL Server 2000 as a named instance rather than the default instance.

Chapter 5: Understanding System and User Databases

Page 158

1. Describe the difference in the ordering of data pages from a table caused by using either a clustered index or a nonclustered index.

   A clustered index on a table causes the data pages (and the index pages) to be physically ordered in the data file based on the key value in the clustered index. A nonclustered index does not physically order the data pages. Only the index pages of the nonclustered index are physically ordered.

2. Which recovery model does not require regular backups of the transaction log?

   The Simple Recovery model does not rely on transaction log backups to truncate the transaction log. Rather, the checkpoint process automatically truncates the inactive portion of the logical log at the end of each checkpoint.

3. Why should you not create scripts that use Transact-SQL statements to directly query system tables?

You should not create scripts that use Transact-SQL statements to query system tables directly because the underlying system tables might change between releases of SQL Server. If such a change does occur, you would have to rewrite those scripts. Microsoft sometimes modifies system tables with new releases to add new functionality.

Chapter 6: Creating and Configuring User Databases

Page 196

1. You want to create a user database containing multiple data files on separate physical disks. You are not experienced at writing Transact-SQL statements. What is the simplest method you can use to create this database?

   Use the direct method in SQL Server Enterprise Manager. The Create Database Wizard does not allow you to create a database with multiple data files on separate disks, but the direct method does.

2. Describe the two methods you can use to change the database recovery model for a database.

   You can change the database recovery model for a database on the Options tab in the Properties dialog box for the database. You can also use the *ALTER DATABASE* Transact-SQL statement.

3. You created a new database on your system. You used the default properties for the transaction log file. You backed up the new database and the master database. After you performed a bulk load of data into your new database, you notice that the transaction log is quite large. Why did it grow so large and what must you do to reduce the size of the transaction log?

   The transaction log file grew so large because it was set to autogrow and because the recovery model was set to full. The bulk load operation was fully logged and generated many transaction log records. To reduce the size of the transaction log, you should first back up the transaction log file and then use the DBCC SHRINKFILE or DBCC SHRINKDATABASE command. You cannot shrink the transaction log using SQL Server Enterprise Manager.

4. You are managing a small database system running on Windows 2000 Server. Although the database is under 1 GB in space, it is very busy (primarily performing writes), and you want to improve its performance. You do not have the budget for a hardware RAID system and are not aware of specific database access patterns. You have already placed the transaction log file on a separate disk from the data file. What is an inexpensive solution?

   You can procure between three and six small disks. Set up a mirror of the transaction log files using the software RAID capabilities of Windows 2000 Server. Combine the remaining disks using RAID 0 and move the data file to this array. Because you have fault tolerance on the transaction log, the

lack of fault tolerance on the data files may be acceptable if the performance gain is significant.

Chapter 7: Populating a Database

Page 244

1. You are analyzing the data in a text file containing data that you want to import into your database. You have determined that the data is internally consistent but contains fields that are inconsistent with existing data in your database. The text file is representative of data that you will be importing weekly. What is your best solution for achieving the necessary data consistency? You have already determined that you cannot change the original data source.

   You have a number of options. You can use DTS to perform transformations of data during the import. You can use a text editor and manually perform a search and replace. You can import the data into a temporary table and use Transact-SQL to massage and scrub the data. Although each of these methods will work, DTS provides the most automated method and, because this is a task you will have to perform repeatedly, DTS provides the best solution.

2. Describe the difference between the On Success precedence constraint and the On Completion precedence constraint.

   A task that follows the On Success precedence constraint will only execute if the preceding task completes the task it intended to complete. A task that follows the On Completion precedence constraint will execute when the preceding task completes, regardless of whether that task achieved the task it intended to complete.

3. You have created and saved a simple data import and transform package that imports data from the spreadsheets maintained by your salespeople for expense reports. However, you want to add additional functionality to the package, including notifying an administrator after the entire sales staff has uploaded their expense reports. How might you accomplish this?

   You could use DTS Designer to edit the existing package to connect to multiple data sources (each salesperson's notebook) once per week and upload the expense report. You could use Message Queuing to queue a spreadsheet upload task that occurred weekly for each salesperson. When the last salesperson has uploaded data, the package could notify an administrator using the Send Mail task.

4. You have created a package that collects completed sales information from several different spreadsheet files used by salespeople in your company. After it collects this information, it inserts the collected information in one of your sales reporting databases. You want to distribute this package to your salespeople to execute regularly as part of their weekly reports. However, you do not want them to be able to open or edit the package. How should you save this package and how should you secure it?

You should save it as a structured storage file, using both an owner and a user password. You can then mail or otherwise distribute the package to your salespeople without the package being viewable or editable.

5. You want to import a large amount of data from a text file into a table that contains a clustered and a nonclustered index. The data being inserted exists in the text file in the same order as the clustered index. As part of the process, you first truncate the existing table to replace it with this new data. Should you drop each of the indexes before you insert the new data?

Because the table will be truncated prior to new data being inserted, you should drop the nonclustered index and rebuild it after the data insert is complete. However, you should not drop the clustered index. Rather, you should specify in your Bcp command or *BULK INSERT* statement that the data is already ordered.

Chapter 8: Developing a Data Restoration Strategy

Page 264

1. You are using RAID 1 for your transaction log and RAID 10 for your database. With this level of fault tolerance, why is it still critical to have a data restoration plan?

Using fault tolerance for your disk subsystem does not protect your data from all forms of disaster. For example, multiple disks could fail simultaneously, your disk subsystem could be stolen, or a natural disaster could strike. In addition, you might need to roll your database back to an earlier point in time because of user or application error.

2. You are developing your data recovery plan. You have tested the length of time required to perform a full database backup and determined that you can back up the entire database in six hours. You have decided to perform full database backups every night. You have also determined that you need to perform transaction log backups every 15 minutes to minimize the risk of data loss. Should you also use regular differential database backups as part of your data recovery plan?

It depends. The benefit of regular differential database backups is to speed the restoration process. If your database fails at 5:00 P.M., you will need to restore each transaction log backup since the full database backup the night before. If the transaction log backups are reasonably small and are either on a network file server or only on a few tapes, the benefit of differential database backups might not be significant. However, if you must

insert a separate tape for each transaction log backup or if each transac-tion log backup is large, performing a differential database backup every two hours could substantially reduce your data restoration time.

3. You are responsible for maintaining and restoring, if needed, a decision support database. Several different data sources regularly populate this database using DTS packages. What is the restoration benefit, if any, to using the Full Recovery model for this database given the substantial increase in the number and size of the transaction log backups required?

There is little restoration benefit in this scenario. All of the data in this database comes from existing data sources. If the Full Recovery model is not used and the entire database is lost because of some disaster, you can restore data to the point of the most recent transaction log backup. You can regenerate any more recent data relatively easily from the original data sources.

Chapter 9: Backing Up and Restoring SQL Server

Page 314

1. You regularly perform full, differential, and transaction log backups to disk. Are there any other backup tasks that you should perform regularly to protect your database from data loss?

Yes, you should regularly archive the backups from disk to tape for perma-nent storage. This will protect your backups in case the disk containing the backup files should fail.

2. You are a new database administrator. You want to create Transact-SQL scripts to automate the backup of your database. However, the syntax is imposing. What are several good methods for familiarizing yourself with the Transact-SQL syntax and the various backup options?

There are two excellent ways to become familiar with the available backup options and the Transact-SQL syntax. The first is to use SQL Server Enterprise Manager, including the Create Database Backup Wizard. This will assist you in understanding how each backup option works. The sec-ond is to use the sample Transact-SQL scripts in this chapter as well as SQL Server Books Online on a sample database and practice modifying and running backup scripts.

3. What is a major advantage to using SQL Server Enterprise Manager for per-forming database restorations, rather than Transact-SQL?

A major advantage to using SQL Server Enterprise Manager rather than Transact-SQL (other than not having to learn the Transact-SQL syntax) is

that SQL Server Enterprise Manager will use the backup history in the msdb database to assist you in selecting the necessary backup sets to perform a complete database restoration as quickly as possible.

4. What is the major difference between performing a restoration of the master database and all other databases?

You must start SQL Server 2000 in single-user mode to perform a master database restoration.

Chapter 10: Managing Access to SQL Server 2000

Page 355

1. You are concerned about keeping the data stored within your SQL Server 2000 installation extremely secure. All of the users who will access this data are Windows 2000 users. Should you permit SQL Server authentication? Why or why not?

Given the information in the question, the answer is no. The primary benefit to enabling SQL Server authentication is to permit users who will not be previously authenticated by the Windows operating system to access a SQL Server 2000 installation. The downside to permitting SQL Server authentication is significantly weaker security. This is primarily because of the lack of account policy protections that are enforced by Windows 2000 (or Windows NT 4.0) and the lack of encryption for user names and passwords on the wire (unless SSL is enabled for the entire session).

2. A member of the help desk staff has complained that although she can log on to SQL Server 2000 and access the Northwind and Pubs databases, she cannot even see the Northwind Reports database. How is this possible?

A user cannot see databases to which he or she has no access rights. In general, for this member of the help desk staff to see and access the Northwind Reports database, she must be granted direct rights to the database, be added to a Windows group that has access, or be added to a database role in that database. Enabling the guest user account in the Northwind Reports database will also enable the member of the helpdesk staff to see and access the Northwind Reports database.

3. You are creating a new SQL Server 2000 installation. Hundreds of users will require access to several different databases on this SQL Server 2000 instance. Should you use SQL Server Enterprise Manager or Transact-SQL system stored procedures for creating these login and user accounts? Why?

You should create Transact-SQL scripts rather than use SQL Server Enterprise Manager because you can create many users with a single script, whereas SQL Server Enterprise Manager would require hundreds of separate clicks to create this many users.

Chapter 11: Managing SQL Server Permissions

Page 389

1. You created a Windows 2000 security group for users of the SalesReporting database on your SQL Server 2000 installation and placed the sales managers in this group. You then granted this group access to SQL Server 2000 and the SalesReporting database. In addition, you made this group a member of the db_datawriter and db_datareader fixed database roles. Several members have complained that although they can access the data in each table and view in the database, they are only able to execute certain stored procedures, but not all. To make matters more complicated, one of the members of this group can execute all of the stored procedures without a problem. What are the likely causes of this problem?

   The problem begins with the fact that membership in the db_datawriter and db_datareader fixed database roles does not grant any permissions to execute stored procedures. Therefore, the problem must relate to permissions on the stored procedures themselves. It is likely that the public role has been granted execution rights on the stored procedures they are able to execute. With respect to the remaining stored procedures, either the member of the group that can execute them is receiving permission through membership in another group, or the members that cannot execute them belong to a group that has been denied the right to execute those specific stored procedures.

2. You need to grant certain users the ability to insert new data into a highly secure database. They also require very limited lookup rights to the data. You are concerned about security for this data. What is the most secure method you can use to allow the users to perform their task?

   You can create an application role with very specifically delimited rights to the database. You can work with a developer to create an application that only allows the users to perform the specific tasks they need to perform and have the custom application access the database using the application role and an encrypted password. Finally, you can ensure that none of the users of the application have any access rights to the SQL Server 2000 installation other than through the custom application.

3. You are designing a security strategy for your SQL Server 2000 installation. You are only allowing access to Windows 2000 users and groups. Is there any advantage to applying permissions to user-defined database groups rather than directly to Windows groups?

Possibly. If each different grouping of permissions maps directly to a single Windows 2000 group and you will never allow SQL Server logins, there is no advantage. However, if you might need to permit SQL Server logins in the future, or if there are multiple Windows 2000 groups that need the same grouping of permissions, assigning permissions to a user-defined database group will ease the administrative task over the life cycle of the SQL Server 2000 installation.

Chapter 12: Performing Administrative Tasks

Page 440

1. You are running a number of server applications on the same computer. You observe that the performance of SQL Server 2000 is initially poor after a period of low activity. What can you do to improve its responsiveness?

   You can configure a minimum memory setting guaranteeing that a sufficient minimum amount of physical memory will always be available to the SQL Server 2000 instance.

2. You want to configure the SQL Server Agent service to send mail to administrators in response to alerts. What is the first task you must perform?

   You must configure the SQL Server Agent service to use a domain user account.

3. You want to enable one of your databases to be queried using XML. What must you do?

   You must configure a virtual directory in IIS pointing to the database and specify the security context of connecting users. You must also specify the types of XML queries that will be permitted.

Chapter 13: Automating Administrative Tasks

Page 507

1. The database administrator who has been designated as the fail-safe operator is leaving the company. What must you do before you delete this person as an operator?

   You must either assign another person as the fail-safe operator or disable the fail-safe operator feature.

2. If a job fails to execute when scheduled, what are some troubleshooting steps you can follow?

   Verify that the schedule is enabled; verify that the job is enabled; and verify that SQL Server Agent is running.

3. You have defined an alert that backs up the transaction log when it is 90 percent full. However, occasionally the transaction log fills up before the job executes. Why is this occurring and what can be done to solve this problem?

Performance condition alerts sample the performance object counters every few seconds. If your transaction log fills up very quickly, this sampling rate is not frequent enough to back up the transaction log before it fills. Set a lower threshold for the alert to solve the problem.

4. You are in charge of managing a small database for your company. This is a part-time responsibility. You are also managing your company's domain controllers, Web site, and e-mail server. You want to automate as many tasks as possible. Where should you start?

The first automation task is backup. Use the Database Maintenance Plan Wizard to automate the backup of all system and user databases. Next, consider the other tasks you can automate with the Database Maintenance Plan Wizard and automate those that apply. Next, evaluate the types of events and conditions for which you should define alerts. This will provide you with advance notice of potential problems.

5. You want to create a single job that backs up the system databases nightly on every SQL Server instance within your company. You want to ensure that this happens automatically, with notice to you only if there is a problem. Can this be done?

Yes. You can create a multiserver job to perform this task and notify you as the MSXOperator only if a job fails. If you do not receive notification, you can generally assume that the job completed successfully on all servers. However, if the e-mail system within your company fails or the Messenger service stops running, you might not receive notification of failure.

Chapter 14: Monitoring SQL Server Performance and Activity

Page 546

1. You have recently been hired as the new database administrator for a medium-sized database. You have been tasked with improving the performance of the database, although no specific problems are apparent. Where should you start?

You should start by reviewing any performance baseline information that is available. You need to determine whether there are any immediate resource limitations affecting performance. Thereafter, you can begin identifying more subtle performance issues, such as inadequate indexes and long-running queries.

2. You want to be able to quickly view overall levels of resource use on a computer running SQL Server to determine whether resources are adequate. What is the most appropriate tool for the task?

Task Manager is the most appropriate tool for this task. It can be placed in the system tray and used to quickly display overall processor, memory, and I/O activity on the computer.

3. You have been viewing current server activity through SQL Server Enterprise Manager. You have noticed a number of blocking locks. What steps should you take to determine whether this is a serious problem?

You should use SQL Profiler to determine the number and frequency of blocking locks. By performing this step over time, you can determine whether the number of blocking locks is stable or increasing (or perhaps decreasing). You also capture sufficient information to determine whether specific SQL batches or stored procedures are causing the majority of the blocking locks. You can then determine the necessary steps to improve concurrency and performance, such as rewriting scripts and stored procedures, or changing the design of the database.

Chapter 15: Using SQL Server Replication

Page 629

1. You have a number of users in Brazil who need to access data for the purpose of sales analysis. The data is stored in a centralized database in New York. They have been accessing the database in New York over a 56K dedicated link that is also supporting a variety of other interoffice traffic. You want to implement a replication solution between your New York office and your Brazil office. What type of replication would you implement and what additional information do you need to know?

Because this information is for sales analysis, the users probably do not need up-to-the-minute data. Depending upon the size of the database and the number of changes, you would implement either snapshot or transactional replication. Replication could occur once a day, probably late in the evening.

2. You have implemented a merge replication solution. Each Subscriber running on Windows 2000 and Windows NT 4.0 is able to initialize the subscription and replicate data successfully with the Publisher. However, your Windows Me and Windows 98 Subscribers are unable to successfully replicate with the Publisher. What is a likely source of this problem? How would you solve this problem?

The Windows Me and Windows 98 Subscribers probably cannot access the initial snapshot folder. By default, the initial snapshot folder is accessible only using the hidden administrative share. This share is accessible only to users that are members of the local Administrators group of the Distributor. Solve this problem by using an explicitly created share for the snapshot folder and grant the required permissions to this share.

3. You are planning to implement a merge replication solution. What is the benefit of using a dedicated Distributor?

There is little benefit to a dedicated server because the Distributor plays a very limited role in merge replication. It serves primarily as a storage location for history information.

4. You have implemented transactional replication. You have been monitoring the size of the distribution database on the Distributor and notice that its size seems to be larger than anticipated. What might be the cause of this? What Distributor setting could you modify to affect its size?

The cause of the distribution database being larger than anticipated could be the retention of transactions in the database for longer than anticipated. By default, they are held in the distribution database until all Subscribers have downloaded the transactions or a default period of 72 hours. You should check the maximum retention period to verify the maximum retention period. You should also check whether one or more Subscribers is taking a long time to download changes. Also, if anonymous Subscribers are permitted, all transactions will be kept for the maximum length of time.

Chapter 16: Maintaining High Availability

Page 659

1. You are the database administrator for a number of SQL Server installations that generally must be available 24 x 7. What are the major failover differences between the use of standby servers with log shipping and the use of failover clustering?

With failover clustering, failover to a secondary node occurs automatically with only a brief delay and without the need for users to connect to another server and restart incomplete transactions. With standby servers, a database administrator must manually promote the standby server to primary and demote the primary server. During this time, the database is unavailable. In addition, users must connect to a different server (or the standby server must be renamed to the original server name) and incomplete transactions must be restarted.

2. You are administering 10 production servers. You are planning to implement log shipping to provide for a quick restore of each production server in the case of a system failure. What is the minimum number of computers you can use to accomplish this task? What is the minimum number of computers you would recommend be used?

The minimum number of computers is one. You could copy all transaction logs to a single server, which could also function as a monitoring server. If a production server fails, you can create the necessary logins and promote the standby server to primary for the databases affected. The standby server would continue to function as the standby server for the other production servers. Obviously, the capacity of a single server to handle this load is an issue. Also, this is a single point of failure, which is not advisable. The recommended number of servers will vary depending upon additional facts not presented here, such as size of databases and capacity of each server. However, you would probably want to have at least two standby servers and a separate monitoring server to eliminate single points of failure and provide excess capacity.

Glossary

Symbol

% User Time   A processor object counter that reports the percentage of time the processor is spending executing user processes, such as SQL Server.

A

ACID properties   The four properties (atomicity, consistency, isolation, durability) of a transaction. Atomicity means that all of a transaction's data modifications are performed, or none of them is performed. Consistency means that all data must be left in a consistent state. Isolation means that modifications made by concurrent transactions must be isolated from the modifications made by any other concurrent transactions. Durability means that the effects of a transaction must be permanent (even after a system failure).

active statement   A SQL statement that has been executed but whose result set has not yet been canceled or fully processed.

ActiveX Data Objects (ADO)   An easy-to-use application programming interface (API) that wraps OLE DB for use in languages such as Visual Basic, Visual Basic for Applications, Active Server Pages (ASP), and Microsoft Internet Explorer Visual Basic Scripting.

ActiveX Data Objects (Multidimensional) (ADO MD)   A high-level, language-independent set of object-based data access interfaces optimized for multidimensional data applications. Visual Basic and other automation languages use ADO MD as the data access interface to multidimensional data storage. ADO MD is a part of ADO 2.0 and later.

ActiveX script   Scripts that can be written in several scripting languages, such as Microsoft Visual Basic Scripting Edition, Microsoft JScript, or PerlScript, that can utilize the objects, methods, properties, and collections of the DTS object model and code transformations of source data to destination data, create COM objects, dynamically change properties of a DTS object, or create and set DTS package global variables.

ADO *See* **ActiveX Data Objects**

ADO MD *See* **ActiveX Data Objects (Multidimensional) (ADO MD)**

alert   A user-defined response to a SQL Server event. Alerts can either execute a defined task or send an e-mail, pager, or NET SEND message to a specified operator.

ALTER TABLET   SQL command that enables users with the appropriate permissions to modify a table's definition.

ALTER TRIGGER   SQL command that enables users with the appropriate permissions to modify a previously created trigger.

ALTER VIEW   SQL command that enables users with the appropriate permissions to modify a previously created view.

American National Standards Institute (ANSI)   An organization of American industry and business groups that develops trade and communication standards for the United States. Through membership in the International Organization for Standardization (ISO) and the International Electrotechnical Commission (IEC), ANSI coordinates American standards with corresponding international standards.

Analysis Server   The server component of Analysis Services that is specifically designed to create and maintain multidimensional data structures and provide multidimensional data in response to client queries.

anonymous subscription   An anonymous subscription is a type of pull subscription for which detailed information about the subscription and the Subscriber is not stored.

ANSI *See* **American National Standards Institute (ANSI)**

ANSI-to-OEM conversion   The conversion of characters that must occur when data is transferred from a database that stores character data using a specific code page to a client application on a computer that uses a different code page. Typically, Windows-based client computers use ANSI/ISO code pages, and some databases (for compatibility reasons) might use OEM code pages, such as the MS-DOS 437 code page or code page 850.

API *See* **application programming interface (API)**

API server cursor   A server cursor built to support the cursor functions of an application programming interface (API), such as ODBC, OLE DB, ADO, and DB-Library. An application does not usually request a server cursor directly; it calls the cursor functions of the API. The SQL Server interface for that API implements a server cursor if that is the best way to support the requested cursor functionality. *See also* **server cursor**

application programming interface (API)   A set of routines available in an application, such as ADO, for use by software programmers when designing an application interface.

application role   A SQL Server role created to support the security needs of an application.

Article   An object specified for replication. An article is a component in a publication and can be a table, specified columns (using a column filter), specified rows (using a row filter), a stored procedure or view definition, the execution of a stored procedure, a view, an indexed view, or a user-defined function.

Atomic   Either all of the transaction data modifications are performed or none of them are performed.

Authentication   The process of validating that the user attempting to connect to SQL Server is authorized to do so. *See also* **SQL Server authentication**

authentication modes   Microsoft SQL Server 2000 can be configured to support one of two authentication modes: Mixed Mode or Windows Authentication.

Authorization   The operation that verifies the permissions and access rights granted to a user.

AUTO_CLOSE   A database option used to control the behavior of a database when the last user of the database exits and all processes in the database complete.

AUTO_CREATE_STATISTICS   A database option used to control the behavior of statistics being automatically created on columns used in a predicate.

AUTO_UPDATE_STATISTICS   A database option used to control the behavior of statistics being automatically updated when the statistics become out of date because the data in the tables has changed.

automatic recovery   Recovery that occurs every time SQL Server is restarted. Automatic recovery protects your database if there is a system failure.

Autonomy   The independence one site has from other sites when performing modifications to data.

B

Backup   A copy of a database, transaction log, file, or filegroup used to recover data after a system failure.

BACKUP DATABASE   T-SQL command used to back up a database.

backup device   A tape or disk used in a backup or restore operation.

backup file   A file that stores a full or partial database, transaction log, or file and/or filegroup backup.

BACKUP LOG   T-SQL command used to back up a transaction log.

backup media   The tape, disk, or named pipe used to store a backup set.

backup set   The output of a single backup operation.

base data type   Any system-supplied data type, for example, char, varchar, binary, and varbinary. User-defined data types are derived from base data types. *See also* **data type, user-defined data type**

batch   A set of SQL statements submitted together and executed as a group. A script is often a series of batches submitted one after the other.

Bcp files   Files that store bulk copy data created by the bulk copy utility or synchronization.

Bcp utility *See* **Bulk Copy (Bcp) Utility**

binary data type   Fixed-length binary data with a maximum length of 8,000 bytes.

Buffer Cache Hit Ratio   A Buffer Manager object counter that reports the percentage of pages found in the buffer cache without having to read from a disk.

Buffer Manager object   Provides counters to monitor how SQL Server uses memory to store data pages, internal data structures, and the procedure cache.

Bulkadmin   A fixed server role that enables members of the role to execute BULK INSERT statements.

Bulk Copy (Bcp) Utility   A command-prompt bulk copy utility that copies SQL Server data to or from an operating system file in a user-specified format.

built-in functions   A group of predefined functions provided as part of the Transact-SQL and Multidimensional Expressions (MDX) languages.

business rules   The logical rules that are used to run a business. Business rules can be enforced in the .com objects that make up the middle tier of a Windows DNA system; they can also be enforced in a SQL Server database using triggers, stored procedures, and constraints.

C

CA *See* **certification authority (CA)**

cache aging   The mechanism of caching that determines when a cache row is outdated and must be refreshed.

calculated column   A column in a table that displays the result of an expression rather than stored data. For example, CalculatedCostColumn = Price * Quantity.

calculated field   A field defined in a query that displays the result of an expression rather than stored data.

call-level interface (CLI)   The interface supported by ODBC for use by an application.

cascading delete   An operation that deletes a row containing a primary key value that is referenced by foreign key columns in existing rows in other tables. On a cascading delete, all of the rows whose foreign key values reference the deleted primary key value are also deleted.

cascading update   An operation that updates a primary key value that is referenced by foreign key columns in existing rows in other tables. On a cascading update, all of the foreign key values are updated to match the new primary key value.

CAST   Explicitly converts an expression of one data type to another. Cast is based on the SQL-92 standard.

catalog (database) *See* **database catalog**

catalog (system) *See* **system catalog**

certificate   A collection of data used for authentication and secure exchange of information on nonsecured networks, such as the Internet. A certificate securely binds a public encryption key to the entity that holds the corresponding private encryption key. Certificates are digitally signed by the issuing certification authority and can be managed for a user, a computer, or a service.

certification authority (CA)   An entity responsible for establishing and vouching for the authenticity of public keys belonging to users (end entities) or other certification authorities. Activities of a certification authority may include binding public keys to distinguished names through signed certificates, managing certificate serial numbers and certificate revocation.

char data type   Fixed-length non-Unicode character data that holds a maximum of 8,000 characters.

character format   Data stored in a bulk copy data file using text characters. *See also* **native format**

character set   A character set determines the types of characters that SQL Server recognizes in the char, varchar, and text data types. Each character set is a set of 256 letters, digits, and symbols specific to a country or language. The printable characters of the first 128 values are the same for all character sets. The last 128 characters, some-

times referred to as extended characters, are unique to each character set. A character set is related to, but separate from, Unicode characters.

CHECK constraints   A constraint that defines which data values are acceptable in a column. You can apply CHECK constraints to multiple columns, and you can apply multiple CHECK constraints to a single column. When a table is dropped, CHECK constraints are also dropped.

Checkpoint   An event in which the database engine writes dirty buffer pages to disk. Dirty pages are pages that have been modified, but the modifications have not yet been written to disk. Each checkpoint writes to disk all pages that were dirty at the last checkpoint and still have not been written to disk. Checkpoints occur periodically based on the number of log records generated by data modifications, or when requested by a user or a system shutdown.

CLI *See* **call-level interface (CLI)**

client cursor   A cursor implemented on the client. The entire result set is first transferred to the client, and the client application programming interface (API) software implements the cursor functionality from this cached result set.

clustered index   An index in which the logical order of the key values determines the physical order of the corresponding rows in a table.

CmdExec   Operating system commands or executable programs ending with .bat, .cmd, .com, or .exe.

CNFGSVR.EXE   An application that runs during the configuration portion of SQL Server setup to execute the initial installation scripts.

code page   For character and Unicode data, a definition of the bit patterns that represent specific letters, numbers, or symbols (such as 0x20 representing a blank space and 0x74 representing the character "t"). Some data types use 1 byte per character; each byte can have 1 of 256 different bit patterns.

Collation A set of rules that determine how data is compared, ordered, and presented. Character data is sorted using collation information, including locale, sort order, and case sensitivity. *See also* **locale, SQL collation**

Column In a SQL table, the area in each row that stores the data value for some attribute of the object modeled by the table. For example, the Employees table in the Northwind sample database models the employees of the Northwind Traders company. The LastName column in each row of the Employees table stores the last name of the employee represented by that row, the same way a LastName field in a window or form would contain a last name. *See also* **row**

column filter Column filters restrict the columns to be included as part of a snapshot, transactional, or merge publication.

column-level collation The ability of SQL Server 2000 to support multiple collations in a single instance. Databases can have default collations different from the default collation of the instance. Individual columns and variables can be assigned collations different from the default collation for the instance or database. Each column in a table can have a different collation.

column-level constraint A constraint definition that is specified within a column definition when a table is created or altered. The constraint applies only to the associated column. *See also* **constraint**

COM *See* **Component Object Model (COM)**

COM-structured storage file A component object model (COM) compound file used by Data Transformation Services (DTS) to store the version history of a saved DTS package.

commit An operation that saves all changes to databases made since the start of a transaction. A commit guarantees that all of the transaction's modifications are made a permanent part of the database. A commit also frees resources, such as locks, used by the transaction. *See also* **roll back**

Component Object Model (COM) A Microsoft specification for developing component software. Several SQL Server and database application programming interfaces (APIs) such as SQL-DMO, OLE DB, and ADO are based on COM. Some SQL Server components, such as Analysis Services and English Query, store objects as COM objects. *See also* **method**

composite index An index that uses more than one column in a table to index data.

composite key A key composed of two or more columns.

computed column A virtual column in a table whose value is computed at run time. The values in the column are not stored in the table, but are computed based on the expression that defines the column. An example of the definition of a computed column is: Cost as Price * Quantity.

Concurrency A process that allows multiple users to access and change shared data at the same time. SQL Server uses locking to allow multiple users to access and change shared data at the same time without conflicting with each other.

Connection An interprocess communication (IPC) linkage established between a SQL Server 2000 application and an instance of SQL Server 2000. The connection is a network link if the application is on a computer different from the SQL Server 2000 instance. If the application and the SQL Server 2000 instance are on the same computer, the linkage is formed through a local IPC mechanism, such as shared memory. The application uses the IPC linkage to send Transact-SQL statements to SQL Server and to receive result sets, errors, and messages from SQL Server.

constraint A property assigned to a table column that prevents certain types of invalid data values from being placed in the column. For example, a UNIQUE or PRIMARY KEY constraint prevents you from inserting a value that is a duplicate of an existing value, a CHECK constraint prevents you from inserting a value that does not match a search condition, and NOT NULL prevents you from inserting a NULL value. *See also* **column-level constraint**

continuation media The backup media used when the initial medium becomes full, allowing continuation of the backup operation.

CONVERT Explicitly converts an expression of one data type to another.

Copy Database Wizard Allows you to copy or move databases between servers.

CPU busy A SQL Server statistic that reports the time, in milliseconds, the central processing unit (CPU) spent on SQL Server work.

Create Database Wizard Wizard used to simplify the creation of a SQL Server database.

Create Login Wizard Wizard used to simplify the process of granting logon access to SQL Server and databases.

cube A set of data that is organized and summarized into a multidimensional structure. *See also* **multidimensional structure**

Current Activity window Graphically displays information about processes currently running on an instance of SQL Server, blocked processes, locks, and user activity.

Cursor An entity that maps over a result set and establishes a position on a single row within the result set. After the cursor is positioned on a row, operations can be performed on that row, or on a block of rows starting at that position. The most common operation is to fetch (retrieve) the current row or block of rows.

D

data block In text, ntext, and image data, a data block is the unit of data transferred at one time between an application and an instance of SQL Server 2000. The term is also applied to the units of storage for these data types. In tape backup files, data block is the unit of physical I/O.

data connection A collection of information required to access a specific database. The collection includes a data source name and logon information. Data connections are stored in a project and are activated when the user performs an action that requires access to the database. For example, a data connection for a SQL Server database consists of the name of the database, the location of the server on which it resides, network information used to access that server, and a user ID and password.

Data Control Language (DCL) The subset of SQL statements used to control permissions on database objects. Permissions are controlled using the GRANT and REVOKE statements.

data definition The process of specifying the attributes, properties, and objects in a database.

data definition language (DDL) A language, usually part of a database management system, that is used to define all attributes and properties of a database, especially row layouts, column definitions, key columns (and sometimes keying methodology), file locations, and storage strategy.

data dictionary A set of system tables, stored in a database catalog, that includes definitions of database structures and related information, such as permissions.

data dictionary view A system table.

data file In bulk copy operations, the file that transfers data from the bulk copy out operation to the bulk copy in operation. In SQL Server 2000 databases, data files hold the data stored in the database. Every SQL Server 2000 database has at least one primary data file, and can optionally have multiple secondary data files to hold data that does not fit on the primary data file. *See also* **log file**

data integrity A state in which all the data values stored in the database are correct. If incorrect data values have been stored in a database, the database is said to have lost data integrity.

data lineage Information used by Data Transformation Services (DTS), in conjunction with Meta Data Services, that records the history of package execution and data transformations for each piece of data.

data manipulation language (DML) The subset of SQL statements used to retrieve and manipulate data.

data mart A subset of the contents of a data warehouse. A data mart tends to contain data focused at the department level, or on a specific business area. *See also* **data warehouse**

data modification An operation that adds, deletes, or changes information in a database using Transact-SQL statements such as INSERT, DELETE, and UPDATE.

data pump An OLE DB service provider that provides the infrastructure to import, export, and transform data between heterogeneous data stores using Data Transformation Services (DTS).

data scrubbing Part of the process of building a data warehouse out of data coming from multiple online transaction processing (OLTP) systems. The process must address errors such as incorrect spellings, conflicting spelling conventions between two systems, and conflicting data (such as having two part numbers for the same part).

data source In ADO and OLE DB, the location of a source of data exposed by an OLE DB provider. *See also* **ODBC data source**

data source name (DSN) The name assigned to an ODBC data source. Applications can use DSNs to request a connection to a system ODBC data source, which specifies the computer name and (optionally) the database to which the DSN maps.

Data Transformation Services (DTS) The SQL Server tool for transferring and transforming data between disparate data sources.

data type An attribute that specifies what type of information can be stored in a column, parameter, or variable. System-supplied data types are provided by SQL Server; user-defined data types can also be created. *See also* **base data type**

data warehouse A database specifically structured for query and analysis. A data warehouse typically contains data representing the business history of an organization. *See also* **data mart, fact table**

database A collection of information, tables, and other objects organized and presented to serve a specific purpose, such as searching, sorting, and recombining data. Databases are stored in files.

database backup A copy of a database used to recover data after a system failure.

database catalog The part of a database that contains the definition of all the objects in the database, as well as the definition of the database. *See also* **system catalog**

Database Consistency Checker (DBCC) A Microsoft SQL Server utility that can be run to check the consistency of a specified database. DBCC can be run through the Database Maintenance Plan Wizard or as a T-SQL command. The DBCC command can be used to run integrity checks of all the objects in a database or of specific objects, such as indexes only.

database diagram   A graphical representation of the objects in a database. A database diagram can be either a whole or a partial picture of the structure of a database; it includes objects for tables, the columns they contain, and the relationship between them.

database file   One of the physical files that make up a database.

database language   The language used for accessing, querying, updating, and managing data in relational database systems. Structured Query Language (SQL) is a widely used database language. The Microsoft SQL Server implementation of SQL is called Transact-SQL.

Database Maintenance Plan Wizard   A built-in Microsoft SQL Server tool that allows administrators to schedule core maintenance tasks, such as database backups, integrity checks, and setting up log shipping.

database object   A database component. A table, index, trigger, view, key, constraint, default, rule, user-defined data type, or stored procedure in a database. May also refer to a database.

database owner   A member of the database administrator role of a database. There is only one database owner. The owner has full permissions in that database and determines the access and capabilities provided to other users.

database schema   The names of tables, fields, data types, and primary and foreign keys of a database. Also known as the database structure.

database script   A collection of statements used to create database objects. Transact-SQL scripts are saved as files, usually ending with .sql.

datetime data type   A SQL Server system data type that stores a combined date and time value from January 1, 1753 through December 31, 9999 with an accuracy of three-hundredths of a second, or 3.33 milliseconds.

db_accessadmin   A fixed database role that enables members of the role to add or remove Windows NT 4.0 or Windows 2000 groups and users and SQL Server users in the database.

db_backupoperator   A fixed database role that enables members of the role to back up the database.

DBCC   *See* Database Consistency Checker

DBCC CHECKALLOC   This command checks page usage in a database and indexed views. If you have executed DBCC CHECKDB, it is not necessary to execute DBCC CHECKALLOC because it is a subset of the DBCC CHECKDB command.

DBCC CHECKCONSTRAINTS   This command verifies the integrity of each constraint if you have a database that has constraints created for it.

DBCC CHECKDB   This command verifies the integrity of everything in a database including views, indexes, and tables. If you are unsure of any specific problems with a single database, you can run DBCC CHECKDB.

DBCC DBREINDEX   Rather than deleting and recreating a suspect index, you can execute DBCC DBREINDEX to attempt to rebuild it.

DBCC INDEXDEFRAG   This command defrags the index if fragmentation is apparent for a clustered or nonclustered index.

DBCC INPUTBUFFER   Displays the last statement sent from a client to SQL Server.

DBCC NEWALLOC   Different than the DBCC CHECKALLOC command, this command verifies the allocation of data and index pages for each table within a specified database.

DBCC OPENTRAN   Displays information about the oldest active transaction and the oldest distributed and nondistributed replicated transaction, if any, within the specified database.

Dbcreator   A fixed server role that enables members of the role to create and alter databases.

db_datareader   A fixed database role that enables members of the role to see all data from all user tables in the database.

db_datawriter   A fixed database role that enables members of the role to add, change, or delete data from all user tables in the database.

db_ddladmin   A fixed database role that enables members of the role to add, modify, or drop objects in the database.

db_denydatareader   A fixed database role that denies members of the role from selecting data from the database.

db_denydatawriter   A fixed database role that denies members of the role from changing data in the database.

Db-Lib *See* **DB-Library (DB-Lib)**

DB-Library (DB-Lib)   A series of high-level language (including C) libraries that provide the application programming interface (API) for the client in a client/server system. Supported only for backward compatibility.

db_owner   A fixed database role that enables members of the role to perform activities of all database roles as well as other maintenance and configuration activities in the database. The permissions of this role span all of the other fixed database roles.

db_securityadmin   A fixed database role that enables members to manage roles and member objects of a SQL Server 2000 database. It also enables members to manage statement and object permissions in the database.

DCL *See* **Data Control Language (DCL)**

DDL *See* **data definition language (DDL)**

Deadlock   A situation in which two users, each having a lock on one piece of data, attempt to acquire a lock on the other's piece. Each user would wait indefinitely for the other to release the lock, unless one of the user processes is terminated. SQL Server detects deadlocks and terminates one user's process. *See also* **livelock**

decimal data type   Contains fixed precision and scale numeric data from -10^38 +1 through 10^38 -1.

decision support   Systems designed to support the complex analytic analysis required to discover business trends. The information retrieved from these systems allows managers to make business decisions based on timely and accurate analysis of business trends.

declarative referential integrity (DRI)   FOREIGN KEY constraints defined as part of a table definition that enforce proper relationships between tables. The constraints ensure that proper actions are taken when DELETE, INSERT, and UPDATE statements remove, add, or modify primary or foreign key values. The DRI actions enforced by FOREIGN KEY constraints can be supplemented with additional referential integrity logic defined in triggers on a table.

default   A data value, option setting, collation, or name assigned automatically by the system if a user does not specify the value, setting, collation, or name. An action taken automatically at certain events if a user has not specified the action to take.

DEFAULT constraint   A property defined for a table column that specifies a constant to be used as the default value for the column. If any subsequent INSERT or UPDATE statement specifies a value of NULL for the column, or does not specify a value for the column, the constant value defined in the DEFAULT constraint is placed in the column.

default database The database the user is connected to immediately after logging in to SQL Server.

default instance The copy of SQL Server that uses the computer name on which it is installed as its name. *See also* **multiple instances, named instance**

default language The language that SQL Server 2000 uses for errors and messages if a user does not specify a language. Each SQL Server 2000 login has a default language.

delimiter In Transact-SQL, characters that indicate the start and end of an object name, using either double quotation marks ("") or brackets ([]).

denormalize To introduce redundancy into a table in order to incorporate data from a related table. The related table can then be eliminated. Denormalization can improve efficiency and performance by reducing complexity in a data warehouse schema.

deny To remove a permission from a user account and prevent the account from gaining permission through membership in groups or roles within the permission.

dependencies The views and procedures that depend on the specified table or view.

device *See* **file**

differential database backup A database backup that records only those changes made to the database since the last full database backup. A differential backup is smaller, is faster to restore than a full backup, and has minimal effect on performance.

direct response mode The default mode in which SQL Server statistics are gathered separately from the SQL Server Statistics display. Data is available immediately to SQL Server Performance Monitor; however, the statistics displayed are one period behind the statistics retrieved.

dirty pages Buffer pages that contain modifications that have not been written to disk.

dirty read Reads that contain uncommitted data. For example, transaction1 changes a row. Transaction2 reads the changed row before transaction1 commits the change. If transaction1 rolls back the change, transaction2 has read a row that never logically existed.

Diskadmin A fixed server role that enables members of the role to manage disk files.

Distribute To move transactions or snapshots of data from the Publisher to Subscribers, where they are applied to the destination tables in the subscription databases.

distributed query A single query that accesses data from multiple data sources.

distributed transactions Transactions that involve the use of two or more data sources.

distributed views SQL Server views that must be created when implementing a federated database.

distribution database A database on the Distributor that stores data for replication including transactions, snapshot jobs, synchronization status, and replication history information.

distribution retention period The distribution retention period determines the amount of information stored for a replication agent and the length of time subscriptions will remain active in the distribution database. When the distribution retention period is exceeded, the Distribution Clean Up Agent runs.

Distributor A server for SQL Server replication that hosts the distribution database and stores history data, and/or transactions and metadata. *See also* **local Distributor, remote Distributor**

DML *See* **data manipulation language (DML)**

Domain In Windows 2000 security, a collection of computers grouped for viewing and administrative purposes that share a common security database. In relational databases, the set of valid values allowed in a column.

domain integrity An integrity mechanism that enforces the validity of entries for a given column. The mechanism, such as the CHECK constraint, can restrict the possible data values by data type, format, or range of values allowed.

DRI *See* **declarative referential integrity (DRI)**

DSN *See* **data source name (DSN)**

DTS *See* **Data Transformation Services (DTS)**

DTS package An organized collection of connections, Data Transformation Services (DTS) tasks, DTS transformations, and workflow constraints defined by the DTS object model and assembled either with a DTS tool or programmatically.

DTS package template A model Data Transformation Services (DTS) package. The template is used to help create and configure a particular type of package.

dump *See* **backup**

dump file *See* **backup file**

dynamic filter Merge replication filters that restrict data based on a system function or user-defined function (for example: SUSER_SNAME()).

dynamic locking The process used by SQL Server to determine the most cost-effective locks to use at any one time.

dynamic recovery The process that detects and/ or attempts to correct software failure or loss of data integrity within a relational database management system (RDBMS).

dynamic snapshot A snapshot of a merge publication with dynamic filters that is applied using bulk copy files to improve performance.

E

e-mail notification notification sent as an e-mail message that contains information about an event or an alert that took place on the SQL Server.

Encryption A method for keeping sensitive information confidential by changing data into an unreadable form.

English Query Refers to a Microsoft application development product that allows users to ask questions in English, rather than in a computer language such as SQL. For example, you might ask, "How many customers bought products last year?" rather than prepare an equivalent SQL statement.

error log A text file that records system information from SQL Server.

error state number A number associated with SQL Server 2000 messages that helps Microsoft support engineers find the specific code location that issued the message. This can be helpful in diagnosing errors that may be generated from multiple locations in the SQL Server 2000 code.

exclusive lock A lock that prevents any other transaction from acquiring a lock on a resource until the original lock on the resource is released at the end of the transaction. An exclusive lock is always applied during an update operation (INSERT, UPDATE, or DELETE).

explicit transaction A group of SQL statements enclosed within transaction delimiters. The first delimiter must be either BEGIN TRANSACTION or BEGIN DISTRIBUTED TRANSACTION, and the end delimiter must be one of the following: COMMIT TRANSACTION, COM-

MIT WORK, ROLLBACK TRANSACTION, ROLLBACK WORK, SAVE TRANSACTION.

extended stored procedure   A function in a dynamic-link library (DLL) that is coded using the SQL Server 2000 Extended Stored Procedure API. The function can then be invoked from Transact-SQL using the same statements that are used to execute Transact-SQL stored procedures. Extended stored procedures can be built to perform functionality not possible with Transact-SQL stored procedures.

extent   The unit of space allocated to a SQL Server object, such as a table or index, whenever the object needs more space. In SQL Server 2000, an extent is eight contiguous pages.

F

fact table   A central table in a data warehouse schema.

fail-safe operator   The fail-safe operator is notified about an alert after all pager notifications to the designated operators have failed.

field   An area in a window or record that stores a single data value. Some databases, such as Microsoft Access, use field as a synonym for column.

field length   In bulk copy, the maximum number of characters needed to represent a data item in a bulk copy character format data file.

field terminator   In bulk copy, one or more characters marking the end of a field or row, separating one field or row in the data file from the next.

file   In SQL Server databases, a basic unit of storage for a database. One database can be stored in several files. SQL Server uses three types of files: data files (which store data), log files (which store transaction logs), and backup files (which store backups of a database).

file DSN   Stores connection information for a database in a file that is saved on your computer. The file is a text file with the extension .dsn. The connection information consists of parameters and corresponding values that the ODBC Driver Manager uses to establish a connection.

file storage type   Defines the storage format used in the data file that transfers data from a bulk copy out operation to a bulk copy in operation. In native mode files, all data is stored using the same internal structures that SQL Server 2000 uses to store the data in a database. In character mode files, all data is converted to character strings.

filegroup   In SQL Server, a named collection of one or more files that forms a single unit of allocation or that is used for administration of a database.

fill factor   An attribute of an index that defines the amount of free space on each page of the index. FILLFACTOR accommodates future expansion of table data and reduces the potential for page splits. FILLFACTOR is a value from 1 through 100 that specifies the percentage of the index page to be left empty.

filter   A set of criteria that controls the set of records returned as a result set. Filters can also define the sequence in which rows are returned.

filtering   The ability to restrict data based upon criteria set in the WHERE clause of a SQL statement. For replication, filtering occurs on table articles defined in a publication. The result is partitions of data that can be published to Subscribers. *See also* **partitioning, vertical filtering**

fixed database role   A predefined role that exists in each database. The scope of the role is limited to the database in which it is defined.

fixed server role   A predefined role that exists at the server level. The scope of the role is limited to the SQL Server instance in which it is defined.

FK *See* **foreign key (FK)**

foreign key (FK)   The column or combination of columns whose values match the primary key (PK) or unique key in the same or another table. Also called the referencing key.

foreign table   A table that contains a foreign key.

fragmentation   Occurs when data modifications are made. You can reduce fragmentation and improve read-ahead performance by dropping and re-creating a clustered index.

full-text catalog   Stores all of the full-text indexes for tables within a database.

full-text enabling   The process of allowing full-text querying to occur on the current database.

full-text index   The portion of a full-text catalog that stores all of the full-text words and their locations for a given table.

full-text query   As a SELECT statement, a query that searches for words, phrases, or multiple forms of a word or phrase in the character-based columns (of char, varchar, text, ntext, nchar, or nvarchar data types). The SELECT statement returns those rows meeting the search criteria.

full-text service   The SQL Server component that performs the full-text querying.

function   A piece of code that operates as a single logical unit. A function is called by name, accepts optional input parameters, and returns a status and optional output parameters. Many programming languages support functions, including C, Visual Basic, and Transact-SQL. Transact-SQL supplies built-in functions, which cannot be modified, and supports user-defined functions, which can be created and modified by users.

G

global default   A default that is defined for a specific database and is shared by columns of different tables.

global rule   A rule that is defined for a specific database and is shared by columns of different tables.

global subscriptions   A subscription to a merge publication with an assigned priority value used for conflict detection and resolution.

grant   Applies permissions to a user account, which allows the account to perform an activity or work with data.

guest   A special user account that is present in all SQL Server 2000 databases and cannot be removed from any database. If a connection is made using a login that has not been assigned a user account in a database and the connection references objects in that database, it has the permissions assigned only to the guest account in that database.

H

heterogeneous data   Data stored in multiple formats. For example, data stored in a SQL Server database, a text file, and an Excel spreadsheet.

homogeneous data   Data that comes from multiple data sources that are all managed by the same software (for example, data that comes from several Excel spreadsheets, or data that comes from several SQL Server 2000 instances). A SQL Server 2000 distributed query is homogeneous if all the data comes from SQL Server 2000 instances.

horizontal partitioning   To segment a single table into multiple tables based on selected rows. Each of the multiple tables has the same columns but fewer rows. *See also* **partitioning**

HTML *See* **Hypertext Markup Language (HTML)**

Hypertext Markup Language (HTML)   A system of marking up, or tagging, a document so that it can be published on the World Wide Web

(WWW). Documents prepared in HTML include reference graphics and formatting tags. You use a Web browser (such as Microsoft Internet Explorer) to view these documents.

HTTP Abbreviation for Hypertext Transfer Protocol. It is the application-level Internet protocol used by World Wide Web clients and servers to exchange information. The protocol makes it possible for a user to use a client program (browser) to enter a Uniform Resource Locator (or click a hyperlink) and retrieve data, such as text, graphics, sound, and other digital information, from a Web server.

I

identifier The name of an object in a database. An identifier can be from 1 through 128 characters.

identity column A column in a table that has been assigned the identity property. The identity property generates unique numbers.

identity property A property that generates values that uniquely identify each row in a table. When inserting rows into a table that has an identity column, SQL Server generates the next identity value automatically based on the last used identity value and the increment value specified during column creation.

idle time A SQL Server 2000 Agent condition that defines the level of CPU usage by the SQL Server 2000 database engine that constitutes an idle state. SQL Server 2000 Agent jobs can then be created to run whenever the database engine CPU usage falls below the level defined in the idle time definition. This minimizes the impact the SQL Server Agent jobs may have on other tasks accessing the database.

IEC *See* **International Electrotechnical Commission (IEC)**

IIS Virtual Directory Management for SQL Server Utility A utility used to define and register a new, SQL Server 2000–specific virtual directory, also known as the virtual root, on a computer running Internet Information Server (IIS).

image data type A SQL Server variable-length binary data type with a maximum length of 2^31 - 1 (2,147,483,647) bytes.

immediate updating An option available with snapshot replication and transactional replication that allows data modifications to be made to replicated data at the Subscriber. The data modifications are then immediately propagated to the Publisher using two-phase commit protocol (2PC).

immediate updating Subscribers *See* **immediate updating subscriptions**

immediate updating subscriptions A subscription to a snapshot or transactional publication for which the user is able to make data modifications at the Subscriber. The data modifications are then immediately propagated to the Publisher using two-phase commit protocol (2PC).

implicit transaction A connection option in which each SQL statement executed by the connection is considered a separate transaction.

implied permission Permission to perform an activity specific to a role. Implied permissions cannot be granted, revoked, or denied.

index In a relational database, a database object that provides fast access to data in the rows of a table, based on key values. Indexes can also enforce uniqueness on the rows in a table. SQL Server supports clustered and nonclustered indexes. The primary key of a table is automatically indexed. In full-text search, a full-text index stores information about significant words and their location within a given column.

index page A database page containing index rows.

information model An object-oriented schema that defines metadata constructs used to specify the structure and behavior of an application, process, component, or software artifact.

initial media The first medium in each media family.

initial snapshot Files including schema and data, constraints, extended properties, indexes, triggers, and system tables necessary for replication. The initial snapshot is transferred to Subscribers when implementing replication. *See also* **synchronization**

instance A copy of SQL Server running on a computer. A computer can run multiple instances of SQL Server 2000. A computer can run only one instance of SQL Server version 7.0 or earlier, although in some cases it can also be running multiple instances of SQL Server 2000.

int (integer) data type A SQL Server system data type that holds whole numbers from -2^31 (-2,147,483,648) through 2^31 - 1 (2,147,483,647).

integrated security *See* **Windows authentication**

integrity constraint A property defined on a table that prevents data modifications that would create invalid data.

intent lock A lock placed on one level of a resource hierarchy to protect shared or exclusive locks on lower-level resources. For example, before a SQL Server 2000 database engine task applies shared or exclusive row locks within a table, it places an intent lock on the table. If another task tries to apply a shared or exclusive lock at the table level, it is blocked by the table-level intent lock held by the first task. The second task does not have to check for individual page or row locks before locking the table; it only has to check for an intent lock on the table.

interactive structured query language (ISQL) An interactive command-prompt utility provided with SQL Server that allows users to execute Transact-SQL statements or batches from a server or workstation and view the results returned.

internal identifier A more compact form of an object identifier in a repository. An internal identifier is guaranteed to be unique only within a single repository. *See also* **object identifier**

International Electrotechnical Commission (IEC) One of two international standards bodies responsible for developing international data communications standards. The International Electrotechnical Commission (IEC) works closely with the International Organization for Standardization (ISO) to define standards of computing. They jointly published the ISO/IEC SQL-92 standard for SQL.

International Organization for Standardization (ISO) One of two international standards bodies responsible for developing international data communications standards. International Organization for Standardization (ISO) works closely with the International Electrotechnical Commission (IEC) to define standards of computing. They jointly published the ISO/IEC SQL-92 standard for SQL.

Internet-enabled A publication setting that enables replication to Internet Subscribers.

interprocess communication (IPC) A mechanism through which operating system processes and threads exchange data and messages. IPCs include local mechanisms such as Windows shared memory, or network mechanisms such as Windows Sockets.

IPC *See* **interprocess communication (IPC)**

ISO *See* **International Organization for Standardization (ISO)**

ISQL *See* **interactive structured query language (ISQL)**

J

job   A specified series of operations, called steps, performed sequentially by SQL Server Agent.

join   As a verb, to combine the contents of two or more tables and produce a result set that incorporates rows and columns from each table. Tables are typically joined using data that they have in common. As a noun, the process or result of joining tables, as in the term "inner join" to indicate a particular method of joining tables.

join filter   A row filter used in merge replication that defines a relationship between two tables that will be enforced during synchronization, which is similar to specifying a join between two tables.

join operator   A comparison operator in a join condition that determines how the two sides of the condition are evaluated and which rows are returned.

K

kernel   In SQL Server 2000, a subset of the storage engine that is referenced in some error messages. In Windows 2000, the core of the operating system that performs basic operations.

key   A column or group of columns that uniquely identifies a row (PRIMARY KEY), defines the relationship between two tables (FOREIGN KEY), or is used to build an index. *See also* **key column**

key column   A column referenced by a primary, foreign, or index key. *See also* **key**

keyword   A reserved word in SQL Server that performs a specific function, such as to define, manipulate, and access database objects.

L

latency   The amount of time that elapses when a data change is completed at one server and when that change appears at another (for example, the time between when a change is made at a Publisher and when it appears at the Subscriber).

LCID *See* **locale identifier (LCID)**

leaf   In a tree structure, an element that has no subordinate elements. *See also* **nonleaf**

leaf level   The bottom level of a clustered or nonclustered index. In a clustered index, the leaf level contains the actual data pages of the table. In a nonclustered index, the leaf level either points to data pages or points to the clustered index (if one exists), rather than containing the data itself.

linked server   A definition of an OLE DB data source used by SQL Server 2000–distributed queries. The linked server definition specifies the OLE DB provider required to access the data, and includes enough addressing information for the OLE DB provider to connect to the data. Any rowsets exposed by the OLE DB data source can then be referenced as tables, called linked tables, in SQL Server 2000–distributed queries. *See also* **local server**

livelock   A request for an exclusive lock that is repeatedly denied because a series of overlapping shared locks keeps interfering. SQL Server detects the situation after four denials and refuses further shared locks. A livelock also occurs when read transactions monopolize a table or page, forcing a write transaction to wait indefinitely. *See also* **deadlock**

local Distributor   A server that is configured as both a Publisher and a Distributor for SQL Server replication. *See also* **Distributor, remote Distributor**

local group   A group in Windows NT 4.0 or Windows 2000 containing user accounts and global groups from the domain group in which they are created and any trusted domain. Local groups cannot contain other local groups.

local login identification   The identification (ID) a user must use to log in to a local server. A login ID can have up to 128 characters. The characters can be alphanumeric; however, the first character must be a letter (for example, CHRIS or TELLER8).

local server   In SQL Server 2000 connections, an instance of SQL Server 2000 running on the same computer as the application. When resolving references to database objects in a Transact-SQL statement, the instance of SQL Server 2000 executing the statement. In SQL Server 2000–distributed queries, the instance of SQL Server 2000 executing the distributed query. The local server then accesses any linked servers referenced in the query. In SQL Server 2000 remote stored procedures, the instance of SQL Server executing an EXEC statement that references a remote stored procedure. The local server then passes the execution request to the remote server on which the remote stored procedure resides. *See also* **linked server, remote server**

local subscription   A subscription to a merge publication using the priority value of the Publisher for conflict detection and resolution.

locale   The Windows operating system attribute that defines certain behaviors related to language. The locale defines the code page, or bit patterns, used to store character data, and the order in which characters are sorted. It also defines language-specific items such as the format used for dates and time and the character used to separate decimals in numbers. Each locale is identified by a unique number, called a locale identifier or LCID. SQL Server 2000 collations are similar to locales in that the collations define language-specific types of behaviors for instances of SQL Server 2000. *See also* **collation, locale identifier (LCID)**

locale identifier (LCID)   A number that identifies a Windows-based locale. *See also* **locale**

lock   A restriction on access to a resource in a multiuser environment. SQL Server locks users out of a specific row, column, or file automatically to maintain security or prevent concurrent data modification problems.

lock escalation   The process of converting many fine-grain locks into fewer coarse-grain locks, thereby reducing system overhead.

log file   A file or set of files containing a record of the modifications made in a database. *See also* **data file**

logical name   A name used by SQL Server to identify a file. A logical name for a file must correspond to the rules for identifiers and can have as many as 30 characters (for example, ACCOUNTING or LIBRARY).

login (account)   An identifier that gives a user permission to connect to SQL Server 2000 using SQL Server Authentication. Users connecting to SQL Server 2000 using Windows NT Authentication are identified by their Windows 2000 login, and do not need a separate SQL Server 2000 login.

login security mode   A security mode that determines the manner in which a SQL Server 2000 instance validates a login request. There are two types of login security: Windows authentication and SQL Server authentication.

lookup table   A table, either in a database or hard-coded in the English Query application, that contains codes and the English word or phrase they represent. For example, a gender lookup table contains the following code and English descriptions: M, Male, F, Female.

M

machine DSN   Connection information for a database, stored in the system registry. The connection information consists of parameters and corresponding values that the ODBC Driver Manager uses to establish a connection.

MAPI *See* **Messaging Application Programming Interface (MAPI)**

master database   The database that controls the operation of each instance of SQL Server. It is installed automatically with each instance of SQL Server and keeps track of user accounts, remote user accounts, and remote servers that each instance can interact with. It also tracks ongoing processes, configurable environment variables, system error messages, tapes and disks available on the system, and active locks.

master definition site *See* **Publisher**

master file   The file installed with earlier versions of SQL Server used to store the master, model, and tempdb system databases and transaction logs and the pubs sample database and transaction log.

master site *See* **Distributor**

MDX *See* **Multidimensional Expressions (MDX)**

media description   The text describing the media set. *See also* **media set**

media family   All media in a set written by a single device (for example, an initial medium and all continuation media, if any). *See also* **media set**

media header   Information about the backup media.

media name   The descriptive name for the entire backup media set.

media set   All media involved in a backup operation. *See also* **media description, media family**

Memory Manager object   Provides counters to monitor overall server memory usage.

merge   The operation that combines two partitions into a single partition.

merge replication   A type of replication that allows sites to make autonomous changes to replicated data, and at a later time, merge changes and resolve conflicts when necessary. *See also* **snapshot replication, transactional replication**

message number   A number that identifies a SQL Server 2000 error message.

Messaging Application Programming Interface (MAPI)   An e-mail application programming interface (API).

metadata   Information about the properties of data, such as the type of data in a column (numeric, text, and so on) or the length of a column. It can also be information about the structure of data or information that specifies the design of objects.

method   A function that performs an action by using a COM object, as in SQL-DMO, OLE DB, and ActiveX Data Objects (ADO). *See also* **Component Object Model (COM)**

mirroring   The process for protecting against the loss of data because of disk failure by maintaining a fully redundant copy of data on a separate disk. Mirroring can be implemented at several levels: in SQL Server 2000, in the operating system, and in the disk controller hardware.

Mixed Mode   A mode that combines Windows Authentication and SQL Server Authentication. Mixed Mode allows users to connect to an instance of SQL Server through either a Windows NT 4.0 or Windows 2000 user account or a SQL Server login.

model database   A database installed with SQL Server that provides the template for new user databases. SQL Server 2000 creates a new database by copying in the contents of the model database and then expanding it to the size requested.

Multidimensional Expressions (MDX)   A syntax used for defining multidimensional objects and querying and manipulating multidimensional data.

multidimensional structure   A database paradigm that treats data not as relational tables and columns, but as information cubes. *See also* **cube**

multiple instances   Multiple copies of SQL Server running on the same computer. There can be one default instance, which can be any version of SQL Server. There can be multiple named instances of SQL Server 2000. *See also* **default instance, named instance**

multithreaded server application   An application that creates multiple threads within a single process to service multiple user requests at the same time.

multiuser   The ability of a computer to support many users operating at the same time, while providing the computer system's full range of capabilities to each user.

N

named instance   An installation of SQL Server 2000 that is given a name to differentiate it from other named instances and from the default instance on the same computer. A named instance is identified by the computer name and instance name. *See also* **default instance**, **multiple instances**

named pipe   An interprocess communication (IPC) mechanism that SQL Server uses to provide communication between clients and servers. Named pipes permit access to shared network resources.

native format   Bulk copy data files in which the data is stored using the same internal data structures SQL Server uses to store data in SQL Server databases. Bulk copy can quickly process native mode files because it does not have to convert data when transferring it between SQL Server and the bulk copy data file. *See also* **character format**

Net-Library   A SQL Server communications component that isolates the SQL Server client software and database engine from the network APIs. The SQL Server client software and database engine send generic network requests to a Net-Library, which translates the request to the specific network commands of the protocol chosen by the user.

net send notification   Sends out a broadcast to all registered users of the local domain. Net send is one of the three ways that SQL Server administrators can send alert notifications to specified users.

network libraries   A set of dynamic link libraries (DLLs) that enable SQL Server to communicate over a variety of protocols.

nickname   When used with merge replication system tables, a name for another Subscriber that is known to already have a specified generation of updated data. Used to avoid sending an update to a Subscriber that has already received those changes.

niladic functions   Functions that do not have any input parameters. Most niladic SQL Server functions return system information.

nonclustered index   An index in which the logical order of the index is different from the physical, stored order of the rows on disk.

nonleaf   In a tree structure, an element that has one or more subordinate elements. In SQL Server indexes, an intermediate index node that points to other intermediate nodes or leaf nodes. *See also* **leaf**

normalization rules   A set of database design rules that minimize data redundancy and results in a database in which the database engine and application software can easily enforce integrity.

NULL   An entry that has no explicitly assigned value. NULL is not equivalent to zero or blank. A value of NULL is not considered to be greater than, less than, or equivalent to any other value, including another value of NULL.

nullability   The attribute of a column, parameter, or variable that specifies whether it allows null data values.

O

object   In databases, one of the components of a database: a table, index, trigger, view, key, constraint, default, rule, user-defined data type, or stored procedure.

object dependencies   References to other objects when the behavior of the first object can be affected by changes in the object it references. For example, if a stored procedure references a table, changes to the table can affect the behavior of the stored procedure.

object identifier   A unique name given to an object. In Meta Data Services, a unique identifier constructed from a globally unique identifier (GUID) and an internal identifier. All objects must have an object identifier. *See also* **internal identifier**

object owner   The security account that controls the permissions for an object, usually the creator of the object. Object owner is also called the database object owner.

object permission   An attribute that controls the ability to perform operations on an object. For example, table or view permissions control which users can execute SELECT, INSERT, UPDATE, and DELETE statements against the table or view.

ODBC *See* **Open Database Connectivity (ODBC)**

ODBC data source   The location of a set of data that can be accessed using an ODBC driver. Also, a stored definition that contains all of the connection information an ODBC application requires to connect to the data source. *See also* **data source**

ODBC driver   A dynamic-link library (DLL) that an ODBC-enabled application, such as Excel, can use to access an ODBC data source. Each ODBC driver is specific to a database management system (DBMS), such as SQL Server, Access, and so on.

ODS *See* **Open Data Services (ODS)**

OIM *See* **Open Information Model (OIM)**

OLAP *See* **online analytical processing (OLAP)**

OLE DB   A COM-based application programming interface (API) for accessing data. OLE DB supports accessing data stored in any format (databases, spreadsheets, text files, and so on) for which an OLE DB provider is available. *See also* **OLE DB for OLAP**

OLE DB for OLAP   Formerly, the separate specification that addressed OLAP extensions to OLE DB. Beginning with OLE DB 2.0, OLAP extensions are incorporated into the OLE DB specification. *See also* **OLE DB**

OLE DB provider   A software component that exposes OLE DB interfaces. Each OLE DB provider exposes data from a particular type of data source (for example, SQL Server databases, Access databases, or Excel spreadsheets).

OLTP *See* **online transaction processing (OLTP)**

online analytical processing (OLAP)   A technology that uses multidimensional structures to provide rapid access to data for analysis. The source data for OLAP is commonly stored in data warehouses in a relational database.

online transaction processing (OLTP)   A data processing system designed to record all of the business transactions of an organization as they occur. An OLTP system is characterized by many concurrent users actively adding and modifying data.

Online Troubleshooters   Web-based troubleshooters for common problems that can help diagnose what is happening with an installation of SQL Server 2000.

Open Data Services (ODS)   The layer of the SQL Server database engine that transfers client requests to the appropriate functions in the database engine. Open Data Services exposes the extended stored procedure API used to write DLL functions that can be called from Transact-SQL statements.

Open Database Connectivity (ODBC)   A data-access application programming interface (API) that supports access to any data source for which an ODBC driver is available. ODBC is aligned with the American National Standards Institute (ANSI) and International Organization for Standardization (ISO) standards for a database Call Level Interface (CLI).

Open Information Model (OIM)   An information model published by the Meta Data Coalition (MDC) and widely supported by software vendors. The OIM is a formal description of metadata constructs organized by subject area.

optimize synchronization   An option in merge replication that allows you to minimize network traffic when determining whether recent changes have caused a row to move into or out of a partition that is published to a Subscriber.

optimizer *See* **query optimizer**

P

page   In a virtual storage system, a fixed-length block of contiguous virtual addresses copied as a unit from memory to disk and back during paging operations. SQL Server allocates database space in pages. In SQL Server, a page is 8 kilobytes (KB) in size.

Page Reads/sec   A Buffer Manager object counter that reports the number of physical database page reads that are issued per second.

page split   The process of moving half the rows or entries in a full data or index page to two new pages to make room for a new row or index entry.

Page Writes/sec   A Buffer Manager object counter that reports the number of physical database page writes that are issued per second.

pager notification   A notification sent as an e-mail message to a pager that contains information about an event or an alert that took place on the SQL Server.

partitioning   The process of replacing a table with multiple smaller tables. Each smaller table has the same format as the original table, but with a subset of the data. Each partitioned table has rows allocated to it based on some characteristic of the data, such as specific key ranges. The rules that define into which table the rows go must be unambiguous. For example, a table is partitioned into two tables. All rows with primary key values lower than a specified value are allocated to one table, and all keys equal to or greater than the value are allocated to the other. Partitioning can improve application processing speeds and reduce the potential for conflicts in multisite update replication. You can improve the usability of partitioned tables by creating a view. The view, created by a union of select operations on all the partitioned tables, presents the data as if it all resided in a single table. *See also* **filtering, horizontal partitioning, vertical partitioning**

permissions   Authorization that enforces database security. SQL Server permissions specify the Transact-SQL statements, views, and stored procedures each user is authorized to use. There are two types of permissions: object permissions and statement permissions.

physical name   The path where a file or mirrored file is located. The default is the path of the Master.dat file followed by the first eight characters of the file's logical name. For example, if Accounting is the logical name, and the Master.dat file is located in Sql\Data, the default physical name is Sql\Data\Accounti.dat. For a mirrored file, the default is the path of the Master.mir file followed by the first eight characters of the mirror file's logical name. For example, if Maccount is the name of the mirrored file, and the Master.mir file is located in Sql\Data, the default physical name is Sql\Data\Maccount.mir.

physical reads   A request for a database page in which SQL Server must transfer the requested page from disk to the SQL Server buffer pool. All attempts to read pages are called logical reads. If the page is already in the buffer, there is no associated physical read generated by the logical read. The number of physical reads never exceeds the number of logical reads. In a well-tuned instance of SQL Server, the number of logical reads is typically much higher than the number of physical reads.

PK *See* **primary key (PK)**

precision   The maximum total number of decimal digits that can be stored both to the left and right of the decimal point.

primary data file   Files containing the startup information for the database; they can also be used to store data. Every database has one primary data file.

primary filegroup   The filegroup that contains the primary data file and any other files not specifically assigned to another filegroup.

primary key (PK)   A column or set of columns that uniquely identifies all the rows in a table. Primary keys do not allow null values. No two rows can have the same primary key value; therefore, a primary key value always uniquely identifies a single row. More than one key can uniquely identify rows in a table, and each of these keys is called a candidate key. Only one candidate can be chosen as the primary key of a table; all other candidate keys are known as alternate keys. Although tables are not required to have primary keys, it is good practice to define them. In a normalized table, all of the data values in each row are fully dependent on the primary key. For example, in a normalized employee table that has EmployeeID as the primary key, all of the columns should contain data related to a specific employee. The table does not have the column DepartmentName because the name of the department is dependent on a department ID, not on an employee ID.

primary table   The "one" side of two related tables in a one-to-many relationship. A primary table should have a primary key and each record should be unique. An example of a primary table is a table of customer names that are uniquely identified by a CustomerID primary key field.

procedure cache   The part of the SQL Server memory pool that is used to store execution plans for Transact-SQL batches, stored procedures, and triggers. Execution plans record the steps that SQL Server must take to produce the results specified by the Transact-SQL statements contained in the batches, stored procedures, or triggers.

processadmin   A fixed server role that enables members of the role to manage processes running in an instance of SQL Server.

producer   A SQL Profiler process that collects events in a specific event category and sends the data to a SQL Server Profiler queue.

property   A named attribute of a control, field, or database object that you set to define one of the object's characteristics (such as size, color, or screen location) or an aspect of its behavior (such as whether it is hidden).

property pages   A tabbed dialog box in which you can identify the characteristics of tables, relationships, indexes, constraints, and keys. Every object in a database diagram has a set of properties that determine the definition of a database object. Each set of tabs shows only the properties specific to the selected object. If multiple objects are selected, the property pages show the properties of the first object you selected.

provider   An OLE DB provider. An in-process dynamic-link library (DLL) that provides access to a database.

public role   A special database role used to capture all default permissions for users in a database. Every database user belongs to this role.

publication   A publication is a collection of one or more articles from one database. This grouping of multiple articles makes it easier to specify a logically related set of data and database objects that you want to replicate at the same time.

publication database   A database on the Publisher from which data and database objects are marked for replication as part of a publication that is propagated to Subscribers.

publication retention period   A predetermined length of time that regulates how long subscriptions will receive updates during synchronizations and remain activated in databases.

published data   Data at the Publisher that has been replicated.

Publisher   A server that makes data available for replication to other servers, detects changed data, and maintains information about all publications at the site.

publishing table   The table at the Publisher in which data has been marked for replication and is part of a publication.

pubs database   A sample database provided with SQL Server.

pull subscription   A subscription created and administered at the Subscriber. Information about the publication and the Subscriber is stored. *See also* **push subscription**

push subscription   A subscription created and administered at the Publisher. Information about the publication and Subscriber is stored. *See also* **pull subscription**

Q

query optimizer   The SQL Server database engine component responsible for generating efficient execution plans for SQL statements.

queue   A SQL Server Profiler queue provides a temporary holding place for server events to be captured.

R

RAISERROR   A T-SQL statement that enables users to retrieve an existing entry from sysmessages, or it can use a hard-coded (user-defined) message.

RDBMS *See* **relational database management system (RDBMS)**

record   A group of related fields (columns) of information treated as a unit. A record is more commonly called a row in a SQL database.

Recovery   An operation in which SQL Server is restarted after a system failure; the transaction log is used to roll forward all committed transactions and roll back all uncommitted transactions in order to bring the database to the state it was in at the point of failure.

recovery interval   The maximum amount of time that the database engine should require to recover a database. The database engine ensures that the active portion of the database log is small enough to recover the database in the amount of time specified for the recovery interval.

referenced key   A primary key or unique key referenced by a foreign key.

referencing key *See* **foreign key (FK)**

referential integrity (RI)   A state in which all foreign key values in a database are valid. For a foreign key to be valid, it must contain either the value NULL, or an existing key value from the primary or unique key columns referenced by the foreign key.

reflexive relationship   A relationship from a column or combination of columns in a table to other columns in that same table. A reflexive relationship is used to compare rows within the same table. In queries, this is called a self-join.

relational database   A collection of information organized in tables. Each table models a class of objects of interest to the organization (for example, Customers, Parts, Suppliers). Each column in a table models an attribute of the object (for example, LastName, Price, Color). Each row in a table represents one entity in the class of objects modeled by the table (for example, the customer name John Smith or the part number 1346). Queries can use data from one table to find related data in other tables.

relational database management system (RDBMS)   A system that organizes data into related rows and columns. SQL Server is a relational database management system (RDBMS).

remote data   Data stored in an OLE DB data source that is separate from the current instance of SQL Server. The data is accessed by establishing a linked server definition or using an ad hoc connector name.

remote Distributor   A server for SQL Server replication configured as a Distributor that is sepa-

rate from the server configured as the Publisher. *See also* **Distributor, local Distributor**

remote login identification   The login identification (login ID) assigned to a user for accessing remote procedures on a remote server.

remote server   A definition of an instance of SQL Server used by remote stored procedure calls. Remote servers are still supported in SQL Server 2000, but linked servers offer greater functionality. *See also* **local server**

remote stored procedure   A stored procedure located on one instance of SQL Server that is executed by a statement on another instance of SQL Server. In SQL Server 2000, remote stored procedures are supported, but distributed queries offer greater functionality.

remote table   A table stored in an OLE DB data source that is separate from the current instance of SQL Server. The table is accessed by either establishing a linked server definition or using an ad hoc connector name.

replicated data   Data at the Subscriber that has been received from a Publisher.

Replication   A process that copies and distributes data and database objects from one database to another and then synchronizes information between databases for consistency.

Replication Conflict Viewer   Allows users to view and resolve conflicts that occurred during the merge replication process and to review the manner in which conflicts have been resolved.

Replication Monitor   Allows users to view and manage replication agents responsible for various replication tasks and to troubleshoot potential problems at the Distributor.

replication scripting   The generation of .sql scripts that can be used to configure and disable replication.

replication topology   A network layout that defines the relationship between servers and the copies of data and clarifies the logic that determines how data flows between servers.

Repository   A database containing information models that, in conjunction with the executable software, manage the database. The term can also refer to an installation of Meta Data Services.

repository engine   Object-oriented software that provides management support for and customer access to a repository database.

repository object   A COM object that represents a data construct stored in a repository type library.

Repository SQL schema   A set of standard tables used by the repository engine to manage all repository objects, relationships, and collections. Repository SQL schema maps information model elements to SQL schema elements.

Repository Type Information Model (RTIM)   A core object model that represents repository type definitions for Meta Data Services. This object model is composed of abstract classes upon which instances of information models are based.

Republish   For a Subscriber to publish data received from a Publisher to another Subscriber.

Republisher   A Subscriber that publishes data that it has received from a Publisher.

resolution strategy   A set of criteria that the repository engine evaluates sequentially when selecting an object, where multiple versions exist and version information is unspecified in the calling program.

Restore   An operation in which a SQL Server backup file is copied back into the SQL Server database. This operation takes the database back to the state it was in when the backup was created.

RESTORE DATABASE   T-SQL command used to restore a database.

RESTORE LOG   T-SQL command used to restore a transaction log.

result set   The set of rows returned from a SELECT statement. The format of the rows in the result set is defined by the column-list of the SELECT statement.

revoke   To remove a previously granted or denied permission from a user account, role, or group in the current database.

RI *See* **referential integrity (RI)**

role   A SQL Server security account that is a collection of other security accounts that can be treated as a single unit when managing permissions. A role can contain SQL Server logins, other roles, and Windows logins or groups.

roll back   To remove the updates performed by one or more partially completed transactions. Rollbacks are required to restore the integrity of a database after an application, database, or system failure. *See also* **commit**

roll forward   To apply all the completed transactions from a database or log backup in order to recover a database to a point in time or the point of failure (for example, after events such as the loss of a disk).

row   In a SQL table, the collection of elements that form a horizontal line in the table. Each row in the table represents a single occurrence of the object modeled by the table and stores the values for all the attributes of that object. For example, in the Northwind sample database, the Employees table models the employees of the Northwind Traders Company. The first row in the table records all the information (for example, name and title) about the employee who has employee ID 1. *See also* **column**

row filter   A filter that specifies a subset of rows from a table to be published and when specific rows need to be propagated to Subscribers.

row lock   A lock on a single row in a table.

Rowset   The OLE DB object used to contain a result set. It also exhibits cursor behavior depending on the rowset properties set by an application.

RTIM *See* **Repository Type Information Model (RTIM)**

Rule   A database object that is bound to columns or user-defined data types, and specifies which data values are acceptable in a column. CHECK constraints provide the same functionality and are preferred because they are in the SQL-92 standard.

S

sample setup files   SQL Server 2000 contains several sample setup scripts that you can use when running an unattended installation. These scripts include instructions to conduct a typical install, install only client tools, or upgrade from SQL Server 7.0.

Savepoint   A marker that allows an application to roll back part of a transaction if a minor error is encountered. The application must still commit or roll back the full transaction when it is complete.

Scale   The number of digits to the right of the decimal point in a number.

scheduled backup   An automatic backup accomplished by SQL Server Agent when defined and scheduled as a job.

Schema   In the SQL-92 standard, a collection of database objects that are owned by a single user and form a single namespace. A namespace is a set of objects that cannot have duplicate names. For example, two tables can have the same name only if they are in separate schemas; no two tables in the same schema can have the same name. In

Transact-SQL, much of the functionality associated with schemas is implemented by database user IDs. In database tools, schema also refers to the catalog information that describes the objects in a schema or database.

schema rowset   A special OLE DB or Analysis Services rowset that reports catalog information for objects in databases or multidimensional cubes. For example, the OLE DB schema rowset DBSCHEMA_COLUMNS describes columns in tables.

Script   A collection of Transact-SQL statements used to perform an operation. Transact-SQL scripts are stored as files, usually with the .sql extension.

search condition   In a WHERE or HAVING clause, predicates that specify the conditions that the source rows must meet to be included in the SQL statement. For example, the statement SELECT * FROM Employees WHERE Title = 'Sales Representative' returns only those rows that match the search condition: Title = 'Sales Representative'.

secondary data file   Any file other than the primary data file that is used to store data or spread data across multiple disk drives. A database may have multiple secondary data files.

Securityadmin   A fixed server role that enables members of the role to manage server logons.

Security Identifier (SID) A unique value that identifies a user who is logged on to the security system. SIDs can identify either one user or a group of users.

SELECT   The Transact-SQL statement used to return data to an application or another Transact-SQL statement, or to populate a cursor. The SELECT statement returns a tabular result set consisting of data that is typically extracted from one or more tables. The result set contains only data from rows that match the search conditions specified in WHERE or HAVING clauses.

select list   The SELECT statement clause that defines the columns of the result set returned by the statement. The select list is a comma-separated list of expressions, such as column names, functions, or constants.

Serveradmin   A fixed server role that enables members of the role to configure serverwide settings.

server cursor   A cursor implemented on the server. The cursor itself is built at the server, and only the rows fetched by an application are sent to the client. *See also* **API server cursor**

server name   A name that uniquely identifies a server computer on a network. SQL Server applications can connect to a default instance of SQL Server by specifying only the server name. SQL Server applications must specify both the server name and instance name when connecting to a named instance on a server.

Setupadmin   A fixed server role that enables members of the role to add and remove linked servers and execute some stored procedures.

Setup initialization file   A text file, using the Windows .ini file format, that stores configuration information allowing SQL Server to be installed without a user having to be present to respond to prompts from the Setup program.

SETUP.ISS   The SETUP.ISS file is created when you use the Setup screens to install SQL Server 2000. All of the options you select, such as the collation type, are recorded in the SETUP.ISS file. You can then use the SETUP.ISS file to run an unattended installation if you have to reinstall the server or install a similar configuration to another server.

severity level   A number indicating the relative significance of an error generated by the SQL Server database engine. Values range from informational (1) to severe (25).

shared lock   A lock created by nonupdate (read) operations. Other users can read the data concurrently, but no transaction can acquire an exclusive lock on the data until all the shared locks have been released.

showplan   A report showing the execution plan for a SQL statement. SET SHOWPLAN_TEXT and SET SHOWPLAN_ALL produce textual showplan output. SQL Query Analyzer and SQL Server Enterprise Manager can display showplan information as a graphical tree.

SID *See* **Security Identifier (SID)**

SIMPLE   Recovery model that provides recovery up to the point of the last backup.

single-user mode   A state in which only one user can access a resource. Both SQL Server instances and individual databases can be put into single-user mode.

Snapshot Agent   A SQL Server Agent job that prepares snapshot files containing schema and data of published tables, stores the files in the snapshot folder, and inserts synchronization jobs in the publication database.

Snapshot Agent utility   A utility that configures and triggers the Snapshot Agent, which prepares snapshot files containing schema and data of published tables and database objects.

snapshot replication   A type of replication that distributes data exactly as it appears at a specific moment in time and does not monitor for modifications made to the data. *See also* **merge replication, transactional replication**

sort order   The set of rules in a collation that defines how characters are evaluated in comparison operations and the sequence in which they are sorted.

source and target A browsing technique in which a source object is used to retrieve its target object or objects through their relationship.

source database *See* **publication database**

sp_add_alert Stored procedure that creates an alert, which then can be used for the purposes of notifying the SQL Server administrator.

sp_add_job Stored procedure that adds a new job executed by the SQLServerAgent service.

sp_add_jobschedule Stored procedure that creates a schedule for a job.

sp_add_jobstep Stored procedure that adds a step (operation) to a job.

sp_addlogin Stored procedure that creates a new SQL Server logon that allows a user to connect to an instance of SQL Server using SQL Server Authentication.

sp_add_notification Stored procedure that sets up a notification for an alert.

sp_add_operator Stored procedure that creates an operator (notification recipient) for use with alerts and jobs.

sp_addtype Stored procedure that creates a user-defined data type.

sp_attach_db Microsoft SQL Server system stored procedure that enables administrators to create a new database by attaching specified .mdf and .ldf database files to the database. The command can also be used to attach the database files to an existing database.

sp_denylogin Stored procedure that prevents a Windows NT or Windows 2000 user or group from connecting to SQL Server.

sp_detach_db Microsoft SQL Server system stored procedure that removes a database from the server. The command does not delete the .mdf and .ldf files from the server, which allows an administrator to move or copy the files to another Microsoft SQL Server.

specialized setup file A specialized setup file is created when you use the Record Unattended .iss option in the Setup program. This specialized setup file can be used as an alternative to the SETUP.ISS file. It allows you to specify domain user accounts that should be used for the SQL Services.

sp_grantdbaccess Stored procedure that adds a security account in the current database for a SQL Server logon or Windows NT or Windows 2000 user or group and enables it to be granted permissions to perform activities in the database.

sp_grantlogin Stored procedure that allows a Windows NT or Windows 2000 user or group account to connect to SQL Server using Windows Authentication.

sp_help_job Stored procedure that returns information about jobs that are used by SQLServerAgent service to perform automated activities in SQL Server.

sp_help_jobhistory Stored procedure that provides information about the jobs for servers in the multiserver administration domain.

sp_lock Stored procedure that displays information about locks.

sp_manage_jobs_by_login Stored procedure that deletes or reassigns jobs that belong to the specified logon.

sp_monitor Stored procedure that displays statistics about SQL Server, such as the number of seconds the SQL Server has been idle.

sp_processmail Stored procedure that uses extended stored procedures to process incoming mail messages from the inbox for SQL Server.

sp_revokelogin   Stored procedure that removes the logon entries for SQL Server for a Windows NT or Windows 2000 user or group created with sp_grantlogin or sp_denylogin.

sp_who   Stored procedure that provides information about current Microsoft SQL Server users and processes.

SQL *See* **Structured Query Language (SQL)**

SQL collation   A set of SQL Server 2000 collations whose characteristics match those of commonly used code page and sort order combinations from earlier versions of SQL Server. SQL collations are compatibility features that let sites choose collations that match the behavior of their earlier systems. *See also* **collation**

SQL database   A database based on Structured Query Language (SQL).

SQLDIAG.EXE   A utility that gathers and stores diagnostic information and the contents of the query history trace (if it is running).

SQL expression   Any combination of operators, constants, literal values, functions, and names of tables and fields that evaluates to a single value. For example, use expressions to define calculated fields in queries.

SQL Mail   A component of SQL Server that allows SQL Server to send and receive mail messages through the built-in Windows NT 4.0 or Windows 2000 Messaging Application Programming Interface (MAPI). A mail message can consist of short text strings, the output from a query, or an attached file.

SQL Profiler   A SQL Server utility that is used to monitor server performance and activity. SQL Profiler is used for tracking events within SQL Server.

SQL query   A SQL statement such as SELECT, INSERT, UPDATE, DELETE, or CREATE TABLE.

SQL Query Analyzer   SQL Query is a graphical user interface for designing and testing Transact-SQL statements, batches, and scripts interactively.

SQL Server Agent   A Windows service that performs background tasks, such as scheduling SQL Server jobs and notifying the appropriate person of problems within SQL Server.

SQL Server authentication   One of two mechanisms for validating attempts to connect to instances of SQL Server. Users must specify a SQL Server login ID and password when they connect. The SQL Server instance ensures that the login ID and password combination are valid before allowing the connection to succeed. Windows authentication is the preferred authentication mechanism. *See also* **Authentication, Windows authentication**

SQL Server Event Forwarding Server   A central instance of SQL Server that manages SQL Server Agent events forwarded to it by other instances. Enables central management of SQL Server events.

SQL Server login   An account stored in SQL Server that allows users to connect to SQL Server.

SQL Server role *See* **role**

SQL Server user *See* **user (account)**

SQL statement   A SQL or Transact-SQL command, such as SELECT or DELETE, that performs some action on data.

SQL-92 The version of the SQL standard published in 1992. The international standard is ISO/IEC 9075:1992 Database Language SQL. The American National Standards Institute (ANSI) also published a corresponding standard (Data Language SQL X3.135-1192), so SQL-92 is sometimes referred to as ANSI SQL in the United States.

standard security *See* **SQL Server authentication**

statement permission An attribute that controls whether a user can execute CREATE or BACKUP statements.

step object A Data Transformation Services (DTS) object that coordinates the flow of control and execution of tasks in a DTS package. A task that does not have an associated step object is never executed.

store-and-forward database *See* **distribution database**

stored procedure A precompiled collection of Transact-SQL statements stored under a name and processed as a unit. SQL Server supplies stored procedures for managing SQL Server and displaying information about databases and users. SQL Server-supplied stored procedures are called system stored procedures.

string A set of contiguous bytes that contain a single character-based or binary data value. In character strings, each byte, or pair of bytes, represents a single alphabetic letter, special character, or number. In binary strings, the entire value is considered to be a single stream of bits that do not have any inherent pattern. For example, the constant 'I am 32.' is an 8-byte character string, whereas the constant 0x0205efa3 is a 4-byte binary string.

Structured Query Language (SQL) A language used to insert, retrieve, modify, and delete data in a relational database. SQL also contains statements for defining and administering the objects in a database. SQL is the language supported by most relational databases, and is the subject of standards published by the International Standards Organization (ISO) and the American National Standards Institute (ANSI). SQL Server 2000 uses a version of the SQL language called Transact-SQL.

structured storage file *See* **COM-structured storage file**

subscribe To request data from a Publisher.

Subscriber A server that receives copies of published data.

subscription An order that defines what data will be published, when, and to what Subscriber.

subscription database A database at the Subscriber that receives data and database objects published by a Publisher.

synchronization In replication, the process of maintaining the same schema and data at a Publisher and at a Subscriber. *See also* **initial snapshot**

system administrator The person or group of people responsible for managing an instance of SQL Server. System administrators have full permissions to perform all actions in an instance of SQL Server. System administrators either are members of the sysadmin fixed server role, or log in using the sa login ID.

system catalog A set of system tables that describe all the features of an instance of SQL Server. The system catalog records metadata such as the definitions of all users, all databases, all objects in each database, and system configuration information such as server and database option settings. *See also* **database catalog**

system databases A set of four databases present in all instances of SQL Server that are used to store system information: The master database stores all instance-level metadata, and records the location of all other databases. The tempdb database stores transient objects that exist only for the length of a single statement or connection, such as worktables and temporary tables or stored procedures. The model database is used as a template for creating all user databases. The msdb database is used by the SQL Server Agent to record information on jobs, alerts, and backup histories. *See also* **user database**

system functions A set of built-in functions that perform operations on and return the information about values, objects, and settings in SQL Server.

system stored procedures A set of SQL Server–supplied stored procedures that can be used for actions such as retrieving information from the system catalog or performing administration tasks.

system tables Built-in tables that form the system catalog for SQL Server. System tables store all the metadata for an instance of SQL Server, including configuration information and definitions of all the databases and database objects in the instance. Users should not directly modify any system table.

T

table A two-dimensional object, consisting of rows and columns, used to store data in a relational database. Each table stores information about one of the types of objects modeled by the database. For example, an education database would have one table for teachers, a second for students, and a third for classes. The columns of a table represent an attribute of the modeled object (for example, first name, last name, and address). Each row represents one occurrence of the modeled object. For example, one row in the Class table would record the information about an Algebra 1 class taught at 9:00 A.M. and another would record the information about a World History class taught at 10:00 A.M.

table lock A lock on a table including all data and indexes.

table scan A data retrieval operation in which the database engine must read all the pages in a table to find the rows that qualify for a query.

table-level constraint Constraints that allow various forms of data integrity to be defined on one column (column-level constraint) or several columns (table-level constraints) when the table is defined or altered. Constraints support domain integrity, entity integrity, and referential integrity, as well as user-defined integrity.

tabular data stream (TDS) The SQL Server internal client/server data transfer protocol. TDS allows client and server products to communicate regardless of operating system platform, server release, or network transport.

tape backup A backup operation to any tape device supported by Windows NT 4.0 and Windows 2000. If you are creating a tape backup file, you must first install the tape device by using Windows NT 4.0 and Windows 2000. The tape device must be physically attached to the SQL Server computer that you are backing up.

target object *See* **source and target**

Target Server Memory A Memory Manager object counter that reports the total amount of dynamic memory the server can consume.

task *See* **job**

task object A Data Transformation Services (DTS) object that defines pieces of work to be performed as part of the data transformation process. For example, a task can execute a SQL statement or move and transform heterogeneous data from an OLE DB source to an OLE DB destination using the DTS Data Pump.

TDS *See* **tabular data stream (TDS)**

tempdb database The database that provides a storage area for temporary tables, temporary stored procedures, and other temporary working storage needs.

text data type A SQL Server system data type that specifies variable-length non-Unicode data with a maximum length of 2^31 -1

(2,147,483,647) characters. The text data type cannot be used for variables or parameters in stored procedures.

thread   An operating system component that allows the logic of multiuser applications to be performed as several separate, asynchronous execution paths. The SQL Server relational database engine executes multiple threads in order to make use of multiple processors. The use of threads also helps ensure that work is being performed for some user connections even when other connections are blocked (for example, when waiting for a disk read or write operation to complete).

tool   A SQL Server application with a graphical user interface used to perform common tasks.

Total Server Memory   A Memory Manager object counter that reports the total amount of dynamic memory that the server is currently using.

trace file   A file used by SQL Profiler to record monitored events.

Transact-SQL   The language containing the commands used to administer instances of SQL Server, create and manage all objects in an instance of SQL Server, and to insert, retrieve, modify, and delete all data in SQL Server tables. Transact-SQL is an extension of the language defined in the SQL standards published by the Organization for International Standardization (ISO) and the American National Standards Institute (ANSI).

Transact-SQL cursor   A server cursor defined by using the Transact-SQL DECLARE CURSOR syntax. Transact-SQL cursors are intended for use in Transact-SQL batches, stored procedures, and triggers.

transaction   A group of database operations combined into a logical unit of work that is either wholly committed or rolled back. A transaction is atomic, consistent, isolated, and durable.

transaction log   A database file in which all changes to the database are recorded. It is used by SQL Server during automatic recovery.

transaction processing   Data processing used to efficiently record business activities, called transactions, that are of interest to an organization (for example, sales, orders for supplies, or money transfers). Typically, online transaction processing (OLTP) systems perform large numbers of relatively small transactions.

transaction rollback   Rollback of a user-specified transaction to the last savepoint inside a transaction or to the beginning of a transaction.

transactional replication   A type of replication in which an initial snapshot of data is applied at Subscribers, and then when data modifications are made at the Publisher, the individual transactions are captured and propagated to Subscribers. *See also* **merge replication, snapshot replication**

transformable subscription   A subscription that allows data movement, transformation mapping, and filtering capabilities of Data Transformation Services (DTS) during replication.

transformation   In data warehousing, the process of changing data extracted from source data systems into arrangements and formats consistent with the schema of the data warehouse.

trigger   A stored procedure that executes when data in a specified table is modified. Triggers are often created to enforce referential integrity or consistency among logically related data in different tables.

trusted connection   A Windows network connection that can be opened only by users who have been authenticated by the network. The users are identified by their Windows login ID and do not have to enter a separate SQL Server login ID. *See also* **Windows authentication**

two-phase commit A process that ensures transactions that apply to more than one server are completed on all servers or on none.

U

unattended installation Microsoft SQL Server 2000 installation scripts can be created enabling administrators to run unattended installations of SQL Server 2000. Unattended installations are particularly useful for those administrators deploying Microsoft SQL Server 2000 within an enterprise environment.

Unicode Unicode defines a set of letters, numbers, and symbols that SQL Server recognizes in the nchar, nvarchar, and ntext data types. It is related to but separate from character sets. Unicode has more than 65,000 possible values compared to a character set's 256, and takes twice as much space to store. Unicode includes characters for most languages.

Unicode collation A set of rules that determines how SQL Server compares, collates, and presents Unicode data in response to database queries. It acts as a sort order for Unicode data.

Unicode format Data stored in a bulk copy data file using Unicode characters.

unique indexes An index in which no two rows are permitted to have the same index value, thus prohibiting duplicate index or key values. The system checks for duplicate key values when the index is created and checks each time data is added with an INSERT or UPDATE statement.

update To modify one or more data values in an existing row or rows, typically by using the UPDATE statement. Sometimes, the term update refers to any data modification, including INSERT, UPDATE, and DELETE operations.

update lock A lock placed on resources (such as row, page, table) that can be updated. Updated locks are used to prevent a common form of deadlock that occurs when multiple sessions are locking resources and are potentially updating them later.

update query A query that changes the values in columns of one or more rows in a table.

update statistics A process that recalculates information about the distribution of key values in specified indexes. These statistics are used by the query optimizer to determine the most efficient way to execute a query.

URL Abbreviation for Uniform Resource Locator. URLs are formatted strings or streams that an Internet application can use to reference resources on the Internet or on an intranet.

user (account) A SQL Server security account or identifier that represents a specific user in a database. Each user's Windows account or SQL Server login is mapped to a user account in a database. Then the appropriate permissions are granted to the user account. Each user account can only access data with which it has been granted permission to work.

user database A database created by a SQL Server user and used to store application data. Most users connecting to instances of SQL Server reference user databases only, not system databases. *See also* **system databases**

user-defined data type A data type, based on a SQL Server data type, created by the user for custom data storage. Rules and defaults can be bound to user-defined data types (but not to system data types). *See also* **base data type**

user-defined event A type of message, defined by a user, that can be traced by SQL Profiler or used to fire a custom alert. Typically, the user is the system administrator.

user-defined function In SQL Server, a Transact-SQL function defined by a user. Functions encapsulate frequently performed logic in a named entity that can be called by Transact-SQL statements instead of recoding the logic in each statement.

utility   A SQL Server application run from a command prompt to perform common tasks.

V

vertical filtering   Filtering columns from a table. When used as part of replication, the table article created contains only selected columns from the publishing table. *See also* **filtering, vertical partitioning**

vertical partitioning   Segmenting a single table into multiple tables based on selected columns. Each of the multiple tables has the same number of rows but fewer columns. *See also* **partitioning, vertical filtering**

view   A database object that can be referenced the same way as a table in SQL statements. Views are defined using a SELECT statement and are analogous to an object that contains the result set of this statement.

Vswitch   A utility used to switch between SQL Server 2000, SQL Server 6.5, and SQL Server 6.0 as the active version of SQL Server.

W

WHERE clause   The part of a SQL statement that specifies which records to retrieve.

Windows authentication   One of two mechanisms for validating attempts to connect to instances of SQL Server. Users are identified by their Windows user or group when they connect. Windows authentication is the most secure mechanism for connecting to SQL Server. *See also* **SQL Server authentication, trusted connection**

Windows collation   A set of rules that determine how SQL Server sorts character data. It is speci-

fied by name in the Windows Control Panel and in SQL Server 2000 during Setup.

write-ahead log   A transaction logging method in which the log is always written prior to the data.

X

XDR schema   XML Data Reduced schemas represent a logical view of tables in a database.

XML   Extensible Markup Language is a hypertext programming language used to describe the contents of a set of data and how the data should be output to a device or displayed in a Web page.

Xpath   A query language defined for XML that provides syntax to select a specific node, or subset of nodes, in an XML document.

xp_deletemail   Extended stored procedure that deletes a message from the SQL Server inbox.

xp_findnextmsg   Extended stored procedure that accepts a message ID for input and returns the message ID for output.

xp_logevent   Extended stored procedure that logs a user-defined message in the Microsoft SQL Server log file and in the Microsoft Windows NT Event Viewer.

xp_readmail   Extended stored procedure that reads a mail message for the SQL Server mail inbox.

xp_sendmail   Extended stored procedure that sends a message and a query result set attachment to the specified recipients.

xp_startmail   Extended stored procedure that starts a SQL Server mail client session.

xp_stopmail   Extended stored procedure that stops a SQL Server mail client session.

Index

A

R

W

X-Z

At Microsoft Press, we use tools to illustrate our books for software developers and IT professionals. Tools very simply and powerfully symbolize human inventiveness. They're a metaphor for people extending their capabilities, precision, and reach. From simple calipers and pliers to digital micrometers and lasers, these stylized illustrations give each book a visual identity, and a personality to the series. With tools and knowledge, there's no limit to creativity and innovation. Our tag line says it all: *the tools you need to put technology to work*.

Cover Designer:	Methodologie, Inc.
Interior Graphic Designer:	James D. Kramer
Principal Desktop Publisher:	Kerri DeVault
Principal Copyeditor:	nSight, Inc.
Indexer:	Ginny Bess

Inside *security information* you can trust

Microsoft® Windows® Security Resource Kit
ISBN 0-7356-1868-2   Suggested Retail Price: $59.99 U.S., $86.99 Canada

Comprehensive security information and tools, straight from the Microsoft product groups. This official RESOURCE KIT delivers comprehensive operations and deployment information that information security professionals can put to work right away. The authors—members of Microsoft's security teams describe how to plan and implement a comprehensive security strategy, assess security threats and vulnerabilities, configure system security, and more. The kit also provides must-have security tools, checklists, templates, and other on-the-job resources on CD-ROM and on the Web.

Microsoft Encyclopedia of Security
ISBN 0-7356-1877-1   Suggested Retail Price: $49.99 U.S., $72.99 Canada

The essential, one-of-a-kind security reference for computer professionals at all levels. This encyclopedia delivers 2000+ entries detailing the latest security-related issues, technologies, standards, products, and services. It covers the Microsoft Windows platform as well as open-source technologies and the platforms and products of other major vendors. You get clear, concise explanations and case scenarios that deftly take you from concept to real-world application—ideal for everyone from computer science students up to systems engineers, developers, and managers.

Microsoft Windows Server 2003 Security Administrator's Companion
ISBN 0-7356-1574-8   Suggested Retail Price: $49.99 U.S., $72.99 Canada

The in-depth, practical guide to deploying and maintaining Windows Server 2003 in a secure environment. Learn how to use all the powerful security features in the latest network operating system with this in-depth, authoritative technical reference—written by a security expert on the Microsoft Windows Server 2003 security team. Explore physical security issues, internal security policies, and public and shared key cryptography, and then drill down into the specifics of the key security features of Windows Server 2003.

Microsoft Internet Information Services Security Technical Reference
ISBN 0-7356-1572-1   Suggested Retail Price: $49.99 U.S., $72.99 Canada

The definitive guide for developers and administrators who need to understand how to securely manage networked systems based on IIS. This book presents obvious, avoidable mistakes and known security vulnerabilities in Internet Information Services (IIS)—priceless, intimate facts about the underlying causes of past security issues—while showing the best ways to fix them. The expert author, who has used IIS since the first version, also discusses real-world best practices for developing software and managing systems and networks with IIS.

To learn more about Microsoft Press® products for IT professionals, please visit:

microsoft.com/mspress/IT

In-depth, daily administration guides
for Microsoft Windows Server 2003

Microsoft® Windows® Server 2003 Administrator's Companion
ISBN 0-7356-1367-2

The in-depth, daily operations guide to planning, deployment, and maintenance. Here's the ideal one-volume guide for the IT professional who administers Windows Server 2003. This ADMINISTRATOR'S COMPANION offers up-to-date information on core system-administration topics for Windows, including Active Directory® services, security, disaster planning and recovery, interoperability with NetWare and UNIX, plus all-new sections about Microsoft Internet Security and Acceleration (ISA) Server and scripting. Featuring easy-to-use procedures and handy workarounds, this book provides ready answers for on-the-job results.

Microsoft Windows Server 2003 Security Administrator's Companion
ISBN 0-7356-1574-8

The in-depth, daily operations guide to enhancing security with the network operating system. With this authoritative ADMINISTRATOR'S COMPANION—written by an expert on the Windows Server 2003 security team—you'll learn how to use the powerful security features in the latest network server operating system. The guide describes best practices and technical details for enhancing security with Windows Server 2003, using the holistic approach that IT professionals need to grasp to help secure their systems. The authors cover concepts such as physical security issues, internal security policies, and public and shared key cryptography, and then drill down into the specifics of key security features of Windows Server 2003.

To learn more about the full line of Microsoft Press® products for IT professionals, please visit:

microsoft.com/mspress/IT

Get a **Free**
e-mail newsletter, updates,
special offers, links to related books,
and more when you

register on line!

Register your Microsoft Press® title on our Web site and you'll get a FREE subscription to our e-mail newsletter, *Microsoft Press Book Connections.* You'll find out about newly released and upcoming books and learning tools, online events, software downloads, special offers and coupons for Microsoft Press customers, and information about major Microsoft® product releases. You can also read useful additional information about all the titles we publish, such as detailed book descriptions, tables of contents and indexes, sample chapters, links to related books and book series, author biographies, and reviews by other customers.

Registration is easy. Just visit this Web page and fill in your information:

http://www.microsoft.com/mspress/register

Microsoft®

MICROSOFT LICENSE AGREEMENT

Book Companion CD

IMPORTANT—READ CAREFULLY: This Microsoft End-User License Agreement ("EULA") is a legal agreement between you (either an individual or an entity) and Microsoft Corporation for the Microsoft product identified above, which includes computer software and may include associated media, printed materials, and "online" or electronic documentation ("SOFTWARE PRODUCT"). Any component included within the SOFTWARE PRODUCT that is accompanied by a separate End-User License Agreement shall be governed by such agreement and not the terms set forth below. By installing, copying, or otherwise using the SOFTWARE PRODUCT, you agree to be bound by the terms of this EULA. If you do not agree to the terms of this EULA, you are not authorized to install, copy, or otherwise use the SOFTWARE PRODUCT; you may, however, return the SOFTWARE PRODUCT, along with all printed materials and other items that form a part of the Microsoft product that includes the SOFTWARE PRODUCT, to the place you obtained them for a full refund.

SOFTWARE PRODUCT LICENSE

The SOFTWARE PRODUCT is protected by United States copyright laws and international copyright treaties, as well as other intellectual property laws and treaties. The SOFTWARE PRODUCT is licensed, not sold.

1. **GRANT OF LICENSE.** This EULA grants you the following rights:

   a. **Software Product.** You may install and use one copy of the SOFTWARE PRODUCT on a single computer. The primary user of the computer on which the SOFTWARE PRODUCT is installed may make a second copy for his or her exclusive use on a portable computer.

   b. **Storage/Network Use.** You may also store or install a copy of the SOFTWARE PRODUCT on a storage device, such as a network server, used only to install or run the SOFTWARE PRODUCT on your other computers over an internal network; however, you must acquire and dedicate a license for each separate computer on which the SOFTWARE PRODUCT is installed or run from the storage device. A license for the SOFTWARE PRODUCT may not be shared or used concurrently on different computers.

   c. **License Pak.** If you have acquired this EULA in a Microsoft License Pak, you may make the number of additional copies of the computer software portion of the SOFTWARE PRODUCT authorized on the printed copy of this EULA, and you may use each copy in the manner specified above. You are also entitled to make a corresponding number of secondary copies for portable computer use as specified above.

   d. **Sample Code.** Solely with respect to portions, if any, of the SOFTWARE PRODUCT that are identified within the SOFTWARE PRODUCT as sample code (the "SAMPLE CODE"):

   i. **Use and Modification.** Microsoft grants you the right to use and modify the source code version of the SAMPLE CODE, *provided* you comply with subsection (d)(iii) below. You may not distribute the SAMPLE CODE, or any modified version of the SAMPLE CODE, in source code form.

   ii. **Redistributable Files.** Provided you comply with subsection (d)(iii) below, Microsoft grants you a nonexclusive, royalty-free right to reproduce and distribute the object code version of the SAMPLE CODE and of any modified SAMPLE CODE, other than SAMPLE CODE, or any modified version thereof, designated as not redistributable in the Readme file that forms a part of the SOFTWARE PRODUCT (the "Non-Redistributable Sample Code"). All SAMPLE CODE other than the Non-Redistributable Sample Code is collectively referred to as the "REDISTRIBUTABLES."

   iii. **Redistribution Requirements.** If you redistribute the REDISTRIBUTABLES, you agree to: (i) distribute the REDISTRIBUTABLES in object code form only in conjunction with and as a part of your software application product; (ii) not use Microsoft's name, logo, or trademarks to market your software application product; (iii) include a valid copyright notice on your software application product; (iv) indemnify, hold harmless, and defend Microsoft from and against any claims or lawsuits, including attorney's fees, that arise or result from the use or distribution of your software application product; and (v) not permit further distribution of the REDISTRIBUTABLES by your end user. Contact Microsoft for the applicable royalties due and other licensing terms for all other uses and/or distribution of the REDISTRIBUTABLES.

2. **DESCRIPTION OF OTHER RIGHTS AND LIMITATIONS.**

   • **Limitations on Reverse Engineering, Decompilation, and Disassembly.** You may not reverse engineer, decompile, or disassemble the SOFTWARE PRODUCT, except and only to the extent that such activity is expressly permitted by applicable law notwithstanding this limitation.

   • **Separation of Components.** The SOFTWARE PRODUCT is licensed as a single product. Its component parts may not be separated for use on more than one computer.

   • **Rental.** You may not rent, lease, or lend the SOFTWARE PRODUCT.

- **Support Services.** Microsoft may, but is not obligated to, provide you with support services related to the SOFTWARE PRODUCT ("Support Services"). Use of Support Services is governed by the Microsoft policies and programs described in the user manual, in "online" documentation, and/or in other Microsoft-provided materials. Any supplemental software code provided to you as part of the Support Services shall be considered part of the SOFTWARE PRODUCT and subject to the terms and conditions of this EULA. With respect to technical information you provide to Microsoft as part of the Support Services, Microsoft may use such information for its business purposes, including for product support and development. Microsoft will not utilize such technical information in a form that personally identifies you.

- **Software Transfer.** You may permanently transfer all of your rights under this EULA, provided you retain no copies, you transfer all of the SOFTWARE PRODUCT (including all component parts, the media and printed materials, any upgrades, this EULA, and, if applicable, the Certificate of Authenticity), **and** the recipient agrees to the terms of this EULA.

- **Termination.** Without prejudice to any other rights, Microsoft may terminate this EULA if you fail to comply with the terms and conditions of this EULA. In such event, you must destroy all copies of the SOFTWARE PRODUCT and all of its component parts.

3. **COPYRIGHT.** All title and copyrights in and to the SOFTWARE PRODUCT (including but not limited to any images, photographs, animations, video, audio, music, text, SAMPLE CODE, REDISTRIBUTABLES, and "applets" incorporated into the SOFTWARE PRODUCT) and any copies of the SOFTWARE PRODUCT are owned by Microsoft or its suppliers. The SOFT-WARE PRODUCT is protected by copyright laws and international treaty provisions. Therefore, you must treat the SOFTWARE PRODUCT like any other copyrighted material **except** that you may install the SOFTWARE PRODUCT on a single computer provided you keep the original solely for backup or archival purposes. You may not copy the printed materials accompanying the SOFTWARE PRODUCT.

4. **U.S. GOVERNMENT RESTRICTED RIGHTS.** The SOFTWARE PRODUCT and documentation are provided with RESTRICTED RIGHTS. Use, duplication, or disclosure by the Government is subject to restrictions as set forth in subparagraph (c)(1)(ii) of the Rights in Technical Data and Computer Software clause at DFARS 252.227-7013 or subparagraphs (c)(1) and (2) of the Commercial Computer Software—Restricted Rights at 48 CFR 52.227-19, as applicable. Manufacturer is Microsoft Corporation/One Microsoft Way/Redmond, WA 98052-6399.

5. **EXPORT RESTRICTIONS.** You agree that you will not export or re-export the SOFTWARE PRODUCT, any part thereof, or any process or service that is the direct product of the SOFTWARE PRODUCT (the foregoing collectively referred to as the "Restricted Components"), to any country, person, entity, or end user subject to U.S. export restrictions. You specifically agree not to export or re-export any of the Restricted Components (i) to any country to which the U.S. has embargoed or restricted the export of goods or services, which currently include, but are not necessarily limited to, Cuba, Iran, Iraq, Libya, North Korea, Sudan, and Syria, or to any national of any such country, wherever located, who intends to transmit or transport the Restricted Components back to such country; (ii) to any end user who you know or have reason to know will utilize the Restricted Components in the design, development, or production of nuclear, chemical, or biological weapons; or (iii) to any end user who has been prohibited from participating in U.S. export transactions by any federal agency of the U.S. government. You warrant and represent that neither the BXA nor any other U.S. federal agency has suspended, revoked, or denied your export privileges.

DISCLAIMER OF WARRANTY

NO WARRANTIES OR CONDITIONS. MICROSOFT EXPRESSLY DISCLAIMS ANY WARRANTY OR CONDITION FOR THE SOFTWARE PRODUCT. THE SOFTWARE PRODUCT AND ANY RELATED DOCUMENTATION ARE PROVIDED "AS IS" WITHOUT WARRANTY OR CONDITION OF ANY KIND, EITHER EXPRESS OR IMPLIED, INCLUDING, WITHOUT LIMITA-TION, THE IMPLIED WARRANTIES OF MERCHANTABILITY, FITNESS FOR A PARTICULAR PURPOSE, OR NONINFRINGEMENT. THE ENTIRE RISK ARISING OUT OF USE OR PERFORMANCE OF THE SOFTWARE PRODUCT REMAINS WITH YOU.

LIMITATION OF LIABILITY. TO THE MAXIMUM EXTENT PERMITTED BY APPLICABLE LAW, IN NO EVENT SHALL MICROSOFT OR ITS SUPPLIERS BE LIABLE FOR ANY SPECIAL, INCIDENTAL, INDIRECT, OR CONSEQUENTIAL DAM-AGES WHATSOEVER (INCLUDING, WITHOUT LIMITATION, DAMAGES FOR LOSS OF BUSINESS PROFITS, BUSINESS INTERRUPTION, LOSS OF BUSINESS INFORMATION, OR ANY OTHER PECUNIARY LOSS) ARISING OUT OF THE USE OF OR INABILITY TO USE THE SOFTWARE PRODUCT OR THE PROVISION OF OR FAILURE TO PROVIDE SUPPORT SERVICES, EVEN IF MICROSOFT HAS BEEN ADVISED OF THE POSSIBILITY OF SUCH DAMAGES. IN ANY CASE, MICROSOFT'S ENTIRE LIABILITY UNDER ANY PROVISION OF THIS EULA SHALL BE LIMITED TO THE GREATER OF THE AMOUNT ACTUALLY PAID BY YOU FOR THE SOFTWARE PRODUCT OR US$5.00; PROVIDED, HOWEVER, IF YOU HAVE ENTERED INTO A MICROSOFT SUPPORT SERVICES AGREEMENT, MICROSOFT'S ENTIRE LIABILITY REGARDING SUPPORT SERVICES SHALL BE GOVERNED BY THE TERMS OF THAT AGREEMENT. BECAUSE SOME STATES AND JURISDICTIONS DO NOT ALLOW THE EXCLUSION OR LIMITATION OF LIABILITY, THE ABOVE LIMITATION MAY NOT APPLY TO YOU.

MISCELLANEOUS

This EULA is governed by the laws of the State of Washington USA, except and only to the extent that applicable law mandates govern-ing law of a different jurisdiction.

Should you have any questions concerning this EULA, or if you desire to contact Microsoft for any reason, please contact the Microsoft subsidiary serving your country, or write: Microsoft Sales Information Center/One Microsoft Way/Redmond, WA 98052-6399.

System Requirements

To get the most out of the Training Kit, you will need a computer equipped with the following minimum configuration:

- 166-MHz or higher Pentium processor
- 128 MB RAM (minimum), 256 MB or more recommended
- SQL Server database components: 95 MB to 270 MB of free hard disk space, 250 MB typical
- CD-ROM drive
- Super VGA display with at least 256 colors
- Microsoft Mouse or compatible pointing device
- Microsoft Internet Explorer 5.01 or later

To use the electronic assessment program on the Supplemental Course Materials CD-ROM, you need a computer equipped with the following minimum configuration:

- Microsoft Windows NT 4 with Service Pack 3 or later, Microsoft Windows 98, Windows Me, Windows XP, Windows 2000 Server, or Windows 2003
- Multimedia PC with a 75-MHz Pentium or higher processor
- 32 MB RAM for Windows Me or Windows NT, or
- 64 MG RAM for Windows 2000 or Windows XP
- Super VGA display with at least 256 colors
- Microsoft Mouse or compatible pointing device and keyboard
- Microsoft Internet Explorer 5.01 or later (additional 13 MB minimum hard disk space to install Internet Explorer 6 from this CD-ROM)
- 17 MB of available hard drive space for installation
- A double-speed CD-ROM drive or faster

The latest version of the HCL can be downloaded from the Hardware Compatibility List Web page at *http://www.microsoft.com/hwdq/hcl/*.